李崇峰 著

CHONGFENG LI

佛教考古

从印度到中国

BUDDHIST ARCHAEOLOGY

FROM INDIA TO CHINA

修订本

II

上海古籍出版社

Shanghai Chinese Classics Publishing House

龙门石窟唐代窟龛分期试论

以大型窟龛为例

一、引　言

洛阳，位于河南省西部黄河中游南岸，背依邙山，面临龙门，西扼函谷，东接虎牢；山河拱卫，物产丰富。隋统一后，全国经济迅速恢复。为了进一步控制关东和江南，隋炀帝于大业元年(605年)三月诏尚书令杨素、将作大匠宇文恺等人在洛阳"营建东京，徙豫州郭下居人以实之……徙天下富商、大贾数万家于东京"[1]。唐"武德九年(626年)复为洛州都督府，贞观六年(632年)改为东都，旧宫为洛阳宫"[2]。高宗显庆元年(656年)又诏建东都，因"此都心兹宇宙，通赋贡于四方……岂得宅帝之乡独称雄于四塞？里王之邑匪建国于三川？宜改洛阳宫为东都"[3]。乾封二年(667年)在东都苑东部修建上阳宫。据《太平御览》卷一七三引《东京记》，"上阳宫在皇城西南东苑，前苑东垂，南临洛水，西亘榖水。上元中，韦机充使所造，列岸修廊连垣……高宗末年，常居此宫，以听政也"[4]。由于交通方便、四方(事实上以江淮为主)租赋易于集中，东都建立之后，高宗在显庆二年以后的

---

[1]《隋书》卷三《炀帝纪》，点校本，北京：中华书局，1973年，第63页。

[2]《太平御览》卷一百五十六《州郡部·叙京都》下引《两京记》，影印宋本，北京：中华书局，1960年，第760页。

[3][明]陈耀文《天中记》卷十三引《建东都诏》，明隆庆三年刻本(北京大学图书馆藏)。参见《全唐文》卷十二《高宗皇帝》，影印本，北京：中华书局，1983年，第147页。

[4]《太平御览》卷一百七十三《居处部·宫》引《东京记》，影印宋本，北京：中华书局，1960年，第848页。又，[清]缪荃孙编《藕香零拾》所收《元河南志》卷四有相似记载："上阳宫，在皇城之西南隅，上元(674-676年)中置。南临洛水，西距榖水，东面即皇城右掖门之南。上元中，司农卿韦机造。大帝末年，常居此宫听政。"缪荃孙编《藕香零拾》，影印本，北京：中华书局，1999年，第225页。

二十六七年之内，行幸洛阳的时间几占一半，其“所以屡次行幸洛阳，实以经济的原因为主”[1]。高宗死后，武则天临朝称制，独揽大权，于光宅元年(684年)九月“改东都为神都”[2]，“遂定都于此，日巳营构，而宫府备矣”[3]。据统计，在武则天执政的二十余年里，除大足元年(701年)十月至长安三年(703年)十月临朝长安外，其余都居洛阳。武则天之所以长期留居神都，虽与其政治野心[4]和个人迷信[5]有关，但当时两京的不同经济状况，应是很重要的因素[6]。“神都帑藏储粟，积年充实，淮海漕运，日夕流衍，地当六合之中，人悦四方之会……长安府库及仓，庶事空缺，皆借洛京。”[7]“文献记载和考古发现都表明了洛阳含嘉仓存储、租粮最多的时期，是在武则天和玄宗时期。据仓内所出窖砖上的刻铭，知窖粮多从江淮运来。唐王朝经济来源逐渐依赖江淮，这是唐前期即已重视洛阳，武则天掌权后，更长期在洛阳听政的主要原因。”[8]

一个朝代的都城，既是该朝政治、经济和文化的集中表现，也是该朝君主威势和思想观念的反映。唐初，高宗、武则天并称“二圣”；而“武后擅权”[9]，“素多智计，兼涉文史。帝(高宗)自显庆已后，多苦风疾，百司表奏皆委天后详决。自此内辅国政数十年，威势与帝无异，当时称为‘二圣’”[10]，“皇曰纳辅，后其谋咨。谋咨攸俟，

[1] 全汉昇《唐宋帝国与运河》，重排版，台北：中研院历史语言研究所，1995年，第20页。

[2]《旧唐书》卷六《则天皇后纪》，点校本，北京：中华书局，1975年，第117页。参见:《新唐书》卷三十八《地理志》，点校本，北京：中华书局，1975年，第981页。

[3]《太平御览》卷一百五十六《州郡部·叙京都》下引《两京记》，影印宋本，北京：中华书局，1960年，第760页。

[4] 陈寅恪《唐代政治史略稿》(手写本)，上海：上海古籍出版社，1988年，第33-34、82-84页。

[5] 据《旧唐书》卷五十一《后妃·高宗废皇后王氏传》，“永徽六年(655年)十月，废后(王氏)及萧良娣皆为庶人，囚之别院”。“武后知之，令人杖庶人及萧氏各一百，截去手足，投于酒瓮中，曰：‘令此二妪骨醉’，数日而卒。后则天频见王、萧二庶人披发沥血，如死时状。武后恶之，祷以巫祝，又移居蓬莱宫，复见，故多在东都。”《旧唐书》，点校本，北京：中华书局，1975年，第2170页。

[6] 参见：1) 陈寅恪《隋唐制度渊源略论稿》，上海：上海古籍出版社，1982年，第146页；2) 全汉昇，上引书，第22页；3) 唐长孺《魏晋南北朝隋唐史三论》，武汉：武汉大学出版社，1993年，第339-340页。

[7]《唐会要》卷二十七《行幸》，影印《丛书集成》本，北京：中华书局，1955年，第518页。

[8] 宿白《隋唐长安城和洛阳城》，见宿白《魏晋南北朝唐宋考古文稿辑丛》，北京：文物出版社，2011年，第56页。

[9] 严耕望《唐人习业山林寺院之风尚》，见《严耕望史学论文选集》，北京：中华书局，2006年，第234页。

[10]《旧唐书》卷六《则天皇后纪》，点校本，北京：中华书局，1975年，第115页。

皇用嘉止。亦既顾命,聿怀代已。圣后谦冲,辞不获已。从宜称制,于斯为美。仗义当责,忘躯济厄。神器权临,大运匪革。宗祧永固……英才远略,鸿业大勋。雷霆其武,日月其文。洒以甘露,覆之庆云"[1]。另据中宗《答敬晖请削武氏王爵表敕》,"则天大圣皇帝内辅外临,将五十载。在朕躬则为慈母,于士庶即是明君"[2]。据研究,武则天"其人本无坚定之宗教信仰,先以神皇自居。继又自比于转轮王,特攘借释氏之号,妄自尊大而已。早年重儒术,登基时利用佛典为符谶,虽出僧徒辈与薛怀义等之谋,然后之思想早已有'金轮'二字,形之吟咏。晚岁多病,转而好言长生久视之术……其思想及信仰非释、道之所能囿,晚岁至欲牢笼三教"[3]。不过,"凡武则天在政治上新取得之地位,悉与佛典之教义为证明"[4]。因此"自古君臣事佛,未有如武氏之时盛也"[5]。

龙门"地耸双阙,壁映千寻;前岸清流,却倚重岫;萦带林薄,密迩京华;似耆山之接王城,给园之依卫国也。既资胜地,又属神工,疏凿雕镌,备尽微妙"[6]。7世纪中叶,随着唐王朝政治和经济中心东移,高宗、武则天佞佛,中国的佛教中心也转移到洛阳,龙门石窟在北朝原有基础上迎来了更大规模的开窟造像活动,由此成为这一时期最具代表性的佛教遗迹,堪称中国唐代前期佛教石窟寺之精髓。

---

[1] 崔融《高宗则天皇后哀册文》,参见姚铉纂《唐文粹》卷三十二《文·后妃·哀册》,载《四部丛刊》初编缩印本,上海:商务印书馆,1936年,第258页。

[2]《旧唐书》卷一百八十三《武承嗣传》附,参见:1)《旧唐书》,点校本,北京:中华书局,1975年,第4732页;2)《全唐文》卷十七《中宗皇帝》,影印本,北京:中华书局,1983年,第204页。

[3] 饶宗颐《从石刻论武后之宗教信仰》,见《中研院历史语言研究所集刊》,台北:中研院历史语言研究所,1974年,第45卷第3本,第411页。

[4] 陈寅恪《武则天与佛教》,见陈寅恪《金明馆丛稿二编》,上海:上海古籍出版社,1980年,第151页。

[5] 欧阳修于宋嘉祐八年(1063年)重阳后一日,题跋于长安二年(702年)《唐司刑寺大脚迹敕》:"右司刑寺大脚迹并碑铭二,阎朝隐撰,附诗曰:匪手携之,言示之事,盖谕昏愚者不可以理晓,而决疑惑者难用空言。虽示之已验之事,犹惧其不信也。此自古圣贤以为难,语曰:中人以下不可以语上者,圣人非弃之也,以其语之难也。佛为中国大患,非止中人以下,聪明之智一有惑焉,有不能解者矣。方武氏之时,毒被天下;而刑狱惨烈,不可胜言。而彼佛者遂见光迹于其间,果何为哉?自古君臣事佛,未有如武氏之时盛也。视《朝隐》等碑铭,可见矣。然祸及生民,毒流王室,亦未有若斯之甚也。碑铭文辞不足录,录之者,所以有警也。俾览者知无佛之世,诗书雅颂之声;斯民蒙福者,如彼有佛之盛。其金石文章与其人之被祸者如此,可以少思焉。"欧阳修《集古录跋尾》卷六,参见《欧阳修全集》,影印本,北京:中国书店,1986年,第1161页。

[6] 龙门贞观二十二年《弥勒像之碑》,参见刘景龙、李玉昆主编《龙门石窟碑刻题记汇录》,北京:中国大百科全书出版社,1998年,第22页。

龙门石窟现存编号窟龛2345座[1]，其中唐代遗迹约占总数的2/3[2]，大约1600余座。据我们现场调查，龙门遗存的唐代大型窟龛39座[3]，其余皆为小型窟龛（参见龙门石窟西山、东山立面示意图）。由于种种原因，迄今学界研讨龙门唐代窟

[1] 龙门石窟的编号始于20世纪初法国汉学家沙畹，后来日本学者常盘大定和关野贞，以及水野清一和长广敏雄等，也都为了调查和记录方便，各自临时做了编号。1954年，龙门保管所曾组织人力对龙门石窟做了系统调查，统计出2161个窟龛。1962年，北京大学阎文儒曾采用分区方法做过编号尝试。1974、1983-1985年，龙门保管所进一步做了编号工作。1988-1991年，龙门石窟研究所与中央美术学院美术史系共同对龙门石窟做了现场调查，依据窟龛地理位置，自西山北端开始至南端，再顺延到东山南端起至北端，顺序编排，共编2345个号。当时采用的编号原则是："凡开凿在崖面上的窟龛，高度超过30厘米者均予编号，不足30厘米者及洞窟内部小龛不予编号；凡某窟窟门外原设计为此窟形制的组成部分，如建筑形式、力士龛等，其间有后世增开的小龛不予编号。"这次编号为龙门石窟的保护、研究和旅游提供了一定方便，但也明显存在不足，致使窟、龛界限不清，未考虑彼此间之关系。如，东山看经寺（编为2194号）是武周时期开凿的一座大窟，由前庭和主室两部分构成。然而编号时没有考虑这个因素，只以高30厘米为准，导致该窟前庭左右侧壁开窟后补凿的小龛皆分别编号，从2185排到2204号。在号码上，前庭小龛与看经寺窟本体并列，无法反映出其相互关系，出现了"窟中窟"现象，既与当时石窟寺的"经营"规制或布局相悖，也不符合编号者预先制定的编号原则。我们认为这种编号原则不适于龙门石窟现存遗迹。比较可行的办法是，先划分出大的区域，然后采用大窟附带小龛的办法加以编排，即分区后，每个大窟编排一个号，然后把大窟周围的诸多小龛作为大窟的附属加以编排。这样，相对来说既能防止"窟中窟"编号现象的出现，也会减少许多不必要的排号，便于石窟寺的管理、保护和研究。参见：1) 水野清一、長廣敏雄《龍門石窟の研究》，東京：座右寳刊行會，1941年：附表第二《龙门石窟洞名对照表并造窟年代表》；2)《文物参考资料》，1954年第4期，第121页；3)《光明日报》，1962年9月28日；4) 龙门石窟研究所、中央美术学院美术史系《龙门石窟窟龛编号图册》前言，北京：人民美术出版社，1994年。

[2] 龙门文物保管所《龙门石窟》，北京：文物出版社，1980年，第4页。

[3] 这里所指的唐代大型窟龛，系指洞窟进深、面阔或高在3米以上、保存较为完好的窟龛，且多为国内外学者所熟知。据我们统计，这类窟龛保存较完好者有33座，即八作司洞（现编1628号）、宝塔洞（现编1720号）、宾阳北洞（现编104号）、宾阳南洞（现编159号）、二莲花北洞（现编2214号）、二莲花南洞（现编2211号）、奉南洞（现编1282号）、大卢舍那像龛（即奉先寺，现编1280号）、高平郡王洞（即东山第一窟，现编2144号）、惠简洞（现编565号）、火上洞（即火顶洞，现编1524号）、火下洞（现编1559号）、极南洞（现编1955号）、敬善寺（现编403号）、净土堂（即北市彩帛行净土堂，现编1896号）、看经寺（现编2194号）、老龙洞（即老龙窝，现编669号）、擂鼓台北洞（现编2062号）、擂鼓台南洞（现编2050号）、擂鼓台中洞（即大万伍千佛龛，现编2055号）、龙华寺（现编1931号）、摩崖三佛（现编435号）、破窑（即破洞，现编1069号）、潜溪寺（即斋祓堂，现编20号）、清明寺（现编557号）、三佛洞（现编2150号）、双窑北洞（现编521号）、双窑南洞（现编522号）、四雁洞（现编2220号）、唐字洞（现编1192号）、万佛洞（现编543号）、药方洞（现编1381号）、赵客师洞（现编1038号）等。此外，还应包括火左洞（火烧洞左侧窟，现编1517号）、鷩上洞（鷩骧将军洞上方窟，现编1729号）、弥上洞（弥勒像龛上方窟，现编1071号）、破上洞（破窑上方窟，现编1070号）、普上洞（普泰洞上方窟，现编1019号）和赵上洞（赵客师洞上方窟，现编1045号）等6座。上述39座窟龛中，老龙洞和破窑系利用前代大窟雕造数量众多的小龛，主体造像不清，故暂不列入类型分析。火左洞、弥上洞、破上洞、普上洞和赵上洞位居高处，现难以登临，只有凭借望远镜观察并根据（北京）中国大百科全书出版社1999年9月出版的《龙门石窟总录》补录，其余洞窟皆据笔者实地调查所作记录整理。

龛造像之论著不少[1],但真正从考古学角度对龙门石窟中唐代窟龛作类型研究的则不多[2]。

鉴于龙门石窟中小型窟龛数量极为庞大,且许多不易登临,故本文在前人工作基础上,基于实地考察所得,拟用考古学方法,首先选择龙门石窟中的大型窟龛试做分期研究;将来一旦时机成熟,再扩展到全部小型龛像[3]。不当之处,尚待方家指正。

---

[1] 百年来关于龙门唐代石窟较重要的论著有:1) 路朝霖撰《洛阳龙门志》,光绪十三年(1887年)刊本;2) Édouard Chavannes(沙畹), *Mission archéologique dans la Chine septentrionale.* Paris: Leroux, Publications de l'Ecole française d'Extréme-Orient, 1909-15, Vol. text, 2 portfolios pls., Tome I, 321 ff; 3) Osavld Siren(喜龙仁), *Chinese sculpture from the fifth to the fourteenth century.* London: E. Benn, 1925, Vol. I: C-Cii, 123-126; Pls. 452-462; 4) 常盤大定、關野貞《支那佛教史蹟》第二輯,東京:佛教史蹟研究會,1926年:圖版51-103;常盤大定、關野貞《支那佛教史蹟評解》第二集,東京:佛教史蹟研究會,1926年,第65-115页;5) 关百益《伊阙石刻图表》,开封:河南博物馆,1935年;6) 水野清一、長廣敏雄《龍門石窟の研究》,東京:座右寶刊行會,1941年;7) 龙门保管所编《龙门石窟》,北京:文物出版社,1961年;8) 宫大中《龙门石窟艺术》,上海:上海人民出版社,1981年;9) 曽布川寛《龍門石窟における唐代造像の研究》,見《東方學報》,第60冊,京都:京都大学人文科学研究所,1988年,第199-397页;颜娟英汉译本见《艺术学》第七期(1992年),第163-234页,第八期(1993年),第99-140页;10)《中国石窟·龙门石窟》二,北京:文物出版社,1992年;11) 阎文儒、常青《龙门石窟研究》,北京:书目文献出版社,1995年;12) 龙门石窟研究所编《龙门石窟志》,北京:中国大百科全书出版社,1996年;13) 刘景龙、李玉昆主编《龙门石窟碑刻题记汇录》,北京:中国大百科全书出版社,1998年;14) 刘景龙、杨超杰编《龙门石窟总录》,北京:中国大百科全书出版社,1999年;15)Amy McNair(马嘉德), *Donors of Longmen: Faith, Politics and Patronage of Medieval Chinese Buddhist Sculpture,* Honolulu: University of Hawaii Press, 2007.

[2] 参见:1) 丁明夷《龙门石窟唐代造像的分期与类型》,见《考古学报》,1979年第4期,第519-545页;2) 温玉成《龙门唐窟排年》,见《中国石窟·龙门石窟》二,北京:文物出版社,1992年,第172-216页。

丁明夷认为:龙门唐代前期各种造像的变化均较规整;唐代后期护法类(天王、力士)及弟子等造像形式的变化,较之佛、菩萨等主像更为明显、自由。不过由于当时条件和其他客观原因,他仅对佛和菩萨像进行了分期和类型研究,同时涉及了窟龛构造和造像布局。在分期排队时,丁明夷分小像和大像两部分进行。"小像以龛像为主,辅以小窟的造像";"大像系指大窟中佛与菩萨两种造像"。其中,佛以结跏趺坐类、菩萨以立式类为例加以排比。

温玉成的大作,可谓迄今有关龙门唐代窟龛最为全面的排年。作者认为:"龙门唐窟的排年,因有许多窟龛具有纪年铭,所以是有可靠的年代依据的。我们的排年工作,第一个方法就是依年代序列找出洞窟在结构方面和各种形象演变方面的时代特征,将被研究的洞窟与之相比较分析;第二个方法是就洞窟本身作考古调查,找出其时代的上限或下限。"限于时间和其他因素,该文没有延续作者有关龙门北朝小龛的分期方法,对龙门唐代窟龛未做系统的考古类型学分析。

[3] 由于龙门石窟遗存的小型窟龛众多,而考古类型学分析又不允许做主观遴选,因此有些重要窟龛,如唐高宗时期开凿的一批小型窟龛和当时流行的优填王像等,无法纳入我们的分期排队系列,只有留待来日再做全面、系统的勘察和整理。关于这批材料,参见:温玉成《龙门唐窟排年》,上引书,第172-216页。

二、龙门石窟唐代窟龛的类型

龙门石窟上述39座唐代大型窟龛，通常具前后两部分，即前庭（前室）和主室（后室）。前庭进深一般较短且保存不好，主室则保存相对完整。主室平面多作方形，穹隆顶；一般于正壁及两侧壁造像，窟顶浮雕纹饰或天空。依据洞窟结构及像设，我们分别对上述窟龛的建筑形制、造像题材及组合、造像特征、装饰纹样以及技法等进行考古类型学分析，而后分组排比，找出洞窟的先后发展演变序列，在此基础上进行考古学研究。

（一）窟龛形制

1. 平面

依据洞窟主室的平面布局，可将唐代窟龛分作三型。

A型：正壁佛坛窟 / 正壁一龛窟[1]，洞窟平面前半近方形，后半部略作半圆状，正壁及两侧壁后端造像（图1）。13个，即宾阳北洞[2]、宾阳南洞、惠简洞[3]、敬善寺、摩崖三佛[4]、破上洞、清明寺、双窑北洞[5]、双窑南洞[6]、唐字洞、万佛洞[7]、药方洞[8]、赵客师洞。

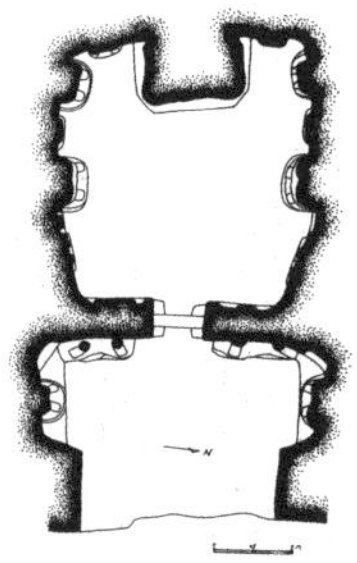

图1　敬善寺平面图

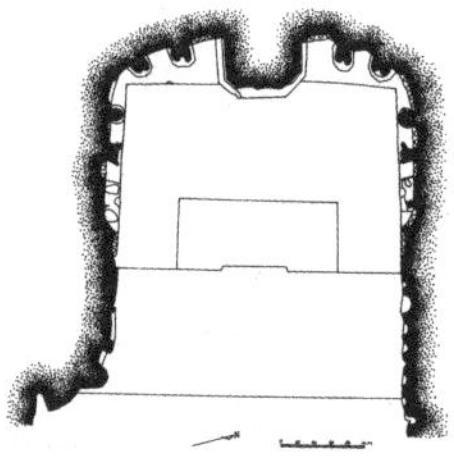

图2　大卢舍那像龛平面图

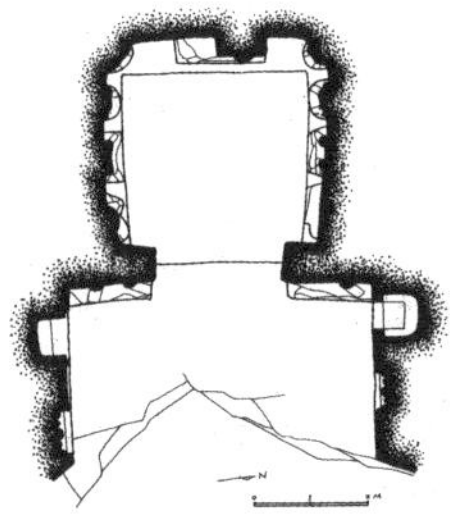

图3　极南洞平面图

[1] 这种正壁佛坛窟或正壁一龛窟，有些不是严格意义上的佛坛或龛，仅在正壁造像一铺。为了行文方便，暂时归入一类。

[2] 宾阳北洞后半部略作半圆形。

[3] 惠简洞后半部略作半圆形，有一高20厘米的低坛，上造像。

[4] 摩崖三佛为敞口式大龛。暂入此式。

[5] 双窑北洞后端，凿出高约20厘米的低坛，上造像。

[6] 双窑南洞后半略作半圆形，有一高12厘米的低坛，上造像。

[7] 万佛洞后半部方整。暂入此式。

[8] 药方洞后半部略作半圆形。

B 型：三壁环坛窟，平面方形，或横长方形，或多边形，正壁略弧，与侧壁相交处多圆角；环左、右、后三壁设高坛，坛上造像（图 2、3、4）。20 个，即八作司洞、宝塔洞、大卢舍那像龛[1]、二莲花北洞、二莲花南洞、奉南洞、高平郡王洞[2]、火上洞、火下洞、火左洞、极南洞、净土堂、擂鼓台北洞[3]、龙华寺[4]、鸗上洞、弥上洞、普上洞、潜溪寺[5]、三佛洞、四雁洞[6]、赵上洞。

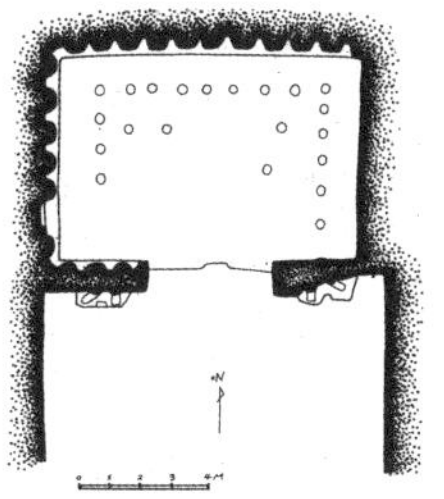

图 4　高平郡王洞平面图

C 型：中心方坛窟，平面方形，正中设坛（图 5）。3 个，即看经寺[7]、擂鼓台南洞、擂鼓台中洞。

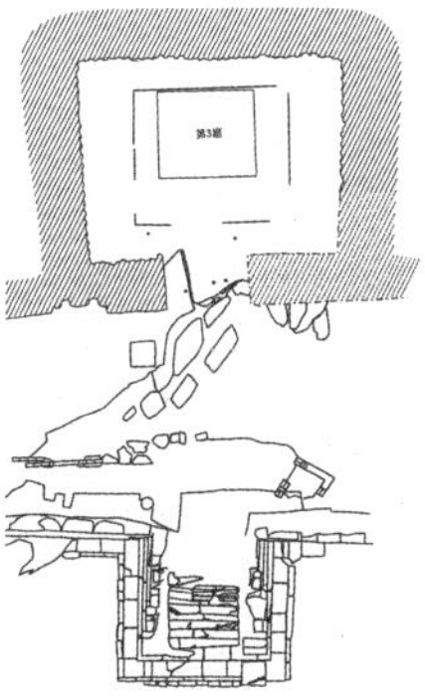

图 5　擂鼓台南洞平面图

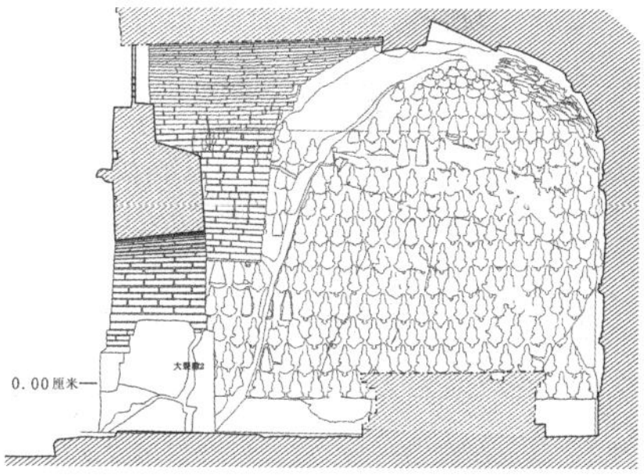

图 6　擂鼓台南洞纵向垂直剖面图

2. 窟顶

依据主室窟顶结构[8]，可将唐代窟龛分作三型。

A 型：穹隆顶（图 6）。23 个，即宝塔洞[9]、八作司洞、宾阳北洞、宾阳南洞[10]、二莲花北洞、奉南洞、火下洞、火左洞、极南洞、敬善寺、擂鼓台南洞、擂鼓

[1] 大卢舍那像龛为敞口式大龛。暂入此式。

[2] 高平郡王洞平面横长方形，正壁、右壁及前壁右侧造形体较大的坐佛，未按原计划完工。暂入此式。

[3] 擂鼓台北洞平面近五边形，窟内左右后三面设一高约 13 厘米的低坛，上造像。暂入此式。

[4] 龙华寺平面近圆形。

[5] 潜溪寺平面横长方形，四角皆圆作；环三壁设低坛，坛上造像。

[6] 四雁洞平面近圆形，窟内后半部凿一高约 70 厘米的佛坛，上置像。暂入此式。

[7] 看经寺现存窟内方坛，系 2001 年砌造。坛所在地面原有一凹凸不平的地方，呈方形，原应置坛，形如擂鼓台中洞中央残坛内芯及周围地面。此承龙门石窟研究院王振国见告。谨此致谢。

[8] 大卢舍那像龛和摩崖三佛系依山开凿的露天大龛，无顶。

[9] 此窟未按计划完工。暂入此式。

[10] 宾阳北洞和宾阳南洞的窟顶纹饰系北魏开窟时原作，后整个洞窟因故中辍。暂入此式。

台中洞、龙华寺、鸑上洞、弥上洞、破上洞、普上洞、潜溪寺、清明寺、双窑北洞、双窑南洞[1]、药方洞、赵客师洞。

B型：平顶，顶与侧壁连接处较圆缓。7个，即惠简洞、净土堂、看经寺[2]、擂鼓台北洞、唐字洞、万佛洞[3]、赵上洞[4]。

C型：浅穹顶与平顶混合式，窟顶边缘与斜坡门道顶部交接处略高出后者或与之几乎持平，有的顶部直接通至窟外。5个，即二莲花南洞、高平郡王洞[5]、火上洞、三佛洞、四雁洞。

（二）造像题材及组合

1. 造像题材

依据窟内主要造像可以将唐代窟龛分作三型。

A型：一佛，主尊雕造于正壁中央，两侧为胁侍像（图7）。31个，即八作司洞、宝塔洞、宾阳北洞、宾阳南洞、大卢舍那像龛、二莲花北洞、二莲花南洞、奉南洞、高平郡王洞、惠简洞、火上洞、火下洞、火左洞、极南洞、敬善寺、净土堂、擂鼓台南洞[6]、擂鼓台中洞[7]、鸑上洞、弥上洞、破上洞、普上洞[8]、潜溪寺、清明寺、双窑南洞、四雁洞[9]、唐字洞、万佛洞、药方洞、赵客师洞、赵上洞。

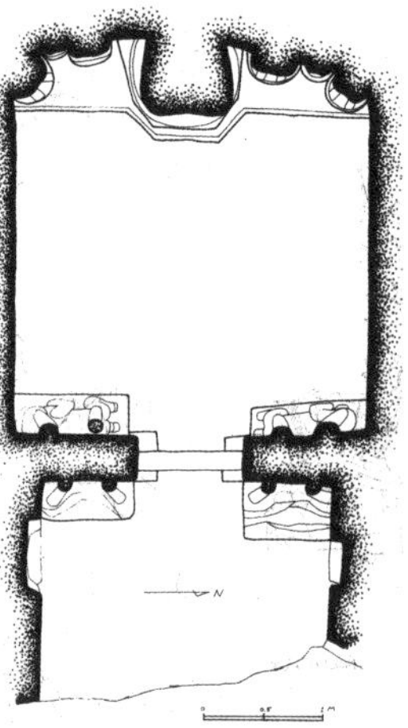

图7　万佛洞造像题材示意图

B型：三佛，左、右、后三壁各造一佛，个别窟在正壁与侧壁间再造二佛（图8）。5个，即擂鼓台北洞、龙华寺[10]、摩崖三佛、三佛洞、双窑北洞。

C型：多佛。窟壁上雕造数量众多或成千上万尊小型坐佛（图9）。5个，即高

[1] 双窑南洞窟顶前半为筒拱（纵券），后半作穹隆形，表面无饰。暂入此式。

[2] 看经寺窟顶与侧壁连接作直角。暂入此式。

[3] 万佛洞窟顶与侧壁连接作直角。暂入此式。

[4] 赵上洞窟顶近横券。暂入此式。

[5] 此窟未按计划完工，窟顶表面处理粗糙。暂入此式。

[6] 擂鼓台南洞中央佛坛上主尊，传说从附近寺院移入，因此该像是否为窟内原作，尚不能肯定。不过，依据日人关野贞等1906-1908年间（一说1918年）拍摄的擂鼓台南洞内景照片，该像已置坛上。暂入此式。

[7] 擂鼓台中洞佛坛上原应有造像，但内容现无从知晓。该窟正壁造像为一佛二菩萨，暂入此式。

[8] 普上洞正壁主尊为二佛并坐，表现的可能是释迦多宝这一特定题材。暂入此式。

[9] 四雁洞造像不存，据其坛上现存像座槽判断，应为一佛。暂入此式。

[10] 龙华寺造像为五佛，即一坐佛、二弟子、二立佛、二菩萨、二坐佛、二神王、金刚力士、二狮子。暂入此式。

平郡王洞、擂鼓台南洞[1]、擂鼓台中洞、双窑南洞、万佛洞。

图 8　龙华寺造像题材示意图

图 9　擂鼓台中洞造像题材示意图

2. 造像组合

依据主体造像组合形式，可将唐代窟龛分作二型。

A 型：一铺像，即正壁中央造主尊，两侧雕胁侍像。依据组合不同，下分三式。

Ai 式：一铺三身或五身像，即一佛二菩萨或一佛二弟子二菩萨；有的在菩萨像外侧各加雕一狮子[2]（图 10)。4 个，即宾阳南洞、清明寺[3]、唐字洞[4]、赵客师洞。

Aii 式：一铺七身像，即一佛二弟子二菩萨二神王[5]或金刚力士[6]（图

[1] 擂鼓台南洞四壁及窟顶雕造的小坐像，目前学界有两种看法：一种认为是菩萨像，一种认为是佛像。另外，该洞正壁未设置主像。暂入此式。参见李崇峰《地婆诃罗、香山寺与"石像七龛"》（见本书）。

[2] 依据龙门石窟造像题铭，当时甚至把狮子也列入造像题材之中，如赵客师洞一则题记作："显庆五年（660 年）□月□日刘□□于赵客师龛内敬造阿弥陀佛像一躯并二菩萨、二圣僧、狮子、香炉……"。参见刘景龙、李玉昆主编《龙门石窟碑刻题记汇录》，北京：中国大百科全书出版社，1998 年，第 326 页。

[3] 清明寺造像为一佛二菩萨，另外加雕二狮子。

[4] 唐字洞造像为一佛二菩萨。

[5] 这种身着铠甲的武士像，通常称作天王。结合现存造像并依照相关题铭，这种"天王"形象，当时皆称作"神王"，如唐咸亨四年（673 年）完工的惠简洞题铭和上元二年（675 年）完工的大卢舍那像龛（今称奉先寺）题铭。参见：刘景龙、李玉昆主编，上引书，第 179、381 页。又，上海博物馆收藏的一件开元九年 (722) 十二月造像碑，倚坐主尊两侧龛边及龛楣镌刻的铭文作"……行并州辽城府长史后任沁州安府□长史……皇帝 / 皇后□ / □亡父 / 母□□ / 家口造 / 石碑阿 / 弥陀 / 佛一塔 / 弥勒佛一 / 塔左右二 / 菩萨二 / 圣僧余 / □□□先 / 造石碑像一铺二独立菩萨二神王二师子　开元九年十二月……"

关于这种护法形象，参见李聿骐《试述李治武则天时期龙门石窟中的神王像：以典型窟龛为例》，载《石窟寺研究》第 2 辑，北京：文物出版社，2011 年，第 178-190 页。

[6] 据宾阳南洞前壁刘玄意题记和大卢舍那像龛题铭，这种威风凛凛的护法形象当时称作"金刚力士"或"金刚"。参见：刘景龙、李玉昆主编，上引书，第 51、381 页。关于金刚力士，参见李崇峰《金刚力士钩稽》（见本书）。

11)。9个，即宾阳北洞、高平郡王洞、擂鼓台中洞[1]、弥上洞、破上洞、潜溪寺、双窑南洞、药方洞、赵上洞[2]。

Aiii式：一铺九身像，即一佛二弟子二菩萨二神王和金刚力士（参见图2）；有的在神王与金刚力士间各加雕一狮子，构成所谓的一铺十一身像，即一佛二弟子二菩萨二神王二狮子和金刚力士（图12）。16个，即八作司洞[3]、宝塔洞[4]、大卢舍那像龛、二莲花北洞、二莲花南洞、奉南洞[5]、惠简洞[6]、火上洞、火下洞[7]、极南洞[8]、敬善寺[9]、净土堂[10]、鷰上洞、普上洞[11]、四雁洞[12]、万佛洞[13]。

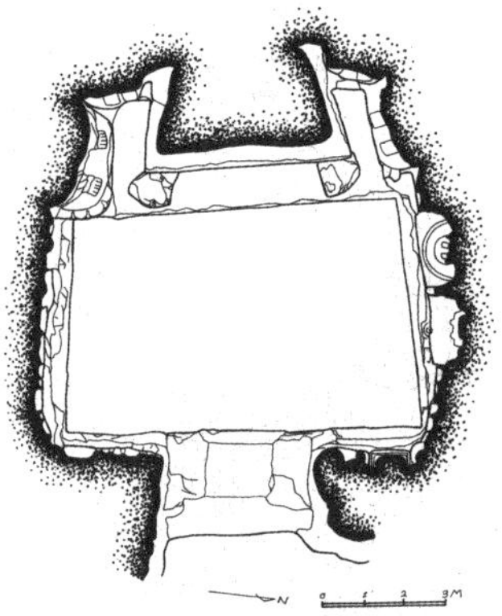

图10　宾阳南洞造像组合示意图

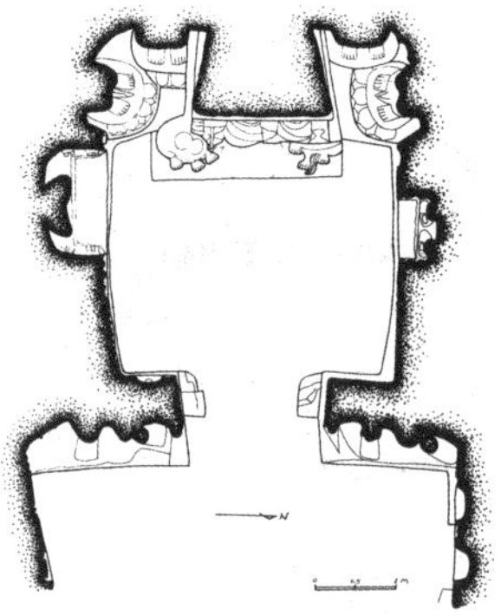

图11　药方洞造像组合示意图

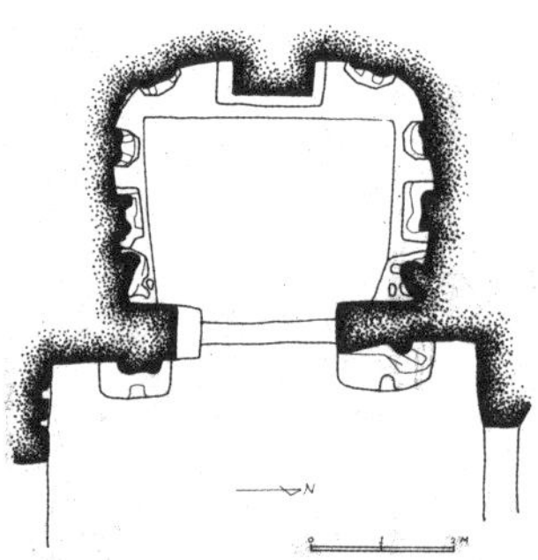

图12　八作司洞造像组合示意图

[1] 擂鼓台中洞正壁主尊为一佛二菩萨，但前庭正壁门道两侧雕金刚力士（右侧雕像已毁）。暂入此式。

[2] 赵上洞窟内造像为一佛二弟子二菩萨二地藏，组合特别。暂入此式。

[3] 八作司洞雕造一佛二弟子二菩萨二神王二狮子和金刚力士。暂入此式。

[4] 宝塔洞雕造一佛二弟子二菩萨二神王二狮子和金刚力士。暂入此式。

[5] 奉南洞雕造一佛二弟子二菩萨二神王二狮子和金刚力士。暂入此式。

[6] 惠简洞左右侧壁外端的两身造像不存，据开窟题记，应为神王和金刚力士像。

[7] 火下洞主室正壁主尊尚存，两侧胁侍已失。从侧壁残存的头光判断，主室应为一坐佛二弟子二菩萨二神王，前庭为金刚力士及二狮子，即一铺十一身像。暂入此式。

[8] 极南洞雕造一佛二弟子二菩萨二神王二狮子和金刚力士。暂入此式。

[9] 敬善寺前庭两侧壁的二菩萨像，似不在原设计之内，应为后来补作而成。其补作时间可能在该窟完工前后，因该窟前庭地面的原设计与双窑前庭相似。暂入此式。

[10] 净土堂内造像不存，依据门楣上题额和正壁造像铭记，主室内原主像应为阿弥陀和观世音、大势至西方三圣像，加胁侍共十一身。暂入此式。

[11] 普上洞造像为二坐佛二弟子二菩萨二神王和金刚力士。暂入此式。

[12] 四雁洞主室内造像不存，仅在坛上存原像座槽；前庭正壁两侧雕金刚力士。暂入此式。

[13] 万佛洞雕造一佛二弟子二菩萨二神王二狮子和金刚力士。暂入此式。

B 型：三铺像，即以三佛为中心的造像（图 13）。5个，即擂鼓台北洞[1]、龙华寺[2]、摩崖三佛、三佛洞、双窑北洞[3]。

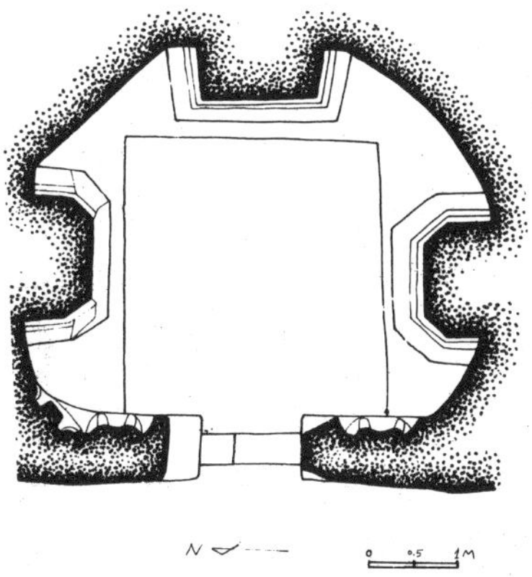

图 13　擂鼓台北洞造像组合示意图

（三）造像特征

1. 佛像

佛像既是寺院（包括石窟寺）像设的核心，又是信徒的主体朝拜对象。佛像特征主要表现在法衣、手印以及姿态等方面。鉴于佛之手印大多残毁，佛像的考古类型学分析仅以洞窟内主尊为例，分法衣与坐姿、头光和像座三部分排比。

(1) 法衣与坐姿

依佛本制，缠缚于佛及僧众身上的法衣或法服，通常有三种，即三衣，制法固定，疑“佛自亲制”[4]。传说释迦牟尼曾用法服、钵和锡杖教示信徒如何造塔[5]；而现存视觉艺术中表示佛陀“换衣”的唯一画面是犍陀罗出土的一幅浮雕，现为比利时克洛德·德马尔托 (Claude de Marteau) 收藏。该浮雕表现悉达多出家“剃除须发，向猎师边，以憍奢耶衣贸易袈裟清净法服”[6]场景，为太子下系内衣、披覆上衣之瞬间（图 14a）[7]。其中，憍奢耶衣 (kāśikā-vastra/kāśikāni-vastrāṇi/kauśeya) 系以迦尸 (Kāśi) 生产的细棉或“用野蚕丝棉作衣者”[8]，汉译天衣、宝衣、好衣，音写憍奢耶衣、憍尸迦衣、迦尸迦衣、迦尸衣等。“此衣价直百千亿金，复为种种旃檀香等之所熏修”[9]。

---

[1] 擂鼓台北洞左、右、后三壁各一坐佛，前壁门道两侧各一菩萨像。暂入此式。

[2] 龙华寺造像为一铺十五身，即一坐佛二弟子二立佛二菩萨二坐佛二神王金刚力士及二狮子。暂入此式。

[3] 三佛洞和双窑北洞造像皆一铺十三身，即一佛二弟子二菩萨二坐佛二菩萨二神王和金刚力士。

[4] 义净《南海寄归内法传》卷二“着衣法式”，王邦维校注，北京：中华书局，1995 年，第 102 页。

[5] 玄奘《大唐西域记》卷一《缚喝国》，季羡林等校注，北京：中华书局，1985 年，第 122-124 页。

[6] 地婆诃罗译《方广大庄严经》卷七《频婆娑罗王劝受俗利品》，参见《大正藏》第 3 卷，第 578c 页。关于憍奢耶衣与袈裟交换情景，隋阇那崛多译《佛本行集经》卷十八《剃发染衣品》和唐地婆诃罗译《方广大庄严经》卷六《出家品》叙述颇详。参见《大正藏》第 3 卷，第 737c-738a、576c 页。

[7] 栗田功《ガンダーラ美術》，I 佛伝，東京：二玄社，1988 年，図 164。

[8] 玄应《一切经音义》，见《一切经音义：三种校本合刊》，徐时仪校注，上海：上海古籍出版社，2008 年，第 215 页。

唐初高僧玄应，博学字书，曾参与玄奘译场，担当“正字”之职。因此，玄应对佛教法衣之解释，应代表了唐初此土的权威认识。故本文对法衣之阐释，首选玄应字书。

[9] 阇那崛多译《佛本行集经》卷十八《剃发染衣品》，《大正藏》第 3 卷，第 738a 页。

图 14　天竺三衣及僧祇支披覆图

a. 比利时所藏犍陀罗浮雕“换衣”图；b. 下衣折束示意图；c. 上衣披覆示意图；d. 上衣作“右袒式”披覆示意图；e. 上衣作通肩式披覆示意图；f. 上衣作通肩式披覆示意图（背面）；g. 上衣作通肩式披覆示意图；h. 上衣作“右袒式”披覆示意图（正面）；i. 上衣作“右袒式”披覆示意图（背面）；j. 大衣披覆示意图（正面）；k. 大衣（披肩）正面示意图；l. 大衣（披肩、覆背）背面示意图；m. 僧祇支披覆示意图

袈裟 (kāṣāya/kaṣāya)[1]汉译染色衣、染衣、间色衣、法服，音写袈裟衣、袈裟等，“乃是往古诸佛之服”[2]，为“粗弊衣服袈裟色……是解脱圣人衣”[3]。至于中土大多数雕塑和绘画中表示的佛陀法衣，疑为艺术家或工匠“对世俗僧人所着袈裟的摹写，它在某种程度上反映出彼时世俗社会中僧人所着袈裟的一些情况”[4]。对此，格里斯沃尔德 (A. B. Griswold) 在 20 世纪 60 年代以瑞士里特伯格博物馆 (Rietberg Museum) 藏品为基础，参照上座部传统和南亚及东南亚僧人日常穿着，根据巴利语律典和义净《南海寄归内法传》，并与秣菟罗与犍陀罗出土的造像进行对比，对中国雕塑中的佛法衣做了系统梳理 (图 14b-m)[5]，颇具启发。据义净记载，佛教“三衣皆名支伐罗 (cīvara，三衣巴利语作 ti-cīvara，梵语为 traya-cīvara 或 tri-cīvara)，北方诸国多名法衣为袈裟，乃是赤色之义，非律文典语”[6]。因此，袈裟乃北传佛教对三衣之通称[7]。实际上，佛所披着的三衣[8]，包括

[1] 据玄应《一切经音义》卷十四《四分律音义》：“袈裟，举佉反，下所加反。《韵集》音加沙。字本从毛作髦毠二形。葛洪后作《字苑》始改从衣。案：外国通称袈裟，此云不正色也。诸草木中，若皮、若叶、若花等，不成五味、难以为食者，则名迦沙。此物染衣，其色浊赤，故梵本五浊之浊，亦名迦沙。天竺比丘多用此色，或言缁衣者，当是初译之时见其色浊，因以名也。又案：《如幻三昧经》云：晋言无垢秽。又义云离尘服，或云消瘦衣，或称莲华服，或言间色衣，皆随义立名耳。真谛三藏云袈裟，此云赤血色衣，言外国虽有五部不同，并皆赤色，言青黑木兰者，但点之异耳”。玄应，上引书，第 294 页。

[2]《方广大庄严经》卷六《出家品》，《大正藏》第 3 卷，第 576c 页。

[3]《佛本行集经》卷十八《剃发染衣品》，《大正藏》第 3 卷，第 738a 页。

[4] 马世长《汉式佛像袈裟琐议：汉式佛教图像札记之一》，见《艺术史研究》第七辑，中山大学出版社，2005 年，第 250 页。

[5] A. B. Griswold, “Prolegomena to the Study of the Buddha’s Dress in Chinese Sculpture”, in: *Artibus Asiae*, Vol. XXVI (1963), No. 2: 85-131, Vol. XXVII (1964/65), No. 4: 335-348.

[6] 义净《南海寄归内法传》卷二“衣食所须”，王邦维校注，北京：中华书局，1995 年，第 75-76 页。

[7] 慧琳《一切经音义》，《大正藏》第 54 卷，第 317c、381c 页。

[8] 玄应在《一切经音义》卷十四《四分律音义》中，特别对佛法衣作了如下解释：“三衣：僧伽梨，此音讹也，应云僧伽致，或云僧伽胝，译云合成，或云重，谓割之合成又重作也。此一衣必割截成，余二衣或割不割，若法密部、说诸有部等多则不割，若圣辩部、大众部等则割。若不割者，直安怗角及以钩纽而已也。

欝多罗僧，或云郁多啰僧伽，或云优多罗僧，或作沤多罗僧，亦梵言讹转耳，此译云上着衣也。着谓与身相合，言于常所服中最在其上，故以名焉。或云覆左肩衣。

安多会，或作安多卫，或作安多婆娑，或作安陀罗跋萨，此译云中宿衣，谓近身住也。或云里衣也。”

玄应，上引书，第 298 页。

义净《南海寄归内法传》卷二“衣食所须”条所记三衣，则为：“一、僧伽胝，译为复衣也；二、嗢呾啰僧伽，译为上衣也；三、安呾婆娑，译为内衣也。”义净，上引书，第 75 页。

本文关于佛及弟子所着法衣之描述，主要依据义净《南海寄归内法传》卷二相关记述，因为“义净法师所述之袈裟穿着法，是其在印度亲见的标准披着方式”。同时，参照玄奘《大唐西域记》、玄应《一切经音义》、慧琳《一切经音义》及法云《翻译名义集》。值得注意的是，慧琳关于法服的解释似乎主要采纳了义净之说。鉴于迄今讨论佛教法衣的文章多偏重形象比较，本文拟将唐宋关于佛教服饰之重要音义详列出来并附梵语原语 (采用拉丁字母转写形式)，以就正同好。参见：1) 义净，上引书，第 75-76 页；2) 玄奘，上引书，第 122-124、176-180 页；3) 慧琳《一切经音义》卷五十九，《大正藏》第 54 卷，第 700b 页；4) 法云《翻译名义集》卷七，《大正藏》第 54 卷，第 1171a-b 页；5) 荻原雲來《漢訳対照梵和大辭典》，東京：鈴木学術財団，1974 年，第 1386、244、74 页；6) 马世长，上引书，第 250 页。

复衣 (saṃghāṭī 僧伽胝，即大衣)[1]、上衣 (uttarāsaṅga 郁多罗僧，即上着衣)[2] 和内衣 (antarvāsaka 安多会，即里衣、下衣)[3]，属义净记载的天竺内法“衣食所须”之“充身六物”及“十三资具”中前三种[4]。其中，三衣中的复衣/大衣，依照“佛制，入王宫时，入聚落时，摧伏外道时，见猛兽时，应着此衣”，堪称法衣“正装”。不过，现存图像中，除三衣外，佛多内着僧祇支(僧脚崎衣，掩腋衣)[5]，因为“恐汗污三衣，先以此衣掩腋，然后披着三衣”[6]。依据三衣等“披覆”方式[7]，主要是大衣(复衣)的缠绕形式，可将唐代窟龛分作五型。

---

[1] 玄应《一切经音义》卷二十一《大菩萨藏经音义》：“僧伽胝[陟尸反]，旧言僧伽梨，此云合，谓割之合成也。又云重，谓重作也。王宫聚落着之，伏外道衣”；同书卷二十二《瑜伽师地论音义》：“僧伽胝[陟尸反]，此云合，或言重，谓割之合成又重作也。旧经律中作僧伽梨，或作僧伽致，皆讹也。”玄应，上引书，第 432、453 页。

另，据慧琳《一切经音义》卷十二《大宝积经音义》，“僧伽胝[音知]，旧曰僧伽梨，此云复衣，即今僧之大衣是也。下从九条，上至二十五条，但取奇数，九种差别具如律文所说。佛制：入王宫时，入聚落时，摧伏外道时，见猛兽时应着此衣”。《大正藏》第 54 卷，第 380c 页。

[2] 玄应《一切经音义》卷二十五《阿毗达磨顺正理论音义》：“嗢多罗僧[乌没反]，旧云郁多罗，亦云郁多罗，此云上首(着)衣，此谓常着衣中最在上也。”玄应，上引书，第 507 页。

另，据慧琳《一切经音义》卷十五《大宝积经音义》，郁多罗僧伽，梵语僧衣名也。即七条袈裟，是三衣之中常服衣也。亦名上衣，见《南海寄归传》；同书卷六十六《集异门足论音义》：“嗢怛罗僧[上温没反]，梵语。唐云上衣，今之七条也。”《大正藏》第 54 卷，第 397a、700b、744c 页。

又，另一类似的梵语词是 uttarīya，意为上衣、外衣、披覆、覆布等，汉译作衣、衣裳。参见：荻原雲来，上引书，第 245 页。

[3] 玄应《一切经音义》卷二十《四阿含暮抄音义》：“婆喋[丈甲反]，梵言安陀罗婆波，此云五条。”玄应，上引书，第 422 页。

据道宣《四分律删繁补阙行事钞》卷三《二衣总别篇》，“五条者名下衣，从用院内道行杂作衣”。《大正藏》第 40 卷，第 105a 页。另，据法云《翻译名义集》卷七，“安陀会，或安怛罗婆沙，此云中宿衣，谓近身住也。南山云：五条，名下衣，从用云院内行道、杂作衣”。《大正藏》第 54 卷，第 1171b 页。

[4] 义净，上引书，第 75-76 页。

[5] 参见本文菩萨服饰。

[6] 慧琳《一切经音义》卷六十二《根本毗奈耶杂事律音义》，《大正藏》第 54 卷，第 721b 页。参见同书第 581c 页。

[7] 龙门石窟中佛的三衣原皆着色，层次清晰。不过由于自然和人为的破坏，石雕佛像的原始颜色早已退去，三衣的披覆方式不宜辨认。因此，我们在类型分析时参考了敦煌莫高窟彩塑和壁画中与之同时期或稍早(隋代)的佛三衣披覆方式。关于中国雕塑和绘画中表现的佛法衣，参见：1) 马世长《汉式佛像袈裟琐议：汉式佛教图像札记之一》，上引书，第 247-268 页；2)《中国石窟·敦煌莫高窟》二，北京：文物出版社，1984 年，图版 1、43、57、92、97、138、163、165、178 等；3)《中国石窟·敦煌莫高窟》三，北京：文物出版社，1987 年，图版 14、18、27、93、99、104、126、143、179 等。

A 型：褒衣博带式[1]。佛结跏趺坐,内着掩腋衣,上衣覆搭双肩且于胸前束带打结[2]；大衣(复衣)边缘在颈部两侧向下垂至腹部,右侧边缘多上搭左小臂垂下。大衣造型肥大宽博,衣摆褶襞密集、垂于座前(图 15)。3 个,即宾阳北洞[3]、唐字洞[4]、药方洞。

[1] 这种样式的佛衣,指学界习称的"双领下垂式大衣"或"褒衣博带式大衣"。印度传统的僧俗衣,仅仅是一块长方形棉布,既无衣领,也无衣袖,故梵语中似无衣领、衣袖之词,因此颈下衣缘 / 边不能称作衣领。这种颈下垂双衣边之大衣,是佛教传入此土后的一种创新,出现在 5 世纪下半叶,系受南朝汉式服饰影响所致,不见于天竺或佛教律典。依《汉书》卷七十一《隽不疑传》颜师古注"褒衣博带"条,师古曰:"褒,大裾也。言着褒大之衣,广博之带也。而说者乃以为朝服垂褒之衣,非也。"另据《颜氏家训》卷下《涉务》第十一,"梁世士大夫,皆尚褒衣博带,大冠高履"。至于佛教造像中之褒衣博带式大衣,系宿师季庚先生依据其显著外观所拟定,亦作冕服式,可称汉式袈裟,日本学者作"北魏式服制"。

参见：1) 班固《汉书》,颜师古注,点校本,北京：中华书局,1962 年,第 3035-3036 页；2) 颜之推《颜氏家训》,周法高汇注,二版,台北：中研院历史语言研究所,1993 年,第 71 页；3) 宿白《参观敦煌莫高窟第 285 号窟札记》,载宿白《中国石窟寺研究》,北京：文物出版社,1996 年,第 206-213 页；4) 長廣敏雄《雲岡石窟における仏像の服制》,載長廣敏雄《中國美術論集》,東京：株式会社講談社,1984 年,第 431-445 頁；5)《中国石窟・敦煌莫高窟》二,北京：文物出版社,1984 年,图版 182。

[2] 关于束带打结,有的图像似作内衣束带,即迄今所说的僧祇支于胸前束带打结；有些似为上衣覆搭双肩后于胸前以带系之。在这点上,麦积山石窟中的彩绘佛像,对我们认识三衣的披衣方式大有裨益。麦积山第 142 窟开凿于北魏时期,左壁坐佛,内着僧祇支,上衣覆搭双肩后两衣边缘自颈侧垂下,于胸前以黑色大带系之,打蝴蝶结；大衣自右腋下伸出后,上搭左肩作"右袒式"披覆。同窟正壁坐佛僧祇支及上衣的披衣方式同左侧坐佛,唯大衣作汉式披覆,右衣缘自颈侧垂至腹前后上搭左肩。大约雕造于西魏的 135 窟立佛,三衣披覆方式与第 142 窟正壁主尊坐佛完全相同。至于麦积山第 20 窟正壁及侧壁的彩塑坐佛,应雕造于西魏时期,保存完好,三衣的"披衣"方式清晰。正壁坐佛内着僧祇支；上衣覆搭双肩后两衣缘自颈侧垂下,于胸前以带系之并打结,长带垂至腹前；大衣作汉式披覆,右衣缘自颈侧垂至腹前后上搭左臂垂下,大衣下摆垂覆座前。雕造于北周的第 62 窟正壁坐佛,内着僧祇支,上衣覆搭双肩后自颈侧垂下,于胸前以带系之；大衣自右腋下伸出后上搭左肩后垂,作"右袒式"披覆。参见天水麦积山石窟艺术研究所编《中国石窟・天水麦积山》,北京：文物出版社,1998 年,图版 108、109、173、180、181、218。因此,这些清晰的披衣方式,尤其是上衣于胸前系带打结,可能是佛教法服汉化的一种反应。参见本书《敦煌莫高窟北朝晚期洞窟的分期与研究》中关于佛像"法衣束带"的注释。

[3] 宾阳北洞主尊上衣未束带打结,大衣边缘自颈部两侧向下垂至腹部后不清。暂入此式。

[4] 唐字洞主尊左手施无畏印,右手抚于大腿之上；大衣右边缘与腹前斜向褶襞交待不清。暂入此式。

B型：钩纽式[1]。佛结跏趺坐，内着掩腋衣，上衣覆搭双肩后于胸前束带打结，右侧衣缘垂下遮掩大衣；大衣由左肩覆背披至右胁下后衣尾伸出，与左肩处衣头用芹纽扣挂[2]，下摆垂覆座前，腿部衣纹近横向，摆边平缓（图16）。1个，即宾阳南洞。

图15　药方洞主尊佛像

图16　宾阳南洞主尊佛像

C型：偏覆式[3]。佛结跏趺坐，内着掩腋衣；上衣覆搭双肩，两衣缘自颈侧垂下后于胸前以带系之，唯左衣缘被大衣遮覆；大衣由左肩覆背披至右肘后衣尾上搭左肩，仅在右肩上略遮覆上衣[4]，下摆垂覆座前，腿部衣纹近横

---

[1] 钩纽式大衣，乃佛允许僧众"搭衣"之一种。据《四分律》卷四十《衣揵度》，"尔时舍利弗入白衣舍，患风吹，割截衣堕肩。诸比丘白佛，佛言：听肩头安钩纽"。参见《大正藏》第22卷，第855c页。

另，据《弥沙塞部和醯五分律》卷二十六《杂法》，"有诸比丘着轻衣入聚落，风吹露形，诸女人笑羞耻。佛言：听作衣纽钩钩之。应用铜、铁、牙、角、竹、木作钩，除漆树；乃至作带带之。诸比丘一向着衣，下易坏。佛言：听颠倒着衣，上下皆安钩纽及带"。参见《大正藏》22卷，第174b-c页。又，同律卷二十九《比丘尼法》，"有诸比丘尼，着轻衣入聚落，风吹露形。佛言：听上下安钩纽带系之"。参见《大正藏》第22卷，第190a页。

[2] 参见：1)《中国石窟·敦煌莫高窟》二，北京：文物出版社，1984年，图版165；2)《中国石窟·敦煌莫高窟》三，北京：文物出版社，1987年，图版179。

[3] 这种大衣披覆方式，实为下文右袒式之变体。据宋元丰三年（1080年）夏余杭沙门元照于天宫院所编《佛制比丘六物图》卷一："初制意者，尼女报弱，故制祇支，披于左肩，以衬袈裟。又制覆肩，掩于右膊，用遮形丑。是故，尼众必持五衣……梵语僧祇支，此云上狭下广衣（此据律文，以翻全乖衣相。若准应法师音义，翻云掩腋衣，颇得其实）；覆肩华语，未详梵言……着用世多纷诤，今为明之。此方往古，并服祇支。至后魏时，始加右袖。两边缝合，谓之偏衫。截领开裾，犹存本相。故知偏衫左肩，即本祇支，右边即覆肩也。今人迷此，又于偏衫之上，复加覆肩。谓学律者，必须服着。但西土人多袒膊，恐生讥过，故须掩之。此方袄褶重重，仍加偏袖，又覆何为？"参见《大正藏》第45卷，第901b页。关于偏覆式大衣的出现及流行，参见：马世长，上引书，第254-259页。

[4] 参见《中国石窟·敦煌莫高窟》三，北京：文物出版社，1987年，图版14、27、93。

向，摆边较平缓（图 17）。2 个，潜溪寺，赵客师洞。

D 型：右袒式[1]，亦称偏袒右肩，略作偏袒，即披着法衣时袒露右肩，覆盖左肩，原为古代天竺表示尊敬之礼法，佛教沿用之。依据法衣披覆方式可分为二式。

图 17　潜溪寺主尊佛像

Di 式：佛结跏趺坐或善跏趺坐，内着僧祇支；上衣覆搭双肩后两衣缘自颈侧垂于腹前，有的于胸前束带打结，唯左衣缘多被大衣遮覆；大衣右角宽搭左肩，垂之背后，左侧边缘自颈外垂下，右侧边缘自右胁下绕出覆腹后衣尾上搭左臂或左肩，作“右袒式”披覆[2]。其中，结跏趺坐者，双腿间弧形衣纹多近横向，摆边呈倒三角形或半圆状垂覆座前或座上（图 18）；善跏趺坐（倚坐）者，大衣下摆垂覆脚面，双腿间衣纹呈水波状（图 19）。13 个，即宝塔洞[3]、惠简洞[4]、敬善寺、擂鼓台中洞[5]、摩崖三佛、破上洞、普上洞、清明寺、三佛洞、双窑北洞、双窑南洞[6]、万佛洞、赵上洞。

---

[1] 右袒式即佛典中的“偏袒右肩”。梵语词有不同表示，如 ekāṃsam uttarāsaṅgaṃ kṛtvā 或 ekāṃsenacīvarāṇi prāvṛtya（偏袒右肩），ekāṃśam uttarāsaṅgaṃ kṛtvā（偏袒一肩 / 偏袒右肩），ekāṃsāny uttarāsaṅgāni kṛtvā 或 ekāṃsacīvaraṃ prāvṛtya（偏覆左肩 / 偏袒右肩）。参见：荻原雲來，上引书，第 296a、476a 页。

据道世《法苑珠林》卷二十《致敬篇 · 仪式部》：“偏袒者，依律云：偏露右肩，或偏露一肩，或偏露一膊。所言袒者，谓肉袒也。示从依学，有执作之务。俗中袖狭右袂，便稳于事是也。今诸沙门但出一肩，仍有衫袄，非袒露法。如大庄严论云：‘沙门释子者，肩黑是也’。外道通黑，沙门露右，故有不同。律中但有三衣通肩被服，如见长老乃偏袒之。设以衣遮，名为偏袒，一何可笑也。故知肉袒肩露，乃是立敬之极。然行事之时，量前为袒。如在佛前及至师僧忏悔礼拜，并须依前右袒为恭。若至寺外街衢路行，则须以衣覆肩，不得露肉。西国湿热，共行不怪；此处寒地，人多讥笑。”参见道世《法苑珠林》，周叔迦、苏晋仁校注，北京：中华书局，2003 年，第 654-655 页。

[2] 敦煌莫高窟初唐时期的彩塑和壁画佛像大多采用这种搭衣方式，系受到当时两京造型艺术影响所致，只是敦煌佛像大衣之衣尾皆上搭左肩。参见《中国石窟 · 敦煌莫高窟》三，北京：文物出版社，1987 年，图版 8、16、18、27、42、73、126、143 等。

[3] 宝塔洞主尊双腿以下残毁。暂入此式。

[4] 惠简洞主像背屏，上部半圆形，下部方形。下半部两边似雕“六拏具”，上半两边饰垂带和花饰，顶部中央为摩尼宝珠，两侧各一飞天。参见工布查布《佛说造像量度经解》，载《大正藏》第 21 卷，第 941b-945b 页。

[5] 擂鼓台中洞主尊背屏，形同惠简洞主尊背屏。

[6] 双窑北洞主尊为结跏趺坐，而双窑南洞主尊则为善跏趺坐。

图 18　万佛洞主尊佛像

图 19　惠简洞主尊佛像

图 20　擂鼓台北洞主尊佛像

Dii 式：佛结跏趺坐，戴宝冠，佩项饰、臂钏；“以衣右角宽搭左肩，垂之背后，勿安肘上”[1]，即佛典中的“偏袒右肩 (ekāṃsena-cīvarāṇi prāvṛtya)”[2]，或大衣偏袒右肩 (ekāṃśikasaṃghāṭī/ekāṅsikaśaṅghāṭī)，或上衣偏袒右肩 (ekāṃśam-uttarāsaṅgaṃ kṛtvā)；左手平伸置于腹前腿上，右手抚膝作触地印 (图 20)。2 个，即擂鼓台北洞、擂鼓台南洞[3]。

E 型：通肩式，“以角搭肩，衣便绕颈，双手下出，一角前垂。阿育王像正当其式”[4]。通肩用以表示福田之相，于乞食、坐禅、诵经或经行时披着。佛

[1] 义净，上引书，第 98 页。

[2] “偏袒右肩”之制，在现存汉译《弥沙塞部和醯五分律》、《摩诃僧祇律》、《四分律》、《十诵律》、《根本说一切有部毗奈耶》、《根本说一切有部毗奈耶药事》、《根本说一切有部毗奈耶破僧事》、《根本说一切有部毗奈耶杂事》、《善见律毗婆沙》和道宣《四分律删繁补阙行事钞》等都有记载。参见《大正藏》第 22 卷，第 14b、228c、816a 页；第 23 卷，第 3a、801b 页；第 24 卷，第 3c、138a、261a、675b 页；第 40 卷，第 23b 页。至于图像，参见《中国石窟·敦煌莫高窟》三，北京：文物出版社，1987 年，图版 19、32、53、100、106 等。

[3] 擂鼓台南洞主尊是否为此洞原作，尚不能肯定。暂入此式。

[4] 义净，上引书，第 98 页。荷兰学者 Johanna E. van Lohuizen-de Leeuw 早年推测：“通肩”之观念可能源自秣菟罗 (Mathurā)，否则它是我们辨识出的秣菟罗艺术受到西北印度影响的最早征兆。现在一般认为佛教造像中大衣作“通肩式”披覆，是受犍陀罗佛像影响出现的。参见：1) Johanna E. van Lohuizen-de Leeuw, *The “Scythian” Period: An approach to the history, art, epigraphy and palaeography of north India from the 1st century BC to the 3rd century AD*. Leiden: E. J. Brill, 1949: 183; 2) R. C. Sharma, “Mathurā and Gandhāra: The Two Great Styles” , in: *Buddhism and Gandhāra Art*, ed R. C. Sharma, Simla: Indian Institute of Advanced Study et al, 2004: 66-72, esp. 68.

上衣隐现，大衣（复衣）披搭双肩、通体遮覆[1]，即律典规定的“通肩披衣”[2]、“通肩被服”[3]或“通肩覆”[4]。佛结跏趺坐者，大衣衣纹自颈下呈水波状垂下，双腿间衣纹斜向、呈倒八字形，下摆多呈三瓣形垂覆座前（图21、33）；善跏趺坐者，衣纹走向与前者相似，唯双腿间衣纹亦作水波状（图22）。11个，即八作司洞[5]、大卢舍那像龛[6]、二莲花南洞、奉南洞、高平郡王洞[7]、火上洞、火下洞[8]、火左洞、极南洞、龙华寺、鹰上洞。

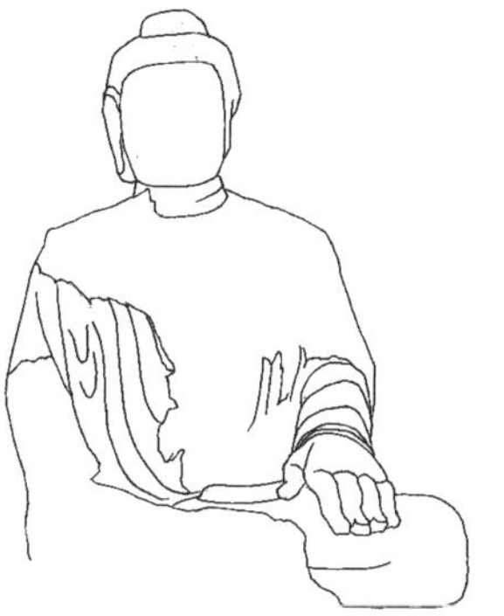
图21　八作司洞主尊佛像

图22　极南洞主尊佛像

(2) 头光

依据佛像头光的主体纹饰，可将唐代窟龛分作三型。

A型：椭圆形。头光由缠枝花卉构成，有的加饰莲花；有的于缠枝花卉中加雕小坐佛（图23）。2个，即宾阳南洞[9]、药方洞[10]。

B型：圆形。头光分内外二匝，内匝雕饰莲花，外匝为圆环带。有的在外匝周围饰火焰纹。依据莲瓣和外匝样式，下分三式。

图23　药方洞佛像头光

[1] 参见《中国石窟·敦煌莫高窟》三，北京：文物出版社，1987年，图版27、94等。

[2] “通肩披衣”之制，在汉译《四分律》、道宣《四分律删繁补阙行事钞》等有记载。参见《大正藏》第22卷，第836c页；第40卷，第108a页。

[3] “通肩被服”之称，参见：道世，上引书，第654页。

[4] “通肩覆”之称，在汉译《弥沙塞部和醯五分律》有记载。参见《大正藏》第22卷，第181b页。

[5] 八作司洞主尊残损较甚。暂入此式。

[6] 大卢舍那像龛主尊双腿以下残毁。暂入此式。

[7] 高平郡王洞主尊袈裟衣摆垂覆座上。暂入此式。

[8] 火下洞主尊双腿以下残毁。暂入此式。

[9] 宾阳南洞的主尊头光系绘制而成。

[10] 药方洞缠枝花卉中雕造七尊小坐佛。

Bi 式：莲瓣为单方圆尖莲瓣，外匝素面（图 24），有的外匝雕饰七身小坐佛（参见图 18）。7 个，即宾阳北洞、敬善寺[1]、潜溪寺[2]、双窑北洞[3]、双窑南洞[4]、万佛洞[5]、赵客师洞[6]。

Bii 式：莲瓣作如意头形，外匝雕饰七身小坐佛（图 25）。9 个，即八作司洞、大卢舍那像龛[7]、二莲花南洞[8]、惠简洞、火左洞、擂鼓台北洞、擂鼓台中洞、龙华寺[9]、清明寺[10]。

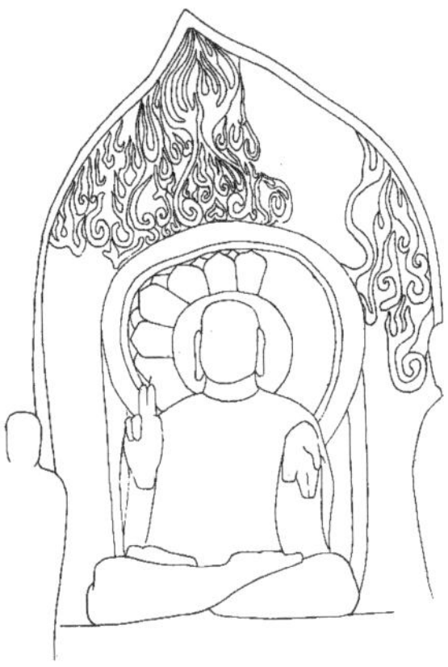

图 24　宾阳北洞佛像头光

图 25　大卢舍那像龛佛像头光

C 型：桃形（图 26）。4 个，即奉南洞[11]、净土堂[12]、鷪上洞、弥上洞[13]。

(3) 佛座

依据佛座结构和样式，可将唐代窟龛分作五型。

A 型：等腰梯形方座，座前雕饰双狮和一香炉（图 27）。2 个，即唐字洞、药方洞。

[1] 敬善寺佛像头光外匝雕七身小坐佛。

[2] 潜溪寺佛像头光外匝雕七身小坐佛。

[3] 双窑北洞主尊头光外缘饰火焰纹。暂入此式。

[4] 双窑南洞主尊头光外缘饰火焰纹。暂入此式。

[5] 万佛洞佛像头光外匝雕七身小坐佛。

[6] 赵客师洞主尊头光较大，内匝似雕单方圆莲瓣。暂入此式。

[7] 大卢舍那像龛主尊头光内匝雕如意头莲瓣；外匝雕缠枝花卉和小坐佛，小坐佛每铺皆作一佛二菩萨；再外为火焰纹。暂入此式。

[8] 二莲花南洞主尊头光较小，似内雕如意头莲瓣，外刻小坐佛。暂入此式。

[9] 龙华寺主尊头光内匝雕如意头莲瓣，外匝刻七身小坐佛和缠枝花卉。暂入此式。

[10] 清明寺主尊头光莲瓣作如意头形，外匝素面。暂入此式。

[11] 奉南洞主尊佛像头光边缘雕三小坐佛，与身光四小坐佛一道合成七佛。

[12] 净土堂主尊头光内匝雕单方圆尖莲瓣。

[13] 弥上洞主尊佛像头光内为二同心圆。

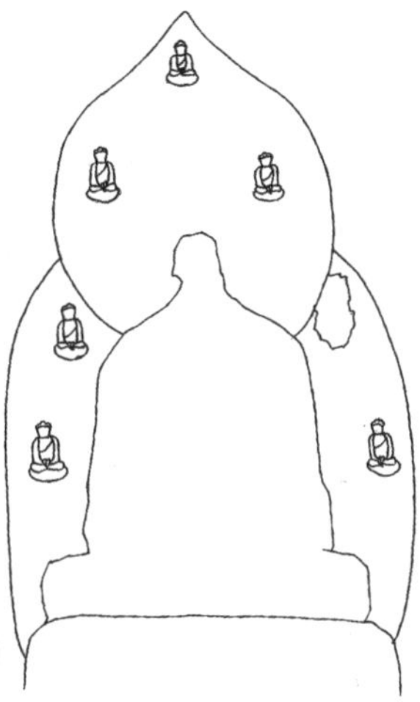

图26　奉南洞佛座头光

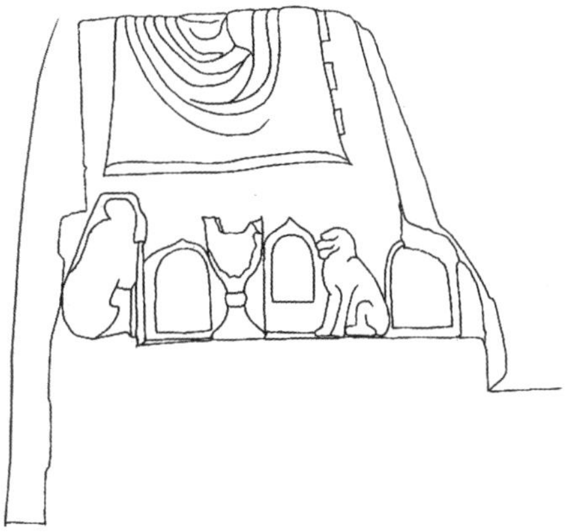

图27　唐字洞佛座

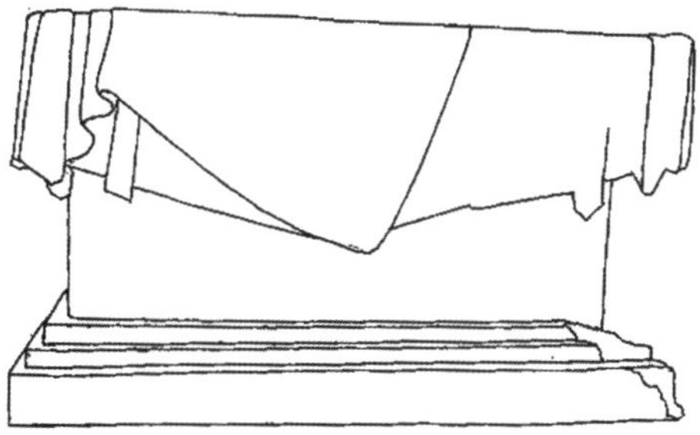

图28　潜溪寺佛座

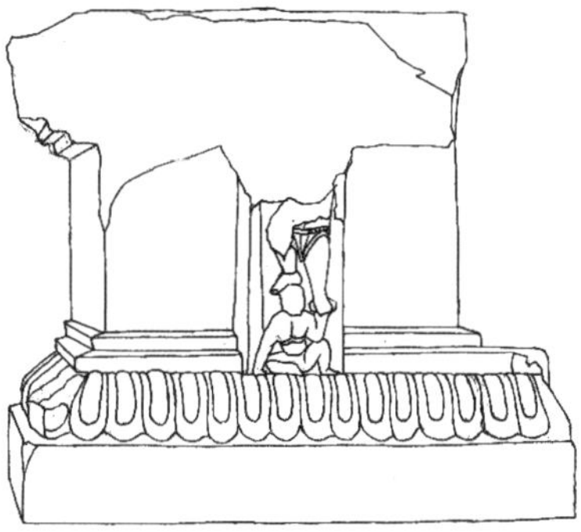

图29　二莲花北洞佛座

B型：方形须弥座。依据装饰下分二式。

Bi式：束腰下叠涩三层，有的在束腰部位雕刻力士，有的座前饰双狮（图28）。3个，即宾阳北洞[1]、宾阳南洞[2]、潜溪寺。

Bii式：束腰部位雕刻神王，束腰下部依次为二层叠涩、双圆翘角合莲（覆莲）、基座（图29）。7个，即八作司洞[3]、二莲花北洞、火下洞、火左洞、极南洞[4]、擂鼓台北洞[5]、擂鼓台南洞。

[1] 宾阳北洞佛座束腰部位刻出壸门，每一壸门内雕一力士。

[2] 宾阳南洞主尊佛座前雕饰双狮。

[3] 八作司洞主尊佛座下另有一须弥基座，其束腰部分有四力士托扛。暂入此式。

[4] 极南洞主尊佛座为束腰方形须弥座，束腰下部依次为二层叠涩、双圆翘角合莲、基座。唯合莲中央伸出二莲踏。暂入此式。

[5] 擂鼓台北洞主尊佛座束腰部位无神王。暂入此式。

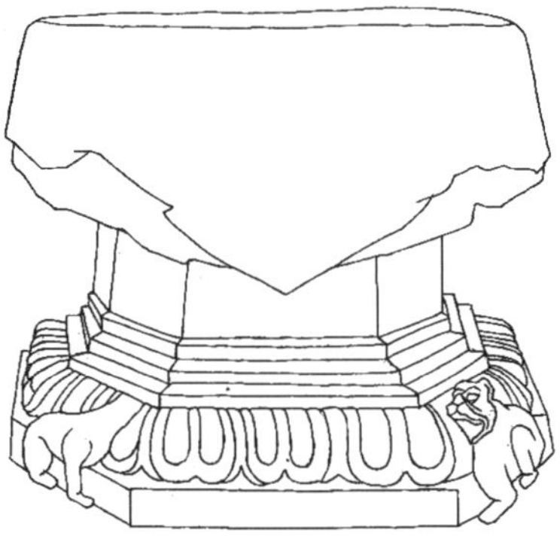

图 30　敬善寺佛座

图 31　万佛洞佛座

C 型：八角须弥座，三面隐现。依据细部和装饰下分三式。

Ci 式：束腰下部依次为二或三层叠涩、双圆合莲、基座。两侧抹角处各雕一形体较小的狮子（图 30)。3 个，即敬善寺、双窑北洞、赵客师洞[1]。

Cii 式：上半部为双层单圆翘角仰莲，束腰部位雕出力士，下部依次为三层叠涩、如意头莲瓣、基座(图31)。5个，即宝塔洞[2]、大卢舍那像龛、龙华寺[3]、清明寺[4]、万佛洞。

Ciii 式：束腰下部依次为一或二层叠涩、双圆翘角合莲、基座（图 32)。8 个，即二莲花南洞、奉南洞、火上洞[5]、鸗上洞、弥上洞、破上洞[6]、普上洞[7]、赵上洞。

D 型：高方座或高须弥座，前有踏座，整体平面作凸字形（参见图 19)。5 个，即惠简洞、擂鼓台中洞、摩崖三佛[8]、三佛洞、双窑南洞。

E 型：半圆形莲座，为二层单圆翘角仰莲（图 33)。1 个，即高平郡王洞。

2. 弟子像

弟子像位于主尊两侧，依据大卢舍那像龛等原始题铭，通常表现迦叶 (Mahākāśyapa)

---

[1] 赵客师洞主尊佛座为八角形，唯因衣摆覆盖，束腰情况不清。暂入此式。

[2] 宝塔洞主尊佛座的束腰部位无力士像。暂入此式。

[3] 龙华寺佛座为束腰八角须弥座，三面隐现。束腰部位雕刻力士，束腰下部依次为三层叠涩、双圆翘角莲瓣、基座。暂入此式。

[4] 清明寺主尊佛座束腰下部依次为叠涩、如意头莲瓣、基座。暂入此式。

[5] 火上洞主尊佛座近束腰圆莲座。暂入此式。

[6] 破上洞主尊佛座为束腰圆莲座，下有叠涩二层，但未雕出莲瓣。暂入此式。

[7] 普上洞主尊为二佛并坐，二佛座同型。

[8] 摩崖三佛中央主尊佛座为高方座，座前有二踏座，整体近似凸字形。暂入此式。

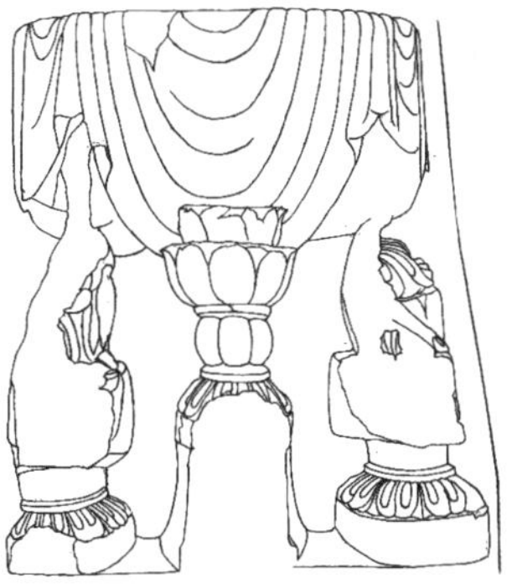

图 32　奉南洞佛座

图 33　高平郡王洞佛座

和阿难(Ānanda)[1]。为客观排比弟子类型,将分左侧弟子、右侧弟子、头光和像座四项分别做考古类型学分析。

(1) 左侧弟子[2]

弟子法服基本同佛像[3]。依据弟子法服“搭衣”方式及姿态,可将唐代窟龛分作三型。

A 型:弟子内着掩腋衣,上衣覆搭双肩后两衣缘自颈侧垂于腹前;大衣(复衣)作“右袒式”披覆[4],外观呈筒状;内衣(下衣)下摆长于大衣;身体直立,双手合十于胸前(图 34)。2 个,即宾阳南洞、药方洞。

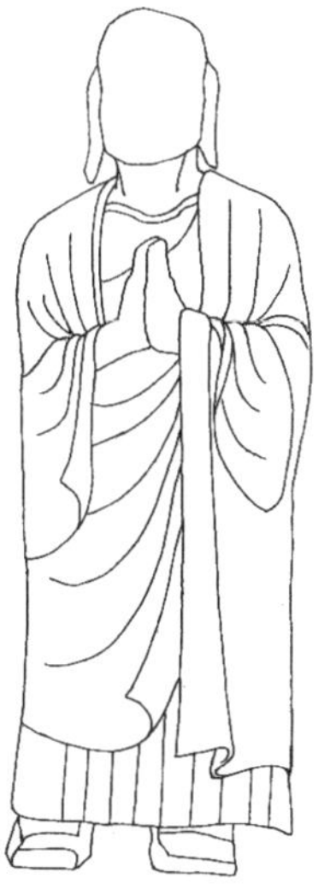

图 34　宾阳南洞左侧弟子

B 型:弟子内着“交领衫”;上衣覆搭双肩后两衣缘自颈侧垂至腹前,唯左衣缘多被大衣遮覆;大衣右角宽搭左肩,垂之背后,左侧边缘自颈外垂下,右

[1] 参见刘景龙、李玉昆主编《龙门石窟碑刻题记汇录》,北京:中国大百科全书出版社,1998 年,第 379-381、549 页。

[2] 本文中的左侧弟子,系指佛像左侧的弟子,右侧弟子系指佛像右侧的弟子。下文中的菩萨、神王和金刚力士等像的左、右侧含义相同,不赘。

[3] 玄奘在《大唐西域记》卷二“印度总述”条中明确记载:“沙门法服,唯有三衣及僧却崎(掩腋),泥缚些[桑个反]那(裙)”。参见:玄奘,上引书,第 176 页。又,《酉阳杂俎》续集之六《寺塔记》下“招国坊崇济寺”条,有善继所作《辞宣律和尚袈裟绝句》:“共覆三衣中夜寒,披时不镇尼师坛。无因盖有龙宫地,畦里尘飞业相残。”这说明“三衣”迄唐初还是出家僧众的基本法服。参见:段成式撰《酉阳杂俎》,方南生点校,北京:中华书局,1981 年,第 260 页。不过,现存石窟雕塑和壁画中似乎很难辨识出弟子披覆五衣。

[4] 参见《中国石窟·敦煌莫高窟》三,北京:文物出版社,1987 年,图版 49、93、113、128、147 等。

侧边缘自右胁下绕出覆腹后衣尾上搭左臂，作 “右袒式” 披覆[1]；个别 “通肩披衣”；内衣下摆长于大衣，垂覆脚面。依体态、手势及大衣外观，下分三式。

Bi 式：身体比例适中、直立，双手合十于胸前，大衣外观呈筒状（图 35）。2 个，即宾阳北洞、潜溪寺。

Bii 式：身体比例适中、直立，双手多于胸前合十，个别双手于胸前托持一物；大衣下半部渐窄（图 36）。7 个，即大卢舍那像龛[2]、敬善寺、破上洞[3]、双窑北洞、双窑南洞、赵客师洞、赵上洞。

Biii 式：多上身短、下身长，身体直立，双手合十于胸前或托持珠形物或作叉手状；内衣下摆外张（图 37、38）。12 个，即宝塔洞、二莲花北洞、二莲花南洞[4]、奉南洞、高平郡王洞、火上洞、极南洞、鷰上洞、弥上洞、普上洞、三佛洞、万佛洞。

C 型：弟子上衣作 “交领式”[5]，唯右臂前带状物不明；大衣作 “右袒式” 披覆，

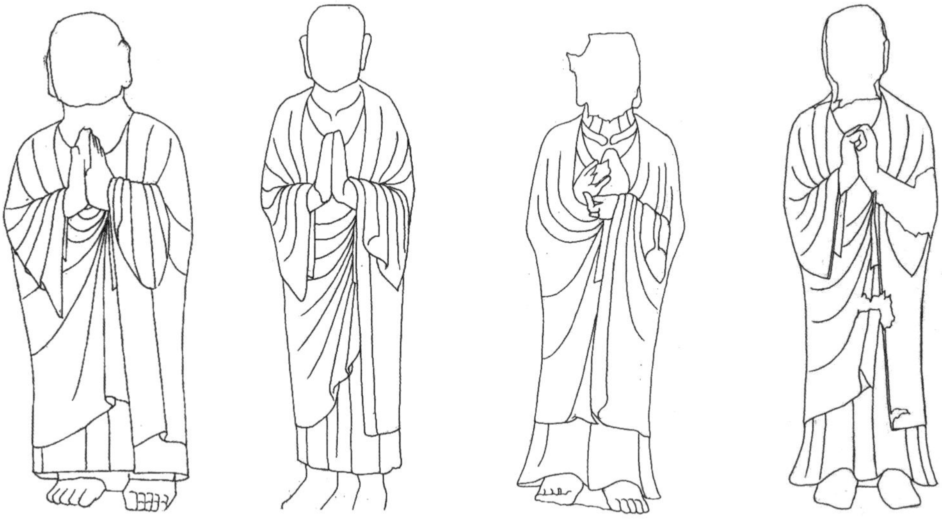

图 35　潜溪寺左侧弟子　　图 36　敬善寺左侧弟子　　图 37　二莲化南洞左侧弟子　　图 38　极南洞左侧弟子

[1] 参见：上引书，图版 96、154、169 等。

[2] 大卢舍那像龛左胁侍弟子残损较甚。暂入此式。

[3] 破上洞左侧弟子上半身残毁。暂入此式。

[4] 二莲花南洞左侧弟子大衣覆搭双肩后，右衣缘包遮右臂后上搭左肘垂下，样式较特别，似介于 “通肩” 与 “垂领” 样式之间，暂入此式。

[5] 这种交领式上衣，疑为唐初高僧道世所记之 “衫袄”。据前引《法苑珠林》卷二十《致敬篇 · 仪式部》：“今诸沙门但出一肩，仍有衫袄，非袒露法。” 尽管这种法服与律相悖，即大衣作右袒式，肩有衫袄，但图像表明 “当时已有沙门着衣不合规制”，且忠实地反映在彼时佛教造型艺术之中。参见：1) 道世，上引书，第 654-655 页；2) 马世长，上引书，第 253-254 页。

即由左肩覆背披至右胁下后上搭左小臂，左手于腹前勾持衣尾；内衣下摆长出大衣，且外张。上身短、下身长，胯部略扭（图 39）。1 个，即八作司洞。

(2) 右侧弟子

依据弟子“搭衣”方式及姿态并参照左侧弟子样式，可将唐代窟龛分作三型。

A 型：同左侧弟子 A 型，唯双手于胸前托持宝珠或合十（图 40）。2 个，即宾阳南洞、药方洞。

B 型：法服同左侧弟子 B 型，下分三式。

Bi 式：基本同左侧 Bi 式弟子，唯双手于胸前托持一宝珠，大衣下部略窄（图 41）。2 个，即宾阳北洞、潜溪寺。

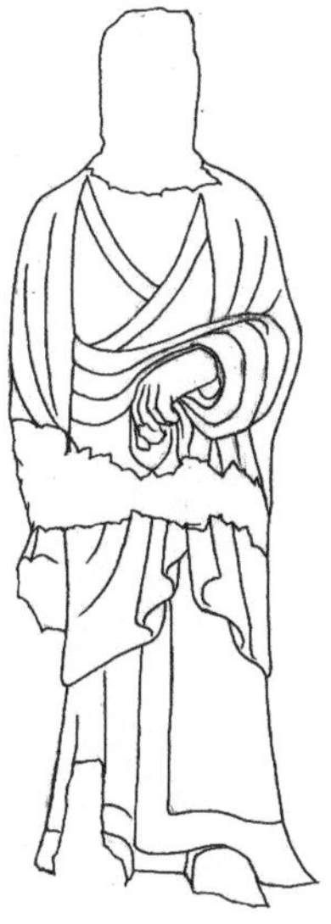

图 39　八作司洞左侧弟子

图 40　宾阳南洞右侧弟子

图 41　宾阳北洞右侧弟子

Bii 式：基本同左侧 Bii 式弟子，唯双手多于胸前托持宝珠，个别双手合十（图 42）。6 个，即惠简洞、敬善寺、破上洞、双窑北洞、双窑南洞、赵客师洞。

Biii 式：基本同左侧 Biii 式弟子，唯身体比例适中、胯部多略扭；内衣下摆略外张（图 43）。3 个，即大卢舍那像龛[1]、万佛洞、赵上洞[2]。

[1] 大卢舍那像龛右胁侍弟子双手已残损，但不作合十状。暂入此式。

[2] 赵上洞右侧弟子像残损较甚。暂入此式。

C型：基本同左侧弟子C型[1]，唯少数大衣作钩钮式，内衣下摆外张；双手交搭于腹前，多右手压左手（图44、45）。12个，即八作司洞[2]、宝塔洞[3]、二莲花北洞[4]、二莲花南洞、奉南洞[5]、高平郡王洞、火上洞、极南洞、鷰上洞、弥上洞[6]、普上洞[7]、三佛洞。

图42　惠简洞右侧弟子

图43　万佛洞右侧弟子

图44　二莲花南洞右侧弟子

图45　极南洞右侧弟子

(3) 头光

依据弟子头光样式，可将唐代窟龛分作二型。

A型：头光圆形，素面（参见图43）。8个，即宾阳北洞、敬善寺、弥上洞、双窑北洞、双窑南洞、万佛洞、赵客师洞[8]、赵上洞。

B型：头光作双同心圆，按装饰可分二式。

Bi式：素面（图46）。4个，即大卢舍那像龛、惠简洞、龙华寺、鷰上洞。

Bii式：凸缘，外缘为火焰纹（图47）。2个，即八作司洞、奉南洞。

---

[1] 敦煌莫高窟初、盛唐洞窟正壁主尊右侧的弟子像，多着这种法服，系受到当时两京佛教造型艺术影响所致。参见《中国石窟·敦煌莫高窟》三，北京：文物出版社，1987年，图版16、116、130、143、147等。

[2] 八作司洞右胁侍弟子双手似交搭于腹前，但已残损。暂入此式。

[3] 宝塔洞右胁侍弟子头及身体大部分残损，似双手交搭于腹前。暂入此式。

[4] 二莲花北洞右胁侍弟子上衣似作交领式、外着钩纽式大衣。暂入此式。

[5] 奉南洞右胁侍弟子上衣作交领式、外着钩钮式大衣。暂入此式。

[6] 弥上洞右侧弟子外着钩纽式大衣。

[7] 普上洞右侧弟子外着钩纽式大衣。

[8] 赵客师洞弟子头光与主尊舟形头光同用。暂入此式。

图 46　大卢舍那像龛弟子头光

图 47　奉南洞弟子头光

(4) 像座

依据弟子像座结构可将唐代窟龛分作四型。

A 型：简朴圆座。有的中央雕莲蓬，周围作合莲瓣（图 48）。2 个，即宾阳南洞[1]、药方洞。

B 型：束腰圆莲座。依据细部装饰及莲瓣样式下分三式。

Bi 式：上半部为单方圆仰莲，下半为双圆合莲（图49）。3个，即宾阳北洞、潜溪寺、赵客师洞[2]。

Bii 式：上半部为单圆翘角仰莲，下半部为双圆翘角合莲（图 50）。4 个，即敬善寺、双窑北洞、双窑南洞[3]、赵上洞。

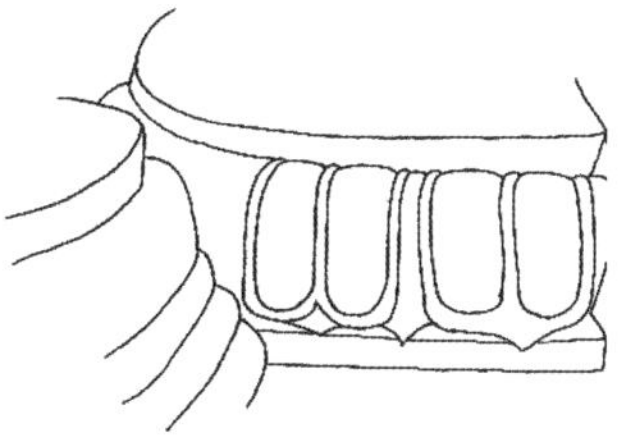

图 48　药方洞弟子像座

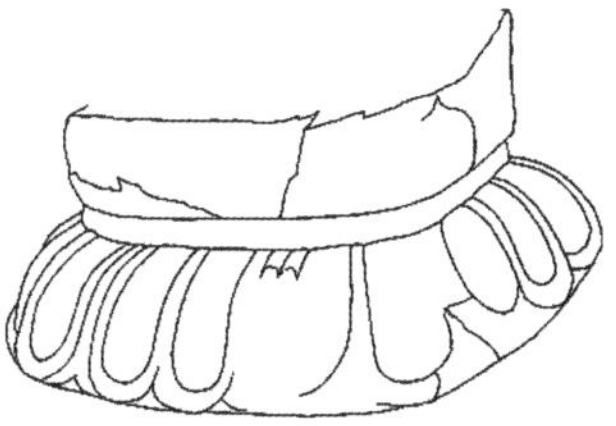

图 49　宾阳北洞弟子像座

Biii 式：基本同 Bii 式，唯束腰上下各一凸缘或叠涩（图 51、52）。12 个，即宝塔洞、二莲花北洞、二莲花南洞、奉南洞、惠简洞[4]、火上洞、极南洞、鸝上洞、破上洞[5]、普上洞、三佛洞、万佛洞[6]。

[1] 宾阳南洞弟子像具简朴圆座，无纹饰。暂入此式。

[2] 赵客师洞弟子像为高圆座，细部未雕。暂入此式。

[3] 双窑南洞弟子像座上半为单圆翘角仰莲，下半为单圆翘角合莲。暂入此式。

[4] 惠简洞仅存右侧弟子，其像座上半部不见莲瓣。暂入此式。

[5] 破上洞弟子像座莲瓣未雕出。暂入此式。

[6] 万佛洞弟子莲座，束腰上下各一凸缘；上半为单圆翘角仰莲，下半为如意头合莲。暂入此式。

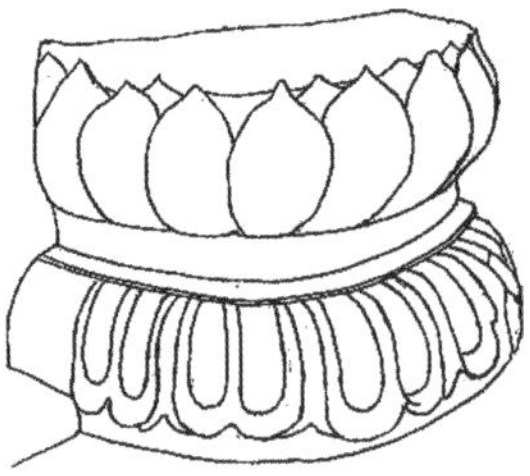

图 50　敬善寺弟子像座

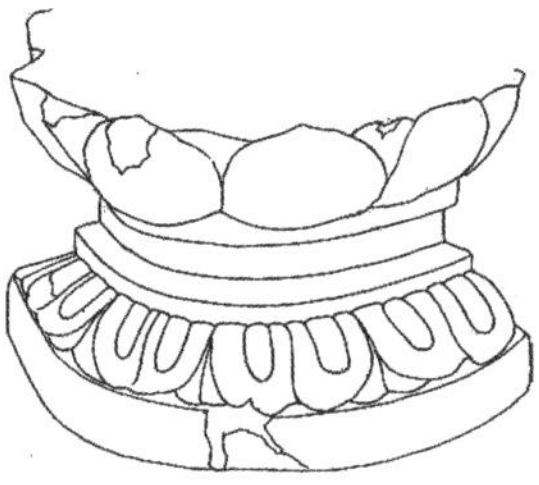

图 51　二莲花北洞弟子像座

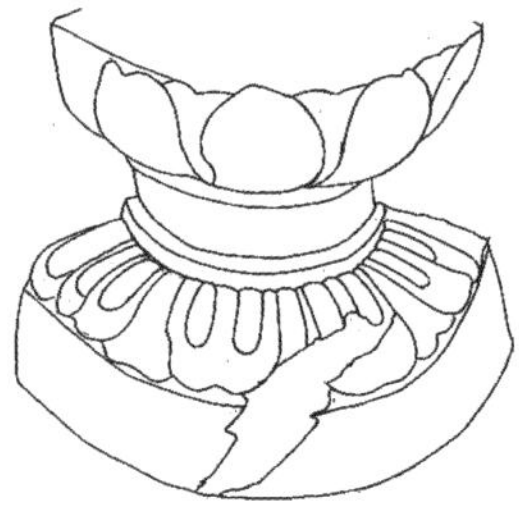

图 52　奉南洞弟子像座

C 型：三面隐现之束腰八角莲座或圆莲座。束腰凸显的五面或圆莲座的凸起部位皆刻尖楣圆拱形壸门，束腰上下皆具叠涩，上半部为仰、覆翘角莲瓣，下半部为双圆翘角合莲（图 53）。4 个，即八作司洞、大卢舍那像龛、龙华寺[1]、弥上洞[2]。

D 型：单圆翘角仰莲座，下为粗莲茎（图 54）。1 个，即高平郡王洞。

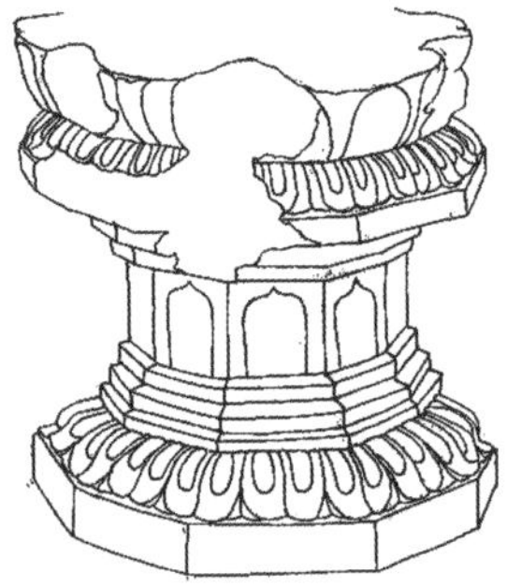

图 53　八作司洞弟子像座

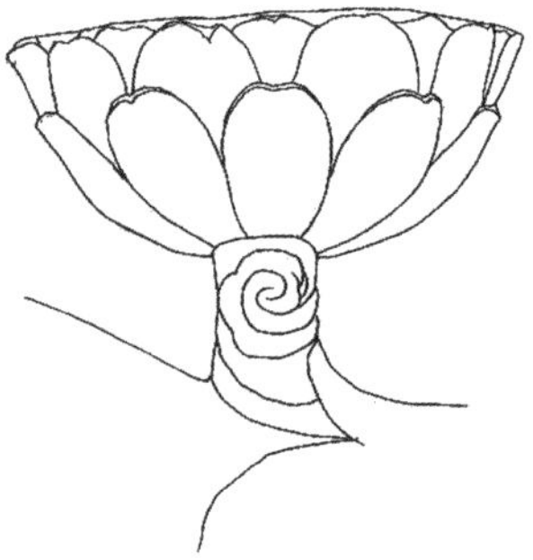

图 54　高平郡王洞弟子像座

3. 菩萨像

菩萨位于主尊两侧或主尊两侧弟子的外侧，是石窟造像组合中的重要内容。菩萨梵语作 bodhisattva，引申为“有觉悟为其本性之人”。“故可以说，菩萨当为尚未成佛的佛”[3]。菩萨所着服饰特征显著，如秣菟罗和犍陀罗出土的菩萨像，似源自印度王公大臣，主要有掩腋衣、裙及宝冠、项饰、披巾、璎珞等，因为印度“国王、大臣，服玩

[1] 龙华寺弟子像具束腰圆莲座。束腰部分刻出三个尖楣圆拱形壸门，束腰上下皆有二层叠涩，上半为单圆翘角仰莲，下半为双圆翘角合莲。暂入此式。

[2] 弥上洞弟子像座上半似为单圆翘角仰莲。暂入此式。

[3] 汤用彤《佛与菩萨》，载《汤用彤学术论文集》，北京：中华书局，1983 年，第 316-318 页。又，金克木认为：“‘佛’字的本意是觉悟了的人。‘菩萨’的字义是有觉悟的人。‘阿罗汉（罗汉）’的字义是应当受尊敬的人。”金克木《再阅〈楞伽〉》，见：金克木《梵佛探》(413-421 页)，石家庄：河北教育出版社，1996 年，第 414 页。

良异。花鬘宝冠,以为首饰；环钏璎珞,而作身佩”[1]。其中,“掩腋衣”和“裙”,乃义净《南海寄归内法传》卷二“衣食所须・十三资具”中第七、五种,同卷“尼衣丧制”中第四、五种[2]。中土出现的菩萨像造型似受其影响,只是愈晚愈呈现女性化。为了客观排比菩萨类型,将分左侧菩萨、右侧菩萨[3]、头光和像座四项做考古类型学分析。

(1) 左侧菩萨

依据菩萨服饰及体态,可将唐代窟龛分作三型。

A 型：上身着掩腋 (saṃkakṣikā, 僧脚崎,即络腋衣)[4],下身系裙 (nivāsana,泥婆娑,即裹衣)[5],体态多僵直；束裙大带下垂如绅,上多打蝴蝶结。披巾自肩搭下后于腹下交叉,或横于腹下膝前两道,或径直下垂至脚侧；璎珞粗大且多压覆披巾之上。依据体态及掩腋束扎情况下分三式。

Ai 式：身体僵直,无扭动之感,胸前系带打结或无带 (图 55)。 2 个,即宾阳南洞、药方洞。

---

[1] 玄奘《大唐西域记》卷二“印度总述”条,季羡林等校注,北京：中华书局,1985 年,第 177 页。

[2] 义净,上引书,第 6、103-104 页。

[3] 主尊两侧的菩萨像,在造型上有时出现差异,故分作左侧菩萨和右侧菩萨进行类型分析。

[4] 玄奘《大唐西域记》卷二“印度总述”条：“僧却崎,唐言掩腋,旧曰僧祇支,讹也。覆左肩,掩两腋,左开右合,长裁过腰。”参见：玄奘,上引书,第 176 页。

义净在《南海寄归内法传》卷二“尼衣丧制”条记载：“准捡梵本,无覆肩衣名,即是僧脚崎衣。此乃祇支之本号。”“其僧脚崎衣,即是覆髆；更加一肘,始合本仪。其披着法,应出右肩,交搭左髆。房中恒着,唯此与裙。出外礼尊,任加余服。”义净,上引书,第 105、100 页。

据玄应《一切经音义》卷四《观佛三昧海经音义》：“竭支,或作僧祇支者,皆讹也。应言僧迦鵄,此译云覆腋。若着瞿修罗,则不着僧迦鵄。瞿修罗者,此云图也,象其衣形而立名也”；同书卷十四《四分律音义》：“祇袯,《字苑》巨儿[之移反]。法服也。或作竭支,或言僧迦支,又作僧迦鵄,梵言讹转也。正言僧脚崎,此云覆腋衣也。或言瞿修罗,此云图也。像其衣形立二名也。此二衣西国亦着,但非净耳”；同书卷十六《大比丘三千威仪音义》,“僧迦,正言僧脚差。僧,此云掩覆。脚差,此云腋。名掩腋衣。律文作僧迦支,或作祇支,或作竭支,皆讹也”。玄应《一切经音义》,上引书,第 91、309、350 页。

又,慧琳《一切经音义》卷四十一《大乘理趣六波罗蜜多经音义》：“络掖衣,上郎各反,次音亦。正合从肉作腋,又音征石反。络腋衣者,《一切有部律》中名僧脚崎,唐云掩腋衣。本制此衣,恐污汙三衣。先以此衣掩右腋交络于左肩上,然后披着三衣。《四分律》中错用为覆髆者,误行之久矣,不可改也。”见《大正藏》第 54 卷,第 581c 页。

参见荻原雲來《漢訳対照梵和大辭典》,東京：鈴木学術財团,1974 年,第 1380 页。

[5]《大唐西域记》卷二“印度总述”条,“泥缚些那,唐言裙,旧曰涅槃僧,讹也。既无带襻,其将服也,集衣为襵,束带以绦。襵则诸部各异,色乃黄赤不同”。玄奘,上引书,第 176 页。

据玄应《一切经音义》卷十六《大比丘三千威仪音义》：“尼卫,此译云裹衣也。”玄应,上引书,第 350 页。

另据怀海《百丈清规证义记》卷七：“泥缚些罗,即禅裙,俗呼金刚裤,坐禅衲子尤为利用。”怀海集编《百丈丛林清规》,仪润证义,见《卍新纂大日本續藏經》No. 1244,第 63 卷,第 480c 页。

参见：荻原雲來,上引书,第 697 页。

Aii 式：身体基本直立，微扭动，掩腋无带（图 56）。2 个，即宾阳北洞、唐字洞[1]。

Aiii 式：身体略扭动，腹部略鼓，掩腋于胸前扣带（图 57）。2 个，惠简洞、潜溪寺。

B 型：上身着掩腋，下身系裙，体态多扭动，多配繁复项饰。披巾自肩搭下后横于腹下两道，或径直下垂至脚侧；璎珞交叉于腹前。依据体态、掩腋及裙带样式下分四式。

Bi 式：身体略扭动，腹部较鼓；掩腋简朴无饰；束裙大带下垂如绅，上打蝴蝶结（图 58）。5 个，即敬善寺[2]、清明寺、双窑北洞[3]、双窑南洞、赵客师洞[4]。

图 55　宾阳南洞左侧菩萨

图 56　宾阳北洞左侧菩萨

图 57　惠简洞左侧菩萨

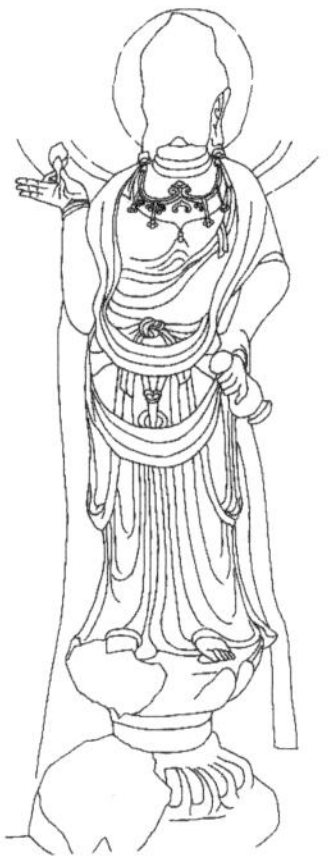
图 58　清明寺左侧菩萨

Bii 式：身体扭动略呈 S 形，掩腋似作带状且多简朴无饰，如绅大带多不见（图 59）。7 个，即八作司洞[5]、大卢舍那像龛、二莲花南洞、龙华寺[6]、破上洞、普上洞、万佛洞。

Biii 式：身体扭动呈 S 形、鼓腹、细腰；掩腋于胸前搭垂一角，似作带状；如绅大带不见（图 60）。5 个，即高平郡王洞、极南洞、擂鼓台北

[1] 唐字洞左侧菩萨雕凿粗糙，无下垂绅带。暂入此式。
[2] 敬善寺前庭和主室各有二菩萨。现以主室菩萨为例作类型分析。
[3] 双窑北洞共有四身菩萨，现以主尊两侧胁侍菩萨为例作类型分析。
[4] 赵客师洞主尊左侧菩萨上身掩腋与一般披法不同，系覆右肩。
[5] 八作司洞左胁侍菩萨双腿间有一如绅大带。暂入此式。
[6] 龙华寺左胁侍菩萨双腿间有一如绅大带。暂入此式。

洞[1]、擂鼓台中洞、鷰上洞。

Biv 式：上身短、下身长，身体扭动略呈 S 形，鼓腹、细腰，掩腋简朴无饰，如绅大带不见（图 61）。1 个，即奉南洞。

C 型：上身袒裸，下身着裙。上身短，下身长；挺胸、鼓腹、细腰，身体扭动呈 S 形。披巾自肩搭下后径直垂下，肩挂璎珞（图 62）。1 个，即火上洞。

图 59　大卢舍那像龛左侧菩萨

图 60　擂鼓台北洞左侧菩萨

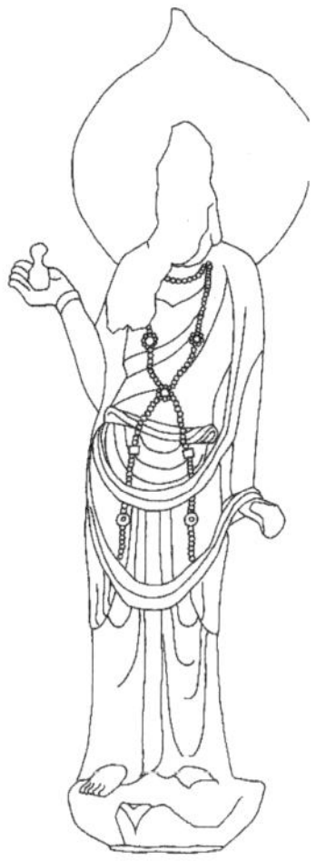

图 61　奉南洞左侧菩萨

图 62　火上洞左侧菩萨

(2) 右侧菩萨

依据服饰、体态并参照左侧菩萨样式，可将唐代窟龛分作三型。

A 型：基本同左侧 A 型菩萨，下分三式。

Ai 式：基本同左侧 Ai 式菩萨，唯胸前无带（图 63）。2 个，即宾阳北洞、宾阳南洞。

Aii 式：同左侧 Aii 式菩萨（图 64）。2 个，唐字洞[2]、药方洞[3]。

Aiii 式：基本同左侧 Aiii 式菩萨，唯掩腋于胸前扣带或无带（图 65）。3 个，敬善寺[4]、潜溪寺、双窑北洞。

B 型：同左侧菩萨 B 型，下分四式。

Bi 式：同左侧 Bi 式菩萨（图 66）。2 个，即惠简洞、清明寺。

---

[1] 此系擂鼓台北洞前壁门道左侧菩萨像。

[2] 唐字洞右菩萨雕造粗糙，无下垂绅带。暂入此式。

[3] 药方洞菩萨掩腋披覆右肩，与常见样式有别。暂入此式。

[4] 如前所述，敬善寺前庭和主室各有二菩萨。现以主室菩萨为例作类型分析。

图 63　宾阳南洞右侧菩萨

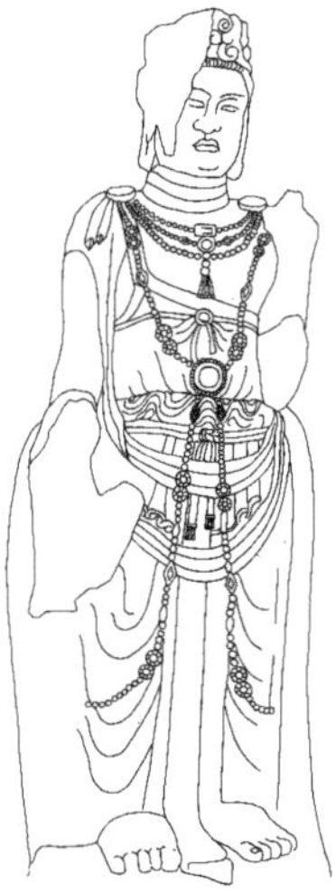

图 64　药方洞右侧菩萨

图 65　敬善寺右侧菩萨

图 66　惠简洞右侧菩萨

Bii 式：同左侧 Bii 式菩萨（图 67）。8 个，即八作司洞[1]、大卢舍那像龛、二莲花南洞、龙华寺、破上洞[2]、普上洞、万佛洞、赵上洞。

Biii 式：同左侧 Biii 式菩萨（图 68）。4 个，即宝塔洞、擂鼓台北洞[3]、擂鼓台中洞、鷰上洞。

Biv 式：同左侧 Biv 式菩萨（图 69）。1 个，即奉南洞[4]。

C 型：基本同左侧 C 型菩萨，唯披巾自肩搭下后径直垂下或横于腹前两道（图 70）。3 个，即高平郡王洞、火上洞、极南洞。

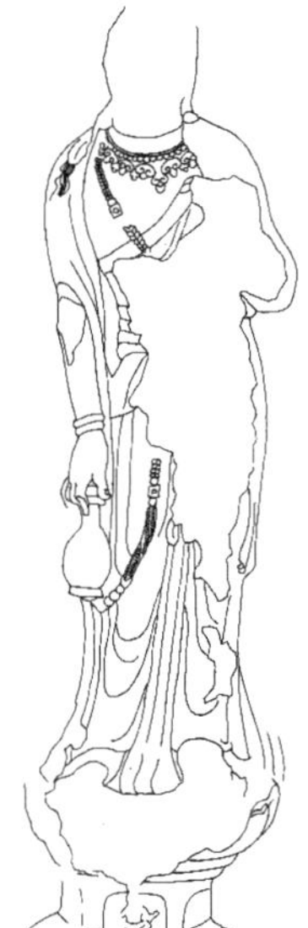

图 67　龙华寺右侧菩萨

(3) 头光

依据菩萨头光的主体纹饰，可将唐代窟龛分作二型。

A 型：圆形火焰状，整体似"桃形"，分为内外两匝，内匝通常雕莲花，外匝刻火焰纹。依据莲瓣样式等，下分三式。

Ai 式：单方圆尖莲瓣（图 71、参见图 66）。10 个，即宾阳北洞、宾阳南洞、

[1] 八作司洞右侧菩萨胸部残损，似着掩腋；膝下绅带清晰可见。暂入此式。

[2] 破上洞右侧菩萨像双腿间似有一如绅长带且打蝴蝶结。暂入此式。

[3] 此系擂鼓台北洞前壁门道右侧菩萨像，胸部略残损。暂入此式。

[4] 奉南洞主尊右侧菩萨，掩腋覆右肩，与一般披法不同。暂入此式。

图 68　擂鼓台北洞右侧菩萨

图 69　奉南洞右侧菩萨

图 70　极南洞右侧菩萨

惠简洞、敬善寺、潜溪寺、清明寺、双窑北洞[1]、双窑南洞、唐字洞、药方洞。

Aii 式：单方圆翘角莲瓣，个别为如意头莲瓣，莲瓣外缘多雕小坐佛七身，再外为火焰纹（图 72、73）。7 个，即八作司洞、大卢舍那像龛[2]、净土堂[3]、擂鼓台中洞、龙华寺、万佛洞、赵上洞[4]。

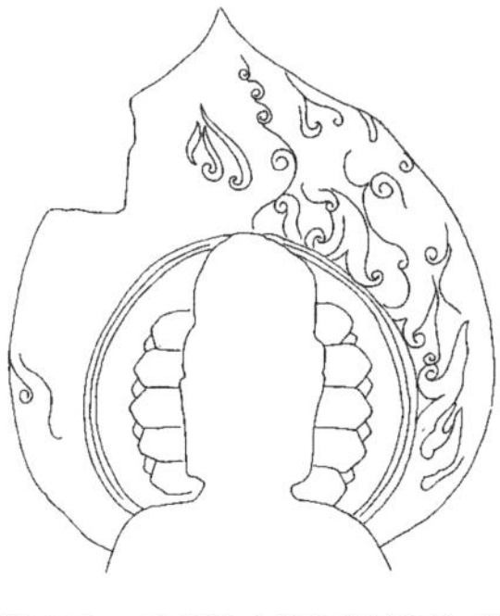
图 71　宾阳南洞菩萨头光

图 72　万佛洞菩萨头光

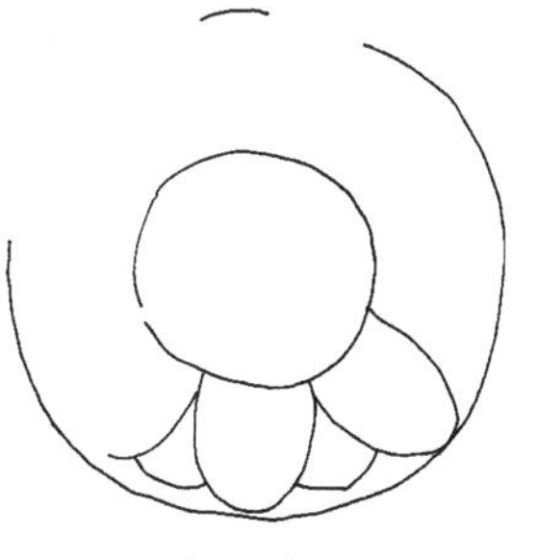
图 73　净土堂菩萨头光

[1] 双窑北洞主室内共四身菩萨。这里仅选择靠近主尊的两身菩萨作类型分析。

[2] 大卢舍那像龛菩萨头光自内而外依次为莲蓬、如意头莲瓣、山花、火焰纹。暂入此式。

[3] 净土堂遗存的菩萨圆形头光外缘似无火焰纹。暂入此式。

[4] 赵上洞胁侍菩萨头光内为单方圆翘角莲瓣，外缘饰火焰纹，无小坐佛。暂入此式。

Aiii 式：内匝素面，外匝雕火焰纹（图 74）。2 个，即二莲花南洞、火下洞。

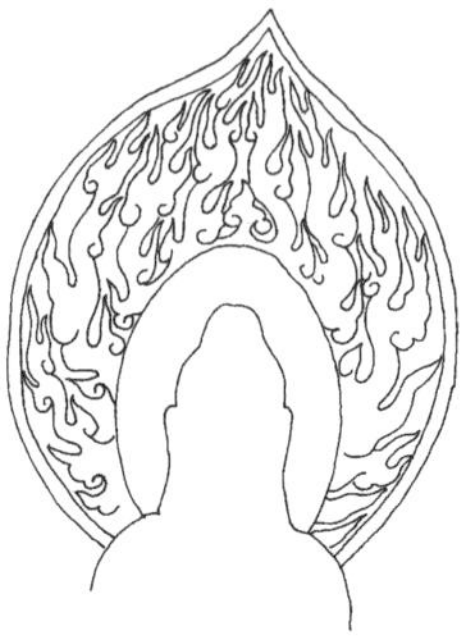

图 74　二莲花南洞菩萨头光

B 型：桃形，素面（参见图 61）。3 个，即奉南洞、弥上洞、鷰上洞。

(4) 像座

依据菩萨像座结构，可将唐代窟龛分作四型。

A 型：圆莲座。中央为莲蓬，周围作合莲瓣（参见图 63）。3 个，即宾阳南洞、唐字洞[1]、药方洞。

B 型：束腰圆莲座。依据细部装饰和莲瓣样式，下分三式。

Bi 式：上半为单方圆仰莲，下半为双圆合莲（图 75）。3 个，即宾阳北洞、潜溪寺、赵客师洞[2]。

Bii 式：上半为单圆翘角仰莲，下半为双圆翘角合莲（图 76）。3 个，即敬善寺、双窑北洞[3]、双窑南洞。

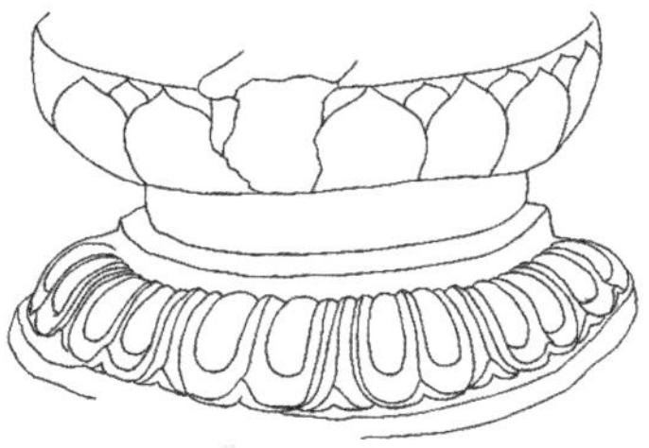

图 75　潜溪寺菩萨像座

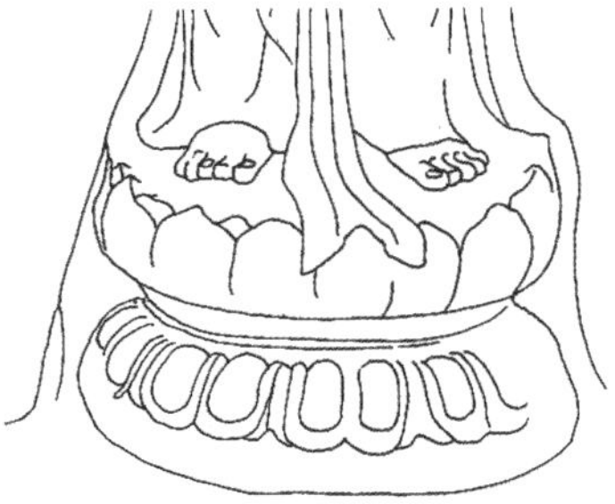

图 76　敬善寺菩萨像座

Biii 式：基本同 Bii 式，唯束腰上下各一凸缘，有的下部二凸缘（图 77、参见图 70）。13 个，即二莲花北洞[4]、二莲花南洞、奉南洞、惠简洞[5]、火上洞、极南洞、鷰上洞、破上洞[6]、普上洞、清明寺、三佛洞、万佛洞[7]、赵上洞。

---

[1] 唐字洞菩萨像座为半圆莲花状，细部未雕。暂入此式。

[2] 赵客师洞菩萨像座为高圆座，细部未雕。暂入此式。

[3] 双窑北洞共雕菩萨像四身，这里仅选择靠近主尊的两身作类型分析。其中，左侧菩萨像座束腰下部为单圆翘角合莲。暂入此式。

[4] 二莲花北洞左侧菩萨已残毁，仅存半圆形座基。右侧菩萨像亦失，仅存像座；像座上半部不见。暂入此式。

[5] 惠简洞菩萨像座上半部未雕出莲瓣。暂入此式。

[6] 破上洞菩萨像座未雕出莲瓣。暂入此式。

[7] 万佛洞菩萨像座束腰上下各一凸缘。上半为单圆翘角仰莲，下半部为如意头合莲。暂入此式。

C型：束腰八角莲座或圆莲座，表面刻尖楣圆拱形壶门，束腰上下皆有叠涩，上半为仰、覆翘角莲瓣，下半为双圆翘角合莲（图78）。5个，即八作司洞、宝塔洞[1]、大卢舍那像龛、龙华寺[2]、弥上洞[3]。

D型：单圆翘角仰莲座，下为粗莲茎（图79）。2个，即高平郡王洞、擂鼓台中洞。

图77　二莲花南洞菩萨像座

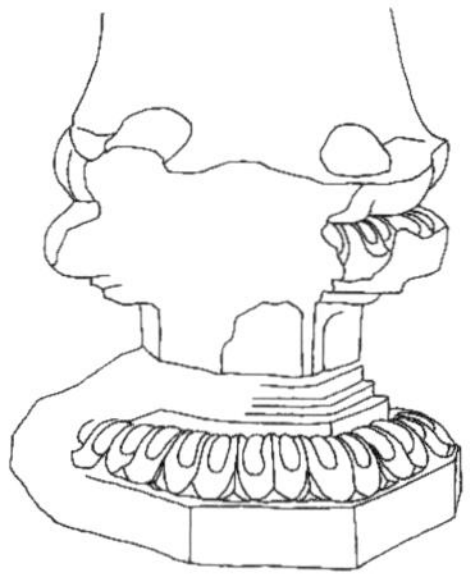

图78　八作司洞菩萨像座

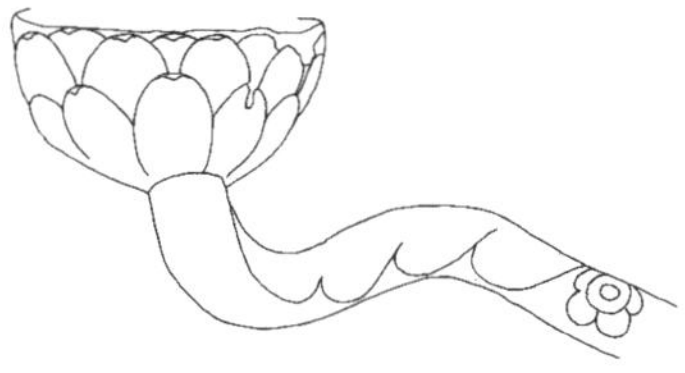

图79　高平郡王洞菩萨像座

4. 神王像

神王，通常位于胁侍菩萨外侧且成对出现，大多头束髻，着铠甲[4]，脚下踏药叉，为威武的护法形像。神王基本呈静态，与金刚力士相邻，后者作忿怒形之动态。“梵（神）王执炉，请转法轮；金刚挥杵，卫护教法。”[5]依据道宣《关中创立戒坛图经》，这二位护法形像疑为金毗罗神王和散脂神将[6]。为客观排比神王样式，将分左侧神王、右侧神王及神王脚下药叉三项作考古类型学分析。

(1) 左侧神王

神王，颈围项护，“上缀披膊”，束臂护。胸护多缀花饰，上缘用带向后与背甲扣联。腰带上多具脐护，腰带下左右各一片膝裙，其表面垂覆一半圆形饰帛，饰帛末端

---

[1] 宝塔洞菩萨像座的束腰未刻壶门，上半为单圆翘角仰莲和底座，下半为双圆合莲。暂入此式。

[2] 龙华寺菩萨像座为束腰圆莲座。束腰部分刻出尖楣圆拱形壶门三个，束腰上下皆有二层叠涩，上半部为单圆翘角仰莲，下半部为双圆翘角合莲。暂入此式。

[3] 弥上洞菩萨像座上半已残损。暂入此式。

[4] 文中所述铠甲各部名称，主要依据［宋］曾公亮等撰《武经总要前集》卷十三《器图》及说明文字和杨泓先生有关论述。参见：1) 曾公亮等《武经总要前集》，影印明本，北京：中华书局，1959年；2) 杨泓《中国古兵器论丛》（增订本），北京：文物出版社，1985年，第54-55页及表三。

[5] 宗鉴集《释门正统》，参见：《卍新纂大日本續藏經》No. 1513，第75卷，第298a页。

[6]《大正藏》第45卷，第809b页。巩县大历山石窟第5窟东端乾封年间(666-667年)雕镌的造像，中央为倚坐佛，右侧为“护法神王”，左侧为“金毗罗神王”；似乎印证了这一推断。参见河南省文化局文物工作队编《巩县石窟寺》，北京：文物出版社，1963年，图版310、311；拓本75、76。

上系两腰后多垂下。膝裙摆边作百褶状，露出战裙。“下属吊腿”[1]，脚着战靴。依据甲带、脐护、膝裙、战裙样式及体态等，可将唐代窟龛分作四型。

A 型：甲带十字形穿环绊在胸前，左右各一较大胸护。脐护作半花形，战裙摆边下垂或略扬向一侧。双腿分开直立（图 80）。2 个，即宾阳北洞[2]、潜溪寺。

B 型：胸甲分左右两片，中间以带或钩相连，每片中心缀凸起花饰；胸腹甲联成一体。脐护作兽面或半花形，多有膝护，战裙下摆有的缚吊腿内。胯部略扭；多一腿弓起，一腿直立（图 81）。5 个，即大卢舍那像龛、敬善寺[3]、弥上洞[4]、普上洞[5]、万佛洞。

C 型：甲带于胸前穿环后与横带相交或自颈下纵束至胸前打结后分束于背后。披膊有的作虎头或龙首状，脐护作半花形或兽面，战裙下摆扬向一侧。胯部扭动，双腿分立（图 82）。3 个，即八作司洞、二莲花北洞、龙华寺[6]。

图 80　宾阳北洞左侧神王

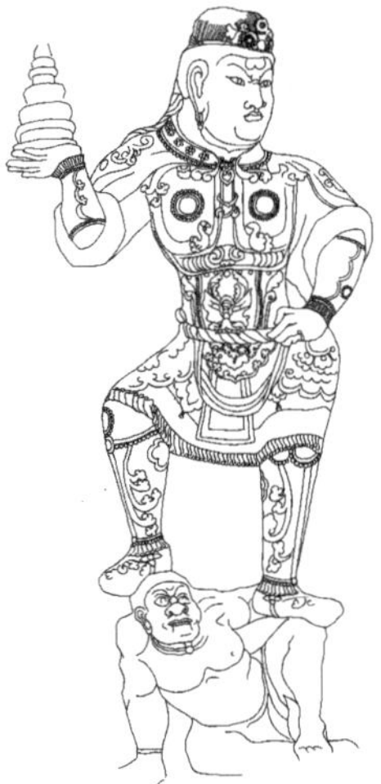

图 81　大卢舍那像龛左侧神王

图 82　八作司洞左侧神王

[1] “上缀披膊、下属吊腿”一语，采自曾公亮等《武经总要前集》卷十三《器图》及说明文字。

[2] 宾阳北洞神王系浮雕而成。

[3] 敬善寺左侧神王像脐护作半花形。

[4] 弥上洞左侧神王膝裙表面有一小长方形垂帘，形同大卢舍那像龛左侧神王。

[5] 普上洞左侧神王像残损严重，唯右手所托佛塔保存完好。暂入此式。

[6] 龙华寺左侧神王像脐护作兽面。

D 型：甲带多倒丁字形绊缚[1]，脐护作半花形，膝裙下摆多无褶，战裙下摆呈尖角扬向一侧。多上身短、下身长。胯部扭动，双腿分立。根据腰带上下饰物可分二式。

Di 式：腰带上仅饰脐护（图 83）。5 个，即宝塔洞[2]、火上洞、极南洞[3]、鷰上洞[4]、三佛洞。

Dii 式：基本同 Di 式，唯腰带下有鹘尾（图 84）。1 个，即奉南洞。

(2) 右侧神王

右侧神王之铠甲基本同左侧神王。参照左侧神王造型，可将唐代窟龛亦分作四型。

A 型：基本同左侧 A 型神王，唯胸护作圆形或花形，脐护作半圆形或半花状，膝裙下摆多饰百褶（图 85、86）。4 个，即宾阳北洞、敬善寺、潜溪寺、双窑北洞。

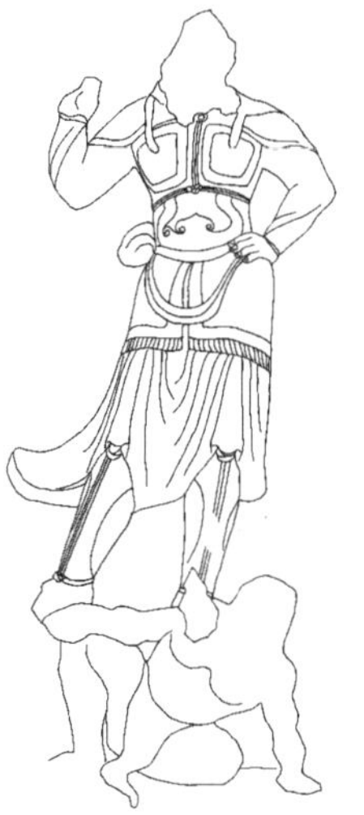

图 83　极南洞左侧神王

图 84　奉南洞左侧神王

图 85　宾阳北洞右侧神王

图 86　敬善寺右侧神王

B 型：基本同左侧 B 型神王，唯披膊有的作龙首状，脐护作兽面，有膝护（图 87）。2 个，即大卢舍那像龛、万佛洞。

C 型：基本同左侧 C 型神王，唯甲带自颈下纵束至胸前打结后再向左右分束于背后，整体作倒丁字形或十字形；脐护作兽面状，咬住腰带，个别作半花

[1] 即甲带由颈下纵束至胸前打结后再向左右分束于背后。

[2] 宝塔洞左侧神王像未按计划完工，倒丁字形束带清晰。暂入此式。

[3] 极南洞左侧神王像膝裙下摆饰百褶。

[4] 鷰上洞左侧神王甲带十字形穿环绊缚于胸前。暂入此式。

形；膝裙下摆作百褶状。胯部扭动，一腿微弓，一腿直立（图 88）。3 个，即八作司洞、龙华寺、弥上洞[1]。

D 型：与左侧 D 型神王相同，下分二式。

Di 式：基本同左侧 Di 式神王，唯甲带有的作十字形扣联于胸前（图 89）。5 个，即宝塔洞[2]、奉南洞[3]、火上洞、鷩上洞[4]、普上洞[5]。

Dii 式：同左侧 Dii 式神王（图 90）。2 个，即极南洞、三佛洞。

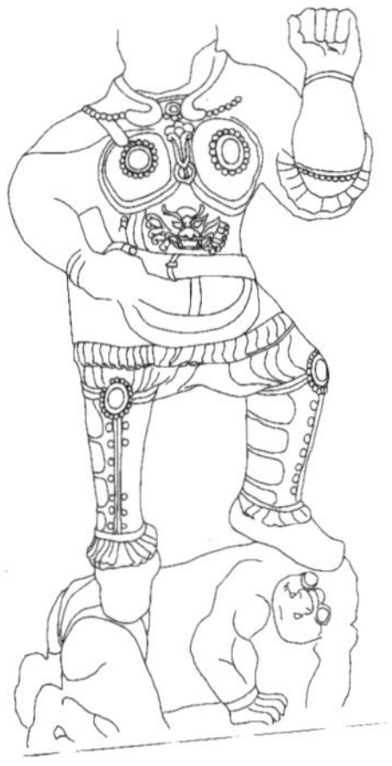

图 87　万佛洞右侧神王

图 88　龙华寺右侧神王

图 89　奉南洞右侧神王

图 90　极南洞右侧神王

(3) 药叉像

药叉[6]被踏神王脚下，托扛神王；有的二药叉合撑一神王。药叉双眼圆睁，三角形塌鼻，颧骨突出，大嘴。略矮胖，挺胸、鼓腹，肌体健壮，袒上身，下着牛鼻裈。依据造型特征可分作三型。

A 型：四肢作爬行状，面部侧向主尊。神王踏其头及臀或腰部（图 91）。3 个，即宾阳北洞[7]、潜溪寺、万佛洞[8]。

[1] 弥上洞右侧神王甲带似倒丁字形绊缚。

[2] 宝塔洞右侧神王像未按计划完工，倒丁字形束带清晰。暂入此式。

[3] 奉南洞右侧神王像甲带十字形扣联。

[4] 鷩上洞右侧神王上半身残毁。暂入此式。

[5] 普上洞右侧神王甲带似十字形扣联。暂入此式。

[6] 药叉有时也称夜叉鬼。参见《贤愚经》卷十，《大正藏》第 4 卷，第 420c 页。

[7] 宾阳北洞神王和药叉系浮雕而成，药叉已残蚀不清，似以臀部托扛神王。暂入此式。

[8] 万佛洞药叉手脚似爪。

B 型：蹲坐。依据发式、四肢等，下分二式。

Bi 式：头发后梳，一腿平放、一腿屈立；上肢作手，下肢多作四爪或蹄。一手拄地或抵膝，以手和头或肩和膝等托扛神王（参见图 81）。4 个，即大卢舍那像龛、二莲花北洞[1]、敬善寺、普上洞。

图 91　潜溪寺药叉像

Bii 式：基本同 Bi 式，唯卷发披肩或竖起，个别似双腿盘坐，一手拄地。有的下肢作爪或蹄形。多以双肩托扛神王，个别以头和臂或肩和膝托举（图 92）。6 个，即八作司洞[2]、奉南洞[3]、火上洞[4]、极南洞[5]、龙华寺、鹮上洞。

C 型：仰卧。头枕山岩，上身略抬起，一腿平放，一腿屈立；一手拄地，一手置膝上；下肢似二蹄。药叉以肩和膝或以头和腿托扛神王（图 93）。1 个，三佛洞。

图 92　龙华寺药叉像

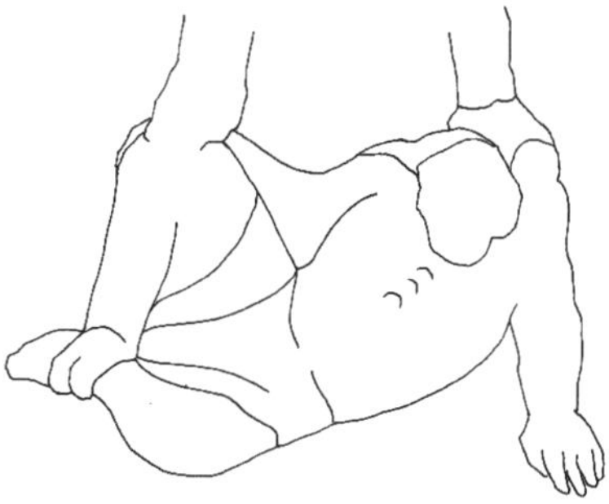

图 93　三佛洞药叉像

[1] 二莲花北洞右侧神王及药叉已毁，左侧神王下踏二药叉。

[2] 八作司洞神王下踏二药叉，药叉坐山岩座。

[3] 奉南洞药叉似双腿盘坐。

[4] 火上洞药叉手脚清晰，无爪。

[5] 极南洞药叉下坐山岩座。

5. 金刚力士像

金刚力士，应分称“金刚”与“力士”为妥，通常位于前庭正壁窟门两侧且对称雕造[1]，但在龙门唐代窟龛的造型上似无差别，通称金刚力士，或简作金刚[2]。为了客观排比这类护法形象，拟分左侧金刚和右侧金刚分别作考古类型学分析。

图94　药方洞左侧金刚

(1) 左侧金刚

金刚双腿叉开立于山岩座上。依据服饰可将唐代窟龛分作二型。

A型：服饰简朴。头束髻，束带自两侧上飘。面相方正，眉骨隆起，眼圆睁，鼻翼较宽，颧骨突出，大嘴、鼓腮。颈部青筋突暴，锁骨显露；一手屈举至肩，一手置于腰部或体侧；胯部扭动，一腿微屈，一腿直立；袒上身，下着裙；裙腰外翻，裙摆呈尖角飘向一侧。依据体态和服饰下分三式：

Ai式：体型较小、单薄但不失健壮；肋骨、双乳、腹肌明显，胸部较鼓，臂、腿肌肉发达。腰带打结隐现。披巾在头后扬成一大圆环，后似于腰侧打结，末端垂于腿侧(图94)。1个，即药方洞[3]。

Aii式：体态雄健有力；胸部隆起，腹部凸显，臂肌略呈块状凸起。披巾有的在头后扬成一大圆环，末端垂至山岩座上，缠绕方式不清；有的于腰带处打结后垂下(图95)。3个，即二莲花北洞[4]、

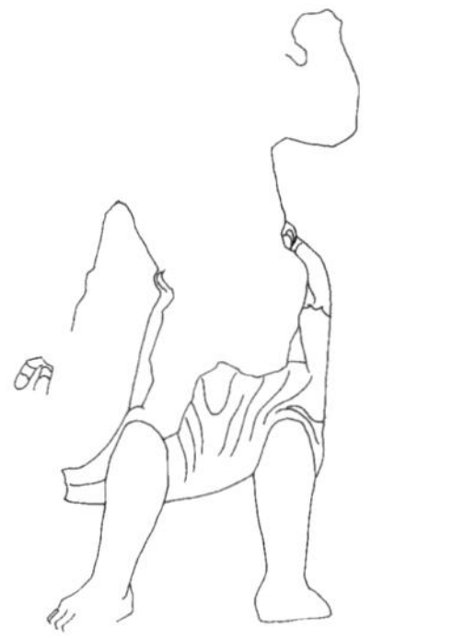

图95　二莲花北洞左侧金刚

[1] 参见李崇峰《金刚力士勾稽》(见本书)。

[2] 唐高宗永徽元年(650年)刘玄意在宾阳南洞前壁所造这种单身护法形象铭文作“金刚力士”，而高宗上元二年(675年)完工的大卢舍那像龛中的同类形象题铭仅称“金刚”。参见：1) 李文生《龙门石窟的新发现及其他》，见李文生《龙门石窟与洛阳历史文化》，上海：上海人民美术出版社，1993年，第16-29页；2) 刘景龙、李玉昆主编《龙门石窟碑刻题记汇录》，北京：中国大百科全书出版社，1998年，第379-381页。

[3] 药方洞前庭正壁两金刚力士面部残蚀，五官不清。

[4] 二莲花北洞左侧金刚上半身残损。暂入此式。

破上洞[1]、普上洞[2]。

Aiii 式：头和上半身多略前倾。体态健壮，胸肌发达，腹肌、臂肌呈圆形或块状凸起。腰带多于腹前打结后呈八字形垂下（图 96-98）。10 个，即宝塔洞[3]、二莲花南洞、奉南洞、高平郡王洞[4]、火上洞[5]、火下洞、火左洞、极南洞[6]、擂鼓台中洞[7]、三佛洞[8]。

图 96　奉南洞左侧金刚

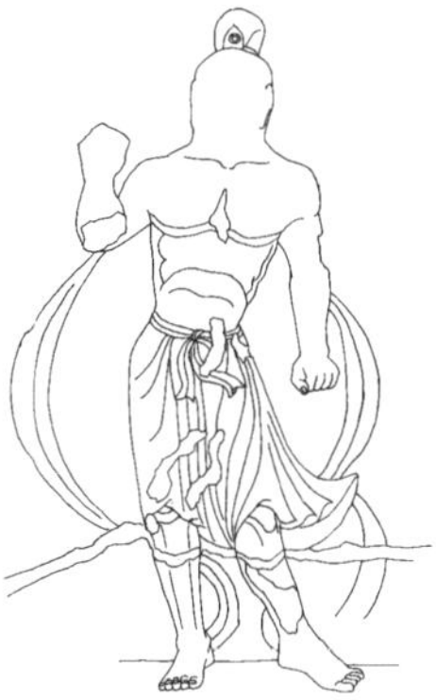

图 97　高平郡王洞左侧金刚

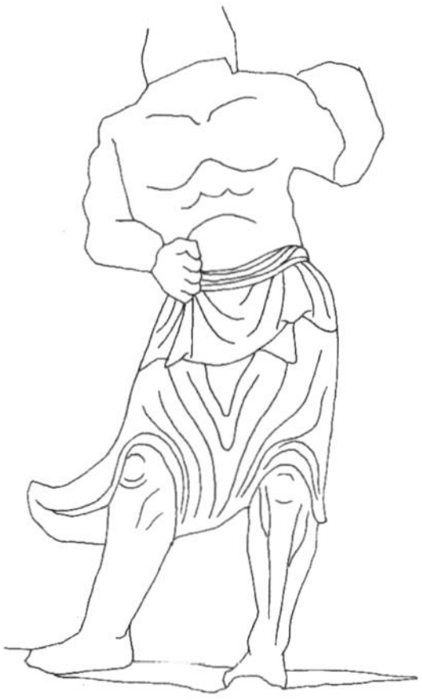

图 98　二莲花南洞左侧金刚

B 型：服饰较多。基本同 A 型，唯力士多戴冠，配项饰，挂璎珞。披巾有的在头后扬成一大圆环，末端垂至山岩座上，缠绕方式不清；个别披巾横于腹下两道。依据体态下分二式：

Bi 式：基本同 Ai 式（图 99）。2 个，即敬善寺、双窑北洞。

Bii 式：基本同 Aii 式，唯双肩较宽，腰带多于腹前打结垂下（图 100）。3 个，即大卢舍那像龛[9]、龙华寺[10]、万佛洞。

(2) 右侧金刚

依据金刚服饰及体态并参照左侧金刚造型，可将唐代窟龛分作二型。

[1] 破上洞左侧金刚像不见披巾。暂入此式。

[2] 普上洞左侧金刚像不见披巾。暂入此式。

[3] 宝塔洞左侧金刚残损较甚。暂入此式。

[4] 高平郡王洞左侧金刚披巾上半被头光遮盖，下半呈弧形飘下。

[5] 火上洞左侧金刚残损较多。暂入此式。

[6] 极南洞左侧金刚头部和臂、腿有残损。

[7] 擂鼓台中洞左侧金刚像残损较甚，腰带打结后呈八字形下垂。暂入此式。

[8] 三佛洞左侧金刚残蚀较甚。暂入此式。

[9] 大卢舍那像龛左侧金刚腰带打半蝴蝶结垂下。

[10] 龙华寺左侧金刚腰带打半蝴蝶结后垂下。

A 型：金刚基本同左侧 A 型金刚，下分三式：

Ai 式：同左侧 Ai 式金刚（图 101）。1 个，即药方洞。

图 99　敬善寺左侧金刚

图 100　万佛洞左侧金刚

图 101　药方洞右侧金刚

Aii 式：基本同左侧 Aii 式金刚，唯腰带于腹前打结后呈八字形垂下（图 102）。4 个，即八作司洞、二莲花北洞、破上洞[1]、普上洞[2]。

Aiii 式：基本同左侧Aiii式金刚，唯腹部较平（图103、104）。7个，即奉南洞、高平郡王洞[3]、火上洞[4]、火左洞、极南洞、看经寺[5]、三佛洞。

B 型：金刚同左侧 B 型金刚，下分二式：

Bi 式：同左侧 Bi 式金刚（图 105、106）。3 个，即敬善寺、双窑北洞、双窑南洞[6]。

Bii 式：同左侧 Bii 式金刚（图 107）。3 个，即大卢舍那像龛[7]、龙华寺[8]、万佛洞。

[1] 破上洞右侧金刚像不见披巾。暂入此式。

[2] 普上洞右侧金刚像不见披巾。暂入此式。

[3] 高平郡王洞右侧金刚像披巾于头后扬成一大圆环后，呈弧形飘垂山岩座上。

[4] 火上洞右侧金刚像残损较多。暂入此式。

[5] 看经寺右侧金刚像头戴火焰冠，身体有残损。披巾在头后扬成一大圆环，末端绕肘或小臂后呈弧形垂下。

[6] 双窑南洞右侧金刚像面部残蚀较重，仅见轮廓。

[7] 大卢舍那像龛右侧金刚像残损较甚。

[8] 龙华寺右侧金刚像残损较甚。暂入此式。

图 102　八作司洞
右侧金刚

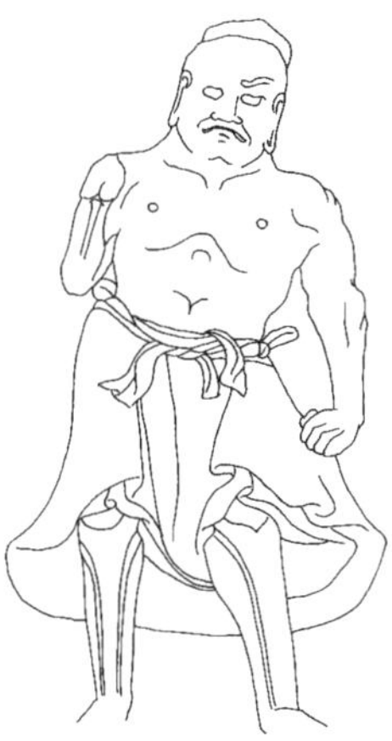

图 103　奉南洞
右侧金刚

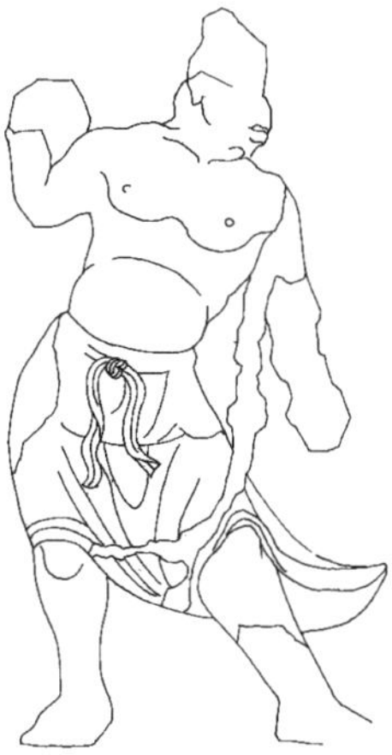

图 104　极南洞
右侧金刚

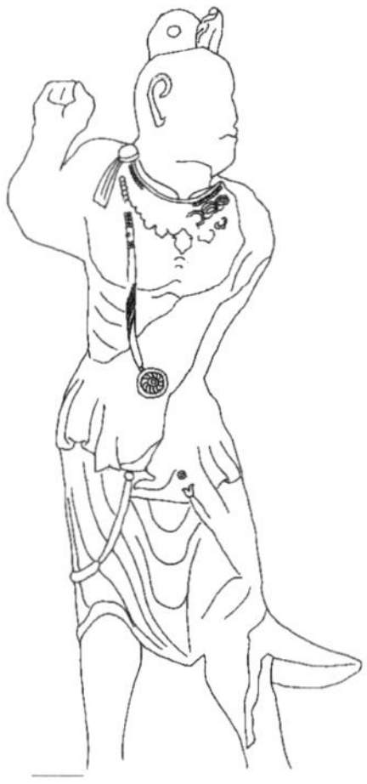

图 105　双窑北洞
右侧金刚

图 106　敬善寺
右侧金刚

图 107　万佛洞
右侧金刚

(四)装饰题材与雕刻技法

1. 窟顶装饰

窟顶装饰可分作二型。

A 型:窟顶中央雕莲花,周围多绕飞天(图 108)。21 个,即八作司洞、宾阳北洞、宾阳南洞[1]、二莲花北洞、二莲花南洞、火下洞、火左洞、极南洞、敬善寺、

[1] 宾阳北洞和宾阳南洞的窟顶纹样系北魏开窟时原作,后整个洞窟因故辍工。暂入此式。

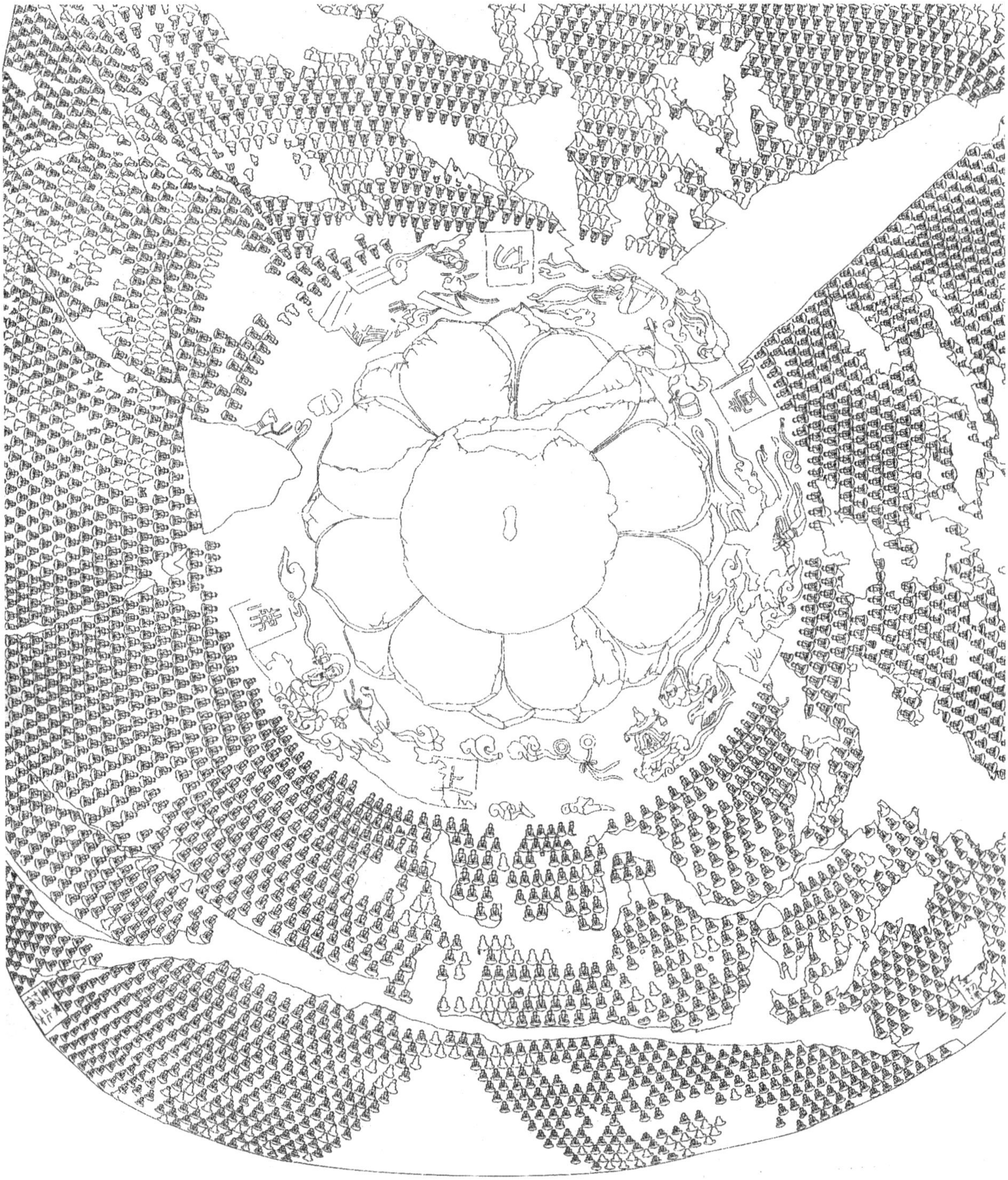

图 108　攞鼓台中洞窟顶装饰

看经寺、擂鼓台北洞、擂鼓台南洞、擂鼓台中洞[1]、龙华寺、普上洞、潜溪寺、清明寺、双窑北洞、万佛洞、药方洞、赵客师洞。

B型：窟顶中央雕莲花，周围绕飞天和大雁(图109)。2个，即奉南洞、四雁洞。

图109　四雁洞窟顶装饰

a

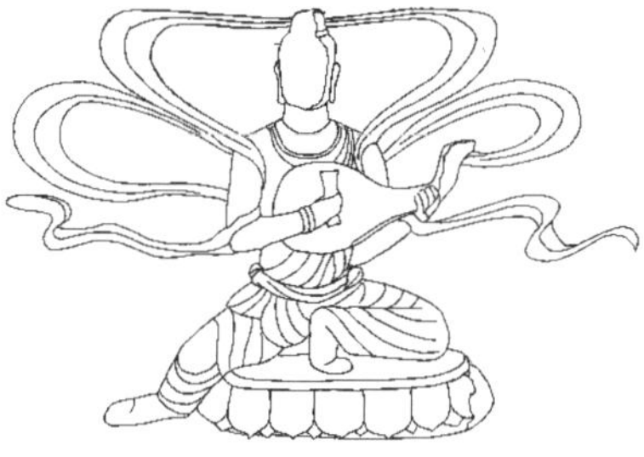

b

图110　万佛洞伎乐

2. 伎乐

伎乐大多雕于基坛表面壸门之内，个别镌于侧壁下部。其中，正壁中央两身作舞蹈状，正壁两端及两侧壁者奏乐。依据造型和服饰，可以分作二型[2]。

A型：头束高髻，宽肩、挺胸、细腰、鼓腹。大多双腿盘坐，或一腿盘坐、一腿垂下。袒上身或着掩腋；下着裙，裙腰外翻。佩项饰、手镯。披巾多在头后扬成三个圆环，呈品字形，末端向两侧飘扬(图110)。2个，即二莲花南洞[3]、万佛洞[4]。

---

[1] 擂鼓台中洞窟顶莲花周围雕镌童子、宝塔、乐器等，是龙门现存石窟中最繁复的窟顶装饰之一。暂入此式。

[2] 二莲花北洞基坛表面的伎乐像残蚀严重，仅见轮廓。故不作类型分析。

[3] 二莲花南洞基坛上的伎乐像有坐有跪，持巾舞动，似无奏乐者。暂入此式。

[4] 万佛洞伎乐像雕刻在两侧壁，故二舞蹈者分居侧壁前端，即靠近正壁与侧壁连接处。

B 型：头多束丫髻，少数作高髻；体态及造型基本同 A 型，唯上身袒裸，奏乐者不见披巾，个别舞蹈者披巾于头后扬成一大圆环后绕臂垂下，持巾而舞，动感较强（图 111、112）。6 个，即八作司洞、奉南洞[1]、火下洞、火左洞、极南洞、龙华寺。

图 111　八作司洞伎乐

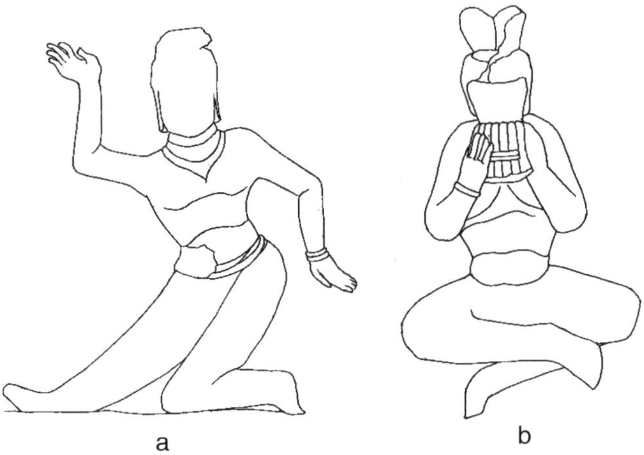

图 112　极南洞伎乐

3. 飞天

飞天多雕于窟顶莲花周围，少数刻在前庭后壁窟门上方；大多俯卧，作飞翔状，身体略呈弧形。飞天束发髻，多戴项饰，袒上身，下着袖腿长裙，披巾多于头后扬成一大圆环，末端自腋下后扬或绕臂后飘。依据手势等可分作四型。

A 型：肉髻较平，双手持乐器（图 113）。2 个，即药方洞、赵客师洞。

B 型：双手合十，或一手前伸、一手于胸前持莲花或宝珠；双腿伸展，或一腿屈起（图 114）。3 个，即敬善寺、双窑北洞、万佛洞。

C 型：双臂张开，一手托盘，一手外扬；一腿弯曲，一腿伸展。少数飞天无披巾（图 115）。7 个，即二莲花北洞[2]、二莲花南洞、火左洞、极南洞[3]、看经寺、龙华寺、四雁洞[4]。

---

［1］奉南洞正壁基坛中央舞蹈者，着披巾。

［2］二莲花北洞窟顶飞天的披巾于头后扬成二个圆环，末端自腋下后飘。

［3］极南洞窟顶飞天无披巾。暂入此式。

［4］四雁洞窟顶飞天无披巾。暂入此式。

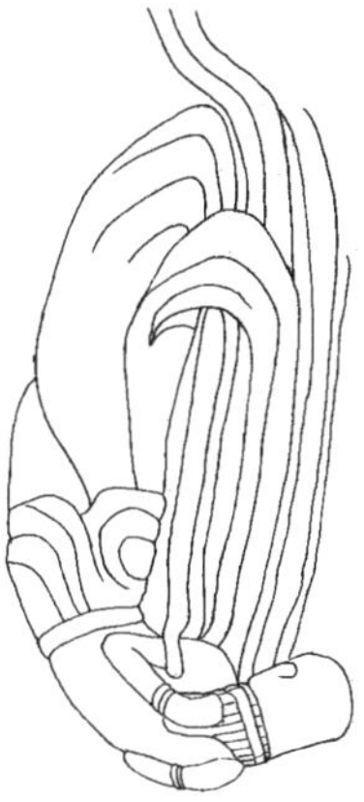

图 113　药方洞飞天

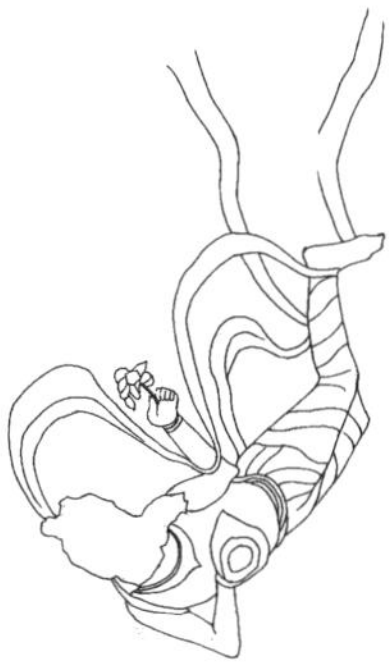

图 114　万佛洞飞天

图 115　龙华寺飞天

D 型：双臂张开、扬掌。裙腰外翻如短裙（图 116）。5 个，即奉南洞、火上洞、看经寺、擂鼓台北洞、普上洞[1]。

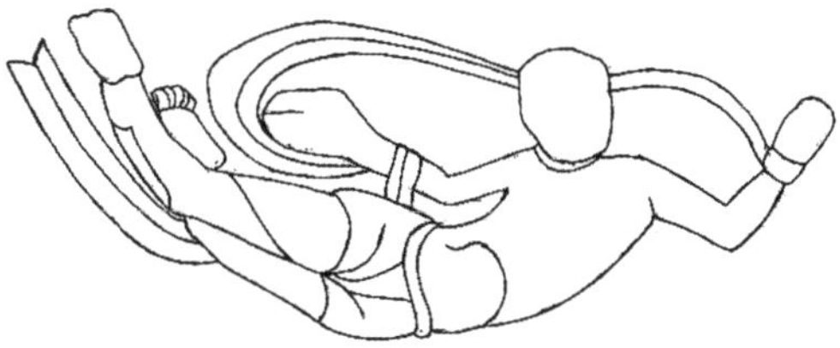

图 116　奉南洞飞天

4. 主像衣纹

依据窟内主尊佛像的衣纹处理方式，可将唐代窟龛分作二型。

A 型：衣纹作“压地隐起”式，断面近似凸棱。8 个，即宾阳北洞、宾阳南洞、敬善寺、潜溪寺、双窑北洞[2]、唐字洞、药方洞、赵客师洞。

B 型：衣纹断面作直平阶梯式。24 个，即八作司洞、宝塔洞、大卢舍那像龛、二莲花南洞、奉南洞、高平郡王洞、惠简洞、火上洞、火下洞、火左洞、极南洞、擂鼓台北洞、擂鼓台南洞[3]、擂鼓台中洞、龙华寺[4]、鸗上洞、摩崖三佛[5]、破上洞、普上洞、清明寺、三佛洞[6]、双窑南洞[7]、万佛洞、赵上洞。

[1] 普上洞窟顶飞天无披巾。暂入此式。

[2] 双窑北洞内共有一坐佛、二立佛。这里仅选正壁佛像衣纹作类型分析。

[3] 擂鼓台南洞坛上主尊是否为原作，尚有争议。暂入此式。

[4] 龙华寺内共有三坐佛、二立佛，这里仅选正壁佛像衣纹作类型分析。

[5] 摩崖三佛龛内共有三尊佛像，这里仅选中央佛像衣纹作类型分析。

[6] 三佛洞内共有三尊佛像，这里仅选正壁佛像衣纹作类型分析。

[7] 双窑南洞主尊服饰衣纹近似阶梯式。暂入此式。

三、龙门石窟唐代窟龛的分期与年代

(一)龙门石窟唐代窟龛的分组

由于自然和人为的破坏,上述39座大型窟龛现存状况不完全一致。列入考古类型学分析的四组24项,有时在一座洞窟中仅存6-7项,难以反映洞窟全貌。据我们统计,其中共有32座10项以上保存相对完好的窟龛。

为了便于归纳、排比和总结龙门唐代窟龛各组成部分类型的异同及演化关系,我们拟选取这32座窟龛作为我们分析和比较的对象。在此基础上,进行分组。其余7座保存相对不完整的窟龛,参照已排定的各组,可以较容易地被归入相应的演化序列之中。为了易于排比前述各项,这32座窟龛的每个组成部分可以列表(表一)如下。

从表一中可以看出,第1-4号所含各窟的绝大多数项目,型式完全相同;个别型式不同,但也极为接近。故这些窟龛应为一组。第29-32号所包括的各个窟龛,各组成部分的型式亦极为接近,应为另一组。第5-28号所含各窟龛,型式大多相同,应为一大组;但仔细排比,可以再分作二小组,即第5-14号所含各窟龛为一组,第15-28号为另一组。

根据上述窟龛型式相同和相近的情况,我们可以把龙门石窟唐代窟龛分作如下四组。

A组:4个,即唐字洞、药方洞、宾阳南洞、宾阳北洞。窟龛平面布局皆作A型;窟顶形制多为A型,个别作B型。造像题材皆为A型,造像组合分Ai和Aii式。至于造像特征,佛法衣分A、B型,以前者为主;佛像头光分A型和Bi式,以前者为多;佛座分为A型和Bi式。弟子像分A型和Bi式,以前者为多;弟子头光作A型;弟子像座亦分A型和Bi式,以前者为多。菩萨像分Ai和Aii式,头光皆作Ai式;菩萨像座分A型和Bi式,以前者占多数。神王及神王脚下的药叉皆作A型,金刚力士像为Ai式。窟顶装饰、飞天造型及主尊衣纹皆作A型。

B组:10个,即潜溪寺、赵客师洞、敬善寺、双窑北洞、双窑南洞、清明寺、惠简洞、大卢舍那像龛、万佛洞、赵上洞。洞窟平面布局绝大多数为A型,个别作B型;窟顶形制多为A型,少数作B型。造像题材分A、B、C三型,以A型占绝大多数;造像组合多样,有Ai、Aii、Aiii式和B型之分。在造像特征方面,佛法衣分C型、Di式和E型,以Di式为多;佛像头光分Bi和Bii式,以Bi式略多;佛座有Bi、Ci、Cii、Ciii式和D型之分。弟子像多作Bii式,少数为Biii式,个别为Bi式;弟子头光绝大多数为A型,

表一 龙门石窟唐代窟龛型式与组合表

序号	窟名	形制		造像		个体造像特征															技法与装饰				组别
						佛			弟子				菩萨				神王			金刚					
		平面	窟顶	题材	组合	法衣	头光	佛座	左侧	右侧	头光	像座	左侧	右侧	头光	像座	左侧	右侧	药叉	左侧	右侧	窟顶	伎乐	飞天	衣纹	
1	唐字洞	A	B	A	Ai	A		A					Aii	Aii	Ai	A						A			A	
2	药方洞	A	A	A	Aii	A	A	A	A	A		A	Ai	Aii	Ai	A				Ai	Ai	A		A	A	A
3	宾阳南洞	A	A	A	Ai	B	A	Bi	A	A		A	Ai	Ai	Ai	A						A			A	
4	宾阳北洞	A	A	A	Aii	A	Bi	Bi	Bi	Bi	A	Bi	Aii	Ai	Ai	Bi	A	A	A			A			A	
5	潜溪寺	B	A	A	Aii	C	Bi	Bi	Bi	Bi		Bi	Aiii	Aiii	Ai	Bi	A	A	A			A			A	
6	赵客师洞	A	A	A	Ai	C	Bi	Ci	Bii	Bii	A	Bi	Bi	×		Bi						A		A	A	
7	敬善寺	A	A	A	Aiii	Di	Bi	Ci	Bii	Bii	A	Bii	Bi	Aiii	Ai	Bii	B	A	Bi	Bi	Bi	A		B	A	
8	双窑北洞	A	A	B	B	Di	Bi	Ci	Bii	Bii	A	Bii	Bi	Aiii	Ai	Bii	×	A		Bi	Bi	A		B	A	
9	双窑南洞	A	A	AC	Aii	Di	Bi	D	Bii	Bii	A	Bii	Bi	×	Ai	Bii				×	Bi				B	B
10	清明寺	A	A	A	Ai	Di	Bii	Cii					Bi	Bi	Ai	Biii						A			B	
11	惠简洞	A	B	A	Aiii	Di	Bii	D	×	Bii	Bi	Biii	Aiii	Bi	Ai	Biii	×	×							B	
12	大卢舍那像龛	B		A	Aiii	E	Bii	Cii	Bii	Biii	Bi	C	Bii	Bii	Aii	C	B	B	Bi	Bii	Bii				B	
13	万佛洞	A	B	AC	Aiii	Di	Bi	Cii	Biii	Biii	A	Biii	Bii	Bii	Aii	Biii	B	B	A	Bii	Bii	A	A	B	B	
14	赵上洞	B	B	A	Aii	Di		Ciii	Bii	Biii	A	Bii	×	Bii	Aii	Biii									B	
15	破上洞	A	A	A	Aii	Di		Ciii	Bii	Bii		Biii	Bii	Bii		Biii				Aii	Aii				B	
16	普上洞	B	A	A	Aiii	Di		Ciii	Biii	C		Biii	Bii	Bii		Biii	B	Di	Bi	Aii	Aii	A		D	B	
17	弥上洞	B	A	A	Aii	×	C	Ciii	Biii	C	A	C	×	×	B	C	B	C							×	
18	八作司洞	B	A	A	Aiii	E	Bii	Bii	C	C	Bii	C	Bii	Bii	Aii	C	C	C	Bii	×	Aii	A	B		B	
19	火下洞	B	A	A	Aiii	E		Bii	×	×		×	×	×	Aiii	×	×	×	×	Aiii	×	A	B		B	
20	火左洞	B	A	A	×	E	Bii	Bii	×	×		×	×	×		×	×	×	×	Aiii	Aiii	A	B	C	B	
21	龙华寺	B	A	B	B	E	Bii	Cii	×	×	Bi	C	Bii	Bii	Aii	C	C	C	Bii	Bii	Bii	A	B	C	B	C
22	二莲花北洞	B	A	A	Aiii	×		Bii	Biii	C		Biii	×	×		Biii	C	×	Bi	Aii	Aii	A		C	×	
23	二莲花南洞	B	C	A	Aiii	E	Bii	Ciii	Biii	C		Biii	Bii	Bii	Aiii	Biii	×			Aiii	×	A	A	C	B	
24	鷰上洞	B	A	A	Aiii	E	C	Ciii	Biii	C	Bi	Biii	Biii	Biii	B	Biii	Di	Di	Bii	×	×				B	
25	擂鼓台北洞	B	B	B	B	Dii	Bii	Bii					Biii	Biii		?						A		D	B	
26	擂鼓台中洞	C	A	AC	Aii	Di	Bii	D					Biii	Biii	Aii	D				Aiii	×	A			B	
27	宝塔洞	B	A	A	Aiii	Di		Cii	Biii	C		Biii	×	Biii		C	Di	Di		Aiii					B	
28	高平郡王洞	B	C	AC	Aii	E		E	Biii	C		D	Biii	C		D				Aiii	Aiii				B	
29	极南洞	B	A	A	Aiii	E		Bii	Biii	C		Biii	Biii	C		Biii	Di	Dii	Bii	Aiii	Aiii	A	B	C	B	
30	奉南洞	B	A	A	Aiii	E	C	Ciii	Biii	C	Bii	Biii	Biv	Biv	B	Biii	Dii	Di	Bii	Aiii	Aiii	B	B	D	B	D
31	火上洞	B	C	A	Aiii	E		Ciii	Biii	C		Biii	C	C		Biii	Di	Di	Bii	Aiii	Aiii			D	B	
32	三佛洞	B	C	B	B	Di		D	Biii	C		Biii	×	×		Biii	Di	Dii	C	Aiii	Aiii				B	
	破窑																									A
	老龙洞																									
	净土堂	B	B	A	Aiii	×	C	×	×	×		×	×	×	Aii	×	×	×	×						×	
	擂鼓台南洞	C	A	AC	×	Dii		Bii														A			B	C
	看经寺	C	B	D	×	×		×												×	Aiii	A		C/D	×	
	摩崖三佛	A		B	B	Di		D																	B	
	四雁洞	B	C	A	Aiii	×		×	×	×		×	×	×		×	×	×		×	×	B		C	×	D

序列号第1-32窟各部分类型中的 × 表示该部分已毁,余同

少数为 Bi 式；弟子像座分 Bi、Bii、Biii 式和 C 型，以 Bii 式为多。菩萨像分 Aiii、Bi 和 Bii 式，以 Bi 式为多，Aiii 式和 Bii 式次之；菩萨头光多数作 Ai 式，少数为 Aii 式；菩萨像座分 Bi、Bii、Biii 式和 C 型，以 Biii 式为多，Bii 式次之。神王像分 A、B 型，以后者略多；神王脚下药叉分 A 型和 Bi 式。金刚像分 Bi 和 Bii 式，以 Bi 式略多。窟顶装饰皆作 A 型。伎乐出现，造型作 A 型。飞天分 A、B 型，以后者为多。主尊服饰衣纹分 A、B 型，后者略多。

C 组：14 个，即破上洞、普上洞、弥上洞、八作司洞、火下洞、火左洞、龙华寺、二莲花北洞、二莲花南洞、鷰上洞、擂鼓台北洞、擂鼓台中洞、宝塔洞、高平郡王洞。窟龛平面布局分 A、B、C 三型，以 B 型占绝大多数；窟顶形制分 A、B、C 三型，以 A 型为主。造像题材分 A、B、C 三型，以 A 型占绝大多数；造像组合分 Aii、Aiii 式和 B 型，以 Aiii 式为主。至于造像特征，佛法衣分 Di、Dii 式和 E 型，以 E 型为多，Di 式次之；佛像头光绝大多数为 Bii 式，个别作 C 型；佛座分 Bii、Cii、Ciii 式和 D、E 型，以 Bii 和 Ciii 式略多。弟子像分 Bii、Biii 式和 C 型，其中，左侧弟子造型主要为 Biii 式，右侧弟子绝大多数为 C 型；弟子头光分 A 型和 Bi、Bii 式；弟子像座分 Biii 式和 C、D 型，以 Biii 式为多，C 型次之。菩萨像分 Bii、Biii 式和 C 型，以 Bii 式为多，Biii 式次之，个别为 C 型；菩萨头光分 Aii、Aiii 式和 B 型，以 Aii 式略多；菩萨像座有 Biii 式和 C、D 型之分，以 Biii 式和 C 型为主。神王像分 B、C 型和 Di 式，以 C 型为多，Di 式次之。神王脚下的药叉，分为 Bi 和 Bii 两式。金刚像分 Aii、Aiii 和 Bii 式，以 Aii 式占绝大多数，Aiii 式次之。窟顶装饰皆作 A 型。伎乐造型多为 B 型，个别作 A 型。飞天造型多为 C 型，少数为 D 型。主尊大衣衣纹处理皆作 B 型。

D 组：4 个，即极南洞、奉南洞、火上洞、三佛洞。窟龛平面布局皆作 B 型，窟顶分 A、C 两型。造像题材分 A、B 两型，以 A 型为多；造像组合分 Aiii 式和 B 型，以 Aiii 式略多。在造像特征方面，佛法衣分 Di 式和 E 型，以 E 型为主；佛像头光为 C 型；佛座分 Bii、Ciii 式和 D 型，以 Ciii 式略多。弟子像分 Biii 式和 C 型，其中，左侧弟子皆为 Biii 式，右侧弟子皆作 C 型。弟子头光为 Bii 式；弟子像座皆为 Biii 式。菩萨像分 Biii、Biv 式和 C 型，以 C 型为多，Biv 式次之；菩萨头光作 B 型；菩萨像座皆为 Biii 式。神王像分 Di、Dii 两式，以 Di 式为多。神王脚下的药叉分 Bii 式和 C 型，以前者为多。金刚像皆作 Aiii 式。窟顶装饰题材分 A、B 型。伎乐皆作 B 型。飞天造型分 C、D 两型，以后者略多。主尊大衣衣纹皆作 B 型。

其余 7 座保存相对不完整窟龛中的 5 座，依据各窟龛组成部分的类型，可以分别归入上述各组之中。

净土堂的 B 型平面，主要见于 C、D 二组中，B 型窟顶见于 B 组，A 型造像题材见于A、B、C组，Aiii型造像组合主要见于C组，C型佛像头光见于C、D组，Aii式菩萨头光亦出现在B、C组。因此，经过综合考虑，我们暂时把净土堂归入C组。

擂鼓台南洞的C型平面、Dii式佛法衣仅见于C组，A/C型造像题材、Bii式佛座和B型主尊大衣衣纹，多见于C、D组。因此，我们暂把擂鼓台南洞归入C组。

看经寺的C型平面仅见于C组，Aiii式金刚、C型或D型飞天见于C、D两组。因此，暂把看经寺归入C组。

摩崖三佛的造像题材及组合皆作B型且多见于C组，Di式佛法衣、D型佛座和B型主尊大衣衣纹，见于B、C、D组。经综合考虑，暂时把摩崖三佛放入C组。

四雁洞的Aiii式造型组合出现在B、C、D三组，C型窟顶和C型飞天造型见于C、D组，而B型窟顶装饰仅见于D组。因此，暂把四雁洞归入D组之中。

（二）龙门石窟唐代窟龛的分期

通过上述类型排比并分析各组成部分型式的异同，我们将龙门唐代窟龛分作四组。下面拟进一步讨论四组的演化序列问题。

实际上，上述四组窟龛代表了龙门唐代窟龛四个先后不同的发展阶段。至于其演化序列，因为B组的大卢舍那像龛、惠简洞和万佛洞皆有唐高宗时期的开窟纪年[1]，C组的擂鼓台中洞保存有武则天创造的具有断代意义的新字[2]，C组高平郡王洞内像座上的题刻[3]和D组极南洞右侧的碑铭[4]也可间接推断出开窟年代（详见后述），所以我们可以比较肯定地说，上述四组窟龛是从A组向D组演化的，不会反其道而行之。A、B、C、D四组可以看作一、二、三、四期。换言之，龙门唐代窟龛可分作四期，一、二、三、四期同上述A、B、C、D四组。至于前述的破窑和老龙洞二窟，没有做类型分析，因为它们是利用前代洞窟补凿而成，壁面布满小龛。破窑现存的最早遗迹，是正壁中央的弥勒像龛，毕工于唐贞观十一年(637年)[5]；老龙洞内现存的最早遗迹，是贞观二十一年(647年)完成的双观音像[6]。因此，暂把破窑和老龙洞归

---

[1] 大卢舍那像龛完工于唐上元二年(675年)，惠简洞完工于唐咸亨四年(673年)，万佛洞完工于唐永隆元年(680年)。参见刘景龙、李玉昆主编《龙门石窟碑刻题记汇录》，北京：中国大百科全书出版社，1998年，第138-139、179、381页。

[2] 参见：刘景龙、李玉昆主编，上引书，第613-625页。

[3] 参见：刘景龙、李玉昆主编，上引书，第639页。

[4] 参见：刘景龙、李玉昆主编，上引书，第610页。

[5] 参见：刘景龙、李玉昆主编，上引书，第332-333页。

[6] 参见：刘景龙、李玉昆主编，上引书，第214-215页。

表二　龙门石窟唐代窟龛分期表

	平面形制	佛像特征	佛座	左侧弟子	右侧弟子	弟子像座	左侧菩萨	右侧菩萨	菩萨像座	左侧神王	右侧神王	药叉	左侧金刚	右侧金刚	飞天
第一期	宾阳北洞	宾阳南洞	唐字洞	宾阳南洞	宾阳南洞	药方洞	宾阳南洞	宾阳南洞	宾阳南洞	宾阳北洞	宾阳北洞		药方洞	药方洞	药方洞
第二期	清明寺 万佛洞	万佛洞 惠简洞	潜溪寺 万佛洞	敬善寺	万佛洞	敬善寺	惠简洞	惠简洞	潜溪寺 敬善寺	大卢舍那像龛	万佛洞	潜溪寺 大卢舍那像龛	万佛洞	万佛洞	万佛洞
第三期	八作司洞 高平郡王洞	八作司洞 擂鼓台北洞	二莲花北洞	二莲花南洞	二莲花南洞	八作司洞 二莲花北洞	擂鼓台北洞	龙华寺	八作司洞 二莲花南洞	八作司洞	龙华寺	八作司洞 龙华寺	高平郡王洞	八作司洞	龙华寺
第四期	三佛洞	极南洞	奉南洞	极南洞	极南洞	奉南洞	火上洞	极南洞	极南洞	极南洞	极南洞	三佛洞	奉南洞	极南洞	奉南洞

入A组之中。

综上所述，我们可以把龙门唐代窟龛分作如下四期（表二）。

第一期：A组的所有窟龛加上破窑和老龙洞，共6个，即唐字洞、药方洞、宾阳南洞、宾阳北洞、破窑和老龙洞；

第二期：包括B组的所有窟龛，10个，即潜溪寺、赵客师洞、敬善寺、双窑北洞、双窑南洞、清明寺、惠简洞、大卢舍那像龛、万佛洞和赵上洞。

第三期：C组的所有窟龛加上4个保存不好的洞窟，共18个，即破上洞、普上洞、弥上洞、八作司洞、火下洞、火左洞、龙华寺、二莲花北洞、二莲花南洞、鹰上洞、擂鼓台北洞、擂鼓台中洞、宝塔洞、高平郡王洞、净土堂、擂鼓台南洞、看经寺和摩崖三佛。

第四期：D组的所有窟龛加上1个保存不好的洞窟，共5个，即极南洞、奉南洞、火上洞、三佛洞和四雁洞。

（三）龙门唐代各期窟龛的主要特点及年代

经过类型排比与分析，我们发现，龙门唐代各期窟龛在建筑形制、造像题材及组合、个体特征、装饰内容及雕刻技法等方面，相互间既有继承关系，彼此又有许多不同之处。现按四期先后序列，分述各期窟龛的主要特点及相互关系。而后，对各期窟龛的相对年代及反映的历史问题试作初步探讨。

1. 第一期

(1) 窟龛形制及造像特征

第一期窟龛形制，既有利用前代大窟雕凿众多小龛之集合体，也有利用北朝方形平面窟（A型）补凿的主像。其中，正壁佛坛窟或正壁一龛窟后半部作半圆形，正壁及侧壁后端造像。窟顶多作穹隆顶（A型），个别为平顶（B型）。

主尊雕造于正壁中央，两侧为胁侍像（A型）；造像组合为一铺三身或一铺五身（Ai式），即一佛、二菩萨或一佛、二弟子、二菩萨；有的为一铺七身（Aii式），即一佛、二弟子、二菩萨及金刚力士或二神王。

佛像结跏趺坐，多作施无畏印，佛衣作褒衣博带式。内着掩腋衣，上衣覆搭双肩且多于胸前束带打结，大衣边缘自颈侧向下垂至腹部，右侧边缘多上搭左小臂垂下。双腿间弧形衣纹多近横向，摆边呈倒三角形或半圆状垂覆座前或座上（A型）。个别大衣作“右袒式”披覆，衣尾与衣头以钩钮系扣（B型）。这些大多系延续北朝晚期以降的法衣旧式。主尊大衣褶襞皆作“压地隐起”式，衣纹断面近似凸棱（A型）。佛头光多为椭圆形，表面绘画或刻出缠枝花卉，有的加饰莲花，有的在缠枝花卉中加雕小坐佛（A型）。个别作圆形，分内外二匝，内匝雕单方圆尖莲瓣，外匝为素面圆环带（Bi式）。佛座分两种，一为等腰梯形方座，座前雕双狮和一香炉（A型）；另一种为束腰方形须弥座，束腰下叠涩三层，有的在束腰部位雕刻药叉，有的座前雕出双狮（Bi式）。

弟子像置于主尊两侧，身体直立，双手合十于胸前。弟子内着掩腋衣，上衣覆搭双肩后两衣缘自颈侧垂于腹前；大衣作"右袒式"披覆，外观呈筒状；内衣下摆长于大衣（A型）。少数弟子内着"交领衫"，颈下衣边呈V字形；余同前者（Bi式）。弟子多无头光；有者，作圆形素面（A型）。弟子像座多为简朴圆座，有的中央雕出莲蓬，周围作合莲（A型）。个别为束腰圆莲座，束腰上半为单方圆仰莲，下为双圆合莲（Bi式）。

菩萨像身体僵直，无扭动之感。上身着掩腋衣，下身系裙；掩腋衣胸前系带打结或无带，束裙大带下垂如绅，上多打蝴蝶结。披巾自肩搭下后于腹下交叉，或横于腹下膝前两道，或径直下垂至脚侧，璎珞粗大且多压覆披巾之上，这应是模仿北朝菩萨像服饰的做法（Ai式）。有的菩萨身体微扭动，掩腋衣无带，余同前者（Aii式）。菩萨头光作圆形火焰状，整体似桃形，皆内雕单方圆尖莲瓣，外为火焰纹（Ai式）。菩萨像座主要为圆莲座，中央为莲蓬，周围作合莲（A型）；个别为束腰圆莲座，上半为单方圆仰莲，下半为双圆合莲（Bi式）。

龙门石窟中新出现的神王，颈围项护，"上缀披膊"，束臂护。胸护多有花饰，上缘用带向后与背甲扣联。腰带上多具脐护，腰带下左右各一片膝裙，其表面垂覆一半圆形饰帛，饰帛末端上系两腰后多垂下。膝裙下摆饰百褶，露出战裙，"下属吊腿"，脚着战靴。本期神王甲带十字形穿环绊在胸前，左右各一较大的胸护。脐护作半花形，战裙摆边下垂或略扬向一侧。双腿分开直立（A型）。神王脚下的药叉，已残蚀不清，似以臀部托扛神王（A型）。

金刚力士双腿叉开立于山岩座上，头束髻，束带自两侧上飘。面相方正，眉骨隆起，眼圆睁，鼻翼较宽，颧骨突出，大嘴、鼓腮。颈部青筋突暴，锁骨显露；一手屈举至肩，一手置于腰部或体侧；胯部扭动，一腿微屈，一腿直立；袒上身，下着裙；裙腰外翻，裙摆呈尖角飘向一侧。金刚力士像，本期仅见于宾阳南洞和药方洞，体型较小，略显单薄；肋骨、双乳、腹肌明显，胸部较鼓，臂、腿肌肉发达。腰带打结隐现，披巾在头后扬成一大圆环，后似于腰侧打结，末端垂于腿侧（Ai式）。

窟顶中央雕莲花，周围环绕飞天（A型）。飞天多雕于窟顶莲花周围，少数镌在前庭后壁窟门上方；多身体俯卧，作飞翔状，身体略呈弧形。飞天束发髻，多戴项饰，袒上身，下着袖腿长裙，披巾多于头后扬成一大圆环，末端自腋下或绕臂后飘。本期飞天仅出现在药方洞前庭后壁和主室窟顶，发髻较平，双手持乐器(A型)。

(2) 相关问题及年代推定

龙门唐代第一期窟龛中没有明确的开窟题记，但有些碑铭和后代补凿的纪年小龛，为我们推断这一期窟龛的年代提供了许多信息。

破窑内雕凿小龛约43座，没有主体朝拜对象，不过正壁中央的善跏趺坐佛像位置显要，或许为此窟最早开凿的龛像。龛外右侧榜题作“大唐贞观十一年岁次丁酉十月五日(637年10月28日)□/道国王母刘□妤为道王元庆向洛州咸/礼心中忧悴恐有灾鄣仰凭三宝请乞□/护蒙佛慈恩内外平善敬造弥勒像一区/以报大圣上资　皇帝下及含生同出苦源俱登正觉”[1]。文中的“道国王母刘□妤”，应为“道国王母刘婕妤”，乃唐高祖妃嫔[2]。刘婕妤于贞观十一年为其子(即唐高祖第十六子道王元庆)敬造的弥勒像位于正壁中央，说明她与破窑的开凿活动有某种必然的联系[3]。需要指出的是，该像也是龙门石窟中现存最早的唐代纪年龛像之一[4]。

老龙洞北壁现存《新息县令田弘道等造菩萨像记》，时间是贞观廿一年四月七日(647年5月16日)[5]。

唐字洞是北魏末期始凿的一座洞窟，但未按计划完工；窟内左、右、后三壁现存龛像皆为唐代雕造[6]。正壁龛系草就完成，龛内三像雕刻粗拙，二狮仅雕出轮廓，菩萨座细部未刻。南壁有永徽二年七月六日(651年7月28日)、永州郭孝阵造观世音像[7]，从其位置推断，应晚于正壁龛像。

药方洞前庭后壁右侧力士的披巾外侧，有王师亮所造阿弥陀像，完工于永徽四年八月十日(653年9月7日)[8]。这表明金刚力士像的雕造不会晚于永徽四年[9]，而窟内主像的年代，也应早于永徽四年。

---

[1] 参见：刘景龙、李玉昆主编，上引书，第332-333页。

[2]《旧唐书·高祖二十二子》，点校本，北京：中华书局，第2414、2432页。

[3] 曾布川寛《龍門石窟における唐代造像の研究》，见《東方學報》，第60册，京都：京都大学人文科学研究所，1988年，第208页。

[4] 龙门现存最早的唐代纪年造像，是《洛州乡城老人佛碑》所记龛像，为贞观十一年正月廿一日，仅比刘婕妤所造龛像早九个月。参见：刘景龙、李玉昆主编，上引书，第13-14页。

[5] 参见：刘景龙、李玉昆主编，上引书，第214-215页。

[6] 阎文儒、常青，上引书，第80-81页。

[7] 参见：刘景龙、李玉昆主编，上引书，第364页。

[8] 参见：刘景龙、李玉昆主编，上引书，第412页。

[9] 温玉成《龙门唐窟排年》，见龙门文物保管所、北京大学考古系编《中国石窟·龙门石窟》二，北京：文物出版社，1992年，第178页。

宾阳南洞是北魏皇室出资开凿的宾阳三洞之一，但未按原计划完工[1]。该窟左右壁现存唐贞观年间开凿的纪年龛像约20座，最早者乃贞观十五年三月十日（641年4月25日）豫章公主敬造，此外还有五龛亦同年毕功[2]。这说明贞观十五年前后应是宾阳南洞唐代造像的高潮。唐太宗贞观十五年“十一月，蒐于伊阙，诏所经之县，遣使存问高年，赐帛各有差”[3]。值得注意的是，《伊阙佛龛之碑》立于贞观十五年十一月，这或许不是巧合。据学者近年研究，宾阳南洞正壁一铺五身像，就是《伊阙佛龛之碑》记载的魏王李泰为生母文德皇后长孙氏所造[4]。

从上述纪年铭刻来看，第一期窟龛大约始凿于贞观十一年前后，且主要利用原有遗存进行补造，目的是祈福、供养和做功德，没有大规模的斫岩开窟活动。此前的龙门没有确切的唐代纪年龛像。这种状况，应与当时的历史背景有关。武德四年（621年），唐军攻克隋朝和郑王朝的都城洛阳，标志着李唐王朝取得了全国政权。不过，隋末唐初的战争，也使当时的洛阳及周边地区遭到了较大的破坏。文献记载“隋末土崩，洛中云扰，米遂腾跃，斗至十千。顿碚于是成行，骨肉不能相救”[5]。至贞观六年（632年），魏征尚言：“今自伊、洛之东，暨乎海、岱，灌莽巨泽，茫茫千里，人烟断绝，鸡犬不闻。道路萧条，进退艰阻。”[6]洛阳的再度兴盛，或许与唐太宗首次巡幸有关。据《旧唐书·太宗纪》下，“（贞观十一年二月）甲子（637年3月10日），幸洛阳宫……（三月）丁亥（4月2日），车驾至洛阳。丙申，改洛州为洛阳宫……夏四月……丙寅，诏河北、淮南举孝弟淳笃，兼闲时务；儒术该通，可为师范；文辞秀美，才堪著述；明识政体，可委字人；并志行修立，为乡闾所推者，给传诣洛阳宫”[7]。驾巡洛邑后不久，太宗

[1] 1) 刘汝醴《关于龙门三窟》，见龙门石窟研究所编《龙门石窟研究论文选》，上海：上海人民美术出版社，1993年，第56-61页；2) 宿白《洛阳地区北朝石窟的初步考察》，见宿白《中国石窟寺研究》，北京：文物出版社，1996年，第155-158页。

[2] 参见：刘景龙、李玉昆主编，上引书，第21-41页。

[3]《册府元龟》卷五十五《帝王部·养老》，影印明本，北京：中华书局，1960年，第617页。

[4] 1) 李文生《龙门石窟的新发现及其他》，见李文生《龙门石窟与洛阳历史文化》，上海：上海人民美术出版社，1993年，第16-29页；2) 张若愚《伊阙佛龛之碑和潜溪寺、宾阳洞》，见《文物》，1980年第1期，第19-24页。

[5]《大唐曹州离狐县盖赞君故妻孙夫人墓志之铭》，见周绍良主编《唐代墓志汇编》，永徽108条，上海：上海古籍出版社，1992年，第201页。

[6] 吴兢《贞观政要》卷二《纳谏》，点校本，上海：上海古籍出版社，1978年，第70页。

[7]《旧唐书·太宗纪下》，点校本，北京：中华书局，1975年，第46-48页。

下《道士女冠在僧尼之上诏》，由此引发佛道先后问题之争[1]。唐太宗后 “遣中书侍郎岑文本宣口敕，云语诸僧等，明诏既下，如也不伏，国有严科”[2]。同年，下敕法恭 “赴洛，常州法宣同时被召……深降恩礼……入侍宴筵”[3]。太宗原意借老君高居万姓之上，后来发现佛教更有利于自己的统治。据道宣《集古今佛道论衡》卷三《文帝幸弘福寺立愿重施叙佛道先后事》，“贞观十五年五月十四日 (641 年 6 月 27 日)，太宗文帝躬幸弘福寺……帝曰……自有国已来，何处别造道观？凡有功德，并归寺家。国内战场之始，无不一心归命于佛。今天下大定，战场之地并置佛寺，乃至本宅先妣唯置佛寺。朕敬有处，所以尽命归依”[4]。据文献记载，贞观中前后，唐太宗曾多次下诏度僧传法。如《度僧于天下诏》曰：“天下诸州有寺之处，宜令度人为僧尼，总数以三千为限”[5]，《诸州寺度僧诏》：“京城及天下诸州寺宜各度五人，宏福寺宜度五十人”[6]，《令诸州寺观转经行道诏》：“可于京城及天下诸州寺观，僧尼道士等七月 (日) 七夜转经行道，每年正月、七月，例皆准此”[7]。

因此，龙门唐代开窟造像活动始于此后不久，且规模有限，应是情理中事。至于本期窟龛之下限，依据上述纪年题铭，我们认为：唐字洞正壁主像应早于永徽二年 (651 年) 完工，药方洞前庭后壁金刚力士及窟内主像应完工于永徽四年 (653 年) 之前。至于 “永徽元年十月五日 (650 年 11 月 3 日)，汝州刺史、驸马都尉、渝国公刘玄意敬造金刚力士” 像于宾阳南洞前壁[8]，疑为该窟最晚的造像活动，当时宾阳南洞已无多少可以利用的壁面或空间了。又，宾阳南洞与宾阳北洞有若干相似之处，如佛座、右侧菩萨、菩萨头光的类型等。因此，我们将第一期窟龛的下限暂定在 650 年前后。这样，龙门唐代第一期龛像主要完工于唐太宗后期，即 637 年至 649 年左右。

2. 第二期

(1) 窟龛形制及造像特征

第二期窟龛形制仍以正壁佛坛窟 / 正壁一龛窟 (A 型) 为主，但新出现了三壁环

---

[1] 道宣《集古今佛道论衡》卷三《太宗下敕道先佛后僧等上谏事》，见《大正藏》第 52 卷，第 382b-383a 页。参见宋敏求《唐大诏令集》卷一百十三《政事 · 道释 · 道士女冠在僧尼之上诏》，点校本，北京：商务印书馆，1959 年，第 586-587 页。

[2] 彦悰《唐护法沙门法琳别传》卷中，《大正藏》第 50 卷，第 204a 页。

[3]《续高僧传 · 法恭传》，《大正藏》第 50 卷，第 536b 页。

[4]《大正藏》第 52 卷，第 385c-386a 页。

[5]《广弘明集》卷二十八《启福篇 · 唐太宗度僧于天下诏》，《大正藏》第 52 卷，第 329b 页。

[6]《全唐文》卷八《太宗皇帝》，影印本，北京：中华书局，1983 年，第 104 页。

[7]《全唐文》卷九《太宗皇帝》，影印本，北京：中华书局，1983 年，第 108 页。

[8] 李文生《龙门石窟的新发现及其他》，上引书，第 16-29 页。

坛窟（B 型）。窟顶仍以穹隆顶（A 型）为主，少量为平顶（B 型）。

造像题材仍以一佛为主，即主尊雕造于正壁中央，两侧为胁侍（A 型）；个别为三佛，即左、右、后三壁各造一佛（B 型）；少数窟龛除正壁主尊外，还在侧壁雕造数量众多的小型坐佛（C 型）。造像组合多样，有一铺三身或五身像（Ai 式），即一佛、二菩萨或一佛、二弟子、二菩萨，有的加雕二狮子如清明寺；一铺七身像（Aii 式），即一佛、二弟子、二菩萨、二神王或金刚力士；一铺九身像（Aiii 式），即一佛、二弟子、二菩萨、二神王及金刚力士，如大卢舍那像龛，有的加雕二狮子，如万佛洞。此外，还出现了三铺像，即以三佛为中心的造像组合（B 型）。其中，后三种是新出现的。在上述组合中，以一铺九身像为多，一铺七身像次之，整体模拟地面佛寺的佛殿像设。

关于造像特征，佛像多结跏趺坐，施无畏印。少数内着掩腋衣，上衣覆搭双肩后，两衣缘于胸前系带打结；大衣由左肩覆背披至右肘后，衣尾上搭左肩，仅在右肩上略作遮覆，下摆垂覆座前，腿部衣纹近横向，摆边较平缓（C 型），多数上衣覆搭双肩，两衣缘自颈侧垂于腹前；大衣右角宽搭左肩，垂之背后，左侧边缘自颈外垂下，右侧边缘自右胁下绕出、覆腹后衣尾上搭左臂，作“右袒式”披覆；双腿间弧形衣纹多近横向，摆边呈倒三角形或半圆状垂覆座前或座上，其中佛善跏趺坐者，大衣下摆垂至脚面，双腿间衣纹呈水波状（Di 式）。这种新型“着衣法式”，即上衣遮搭双肩、大衣作“右袒式”披覆，是不符合佛制的，疑与唐初道世所记当时沙门着衣不合规制有关：“今诸沙门但出一肩，仍有衫袄，非袒露法。”[1]由此看出，石窟中的佛法衣，确为当时僧人所着法服的摹写。从这一角度来说，所谓的上衣或许应称作衫袄更贴切些。此外，个别窟龛还出现了佛结跏趺坐，通肩披衣（E 型）之做法。主尊大衣褶襞方面，少数延续前期旧制，即衣纹“压地隐起”，断面近似凸棱（A 型）；多数衣纹断面作直平阶梯式（B 型）。佛像头光皆圆形，多数延续第一期旧制（Bi 式），少数佛像头光内匝莲瓣作如意头形，外匝雕七身小坐佛（Bii 式）。佛座个别延续前期旧式（Bi 式），多数为束腰八角须弥座，三面隐现，有的束腰下部依次为二或三层叠涩、双圆合莲、基座，两侧抹角处各雕一形体较小的狮子（Ci 式）；有的上半部为双层单圆翘角仰莲，束腰部位雕出力士，下半部依次为三层叠涩、如意头合莲、基座（Cii 式）；个别束腰下部依次为叠涩、双圆翘角合莲、基座（Ciii 式）。同时，新出现了前置踏座之高方座（D 型）。

弟子内着交领衫；上衣覆搭双肩后两衣缘自颈侧垂于腹前；大衣多作“右袒式”披覆，个别“通肩披衣”；内衣下摆长出大衣，垂覆脚面。个别延续第一期旧制（Bi 式），多数身体比例适中、直立；双手多于胸前合十，个别双手于胸前托持一物；

---

[1] 道世《法苑珠林》，周叔迦、苏晋仁校注，北京：中华书局，2003 年，第 654 页。

大衣下半部渐窄（Bii 式）。少数上身短、下身长，身体直立，双手合十于胸前，或托持珠形物，或作叉手状；内衣下摆外张（Biii 式）。弟子头光多延续前期旧制（A 型），少数作双同心圆，素面（Bi 式）。弟子像座绝大多数为束腰圆莲座，有的延续第一期旧式（Bi 式）；流行上半部作单圆翘角仰莲，下半部为双圆翘角合莲（Bii 式）；少数上半部为单圆翘角仰莲，下半部为双圆翘角合莲，唯束腰上下各有一凸棱（Biii 式）。此外，个别窟龛还出现了束腰八角莲座（C 型）。

第二期菩萨像样式皆不见第一期，部分左右侧菩萨像出现造型差异，共有两种类型：一种身体略扭动，腹部略鼓；上身着掩腋衣，下身系裙；掩腋衣于胸前扣带，束裙大带下垂如绅，上打蝴蝶结；披巾自双肩搭下后沿体侧自然下垂，璎珞交叉于腹前（Aiii 式）。另一种身体略扭动，腹部较鼓；上身着掩腋，下身系裙，多配繁复项饰，掩腋简朴；束裙大带下垂如绅，上打蝴蝶结；披巾自肩搭下后横于腹下两道或径直下垂至脚侧；璎珞交叉于腹前（Bi 式）；少数身体扭动略呈 S 形，腹部较鼓；掩腋多简朴无饰，如绅大带多不见（Bii 式）。菩萨头光多延续一期旧式（Ai 式），新出现圆形头光内匝雕单方圆翘角莲瓣，个别为如意头莲瓣，莲瓣外缘有的雕小坐佛，外匝为火焰纹（Aii 式）。菩萨像座绝大多数为束腰圆莲座，个别延续一期旧式（Bi 式），流行上半为单圆翘角仰莲，下半作双圆翘角合莲（Bii 式），或上半为单圆翘角仰莲，下半为双圆翘角合莲，束腰上下各一凸棱（Biii 式）。此外，个别窟龛新出现了束腰八角座（C 型）。

神王形象基本同第一期，铠甲分两种。一种延续前期旧式（A 型），另一种是新出现的，即披膊有的作龙首状，胸甲分左右两片，中间以带或钩相连，每片中心缀凸起花饰。胸腹甲联成一体，脐护作兽面或半花形，多有膝护，战裙下摆有的缚吊腿内。胯部略扭，多一腿弓起，一腿直立（B 型）。神王脚下的药叉，双眼圆睁、三角形塌鼻、颧骨突出、大嘴。略矮胖，挺胸、鼓腹，肌体健壮，袒上身，下着牛鼻裈。有的四肢作爬行状，面部侧向主尊，神王踏其头及臀或腰部（A 型）；有的蹲坐，头发后梳，一腿平放，一腿屈立；上肢作手，下肢为爪。一手拄地或抵膝，以手和头或肩和膝等托扛神王（Bi 式）。

金刚造型皆为新样，体态基本同前期，唯服饰较多。金刚多戴冠，配项饰，挂璎珞。披巾有的在头后扬成一大圆环，末端垂至山岩座上，缠绕方式不清；个别披巾横于腹下两道。有的体型较小，单薄但不失健壮，肋骨、双乳、腹肌明显，胸部较鼓，臂、腿肌肉发达，腰带打结隐现（Bi 式）；有的体态雄健有力，双肩较宽，肋骨、双乳、腹肌明显，胸部隆起，腹部凸显，臂肌略呈块状凸起，腰带多于腹前打结垂下（Bii 式）。

窟顶装饰题材仍延续第一期旧制，顶部中央雕莲花，周围绕飞天（A 型）。个别洞窟侧壁雕镌伎乐，其中里端两身作舞蹈状，余奏乐。伎乐头束高髻，宽肩、挺胸、细腰、鼓腹。大多双腿盘坐，或一腿盘坐、一腿垂下。上身袒裸或着掩腋，佩项饰、手镯；下着裙，裙腰外翻。披巾多在头后扬成三个圆环，呈品字形，末端向两侧飘扬（A型）。飞天造型个别延续前期旧式（A型），多数双手合十，或一手前伸、一手于胸前持莲花或宝珠；双腿伸展，或一腿屈起（B型）。

(2) 相关问题及年代推定

第二期窟龛中，有明确开窟纪年者达3座之多，即惠简洞、大卢舍那像龛和万佛洞，是我们排比龙门唐代窟龛年代的标尺。

惠简洞右侧壁前端，镌刻"大唐咸亨四年十一月七/日（673年12月20日）西京海寺法[1]僧惠简/奉为皇帝皇后太子周/王敬造弥勒像一龛二菩/萨神王等并德成就伏愿/皇业圣花无穷殿下诸王福延万代"[2]。

大卢舍那像龛主尊像座正面右侧（南侧），有唐高宗调露二年（680）所刻《大卢舍那像龛记》，唯字迹大部泯灭，现存20行。幸运的是，唐开元十年（722年）重刻于佛座左侧面（北侧面）里端的同一内容碑铭保存完整，并附刻牒文：大卢舍那像龛系"大唐高宗天皇大帝之所建也佛身通光座高八十五尺二菩萨七十尺/迦叶阿难金刚神王各高五十尺粤以咸亨三年壬申之岁四月一日（672年5月3日）/皇后武氏助脂粉钱二万贯奉敕检校僧西京实际寺善道禅师法/海寺主惠暕（简）法师大使司农卿韦机副使东面监上柱国樊玄则支料/匠李君瓒成仁威姚师积等至上元二年乙亥十二月卅日（676年1月20日）毕功……"[3]

万佛洞窟顶莲花周围镌刻"大监/姚神表/内/道场/运禅/师一/万五/千尊/像龛/大唐/永隆/元年/十一/月卅/日（680年12月26日）成"[4]；窟门左侧上方，又镌"沙门智运奉为/天皇天后太子/诸王敬造一万/五千尊像一龛"[5]。

此外，第二期有些窟龛中的碑刻铭记，对我们进一步判断龙门唐代第二期窟龛的年代，也具有较大价值。

---

[1] 依据大卢舍那像龛题铭，此"海寺法"应为"法海寺"之误。参见：刘景龙、李玉昆主编，上引书，第179页。

[2] 参见：刘景龙、李玉昆主编，上引书，第179页。

[3] 参见：刘景龙、李玉昆主编，上引书，第379-381页。又，龙门石窟编号1483窟也有一《卢舍那大石像记》，内容与之基本相同，亦记大卢舍那像龛的开凿。参见：刘景龙、李玉昆主编，上引书，第549页。

[4] 参见：刘景龙、李玉昆主编，上引书，第138-139页。

[5] 参见：刘景龙、李玉昆主编，上引书，第143页。

敬善寺前庭左侧壁现存宣德朗守记室参军事李孝伦所撰《敬善寺石像铭》。内云："纪国太妃韦氏，京兆人也……爰择胜畿，聿修灵像。"[1]依据碑文，足证敬善寺乃韦太妃出资敬造而成。韦太妃乃唐太宗妃嫔、太宗十四子纪王慎之母[2]，麟德二年(665年)"纪国太妃时在洛下"[3]。敬善寺的开凿或许在此前后[4]。

赵客师洞左壁东端龛内造一佛、二弟子、二菩萨五身像，龛下雕造香炉、双狮、金刚力士及供养人，龛外左侧题刻："大唐显庆五年岁次庚申七月廿日(660年8月31日)洛州偃师县凤□乡□任县尉杨君……敬造阿弥陀像一龛……"[5]；右壁大龛内亦造一佛、二弟子、二菩萨，龛下雕一炉二狮，龛右侧有长篇题记，字迹多泯灭，但纪年清晰："维大唐显庆五年岁次庚申……"[6]从龙门石窟开窟时正壁与侧壁龛像的经营程序来看，侧壁龛像的开凿通常晚于正壁龛像。因此，赵客师洞主尊造像似应完工于显庆五年(660年)之前。

清明寺门道左侧壁中部现存一阿弥陀像，系"上元二年三月十五日(675年4月15日)弟子王仁恪敬造"[7]。由此证明，清明寺的完工应早于上元二年。

双窑北洞右壁现存一垂拱三年四月八日(687年5月24日)毕功之阿弥陀像龛[8]，窟门亦保存一完工于同年同月同日的观音像[9]；而双窑南洞前庭正壁保存的一尊阿弥陀像，系垂拱二年七月十五日(686年8月9日)造讫[10]。这些小型纪年龛像表明，双窑石窟应完工于垂拱二年之前。

赵上洞右壁菩萨像外侧，有一后补小龛，内造坐佛二身，题铭分别为"弟子王元轨妻/刘氏奉为亡妣/崔夫人敬造/弥陁像一躯"、"弟子王元轨为/亡妻刘氏敬造/阿弥陁像一躯/垂拱三年六月/十六日(687年7月30日)造毕"[11]。

依据上述题记，第二期窟龛的上限应为显庆五年(660年)之前，下限为垂拱三

---

[1] 参见：刘景龙、李玉昆主编，上引书，第100-101页。

[2]《旧唐书·太宗诸子》，点校本，北京：中华书局，1975年，第2647、2664页。

[3] 王昶《金石萃编》卷五十六《纪国陆妃碑》和《敬善寺石像铭》及按语，影印本，北京：中国书店，1985年。

[4] 阎文儒、常青，上引书，第60页。

[5] 参见：刘景龙、李玉昆主编，上引书，第322页。

[6] 参见：刘景龙、李玉昆主编，上引书，第323页。

[7] 参见：刘景龙、李玉昆主编，上引书，第167页。

[8] 参见：刘景龙、李玉昆主编，上引书，第118页。

[9] 参见：刘景龙、李玉昆主编，上引书，第119页。

[10] 参见：刘景龙、李玉昆主编，上引书，第123页。

[11] 参见：刘景龙、李玉昆主编，上引书，第327页。

年 (687 年) 之前，主要完工于唐高宗统治时期。

高宗修正了太宗 "道士、女冠宜在僧、尼之前"[1] 的主张，采用折中办法，于上元元年八月二十四日 (674 年 9 月 29 日) 下诏 "公私斋会及参集之处，道士、女冠在东，僧、尼在西，不须更为先后"[2]，致使佛教较前期有了很大发展。高宗曾于贞观十三年(639 年) 下《谕普光寺僧众令》[3] 和《答沙门慧净辞知普光寺任令》[4]，贞观二十二年(648 年) 下《建大慈恩寺令》[5]；即位后，颁布《僧尼不得受父母拜诏》[6]，显庆元年 (656 年) 又下《检阅新译经论敕》[7] 和《为佛光王度七人敕》[8]，显庆三年 (658 年) 下《造西明寺敕》[9]，龙朔二年 (662 年) 下《令僧尼道士女冠致敬父母诏》[10]，仪凤元年(676 年) 下《废宫立开业寺诏》[11]；同时御制《大慈恩寺碑文》[12]，亲撰《二藏圣教后序》[13]、《隆国寺碑铭》[14] 和《摄山栖霞寺明征君碑》[15]。尤为重要的是，"(咸亨) 三年 (672 年)，敕洛阳龙门山镌石龛卢舍那佛像，高八十五尺"[16]，自

---

[1]《唐会要》卷四十九《僧道立位》，影印《丛书集成》本，北京：中华书局，1955 年，第 859 页。

[2] 出处同上。

[3]《续高僧传 · 慧净传》，见《大正藏》第 50 卷，第 444a-b 页。参见《全唐文》卷十一《高宗皇帝》，影印本，北京：中华书局，1983 年，第 135 页。

[4]《全唐文》卷十一《高宗皇帝》，影印本，北京：中华书局，1983 年，第 135-136 页。

[5] 慧立、彦悰《大慈恩寺三藏法师传》，孙毓棠、谢方点校，北京：中华书局，2000 年，第 155 页。

[6]《唐大诏令集》卷一百十三《政事 · 道释 · 僧尼不得受父母拜诏》，点校本，北京：商务印书馆，1959 年，第 587 页。参见《唐会要》卷四十七《议释教》上，影印《丛书集成》本，北京：中华书局，1955 年，第 836 页。

[7]《全唐文》卷十四《高宗皇帝》，影印本，北京：中华书局，1983 年，第 1164 页。

[8] 慧立、彦悰，上引书，第 201 页。

[9]《大唐故三藏玄奘法师行状》，参见《大正藏》第 50 卷，第 218c 页。

[10] 1)《宋本册府元龟》卷六十《帝王部 · 立制度》，影印本，北京：中华书局，1989 年，第 99 页。2)《全唐文》卷十二《高宗皇帝》，影印本，北京：中华书局，1983 年，第 148 页。

[11]《唐会要》卷四十八《议释教》下，影印《丛书集成》本，北京：中华书局，1955 年，第 845 页。

[12] 慧立、彦悰，上引书，第 185-189 页。

[13]《全唐文》卷十五《高宗皇帝》，影印本，北京：中华书局，1983 年，第 177-178 页。

[14] 1) 道世，上引书，第 2898 页；2)《全唐文》卷十五《高宗皇帝》，影印本，北京：中华书局，1983 年，第 179-180 页。

[15] 原碑今存南京栖霞寺大殿前。参见：1) 赵明诚《金石录》卷四、卷二十四《唐明征君碑》，金文明校证，桂林：广西师范大学出版社，2005 年，第 64、418 页；2)《全唐文》卷十一《高宗皇帝》，影印本，北京：中华书局，1983 年，第 181-184 页。

[16]《佛祖统纪》卷三十九《法运通塞志 · 高宗》、卷五十三《历代会要志 · 设像置经》，见《大正藏》第 49 卷，第 368a、463a 页。

此成为龙门的标志性龛像[1]。

大卢舍那像龛的开凿，疑与高僧法藏有关。据阎朝隐《大唐大荐福寺故大德康藏法师之碑》，法藏早年“闻云华寺俨法师讲《华严经》，投为上足。泻水置瓶之受纳，以乳投水之因缘。名播招提，誉流宸极。属荣国夫人奄捐馆舍，未易齐衰；则天圣后广树福田，大开讲座。法师策名宫禁，落发道场，住太原寺”[2]。关于法藏，海东崔致远结《唐大荐福寺故寺主翻经大德法藏和尚传》叙述尤详：

> 法藏年甫十七（显庆四年己未，659年）志锐择师，遍谒都邑缁英，懊其拙于用大，遂辞亲求法于太白山。饵术数年，敷阅《方等》，后闻亲疾，出谷入京。时智俨法师于云华寺讲《华严经》。（法）藏于中夜忽睹神光来烛庭宇，乃叹曰：“当有异人弘扬大教。”翌旦，就寺膜拜已，因设数问，言皆出意表……藏既飡俨之妙解，以为真吾师也。俨亦喜传炷之得人，自是预流徒中……及总章元年(668年)，俨将化去，藏犹居俗（时年二十六）。俨乃累道成、薄尘二大德，曰：此贤者注意于华严，盖无师自悟；绍隆遗法其惟是人，幸假余光俾沾制度。至咸亨元年(670年，藏年二十八)，荣国夫人奄归冥路，则天皇后广树福田，度人则择上达僧，舍宅乃成太原寺。于是，受顾托者连状荐推。帝诺曰：俞仍頯新刹，周罗遂落夏援常科。此之谓削染因缘，岂非以方便心推求简择趣真方便乎？既出家未进具，承旨于所配寺讲百千经。时属端午，天后遣使送衣五事，其书曰：蕤宾应节，角黍登期，景候稍炎。师道体清适，属长丝之令节。承命缕之嘉辰，今送衣裳五事，用符端午之数。愿师承兹采艾之序，更茂如松之龄，永耀传灯，常为导首……[3]

荣国夫人杨氏佞佛，唐初高僧与之多有交际，如律宗巨匠道宣。唐彦悰纂《集沙门不应拜俗等事》，内收《西明寺僧道宣等重上荣国夫人杨氏请论不合拜见启》一首[4]。关于武则天母亲荣国夫人故去时间，《唐大荐福寺故寺主翻经大德法藏和尚传》作咸亨元年(670年)，《旧唐书·高宗纪》作咸亨元年九月甲申(670年10月3日)[5]，《资

[1] 关于卢舍那大像龛的兴建，有学者认为是唐高宗为唐太宗追福所立，参见温玉成《略谈龙门奉先寺的几个问题》，见《中原文物》，1984年第2期，第53-57页；也有学者认为是高宗和武则天为纪念武后圣母杨氏所建，参见Anotonino Forte[富安敦]，*Political Propaganda and Ideology in China at the End of the Seventh Century: Inquiry into the Nature, Authors and Function fo the Tunhuang Document S. 6502*, Napoli: Istituto Universitario Orientale-Seminario di Studi Asiatici, 1976: 97-98.

[2]《大正藏》第50卷，第280b页。

[3]《大正藏》第50卷，第281b页。

[4] 参见:《大正藏》第52卷，第473a页。

[5]《旧唐书》卷五《高宗纪》下，“（咸亨元年）九月甲申(670年10月3日)，卫国夫人杨氏薨，赠鲁国夫人，谥曰忠烈。闰月壬子，故赠司徒、周忠孝公士彟赠太尉、太子太师、太原郡王，赠鲁国忠烈太夫人赠太原王妃。甲寅，葬太原王妃，京官文武九品已上及外命妇，送至便桥宿次”。《旧唐书》，点校本，北京：中华书局，1975年，第95页。

治通鉴》亦作咸亨元年九月甲申[1]，只有《旧唐书·外戚传》作咸亨二年[2]。因此，可以推定荣国夫人薨于唐咸亨元年。另据《新唐书·高宗则天顺圣皇后传》，“杨氏徙酆、卫二国，咸亨元年卒，追封鲁国，谥忠烈，诏文武九品以上及五等亲与外命妇赴吊，以王礼葬咸阳，给班剑、葆仗、鼓吹”[3]。

对此，新近从《册府元龟》卷三百零三《外戚部·褒宠》检出的资料颇具价值：

> 咸亨元年九月甲申（670年10月3日），后母卫国夫人杨氏薨，赠鲁国太夫人，谥曰“忠烈”。司刑、太常伯卢承庆，摄同文正卿、充使监护、西台侍郎戴至德持节吊祭哀，文武九品以上及亲戚五等以上并外命妇，并听赴宅吊哭。葬及坟茔、卤簿等一事已上并依王礼，给班剑四十人，羽葆鼓吹，仪仗送至墓所往还。其文武官九品以上，并至渭桥宿次；外妇诸亲妇女，并送至墓所。官为立碑，仍令特进许敬宗为其文。壬辰（10月11日），皇后请为夫人度太平公主出家为女官，并请颁政坊民置女宫观，休祥坊宅置僧寺，兼各度人追福。并从之。闰九月壬子（10月31日），又诏故工部尚书、赠司徒、周忠孝公士彟加赠太尉、兼太子太师、太原郡王；鲁国忠烈太夫人加赠太原郡王妃，所司备礼册命[4]。

《册府元龟》除详细介绍武则天母亲故去、葬礼及授封情况外，还记载了武则天奏请为荣国夫人度太平公主出家为女官，并请颁政坊民置女宫观[5]，休祥坊宅置僧寺，兼各度人追福。

---

[1]《资治通鉴》卷二百零一《唐纪》十七：“（咸亨元年九月）甲申（670年10月3日），皇后母鲁国忠烈夫人杨氏卒，敕文武九品以上及外命妇并诣宅吊哭。”《资治通鉴》，标点本，北京：中华书局，1956年，第6365页。

[2]《旧唐书》卷一百八十三《外戚·武承嗣传》：“咸亨二年（671年），荣国夫人卒，则天出内大瑞锦，令敏之造佛像追福，敏之自隐用之。”《旧唐书》，点校本，北京：中华书局，1975年，第4728页。

[3]《新唐书》卷七十六《后妃·高宗则天顺圣皇后传》，点校本，北京：中华书局，1975年，第3476-3477页。

[4]《册府元龟》卷三百零三《外戚部·褒宠》，影印明本，北京：中华书局，1960年，第3572页。

[5] 颁政坊在休祥坊东南，与之毗邻。坊内民置女宫观，位于西北隅，韦述《两京新记》、宋敏求《长安志》和王溥《唐会要》等都有记载。《两京新记》曰：“大崇福观，本杨士达宅。咸亨中，为太平公主立。有道士刘宝概者，京兆三原人，善讲论，为时所重。垂拱中卒，御史中丞李嗣真临哭吊，赋诗申意。”《长安志》：“西北隅昭成观，本杨士达宅。咸亨元年（670年），太平公主立为太平观。寻移于大业坊，改此观为太清观，高宗御书飞白额。至垂拱三年（687年），改为魏国观。载初元年（690年），改为大业崇福观，武太后又御书飞白额。开元二十七年（739年），为昭成太后追福，改立此名。”《唐会要》卷五十《观》：“太平观，大业坊，本徐王元礼宅。太平公主出家，初以颁政坊宅为太平观，寻移于此。公主居之，时颁政坊观改为太清观。”参见：1）韦述《两京新记》，辛德勇辑校，西安：三秦出版社，2006年，第32页；2）宋敏求《长安志》，影印《丛书集成》本，北京：中华书局，1991年，第128页；3）王溥《唐会要》，影印《丛书集成》本，北京：中华书局，1955年，第870页。

"武则天之母杨氏为隋宗室观王雄弟始安侯达之女",而隋司空观王雄之子即杨恭仁[1]。杨恭仁原居休祥坊,贞观十三年(639年)卒,子杨思训及思训妻亦亡于显庆四年(659年),思训孙睿交"少袭爵观国公,尚中宗女长宁公主"[2]。恭仁从孙执柔,"历地官尚书,武后母即恭仁叔父达之女。及临朝,武承嗣、攸宁相继用事,后曰:'要欲我家及外氏常一人为宰相'。乃以执柔同中书门下三品,未几,卒"[3]。因此,武则天母女与杨恭仁一系关系密切。武则天之母杨氏"休祥坊宅",疑为杨恭仁休祥坊旧居。"武则天之母杨氏既为隋之宗室子孙,则其人之笃信佛教,亦不足为异也。"[4]故阎朝隐有"荣国夫人奄捐馆舍,未易齐衰"之词。及"荣国卒,后出珍币建佛庐徼福"[5]。稍后,奏请在休祥坊置僧寺,兼度人追福。武则天所置僧寺,应是韦述《两京新记》及宋敏求《长安志》所记载的西京太原寺[6]。故而,出现了阎朝隐及崔致远的上述记载。

智俨临终,嘱咐弟子道成、薄尘[7]:法藏留意《华严经》,能够无师自悟,绍隆遗法,幸而假你们之余光,使其剃度。咸亨元年(670年),武后舍宅作太原寺(即休祥坊僧寺),因道成、薄尘"联状荐推",法藏出家,受沙弥戒,令隶属太原寺。还没进具,他就得到允许登座讲经,即"承旨于所配寺讲百千经"。这时的法藏,已策名宫禁,名播招提,誉流宸极。时属端午,天后遣使送衣五事,"愿师承兹采艾之序,更茂如松之龄,永耀传灯,常为导首"。因此,两年后开凿的卢舍那大像,既然有皇后武则天赞助脂粉钱,恐与武则天家庙之高僧、华严宗实际创始人法藏不无关系。

---

[1] 陈寅恪《武则天与佛教》,载《金明馆丛稿二编》,上海:上海古籍出版社,1980年,第137-155页。

[2]《旧唐书》卷六十二《杨恭仁传》,点校本,北京:中华书局,1975年,第2382页。

[3]《新唐书》卷一百《杨恭仁传》,点校本,北京:中华书局,1975年,第3928页。

[4] 陈寅恪《武则天与佛教》,上引书,第144页。

[5]《新唐书》卷二百六《外戚·武士彟传》,点校本,北京:中华书局,1975年,第5836页。

[6]《两京新记》卷三:"休祥坊东北隅,崇福寺,本开府仪同三司、观(国)公杨恭仁宅。咸亨元年(670年),以武皇后外氏故宅立";《长安志》卷十《唐京城》四:"(休祥坊)东北隅,崇福寺,本侍中观国公杨恭仁宅,咸亨元年以武皇后外氏故宅,立为太原寺。垂拱三年(687年),改为魏国寺。载初元年(690年),又改为崇福寺;寺额,武太后飞白书";《唐会要》卷四十八《寺》,"崇福寺,休祥坊,本侍中杨恭仁宅。咸亨二年九月二日(671年10月10日),以武后外氏宅立太原寺。垂拱三年十二月(688年1月9日至2月6日),改为魏国寺。载初元年五月六日(690年6月17日),改为崇福寺"。上述记载中,仅《唐会要》把崇福寺立寺时间写作二年,疑有误。参见:1)韦述《两京新记》,辛德勇辑校,西安:三秦出版社,2006年,第44页;2)宋敏求《长安志》,影印《丛书集成》本,北京:中华书局,1991年,第133页;3)王溥《唐会要》,影印《丛书集成》本,北京:中华书局,1955年,第846页。

[7] 道成、薄尘二僧均参与了地婆诃罗译场,这也就不难理解后来法藏参谒地婆诃罗,特请其翻译《华严经》的《入法界品》。据《华严经传记》卷一《传译》:"高宗弘显释门,克隆遗寄,乃诏缁徒龙象、帝邑英髦,道成律师、薄尘法师十大德等,于魏国西寺翻译经论之次。时有贤首法师,先以华严为业,每慨斯经阙而未备,往就问之云:'赍第八会文,今来至此。'贤首遂与三藏对挍,遂获善财、善知识、天主光等十有余人,遂请译新文,以补旧阙。"《大正藏》第51卷,第154c页。

上有好者，下必有甚；“必假时君，弘传声略”[1]。翌年，西京著名高僧、法海寺惠简，“奉为皇帝、皇后、太子周王敬造弥勒像一龛、二菩萨、神王……伏愿皇业圣花无穷，殿下、诸王福延万代”；铭记中尤重周王李显，该窟乃惠简为皇业祈福所造。至于大监姚神表与皇宫内道场智运禅师共造之万佛洞，尽管反映出当时东都盛行礼忏修行并且受到崇重[2]，但也是“奉为天皇、天后、太子、诸王敬造”。两者皆沿袭北魏以来中国之传统：“承继弘福，遮邀冥庆，仰钟皇家，卜世惟永”，即依靠佛家的威力，得到永远的幸福；祝愿皇室，延续长久[3]。在这种背景下，龙门唐代的开窟造像活动达到了第一次高潮。当时皇室、显贵开凿的窟龛，在建筑形制、造像组合及个体造型特征方面，或许源自地面佛寺中的佛殿，因为无论在印度还是在中国，石窟寺皆系同期地面佛寺的模仿[4]或石化形式[5]。这种新型窟龛及其造像，对此后龙门石窟的开窟造像活动产生了较大影响，如大卢舍那像龛中的神王像造型一直沿用到中唐时期。因此，我们把龙门唐代第二期窟龛的雕造年代暂定在唐高宗时期，即649-683年左右。

3. 第三期

(1) 窟龛形制及造像特征

第三期窟龛平面形制多样，除个别延续前期旧制（A型）外，流行三壁环坛窟（B型），这种洞窟平面方形或横长方形，个别作多边形，后两端圆角，正壁略弧，环左、右、后三壁设高坛，坛上造像；出现了中心方坛窟，即窟平面方形，中央设坛（C型）。窟顶仍以前期流行的穹隆顶（A型）为主，少数为平顶（B型）；新出现了浅穹隆顶与平

---

[1] 道宣《大唐内典录》序，见《大正藏》第55卷，第219b页。

[2] 罗炤《宝山大住圣窟刻经中的北方礼忏系统》，见《石窟寺研究》，第一辑，北京：文物出版社，2010年，第161-180页。

[3] 金皇统七年（1147年）曹衍撰《大金西京武州山重修大石窟寺碑》引北魏钳耳庆时镌岩开寺铭，曰“承继弘福，遮邀冥庆，仰钟皇家，卜世惟永”。参见1）宿白《〈大金西京武州山重修大石窟寺碑〉校注》，见宿白《中国石窟寺研究》，北京：文物出版社，1996年，第52-75页；2）宿白《中国佛教石窟寺遗迹——3至8世纪中国佛教考古学》，北京：文物出版社，2010年，第30页。

[4] 即 an imitation of buildings constructed in timber。参见 M. N. Deshpande, “The (Ajanta) Caves: Their Historical Perspective”, in: *Ajanta Murals,* ed. A. Ghosh, New Delhi: Archaeological Survey of India, 1967: 14-21, esp. 17-18.

[5] 即 petrified versions of the contemporary brick-and-timber or the humbler wattle mud-and-thatch structures. *confer* K. R. Srinivasan, “Rock-cut Monuments”, In: *Archaeological Remains, Monuments & Museums,* ed. A. Ghosh, Part I, New Delhi: Archaeological Survey of India, 1964: 110. 最早用“petrified”来表述这一观念，应是印度佛教考古的开创者伯吉斯（James Burgess）。参见：James Fergusson and James Burgess, *The Cave Temples of India* (London: W. H. Allen & Co., 1880), 224.

顶合成型（C 型），即窟顶边缘与斜坡门道顶部交接处低缓，略高出门道或二者几乎持平。另外，为了模仿当时木构佛寺原型，解决洞窟本体与当时路面或通道之高差，有些洞窟在窟前雕砌巨大的石质踏道；踏道与窟体间增建木结构殿堂或窟檐，这是不见于此前的新形式，如擂鼓台中洞、擂鼓台南洞和看经寺等。

造像题材仍延续前期旧制，以一佛为主，即主尊雕造正壁中央，两侧为胁侍像（A 型）；少数为三佛，即左、右、后三壁各造一佛，个别窟在侧壁与正壁之间再增雕二身佛像，成五佛题材，如龙华寺（B 型）；此外，有些窟在侧壁雕造数量众多、形体较小的坐佛（C 型），个别窟还在侧壁下半雕刻高僧像，如擂鼓台中洞和看经寺。造像组合皆延续前期旧式，有一铺七身像，即一佛、二弟子、二菩萨、二神王或金刚力士（Aii 式）；一铺九身像，即一佛、二弟子、二菩萨、二神王及金刚力士，少数加雕二狮子（Aiii 式）；还有以三佛为中心的造像（B 型）。其中，以一铺九身像为主，余为一铺七身像或三铺像。石窟中的造像组合，模似地上寺院佛殿之像设日趋显著[1]。这一时期阿弥陀净土和弥勒净土都受到了重视，如擂鼓台中洞的弥勒和净土堂雕刻等，反映出信徒较普遍地考虑来生，净土信仰愈演愈烈。此外，法相、华严、密宗等也在窟龛造像中有不同程度的反映。

佛多作触地印，少数施无畏印，造型绝大多数延续前期；流行结跏趺坐，通肩披衣，即上衣隐现，大衣覆被两肩，衣纹自颈下呈水波状垂下，双腿间衣纹斜向、呈倒八字型，下摆多呈三瓣形垂覆座前（E 型）；少数结跏趺坐或善跏趺坐者，上衣覆搭双肩，大衣作“右袒式”披覆（Di 式）；新出现佛结跏趺坐，戴宝冠，佩项饰、臂钏，偏袒右肩或上衣偏袒右肩；左手平伸置于腹前腿上，右手抚膝作触地印（Dii 式）。这种新型法服及手印，系“竞模”印度菩提树像，应与当时中印佛教交流频繁、高僧接踵往还有关[2]。主尊大衣褶襞，断面皆作直平阶梯式。半数佛像开始不雕头光，有头光的主要延续前期旧式（Bii 式），新出现了桃形头光（C 型）。佛座变化多样，主要延续前期旧式，有 Bii、Cii、Ciii 式和 D 型之分。新出现了半圆形莲座，表面为二层单圆翘角仰莲（E 型）。

---

[1] 渤海国是唐代东北地区的一个重要政权，其文化大多学习唐朝，首都上京龙泉府位于今黑龙江省宁安县。1963-1964 年，中国科学院考古研究所组织专家对该城址进行了全面调查和大规模发掘，共发现佛寺遗址九座。其中一号佛寺遗址位于宫城朱雀大街东侧，位置显要，可能是上京城中规模最大的佛寺。因限于工作时间，没有将全寺的规模及布局厘清，但发掘出土的正殿遗迹保存较好。正殿包括主殿以及与之相连的东西两配殿，平面略成“凸”字型。主殿佛坛造像遗迹为一铺九身，发掘者推测为一佛、二弟子、二菩萨、二天王、二力士。佛坛遗迹在以前佛寺遗址的发掘中极为少见，这一发现对研究当时佛殿内的主体像设及供奉形式非常重要。这种一铺九身造像遗迹，即一佛、二弟子、二菩萨、二天王（神王）和金刚、力士，与武周时期龙门石窟佛殿内的主体像设非常相似。这既表明渤海国文化与唐朝文化之关系，也印证了石窟寺就是对地面佛寺的模仿。参见：中国社会科学院考古研究所编《六顶山与渤海镇——唐代渤海国的贵族墓地与都城遗址》，北京：中国大百科全书出版社，1997 年，第 76-81 页。

[2] 参见义净《大唐西域求法高僧传》，王邦维校注，附录一《求法僧一览表》，北京：中华书局，1988 年，第 247-252 页。

除个别洞窟外,第三期窟龛中左、右侧弟子的服饰及姿态有别。左侧弟子绝大多数延续前期旧式,上身短,下身长,身体直立,流行内着交领衫,上衣覆搭双肩,两衣缘自颈侧垂于腹前；大衣多作"右袒式"披覆,个别"通肩披衣"；内衣下摆外张(Biii式)。新出现的弟子像上身短,下身长,胯部略扭；上衣作"交领式",覆搭双肩,右臂前有带状物,疑为上衣的一部分；大衣作"右袒式"披覆,内衣下摆长出大衣且外张(C型)。右侧弟子像,除个别沿袭前期旧式(Bii式)外,绝大多数弟子上身短,下身长,胯部略扭；上衣作"交领式",覆搭双肩；大衣多作"右袒式"披覆,少数大衣作钩钮式,内衣下摆长出大衣且外张；双手交搭于腹前,多右手压左手(C型)。C型弟子像是本期新出现的造型[1]。多数弟子不雕头光,少数弟子头光可分圆形素面(A型)、同心圆素面(Bi式)和同心圆凸缘(Bii式)三种。绝大多数弟子像座延续前期旧式,有Biii式和C型之分；新出现了半圆仰莲座,饰单圆翘角莲瓣(D型)。

菩萨像多数延续前期旧式(Bii式),新出现身体扭动呈S形、鼓腹、细腰的形象；上身着掩腋,下身系裙,多配项饰；掩腋于胸前搭垂一角,似作带状；璎珞交叉于腹前,如绅大带不见,披巾自肩搭下后横于腹下两道或径直下垂至脚侧(Biii式)；个别上身短,下身长；挺胸、鼓腹、细腰,身体扭动呈S形；上身袒裸,下身着裙；披巾自肩搭下后径直垂下,肩挂璎珞(C型)。菩萨像近半不雕头光,有头光者多延续前期旧式(Aii式),出现圆形内匝素面外饰火焰纹(Aiii式)和桃形素面(B型)两种新形式。菩萨的像座多延续前期旧式,有Biii式和C型之分；新出现半圆莲座,饰单圆翘角仰莲瓣(D型)。

神王造型同前期,铠甲个别延续前期旧式(B型),新出现披膊作虎头状或龙首状,甲带于胸前穿环后与横带相交,或甲带自颈下纵束至胸前打结后再向左右分束于背后,整体作倒丁字形或十字形；脐护作山花形或兽面,战裙下摆扬向一侧,双腿分立或胯部扭动,一腿微弓,一腿直立(C型)；或上身短,下身长,双腿直立,胯部扭动,甲带倒丁字形绊缚或十字形扣联于胸前,脐护作半花形,膝裙下摆无褶,战裙下摆扬向一侧(Di式)。神王脚下的药叉,有的延续第二期旧式(Bi式),新出现卷发披肩或竖起的形象,多一腿平放、一腿屈立,个别似双腿盘坐；一手拄地,有的下肢作爪或蹄,多以双肩托扛神王(Bii式)。

除个别窟内金刚像延续前期旧式(Bii式),流行体态雄健有力,肋骨、双乳、腹肌明显,胸部隆起,腹部凸显,臂肌略呈块状凸起；袒上身,下着裙,裙腰外翻,腰带于腹前打结后呈八字形垂下；披巾有的在头后扬成一大圆环,末端垂至山岩座上,缠绕方式不清,有的于腰带处打结后垂下(Aii式),新出现Aiii式金刚像。

窟顶装饰同前期。伎乐仅见于少数窟中,多雕于基坛表面壸门之内,个别镌于侧

---

[1] 敦煌莫高窟盛唐洞窟正壁主尊右侧的弟子像似乎都着这种法服,应是受到了两京佛教艺术的影响。参见:《中国石窟：敦煌莫高窟》三,图版116、130。

壁下部。其中,正壁中央两身多作舞蹈状,两侧壁及正壁两端者奏乐。个别伎乐延续前期旧式(A型)。新型伎乐多束丫髻,少数作高髻,双腿多盘坐,上身袒裸,下身着裙,裙腰外翻,佩项饰、手镯。奏乐者不见披巾。个别舞蹈者披巾于头后扬成一圆环后绕臂垂下,持巾而舞,动感较强(B型)。本期飞天造型皆为新式,有两种:一种束发髻,戴项饰,袒上身、下着袖腿长裙;双臂张开,一手托盘,一手外扬;一腿弯曲,一腿伸展;披巾于头后扬成两个圆环,末端自腋下后飘,少数飞天无披巾(C型)。另一种多束髻,面相方圆,戴项饰,袒上身、下着袖腿长裙,裙腰外翻如短裙;双臂张开、扬掌;披巾先在头后扬成一大圆环,末端自腋下或绕臂后飘(D型)。

(2) 相关问题及年代推定

龙门唐代第三期窟龛中大多没有明确的开窟铭记,但有些原始遗迹及后代补造的纪年龛像对我们探讨本期窟龛的年代具有重要价值。

净土堂主室正壁左侧镌刻《王宝泰等造阿弥陀像记》,文中有"佥雕琢之良工,择山川□□□□凿岩开室号之曰西方净土□□□□□□陀佛像三铺并侍卫总□十一□□□□□年岁次甲午八月壬子朔……"[1]文中的年、月,皆为武则天新字。因此,岁次甲午应为武则天延载元年。换言之,净土堂应完工于公元694年8月26日。

擂鼓台中洞左、右、后三壁下部雕造传法高僧像,且采用"左图右史"方式于每一高僧像旁镌刻《付法藏因缘传》片段,经文中出现许多武周新字,如初、天、国、证、圣等。据《资治通鉴》卷二百零四,永昌元年十一月庚辰朔(689年12月18日),即载初元年正月,"凤阁侍郎河东宗秦客改造'天'、'地'等十二字以献,丁亥(12月25日),行之。太后自名'曌',改诏曰制"[2]。神龙元年二月"甲寅(705年3月3日),复国号曰唐,郊庙、社稷、陵寝、百官、旗帜、服色、文字皆如永淳(682年)以前故事"[3]。因此,依据擂鼓台中洞传法高僧像旁之武周新字,该窟,至少是窟中镌刻的《付法藏因缘传》[4],必完工于武则天载初元年[5]正月至中宗神龙元年二月之间[6]。

---

[1] 参见:刘景龙、李玉昆主编,上引书,第631页。

[2]《资治通鉴》卷二百零四《唐纪》,标点本,北京:中华书局,1956年,第6462-6463页。

[3]《资治通鉴》卷二百零八《唐纪》,标点本,北京:中华书局,1956年,第6583页。

[4] 据我们现场观察,当初开窟时雕造高僧像在先,镌刻经文在后,因为现存石刻经文明显避开高僧像,甚至围绕高僧像经营。

[5] 武周新字在龙门石窟中的使用,最早者为载初元年(689年)二月,见龙门石窟第1817号窟题铭。参见:刘景龙、李玉昆主编,上引书,第590页。

[6] 据叶昌炽研究,"以石刻证之,自武后称制,光宅、垂拱、永昌,尚未改字。至载初以后,则无不用新制字矣"。叶昌炽《语石》,柯昌泗评,北京:中华书局,1994年,第24页。

又,龙门石窟研究院焦建辉依据武周新字推测:擂鼓台中洞约完工于武周证圣元年至圣历元年之间,即695-698年。参见焦建辉《武周新字杂识》(待刊)。

擂鼓台北洞外立面窟门周围小龛，应为北洞完工后陆续补凿之作。其中窟门右侧偏上一圆拱龛（原编 2071 号，现编擂鼓台区 5-32 号），内造一佛、二弟子、二菩萨及金刚力士，系阎门冬于“大足元年三月八日（701 年 4 月 20 日）庄严成就”[1]；右上方另一小龛（原编 2076 号，现编擂鼓台区 5-6 号），亦造一佛、二弟子、二菩萨及金刚力士，为张阿双于“长安元年二月八日庄严”[2]。因此，北洞之完工应不晚于武则天大足元年或长安元年，即 701 年。

龙华寺前庭左壁雕一菩萨立像，龛下残记作“……佛慈恩长安三年十二月十二日（704 年 1 月 23 日）功讫”[3]；前庭右侧壁之观世音像，乃“长安四年三月廿七日（704 年 5 月 5 日）中山郡王隆业造功毕”[4]。这说明龙华寺之完工不会晚于长安四年（704 年）。

二莲花北洞前庭右壁一后代补造的圆拱形小龛，题记作“先天二年七月十五日（713 年 8 月 10 日）张庭之为父母造佛一区”[5]。这表明，二莲花北洞之完工不会晚于先天二年（713 年）。

宝塔洞南壁菩萨、神王像间现存一圆拱龛，内造一坐佛，龛下题记为“开元八年（720 年）□□月十五日弟子□□□敬造阿弥陀像一躯……”[6]。虽然宝塔洞未按计划完工，但这说明它的主体工程应至少早于开元八年（720 年）。

火左洞右侧壁千佛上方两立像，分别为“开元廿二年十月廿九日（734 年 11 月 28 日）比丘 / 僧空寂敬造普为法界仓生”和“开元廿四年九月十二日（736 年 10 月 20 日）比 / 丘僧空寂造药师 / 像一躯普为法界 / 仓生一时成□”[7]。两立像系后来补凿，因此，火左洞的开凿应早于开元廿二年（734 年）。

高平郡王洞地面上若干像座上的题铭，证明该窟应凿于武则天天授元年（690 年）之后、中宗神龙元年（705 年）之前[8]；工程未按计划完工，可能因武则天退位、功德主高平郡王武重规失势之故。

---

[1] 参见：刘景龙、李玉昆主编，上引书，第 631 页。

[2] 参见：刘景龙、李玉昆主编，上引书，第 627-628 页。大足元年十月壬寅（701 年 11 月 7 日）改元长安，长安元年二月八日应为 702 年 3 月 10 日。

[3] 参见：刘景龙、李玉昆主编，上引书，第 604 页。

[4] 参见：刘景龙、李玉昆主编，上引书，第 604-605 页。

[5] 参见：刘景龙、李玉昆主编，上引书，第 647 页。

[6] 参见：刘景龙、李玉昆主编，上引书，第 580 页。

[7] 参见：刘景龙、李玉昆主编，上引书，第 559 页。题记中的比丘僧空寂，还在天宝六载十二月廿三日（748 年 1 月 27 日）于同窟前庭左侧壁雕造了药师和观音像各一躯。

[8] 1) 李玉昆《龙门杂考》，见《文物》，1980 年第 1 期，第 26-27 页；2) 李玉昆《龙门碑刻及其史料价值》，载刘景龙、李玉昆主编《龙门石窟碑刻题记汇录》，北京：中国大百科全书出版社，1998 年，第 61 页。

值得注意的是,本期窟龛中有四座,即高平郡王洞、宝塔洞、看经寺和摩崖三佛未按原计划完工。依据中国现存石窟寺之通制,“一座大型洞窟中途停工废置,很有可能与当时统治集团上层的变化有关”[1]。而这一时期重大的政治变化,就是武则天被迫退位、诸武降封。

作为中国历史上唯一的女皇帝,武则天“政治上特殊之地位,既不能于儒家经典中得一合理之证明,自不得不转求于佛教经典……佛教在李唐初期为道教所压抑之后,所以能至武周革命而恢复杨隋时所享之地位者,其原因固甚复杂,而其经典教义可供女主符命附会之利用,要为一主因”[2]。据《旧唐书 · 则天纪》,载初元年(690年)七月,“有沙门十人伪撰《大云经》,表上之,盛言神皇受命之事。制颁于天下,令诸州各置大云寺,总度僧千人……九月九日壬午(690年10月16日),革唐命,改国号为周。改元为天授,大赦天下,赐酺七日。乙酉(10月19日),加尊号曰圣神皇帝”[3]。自此,武则天“政由己出,明察善断”[4]。天授二年四月癸卯(691年5月5日)制文:“朕先蒙金口之记,又承宝偈之文。历数表于当今,本愿标于曩劫。《大云》阐奥,明王国之祯符,《方等》发扬,显自在之丕业。驭一境而敷化,弘五戒以训人。爰开革命之阶,方启惟新之运……自今已后,释教宜在道法之上,缁服处黄冠之前”[5]。制文借用佛教辞句,作为符谶之凭借,以《大云经》中“即以女身当王国土”为女子称帝之理论根据[6]。另据《旧唐书 · 薛怀义传》,“怀义与法明等造《大云经》,陈符命,言则天是弥勒下生,作阎浮提主,唐氏合证。故则天革命称周,怀义与法明等九人并封县公,赐物有差,皆赐紫袈裟、银龟袋。其伪《大云经》颁于天下,寺各藏本,令升高座讲说”[7]。

---

[1] 宿白《洛阳地区北朝石窟的初步考察》,见宿白《中国石窟寺研究》,北京:文物出版社,1996年,第155页。

实际上,佛教石窟寺的发源地——印度的情况也是如此。印度马哈拉施特拉邦奥兰加巴德地区的阿旃陀(Ajaṇṭā)石窟群,现存若干未按计划完工的洞窟,应与Sātavāhanas或Vākāṭaka王朝的兴衰密切相关。参见:1) V. V. Mirashi, ed., *Inscriptions of the Vākāṭakas,* New Delhi: Archaeological Survey of India, 1963: V-X, LXV-LXXVI; 2) M. N. Deshpande, “The (Ajanta) Caves: Their Historical Perspective”, in: *Ajanta Murals,* ed. by A. Ghosh, New Delhi: Archaeological Survey of India, 1967: 14-21; 3) Walter M. Spink, *Ajanta : A Brief History and Guide,* Ann Arbor: Asian Art Archives, University of Michigan, 1994: 40-41.

[2] 陈寅恪《武则天与佛教》,见《金明馆丛稿二编》,上海:上海古籍出版社,1980年,第150页。

[3]《旧唐书》,点校本,北京:中华书局,1975年,第121页。

[4]《资治通鉴》卷二百零五《唐纪》,标点本,北京:中华书局,1956年,第6478页。

[5]《唐大诏令集》卷一百十三《政事 · 道释 · 释教在道法之上制》,点校本,北京:商务印书馆,1959年,第587页。参见《唐会要》卷四十九《僧道立位》,影印《丛书集成》本,北京:中华书局,1955年,第859页。

[6] 饶宗颐《从石刻论武后之宗教信仰》,上引书,第399页。

[7]《旧唐书》,点校本,北京:中华书局,1975年,第4742页。

需要指出的是，《大云经》非为伪造，只可谓伪托，诸沙门大德为了其自身利益，援《弥勒下生经》立说；而当时大臣，不乏亦以则天比之弥勒下生之例[1]。又，《佛说宝雨经》有长寿女蒙佛授记为转轮王事。长寿二年（693年），薛怀义等人把另一符谶羼入新译本中，伪撰日月光天子"于此赡部洲东北方摩诃支那国……现女身为自在主"[2]。稍后，即同年秋九月丁亥（693年10月5日），"魏王承嗣等五千人表请加尊号曰'金轮圣神皇帝'。乙未（10月13日），太后御万象神宫，受尊号，赦天下。作金轮等七宝，每朝会，陈之殿庭"[3]。"七宝"代表转轮王的符命。转轮王乃人间法王，而金轮转轮王则为最尊贵之转轮王。自此，武则天以转轮王自居。证圣元年（695年）五月仲夏，义净自印度取经后还至洛阳。"天后敬法重人，亲迎于上东门外。"[4]"则天尝得玉册，上有名十二字，朝野不能识，义净能读。其文曰：天册神皇万岁忠辅圣母长安。证圣元年五月上之，诏书褒答"[5]。故而，武则天这年的授号与改元，义净似立一功[6]。既然武则天挟佛教之符谶以自量，必然不遗余力地倡导佛教文化[7]。"信心皈依，发宏誓愿，壮其塔庙，广其尊容，已遍于天下久矣……倾四海之财，殚万人之力，穷山之木以为塔，极冶之金以为像"[8]，"役无虚岁"[9]，因为武则天"矜群生迷谬，溺丧无归，欲令像教兼行，睹相生善"[10]。武则天尤偏爱大像[11]和"行像"。证圣元年（695年），薛怀义"造功德堂[12]一千尺于明堂北。其中大像高九百尺，鼻如千斛船，

---

[1] 据《旧唐书》卷九十三《张仁愿传》，"时有御史郭霸上表称则天是弥勒佛身……"《旧唐书》，点校本，北京：中华书局，1975年，第2981页。参见：饶宗颐，上引文，第399-400页。

[2] 达摩流支《佛说宝雨经》，《大正藏》第16卷，第284b页。

[3]《资治通鉴》卷二百零五《唐纪》，标点本，北京：中华书局，1956年，第6492页。

[4] 智昇《开元释教录》卷九，《大正藏》第55卷，第568b页。

[5] 赵明诚《金石录》卷二十五《唐圣教序碑侧》，金文明校证，桂林：广西师范大学出版社，2005年，第434页。

[6] 参见王邦维《义净与〈南海寄归内法传〉——代校注前言》，载义净《南海寄归内法传》，王邦维校注，北京：中华书局，1995年，第20-21页。

[7] 颜娟英《武则天与长安七宝台石雕佛相》，见《艺术学》，1987年第1期，第43-44页。

[8]《旧唐书》卷一百一十《张廷珪传》，点校本，北京：中华书局，1975年，第3151页。

[9]《新唐书》卷一百二十五《苏瓌传》，点校本，北京：中华书局，1975年，第4398页。

[10] 狄仁杰《谏造大像疏》，《唐文粹》卷二十七《奏表书疏》，四部丛刊初编缩印本，上海：商务印书馆，1936年，第219页。

[11]《唐会要》卷四十九《像》，影印《丛书集成》本，北京：中华书局，1955年，第857-858页。

[12] 功德堂即天堂，"天堂五级以贮大像；至三级，则俯视明堂矣"。《资治通鉴》卷二百零四《唐纪》，标点本，北京：中华书局，1956年，第6455页。

中容数十人并坐,夹纻以漆之"[1]。长安二年(702年),从大内请"出等身金铜佛一铺并九部乐,南北两门额。上(武则天)与岐、薛二王亲送至(招福)寺,彩乘象舆,羽卫四和,街中余香,数日不歇"[2]。"长安四年十月九日(704年11月10日)敕,大像宜于白司马阪造为定,仍令春官尚书建安王攸宁充检校大像使。"[3]

在武则天影响下,当时皇室[4]和王公[5]大臣在龙门开窟造像之风盛行。龙门唐代第三期窟龛中盛凿大窟或许与之有关,因为"武后为人,有特殊之生理及过人之精力,而又号大喜功"[6]。龙门这一时期出现的新型窟龛,如擂鼓台中洞和南洞内的方形佛坛、木构殿堂及石质踏道;异彩纷呈的造像题材,如净土堂的西方净土,擂鼓台北洞的"菩提树像"、擂鼓台中洞的"弥勒"、擂鼓台南洞的"密严佛国"[7],以及看经寺内的行僧等,应与武则天佞佛有必然的联系,如当时崇奉弥勒,一是因为《大云经》,二是因为菩提树像[8]。至于本期流行的触地印佛像,或许迎合了这一时期天竺图像再次输入的高潮。此外,这一时期流行的佛衣作右袒式,如擂鼓台北洞和南洞主像所披覆,除了造像内容的自身特征要求之外,或与义净力求改造"披着不称律仪"的"非法衣服"有关[9],因为义净被武则天称作"缁俗之纲维。绀坊之龙象"[10]。至

[1] 张鷟《朝野佥载》,赵守俨点校,北京:中华书局,1979年,第115页。

又据《资治通鉴》卷二百零五《唐纪》,武则天证圣元年正月乙未(694年12月7日)曾"作无遮会于明堂,凿地为坑,深五丈,结彩为宫殿,佛像皆于坑中引出之,云自地涌出。又杀牛取血,画大像,首高二百尺,云(薛)怀义刺膝血为之。丙申(12月8日),张像于天津桥南,设斋。时御医沈南璆亦得幸于太后,怀义心愠,是夕,密烧天堂,延及明堂,火照城中如昼,比明皆尽。暴风裂血像为数百段"。《资治通鉴》,标点本,北京:中华书局,1956年,第6498-6499页。

[2] 段成式《酉阳杂俎续集》卷六《寺塔记》下,方南生点校,北京:中华书局,1981年,第259页。

[3]《唐会要》卷四十九《像》,影印《丛书集成》本,北京:中华书局,1955年,第858页。

不过,由于狄仁杰、李峤、张廷珪等人谏诤,乃罢其役。参见:1)《旧唐书》卷八十九《狄仁杰传》、卷九十四《李峤传》、卷一百一十一《张廷珪传》,点校本,北京:中华书局,1975年,第2893、2994、3151页;2)《资治通鉴》卷二百零七《唐纪》,标点本,北京:中华书局,1956年,第6571页。

[4] 金维诺认为"看经寺是唐武则天皇后为高宗修造的",荆三林亦言"看经寺(系)则天皇后为高宗所建"。两先生大作,不知何据?参见:1)金维诺《中国美术史论集》,北京:人民美术出版社,1981年,第430页;2)荆三林《中国石窟雕刻艺术史》,北京:人民美术出版社,1988年,第91页。

[5] 高平郡王洞乃高平郡王武重规开凿,但工程因故中辍。

[6] 饶宗颐,上引文,第410页。

[7] 参见李崇峰《地婆诃罗、香山寺与石像七龛》(见本书)。

[8] 李崇峰《菩提树像初探》,见《石窟寺研究》第三辑,北京:文物出版社,2012年,第190-211页。

[9] 据义净《南海寄归内法传》卷二《衣食所需》:"且如神州祇支偏袒,覆膊、方裙、禅袴、袍襦,咸乖本制,何但同袖及以连脊。至于披着不称律仪,服用并皆得罪。颇有着至西方,人皆共笑,怀惭内耻,裂充杂用。此即皆是非法衣服也。"参见:义净,上引书,第90页。

[10] 武则天《大周新翻三藏圣教序》,见《大正藏》第15卷,第706a页。

于龙门东山的七座大型洞窟，疑为武氏集团倾心打造的“石像七龛”[1]。神龙元年正月乙巳（705年2月22日），武则天被迫“传位于皇太子”；中宗即位“大赦天下，唯（张）易之党与不在原限”；五月癸卯（6月20日）降封诸武[2]，“以厌人心”[3]；神龙三年七月辛丑（707年8月7日）“杀（武）三思、崇训于其第，并亲党十余人”[4]。因此，武则天及其亲朋大举兴建的佛寺被迫停止[5]，龙门的开窟造像活动受到极大影响，部分窟龛工程中辍，如宝塔洞、高平郡王洞、看经寺、摩崖三佛等。

综上所述，我们将第三期窟龛的年代暂定在高宗统治之末至中宗即位之初，主要当在武则天时期，即684-705年左右。

4. 第四期

(1) 窟龛形制及造像特征

第四期窟龛总数骤减，形制及造型趋于简化。平面皆作三壁环坛（B型），窟顶多作穹隆与平顶混合型，窟顶前缘与斜坡门道顶部交接处低缓，略高出门道或几乎持平，有的顶部直通窟外（C型）；少数窟顶作穹隆形（A型）。造像题材绝大多数为一佛（A型），个别作三佛（B型）。造像组合主要为一铺九身像（Aiii式），个别以三佛为中心（B型）。

至于造像特征，佛多作触地印，结跏趺坐或善跏趺坐，“通肩披衣”（E型）；个别善跏趺坐，上衣覆搭双肩，大衣作“右袒式”披覆（Di式）；衣纹断面皆作直平阶梯式（B型）。多数佛像不雕头光，个别雕出者作桃形（C型）。佛座多样，皆沿袭前期旧式，有Bii、Ciii式和D型之分。

二弟子服饰分明，皆沿袭前期旧式。左侧弟子皆上身短，下身长，身体直立；内着交领衫；上衣覆搭双肩，两衣缘自颈侧垂于腹前；大衣作“右袒式”披覆；双手合十于胸前或托持珠形物或作叉手状，内衣下摆外张（Biii式）。右侧弟子亦上身短，下身长，胯部略扭；上衣作“交领式”，大衣作“右袒式”披覆，内衣下摆长出大衣且外张；双手交搭于腹前，多右手压左手（C型）。弟子大多不雕头光，像座皆为束腰圆莲座（Biii式）。

本期菩萨像的造型主要延续前期旧式，分Biii式和C型，新出现上身短，下身长，

---

[1] 参见李崇峰《地婆诃罗、香山寺与石像七龛》（见本书）。

[2]《旧唐书》卷七《中宗传》，点校本，北京：中华书局，1975年，第136-139页。

[3]《资治通鉴》卷二百零八《唐纪》，标点本，北京：中华书局，1956年，第6593页。

[4] 同上书，第6611页。

[5] 汪篯《武则天》，见《汪篯隋唐史论稿》，北京：中国社会科学出版社，1981年，第131页。

身体扭动略呈 S 形,鼓腹、细腰的形象；上身着掩腋,下身系长裙,掩腋简朴无饰,如绅大带不见 (Biv 式)。菩萨大多不雕头光,个别有头光者作桃形素面 (B 型),菩萨像座皆为束腰圆莲座 (Biii 式)。

神王像沿袭前期旧式 (Di 式),新出现上身短,下身长,双腿分立,胯部扭动,甲带倒丁字形绊缚,脐护作半花形,腰带下饰鹘尾,膝裙下摆多无褶,战裙下摆呈尖角扬向一侧的形象 (Dii 式)。神王脚下的药叉,多数延续前期旧式 (Bii 式),新出现仰卧药叉,即头枕山岩,上身略抬起,一腿平放,一腿屈立,一手拄地,一手置膝上,似具二蹄,以肩和膝或以头和腿托扛神王 (C 型)。

金刚造型沿袭第三期旧式,皆体态健壮,胸肌发达,腹肌、臂肌呈圆形或块状凸起；头及上半身略前倾,胯部扭动,一腿微屈,一腿直立；头束髻,束带自两侧上飘,面相方正,眉骨隆起,眼圆睁,鼻翼较宽,颧骨突出,大嘴、鼓腮；颈部青筋突暴,锁骨显露。服饰简朴,袒上身,下着裙,裙腰外翻,裙摆呈尖角飘向一侧,腰带多于腹前打结后呈八字形垂下 (Aiii 式)。

窟顶装饰有两种,一种延续前期旧式 (A 型)；另一种是新出现的,即窟顶中央雕莲花,周围绕飞天和大雁 (B 型)。伎乐同三期 (B 型),飞天造型亦沿袭前期旧式 (C 型或 D 型)。

(2) 相关问题及年代推定

第四期窟龛数量较少,仅极南洞残存铭记。该题铭位于前庭右壁,现多漫漶不清。清人陆增祥称之《姚夫人残刻》[1],陆心源写作《都督长沙姚意妻造像记》[2],李宗莲作《都督姚懿妻造像》跋[3],内容述及姚懿妻刘氏发心,子女姚崇等“各抽赀俸”,似合家开窟造像。后来,龙门石窟研究院同仁定为《姚崇为亡母刘氏造像记》[4]。近年,姚学谋等人依据旧本,重新作了整理[5]。

鉴于残刻拓本属地不清,陆增祥疑铭“文似述舍宅为寺之事,或亦造像之刻

[1] 陆增祥《八琼室金石补证》卷三十二“姚夫人残刻”条,影印本,北京：文物出版社,1985 年,第 213 页。

[2] 陆心源《唐文续拾》卷十一《都督长沙姚意妻造像记》,参见《全唐文》附《唐文续拾》,影印本,北京：中华书局,1983 年,第 11291 页。

[3] 李宗莲《怀岷精舍金石跋尾》,参见《石刻史料新编》第二辑第十九册,台北：新文丰出版公司,1979 年,第 14205 页。

[4] 参见：刘景龙、李玉昆主编,上引书,第 610 页。

[5] 姚学谋、杨超杰《龙门石窟极南洞新考》,刊《石窟寺研究》第一辑,北京：文物出版社,2010 年,第 74-81 页。

也……据《姚懿碑》,夫人刘氏,以神龙二年(706年)[1]正月殁于洛阳,景龙二年(708年)九月,葬于万安山之南阳。万安距龙门不远,碑刻当在其时"[2]。温玉成认为:该残刻系姚崇等为其亡母刘氏所做功德之碑,极南洞系唐中宗神龙二年(706年)启造,约景龙四年(710年)完工[3]。

姚崇曾于长安三年(703年)9月在武则天敕名之寺——七宝台寺造像,其兄元景翌年也于同寺造像[4]。不过,姚崇或许鉴于武则天之失,后来反对佛教最为剧烈。

> (晚年)遗令诫子孙,其略曰:……近日,孝和皇帝发使赎生,倾国造寺。太平公主、武三思、悖逆庶人、张夫人等皆度人造寺,竟术弥街,咸不免受戮破家,为天下所笑……抄经写像,破业倾家,乃至施身,亦无所恡,可谓大惑也。亦有缘亡人造经像,名为追福。方便之教,虽则多端,功德须自发心,旁助宁应获报?递相欺诳,浸成风俗,损耗生人,无益亡者。假有通才、达识,亦为时俗所拘。如来普慈,意存利物。损众生之不足,厚豪僧之有余,必不然矣。且死者是常,古来不免,所造经像,何所施为?夫释迦之本法,为苍生之大弊。汝等各宜警策,正法在心,勿效儿女子曹,终身不悟也。吾亡后,必不得为此弊法……不得辄用余财,为无益之枉事;亦不得妄出私物,徇追福之虚谈……汝等身没之后,亦教子孙依吾此法[5]。

姚崇开元二年(714年)曾上言检责天下僧尼(见后述),因此,位于龙门西山最南端的极南洞,应早于唐玄宗开元二年开凿,开工之时或为706年左右[6]。

本期窟龛数量骤减之原因,应与当时的历史背景有关。

中宗复辟后直至玄宗前期,都城迁往长安,国家的政治、经济和文化中心西移,洛阳地位骤降。"神龙元年三月十二日(705年4月9日),敕太平公主为天后立罔极

---

[1]《全唐文》卷三百二十八《巂州都督赠幽州都督吏部尚书谥文献姚府君碑铭并序》作"三年",影印本,北京:中华书局,1983年,第3326-3327页。

[2] 陆增祥,上引书,第213页。

[3] 参见:1)温玉成《龙门唐窟排年》,上引书,第200-201页;2)温玉成《龙门所见两〈唐书〉中人物造像概说》,见龙门石窟研究所编《龙门石窟一千五百周年国际学术讨论会论文集》,北京:文物出版社,1996年,第134-135页。温玉成后文推测:"龙门极南洞铭当作于神龙元年正月壬午至二月甲寅间,石窟亦是当年完工。"

[4] 参见:1)王昶《金石萃编》卷六十五,影印本,北京:中国书店,1985年;2)颜娟英《武则天与长安七宝台石雕佛相》,上引书,第53-54、59页。

[5]《宋本册府元龟》八百九十八《总录部·治命》,影印本,北京:中华书局,1989年,第3511-3512页。参见《新唐书》卷一百二十四《姚崇传》,点校本,北京:中华书局,1975年,第4384-4387页。

[6] 关于龙门石窟极南洞的完工时间,许多学者做过有益探讨,通常定在705-713年之间。参见:姚学谋、杨超杰《龙门石窟极南洞新考》,上引书,第75页。

寺"[1];"武太后、孝和朝,太平公主、武三思、悖逆庶人,恣情奢纵,造罔极寺、太平观、香山寺、昭成寺,遂使农功虚费,府库空竭矣"[2]。"中宗时,公主及外戚皆奏请度人为僧尼,亦有出私财造寺者;富户强丁,皆经营避役,后远近充满。"[3]"造寺不止,枉费财者数百亿,度人不休,勉租庸者数十万。"[4]尽管如此,开窟造像活动减少[5]。睿宗时"盛兴佛寺"[6],开窟造像活动反之更少[7]。另外,睿宗在佛道先后的问题上,采用了愈加折中的办法。景云二年(711年)"四月,手制曰:'朕闻释及玄宗,理均迹异,拯人救俗,教别功齐。岂于中间,妄生彼我,不遵善下之旨,相高无上之法,有殊圣教,颇失彝章。自今每缘法事、集会,僧、尼、道士、女冠等,宜令齐行并进。'"[8]由于佛道并举,致使佛教较武周时受到了极大制约。玄宗"初即位,务修德政,军国庶务,多访于(姚)崇"[9]。开元二年正月丙寅(714年1月27日),"姚崇上言请检责天下僧尼,以伪滥还俗者二万余人"[10]。二月"丁未(3月9日),敕:'自今所在毋得创建佛寺,旧寺颓坏应葺者,诣有司陈牒检视,然后听之'……(七月)戊申(9月6日),禁百官家毋得与僧尼、道士往还。壬子(9月10日),禁人间铸佛、写经"[11]。对于这次大规模的抑制佛教政策,《册府元龟》卷一百五十九《帝王部·革弊》有较详细的记载,兹录如下:

(开元)二年正月丙寅,紫微令姚崇上言,请检责天下僧尼,以伪滥还俗二万余人……七月戊申,制曰:"如闻百官家,多以僧尼、道士等为门徒往还,妻子等无所避忌。或诡托禅观,妄陈祸福,事涉左道,深斁大猷。自今已后,百

---

[1]《唐会要》卷四十八《寺》,影印《丛书集成》本,北京:中华书局:1955年,第846页。

[2]杜佑《通典》卷七《食货·历代盛衰户口》,王文锦等点校,北京:中华书局,1988年,第149页。

[3]《册府元龟》卷三百十三《宰辅部·谋猷》,影印明本,北京:中华书局,1960年,第3690页。参见《旧唐书》卷九十六《姚崇传》,点校本,北京:中华书局,1975年,第3023页。

[4]《旧唐书》卷一百零一《辛替否传》,点校本,北京:中华书局,1975年,第3155-3159页。

[5]以龙门石窟为例,据龙门石窟研究院统计,仅武则天长安年间(701-704年),就有纪年造像题记25品,而神龙、景龙(705-710年)年间造像铭记加起来才16品。参见李玉昆《龙门碑刻及史料价值》附表三《隋唐纪年题记分布》,见刘景龙、李玉昆主编,上引书,第67页。

[6]《旧唐书》卷一百零一《辛替否传》,点校本,北京:中华书局,1975年,第3155页。

[7]睿宗时期龙门的开窟造像活动,即景云和延和年间(710-712年)的纪年造像题记,仅存5品。由此看出,当时信徒的宗教旨趣已从开窟造像转向修建地面佛寺。参见:李玉昆,上引书,第67页。

[8]《册府元龟》卷五十三《帝王部·尚黄老》,影印明本,北京:中华书局,1960年,第589页。参见《唐大诏令集》卷一百十三《政事·道释·僧道齐行并进制》,点校本,北京:商务印书馆,1959年,第587页。

[9]《旧唐书》卷九十六《姚崇传》,点校本,北京:中华书局,1975年,第3025页。

[10]《旧唐书》卷八《玄宗传》,点校本,北京:中华书局,1975年,第172页。《唐会要》卷四十七《议释教》上作三万余人,影印《丛书集成》本,北京:中华书局,1955年,第837页。

[11]《资治通鉴》卷二百一十一《唐纪》,标点本,北京:中华书局,1956年,第6696,6703页。

官家不得辄容僧尼、道士等至家。缘吉凶要须设斋者，皆于州县陈牒寺观，然后依数听去。仍令御史金吾明加捉搦。”壬子，诏曰：“佛教者，在于清静，存乎利益。今两京城内，寺宇相望，凡欲归依，足申礼敬。下人浅近，不悟精微，睹叶希金，逐焰思水，浸以流荡，颇成蠹弊。如闻坊巷之内，开铺写经，公然铸佛，口食酒肉，手漫膻腥，尊敬之道既亏，慢狎之心斯起。百姓等或缘求福，因致饥寒，言念愚蒙，深用嗟悼。殊不知佛非在外，法本居心，近取诸身，道则不远。溺于积习，实藉申明。自今已后，林坊市等[1]不得辄更铸佛、写经为业。须瞻仰尊容者，任就寺礼拜；须经典读诵者，勒于寺赎取。如经本少，僧为写供，诸州寺观并准此。”[2]

本期窟龛数量的急剧减少，除了当时的政治环境，恐与佛教分宗立派及其世俗化、功利化不无关系。据文献记载和窟内题铭，龙门石窟从初唐开始流行净土信仰，既有阿弥陀净土，也有弥勒净土[3]。这说明“石窟的性质逐渐从单一的僧人的禅观，转化为除了禅观以外，还要起延寿却病的作用。少数‘观音变’的出现也是同样道理。这种转化的意义，既要对理想的净土通过复杂的形象要求更具体[4]，同时也表现了对现世的众多愿望。这样，礼拜石窟的主要对象，除了禅观的僧人以外，也将包括俗人了”[5]。因此，龙门出现不少家窟，如高平郡王洞；行会社邑[6]开窟，如净土堂[7]和北市香行像龛[8]。“北市香行社铭记说明至迟至武则天时，洛阳北市即有以

[1]《唐大诏令集》卷一百十三《政事·道释·断书经及铸佛像敕》作“州县坊市等”，点校本，北京：商务印书馆，1959年，第588页。

[2]《宋本册府元龟》，影印本，北京：中华书局，1989年，第331页。参见《唐大诏令集》卷一百十三《政事·道释·断书经及铸佛像敕》，点校本，北京：商务印书馆，1959年，第588页。

[3] 丁明夷《龙门石窟唐代造像的分期与类型》，见《考古学报》，1979年第4期，第544页。

[4] 龙门石窟净土堂窟内为阿弥陀雕像，窟外前庭左侧壁雕镌净土细节。

[5] 宿白《敦煌七讲》之四《唐窟性质的逐渐变化·贞观—天宝时期流行的净土变相》，油印本，敦煌：敦煌文物研究所，1963年，第49页。

[6] 社邑是以工商业行会为单位的一种佛教组织。龙门石窟唐代社邑造像，主要是阿弥陀佛，其次是优填王和弥勒像。这说明唐代洛阳地区主要流行净土宗。净土宗在佛教诸宗中，是讲成佛最快、最容易的宗派。它教人一心念佛，广种福田，大造塔寺，无需学习高深的佛理。因此，在社会上尤其是下层民众中广泛流传。参见李文生《龙门石窟佛社研究》，载龙门石窟研究院编《龙门石窟研究院论文选》，郑州：中州古籍出版社，2004年，第77页。

[7] 李玉昆《龙门碑刻及其史料价值》，刘景龙、李玉昆主编，上引书，第16-19页。

[8] 参见张丽明《龙门石窟北市香行像窟的考察》，载龙门石窟研究院编《龙门石窟研究院论文选》，郑州：中州古籍出版社，2004年，第360-371页。

工商业的行为单位组成佛教组织——社”,并参与到龙门石窟的营造中来[1]。“不管某家建窟也好,‘社邑’建窟也好,它都说明这时期石窟的俗人性质越来越增加,越来越接近近代寺院的情况了……各地已不建石窟而只修寺了,而寺的变化也和石窟情况相同。晚唐、五代以降,许多城市中的寺院变成了商肆中心,甚至寺院附设了商肆,定期开张,这就更突出地反映了寺院在这个时期变化的方向……某家建窟、某社建窟,他们的目的主要在求现世问题,可以想见他们之中,不要说像以前的禅观入定,就是贞观以后观念净土、祈求免灾也不可能了。他们的目的明确,行动简单——化钱即可。这是这时中国佛教的一般规律。”[2]另外,净土宗三祖善导鼎立弘教,其“最要之方法,则在称名念佛,禅定之念佛反不重要”[3]。这一时期,信徒已经脱离传统的宗教行为,石窟不再成为禅修的唯一场所,信徒尤其是在俗弟子往往通过舍财免灾、烧香求保,口念阿弥陀佛七日即可成佛。因此,信徒“须瞻仰尊容者,任就寺礼拜”,而非跋山涉水去石窟求佛。此外,作为唐代佛教重要派系,尽管密教杂典及咒术早已传入此土,但直到武则天时密教才渐兴盛[4]。“至盛唐之世,斯教始完成;两部纯密,一时备足。”[5]密宗奉真言和咒语,讲求法术,特重传承。学习密宗,必须由金刚阿阇黎建大曼荼罗,进行秘密授法。“当时洛阳地区的密教可能不在石窟,而在庙里。”[6]至于禅宗,可称中国化了的佛教;自谓“教外别传,不立文字,直指人心,见性成佛”[7]。

---

[1] 宿白《隋唐长安城和洛阳城》,见宿白《魏晋南北朝唐宋考古文稿辑丛》,北京:文物出版社,2011年,第56-57页。

[2] 宿白《敦煌七讲》之四《唐窟性质的逐渐变化·贞观—天宝时期流行的净土变相》,油印本,敦煌:敦煌文物研究所,1963年,第52页。

[3] 汤用彤《隋唐佛教史稿》,北京:中华书局,1983年,第191页。

[4] 现存擂鼓台北洞前壁所造多臂菩萨像和中洞前壁所刻玄奘译本《六门陀罗尼经》,说明武则天时期密教地位大大提升。

[5] 大村西崖《密教發達志》卷三,東京:佛書刊行會圖像部,1918年,第353页。

[6] 此承宿师季庚先生2006年5月17日见告。

又,吕建福认为:“开元后大日如来像流行于密宗中,但并不多见于石窟造像中。这主要是因为善(无畏)、金(刚智)所传的新密教只限于本宗内部传持,曼荼罗修持严格限制在密宗寺院、坛场和宫廷内道场;又密宗注重三密修行,尤重瑜伽观想,这样就与持明密教的公开传扬方式和注重承事供养的修法有很大的不同,所以也就很少出现于一般的寺院和公开让广大信众顶礼膜拜的石窟中。”吕建福《中国密教史》,北京:中国社会科学出版社,1995年,第199页。

[7] 据南宋绍兴壬子(1132年)初冬十日长乐郑昂《〈景德传灯录〉跋》:“达磨具正遍知,华、竺之言盖悉通晓。观其答问,安有传译哉?此如世愚人谓:教外别传,不立文字。”《大正藏》第51卷,第465b页。

又,元大德二年(1298年),前监察御史郭天锡《临济慧照玄公大宗师语录序》:“……二十八祖菩提达磨,提十方三世诸佛密印而来震旦。是时,中国始知佛法,有教外别传,不立文字,直指人心,见性成佛。”《大正藏》第47卷,第495a-b页。

又，此土传统称佛教为像教，即立像设教。据《唐会要》卷四十七引唐武宗《拆寺制》："朕闻三代已前，未常言佛；汉魏之后，像教寖兴。"[1]《广弘明集》卷十一法琳等《上秦王论启》："梦见金人已来，像教东流。"[2]同书卷二十二征引唐李俨《金刚般若经集注序》："自真容西谢，像教东流。"[3]故《六臣注文选》卷五十九《头陀寺碑文》明确指出："'象教'，谓为形象以教人也。"[4]

因为净土崇拜的简化、密宗及禅宗的兴起，"使原来作为像教的佛教，不大重视造像而注重宗教仪式与活动，人们对宗教的要求发生一定变化，寺院崇拜超过了石窟崇拜"[5]。

由于中宗复辟后国家政治、经济和文化中心西移，唐玄宗初期检责僧尼、抑制佛教[6]，以及佛教宗派的发展、信众志趣的转移和功利主义思潮的蔓延，龙门石窟大型窟龛的营造活动，或更准确地说，当时统治阶层在龙门的开窟造像活动便戛然中止了。[7]

基于上述情况，我们将第四期窟龛的年代暂定在中宗、睿宗和玄宗初期，即705-714年前后。

四、结　语

综上所述，我们将龙门唐代大型窟龛分作四期，分期与分区关系明显：

第一期窟龛，包括唐字洞、药方洞、宾阳南洞、宾阳北洞及破窑、老龙洞等，多在北朝未完工的大窟内补作或利用天然溶洞加工雕造，尽管分布范围零散，但全部在西山，主要完工于唐太宗后期，即637-649年左右，是龙门唐代窟龛的创始期。

第二期窟龛，包括潜溪寺、赵客师洞、敬善寺、双窑北洞、双窑南洞、清明寺、惠简

---

[1]《唐会要》卷四十七《议释教》上，影印《丛书集成》本，北京：中华书局，1955年，第840页。参见《唐大诏令集》卷一百十三《政事·道释·拆寺制》，点校本，北京：商务印书馆，1959年，第591页。

[2]《大正藏》第52卷，第161b页。

[3]《大正藏》第52卷，第259c页。

[4]《六臣注文选》，影印《四部丛刊》本，北京：中华书局，1987年，第1089页。

[5] 丁明夷《龙门石窟唐代造像的分期与类型》，上引书，第544页。

[6] 现存文献和遗迹说明，尽管唐玄宗较武则天佞佛程度大减，但他也重视并利用佛教，只是在某些方式上做了若干改变。

[7] 据我们调查，龙门石窟现存开元二年以后的纪年龛像，体量较小，多是妇女或无官职人士敬造的，这种情况一直延续到开元十八年前后才有所改观。开元十八年二月，高力士、杨思勖等"一百六十人奉为大唐开元神武皇帝……敬造西方无量寿佛一铺一十九事"。参见阎文儒《龙门奉先寺三造像碑铭考释》，见《中原文物》特刊《魏晋南北朝佛教史及佛教艺术讨论会论文选集》，郑州：河南省博物馆，1985年，第154-157页。

洞、大卢舍那像龛、万佛洞、赵上洞等，主要集中在西山中部，大约完成于唐高宗时期，即 649-683 年左右，是龙门唐代窟龛的发展期。

第三期窟龛，包括破上洞、普上洞、弥上洞、八作司洞、火下洞、火左洞、龙华寺、二莲花北洞、二莲花南洞、鷩上洞、擂鼓台北洞、擂鼓台中洞、宝塔洞、高平郡王洞以及净土堂、擂鼓台南洞、看经寺、摩崖三佛等，主要雕造于西山南部和东山，其中东山石窟大多位于崖面下层且体量较大，多仿木构佛寺原型雕造，主要完工于武周时期，即 684-705 年左右，是龙门唐代窟龛的繁盛期。

第四期窟龛，包括极南洞、奉南洞、火上洞、三佛洞以及四雁洞等，雕造范围同第三期，但显得零散，大约完工于中宗、睿宗和玄宗初期，即 705-714 年左右，是龙门唐代窟龛的衰落期。

附　录

大型窟龛与小型窟龛之关系

如前所述,龙门石窟现存编号窟龛 2345 个,其中唐代窟龛约占总数的 2/3。在唐代遗存中,现存大型窟龛仅 39 座,其余皆为小型窟龛。由于小型窟龛数量众多且许多不易登临,目前不具备系统调查和分期排队的条件,因此,现仅以典型的纪年小窟为例,参照大型窟龛各组成部分的类型进行分析,进而试述大型窟龛与小窟之关系[1]。

龙门唐高宗时期开凿的小型纪年窟龛,现存较好者有第 101 和 331 号二座。

第 101 号俗称王师德龛,是王师德等卅人于“大唐永徽元年(650 年)建造”[2]的一座横长方形敞口龛,面阔 3.2 米、进深 1.5 米、高 3.17 米。龛正壁设坛(平面 A 型),上造一佛、二弟子、二菩萨及金刚力士,即一铺七身像(Aii 式),但多有残蚀。此外,主尊座前雕出双狮一炉(图 117)。

图 117　龙门第 101 龛(王师德龛)造像

佛内着掩腋衣,上衣覆搭双肩后两衣缘自颈侧垂至腹前,唯左侧衣缘隐现;大衣作“右袒式”披覆,左手曲举施无畏印[3],右手置放右膝,结跏趺坐于束腰莲座上(Di 式)。二弟子皆双手合十于胸前,上衣被服双肩,大衣作“右袒式”披覆,外观呈筒状,下摆略内收(A 型)。菩萨似上身着掩腋,胸前束带;下身系裙,披巾自肩搭下后横于腹下膝前两道(Aiii 式)。金刚力士袒上身,下着裙,披巾在头后扬成圆环后垂下(Aii 式)[4]。

第 331 号俗称韩氏洞[5],系唐“龙

---

[1] 关于大型窟龛与小型窟龛之关系,拟从唐高宗时期的遗迹开始,因为此前的唐太宗后期,龙门无大型窟龛的营造,均在前代原有窟龛的基础上补凿或续雕。

[2] 刘景龙、李玉昆主编《龙门石窟碑刻题记汇录》,北京：中国大百科全书出版社,1998 年,第 8-9 页。

[3] 左手施无畏印,疑工匠之误。

[4] 参见刘景龙、杨超杰编《龙门石窟总录》,北京：中国大百科全书出版社,1999 年,第壹卷《文字著录》第 28-29 页、《实测图》第 175-178 页、《图版》第 161-164 页。

[5] 温玉成《龙门唐窟排年》,见《中国石窟·龙门石窟》二,北京：文物出版社,1992 年,第 181 页。

朔元年(661年)洛州人杨妻韩敬造阿弥陀像一龛"[1]。窟分前庭和主室两部分,主室面阔1.25米、进深1.98米、高1.60米(A型平面)。主室正壁造一佛、二弟子、二菩萨,前庭两侧壁造二神王和金刚力士,即一铺九身像(Aiii式)。

佛头残,内着掩腋衣,上衣覆搭双肩后两衣缘自颈侧垂于腹前,唯左侧衣缘被大衣遮覆;大衣作"右袒式"披覆,双腿间衣纹横向,下摆呈倒三角形垂覆座前;右手残,左手置膝上,结跏趺坐于束腰莲座(Di式)。弟子像浮雕而成,直立。左侧弟子内着掩腋衣,上衣似覆搭双肩;大衣包裹双肩及右臂,外观近筒形;双手合十于胸前(A型)。右侧弟子身体比例适中,直立;内着交领衫,上衣覆搭双肩,右侧衣缘垂覆胸前及右臂,左侧衣缘隐现;大衣作"右袒式"披覆,下半部渐窄(Bii式)。菩萨身体略扭动,腹部略鼓,袒上身,下着长裙,璎珞交叉于腹前,披巾沿体侧下垂或横于腹下两道(Aiii式与C型合成)(图118)。前庭右侧神王和金刚残损较甚。左侧神王围项护,上缀虎头披膊,束臂护,甲带十字形绊缚于胸前,左右各缀一较大胸护,膝裙饰百褶,战裙摆边下垂,"下属吊腿",双腿分开踏药叉(A型与C型合成);药叉蹲坐(Bi式)。左侧金刚体态健壮,肋骨、双乳明显,胸部隆起,腹部凸显;袒上身,下着裙;腰带打结后呈八字形斜下,披巾于头后扬成一大圆环,末端至腿侧下垂(Aii式)[2]。

图118 龙门第331龛(韩氏洞)内景

经与前述《龙门石窟唐代窟龛型式与组合表》(表一)对比,我们发现王师德龛和韩氏洞的平面形制(A型)、造像组合(Aii或Aiii式)、佛像特征(Di式)以及弟子(A型或Bii式)、神王(A型与C型合成)和金刚(Aii式)的造型,多与第二期大型窟龛的相关部分相同或接近。不过,两窟的左侧弟子像似沿用第一期旧式,韩氏洞的袒上

[1] 刘景龙、李玉昆主编,上引书,第85页。

[2] 参见:刘景龙、杨超杰编,上引书,第贰卷《文字著录》第59页、《实测图》第404-410页、《图版》第348-352页。

身菩萨甚至尚存北朝遗风；至于韩氏洞神王的虎头披膊(C型)和二窟的金刚力士造型(Aii式),则又属于超前使用。

龙门武则天时期开凿的小型纪年窟龛,保存较完整者有如下三座。

第1058号,系“大唐垂拱元年十月廿日(685年11月20日)孤子坚观亘之寿□并□女奉为亡考敬造石像一龛”[1]。窟前庭进深较短,主室平面横长方形,面阔1.93米、进深1.01米、高1.85米。主室三壁环坛(平面B型),正壁造一佛二弟子,佛座下雕二狮子;侧壁雕二菩萨、二神王和金刚力士,即一铺九身像(Aiii式)。

佛内着掩腋衣,上衣覆搭双肩后两衣缘于胸前系带打结;大衣作“右袒式”披覆,下摆呈倒三角形垂下;左手横置腹前,右手作触地印,结跏趺坐于束腰八角座上(Di式)。弟子身体比例适中,直立,双手合十于胸前,左侧弟子胸部以上剥蚀严重。右侧弟子内着交领衫;上衣覆搭双肩后两衣缘自颈侧垂于腹前;大衣尾自右胁下上搭左肩,作“右袒式”披覆,内衣下摆略外张(Bii式与Biii式合成)(图119a)。菩萨身体扭动略呈S形,腹部较鼓。戴项饰、手镯,饰璎珞,上身着掩腋衣,下身系裙;掩腋简朴无饰,裙腰外翻,披巾自肩搭下后以手牵持垂下(Bii式)。左侧神王、金刚多漫漶,仅见大体轮廓。神王一腿弓起,一腿直立,右手托塔,形同大卢舍那像龛神王,姿态亦同(B型);金刚体态雄健,肋骨、双乳、腹肌明显,胸部隆起,腹部凸显,臂肌略呈块状凸起,袒上身,下着裙(Aii式)。右侧神王一腿弓起,一腿直立,颈围项护,上缀披

a　　　　　　　　　　　　　　　　　　　b

图119　龙门第1058窟

a. 西壁立面；b. 北壁立面

[1] 刘景龙、李玉昆主编的《龙门石窟碑刻题记汇录》把此题铭误作第1089龛,参见：刘景龙、李玉昆主编,上引书,第343-344页。

膊，甲带十字形穿环绊缚于胸前，左右各一较大胸护，膝裙细部漫漶，战裙下摆斜下，脚踏药叉（A 型与 B 型合成）；药叉蹲坐（Bi 式）。右侧金刚残毁（图 119b）[1]。

第 1817 号原误军元庆洞[2]，系“大唐载初元年二月十日（690 年 3 月 25 日）右玉钤卫大将军行皋兰州都督兼使持节左卫将军上下灵丘县开国伯浑元庆并夫人京兆史敬佛龛一所”[3]。窟平面近方形，面阔 1.56 米、进深 1.90 米、高 1.57 米。窟内三壁环坛（平面 B 型），上造一佛（正壁）、二弟子、二菩萨、二神王（侧壁），前庭正壁门道两侧雕金刚力士，即一铺九身像（Aiii 式）。正壁佛座下雕出双狮。

佛结跏趺坐，内着掩腋衣，上衣覆搭双肩后两衣缘自颈侧垂于腹前；大衣尾自右胁伸出上搭左肩，作“右袒式”披覆，双腿间衣纹斜向，摆边垂覆束腰八角莲座前；左手抚膝，右手横置腹前（Di 式）（图 120a）。左侧弟子头残，上身短，下身长，身体直立，

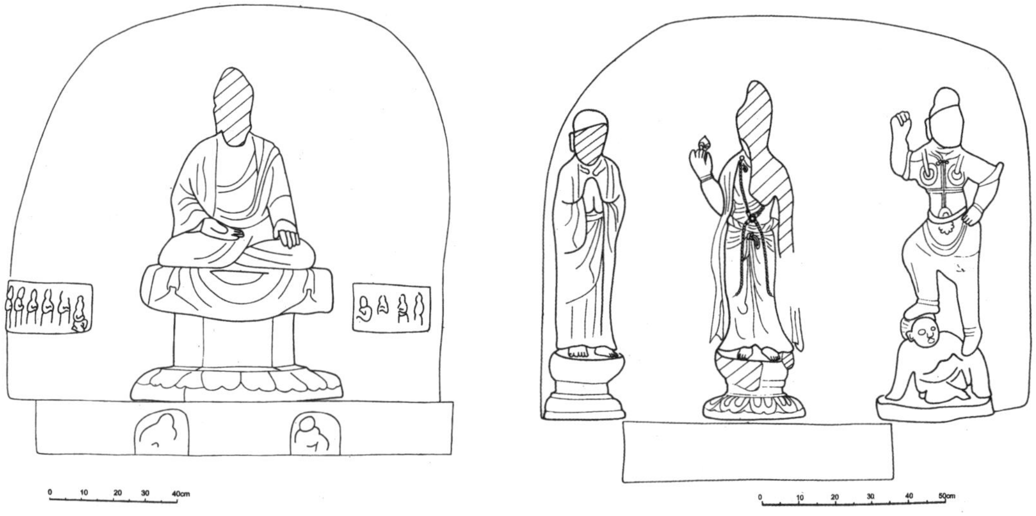

a　　　　　　　　　　　　　　　　　　　　　　b

图 120　龙门第 1817 窟

a. 西壁立面；b. 北壁立面

［1］参见刘景龙、杨超杰编，上引书，第陆卷《文字著录》第 77-78 页、《实测图》第 396-399 页、《图版》第 490-495 页。

［2］温玉成《龙门唐窟排年》，上引书，第 197-198 页。

［3］参见：刘景龙、李玉昆主编，上引书，第 590 页。铭文中已经使用武则天新字，框内字系笔者据《旧唐书》卷一百三十四和卷一百九十四相关部分及宋人邓名世《古今姓氏书辨证》卷七补。浑元庆，《旧唐书》卷一百三十四《浑瑊传》中附传，为皋兰州人，本铁勒九姓部落之浑部也。另据《旧唐书》卷一百九十四下《突厥传》下“则天临朝……垂拱初，遂擢授（阿史那）弥射子左豹韬卫翊府中郎将，元庆为左玉钤卫将军兼昆陵都护……寻进授元庆左卫大将军”。见中华书局点校本《旧唐书》第 3703、5189 页，及中华书局点校本《新唐书》卷七十五下《宰相世系表》五下，第 338 页。另见赵超《新唐书宰相世系表集校》，北京：中华书局，1998 年，第 842-845 页。

双手合十于胸前；内着交领衫，上衣覆搭双肩后两衣缘自颈侧垂于腹前；大衣尾自右胁伸出上搭左臂，作“右袒式”披覆，内衣下摆略外张（Biii 式）。右侧弟子头残毁，上身短，下身长，胯部略扭动，双手交搭于腹前，右手压左手；上衣为“交领式”，大衣作“右袒式”披覆，内衣下摆略外张（C 型）。左侧菩萨左上半残损，身体扭动略呈 S 形，腹部较鼓；上身着掩腋衣，下身系裙，掩腋简朴无饰；披巾沿体侧垂下，璎珞交叉于腹前，右手持莲花（Bii 式）。右侧菩萨头及左臂残，造型基本同左侧（Bii 式）。左侧神王尚完好，颈围项护，上缀披膊，甲带十字形绊缚胸前，左右各一胸护；半圆形脐护，下有半花形饰（鹘尾？）；膝裙饰百褶，战裙下摆缚吊腿内；右手持剑，一腿弓起，一腿直立，下踏药叉（A 型与 B 型混成式）；药叉蹲坐（Bii 式）（图 120b）。右侧神王上半身残毁。左侧金刚体态健壮，胯部扭动较甚，胸部隆起，腹部凸显，臂肌略呈块状凸起；头束髻，袒上身，下着裙（Aii 式）。右侧金刚残蚀严重[1]。

第 1674 号系郭玄奭于武周“万岁通天元年肆月捌日（696 年 5 月 14 日）□□于龙门秀岭造此尊龛”[2]。窟由凸字形平面前庭和长方形平面主室构成，主室面阔 1.53 米、进深 1.35 米、高 1.45 米。主室三壁环坛（平面 B 型），正壁造一佛二弟子，侧壁各造二菩萨一神王；前庭正壁门道两侧雕金刚力士（图 121a），即一铺十一身像组合，系前述 Aiii 式的拓展[3]。此外，前庭两侧壁雕造小型菩萨坐像。

佛头残，结跏趺坐，左手抚膝，右手残；上衣隐现，大衣“通肩被服”（E 型），衣纹自颈下呈水波状垂下，双腿间衣纹斜向，呈八字形，下摆垂覆座上；佛座为束腰莲座，束腰部位饰一圈凸起的莲蕾状物（Ci 型）。左侧弟子上身短，下身长，身体直立，双手合十作叉手状；内着交领衫，上衣覆搭双肩后两衣缘自颈侧垂于腹前；大衣尾自右腋下伸出上搭左臂，作“右袒式”披覆，内衣下摆外张（Biii 式）。右侧弟子上身短，下身长，胯部略扭；双手交搭于腹前，右手压左手，左手提净瓶；上衣作“交领式”，大衣作“右袒式”披覆，内衣下摆长出大衣且外侈（C 型）。左侧二菩萨像及右侧内身菩萨像残毁。右侧外身菩萨身体扭动略呈 S 形，上身着掩腋衣，唯反向，掩腋简朴无饰；下身系裙，裙腰外翻，如绅大带不见；璎珞交叉于腹前（Bii 式）。左侧神王尚完好，甲带十字形穿环绊缚胸前，左右各缀一较大胸护，脐护作半花形，膝裙下摆呈百褶状，战裙下摆呈尖角后扬，“下属吊腿”；胯部略扭动，双腿直立踏药叉（A、B、C 型混成式）；

[1] 参见：刘景龙、杨超杰编，上引书，第拾壹卷《文字著录》第 38-39 页、《实测图》第 358-363 页、《图版》第 347-358 页。

[2] 参见：刘景龙、李玉昆主编，上引书，第 576-578 页。

[3] 如前所述，龙门唐代大型窟龛中的一铺十一身造像组合，通常包括一佛、二弟子、二菩萨、二神王及金刚力士，外加二狮子。

图 121　龙门第 1674 窟
a. 前庭正壁　b. 南壁立面

药叉半仰卧,头发直立 (Bii 式与 C 型合成)(图 121b)。左侧金刚,上半身残,体态雄健,臂肌略呈块状凸起;披巾上端缠绕不清,下半缠臂垂至山岩座上;左手似托山 (Aii 式)。右侧金刚基本同左侧,胸肌发达,腹肌、臂肌呈块状凸起,腹部略鼓;腰带于腹前打结后呈八字形垂下,披巾自肩搭下后,以左手牵持并垂至山岩座上,右侧缠绕方式不清 (Aii 式与 Aiii 式合成)[1]。

经与《龙门石窟唐代窟龛型式与组合表》(表一) 对比,我们发现第 1058 号、1817 号和 1674 号窟龛的平面形制 (B 型)、造像组合 (Aiii 式)、佛像特征 (Di 式或 E 型)、弟子 (Bii 式与 Biii 式合成或 C 型)、菩萨 (Bii 式)、神王 (A、B、C 型混成式) 以及金刚力士 (Aii 或 Aiii 式) 的类型相同或相似,且多与第三期大窟的相关部分相同或接近,不过第 1058 号右侧神王造型、1817 号和 1674 号左侧神王的十字形甲带绊缚式样,系沿用第二期旧制。此外,第 1817 号窟左侧神王脐护下的半花饰,明显仿效第二期大卢舍那像龛左侧神王的脐护式样。至于第 1674 号窟神王脚下之仰卧式药叉和造像组合中的四菩萨像,则是新出现的。

中宗以后开凿的纪年小窟,以第 1950 号最为典型。

[1] 参见:刘景龙、杨超杰编,上引书,第拾卷《文字著录》第 97-98 页、《实测图》第 683-689 页、《图版》第 675-680 页。

第 1950 号俗称徐恽洞[1]，系“郎中徐恽”[2]于唐“开元廿一年十月四日 (733 年 11 月 14 日) 建”[3]，为一长方形小窟，面阔 1.20 米、进深 1.27 米、高 1.23 米。窟三壁环坛，坛边延至窟外 (B 型平面)，上造一佛二弟子 (正壁)、二菩萨、二神王 (侧壁)，前庭正壁门道两侧雕金刚力士，即一铺九身像 (Aiii 式)。

a　　　　　　　　　　　　　　　　　　b

图 122　龙门第 1950 窟

a. 西壁立面；b. 南壁立面

佛头残毁，结跏趺坐，左手抚膝，右手横置腹前；上衣隐现，大衣“通肩被服”，褶襞自颈下呈水波状垂下，下摆垂覆束腰莲座上 (E 型)。左侧弟子大部残 (图 122a)。右侧弟子头残，上身短，下身长，胯部略扭；双手交搭于腹前，右手压左手；上衣为“交领式”，大衣作“右袒式”披覆，内衣下摆长出大衣且外张 (C 型)。二菩萨像均残毁。左侧神王头束髻，上身短，下身长，胯部扭动，一腿微弓，一腿直立；甲带倒丁字形绊缚胸前，脐护作半花形，膝裙摆边无褶，战裙下摆呈尖角扬向一侧 (B 型与 Di 式合成)。脚下药叉仰卧 (C 型)。右侧神王头束髻，体态健壮，上身短，下身长，胯部略扭动，一腿微弓，一腿直立，脚踏药叉；颈围项护，上缀披膊，甲带倒丁字形绊缚，脐护半花形，膝裙摆边无褶，战裙下摆扬向后方 (C 型与 Di 式合成)。药叉作爬行状 (A 型)(图 122b)。

[1] 温玉成《龙门唐窟排年》，上引书，第 208 页。

[2] 徐恽，正史无传，曾任吏部员外郎、御史中丞、陈留太守、河南采访使、江西采访使等。参见：1) [清] 劳格、赵钺《唐尚书省郎官石柱题名考》，徐敏霞、王桂珍点校，北京：中华书局，1992 年，第 126、213 页；2) 赵钺、劳格《唐御史台精舍题名考》，张忱石点校，北京：中华书局，1997 年，第 53、65 页；3) 岑仲勉《元和姓纂四校记》，景印二版，台北：中研院历史语言研究所，1991 年，第 193 页。

[3] 参见：刘景龙、李玉昆主编，上引书，第 608-609 页。

左侧金刚头残，体态健壮，头及上半身略前倾，胸肌发达，腹肌、臂肌呈块状凸起；袒上身，下着裙，腰带于腹前打结后呈八字形垂下（Aiii 式）。右侧金刚残毁[1]。

尽管 1950 号窟左侧神王脚下的仰卧型药叉（C 型）为第四期大窟所特有，但其平面（B 型）、造像组合（Aiii 式）、佛像（E 型）以及右侧弟子（C 型）、神王（B 型与 Di 式合成）和左侧金刚（Aiii 式）的类型都是第三期出现并延续到第四期的。有些特征，如神王一腿弓起、一腿直立的做法还是第二期旧式，而右侧神王脚下的爬行药叉，早在第一期就已出现。

从上述唐代大型窟龛与纪年小窟的对比情况来看，有如下几点值得我们特别关注。

1. 大型窟龛与小型窟龛在建筑形制、造像题材、组合及个体特征方面，几乎同步演进，但彼此保守因素也有，超前趋势亦存。

2. 尽管大窟营造时间较长，但由于是皇室、显贵以及高僧大德所建，敕令或邀请当时佛教权威及造型艺术大师参与联合设计，因而在窟龛形制、造像题材及组合和个体样式上多有创新，反映了当时佛教的流行趋势、最新的艺术潮流，且雕造精致而华丽[2]。如大卢舍那像龛、看经寺、高平郡王洞、擂鼓台三洞等都是不见于此前的新形制、新组合、新题材、新形象及新样式，故而成为当时佛教信徒竞相仿效的楷模。以大卢舍那像龛为例，高宗所“敕检校僧”善道和惠暕（简）皆来自西京长安；“大使”韦机长于设计，曾负责营造东都上阳宫[3]；石作似来自各地巧匠，如支料匠李君瓒在完成卢舍那大像龛后又奉命修建紫桂宫[4]，应为时下名手。当时各方通力协作，共同完成了龙门唐代标志性形象——大卢舍那像龛。龙门石窟此后流行的通肩式大衣及老龙洞上方及西侧的龛形及主尊，可能都受到了大卢舍那像龛的影响。此外，擂鼓台北洞大衣作“右袒式”披覆、手施触地印（残）的主尊，在北洞周围乃至西山清明寺附近都有类似的形象；而擂鼓台南洞众多的小坐佛，则成为 2093 号窟效仿的典型。此外，大型窟龛之间在形制和题材上缺乏相似性，可能与窟主的个人喜好或宗教信仰旨趣相称。至于大窟间的相似，疑与开窟者或造像人的身份有关，如二莲花洞在建筑形制、题材内容及造像特征上的相似，可能缘于它们是一组双窟。

[1] 参见：刘景龙、杨超杰编，上引书，第拾壹卷《文字著录》第 85-86 页、《实测图》第 720-724 页、《图版》第 680-683 页。

[2] 丁明夷《龙门石窟唐代造像的分期与类型》，上引书，第 534 页。

[3]《旧唐书》卷一百八十五上《良吏・韦机传》，点校本，北京：中华书局，1975 年，第 4796 页。

[4] 刘景龙、李玉昆主编，上引书，第 549 页。

3. 小型窟龛之供养人，总的说来不如大型窟龛的地位显赫。他们有的迫于形势，趋炎附势；有的系装点门面，附庸风雅；有的因为种种缘由，所做功德带有极强的功利色彩。因此，小型窟龛在建筑形制、造像组合、题材内容及个体特征等方面不甚讲究，多仿效或因循大型窟龛样式[1]，吸收并融合此前造像之局部特征，但常会简化，他们目的大多单一，有的仅为誓愿、供养。尽管如此，小型窟龛的开凿，由于供养人身份和地位之差，常有两种情况：①供养人为显贵者，所造龛像样式常与大型窟龛相同，且偶有超前现象。如载初元年（690年）开凿的浑元庆窟，神王铠甲部分雕造得极为写实，脐护下的半花形饰系仿大卢舍那像龛，疑为第四期铠甲鹘尾之雏形[2]，这或许与功德主身为武周大将军有关。②一般信徒所造小型龛像，题材、内容单一，甚至保守、退化，新样少见。这可能与供养人的盲目信仰以及财力有关。他们发愿营造时，只能选择技艺较差之本地工匠，至于龛像的样式、特征等均可忽略不计，因此出现了许多在样式上相同、但题铭内容有异的小型龛像。这种情况，似乎是北魏以降中国佛教造像的一般规律。偶尔，有些小型窟龛由于供养人之要求或工匠之喜好，在设计上也会做些许变通，如郭玄奭窟的一铺十一身造像组合。

附记：为编写《龙门石窟擂鼓台区窟群考古报告》，受宿师季庚先生委派，自2004年秋季迄今多次往还京洛两地。2006年利用暑假对龙门石窟做了系统考察，回京后在向季庚师汇报考察心得时，先生即命马上整理唐代部分，为编写石窟考古报告做准备。本文初稿草就于2006年9月，2008年春夏之际，受命主持擂鼓台窟前遗址考古发掘，利用工作闲暇对初稿作了较大改动，完成《龙门唐代窟龛分期试论》，最后一次修订于2013年4月。本文草就后承蒙李裕群、焦建辉提出宝贵意见，谨此致谢。

2013年5月1日凌晨

（本文原刊《石窟寺研究》第4辑，第58-150页。）

［1］丁明夷，上引书，第534页。

［2］洛阳地区神王像或天王铠甲出现鹘尾，似应在武则天晚期至玄宗初期，因为2003年11月在巩义市北山口常庄变电站扩建中出土的长安二年（702年）墓葬中发现的“天王俑”，腰带下仅有一半圆形装饰，尚未出现后来标准的鹘尾；而河南偃师县北窑村五号墓出土的长安三年（703年）天王俑铠甲，和巩义市所出相似，与后来典型的铠甲鹘尾有别。参见：1）郑州市文物考古研究所、巩义市文物保护管理所《巩义常庄变电站大周时期墓葬发掘简报》，刊《中原文物》，2005年第1期，第4-11页，图三、四；2）偃师商城博物馆《河南偃师县四座唐墓发掘简报》，刊《考古》，1992年第11期，第1004-1017页，图版五、六。

地婆诃罗、香山寺与“石像七龛”

据我们实地踏察并参考前人记述，龙门东山在武周以前尚无大型窟龛的营造。由于武氏佞佛空前绝后，西山适于大面积开窟造像之崖面使用殆尽，致使当时主持龛像雕造的规划者另辟蹊径，开窟造像活动届时移至东山；而武则天于东山“置伽蓝，敕内注名为香山寺”，堪称这次开窟造像区域变迁之发端。

一、地婆诃罗与香山寺

香山寺乃武则天为纪念三藏法师地婆诃罗而建。依法藏（643-712年）所集《华严经传记》卷一：

> 中天竺国三藏法师地婆诃罗，唐言日照，婆罗门种。幼而出家，住摩诃菩提及那兰陀寺。三藏风仪温雅，神机朗俊。负笈从师，研精累岁，器成瑚玉，学擅青蓝。承沙门玄奘传教东归，思慕玄门，留情振旦，既而占风圣代，杖锡来仪，载阐上乘，助光神化。爰以永隆初岁（680年），言届京师。高宗弘显释门，克隆遗寄，乃诏：缁徒龙象，帝邑英髦。道诚律师、薄尘法师十大德等，于魏国西寺翻译经论之次。时有贤首法师，先以华严为业，每慨斯经阙而未备，往就问之。云：赍第八会文，今来至此。贤首遂与三藏对校，遂获善财、善知识、天主光等十有余人，遂请译新文，以补旧阙。沙门复礼执笔，沙门慧智译语，更译《密严》等经论十有余部，合二十四卷，并皇太后御制序文，深加赞述，今见流行于代焉。三藏辞乡之日，其母尚存。无忘鞠育之恩，恒思顾复之报，遂诣神都，抗表天阙，乞还旧国。初未之许，再三固请，有敕从之。京师诸德，造绯罗珠宝袈裟，附供菩提树像，敕锡神钟一口，及请幡像供具遵途。以垂拱三年十二月二十七日（688年2月4日），体甚康体。告门人曰：吾当逝矣。右胁而卧，无疾而终于神都魏国东寺，会葬者数千万人。圣母闻之，深加悲悼，施绢千匹，以充殡礼。道俗悲慕，如丧所亲，香华辇舆瘗于龙门山阳，伊水之左。门人修理灵龛，加饰重阁，因起精庐其侧，扫洒供养焉。后因梁王所奏，请置伽蓝，敕内注名为香山寺。危楼切汉，飞阁凌云，石像七龛，浮图八角。驾亲游幸，具题诗赞云尔[1]。

---

[1]《大正藏》第51卷，第154c-155a页。

据《开元释教录》卷九，地婆诃罗"洞明八藏，博晓四含；戒行清高，学业优赡；尤工咒术，兼洞五明；志在利生，来游此国"[1]。地婆诃罗来华后深受唐高宗，尤其武则天礼待，被安置在武后家庙——魏国寺[2]并"仍准玄奘例，于一大寺别院安置[3]，并大德三、五人同译"[4]。魏国寺分东、西二寺。其中，魏国西寺位于长安城休祥坊，原为侍中杨恭仁宅，咸亨元年（670年）立为太原寺[5]。垂拱三年（687年）改为魏国寺，载初元年（689年）又改为崇福寺，为当时西京长安一座大寺[6]，亦称魏国西寺、西京太原寺或西太原寺[7]。魏国东寺位于洛阳城"游艺坊，武太后母杨氏宅。上元二年（675年）立为太原寺，垂拱三年（687年）二月改为魏国寺，天授二年（691年）改为福先寺"[8]，

[1]《大正藏》第55卷，第564a页。

[2] 据彦悰永淳元年（682年）《佛顶最胜陀罗尼经序》，高宗、武则天"敕中天法师地婆诃罗，于东西二京太原、弘福寺等传译法宝"。见《大正藏》第19卷，第355b页。

[3] 擂鼓台窟前遗址发掘出土的碑铭等表明：擂鼓台区域，系香山寺别院，或为纪念地婆诃罗所特设。参见龙门石窟研究院、北京大学考古文博学院、中国社会科学院世界宗教研究所编著《龙门石窟考古报告：东山擂鼓台区》下编（待刊）。

[4] 赞宁《宋高僧传》卷二《日照传》，范祥雍点校，北京：中华书局，1987年，第32页。

[5] 关于太原寺，参见李崇峰《龙门唐代窟龛分期试论》（见本书）。

[6] 西太原寺在唐代长安寺院等级中，可能属于第三等，即规模较大者。这种大型佛寺通常应有别院设置，《宋高僧传》卷二《日照传》明确记载地婆诃罗"仍准玄奘例，于一大寺别院安置"。地婆诃罗在西太原寺先后翻译了《大乘百福相经》、《大乘离文字普光明藏经》、《金刚般若波罗蜜经破取著不坏假名论》、《方广大庄严经》、《七俱胝佛大心准提陀罗尼经》、《大方广佛华严经续入法界品》和《大乘广五蕴论》等。地婆诃罗在西太原寺译经时，法藏也在该寺（魏国西寺/西崇福寺）潜心研究佛法，其间曾参谒地婆诃罗，撰写了《华严经探玄记》及《维摩诘经疏》和《般若心经疏》等。与此同时，沙门怀素则在西太原寺撰写了《四分律疏》、《略羯磨》和《羯磨文》，抄集了《四分比丘尼戒本》、《四分比丘戒本》、《四分尼羯磨》和《四分僧羯磨》等。这说明：唐初不同派系的僧人可以居住同一寺院，讲授不同的经典，有时彼此间还会有些交流，如地婆诃罗与法藏。这点或许受到了印度那烂陀寺院制度的影响。参见：1) 宿白《试论唐代长安佛寺的等级问题》，见宿白《魏晋南北朝唐宋考古文稿辑丛》，北京：文物出版社，2011年，第255-269页；2) 周一良《唐代密宗》附录二十，钱文忠译，上海：上海远东出版社，1996年，第119页。

[7] 据《开元释教录》卷九《总括群经录》上"沙门地婆诃罗"条，"西太原寺即今西崇福寺是也，东太原寺即今大福先寺是也"。见《大正藏》第55卷，第564a页。

[8]《唐会要》卷四十八"寺"条，影印《丛书集成》本，北京：中华书局，1955年，第848页。[清]缪荃孙编《藕香零拾》所收《元河南志》卷一有如下记载："教义坊，唐有武后母荣国夫人宅，后立太原寺。武后登上阳宫遥见之，辄悽感，乃徙于积德坊。此坊唐与禁苑连接"。缪荃孙编《藕香零拾》，影印本，北京：中华书局，1999年，第191页。据《两京新记》卷三，西京"义宁坊南门之东，化度寺……内有无尽藏院，即信行所立。京城施舍，后渐崇盛。贞观之后，钱帛金玉积聚，不可胜计。常使名僧监藏，供天下伽蓝修理。藏内所供，燕、凉、蜀、赵，咸来取给，每日所出，亦不胜数……武太后移此藏于东都福先寺，天下物产，遂不复集。乃还移旧所"。由此看出武后对福先寺的重视与信任。韦述《两京新记》，辛德勇辑校，西安：三秦出版社，2006年，第57页。又，武则天曾于神龙元年（705年）7月撰、武三思正书《大福先寺浮图碑》。参见：1) 赵明诚撰《金石录》卷五《伪周》，金文明校证，桂林：广西师范大学出版社，2005年，第80页；2)《全唐文》卷九十八《高宗武皇后》，影印本，北京：中华书局，1983年，第1010-1012页。

“后改大周东寺”[1]。它既是武则天家庙[2],也是当时“国寺”或“朝寺”[3],还是东都译经中心之一[4],亦称魏国东寺[5]或东/中太原寺[6]。地婆诃罗“于两京东西太原寺及西京弘福寺[7],译《方广大庄严经》(一部二十二卷)、《大乘密严经》(一部三卷)、《大乘显识经》(一部二卷)、《证契大乘经》(一部二卷)、《大方广佛花严经续入法界品》(一卷)、《大乘离文字普光明藏经》(一卷)、《大乘遍照光明藏无字法门经》(一卷)、《大方广师子吼经》(一卷)、《大乘百福相经》(一卷)、《大乘百福庄严相经》(一卷)、《大乘四法经》(一卷)、《菩萨修行四法经》(一卷)、《七俱胝佛大心准提陀罗尼经》(一卷)、《佛顶最胜陀罗尼经》(一卷)、《最胜佛顶陀罗尼净除业障经》(一卷)、《造塔功德经》(一卷)、《金刚般若波罗蜜经破取著不坏假名论》(一部二卷)、《大乘广五蕴论》(一卷),凡一十八部合三十四卷。沙门战陀般若提婆译,沙门慧智证梵语,敕召名德十人助其法化,沙门道成、薄尘、嘉尚、圆测、灵辩、明恂、怀度等证义,沙门思玄、复礼等缀文笔受。天后亲敷睿藻,制序标首;光饰像教,传之不朽也”[8]。

---

[1] 赞宁《宋高僧传》卷二《天智传》,范祥雍点校,北京:中华书局,1987年,第33页。

[2] 伪撰《大云经》的法明,一作法朗,就是魏国东寺的和尚。据《资治通鉴》卷二百零四,“东魏国寺僧法明等撰《大云经》四卷,表上之,言太后乃弥勒佛下生,当代唐为阎浮提主,制颁于天下”。《资治通鉴》,标点本,北京:中华书局,1956年,第6466页。由此可见该寺在武周时期的特殊地位。

[3] [意]富安敦《龙门大奉先寺的起源及地位》,见《中原文物》,1997年第2期,第86-89页。

[4] 地婆诃罗、菩提流志、义净、宝思维和善无畏等先后在此寺译经。参见王振国《唐宋洛阳佛寺、名僧史迹钩沉》,载王振国《龙门石窟与洛阳佛教文化》,郑州:中州古籍出版社,2006年,第196-197页。

[5] 据志静《佛顶尊胜陀罗尼经序》,“垂拱三年(687年),定觉寺主僧志静,因停在神都魏国东寺,亲见日照三藏”。见《大正藏》第19卷,第349c页。

[6] 子璿《起信论疏笔削记》卷一:“西太原寺者,即长安崇福寺也。以天下有五寺,俱名太原,为拣余四故言西也;东即扬州,南即荆南府,西即长安,北即太原(亦名崇福),中即东都(今之福先),俱称太原者,以则天生于太原。此既皆彼舍宅所置,为敌生处。故以为名。”见《大正藏》第44卷,第298a页。

[7] 据宋敏求《长安志》卷十,弘福寺应为长安修德坊西北隅兴福寺,原称宏福寺,“本右领军大将军彭国公王君廓宅。贞观八年(634年),太宗为太穆皇后追福,立为宏福寺。神龙中(702年),改为兴福寺……沙门玄奘于西域回,居此寺西北禅院翻译。”宋敏求《长安志》,《丛书集成初编》本,北京:中华书局,1991年,第127页。参见小野胜年《中国隋唐長安寺院史料集成》,京都:法藏館,1989年,“史料篇”,第198-211页;“解説篇”,第129-136页。

[8] 智昇《续古今译经图记》,见《大正藏》第55卷,第368b-c页。参见《开元释教录》卷九《总括群经录》上“沙门地婆诃罗”条,载《大正藏》第55卷,第563c-564a页。

武则天既崇佛、道，又尚神异、巫祝[1]；地婆诃罗既“洞明八藏、博晓四含”，又“尤工咒术，兼洞五明，志在利生”，自然成为武后最青睐人才[2]。“垂拱元年乙酉岁(685年)，地婆诃罗三藏随驾于东都。”[3]此前高僧随驾之举，仅有三藏法师玄奘贞观廿二年(648年)冬十月随驾还京[4]。由此可见其备受武后推重。此外，“天后时，符瑞图谶为上下所同好，自后秘密、神异之说风行。万回一日行万里，一行之东水西流，均为当时所乐道。道宣之记感应，道世之申冥报，亦可见其时之风尚”[5]。故地婆诃罗卒后，武则天“深加悲悼……香华辇舆瘗于龙门山阳……置伽蓝，敕内注名为香山寺……驾亲游幸，具题诗赞云尔”[6]。

关于香山寺，清康熙四十七年(1708年)杨右曾《重建香山寺记》记载道：“考郡、县志皆不详寺兴废所由。宋陈振孙为公(白居易)作年谱，谓寺在龙门山，后魏熙平元年(516年)建……则寺之创于熙平，其信然欤？历周、隋至唐以公故而始大显于世。自后名人游眺所至，辄见篇咏。”[7]实际上，香山寺之建或重兴，应与地婆诃罗瘗葬有关。因梁王武三思之奏，武则天于东山“置伽蓝，敕内注名为香山寺”。武三思于武周天授元年九月乙酉(690年10月19日)被封梁王，中宗神龙元年五月癸卯(705年6月20日)降为德静郡王[8]。因此，香山寺之设，必在天授元年之后、中宗神龙元年之前。由于香山寺的建立，这一区域遂成为帝王、宠臣乃至文人墨客游览和避暑胜地，且一直延续到北宋不衰[9]，尤以武周时期为盛。据《旧唐书·宋之问传》，

---

[1] 1) 汤用彤《从〈一切道经〉说到武则天》，载《汤用彤全集》七，石家庄：河北人民出版社，2000年，第42-47页；2) 宿白《敦煌莫高窟密教遗迹札记》，见宿白《中国石窟寺研究》，北京：文物出版社，1996年，第280页。

又，史载武后梦见王、萧皇后披发沥血场面时，曾“祷以巫祝”。参见《旧唐书》卷五十一《高宗废后王氏传》，点校本，北京：中华书局，1975年，第2170页。

[2] 深得武后重视、后尊称贤首国师的法藏，虽以新译八十卷《华严经》著名，但也长于咒法。据崔致远《唐大荐福寺故寺主翻经大德法藏和尚传》：“神功元年(697年)，契丹拒命，出师讨之，特诏藏依经教遏寇虐。乃奏曰：若令摧伏怨敌，请约左道诸法。诏从之。法师盥浴更衣，建立十一面道场，置光(观)音像，行道。始数日，羯虏睹王师无数神王之众，或瞩观音之像浮空而至，犬羊之群相次逗挠，月捷以闻。天后优诏劳之，曰：蒯城之外，兵士闻天鼓之声；良乡县中，贼众睹观音之像；醴酒流甘于陈塞，仙驾引纛于军前，此神兵之扫除，盖慈力之加被。”见《大正藏》第50卷，第283c页。

[3] 慧琳《记佛顶尊胜陀罗尼经翻译年代先后》，见《大正藏》第54卷，第544a页。

[4]《大唐故三藏玄奘法师行状》，见《大正藏》第50卷，第218b页。

[5] 汤用彤《隋唐佛教史稿》，北京：中华书局，1982年，第27页。

[6]“武太后、孝和朝，太平公主、武三思、悖逆庶人，恣情奢纵，造罔极寺、太平观、香山寺、昭成寺，遂使农功虚费，府库空竭矣。”见杜佑《通典》，王文锦等点校，北京：中华书局，1988年，第149页。

[7] 龚松林修、汪坚纂《重修洛阳县志》卷十五《记》四十二，乾隆十年(1745年)刻本。

[8]《旧唐书》卷六《则天皇后纪》、卷七《中宗纪》，点校本，北京：中华书局，1975年，第121、139页。

[9] 现存唐宋时期咏赞香山寺的诗词颇多，参见龙门石窟研究所编《龙门石窟志》，北京：中国大百科全书出版社，1996年，第336-349页。

“宋之问……常扈从游宴。则天幸洛阳龙门，令从官赋诗。左史东方虬诗先成，则天以锦袍赐之。及之问诗成，则天称其词愈高，夺虬锦袍以赏之”[1]。对此，《唐诗纪事》尤详：“武后游龙门，命群官赋诗，先成者赐以锦袍。左史东方虬诗成，拜赐。坐未安，之问诗后成，文理兼美，左右莫不称善，乃就夺锦袍衣之。”[2]《大唐传载》则记“龙门香山寺上方，则天时名望春宫。则天常御石楼，坐朝文武、百执事班于外而朝焉”[3]。此外，武三思有《春日幸龙门应制》[4]，沈佺期有《从幸香山寺应制》[5]。由此说明：香山寺乃武周时大寺及游览胜地，武则天常游幸之。这种情形一直延续到中宗时不衰，因为神龙元年“冬十月癸亥（705年11月7日），（中宗）幸龙门香山寺”[6]。

至于香山寺的具体位置，1965年3-5月，龙门石窟保管所为配合洛阳轴承厂疗养院之建设，曾在东山南端，即擂鼓台东南进行了试掘，揭露出部分遗址。尽管整个

---

[1]《旧唐书》，上引书，第5025页。

[2]“其词曰：宿雨霁氛埃，流云度城阙。河堤柳新翠，苑树花初发。洛阳花柳此时浓，山水楼台映几重。群公拂雾朝翔凤，天子乘春幸凿龙。龙门近出王城外，羽从淋漓拥轩盖。云跸才临御水桥，天衣已入香山会。山壁崭岩断复连，清流澄澈俯伊川。塔影遥遥绿波上，星龛奕奕翠微边。层峦旧长千寻木，远壑初飞百丈泉。彩仗蜺旌绕香阁，下辇登高望河洛。东城宫阙拟昭回，南陌沟塍殊绮错。林下天香七宝台，山中春酒万年杯。微风一起祥花落，仙乐初鸣瑞鸟来。鸟来花落纷无已，称觞献寿烟霞里。歌舞淹留景欲斜，石间犹驻五云车。鸟旗翼翼留芳草，龙骑骎骎映晚花。千乘万骑銮舆出，水静山空严警跸。郊外喧喧引看人，倾城南望属车尘。嚣声引扬闻黄道，王气周回入紫宸。先王定鼎三河固，宝命乘周万物新。吾皇不事瑶池乐，时雨来观农扈春。”［宋］计有功《唐诗纪事》卷十一《宋之问》，北京：中华书局，1965年，第165-166页。参见宋之问《驾幸龙门应制》，载《文苑英华》卷一百七十八《诗·应制·杂题》，影印本，北京：中华书局，1966年，第873页。

[3]《文渊阁四库全书》本。《唐语林》有同样记述。

[4]“凤驾临香地，龙舆上翠微。星宫含雨色，月殿抱春晖。碧涧长虹下，雕梁早燕归。云疑浮宝盖，石似拂天衣。露草侵阶长，风花绕席飞。日斜宸赏洽，清吹入重闱。”《文苑英华》卷一百七十八《诗·应制·杂题》，影印本，北京：中华书局，1966年，第872-873页。

[5]“南山奕奕通丹禁，北阙峨峨连翠云。岭上楼台千地起，城中钟鼓四天闻。旃檀晓阁金舆度，鹦鹉晴林彩眊分。愿以醍醐参圣酒，还将祇苑当秋汾。”《文苑英华》卷一百七十八《诗·应制·寺院》，影印本，北京：中华书局，1966年，第869-870页。

[6]《旧唐书》卷七《中宗纪》，点校本，北京：中华书局，1975年，第141页。中宗行幸龙门，疑与此前“复立庐陵”有关。武则天嗣圣元年（684年）二月废中宗后，李显被幽闭于房州（今湖北房县）。圣历元年（698年），庐陵王被秘密接“至神都”。“初，中宗在房陵，而吉顼、李昭德皆有匡复谠言，则天无复辟意。唯仁杰每从容奏对，无不以子母恩情为言，则天亦渐省悟，竟召还中宗，复为诸贰。初，中宗自房陵还宫，则天匿之帐中，召仁杰以庐陵为言。仁杰慷慨敷奏，言发涕流。遽出中宗，谓仁杰曰：还卿储君。仁杰降阶泣贺。既已，奏曰：太子还宫，人无知者，物议安审是非？则天以为然，乃复置中宗于龙门，具礼迎归，人情感悦。仁杰前后匡复奏对，凡数万言。开元（713-741年）中，北海太守李邕撰为《梁公别传》，备载其辞。中宗返正，追赠司空。”（《旧唐书》卷八十九《狄仁杰传》，上引书，第2895页）。因此，中宗返正“幸龙门香山寺”，或有还愿游幸之意。

遗址布局情况不甚清楚，龙门保管所根据地婆诃罗瘗葬“龙门山阳，伊水之左”，推断该遗址为香山寺址[1]。

实际上，据前引《华严经传记》，武周时期的香山寺，应包括灵龛、重阁、精庐、伽蓝、佛塔以及石像七龛等，唯详况不得而知。到了中、晚唐，白居易把为友人元稹撰写墓志款六七十万全部捐出修缮香山寺，并特撰《修香山寺记》：“洛都四郊，山水之胜，龙门首焉；龙门十寺，观游之胜，香山首焉。香山之坏久矣。楼亭骞崩，佛寺暴露……去年秋，微之将薨，以墓志文见托。既而元氏之老，状其藏获、舆马、绫帛，洎银鞍、玉带之物，价当六七十万为谢……回施兹寺，因请悲智僧清闲主张之命，谨干将士复掌理之。始自寺前亭一所、登寺桥一所、连桥廊七间，次至石楼一所、连楼廊六间，次东佛龛大屋十一间，次南宾院堂一所、大小屋共七间。凡支坏、补袂、垒塬、覆漏、圬墁之功必精，赭恶之饰必良。虽一日必葺，越三月而就……于是，龛像无燥湿陊泐之危，寺僧有经行宴坐之安；游者得息肩，观者得寓目。”[2]这次修缮，似主要维修各类建筑，布局上无较大增减。换句话说，白居易的这次捐修，只是对香山寺原始格局建筑做了保护性修缮。白居易捐资修缮香山寺七八年后，即唐开成五年(840年)又于香山寺新建藏经堂，此乃在前述香山寺的基础上之扩建，至此“三宝”俱全[3]，仍居龙门观游之胜十寺之首。

值得注意的是，龙门开窟造像活动从西山移至东山，除武氏集团兴建香山寺及西山崖面局限外，疑与当时南北交通的加强不无关系。

唐代洛阳通往荆南、岭表的主要通行大道，经由龙门、南阳和襄州[4]。据(唐)张说《龙门西龛苏合宫等身观世音菩萨像颂》，“(龙门)北对宫观，南驰荆越；阙路豁开而中断，伊水逶迤而长注。修途交会，车马川流；帝城风俗，是焉游览”[5]。又，龙门西山《唐朝议郎行少府监主簿上柱国巨鹿魏牧谦像龛铭并序》：魏牧谦“于龙门奉先寺北，敬为亡考妣造阿弥陀像、释迦牟尼像、弥勒像，合为三铺，同在一龛，以开元五年龙

---

[1] 参见：1) 洛阳市龙门文物保管所《洛阳龙门香山寺遗址的调查与试掘》，见《考古》，1986年第1期，第40-43页；2) 温玉成《唐代龙门十寺考察》，见《中国石窟·龙门石窟》(二)，北京：文物出版社，1992年，第218-221页。

[2]《文苑英华》卷八百十七《记·释氏》，影印本，北京：中华书局，1966年，第4314-4315页。

[3] 白居易《香山寺新修经藏记》，参见《文苑英华》卷八百十九《记·释氏》，影印本，北京：中华书局，1966年，第4327页。

[4] 1) 王文楚《唐代洛阳至襄州驿路考》，载王文楚《古代交通地理丛考》，北京：中华书局，1996年，第117-133页；2) 严耕望《唐代交通图考》第四卷《山剑滇黔区》，台北：中研院历史语言研究所，1986年，图十五；3) 严耕望遗著、李启文整理《唐代交通图考》第六卷《河南淮南区》，台北：中研院历史语言研究所，2003年，第1840页。

[5]《张说之文集》卷十一，《四部丛刊》本。

集丁巳八月戊辰朔十五日壬午 (717 年 9 月 24 日) 功毕尔。其同成定鼎之故,夏禹疏山之路；削平如砥,正逢绝壁之岩；琢磨为容,不假他山之石；金容相向,初谈贝叶之经；宝座不□,已赴法华之会；前临大道,行李之所往来；密尔名都,众生之所回向。恐□□□,劫尽无闻,海遍桑田,年多不识,乃于龛北自勒铭云……”[1]序中明确记述此龛“前临大道,行李之所往来”。另据龙门西山韦琼造像记,韦琼“以大周长寿□年 (692-693 年) □□岭□□□过此。于时城门□越岭激驻征骖于净土……”[2]这说明当时洛阳通往南方经由龙门伊阙的这条南北交通大动脉,过往人员很多。唐代这条大道,在伊水两岸并未架桥,东、西山间似仅靠渡船相通[3]。至于这条洛阳通襄州之主道到底位于西山脚下还是东山,限于材料,目前尚无定论。据龙门东山万佛沟“卢征题记”,卢征“建中□年 (780-783 年) 自御史谪居,夜郎贞元二祀 (786 年),自□官贬□,南北皆为权臣所忌……夜宿龙门香山寺,灵龛天眼,亿万相对；稽首悲哩,如蹔降临,因发诚愿：归旋之日,于此造等身像一躯。此乃夜郎之黜也。贞元之黜,又过于此,仆夫在后,独行山侧,有白衣路人,随马先后……遂刻全身于此山巅。山既不朽,像亦常存……贞元七年岁次辛未二月八日 (791 年 3 月 17 日)”[4]。卢征失意两过东山,“独行山侧”,似暗示东山脚下即为唐代交通大道。又,龙门地区的唐代僧房,除附近地上寺院之外,东山也开凿不少石室。据 (唐) 刘沧《题龙门僧房》,“静室遥临伊水东,寂寥谁与此身同；禹门山色度寒磬,萧寺竹声来晚风；僧舍石龛残雪在,雁归沙渚夕阳空；偶将心地问高士,坐指浮生一梦中”[5]。龙门东山今香山寺下方的许多空窟龛,或许就是刘沧所记唐代僧舍或静室；而僧房临近大道,也是中外石窟寺之惯例。迄北宋,真宗大中祥符“四年 (1011 年) 三月,上幸洛阳龙门山”[6],御制、御书并篆额《龙

[1] 刘景龙、李玉昆主编《龙门石窟碑刻题记汇录》,北京：中国大百科全书出版社,1998 年,第 316 页。

[2] 刘景龙、李玉昆主编,上引书,第 319 页。

[3] 参见[唐]刘长卿《龙门八咏》。《龙门八咏》包括:《阙口》“秋山向摇落,秋水急波澜。独见鱼龙气,长令烟雨寒。谁穷造化力,空向两崖看”;《水西渡》“伊水摇镜光,纤鳞如不隔。千龛道傍古,一鸟沙上白。何事还山云,能留向城客”;《水东渡》“山叶傍崖赤,千峰秋色多。夜泉发清响,寒渚生微波。稍见沙月上,归人争渡河”;《福公塔》“寂寞对伊水,经行长未还。东流自朝暮,千载空云山。谁见白鸥鸟,无心洲渚间”;《远公龛》“松路向精舍,花龛归老僧。闲云扬锡杖,落日低金绳。入夜翠微里,千峰明一灯”;《石楼》“隐隐见花阁,隔河映青林。水田秋雁下,山寺夜钟深。寂寞群动息,风泉清道心”;《渡水》“日暮下山来,千山暮钟发。不如波上棹,还弄山中月。伊水连白云,东南远明灭”;《下山》“谁识往来意,孤云长自闲。风寒未渡水,日暮更看山。木落众峰出,龙宫苍翠间”。《唐文粹》卷十六《诗 · 古调歌篇 · 胜概》上,《四部丛刊》初编缩印本,上海：商务印书馆,1936 年,第 128-129 页。

[4] 刘景龙、李玉昆主编,上引书,第 643 页。

[5]《全唐诗》卷五百八十六,北京：中华书局,1960 年,第 6788 页。

[6]《佛祖统纪》卷四十四《法运通塞志 · 真宗》,见《大正藏》第 49 卷,第 404b 页。

门铭》[1]于东山二莲花洞南侧，表明北宋时亦循唐代官道。近年在万佛沟前清理出的石凿古道及车辙印痕直通擂鼓台窟前遗址，说明这条大道至迟在武周时已经使用[2]；倘若根据东山擂鼓台南洞上方发现的先秦箭镞和擂鼓台窟前遗址出土的绳纹板瓦及云纹瓦当，或许秦汉以降它就是当时洛阳通往南方的主要交通干道[3]。

二、石像七龛

龙门石窟东山（香山）现存大中型窟龛九座，经过我们排比分析，属于武周时期的有七座，即擂鼓台北洞、擂鼓台中洞、擂鼓台南洞、高平郡王洞、看经寺、二莲花南洞和二莲花北洞（参见本书所载龙门石窟西山、东山立面示意图）[4]。基于对龙门东、西两山现存窟龛的系统考察、分析和排比，结合最近在擂鼓台区窟前遗址的考古发掘（图1），我们怀疑上述七座大型洞窟或为法藏《华严经传记》所记“石像七龛”[5]。其中：

1. 擂鼓台北洞：位于擂鼓台三洞最北侧，故名。从擂鼓台三洞外观看，北洞所在崖面最好[6]。根据中外石窟寺营造通则，一处区域中最早开凿的洞窟往往居于崖面最佳位置。另外，现存的窟前地面，中洞地面较北洞略低、磨礲并局部打破了北洞与之衔接部分[7]；南洞所在崖体最差且高出中洞地面约1米。故我们认为北洞是这一区域中

---

[1] 刘景龙、李玉昆主编，上引书，第646页。

[2] 严耕望认为：“唐代既称东山为香山，即白居易所寓居者，分别言之，西山乃专龙门之名耳。”参见严耕望《洛南三关》，载严耕望遗著、李启文整理《唐代交通图考》第六卷《河南淮南区》，台北：中研院历史语言研究所，2003年，第1831-1843页。

[3] 龙门石窟研究院等编著《龙门石窟考古报告：东山擂鼓台区》下编（待刊）。

[4] 参见李崇峰《龙门唐代窟龛分期试论》（见本书）。

[5] 石像七龛，应为香山寺的重要组成部分，或为七个别院。最早注意到“石像七龛”的学者，是宿师季庚先生。2006年4月18-25日，笔者陪同季庚师考察龙门石窟时，先生曾提出七龛应为七个洞窟。同年5月17日，笔者向季庚师汇报龙门石窟考古工作时，先生再次强调：龙门石窟的研究要注意七龛问题。后来，先生又几次提及此事。

[6] 龙门石窟开凿在中、晚寒武世碳酸盐岩体中，在构造上为四面受断裂切割的近东西向地块，石窟就位于龙门山——香山断块上，主要开凿于上寒武统上部和中寒武统上部的白云岩和灰岩中。经2008年春季考古清理，发现擂鼓台北洞北侧地面有较大岩溶裂隙，影响到上方所谓的“刘天洞”，刘天洞两侧及下方的崖面均有不同程度的溶蚀、开裂，不宜雕造大型窟龛。参见潘别桐、方云、王剑峰《龙门石窟碳酸盐岩体溶蚀病害及防治对策》，载潘别桐、黄克忠主编《文物保护与环境地质》，武汉：中国地质大学出版社，1992年，第99-125页。

[7] 擂鼓台中洞窟外踏道南侧崖壁以条石包边且表面磨礲，踏道北侧崖壁斫砟，表面经人工磨礲，其底部直向凿痕及磨礲面均向北伸入二窟窟外平台表面分界线所显示的北洞范围之内。又，擂鼓台中洞主室右侧壁与左侧壁不完全平行，右壁前端向洞窟中央内收，造成前壁右半部窄于左半部；擂鼓台北洞主室右侧壁与左侧壁对称，且后半部向中洞方向倾斜。依据早期图像资料及近期实测图纸，二窟之间岩体最薄处厚度不足10厘米。我们怀疑擂鼓台中洞主室右侧壁前端内倾，应为躲避北洞主室左侧壁所致。故中洞的开凿应晚于北洞。

a

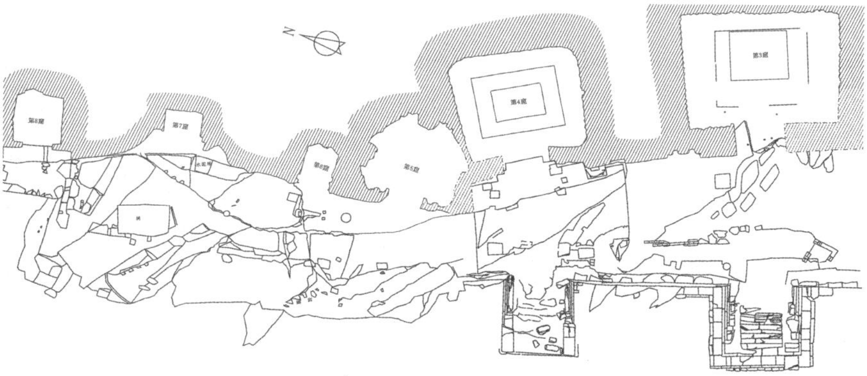

b

图 1　擂鼓台三洞

a. 外立面照片；b. 平面图

开凿最早的洞窟，或许也是龙门东山窟群中最早的[1]。

北洞前室不清，主室平面近五边形，顶作方形；窟顶中央雕莲花，周围绕飞天。正壁和左右侧壁各雕一坐佛，坐佛间雕游戏坐菩萨像；前壁门道两侧各造一多臂菩萨像，其中门道北侧为十一面观音；门道上方雕造千佛。正壁主尊头戴宝冠，颈部三道，宽肩、挺胸、细腰、收腹，戴项饰和臂钏，大衣作“右袒式”披覆；右臂与左小臂残

[1] 2008年于擂鼓台窟前遗址所做的考古发掘，进一步证实了我们的推测。经过清理发现，北洞窟前崖面开窟时没有打剥和斫砟，而是循西山石窟传统做法，仅在通往北洞的岩石表面凿出蹬道台阶或脚窝（图 2），僧俗经过这条简易通道可从地面进入窟中。

图2　擂鼓台北洞窟前岩面蹬道台阶

图3　擂鼓台北洞主尊

损，左手置放脐前，双腿已残毁，下坐方形束腰叠涩须弥座（图3）。

关于这尊造像，目前学界争议较大。考虑到本窟外立面门道上方的小龛铭记和武周时期流行菩提像及其与现存纪年菩提像的相似造型，我们推测北洞主像为菩提树像。从开凿次第看，擂鼓台北洞早于中洞开凿；北洞正壁雕菩提树像，中洞正壁造倚坐弥勒，或许为一固定组合，即"菩提瑞像与弥勒间似乎有着某种微妙的关联"[1]。这种题材组合形式，或许发展了玄奘临终遗愿和地婆诃罗从前梦寐以求的瑜伽行派学说，即于菩提树像前礼忏，祈求往生兜率，值遇弥勒，证得佛果。擂鼓台北洞雕造的菩提树像，疑与地婆诃罗有关[2]，因为地婆诃罗推重佛顶尊胜陀罗尼咒和菩提树像[3]。

值得注意的是，北洞窟门右侧现存一高僧像，连眉、深目、高鼻、大嘴，偏袒右肩，为一域外僧人形象（图4）。经现场观测，此高僧像系打破北洞右侧门框雕造，限于崖面，其头部明显较原有壁面凹陷，疑为后来补雕之作，不在该窟原始设计之中。关于

[1] 李玉珉《四川菩提瑞像窟龛研究》，见重庆大足石刻艺术博物馆编《2005年重庆大足石刻国际学术研讨会论文集》，北京：文物出版社，2007年，第554页。

[2] 经检佛教经论，只有地婆诃罗翻译的二部经，即《佛说七俱胝佛母心大准提陀罗尼经》和《最胜佛顶陀罗尼净除业障咒经》详细记述了菩提树像的功用；而擂鼓台三洞，应在武则天敕建香山寺区域，为纪念地婆诃罗所造"石像七龛"，应包括上述三洞。因此，菩提树像出现在擂鼓台区域，亦情理中事。

[3] 李崇峰《菩提像初探》，见《石窟寺研究》第三辑，北京：文物出版社，2012年，第190-211页。

这身高僧像[1],有人推测是唐代高僧宝思惟[2]。依《华严经传记》所述,我们疑为地婆诃罗。窟内主尊是地婆诃罗推崇备至的菩提树像,窟外则为他的纪念影像[3]。

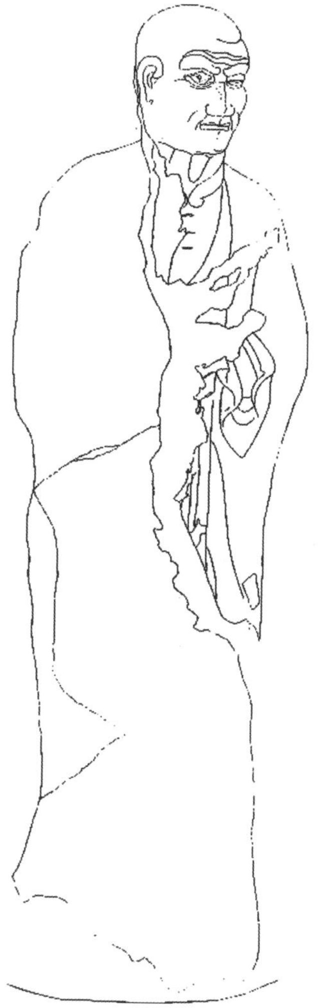

图 4　擂鼓台北洞窟口右侧高僧像

2. 擂鼓台中洞:位于擂鼓台三洞中央,石窟所在崖面较北洞略差,窟前地面打破了北洞窟前地面,主室右壁为避免与擂鼓台北洞打穿而被迫内收,故中洞的开凿晚于北洞。经过 2008 年春夏之际的考古发掘,我们发现:中洞现存窟前下部崖面系人工刻意经营,开窟时正中预留踏道位置,踏道两侧崖面竖向凿齐,表面磨礲,形成一较高的石质殿阶基(台基),上建木构殿堂或窟檐;石雕殿阶基表面岩石状况不好者,以小条石补砌。至于踏道,现踏子不存,副子多损,唯象眼用整石,做工细腻。因此当初策划时,中洞应前有石砌踏道,中建木构殿堂,后凿岩石主室。换言之,岩石主室、窟前平台、木构殿堂、石雕殿阶、石砌踏道、土衬石乃至碎石砖瓦路面系开窟前统一设计,营造时踏道、殿阶基和窟前平台皆磨礲,显得精致细腻(图 5)。这是一种全新形制,完全模拟当时地面佛寺主殿而建,而且为了增加气氛,特在中洞门楣上方仿效地面寺额,镌刻"大万五千佛龛"。

主室平面方形,地面正中置方坛;现仅存石质坛芯,与地面连成一体。正壁中部开一浅龛,内造一佛(倚坐弥勒,图 6)[4]二菩萨像;两侧壁及前壁大部雕造纵成列、横成行的小坐佛,即一万五千佛;正壁及左右侧壁下部雕造 25 身传法高僧像,像旁摘勒《付法藏因缘传》相关内容;前壁下部窟门两侧镌刻《佛顶尊胜陀罗尼》(佛陀波利译本)、《佛

[1] 日人水野清一、长广敏雄认为该像与看经寺洞的祖师像相似,制作精美。参见水野清一、長廣敏雄《龍門石窟の研究》,東京:座右寶刊行會,1941 年,第 123 页,图版 100。

[2] 温玉成《迹旷代之幽潜 托无穷之柄焕——龙门石窟艺术综论》,见龙门石窟研究院编《龙门石窟研究院论文选》,郑州:中州古籍出版社,2004 年,第 38 页。

[3] "在特殊的厅堂里尊奉已逝大师的画像是唐代流行的风俗",如敦煌莫高窟第 17 窟(即藏经洞)北壁坛上有晚唐雕塑的洪䛒影像。擂鼓台北洞门外的高僧像或具此性质。参见周一良《唐代密宗》,钱文忠译,上海:上海远东出版社,1996 年,第 59 页。

[4] 中洞主像整体造型及六拏具式背屏,与西山惠简洞主尊及其装饰极为相似,应为弥勒。又,中洞主尊佛头早年被盗,现藏美国旧金山亚洲艺术博物馆(Asian Art Museum of San Francisco)。

图 5　擂鼓台中洞外立面

图 6　擂鼓台中洞主尊佛像

说阿弥陀经》（鸠摩罗什译本）、《金刚般若波罗蜜经》（菩提流支译本）、《般若波罗蜜多心经》（玄奘译本）和《六门陀罗尼经》（玄奘译本）等[1]；窟顶中央雕巨大莲花，周围绕飞天。

据怀信《释门自镜录》[2]卷二，武周时神都太平寺高僧威整因害蜘蛛疮，全寺徒众，为其求佛，于龙门山造一万五千像一铺[3]。现存龙门石窟中雕造一万五千

[1] 参见：刘景龙、李玉昆主编，上引书，第 613-626 页。

[2]《释门自镜录》似有二本，一为唐高僧慧祥所集，五卷，现缺；一为唐沙门怀信撰，二卷，《大正藏》第 51 卷收入，即《大正藏》，No. 2083，第 802-822 页。参见：1)《日本国承和五年（838 年）入唐求法目录》，载《大正藏》第 55 卷，第 1075 页；2)《大正新脩大藏经勘同目录》，见《昭和法寶總目録》第一卷，第 549 页；3) 吕澂《新编汉文大藏经目录》，济南：齐鲁书社，1980 年，第 148 页。

[3] 此事在《释门自镜录》卷下《害物伤慈录·唐神都太平寺僧威整害蜘蛛事》详记如下："释威整，未详氏族。少出家，修慧解，精勤听习，略无弃日，住神都太平寺，常讲数部大乘，深有弘益。忽于床后壁上见一蜘蛛，以杖狭之，遂误断一脚。遣人送却，至明日还来。整见，又遣人送向水南。经宿又来，整乃以指剔其所患之脚，遂被咬其手指，又遣人送极远之处。他日不觉，复来重咬其指。乃虽小疮，痛不可忍。又令更送，自尔不来。疮后稍增，渐遍身体，体觉渐微痒，以手搔之随手作疮。疮中有蜘蛛丝，出疮皆渐大，二、三寸许。晓夕苦痛，难言难忍。经二年间，涕唾小便，皆有小蜘蛛子出。至今不差，百方推问，莫之能疗。合寺徒众，时时来集，为其求佛，即觉小可，罄舍衣资，于龙门山造一万五千像一铺。像今欲成，其疮稍敛。岂非宿殃，不请之所致耶？"见《大正藏》第 51 卷，第 814b-c 页。

佛者有两处,一为万佛洞,系高宗永淳元年沙门智运与大监姚神表合造[1];另一处就是擂鼓台中洞,即大万五千佛龛。因此,擂鼓台中洞或许就是太平寺“合寺徒众”[2]为高僧释威整生疮痊愈捐资修造的,时间应在唐中宗嗣圣元年九月甲寅(684年10月19日),武后改元光宅,并“改东都为神都”[3]之后、神龙元年二月甲寅(705年3月3日)中宗“复以神都为东都”[4]之前。

正壁雕造主尊弥勒,地面中央置坛(maṇḍala, maṇḍalaka);前壁石刻的《般若波罗蜜多心经》和《六门陀罗尼经》,系印度瑜伽行派中土第一传人玄奘转汉;《金刚般若波罗蜜经》译者菩提流支,学承无著、世亲一系[5];《佛顶尊胜陀罗尼》时为“除病秘方,为世俗所特重”[6],适于释威整祛除“宿殃”。因此,神都太平寺合寺徒众“为其求佛”、“于龙门山造一万五千佛一铺”,“显然属于礼佛、忏悔、灭祸、除殃的宗教行为”[7]。故而,接续北洞开凿的中洞适合僧俗“最上供养”,便于四众“默念弥勒,令傍人称曰:‘南谟弥勒、如来应正等觉,愿与含识,速奉慈颜;南谟弥勒、如来所居内众,愿舍命已,必生其中’”[8]。

又,据(清)缪荃孙《藕香零拾》所收《元河南志》卷一,唐东都归义坊“太平禅院,在福胜院后,唐垂拱二年(686年)太平公主建,号太平寺。后废,复建为太平禅院……”[9]太平寺曾为武周时神都大寺,高僧大德云集[10]。既为太平公主所建,该寺

[1] 参见:刘景龙、李玉昆主编,上引书,第138-143页。

[2] 2008年春夏之季在擂鼓台窟前遗址的发掘中,出土了一残碑碎块,上有“太平寺僧”字样。这或许从另一方面证实了我们的推断。参见龙门石窟研究院等编著《龙门石窟考古报告:东山擂鼓台区》下编(待刊)。

[3]《旧唐书》卷六《则天皇后纪》,点校本,北京:中华书局,1975年,第117页。参见:《资治通鉴》卷二百零三,标点本,北京:中华书局,1956年,第6421页。

[4]《资治通鉴》卷二百零八《唐纪》,标点本,北京:中华书局,1956年,第6583页。

[5] 吕澂认为:“(菩提)流支之学是继承无著、世亲一系的。据他的《金刚经》讲稿《金刚仙论》记载,他还是世亲的四传弟子。因此,他的翻译偏重于这一系。”吕澂《中国佛学源流略讲》第七章《南北各家师说》下,北京:中华书局,1979年,第139页。

[6] 汤用彤《隋唐佛教史稿》,北京:中华书局,1982年,第27页。

[7] 罗炤《宝山大住圣窟刻经中的北方礼忏系统》,见《石窟寺研究》,第一辑,北京:文物出版社,2010年,第172-173页。

[8]《续高僧传》卷四《玄奘传》,见《大正藏》第50卷,第458a页。

[9] 缪荃孙编《藕香零拾》,影印本,北京:中华书局,1999年,第193页。

[10] 除前述高僧释威整外,东都太平寺名僧尚有“上座福庆”、“都维那承办”和“律师道恪”以及利涉等。其中,福庆和承办参与了“大唐天后敕佛授记寺沙门明佺等撰”、天册万岁元年(695年)十月完成的《大周刊定众经目录》的编写,分别担当“刊定真伪经”和“校经目”工作(参见《大正藏》第55卷,第475a、475c页);道恪于唐景龙四年(710年)四月参与义净译场,担当证义之职(参见《大正藏》第24卷,第418b、520a、523c页;《大正藏》第31卷,第81a页)。利涉曾作《成唯识论异义》一卷(参见《大正藏》第55卷,第1142b页)。

大德及僧众参与武氏倡首的香山寺及“皇家龛像”的营造[1]乃情理中事。

2008年春夏之季在龙门擂鼓台窟前遗址的发掘，对我们研究擂鼓台区窟龛乃至擂鼓台与香山寺的关系具有重要价值。

中洞窟前踏道左侧（南侧）原始地面上出土的一座《大佛顶陀罗尼》石幢[2]，系唐“天祐三年岁次丙寅七月丙申朔（应为壬子朔）十七日戊辰（906年8月9日）建”。铭文中有“刻石永记于香山……香山寺主……当寺看经院主……看经徒众”等[3]。此外，中洞窟前踏道左侧岩石殿阶基上镌刻的宋代题铭[4]，再次出现了“看经院”字样。

两铭文中的“看经院”，可能涵盖整个擂鼓台区窟龛，抑或特指擂鼓台中洞，因为该窟采用前殿后窟之制，窟内前壁镌刻当时流行的佛经，左、右壁和正壁下方采用“左图右史”方式向僧俗图释《付法藏因缘传》。因此，疑该窟为香山寺别院——“看经院”或其一部分，至少它应属于香山寺看经院管理。

3. 擂鼓台南洞：位于擂鼓台区窟群最南端，故名。南洞所在崖体较差，现存窟前地面较中洞窟前地面高约1米[5]。从崖面的使用推测，该窟应为擂鼓台三洞中最

[1] 武周时，太平公主、武三思等曾修寺多处。据杜佑《通典》卷七《食货·历代盛衰户口》：“武太后、孝和朝，太平公主、武三思、悖逆庶人，恣情奢纵，造罔极寺、太平观、香山寺、昭成寺，遂使农功虚费，府库空竭矣。”杜佑《通典》，王文锦等点校，北京：中华书局，1988年，第149页。

[2] 这种石质陀罗尼经幢应是佛寺殿堂的供养物。早期佛寺殿外的经幢，质地为木帛，迄开元、天宝时多为石雕。阿弥陀殿通常竖立双幢，即两侧各一幢，弥勒殿前立独幢。中洞踏道旁出土的经幢，或许从另一方面说明主室正壁主尊为弥勒。

[3]《大佛顶陀罗尼》石幢序文如下：“女弟子意者普为四恩三有、巨质微形、水陆飞空、胎卵湿化、三涂八难、受苦众生，弟子若有故杀、悮杀、负命、负财，各怀欢喜之心，莫为宿世冤对，因兹胜利，普及有情。既得道于十方，愿度弟子于八难，更愿普资法界，一切有情，万罪消除，千福圆满，早证月光三昧，速登无上菩提。刻石永记于香山，功德长资于沙界。香山寺主内外临坛大德令表、当寺看经院主内禅大德绪宗、当院内表白大德弘朗、内禅大德智舟、当院权知藏教僧圆辉、当院典座僧自旭、看经徒众……右衔内持念大德智诲书，颖川陈钊镌字。”参见龙门石窟研究院等编著《龙门石窟考古报告：东山擂鼓台区》下编（待刊）。

[4] 全文如下：“内典承制：彭城刘从政仲淑，宝元元年（1038年）仲冬月授西京水北都巡检使兼管勾。太祖、太宗、真宗影殿，应天禅院之命，遂游龙门十有二回，寻幽选胜，终日忘归，而长负不宿山寺之会。庆历改元辛巳岁（1041年），季冬月忝奉帝命解职赴缺。二十三日（1042年1月17日）乃访旧，游得香山、宝应，凡数宵徘徊登眺，不忍轻别，岂敢继古贤仁智之趣聊自足山水之赏？因题于石壁，四明赐紫知白书，太原王德明刊，看经院主赐紫法明，西头供奉官监伊河竹木兼本镇烟火张昭吉。”参见龙门石窟研究院等编著《龙门石窟考古报告：东山擂鼓台区》下编（待刊）。

[5] 龙门东山擂鼓台区域为中寒武统碳酸盐岩体，岩性为石膏化微细晶灰岩。2008年春夏之季的考古发掘，发现中洞与南洞之间窟前殿阶基岩体有一宽约3米、高约1米的岩溶裂隙，充填物主要为土粒和小石块。这种岩体显然不适于雕造龛像，故罗炤认为：南洞地面较中洞地面高出1米乃岩体本身不适宜开凿所致，功德主忌惮其地面下移，系不得已而为之。参见：潘别桐、方云、王剑峰《龙门石窟碳酸盐岩体溶蚀病害及防治对策》，上引书，第99-101页。

晚开凿的。窟前木构殿堂下方崖面仿中洞之制，开窟时在中央预留踏道位置，踏道两侧崖面细漉、斫砟为殿阶基；其中崖体较好者，竖向粗搏、细漉、斫砟；崖体不好者，多用较大石块褊棱、斫砟后垒砌而成。中洞与南洞交接处，现存南洞石作殿阶基打破中洞石作殿阶基，故南洞的开凿较中洞为晚。由于原始路面上距窟前平台多达 4 米，因此石砌踏道显得既陡又高，岩石殿阶基雄伟（图 7)。

图 7　擂鼓台南洞外立面

主室平面方形，穹顶中央雕莲花，地面中央以深蓝色青石块砌出方形佛坛，唯后半局部为原始遗存；窟内四壁及顶部莲花周围雕造小型坐像，横向齐整，上下交错，现存 798 尊，其中能够辨析手势者 545 尊。小坐像偏袒右肩或通肩覆，皆为印度传统披衣方式；除七身为螺发外，皆头戴宝冠，颈饰项圈，肩挂璎珞，胸前佩饰；手印有触地印 (bhūmisparśa mudrā，278 尊)、禅定印 (dhyāna mudrā，153 尊)、施无畏印 (abhaya mudrā，111 尊) 和转法轮印 (dharmacakra mudrā，3 尊) 之分[1]，其中触地印数量过半。窟前半部早已崩毁，现存为石块和青砖补砌[2]。

1906-1908 年间（一说 1918 年）关野贞等所摄照片显示：南洞主室中央坛上所置佛像，结跏趺坐，“顶饰宝冠、身佩璎珞”、偏袒右肩，作触地印。后来此像被移离该窟，现置龙门石窟研究院办公院内。笔者疑此像为南洞开窟时原作，其造型与南洞四壁及窟顶的小型坐像一致（图 8)。

据《开元释教录》卷九《总括群经录》上，地婆诃罗“以天皇仪凤 (676-678 年) 初至天后垂拱 (685-688 年) 末，于两京东、西太原寺（西太原寺即今西崇福寺是也，

---

[1] 参见龙门石窟研究院等编著《龙门石窟考古报告：东山擂鼓台区》下编（待刊）。

[2] 从窟外崖面看，擂鼓台南洞窟门右侧（北侧）有一斜向岩溶裂隙，向下直通中洞窟门前方地面，向上延伸至南洞左侧（南侧）上方，上下贯穿洞窟前半，致使碳酸盐岩体上覆的第四纪土层失去自然平衡。因此，南洞前半塌毁应与之有关。又，南洞窟顶北侧局部未雕，现存四壁多有因岩体不好而补作者，有些小坐佛的莲座甚至部分彩绘而成。推测该窟的营造，系迁就岩体结构不得已而为之。至于窟顶的崩塌或在营造之中或在完工不久，因为该窟门道南侧现存一凸起于地面的未加工岩体。若然，擂鼓台南洞“毕工”之时，或为半雕半砌之作。

图 8　擂鼓台南洞内景

东太原寺即今大福先寺是也）及西京弘福寺，译《大乘显识经》等一十八部，沙门战陀般若提婆译语，沙门慧智证梵语。敕召名德十人助其法化，沙门道成、薄尘、嘉尚、圆测、灵辩、明恂、怀度等证义，沙门思玄、复礼等缀文笔受。天后亲敷睿藻，制序标首，光饰像教，传之不朽也"[1]。《宋高僧传》卷二《日照传》，与《开元释教录》卷九《总括群经录》内容基本相同，只是补充地婆诃罗被高宗敕令"仍准玄奘例，于一大寺别院安置"[2]，由此可见地婆诃罗在当时中土佛教界之崇高地位。前引法藏《华严经传记》，应是迄今关于地婆诃罗最详细、最系统之介绍。法藏参谒地婆诃罗，得《华严经》之《入法界品》，以补《华严经》之缺。因此，法藏熟谙地婆诃罗之思想及译经，记载地婆诃罗除补旧阙外，"更译《密严》等经论十有余部，合二十四卷，并皇太后御制序文，深加赞述，今见流行于代焉"[3]。这里，法藏把《密严经》放在地婆诃罗译经之首，与智昇和赞宁所记地婆诃罗译经次第有别，或许不是偶然。

据吕澂研究：瑜伽行派"护法的主张，重要根据都出于较晚的《密严经》。经中提到有个超世界的地方，即所谓密严净土，佛就住在那里。佛身是无形的，是易变身，虽然可以被看到，但并无形象。这种说法显然带有密教的色彩。护法对这部经很重视"[4]。

---

[1]《大正藏》第 55 卷，第 564a 页。

[2] 赞宁《宋高僧传》卷二《日照传》，范祥雍点校，北京：中华书局，1987 年，第 32-33 页。

[3] 法藏《华严经传记》卷一《传译 · 地婆诃罗》，参见《大正藏》第 51 卷，第 154c 页。

[4] 吕澂《印度佛学源流略讲》第五讲《中期大乘佛学》第四节《瑜伽行学派和中观学派》，上海：上海人民出版社，1979 年，第 206 页。

《密严经》，全称《大乘密严经》[1]，梵名 *Ghana-vyūha-sūtra*，《大周刊定众经目录》仅记“大唐三藏地婆诃罗译”，并无具体出经时间[2]。该经旨在阐说一切法乃心识所变，全经分《密严会》等八品[3]。地婆诃罗逐译《大乘密严经》后，法藏特撰经疏，对《密严经》各品细分科段并详加注解，即《大乘密严经疏》，惟经疏第一卷早已佚失[4]。

《大乘密严经》卷上《密严会品》曰：“一时佛住出过欲色无色无想于一切法自在无碍神足力通密严之国……与诸邻、极修观行者、十亿佛土微尘数菩萨摩诃萨……处离诸有莲花之宫……与诸菩萨入于无垢月藏殿中，升密严场师子之座，诸菩萨众亦皆随坐……密严佛土超诸佛国……尔时世尊现诸国土及佛菩萨胜功德已，复以佛眼遍视十方诸菩萨众，谓如实见菩萨言：‘如实见，今此国土名为密严。’”[5]而后，应如实见菩萨、金刚藏菩萨之请问，佛在密严国宣说法要，示以如来藏不生不灭之理。金刚藏菩萨复对来会之菩萨和诸佛子，宣说阿赖耶识（ālayavijñāna）之能示现重法，染净诸法恒以此识为所依，更阐明阿赖耶识随谜语之缘而别凡圣。

关于密严佛土，卷中《妙身生品》曰：“密严佛土，能净众福，灭一切罪；诸观行人所住之处，于诸佛国最上无比。”[6]又，“密严佛国观行之境，得正定人之所住处，于诸佛刹最胜无比”[7]。卷中《显示自作品》：“密严中，人无有眷属生死之患，其心不为诸业习气之所染着，如莲花出水，如虚空无尘，如日月高升、净无云翳，一切诸佛恒共摄受……密严佛土，是最寂静，是大涅槃，是妙解脱，是净法界。”[8]卷中《分别观行品》：“大心之人疾得生于光明宫殿，离诸贪欲、瞋恚、愚痴，乃至当诣密严佛土。此土广博、微妙、寂静，无诸老、死、衰、恼之患。”[9]卷中《阿赖耶建立品》：“密严佛土，安乐第一；诸佛、菩萨，数如微尘，处莲华藏。”[10]又，“诸佛子转复精进，于莲花藏清净佛土，与诸菩萨、莲花化生入一乘道，离贪等习，乃至降伏欲界天魔。夫精进者，志无怯弱；光隆

---

[1] 参见《大正藏》第 16 卷，第 723-776 页。

[2] 名佺等《大周刊定众经目录》卷一《大乘单译经目》，见《大正藏》第 55 卷，第 379c 页。

[3] 日本大村西崖认为：“《密严经》虽非密经，与《解深密经》同味。其说处则在出过欲、色、无色、无想，于一切法自在无碍神足力通密严国，为无量佛手亲灌顶，从内证智境现法乐、现众色像三昧起而说法。金刚藏菩萨等蒙佛许，而又广说八识等。是实密部说经仪式之蓝本，而又其教相之所沿也。”大村西崖《密教發達志》，東京：佛書刊行會圖像部，1918 年，第 260-261 页。

[4] 参见《卍新纂续藏经》，第 21 卷，第 127-170 页。

[5]《大正藏》第 16 卷，第 723b-c 页。

[6] 同上书，第 732a 页。

[7] 同上书，第 732b 页。

[8] 同上书，第 734b-735a 页。

[9] 同上书，第 736c 页。

[10] 同上书，第 737a 页。

佛家、王诸国土”[1]。

在如来宣说密严佛国期间，不时有“诸佛子各从所住而来此国”[2]。“又有无量佛、菩萨众，从诸国土来此会。”[3]“密严土中诸佛、子众并余佛国来听法者，闻说密严微妙功德，于法尊重，决定转依，恒居此土，不生余处。”[4]“尔时世尊说是经已，金刚藏等无量菩萨摩诃萨，及从他方来此会者无央数众，闻佛所说皆大欢喜，信受奉行。”[5]

《大乘密严经》文中尚有若干描述佛、菩萨及诸佛子服饰之词语，对我们考虑擂鼓台南洞现存遗迹极具价值。如卷中《阿赖耶建立品》：“无量佛子，智慧善巧，众相庄严，顶饰宝冠，身佩璎珞，住兜率陀等诸天之宫。”[6]卷中《妙身生品》：“时螺髻梵王即白佛言：‘世尊，我等今者当何所作而能速诣密严佛土？’”[7]卷下《阿赖耶微密品》：“彼诸菩萨闻说是已……以三昧力见密严土中菩萨之王，首戴宝冠，三十二相，以为严饰。彼诸菩萨便从定起，著上好衣，从他方无量佛国而来此会。”[8]卷下《阿赖耶微密品》：“尔时金刚藏菩萨摩诃萨，三十二相、八十种好庄严其身……佛与金刚藏菩萨，亦复如是等，无有异。”[9]

鉴于密严佛土如此美妙，无老死衰恼之患，《密严经》能净众福，灭一切罪，乃至降伏欲界天魔，甚至光隆佛家及王诸国土；密严佛土超诸佛国，十亿佛土微尘数菩萨摩诃萨及从他方来此会者信受奉行，因此受到当时朝野的推重。《大乘密严经》转汉后，地婆诃罗尤重《密严》，高僧法藏“今见流行于代”[10]，智昇更言“光饰像教，传之不朽”[11]，密严佛国信仰随之影响中土。永泰元年（765年）唐代宗为不空重译《大乘密严经》[12]制序时，写到：

---

[1]《大正藏》第16卷，第737c页。不空译《大乘密严经》卷二《趣入阿赖耶品》作：“必当得解脱，或为彼天主；及以诸粟散，乃至生梵宫；而作转轮王，转生莲花藏；在彼佛会中，莲花而化生；获大精进力，由此降魔众；及欲熏习因，志意无怯弱；证成一道法，绍继于佛事，得王诸国土。”见《大正藏》第16卷，第764b-c页。

[2]《大正藏》第16卷，第732a页。

[3] 同上书，第744b页。

[4] 同上书，第730c页。

[5] 同上书，第747b页。

[6] 同上书，第737b页。

[7] 同上书，第732a-b页。

[8] 同上书，第742b-c页。

[9] 同上书，第746a页。

[10] 法藏《华严经传记》卷一《传译》，见《大正藏》第51卷，第154c页。

[11]《开元释教录》卷九《总括群经录》上，见《大正藏》第55卷，第564a页。

[12] 不空译《大乘密严经》，见《大正藏》第16卷，第747-776页。据《宋高僧传》卷三《飞锡传》，不空永泰元年（765年）奉诏于大明宫内道场重译《大乘密严经》，亦作三卷八品。不空《大乘密严经》译本各品名称，与地婆诃罗译本略有差异，即《密严道场品》、《入密严微妙身生品》、《胎藏生品》、《自作境界品》、《辩观行品》、《趣入阿赖耶品》、《我识境界品》、《阿赖耶即密严品》等八品。参见：赞宁，上引书，第48页。

朕闻西方有圣人焉。演不言之言,垂无教之教。启迪权实,发披聋瞽;迁其善者,不疾而速;阶其益者,即圣自凡;去蒙求以娑婆丘陵,示达观以密严世界。匪染净在我,实是非游。而楚越生于念中,盈缺顿于目下。彼鱼藏鸟逝,其若是乎?钦哉密严,迹超三有;量同乎法界,相离于极微。非声闻之所闻,岂色见之能见?訾洁已至妙,允恭付嘱。是欲泉静识浪,珠清意源。穷赖耶能变之端,照自觉湛然之境。深诣心极,其唯是经[1]。

东晋以降,中土信徒抄写佛经既是功德,也是传播佛教的重要手段之一。据统计,敦煌藏经洞曾出土《大乘密严经》写本五十多件,其中至少有35件为地婆诃罗译本[2];遗憾的是,藏经洞出土的这批《大乘密严经》写本没有一件题署纪年[3]。敦煌不但保存了如此之多的《大乘密严经》写本,而且昔日也绘制了不少《密严经变》。莫高窟现存《密严经变》四铺,即第85窟北壁、150窟北壁、61窟北壁和55窟东壁门北,绘制时代从晚唐到北宋,且原来都有榜题。王惠民曾对敦煌保存的《密严经变》作过介绍。现据王文并结合其他资料综述如下:

第150窟的《密严经变》,"下部被涂改为道教天尊"[4],上部正中为佛说法,两侧各有一大菩萨与二十七身胁侍菩萨,下方为水池,再下有"大乘密严"字样榜题。从经变中的楼阁、水池等画面推断,现存部分表示净土世界——密严佛国。这种构图形式,类似《观无量寿经变》和《阿弥陀经变》等,但无乐舞场景。迄晚唐,各种经变在莫高窟都有绘制,惟构图基本相似,正中一佛说法,两侧各有一大菩萨,众多小菩萨周围环绕听法,下方为净水莲花,楼台亭阁。若无榜题,像150窟这铺具有净土意境的经变或因下部毁失而难以定名。第85、61、55窟《密严经变》的榜题,皆出自地婆诃罗译本。从经营位置看,敦煌莫高窟《密严经变》的基本构图是:中央为密严会,即密严世界,场面较大;上方为赴会诸佛,表现众多佛子"速诣密严佛土";下方

---

[1]《大唐新翻〈密严经〉序》(唐代宗皇帝制),见《大正藏》第16卷,第747b-c页。另参见《全唐文》卷四十九《代宗皇帝·〈密严经〉序》,影印本,北京:中华书局,1983年,第546-547页。

[2]禅叡编著《敦煌宝藏遗书索引》,台北:法鼓文化事业股份有限公司,1996年,第27页;敦煌研究院施萍婷等统计为37件,参见敦煌研究院编《敦煌遗书总目索引新编》,北京:中华书局,2000年,第26页(索引部分)。不过,敦煌研究院王惠民认为敦煌藏经洞出土的《大乘密严经》写本"均属于地婆诃罗译,没有不空译本"。王惠民《敦煌〈密严经变〉考释》,见《敦煌研究》,1993年第3期,第15页。

[3]据薄小莹研究,北京图书馆新1171号写本为《大乘密严经》卷上,题署:垂拱二年正月,北京图书馆疑伪。薄小莹《敦煌遗书汉文纪年卷编年》,长春:长春出版社,1990年,第44页。

[4]石璋如《莫高窟形》一,台北:中研院历史语言研究所,1996年,第30页。不过,敦煌研究院记载为"道教十二星君七身"。参见敦煌研究院编《敦煌石窟内容总录》,北京:文物出版社,1996年,第59页。

为《密严经》相关情节变现，但内容选择较随意[1]。这些经变在创作中显然借鉴了其他经变，构图极为程序化，与同时期其他题材的经变在经营上无大区别；若无原始榜题，恐难以确定其内容。

龙门唐代窟龛多雕大型组像，从一铺三身到一铺九身不等，主旨力图仿效地面佛寺主殿的造像布局[2]，故经变题材少见。龙门石窟中年代明确的净土场景，乃西山南部的“净土堂”，“是北市彩帛行修凿的……北市香行的商人也参加了这座石窟的修凿工程”[3]，完工于694年；该窟主室三壁供奉大型雕像，前庭侧壁似浮雕“九品往生”，整体表现西方净土[4]。万佛沟的“西方净土变”，雕造年代较北市彩帛行净土堂略晚，整个画面以阿弥陀佛为中心经营，构成了庄严的西方极乐世界。

关于擂鼓台南洞的造像题材，迄今学界争议较多[5]。经检索唐高宗、武则天时期新

---

[1] 王惠民《敦煌〈密严经变〉考释》，上引书，第15-25页。

[2] 渤海国是唐代东北地区一个重要政权，其文化大多学习唐朝，首都上京龙泉府位于今黑龙江省宁安县。1963-1964年，中国社会科学院考古研究所对该城址进行了全面调查，并“选择各种有代表性的遗迹作为重点发掘的对象”，共发现佛寺遗址9座。其中一号佛寺位于宫城朱雀大街东侧，位置显赫，有可能是上京城中规模最大的佛寺。因限于工作时间，没有把全寺的规模及布局理清，但发掘出土的正殿遗迹保存较好。正殿包括主殿以及与之相连的东西两配殿，平面布局略成“凸”字形。主殿佛坛造像遗迹为一铺九身，发掘者推测为一佛、二弟子、二菩萨、二天王（神王）、二（金刚）力士。佛坛遗迹在以前地面佛寺遗址发掘中极为少见，这一发现对研究当时佛寺内的像设情形或造像布局非常重要。若当时将其布局全部理清，该寺对探讨唐代两京佛寺的布局应大有裨益。参见中国社会科学院考古研究所编《六顶山与渤海镇——唐代渤海国的贵族墓地与都城遗址》，北京：中国大百科全书出版社，1997年，第76-81页。

[3] 宿白《隋唐长安城和洛阳城》，见宿白《魏晋南北朝唐宋考古文稿辑丛》，北京：文物出版社，2011年，第56页。

[4] 常青《龙门石窟“北市彩帛行净土堂”》，载龙门石窟研究所编《龙门石窟研究论文选》，上海：上海人民美术出版社，1993年，第260-275页。

[5] 关于南洞的造像内容，此前研究的焦点是原置窟内中央方坛上的佛像。

常盘大定、关野贞20世纪初游历龙门石窟时，推断南洞方坛上的本尊为密教像，属于宝冠、佩饰、降魔印佛像系；四壁及顶部为“千体佛”（千佛）。参见：1) 常盤大定、關野貞《支那佛教史蹟》第二輯，東京：佛教史蹟研究會，1926年，圖版第百〇一(1)；2) 常盤大定、關野貞《支那佛教史蹟評解》第二集，東京：佛教史蹟研究會，1926年，第114頁。

水野清一、长广敏雄记载南洞中央佛坛上的圆雕坐佛，戴宝冠，偏袒右肩，左手置足上，右手抚膝，让人联想到戴宝冠、佩璎珞的大日如来或卢舍那。但大日如来像作智拳印，而此像作降魔相之触地印，宝冠也不是五智宝冠。考虑到时代及地域，把该像定作密教尊像之根据尚不够充分。窟四壁及窟顶雕凿千佛，皆坐在莲座上，座下有莲枝。水野清一、長廣敏雄《龍門石窟の研究》，東京：座右寶刊行會，1941年，第121頁。

肥田路美依据文献和实物，对擂鼓台区这种佛像作了系统考察，认为它们是释迦成道像。这种触地印如来像，特别是戴宝冠的触地印如来像是正好处于从印度到中国或者说从显教向密教转折中的一种造像。肥田路美《唐代における仏陀伽耶金剛座真容像の流行について》，載町田甲一先生古稀紀念會編《論叢仏教美術史》，東京：吉川弘文館，1986年，第172頁。

中国学者中，凡涉及龙门这类造像，大多认为是密教的大日如来。21世纪初，常青对这种（转下页注）

出及流行的佛典，尤其是地婆诃罗译经，笔者怀疑南洞主室造像为《密严经》变相，即《大乘密严经·密严会品》之变现。窟内现存遗迹力图反映：佛住密严之国，与诸邻、极修观行者、十亿佛土微尘数菩萨摩诃萨处离诸有莲花之宫。复以佛眼遍视十方诸菩萨众，应如实见菩萨、金刚藏菩萨之请问，在密严国宣说法要，示以如来藏不生不灭之理。

其中，中央佛坛乃狮子座，其上如来结跏趺坐，头戴宝冠，相好庄严，偏袒右肩，与《密严经》菩萨之王的服饰记载相似，即金刚藏菩萨摩诃萨，首戴宝冠，三十二相，以为严饰；而“佛与金刚藏菩萨，亦复如是等，无有异”，造型选取了当时佛像的流行样式。南洞主像与北洞相似，亦和情理，因为当时印度那烂陀寺西北大精舍“中佛像，同菩提树像”[1]。四壁及窟顶小坐像具同样服饰，应与《密严经》所记“无量佛子，智慧善巧，众相庄严，顶饰宝冠，身佩璎珞”相符，诸菩萨着上好衣，从他方无量佛国而来此会；而每一小坐像下的莲茎与窟顶高浮雕大莲花一道，或许表现诸菩萨所住清净莲华之宫。至于窟内现存数量不多的螺发小坐像[2]，可能表现的是期望速诣密严

(接上页注)观点作了集中的论述。常青认为，“现坛上的大日如来石雕像是后来移入的”，不过根据“南洞中部的方形矮坛，就可以想象当年这里可能也有一尊大日如来石像”。窟顶“浮雕大莲花，正壁部位没有主像，而是在四壁面及窟顶雕满了横排齐整、上下交错相对的小坐佛像”。“这种壁面布局，与龙门西山唐代显教窟内的千佛相同，但众小坐佛的形象与服饰却很特殊。”“所以，南洞四壁众多的小像，虽不易断言是否代表着大日如来，但可以确定都是密教化了的佛像。像南洞这样将密教众佛像表现成显教千佛的布局方法，在全国范围内尚属孤例，可能有其特别用意。”参见：1) 李文生《龙门唐代密宗造像》，载李文生《龙门石窟与洛阳历史文化》，上海：上海人民美术出版社，1993 年，第 38-46 页；2) 常青《试论龙门初唐密教雕刻》，见龙门石窟研究院编《龙门石窟研究院论文选》，郑州：中州古籍出版社，2004 年，第 240-279 页。

古正美基于对佛教文献的梳理，在考察擂鼓台三洞后写到：“擂鼓台南洞的主尊头戴天冠，面呈印度人相貌。颈佩璎珞，右臂戴环钏。右手施无畏印，左手作禅定印，结跏趺坐于方形莲花石座上，为身着王装的转轮王造像。”这身造像应是“香王菩萨像”。古正美《龙门擂鼓台三洞的开凿性质与定年：唐中宗的佛王政治活动及信仰》，载《龙门石窟一千五百周年国际学术讨论会论文集》，北京：文物出版社，1996 年，第 166-182 页。

裴珍达 1995 年向韩国弘益大学校大学院提交的美术史学科硕士论文，是《龙门石窟擂鼓台三洞研究》。近年他多次游访龙门，认为：“擂鼓台南洞的图像背景是《华严经》和《梵网经》中提到的莲花藏世界，中央主尊卢舍那佛和周围洞壁上化身千佛的图像结构证明了这一点。即七世纪末作为国家佛教的华严思想通过擂鼓台南洞得到了体现。”换言之，“擂鼓台南洞体现了由主尊法身卢舍那佛和化身释迦牟尼佛组成的《梵网经》莲花藏世界海的千佛图像”。久野美树也基本持类似的观点，认为擂鼓台南洞和中洞是以《华严经》和《梵网经》为中心的华严系受戒的产物。参见：1) 裴珍达《龙门石窟擂鼓台南洞研究》，载《2004 年龙门石窟国际学术研讨会文集》，北京：文物出版社，2006 年，第 165-169 页；2) 久野美樹《龍門石窟擂鼓台南洞中洞試論》，载《美学美术史论集》第 14 辑 (2002 年)，第 93-119 页。

[1] 慧立、彦悰《大慈恩寺三藏法师传》，孙毓棠、谢方点校，北京：中华书局，2000 年，第 73 页。

[2] 据我们统计，擂鼓台南洞窟内现存螺发小坐佛七尊。此外，2008 年春夏之季在擂鼓台窟前遗址的发掘，又出土了两尊。参见龙门石窟研究院等编著《龙门石窟考古报告：东山擂鼓台区》下编 (待刊)。

佛土的螺髻梵王。既然法藏称地婆诃罗译本今见流行于代，那末用造型艺术手段变现《大乘密严经》不更能“光饰像教”吗？

北宋司马光（1019-1086年），曾访游龙门“香山皇龛”。据（宋）邵伯温《闻见录》卷十一，“司马温公居洛时……曾同范景仁过韩城，抵登封，憩峻极下院，登嵩顶，入崇福宫、会善寺。由栅辕道至龙门，游广爱、奉先诸寺，上华严阁、千佛岩，寻高公堂，渡潜溪，入广化寺，观唐郭汾阳铁像，涉伊水至香山皇龛，憩石楼，临八节滩，过白公影堂。凡所经从，多有诗什，自作序曰《游山录》，士大夫争传之”[1]。苏过（1072-1123年），也曾游历伊水东侧的皇龛、看经两寺。据苏过《无题》，“仆以事至洛，言还过龙门，少留一宿。自药寮度广化、潜溪，入宝应。翼日过水东，谒白傅祠，游皇龛、看经两寺，登八节，尤爱之。复至奉先，作此诗，以示同行僧起晖”[2]。此外，张耒（1054-1114年）曾多次游历龙门，其《柯山集》卷七有若干首关于龙门及附近寺院之诗作，如《初望龙门》、《渡伊水》、《白公祠》、《三龛》、《上皇龛》、《石楼》、《广化遇雨》、《晚饭宝应》等。其中“《上皇龛》：升危蹑石梯，已觉毛骨异；玄龛剖山腹，六月霜雪至[3]；佛台磨光瑶，绀滑不留水[4]；巍巍数天人，苍玉刻冠佩[5]；老僧拂高崖，上有昔人字[6]；国都已萧瑟，山泽隐逸事[7]；西轩府空阔，昼夜纳苍翠；卜筑莫后时，林中有余地”[8]。

关于龙门“香山皇龛”，现代学者多认为在擂鼓台一带[9]；而北宋张耒《上皇龛》之诗情与擂鼓台三洞之现状颇相符。既称“皇龛寺”，恐与武则天不无关系。

---

［1］邵伯温《邵氏闻见录》，李剑雄、刘德权点校，北京：中华书局，1983年，第117页。

［2］下文诗作“峥嵘两山门，共挹一秀水。滩声千鼓鼙，石壁万龛窦。何人植翠柏？幽径出尘囿。金银佛寺古，夜籁笙竽奏。僧稀梵呗少，石险松竹瘦。惟当效乐天，早晚弃冠绶”。苏过《斜川集》卷一，见《四部备要》本第9页。

［3］“升危蹑石梯，已觉毛骨异；玄龛剖山腹，六月霜雪至”，系指南洞亦或中洞踏道情景，因为从原始路面仰望窟口，仅见少许窟门，感觉洞窟高耸，好似开在山腹之中。

［4］“佛台磨光瑶，绀滑不留水”，意指深蓝色石块垒砌的南洞或中洞佛坛，表面打磨光滑，类似青瑶，水留不住。

［5］“巍巍数天人，苍玉刻冠佩”，指僧俗一旦步入南洞或中洞窟内，仿佛走进天国，四周及窟顶上的小坐佛，似以苍玉所雕，宝冠华饰，如天神无数，让人难忘。联系上句，似指南洞为妥，因其为密严佛国的再现。

［6］“老僧拂高崖，上有昔人字”，疑指北洞外立面的“高僧像”和中洞门楣上方的“大万五千佛龛”石刻匾额。

［7］“国都已萧条，山泽隐逸事”，指北宋洛阳为西京，情景较武周时神都萧条，但远在城南的香山和伊水尚传颂相关逸事。

［8］张耒《张耒集》卷七《五言古诗》，李逸安、孙通海、傅信点校，北京：中华书局，1990年，第817页。

［9］李玉昆《龙门碑刻及其史料价值》，上引书，第85页。

据李焘《续资治通鉴长编》卷六十五，宋真宗景德四年二月“己卯（1007 年 3 月 3 日），上幸龙门，睹岩崖石佛甚多，经会昌毁废，皆已摧坏。左右曰：‘非官为葺治，不能成此胜迹’。上曰：‘军国用度，不欲以奉外教，恐劳费滋甚也’”[1]。虽然真宗这次婉拒了修缮龙门龛像之建议，但八年后即大中祥符八年（1015 年），还是命人予以修饰。据《佛祖统纪》卷四十四《法运通塞志 · 真宗》，“西京龙门山石龛佛，岁久废坏。上命沙门栖演给工修饰，凡一万七千三百三十九尊”[2]，但未开窟造像。至于擂鼓台南洞窟门北侧元丰二年（1079 年）常景所造阿弥陀像龛，乃私家所为；而此前的五代和中晚唐，不闻有皇室在龙门开龛造像活动乃至修缮之举。

石窟形制，既是容纳雕刻、塑像及壁画之载体，也要满足宗教使用功能之需求。这种三维空间的具象形式，是石窟内涵的重要方面。中国石窟寺前的木构建筑，除栈道外，主要有两种形式：一种为装饰性窟檐，另一种是殿堂建筑，即前殿后窟之制。至于窟前殿堂建筑的式样，当是模拟地面佛寺主殿的建筑形式。

中国的佛教石窟，从十六国迄隋主要为了坐禅观相，绝大多数在崖壁上凌空雕凿，无法于窟前接建体积较大的殿堂建筑，有之多为木构窟檐。“初盛唐时石窟的现世因素逐渐丰富，巡礼石窟除了僧人之外，俗人也就越来越多。这样，俗人的现实要求就必然越来越多地体现在石窟之中”。随着唐代洞窟性质的逐渐变化，除了禅观外，还要起延寿和却病的作用，礼拜对象除了禅观僧人之外，俗人逐渐成为巡礼石窟的主要对象，石窟的俗人性质越来越强[3]。表现在形制上，石窟寺越来越多地模拟地面佛寺布局及形式。根据擂鼓台窟前遗址发掘出土的石作殿阶基及踏道和窟前平台表面的石柱础，结合擂鼓台中洞窟外崖壁上的多重梁孔遗迹，表明该窟在北宋末之前至少曾两次建造过木构殿堂，最早的一次应该与洞窟始凿同时，石砌踏道、木构殿堂与岩石主室系一次性毕工。其中，踏道由土衬石、踏、副子和象眼等构成，经与敦煌初盛唐壁画中的大型佛殿对比，发现擂鼓台石窟寺的踏道工艺极为考究（图 9）。又，在擂鼓台窟前遗址发掘中，中洞原始地面（T3 探方第 7 层地面）曾出土了两件绿釉琉璃残件，似为屋顶建筑构件脊兽的一部分。此外，在北洞北侧另一中型洞窟（现编擂鼓台第 8 窟）窟前遗址也出土了四件绿釉琉璃残件，抑或脊饰的一部分。这表明擂鼓台区窟前木构殿堂等级极高，因为琉璃瓦乃皇家建筑所专用。这些绿釉琉璃残件，疑为武氏营造皇龛寺所用，因为前述“香山寺”遗址也曾出土过若干绿釉莲纹瓦

---

[1] 李焘撰《续资治通鉴长编》，点校本，北京：中华书局，2004 年，第 1445 页。

[2]《大正藏》第 49 卷，第 405c 页。

[3] 宿白《敦煌七讲》，油印本，敦煌：敦煌文物研究所，1962 年，第 40-52 页。

a　　　　b　　　　c

图 9　擂鼓台窟前踏道遗迹

a. 南洞与中洞踏道；b. 中洞踏道南侧面；c. 南洞踏道北侧面

当[1]。长安唐大明宫遗址曾“出土了少数绿琉璃建筑构件，说明当时出现了剪边琉璃屋顶”[2]。根据擂鼓台窟前遗址所出琉璃残件，疑擂鼓台中洞及南洞木构殿堂的顶部采用了同样做法。

龙门石窟这种新型的石窟模式，应该是武则天通过营造香山寺创始的，因为“武后为人，有特殊之生理及过人之精力，而又号大喜功”[3]；武则天“信心皈依，发宏誓愿，壮其塔庙，广其尊容，已遍于天下久矣……倾四海之财，殚万人之力，穷山之木以为塔，极冶之金以为像”[4]。尽管我们已无法从擂鼓台崖面现状去恢复其历史面貌，但昔日擂鼓台外观气势之宏伟还是可以想见的。

---

[1] 参见温玉成《龙门十寺考辨》上，见《中州今古》，1983 年第 2 期，第 31 页。

[2] 宿白《汉唐宋元考古：中国考古学下》，北京：文物出版社，2010 年，第 112-113 页。参见：宿白《中国古建筑考古》，北京：文物出版社，2009 年，第 48 页。

[3] 饶宗颐《从石刻论武后之宗教信仰》，见《中研院历史语言研究所集刊》，第 45 卷第 3 本，第 399 页。

[4]《旧唐书》卷一百一十《张廷珪传》，点校本，北京：中华书局，1975 年，第 3151 页。

图 10　高平郡王洞窟门右侧金刚像

图 11　高平郡王洞主室正壁

因此,我们怀疑擂鼓台三洞,应为武氏营建香山寺时最初开凿的三座窟龛[1],后与高平郡王洞、看经寺和二莲花洞一道合称“石像七龛”[2]。

4. 高平郡王洞:前庭正壁门道两侧雕造金刚力士(图 10),主室平面横长方形,未按原计划完工,仅雕镌了正壁(北壁)、右壁(西壁)和前壁(南壁)部分造像。其中,正壁中央雕一佛(倚坐弥勒?)、二弟子、二菩萨(图 11),其下方的 10 身形体较小的坐佛大部竣工,前壁门道西侧佛像基本完成,右壁佛像多胎形,左壁未雕,窟顶粗糙不平。窟内地面现存 24 个圆形槽孔,原为插置造像之用(图 12)。迄 20 世纪 80 年代,地面上保留许多安置佛像的像座,现皆入藏龙门石窟研究院库房。其中,两件像座上的铭记值得注意。一件作“大唐开元/十六年三/月廿六日(728 年 5 月 9 日)/香山寺/上座比丘/慧澄检/校此龛/庄严功/德记/同检校比丘/张和尚法/号

[1] 龙门石窟研究院王振国认为“皇龛寺有可能就是东山擂鼓台三洞,或三洞之一……擂鼓台三洞,特别是中洞,可能是特为武则天或皇室做功德所开凿的石窟,以皇室定其名,恰如其分”。王振国《唐代洛阳佛寺、名僧史迹钩沉》,上引书,第 234 页。龙门石窟研究院焦建辉进一步推定:“‘皇龛’应为第 4 窟(擂鼓台中洞),即第 4 窟为武周时期皇家洞窟。”焦建辉《龙门东山擂鼓台区第 4 窟相关问题探讨》,见《石窟寺研究》第三辑,文物出版社,2012 年,第 221 页。

[2] 承焦建辉见告,龙门东山 2158 号窟(党晔洞)铭记作“河南尹上柱国赐紫金鱼袋辛秘元和十三年闰五月十三日题”。按:元和十三年无闰月,应为元和十二年,即公元 817 年 7 月 1 日。[宋]朱长文《墨池编》卷六记“唐河南尹辛秘题名,在香山寺”(《文渊阁四库全书》本)。这或许进一步证实:擂鼓台区归香山寺统领,至少北宋初年还是如此。

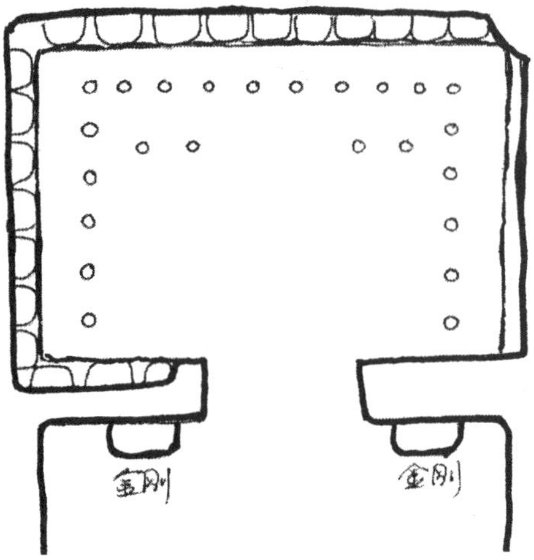

图 12　高平郡王洞平面图

图 13　高平郡王洞像座及铭文

义琬 / 刻字人常 / 思”[1]，另一件为“□周之代高 / 平郡王图像 / 尊仪躯有数 / 十阙功未就 / 掩归四大自 / 兹零露雨洒 / 尘沾遂使 / 佛日沉辉人 / 天福减惟我 / 香山寺上座 / 惠澄法师伤 / 之叹之惭之 / 愧之爰征巧 / 匠尽取其□ / 饰雕翠石焕 / 然紫金即□ / 身之□□□高……（图 13）”[2]第二通题刻中的高平郡王，应是武重规[3]。武重规在武则天天授元年九月丙戌（690 年 10 月 20 日）“周革唐命，盖为从权，子侄封王”[4]中受封为高平郡王，中宗神龙元年五月癸卯（705 年 6 月 20 日）降“高平郡王重规为郐国公”[5]。因此，高平郡王洞的开凿应在武则天天授元年（690 年）之后、中宗神龙元年（705 年）之前。依题刻，当时或稍后的高平郡王洞似归香山寺统领[6]。作为上座，惠澄看到该窟“缺功未就”，“伤之、叹之、惭之、愧之”。因此，“爰征巧匠”，广聚信徒，于开元十六年（728 年）前后“饰雕”、“共妆”高平郡王洞[7]。

[1] 参见：刘景龙、李玉昆主编，上引书，第 639 页。

[2] 参见：刘景龙、李玉昆主编，上引书，第 639-640 页。

[3] 李玉昆《龙门杂考》，见《文物》，1980 年第 1 期，第 26-27 页。

[4] 参见：《旧唐书》卷六《则天皇后纪》、卷一百八十三《外戚・武承嗣传》，点校本，北京：中华书局，1975 年，第 121、4729、4732-4733 页。

[5]《旧唐书》卷七《中宗纪》、卷一百八十三《外戚・武承嗣传》，点校本，北京：中华书局，1975 年，第 139、4732-4733 页。

[6] 温玉成认为：“高平郡王洞是属于香山寺管理的。香山寺是唐‘龙门十寺’之首，梁王武三思为该寺的外护。武则天称帝后曾率群臣登临此寺，命百官赋诗，颂扬大周政权。武重规造窟，又为武家增添一景。”温玉成《迹旷代之幽潜 托无穷之柄焕——龙门石窟艺术综论》，上引书，第 31 页。

[7] 同窟造像记有“佛弟子昌□妻欢心、男寄养妻阿仵，共庄此像，合家供养。开元十六年二月廿六日（728 年 4 月 9 日）”。参见：刘景龙、李玉昆主编，上引书，第 638 页。

5. 看经寺：规模巨大，在龙门全部唐代窟龛中体积仅次于西山大卢舍那像龛。前庭正壁门道两侧雕造金刚力士（图 14），主室地面中央置方坛，左、右、后三壁下部浮雕 29 尊等身高僧像，左右侧壁中部雕造少量千佛（图 15），四壁偏上存一列雕凿整齐的小型孔槽，疑为补造天花所致；整体未按原计划完工。关于看经寺的雕凿年代，现在学界存有争议[1]，我们疑为武周时期始凿[2]，但造像活动因武则天退位而被迫中辍。

图 14　看经寺外立面

图 15　看经寺主室右壁（北壁）

20 世纪 30 年代水野清一与长广敏雄调查看经寺时，特别注意到了侧壁的二十九身高僧像。这二十九身浮雕，相貌既有老年人，也有中年人，还有年轻人。基于擂鼓台中洞二十五身传法高僧像旁镌刻的《付法藏因缘传》经文，水野和长广推想看经寺洞的二十九身罗汉，乃擂鼓台中洞所雕二十五祖续加菩提达摩以下四祖（至

[1] 水野清一与长广敏雄认为：看经寺应开凿于则天武后时期。参见：水野清一、長廣敏雄，上引书，第 115-120 頁，圖版 81-97。

有的学者推测：看经寺开凿于唐开元十年至十五年（722-727 年）。温玉成《龙门唐窟排年》，见《中国石窟·龙门石窟》二，北京：文物出版社，1992 年，第 211 页。

有的学者认为：看经寺的年代，上限是武周时期（684-704 年），下限当不晚于唐玄宗时期（712-756 年）。阎文儒、常青《龙门石窟研究》，北京：书目文献出版社，1995 年，第 128 页。

有的学者推定：看经寺的开凿时间，大约在武周时期，最晚也不会晚于唐玄宗开元、天宝年间（713-756 年），即安史之乱前。宫大中《龙门石窟艺术》（修订本），北京：人民美术出版社，2002 年，第 344 页。

还有的学者进一步推测：看经寺是唐武则天为高宗修造的。参见：1) 金维诺《中国美术史论集》，北京：人民美术出版社，1981 年，第 430 页；2) 荆三林《中国石窟雕刻艺术史》，北京：人民美术出版社，1988 年，第 91 页。

[2] 参见：1) 丁明夷《龙门石窟唐代造像的分期与类型》，见《考古学报》，1979 年第 4 期，第 529 页；2) 龙门石窟研究所编《龙门石窟志》，北京：中国大百科全书出版社，1996 年，第 61 页。

道信）。这些形象，应与当时地面佛寺所造类似题材，如长安千福寺西塔院绕塔板上传法二十四弟子影像及当时的比丘群像，如敬爱寺大院纱廊中门东西壁所绘，多少有些关系，雕造时代当定在则天武后时期较妥[1]。后来，学界通常依据《历代法宝记》考定这群浮雕为西土传法二十九祖[2]。

《历代法宝记》"当在保唐寺无住于唐大历九年（774 年）去世后不久，由其弟子编撰"[3]。因此，其成书与看经寺的始凿相距较大。基于这点，陈清香认为："如果以二十九祖之说的立意而言，那是为了树立南宗的正统地位，开凿石窟雕造二十九尊者像，不也正是为此吗？因此如要肯定看经寺洞是出自南禅的主意，则开窟的年代，势必再向后延至天宝四年（应为"天宝四载"，745 年）之后，则较为合理些。就雕造的艺术题材，以现存的遗侧而言，它应是西天二十八祖，或二十九祖说的最早例证"[4]。若然，天宝四载以后洛阳地区有开凿这样巨型石窟的条件吗？

实际上，看经寺侧壁浮雕的高僧像，有些并非胡貌，如左壁（南壁）西起第二身（图 16）、正壁（东壁）北起第六身、右壁（北壁）西起第三（图 17）和东起第一身，面相似为汉人。有的高僧上衣作"交领式"，大衣作"右袒式"披覆；个别高僧，如左壁西起第三身还著钩钮式束带大衣。这种高僧形象，或许为 7-8 世纪两京地面佛寺中常见的"行僧"像，而非西土传法二十九祖。据唐张彦远《历代名画记》卷三《记两京外州寺观画壁》，西京长安荐福寺西南院佛殿内东壁及廊下"行僧"，并吴画未了；慈恩寺两廊壁间有阎令、李果奴画"行僧"；景公寺东廊南间东门南壁画"行僧，转目视人"[5]；胜光寺西北院小殿南面东西偏门上王定画"行僧"。东都洛阳长寿寺"佛殿两轩行僧亦吴画"；敬爱寺，即佛授记寺"大院纱廊壁'行僧'，中门内以西，并赵武端描，惟唐三藏是刘行臣描，亦成。中门内以东五僧，师奴画。第六僧已东至东行南头第二门已南，并刘行臣描；以北，并赵武端描，或云刘行臣描；中门西边纱廊外面，并圣历已后刘茂德描，陈庶子成"[6]。值得注意的是，东都大敬爱寺这种转目视人的行僧像，主要系刘行臣、刘茂德父子完成，二人皆为武周圣历前后洛阳有名佛画家，

[1] 水野清一、長廣敏雄，上引书，第 115-120 頁。

[2] 1) 温玉成《龙门唐窟排年》，上引书，第 211 页；2) 宫大中，上引书，第 344-348 页。

[3] 杨曾文《唐五代禅宗史》，北京：中国社会科学出版社，1999 年，第 252 页。

[4] 陈清香《龙门看经寺洞罗汉群像考——祖师传承说的石刻例证》，见陈清香《罗汉图像研究》，台北：文津出版社有限公司，1995 年，第 145-146 页。

[5] 看经寺内的行僧像，多具有"转目视人"神态。

[6] 张彦远《历代名画记》卷三《记两京外州寺观画壁》，俞剑华注释，上海：上海人民美术出版社，1964 年，第 60-73 页。

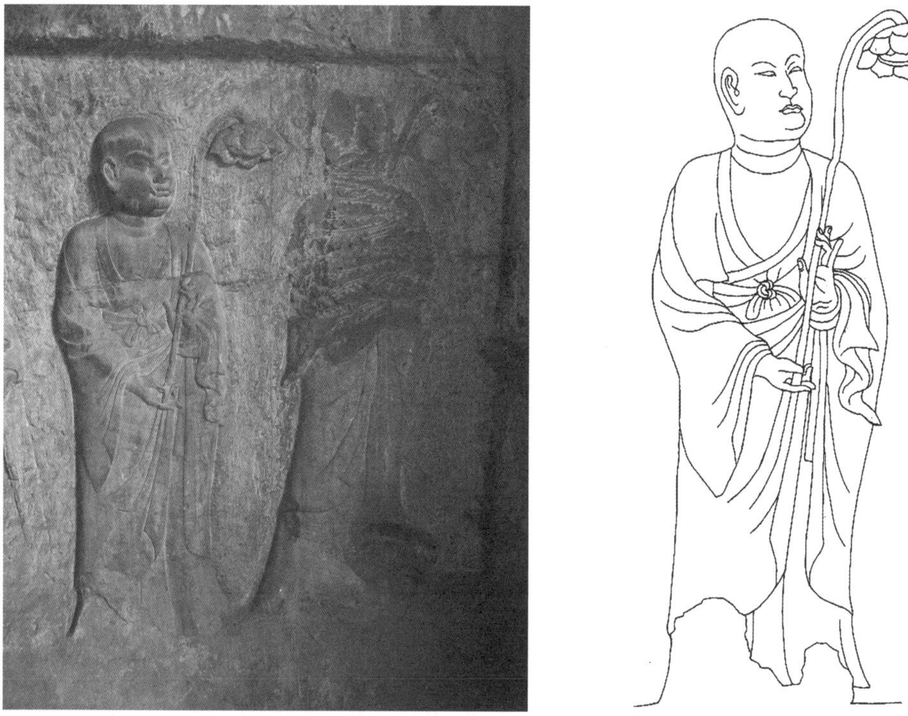

图 16　看经寺主室左壁（南壁）高僧像

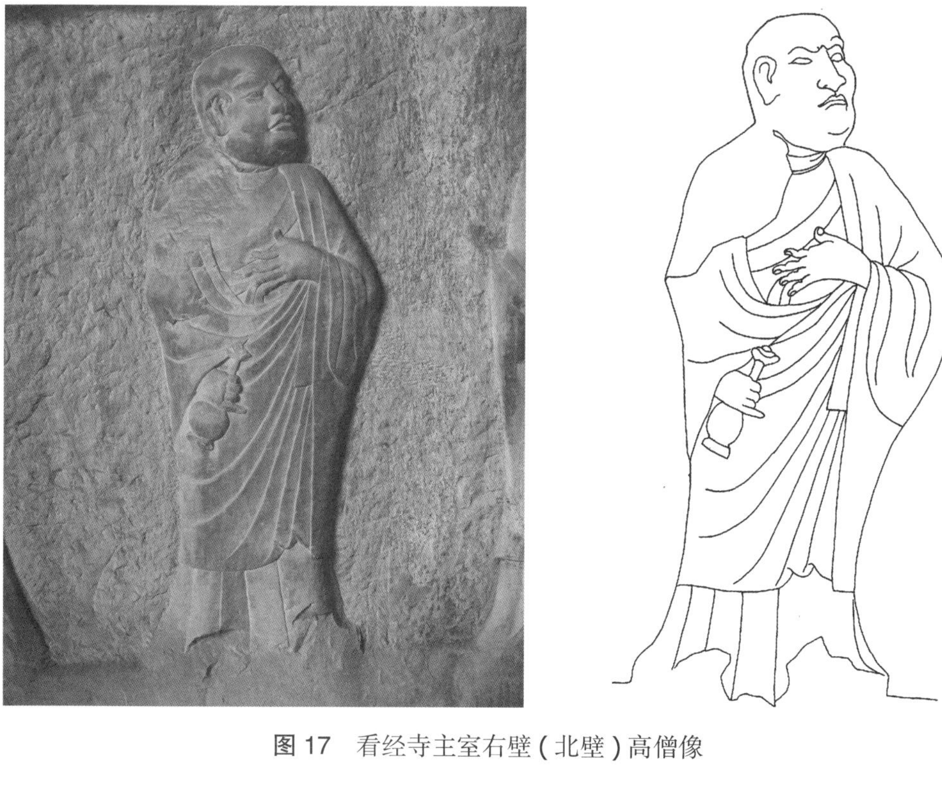

图 17　看经寺主室右壁（北壁）高僧像

"洛下众僧党刘行臣"[1]。大敬爱寺所画行僧像数目众多，且有唐三藏玄奘，说明当时在寺院中为高僧画像极为流行。石窟寺乃地面佛寺的石化形式，因此，看经寺侧壁的浮雕高僧像，或许模仿地面佛寺流行的行僧像，故应称"行僧像"为妥[2]。

6. 二莲花洞：位于看经寺东侧，洞窟形制及题材内容相似，疑为一组双窟（图18)。尽管迄今尚未发现二窟与武家有直接关系，但分期排队表明，它们应属武周时期营造，故疑为香山寺所属"石像七龛"之一部分。

a

b

图 18a　二莲花洞外景
b　二莲花北洞主室窟顶

（本文原为《龙门石窟唐代窟龛分期试论》附录，因涉及问题较多抽出单行。）

[1] 据张彦远记载：大敬爱寺"中门东立神及神之东西两鬼，圣历后，有神英法师令何长寿扫却，欲重描。神英京兆党何生，洛下众僧党刘行臣，时人以何生虽善山水，至于画神，不如刘；刘为关东独步，与西京长寿齐名。洛下之意，抑何进刘，不许神英之请，还遣行臣之子茂德续其父画。今中门东神及两鬼腰已上新接者，亦不迨其父矣"。张彦远，上引书，第 73 页。

[2] 至于地面佛寺中所画传法弟子，文献记载中并不多见，有之则明确说明，如长安千福寺西塔院"绕塔板上传法二十四弟子"，系卢棱伽、韩干画。张彦远，上引书，第 66 页。这种"行道高僧"，不但雕绘于唐代两京，卢楞伽还在益州大圣慈寺画过。参见：[宋]黄休复《益州名画录》卷中"张玄"条，明万历庚寅金陵"王氏淮南书院重刻"《王氏画苑》本。

石窟寺中国化的初步考察

佛教的诞生可谓史诗，佛教文化及艺术在印度的全方位创作与影响亦然。古代摩诃剌侘(今马哈拉施特拉邦)堪称石窟寺的摇篮，自身构成一部伟大的发明、创造史。今天，这一佛教遗迹遍布亚洲，尤其是中国。一位现代游客可以在中国看到许多印度发明的遗迹，就像古代朝圣者在天竺(今南亚次大陆)[1]所能游历的那样。随着塔庙、僧坊、方形窟以及地上寺塔等天竺发明物在天空映衬下于中国形成空中轮廓线，折射出古代中国佛教风景的"天竺式"创作。这种特别现象，说明了中国曾经发生的空前社会—文化变革。因此，佛教艺术从天竺传至中国同样也是一部史诗。

作为一位佛教考古学者，笔者可以肯定地说：在中国发现的佛教遗迹与遗物，其数量远远超过了在印度的发现；而在漫长的历史发展与变革中，在中国境内毁坏的佛教遗迹，其数量也大大超过了印度境内被毁的佛教遗迹之数。仅就石窟寺院的保存数量而言，中国也胜过印度。中国大同云冈、洛阳龙门和敦煌莫高窟堪称世界上规模最大、内容最丰富的佛教石窟群，印度阿旃陀和埃洛拉的佛教石窟寺与中国这些遗迹相比，则要略显逊色。

考虑到这些石窟所在山丘周边恶劣的自然环境和开窟者当时使用的原始工具以及落后的运输和提举能力，这些石窟寺的雕造的确是古代人民一项伟大的工程业绩。如果没有一个万众一心、薪尽火传若干世纪的庞大群体和他们高度虔诚而执着的宗教献身精神，就不可能创造出这样惊人的佛教文化伟绩。当时雕造这样的石窟寺院，需要花费巨大的人力和物力。整个当地社会各阶层，包括统治者、富商、地主以及受压迫的劳苦大众，不得不为此做出巨大的牺牲。

---

[1] 参见：1) P. C. Bagchi, "Ancient Chinese Names of India", in: *India and China: Interactions through Buddhism and Diplomacy; A Collection of Essays by Professor Prabodh Chandra Bagchi*, compiled by Bangwei Wang and Tansen Sen, Delhi: Anthem Press India, 2011: 3-11, esp. 8-9; 2) 钱文忠《印度的古代汉语译名及其来源》，载《十世纪前的丝绸之路和东西文化交流：沙漠路线考察乌鲁木齐国际讨论会(1990年8月19-21日)》，北京：新世界出版社，1996年，第601-611页。

倘若没有强大的社会释罪 (social justification)，就不可能产生如此伟大的牺牲。石窟寺院，一定在那些献身此举的人们脑海中产生了一种神圣动机。我们可以设想在石窟寺完工之时当地人们表现出的心醉神迷状态。为了享受天堂世界，一座神圣的佛殿突然从沉睡的营地中出现，静寂的山岩，突然变成了佛事的场所。石窟寺不仅成为信徒及朝圣者的栖身之处，而且变为佛、菩萨、飞天以及其他超自然生物的家园。你可以设想古人是如何感受的。在微弱的油灯下或烛光中，陆地上这座黑暗之洞变得如此梦幻，让人仿佛看到了人间天堂中的佛与弟子。他们发现岩石在祈祷、说教、微笑和飞跃，听到天乐正从窟顶轻柔地飘来、回荡在他们的心灵深处[1]。

石窟寺堪称深奥、微妙而复杂的建筑艺术品；它的完工，会使人们忘却发狂群体的奋斗与痛苦，去拥抱纯洁的和平气氛所产生的宁静、庄严、怜悯以及其他崇高的目标与理想。石窟寺总是神秘的。那富丽堂皇的雕刻与绘画，创造出尘世任何东西都无法与之比拟的美妙和魔力。它们甚至已把尘世文化生态学，转变为想象的天国。难怪7世纪初中国著名高僧玄奘讲到阿折罗伽蓝 (Acārasaṃghārāma)，即阿旃陀 (Ajaṇṭā) 石窟的创造时，说“斯乃罗汉愿力之所持也，或曰神通之力，或曰药术之功”[2]。

一、天竺石窟的类型

值得注意的是，当初一处大型石窟寺院的所有组成部分，并非同时所雕造，而是逐渐发展完善的。首先应为和尚开凿僧房，即比丘窟 (Bhikṣu-guhā)，尔后逐步将塔庙、方形窟和水窖等引入到这个寺院群体中来[3]。当然，我们认为这是公元前3世纪前后石窟寺创始期的情况。当石窟普遍流行、深受广大僧侣青睐之时，情况就大不一样了。开凿一处石窟寺院，应有它的塔庙、僧坊和其他附属生活设施 (图 1)。

根据洞窟形制和使用性质的不同，天竺佛教石窟可以大体分作僧众栖止、禅修生活用窟和供养、礼忏等佛事用窟[4]两类。前者以僧坊窟为主 (这种石窟晚期也开龛

[1] 唐代诗人宋昱天宝末年之前曾游历大同云冈石窟，并留有诗句吟咏石窟形象：“梵宇开金地，香龛凿铁围；影中群象动，空里众灵飞。簾牖笼朱旭，房廊鍊翠微；瑞莲生佛步，宝树挂天衣。邀福功虽在，兴王代久非；谁知云朔外，更睹化胡归。”宋昱《题石窟寺即魏孝文帝之所置》，见李昉等《文苑英华》，影印本，北京：中华书局，1966 年，第 1181 页。

[2] 玄奘《大唐西域记》，季羡林等校注，北京：中华书局，1985 年，第 897 页。

[3] M. C. Joshi, “Buddhist Rock-cut Architecture: A Survey” , in: *Proceedings of the International Seminar on Cave Art of India and China,* New Delhi: Indira Gandhi National Centre for the Arts, 1991: 1-28, esp. 3-8.

[4] 参见李崇峰《龟兹与犍陀罗的造像组合、题材及布局》(见本书)。

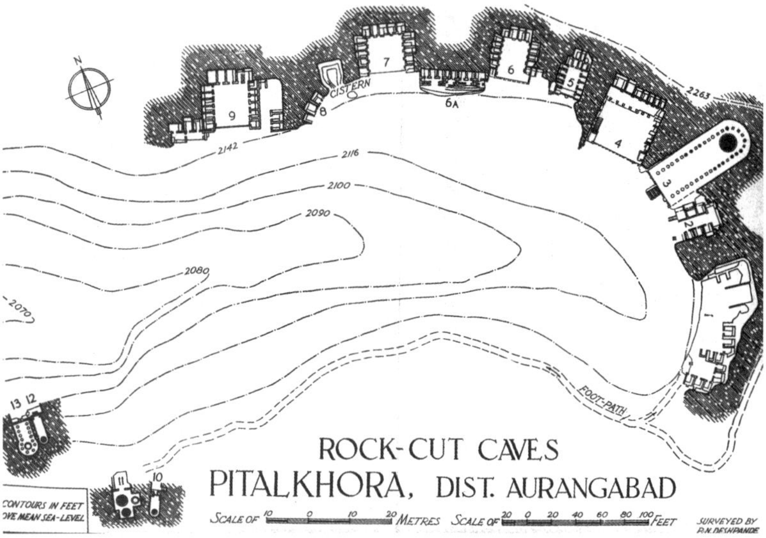

图 1　比德尔科拉石窟连续平面图

造像，兼有礼拜窟的性质），附以方形窟和水窖等；后者主要指塔庙窟[1]。

(1) 僧坊窟，通称 vihāra[2]，不过依据窟内的俗语 (Prākṛta/Prākṛit/Prakrit) 铭文，这种洞窟应称 lēṇa，英文迻译 "cave"[3]，巴利语作 leṇa[4]，梵语对应词为 layana[5]，原意"隐藏"，指苦行者或比丘用作隐居的石窟 (a cave in a rock) 或山洞 (a mountain cave)，尤指凿岩为窟，汉语意为僧坊[6]，"是僧房群式的石

[1] 李崇峰《中印佛教石窟寺比较研究：以塔庙窟为中心》，北京：北京大学出版社，2003 年，第 4-5 页。

[2] 梵语 vihāra 汉译行、行住、游、游步、住、安住、所住、住处、境、静住、修业、所在、(静) 室、静室、舍、房舍、庐舍、寺、寺门、寺舍、寺馆、塔寺、伽蓝、房、僧房、僧坊、精舍、精舍斋堂、大房等，音译毗诃罗、鼻诃罗。参见荻原雲來《漢訳対照梵和大辭典》，東京：鈴木学術財団 / 講談社，1974 年，第 1260a 页。

[3] H. Lüders, "*A List of Brāhmī Inscriptions from the Earliest Times to about A.D. 400 with the Exception of those of Aśōka*", in: *Epigraphia Indica,* Volume X (1909-10), Appendix, Calcutta: Superintendent Government Printing, 1912: Nos. 998, 1000, 1001, 1006, 1007, 1012, 1014, 1016, 1020, 1021, 1024, 1039-1041, 1048, 1051, 1060, 1062, 1063, 1065, 1066, 1073, 1107, 1123-1126, 1131-1133, 1138, 1140, 1144, 1152, 1175, etc.

[4] T. W. Rhys Davids and William Stede, *Pali-English Dictionary,* London: Pali Text Society, 1925: 586.

[5] 梵语 layana 汉译住、怙、归、房、舍、宅、室、住房、房住、房舍、住舍、舍宅、屋宅等。参见：荻原雲來，上引书，第 1147a 页。

[6] 笔者此前曾把这种石窟译作精舍窟，但汉文精舍有广义与狭义之分，广义者指大型地上寺院，如竹林精舍、祇洹精舍等，狭义者指 vihāra。关于精舍，据僧佑《释迦谱》卷三《释迦祇洹精舍缘记》，"祐案：息心所棲是曰精舍"（《大正藏》第 50 卷，第 66b 页）。又，慧琳《一切经音义》卷二十二引慧苑撰《新译大方广佛花严经音义》卷中，"精舍，《艺文类聚》云：'精舍者，非以舍之精妙名为精舍，由有精练行者之所居，故谓之精舍也'"（《大正藏》第 54 卷，第 444b 页）。为避免歧义，这里还是译作僧坊窟。

窟”[1]，为比丘息心所栖之处。传说怀萨罗国“引正王为龙树菩萨凿黑蜂山以为伽蓝诸精舍”[2]，或许就是这种。现存石窟内的有些俗语铭文甚至以开窟时所具禅室之数称谓，如纳西克 (Nāsik) 第 6 窟前廊后壁铭文作：“商人维勒 (Vira) 捐造四室僧坊窟一座，其中一室乃长者之妻纳姆达锡利 (Naṁdasirī) 功德，一室系其小女布里瑟达塔 (Purisadatâ) 施舍，以供养四方僧伽”[3]。此外，郡纳尔地区曼莫迪 (Manmodi, Junnar) 第 21 窟大厅外所刻铭文称该窟为“五室窟” (图 2)[4]，郡纳尔地区伽内什 · 伯哈 (Ganesh Pahar) 第 5 窟左侧明窗上方俗语题铭称该窟为“七室窟”[5]，伽尔拉 (Kārlē) 第 15 窟东壁所刻俗语题铭直接称该窟为九室厅[6]。除个别特例外，这类石窟皆作平顶，平面布局基本分两种[7]：一种由前廊、大厅和一至三个小室构成，小室开凿于大厅的正壁或侧壁 (图 3、4)。这种洞窟主要分布在郡纳尔、根赫里 (Kaṇhēri)、古达 (Kuḍā) 和默哈德

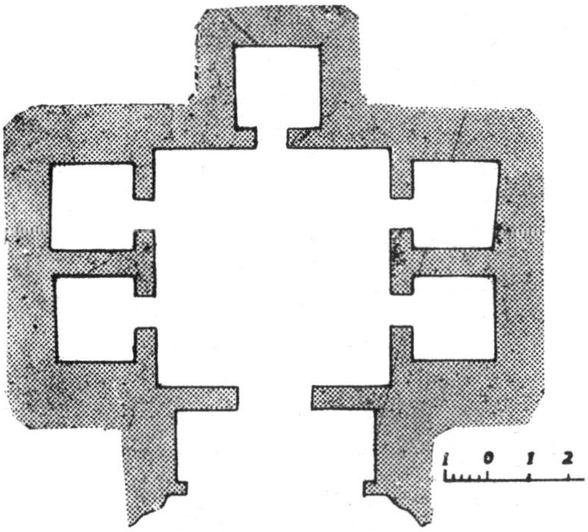

图 2　均讷尔地区门莫迪五室窟 (第 21 窟) 平面图

[1] 1) 宿白《参观敦煌莫高窟第 285 号窟札记》，见《中国石窟寺研究》，北京：文物出版社，1996 年，第 206 页；2) 宿白《调查新疆佛教遗迹应予注意的几个问题》，见《新疆史学》，1980 年第 1 期，第 30 页。

[2] 慧琳《一切经音义》卷六《大般若波罗蜜多经音义》，见《大正藏》第 54 卷，第 342b 页。

[3] 俗语原文可转写为：“Sidhaṃ Viragahapatisa nyegamasa leṇa deyadhama kuṭuṁbiṇiya chasa Naṁdaśrīya ōvarako duhutuya chasa Purisadatâva ovarakâ eva leṇaṁ chatugabhaṁ ṇiyuta bhikusaṁghasa châtudisasa niyâchitaṁ” . 参见：1)Jas. Burgess, *Report on the Buddhist Cave Temples and Their Inscriptions; supplementary to the volume on* “*The Cave Temples of India*” , in: *Archaeological Survey of Western India,* Vol. IV, 1883: 116, No. 24, Plate LV; 2) H. Lüders, *opere citato*: No. 1127.

[4] 1) Jas. Burgess, *opere citato:* 98, No. 31, Plate LI; 2) H. Lüders, *opere citato:* No. 1157.

[5] 1) Jas. Burgess, *opere citato:* 94, No. 10, Plate XLIX; 2) H. Lüders, *opere citato:* No. 1180.

[6] 1) Jas. Burgess, *opere citato:* 113-114, No. 21, Plate LIV; 2) H. Lüders, *opere citato:* No. 1106.

[7] S. Nagaraju, *Buddhist Architecture of Western India* (*C. 250 BC-C. AD 300*), Delhi: Agam Kala Prakashan, 1981: 69-70.

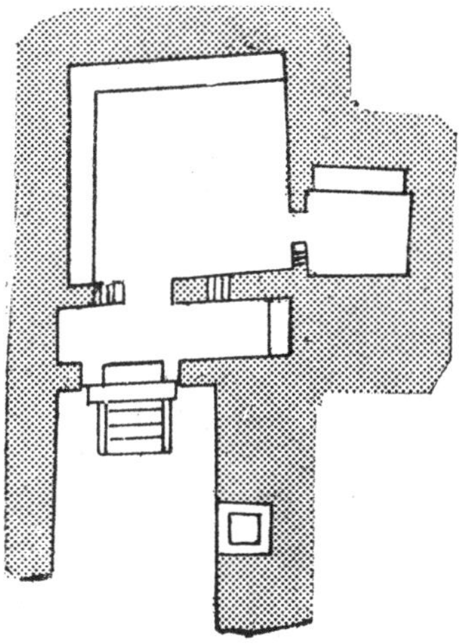

图 3　根赫里第 58 窟平面图

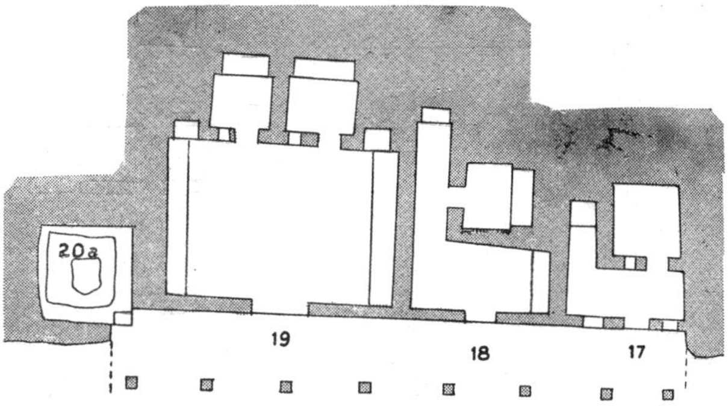

图 4　均讷尔伽内什·伯哈第 17-20a 窟连续平面图

(Mahāḍ) 石窟，少数见于珀贾 (Bhājā)、纳西克和谢拉尔瓦迪 (Śailārwāḍi) 石窟[1]；另一种由前廊、中央大厅 (kodhi/maḍapa) 和多个小室 (ōvaraka/gabha)[2]构成，小室开凿在大厅的左、右、后三壁且多对称排列 (图 5)。到了晚期，通常在方形大厅的正壁向外凿出佛殿 (图 6)。这种僧坊主要分布在阿旃陀、贝德萨 (Beḍsā)、珀贾、埃洛拉 (Ēlūra)、伽尔拉、郡纳尔、纳西克、比德尔科拉 (Pitalkhōrā) 石窟，少数见于郡纳尔的杜尔贾莱纳 (Tūljālēnā)、根赫里、贡德恩 (Kondāṇē)、伯瓦拉 (Pawala) 和谢拉尔瓦迪石窟[3]。其中，第一种平面布局的石窟，创始于公元前 3 世纪，主要流行于公元

[1] 如郡纳尔地区伽内什·伯哈第 1、2、8、11-13、15、17-19、25-28 窟，曼莫迪第 1、27、28 窟，锡万内里 (Sivaneri) 第 33-35、57、60 窟，根赫里第 21、22、32、42、50、53、54、56-59、64、65、70、73、74、78、88、91、93-98 窟，古达第 2、3、5、7、10-12、16-18、23、24 窟，默哈德 (Mahāḍ) 第 4、7、9、11、13、16、19、22-24、26-28 窟，以及珀贾第 15、16 窟，纳西克第 8 窟，谢拉尔瓦迪第 10、11 窟等。

[2] 俗语题铭中关于僧坊窟大厅周匝小室的称谓，多作 ōvaraka，少数为 gabha/gābha。其中 ōvaraka，巴利语作 ovaraka，意为禁室、密室、寝室、内室等，与之相当的梵语词 apavaraka 较之晚出若干世纪，汉译“舍”；gabha/ gābha 似源自吠陀时的 garbha，巴利语作 gabbha，意为内部、洞、内室、私室、寝室，似特指地面建造的 vihāra 内室，即义净所称的“僧房”，与之相当的梵语词是 garbha，汉译胎、藏、胎藏。因此，ōvaraka 与 gabha 意思相同。参见：1) H. Lüders, *opere citato:* Nos. 988, 1078, 1132, 1134, 1180; 2) T. W. Rhys Davids and William Stede, *opere citato:* 171, 244; 3) Monier Monier-Williams, *A Sanskrit-English Dictionary,* London: Oxford University Press, 1899: 52, 349; 4) 荻原雲來，上引书，第 86b、420b 页。

[3] 如阿旃陀第 1、2、4、6、7、11-13、15A、15-17、20-24、27 窟，贝德萨第 11 窟，珀贾第 5-11、13、14、18、22、25 窟，埃洛拉第 1-4 窟，伽内什·伯哈第 5、7、32 窟，曼莫迪第 21、38、43、45 窟，锡万内里第 18、36、42、52 窟，伽尔拉第 4、12-15 窟，以及郡纳尔地区杜尔贾莱纳第 2、4 窟，根赫里第 67 窟，贡德恩第 2、3 窟，伯瓦拉第 1 窟和谢拉尔瓦迪第 3 窟等。

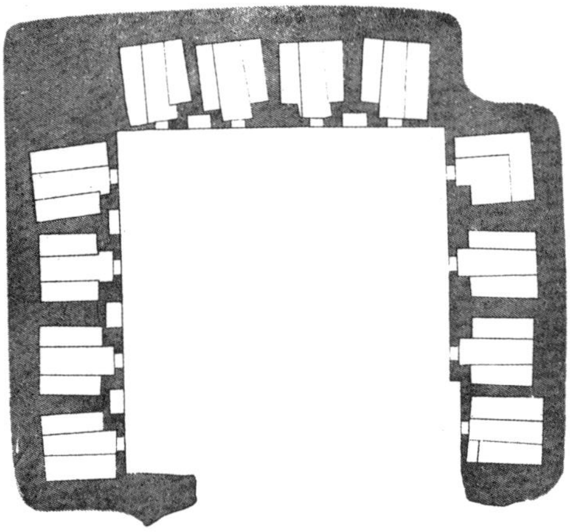

图 5　阿旃陀第 12 窟平面图

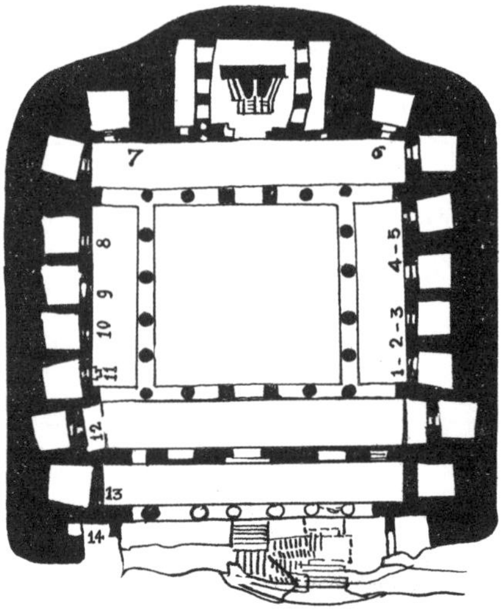

图 6　阿旃陀第 16 窟平面图

1 世纪中叶到 3 世纪中叶；第二种平面布局的僧坊流行地域较广，大约从公元前 2 世纪中叶一直延续使用到公元 7 世纪[1]。

据义净记载，"那烂陀寺，人众殷繁，僧徒数出三千，造次难为详集。寺有八院，房有三百"[2]。"然其寺形，畟方如域，四面直檐，长廊遍匝，皆是砖室。重迭三层，层高丈余，横梁板阗，本无椽瓦，用砖平覆。寺皆正直，随意旋往……其僧房也，面有九焉。一一房中可方丈许，后面通窗户向檐矣。其门既高，唯安一扇，皆相瞻望，不许安帘……于一角头作阁道还往。寺上四角，各为砖堂，多闻大德而住于此。寺门西向，飞阁凌虚，雕刻奇形，妙尽工饰。其门乃与房相连，元不别作，但前出两步，齐安四柱。其门虽非过大，实乃装架弥坚。每至食时，重关返闭，既是圣教，意在防私。寺内之地方三十步许，皆以砖砌。小者或十步，或五步耳……如斯等类，乃有八寺，上皆平通，规矩相似。"[3]

义净文中所称那烂陀寺之"寺"或"院"，应为梵语 vihāra 的汉译。据玄应《一切经音义》卷六《妙法莲华经音义》："塔寺，梵言毗诃罗，此云游行处，谓僧所游履处也。今以寺代之。言寺者，《说文》：廷也，有法度者。《广雅》：寺，治也。《释名》云：寺，

[1] 关于西印度佛教石窟的分期与年代，参见：1) Chongfeng Li, *Chētiyagharas in Indian and Chinese Buddhist Caves: A Comparative Study* (Dissertation submitted to the University of Delhi for the Award of the Degree of Doctor of Philosophy), Delhi: University of Delhi, 1993: 85-172; 2) 李崇峰《中印佛教石窟寺比较研究：以塔庙窟为中心》，北京：北京大学出版社，2003 年，第 63-126 页。

[2] 义净《南海寄归内法传》，王邦维校注，北京：中华书局，1995 年，第 176-177 页。

[3] 义净《大唐西域求法高僧传》，王邦维校注，北京：中华书局，1988 年，第 112-113 页。

嗣也。治事者相嗣续于其中也。”[1]至于“院”,意应同坊,即区院、僧院。唐代高僧一行《大毗卢遮那成佛经疏》卷三《入漫荼罗具缘真言品》:“僧坊,梵音毗诃罗,译为住处,即是长福住处也。”[2]玄应《一切经音义》卷二《大般涅槃经音义》:“僧坊,甫房反。《字林》: 坊,别屋也。”[3]慧琳《一切经音义》卷二十二引慧苑撰《新译大方广佛花严经音义》卷中:“僧坊,坊,甫亡反。《韵林》曰: 坊,区也。谓区院也。”[4]此外,唐代僧寺也称“宝坊”。宋之问《登庄严揔持二寺阁》:“闰月再重阳,仙舆历宝坊。帝歌云稍白,御酒菊尤黄。风铎喧行漏,天花拂舞行。豫游多景福,梵宇自生光。”[5]

因此,义净所言那烂陀“乃有八寺”或“寺有八院”,应指那烂陀寺有八座 vihāra。印度考古调查局 (Archaeological Survey of India)1915 年开始在那烂陀实施的考古发掘,至 1939 年基本上搞清了这处遗址的整体布局。迄今发掘出土的十座僧坊遗址,其中八座坐东朝西,呈一字排开,彼此平面布局基本相同,且僧坊数也与义净所记相符(图 7)[6]。由此可见义净所记不虚。这种 vihāra,系在早期僧坊布局的基础上演化而来,整个那烂陀寺似应称 Nālandā saṃghārāma(僧伽蓝)为妥。据玄应《一切经音义》卷一《大集日藏分经音义》:“僧伽蓝,旧译云村,此应讹也,正言僧伽罗磨,此云众园也。”[7]慧

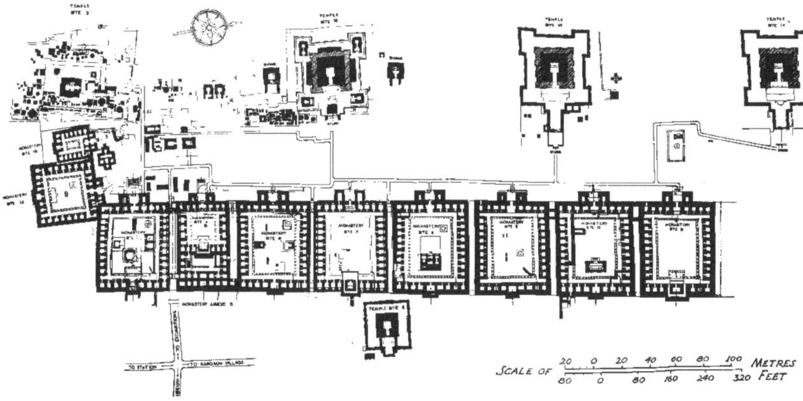

图 7　那烂陀寺遗址平面图

[1]《一切经音义》卷二十四《阿毗达磨俱舍论音义》:“毗诃罗,亦言鼻诃罗,此云游,谓僧游履处也。此土以寺代之。”玄应《一切经音义》,见《一切经音义: 三种校本合刊》,徐时仪校注,上海: 上海古籍出版社,2008 年,第 139、494 页。

[2]《大正藏》第 39 卷,第 615c 页。

[3]《一切经音义》卷六《妙法莲华经音义》:“僧坊,甫亡反。《字林》: 坊,别屋也。”玄应,上引书,第 44、139 页。

[4]《大正藏》第 54 卷,第 443c 页。

[5] 参见: 李昉《文苑英华》卷一七八,影印本,北京: 中华书局,1966 年,第 868 页。

[6] 参见: A Ghosh, *Nālandā*, 6th ed., New Delhi: Archaeological Survey of India, 1986:16.

[7]《一切经音义》卷十四《四分律音义》:“僧伽蓝,此言讹也,正言僧伽啰磨,此云众园。”玄应,上引书,第 17、296 页。

琳《一切经音义》卷二十三引慧苑撰《新译大方广佛花严经音义》卷下："僧伽蓝，具云僧伽罗摩。言僧伽者，此云众也；罗摩，院也。"[1]因此。那烂陀寺系由众院组成。

又，一行《大毗卢遮那成佛经疏》卷十一《悉地出现品》曰："正等觉心，即真言心也；欲作此成就者，当先择处。园苑，谓人所种殖、栽接园苑之处；若不种自成，即是广野非苑也。寺者，毗诃罗，此方译为住处；窟是山间自然石窟，或是人功所穿作之，或复行人心所乐处，亦得于中修道也。若就秘说者，园苑谓大菩提心，此处宽广无所不有，依此修道最为第一上处也；住谓四梵住，或云是大悲以一切菩萨常乐住此中故；窟谓幽邃清闲之处，即是甚深禅定之窟。"[2]

根据文献记载及考古发掘，我们发现这种 lēṇa 从平面布局到窟内立体结构，从中央大厅到周匝长廊及禅室的经营与设置，皆系高度模仿地面砖木结构之毗诃罗/僧坊而建（图8a、8b），是地面毗诃罗的石化形式，故俗称毗诃罗窟[3]。不过据笔者调查，尽管 vihāra（毗诃罗）一词在西印度现存石窟题铭中偶尔出现，但明确指地面砖木结构僧院而非石窟[4]。

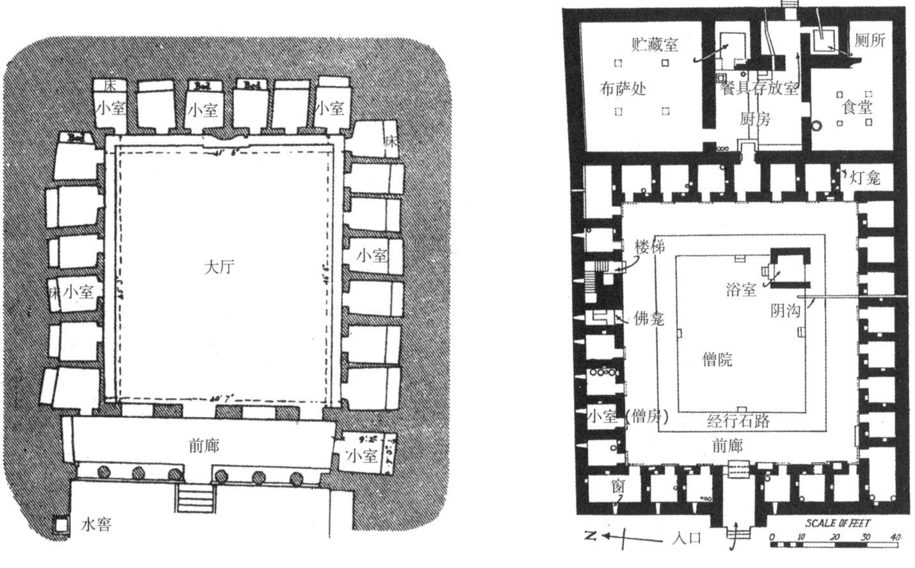

a　　　　　　　　　　　　　　　　　b

图 8a　纳西克第 3 窟平面图
b　呾叉始罗焦莲僧坊遗址平面图

[1]《大正藏》第 54 卷，第 455b 页。

[2]《大正藏》第 39 卷，第 695a-b 页。

[3] 这种洞窟有人也称僧房窟，可能欠妥，因为僧房通常指僧人所居单个房间，如《洛阳伽蓝记》所记永宁寺"僧房楼观一千余间"及瑶光寺"讲殿尼房五百余间"的僧房或尼房似皆具此意。义净《大唐西域求法高僧传》明确指出僧房只是僧坊中的一个房间。因此，僧房不能等同于僧坊。

[4] 参见：H. Lüders, *opere citato:* Nos. 988, 998, 1037.

(2) 塔庙窟，梵语称作 chaityagriha 或 caityagṛha，巴利语作 cetiyaghāra，窟内俗语题铭为 chētiyaghara，英文迻译 “chaitya building”[1]，汉译塔庙窟、支提窟等[2]，是佛陀允许建造的三种佛塔（露塔、无壁塔和屋塔）之一。一般塔庙窟的平面颇似古罗马的巴西利卡（basilica，一译长方形会堂或教堂），窟内空间通常被两列石柱纵向分作三部分，当中部分宽而高，称为主室（nave，一译中厅），两侧部分窄而低，称为侧廊（aisle），主室前端为入口，末端为一半圆形后室（apse）；后室中央雕出佛塔（stūpa），两列石柱于塔后相接。主室之顶，凿成纵向筒拱；侧廊之顶，多作半圆扇形。窟外立面雕饰繁复，入口上方的太阳拱（chaitya arch）系仿原始木构塔庙的外立面雕镌而成。这种窟的主体是后室中央的佛塔，佛教徒绕塔、诵经，以为礼拜（图 9）。其平面与古罗马巴西利卡相似或属偶然，因为塔庙窟的倒 U 字形平面，是为

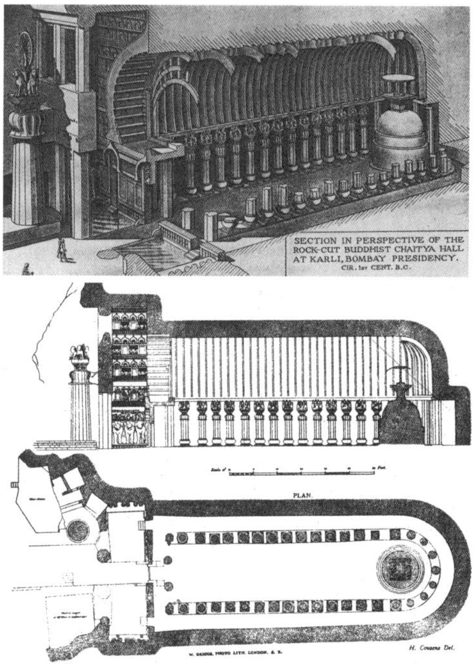

a

b

图 9a　伽尔拉第 8 窟平面及水平剖面、纵向垂直剖面及透视图
　　b　伽尔拉第 8 窟内景

[1] H. Lüders, *opere citato:* Nos. 1050, 1058, 1072, 1141, 1153, 1178, 1179, 1183, etc.

[2] 1) Chongfeng Li, *opere citato:* 29-84; 2) 李崇峰《塔与塔庙窟》（见本书）；3) 李崇峰，上引书，第 25-62 页。

信徒施绕佛涅槃的象征物——塔以及在石窟内进行集会、礼拜而特别设计的[1]。除倒 U 字形平面之外，尚有圆形和长方形平面塔庙窟，但以前者传播范围广、延续时间长[2]。

(3) 方形窟，梵语称作 maṇḍapa，窟内俗语铭刻作 maṭapa[3]，意为殿、舍、亭、庙、台观、延堂、聚所等。洞窟平面方形、平顶；有的凿出前室，有的无前室；有的于主室后壁或侧壁下部凿出凳状物（图 10a、10b）。这种石窟，有些可能为僧侣的住宅或餐厅[4]；有些可能为储藏室。在晚期，有些方形窟在侧壁开龛造像。

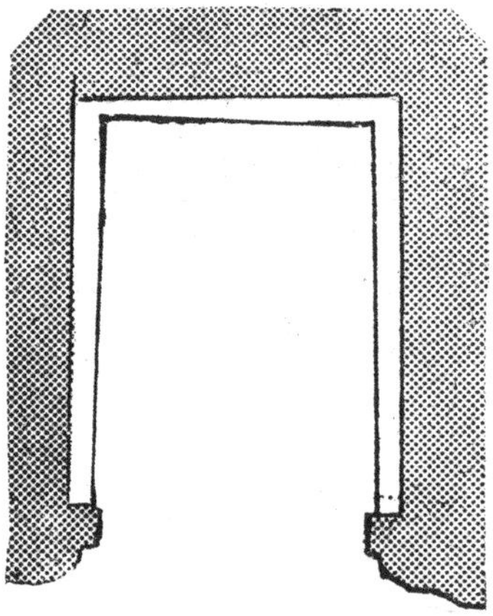

a

b

图 10a　均讷尔地区锡万内里第 64 窟平面图
b　均讷尔地区杜尔贾莱纳第 13 窟内景

(4) 水窖，或称水池，窟内俗语题铭作 pōḍhī[5]，系地下石洞，有足够容积用来蓄水。通常顶部有一小方口，雨水通过一狭窄沟槽流入池内，这样可解决夏季用水问题（图 11）。这种水窖，通常为饮用水窖 (pāṇīapōḍhī/pāṇīyapōḍhī)[6]，个别的为浴池 (sañānapōdhī)[7]。

---

[1] B. Rowland, *The Pelican History of Art; The Art and Architecture of India: Buddhist/Hindu/Jain*, reprinted with revisions and updated bibliography by J. C. Harle, New York: Penguin Books, 1977: 114.

[2] D. Mitra, *Buddhist Monuments*, Calcutta: Sahitya Samsad, 1971: 41.

[3] H. Lüders, *opere citato:* Nos. 1174, 1182.

[4] 根据窟内左壁上的俗语题铭，锡万内里第 64 窟是食堂 (bhōjaṇamaṭapa)。参见：Jas. Burgess, *opere citato:* 94, No. 8, Plate XLIX; 2) H. Lüders, *opere citato:* No. 1182.

[5] H. Lüders, *opere citato:* Nos. 995-996, 1000, 1007, 1013, 1014, 1039, 1041, 1061, 1064, 1072, 1079, 1107, 1119, 1131, 1140, 1148-1150, 1152, 1154, 1155, 1173, 1176, 1177, 1180, etc.

[6] H. Lüders, *opere citato:* Nos. 998, 1006, 1016, 1020.

[7] H. Lüders, *opere citato:* No. 1056.

a

b

图 11 a　贝德萨第 3、4 窟外景
b　贝德萨第 4 窟（水窖）

二、僧坊窟及方形窟的中国化

从某种意义上说，古代摩诃剌侘的佛教石窟，是整个天竺石窟寺的缩影。那里的石窟，以数量巨大、类型齐备、延续时间长久而著称于世。随着佛教的传播和天竺与外族贸易的发展，天竺的佛教石窟，也同其他艺术形式，如佛教雕塑和绘画一道步出国门，逐渐流布于东方世界各地，因为僧侣们发现这种隐逸而幽静的场所有益于健康的寺院生活。事实证明：佛教石雕建筑，即石窟寺是一种极为有效的传播佛教的途径和手段。

一般认为佛教是在公元前传入中国的[1]。随着佛教的传入，天竺的佛教艺术也逐渐东布中土，只是早期“凡宫塔制度，犹依天竺旧状而重构之，从一级至三、五、七、九”[2]。与佛教广被中国的过程一样，开窟造像活动传入中国，首及当时的西域（今新疆地区），尔后逐渐东传，最后遍布大江南北。

在佛教石窟的东布过程中，摩诃剌侘原有的四种主要窟形都先后传入中土；石窟寺的组合形式也对中国早期石窟，尤其新疆和甘肃西部地区的石窟寺有一定影响，如克孜尔第 38 至 40 窟和酒泉文殊山后山区的千佛洞、万佛洞及僧坊窟等。不过如

[1] 汤用彤《汉魏两晋南北朝佛教史》，北京：中华书局，1983 年，第 34-36 页。
[2]《魏书》，点校本，北京：中华书局，1974 年，第 3029 页。

同其他类型的佛教艺术一样，石窟寺作为一种外来形式，为了自身的存在和发展，加之自然因素，不得不与当地的文化传统和审美情趣相结合。这样，各地区形成了富有当地特色的佛教石窟类型。如古龟兹的塔庙窟，既不同于摩诃剌侘原型，又与中原北方的有别；摩诃剌侘原有的方形窟传至中土后，虽然有些尚保持原有属性，但大多数洞窟已演变为佛殿，即由生活用窟变成宗教礼拜活动用窟；至于在摩诃剌侘流行较广、延续时间较长的多室僧坊窟，在中国境内却极为少见。又，西域和内地出现了许多大像窟[1]，而这种窟形则不见于摩诃剌侘。

需要指出的是，摩诃剌侘5世纪中叶到7世纪中叶开凿的僧坊窟，雕造华丽，空间复杂，设施齐备，窟内外雕凿许多龛像，其中大厅正壁向外延伸雕造的佛殿成为礼拜之处（图12）。故而，这种僧坊窟具有双重属性，既是比丘栖止“禅定之窟”，也是四众最上供养之所。这种设计，应该受到了公元1世纪中叶至3世纪中叶流行的塔庙僧坊混成式窟（图13）[2]的强烈影响。

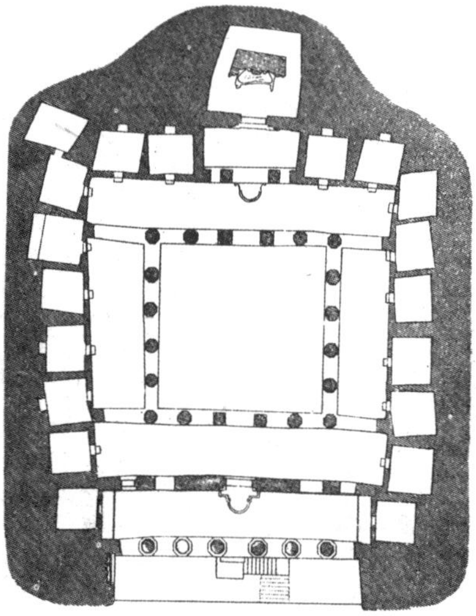

图12　阿旃陀第17窟平面图

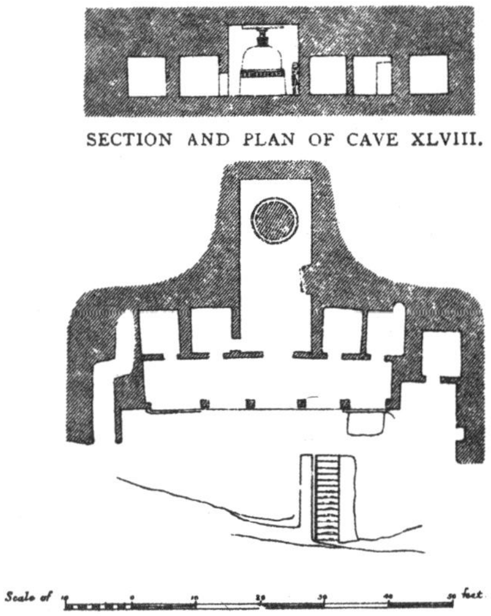

图13　格拉德第48窟平面及横向垂直剖面图

[1] 宿白《新疆拜城克孜尔石窟部分洞窟的类型与年代》，见宿白《中国石窟寺研究》，北京：文物出版社，1996年，第37-38页。

[2] 这种塔庙僧坊混成式窟，在有些窟内原始俗语题铭中仍称 lēṇa（僧坊窟），如古达第1、6窟，谢拉尔瓦迪第8窟；有的则细分为 lēṇa（僧坊）、chētieghara（chētiyaghara 塔庙）和 ōvaraka（小室 / 僧房），如默哈德第8窟。参见：Jas. Burgess, *opere citato:* 84, No. 1, Plate XLV; 85, No. 6, Plate XLV; 92, No. 19, Plate XLVIII; 88, No. 1, Plate XLV I; 2) H. Lüders, *opere citato:* Nos. 1037, 1045, 1072, 1121.

与塔庙窟相比,典型僧坊窟目前仅发现于新疆和甘肃两地,雕造年代大约从 4 世纪到 6 世纪。据笔者调查,新疆库车县的苏巴什(雀离大寺)[1]遗址现存 4 座,即第 1、2、3 和 5 窟(图 14),焉耆县锡克沁(七格星)石窟 1 座,即第 12 窟,吐鲁番地区吐峪沟石窟有 2 座,即第 1、42 窟,雅尔湖 1 座,即第 4 窟;敦煌莫高窟 3 座,即第 268、285(图 15)、487 窟,酒泉文殊山 1 座,即后山区所谓的禅窟群[2]。

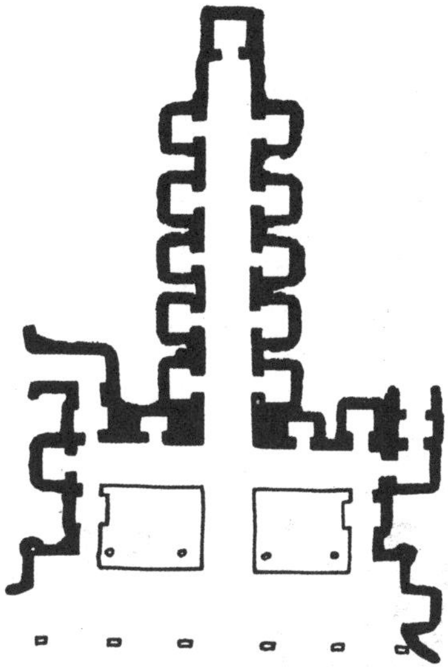

图 14　库车苏巴什第 5 窟平面图

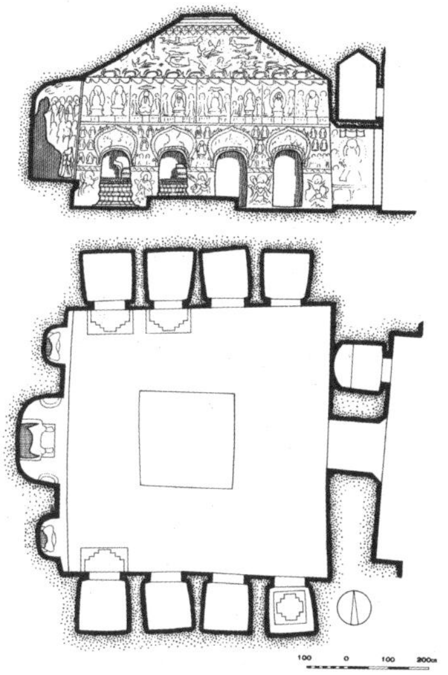

图 15　敦煌莫高窟第 285 窟平面及水平剖面、纵向垂直剖面图

莫高窟第 268 与 285 窟的四壁及窟顶满绘壁画,正壁塑造主尊。其中,第 268 窟为敦煌现存最早的洞窟之一,与左侧的第 272 和 275 窟合为一组;"第 285 号窟自凿绘迄完工,约不出东阳王元荣统治敦煌——当时称瓜州——的时期"[3],其与左侧第 288 窟,"两窟毗邻,时间相同",前庭壁画相应,"一是僧房群(第 285 窟),一是塔庙(第 288 窟)",应为一组双窟[4]。这种洞窟组合,也是摩诃剌侘石窟寺从早到晚最流行的洞窟组合形式[5]。此外,第 285 窟正壁的画

[1] 宿白《调查新疆佛教遗迹应予注意的几个问题》,见《新疆史学》,1980 年第 1 期,第 33 页。

[2] 李崇峰,上引书,第 15 页。

[3] 宿白《参观敦煌莫高窟第 285 号窟札记》,见《中国石窟寺研究》,北京:文物出版社,1996 年,第 211 页。

[4] 宿白,上引书,第 213 页。

[5] 如印度比德尔科拉第 3 窟(塔庙)和第 4 窟(僧坊)可定为公元前 2 世纪,"两窟年代相同、共用一前庭,系同时设计雕造"。参见 M. N. Deshpande, "The Rock-cut Caves of Pitalkhora in the Deccan", in: *Ancient India*, No. 15 (1959): 66-93, esp. 70.

塑内容（图16）尤可注意。中央大龛内塑倚坐佛，龛外两侧绘制形象诡异的护法诸天，如三头八臂的毗瑟纽天(Viṣṇu?)、三头六臂的摩醯首罗天(Maheśvara)、童子相的鸠摩罗天(Kumāra)以及正壁两上角驾马车之日天(Sūrya)与月天(Candradevī)和南侧的婆籔仙(Rishi Vāsu)[1]，皆具有很浓的外来韵味，尤其是人身象头的毗那夜迦(Vināyaka)或谓象头神(Gaṇeśa)[2]颇为特别，应与这一时期和天竺的频繁交往有关[3]。第487窟是20世纪60年代中期发掘出土的，形制与第285窟相似，"与一般住人的僧房不同，有小禅室，有方形低坛，并且原来画有壁画。因此，本窟开凿初期，是为了佛教信徒、僧侣进行佛事之用，则是无可怀疑的"[4]。上述三座僧坊，与这一时期摩诃剌侘习见的僧坊窟在平面布局方面极为相似，雕塑及绘画规制亦相应，皆具双重属性；既是僧侣息心所栖之处，也是四众供养、礼忏之所[5]。

图16　莫高窟第285窟后壁壁画局部

此外，1988-1995年敦煌研究院组织专业人员在莫高窟北区的清理发掘，重新发现了九座"多室禅窟"（僧坊窟）[6]。酒泉以东似不见这种形制的石窟。

僧坊窟在中国境内开凿如此有限，疑与下述因素有关。

(1) 4世纪后半叶，僧纯远赴西域求法；他不但赍经律而返，而且记述了龟兹当

[1] Basil Gray, *Buddhist Cave Paintings at Tun-huang*, photographys by J. B. Vincent, with a preface by Arhthur Waley, London: Faber and Faber Limited, 1959: 43.

[2] 饶宗颐《谈敦煌石窟中的誐尼沙(Ganesa)》，刊《学术研究》，1989年第3期，第62-64页。

[3] 1) 宿白《参观敦煌莫高窟第285号窟札记》，上引书，第213页；2) 宿白《中国佛教石窟寺遗迹——3至8世纪中国佛教考古学》，北京：文物出版社，2010年，第66页。

[4] 潘玉闪、马世长《莫高窟窟前殿堂遗址》，北京：文物出版社，1985年，第93-94页。

[5] 宿师季庚先生把这种窟称之为"禅窟佛殿窟"。参见《中国佛教石窟寺遗迹——3至8世纪中国佛教考古学》，北京：文物出版社，2010年，第64页。

[6] 彭金章、王建军《敦煌莫高窟北区石窟》第一卷，北京：文物出版社，2000年，第343页。

地的佛教情形。据《出三藏记集》卷二《新集撰出经律论录》,"《比丘尼大戒》一卷,右一部,凡一卷。晋简文帝(371-372年)时,沙门释僧纯于西域拘夷国得胡本,到关中,令竺佛念、昙摩持、慧常共译出"[1]。同书卷十一《比丘尼戒本所出本末序》曰:"(拘夷国)寺僧皆三月一易屋、床坐,或易伽蓝者。未满五腊,一宿不得无依止……(比丘尼)亦三月一易房,或易寺。出行非大尼三人不行。"[2]也就说,古龟兹僧人在一座寺庙或一间僧房乃至一张床铺居留三个月后,必须变更居所;出家不满五年者,须与高僧合住。龟兹尼众亦遵奉同样戒律,若非大尼,必须有两人同伴才可出行。据我们调查,克孜尔石窟初期盛凿僧房窟,但有些僧房使用后不久被改造为礼拜窟,如克孜尔第80窟等。"龟兹僧尼三月一易房,或易寺之制,似乎也可引作克孜尔第二阶段以前,多开僧房窟的一种解释。"[3]摩诃剌佗典型的僧坊窟不仅耗费人力、财力巨大,不易雕造,而且系"幽邃清闲之处,即是甚深禅定之窟",乃比丘息心所栖之处。因此,这种石窟,不适于古代龟兹的僧尼戒律。既然雕造这样一所洞窟耗费人力物力巨大,僧尼短期居住后便废弃或改造,无法为龟兹当地信众所接受,那么抽取摩诃剌佗僧坊窟的一部分或一要素改造成适宜当地使用的简朴僧房窟,恐怕是龟兹当时的最佳选择。中原北方与古代龟兹佛教关系密切,石窟雕造规制受其影响颇大。

(2)新疆和中原北方地区位于北温带,这一地区的居民传统上大都使用火炉和炕,尤其是冬季,因为这是最简便的取暖设施。印度僧坊窟"即是甚深禅定之窟",在摩诃剌佗流行,因为该地毗邻印度洋,夏季炎热,冬季凉爽,故而没有必要考虑在窟内取暖。随着石窟寺传入新疆,摩诃剌佗典型僧坊窟因为不便在窟内安置炉、炕不得不作改造,以适应当地习俗。结果,一种具有当地特色的僧房窟在龟兹创造出来,且与当地民居相似(图17)。换言之,龟兹僧房窟可以视作摩诃剌佗僧坊窟每一小室/僧房(ōvaraka)的扩大并增补了甬道和明窗等相关设施。这种僧房窟,可能吸收了印度第一种僧坊窟如伽内什·伯哈(图18)与古达等石窟的若干因素,成为龟兹石窟中僧房的主要类型,并影响了敦煌甚至大同早期兴建的僧房窟,如焦山第11窟[4]。从表象上看,龟兹僧房窟似乎是摩诃剌佗第一种僧坊窟的简单移植,但实质上这应该

[1] 僧佑《出三藏记集》,苏晋仁、萧錬子点校,北京:中华书局,1995年,第46页。

[2] 僧佑,上引书,第410-411页。《比丘尼戒本所出本末序》不记撰人名,中华书局出版的《出三藏记集》的点校者苏晋仁、萧錬子"疑是释道安所撰"。见上引书,第423页注[四二]。

[3] 宿白《新疆拜城克孜尔石窟部分洞窟的类型与年代》,上引书,第36页。

[4] 丁明夷、李治国《焦山、吴官屯(石窟)调查记》,见《中国石窟·云冈石窟》一,北京:文物出版社,1991年,第217-218页。

图 17　拜城克孜尔第 24 窟平面图及第 15 窟炉灶细部

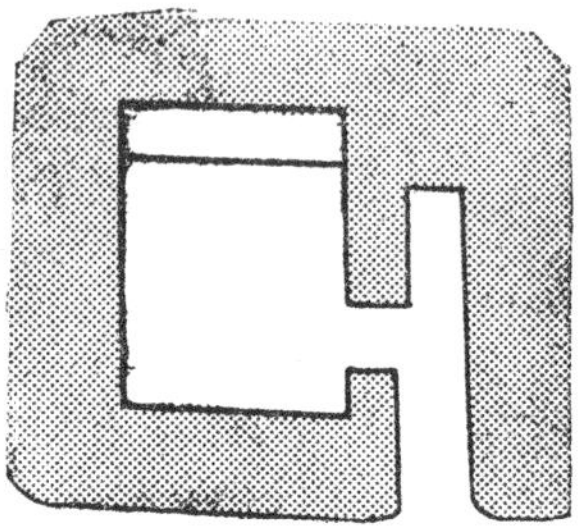

图 18　伽内什 · 伯哈第 24 窟平面图

是从僧坊窟到僧房窟的根本演变。

(3) 据我们调查，新疆以东内地石窟群的营造，有些地点采用供养、礼忏佛事用窟与栖止、禅修生活用窟分区设置之原则。以敦煌莫高窟为例，除了早期部分塔庙或佛殿与僧坊沿袭天竺的石窟寺组合之外，如第 268 与 272、275 窟和 285 与 288 窟分别成组，绝大多数洞窟在营造时把供养、礼忏佛事用窟与栖止、禅修生活用窟分区开凿。经过近年在莫高窟北区的考古发掘，发现“就莫高窟南北两区而言，不同性质的石窟的数量上的差别，反映了不同类型石窟各有其集中分布区，南区是礼佛窟的集中开凿场所，而北区则是以单室禅窟、多室禅窟、僧房窟、僧房窟附设禅窟、瘗窟为主体的多种类型石窟的分布区域”[1]。现存遗迹表明：莫高窟南部窟群主要是四众供养、礼忏区域，北部窟区主要为栖止、禅行之用。又，龙门石窟西山区和东山区南段开凿的窟龛主要为供养、礼忏用窟，而东山区北段即今香山寺下方有许多空窟龛，或许就是刘沧所《题龙门僧房》[2]。这种情况是否也是佛教石窟寺传入中国，尤其是汉地后原始石窟寺院布局方面的一种地方化呢？

(4) 中原北方开凿的石窟，除少数“凿仙窟以聚禅”[3]外，大多数石窟为禅观、礼忏、供养用窟，以满足皇室、显贵、高僧以及普通信众做功德及最上供养之愿望与需

[1] 彭金章、王建军，上引书，第 350 页。

[2]《全唐诗》卷五百八十六，北京：中华书局，1960 年，第 6788 页。

[3] 高允《鹿苑赋》，载《广弘明集》卷二十九，见《大正藏》第 52 卷，第 339b-c 页。

求[1]。僧徒禅修完毕或四众在窟内结束宗教仪式及供养之后，通常回到或投宿于石窟群附近的地面建筑，因为那里设施齐备。如龙门石窟附近唐代有十座大型地面佛寺，那些佛寺乃皇室、显贵及富贾捐资兴造，每寺有大量房舍供僧人或居士居留[2]。这种情况与天竺不同。摩诃剌佗的比丘通常居住在距塔庙窟不远的僧坊窟内，僧坊与塔庙共同构成复杂的石窟寺院。中国内地的石窟寺似主要采用混合营造规制，供养、禅修、礼忏在崖壁石窟之中，日常生活退居地面建筑之内，即石雕窟室与地面建筑合成完整的佛寺。这一规制，疑创始于北魏皇室开凿的武州山石窟寺[3]，稍后为各地石窟寺效仿和延续。

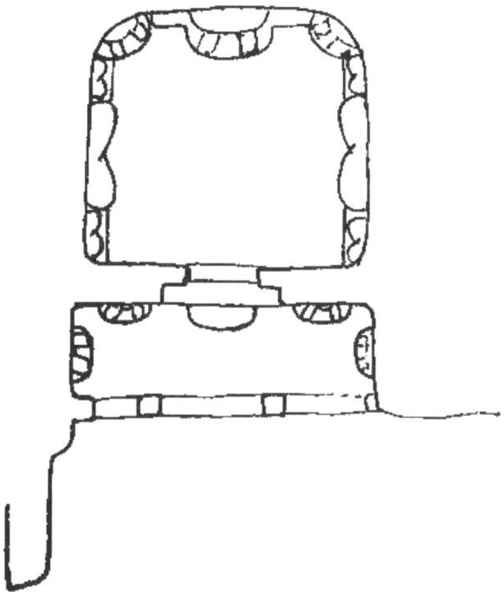

图 19　纳西克第 23 窟平面图及正壁造像

至于方形窟，形制简单，在天竺始见于公元前 2 世纪，5 至 6 世纪时开始在窟内开龛造像（图 19），唯数量有限。不过，这种窟型在中国极为流行，尤其是在中原北方地区，而且后来成为主要的供养、礼忏用窟。尽管在结构上与摩诃剌佗原型（方形窟）相似，但在中国被改造为佛殿，通常具前后室，并于正壁雕造主像（图 20）。这种方形佛殿窟大约 470 年前后首先出现在平城武州山石窟寺，后演变为三壁三龛窟和三壁设坛窟，并在中原北方广为流布[4]，逐渐取代了早期塔庙窟的功能，长期受到僧

[1] 李玉昆《龙门碑刻及其史料价值》，见刘景龙、李玉昆主编《龙门石窟碑刻题记汇录》，北京：中国大百科全书出版社，1998 年，第 20-22 页。

[2] 温玉成《唐代龙门十寺考察》，载《中国石窟・龙门石窟》二，北京：文物出版社，1992 年，第 217-232 页。

[3] 参见李崇峰《从犍陀罗到平城：以地面佛寺布局为中心》（见本书）。

[4] 1) 宿白《云冈石窟分期试论》，载《中国石窟寺研究》，北京：文物出版社，1996 年，第 76-88 页；2) 吕采芷《北魏后期的三壁三龛式窟》，载《中国石窟・云冈石窟》二，北京：文物出版社，1994 年，第 213-218 页。

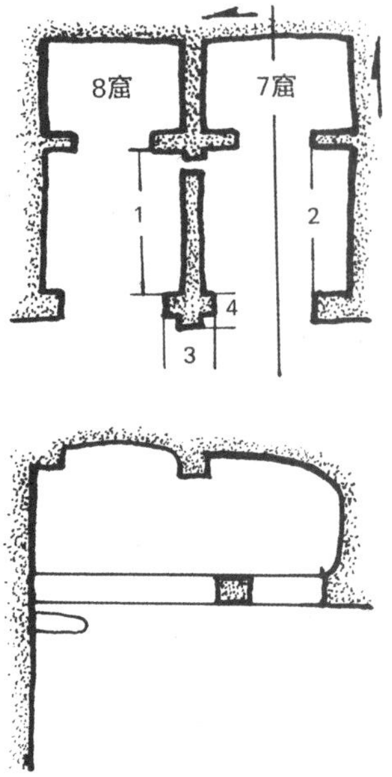

a

b

图 20a　云冈第 7、8 窟平面及纵向垂直剖面图
b　云冈第 7 窟后壁主像

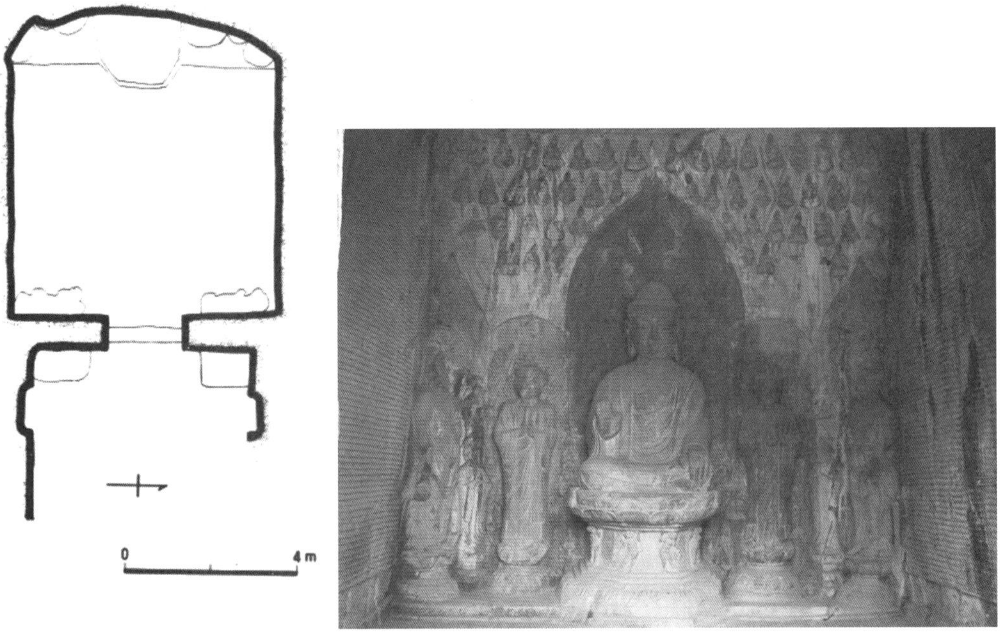

图 21　龙门万佛洞平面图及正壁造像

俗青睐(图 21)。其原型,疑仿效地面木构佛殿的平面布局及像设。

摩诃剌侘石窟群中大量开凿的水窖,传至中国后鲜有发现,目前仅在宁夏须弥山和洛阳龙门石窟发现少量遗迹。

三、塔庙窟之嬗变[1]

如上所述,古代天竺佛教石窟大体可以分作栖止、禅修佛事用窟和供养、礼忏生活用窟两类。作为宗教场所,后者应占主导地位,前者只是为后者服务的;前者以僧坊窟为主,后者以塔庙窟为代表。一座塔庙窟与若干座僧坊窟组成一个院或寺,许多院或寺连在一起,成为大型的石窟寺。作为供养、礼忏的主体,塔庙窟是随着佛教的发展而发展的,如天竺早期塔庙窟内佛塔既不开龛也无造像;到了晚期,由于大乘佛教的兴起,佛教龛像遍布窟内外,佛塔变得复杂起来。因而相对僧坊窟来说,塔庙窟更具有时代气息。

塔庙窟无论是在印度还是在中国的佛教石窟中,都是一种很有代表性的重要窟型。如印度阿旃陀现存石窟 30 座,其中塔庙窟 5 座,即第 9、10、19、26 和 29 窟(该窟未完工),占总数的 1/6。新疆克孜尔现存 60 座中心柱窟(塔庙),约占全部石窟数量的 1/4。敦煌莫高窟现存 36 座北朝洞窟,其中塔洞 15 座,接近整个总数的 2/5。因此,塔庙窟无论在印度还是在中国都是最重要的石雕建筑。

(1) 摩诃剌侘塔庙窟:古代摩诃剌侘,即西印度现存 55 座塔庙窟。通过对洞窟平面、外立面、明窗、窟顶、石柱和佛塔等六部分进行的考古类型学分析,我们把摩诃剌侘塔庙窟分作四期六段。其中,最早的塔庙窟平面为圆形(图 22),开凿于公元前 2 世纪中叶。这种圆形塔庙窟可以看成是早期木构圆形塔殿(图 23)的石化形式。稍后,出现了盛极一时的纵券顶倒 U 字形平面塔庙窟。这种新型塔庙窟通常由一长方形平面主室和一半圆形后室构成,并有一列石柱置于两侧壁和后壁之前,由此形成两个侧廊和一个后廊。在半圆形后室中央,雕有主体朝拜物——石塔,唯塔顶与窟顶不相连接。主室前壁下部辟门道,上部开半圆形明窗(图 24)。这种塔庙当时倍受僧俗青睐,因为它便于四众在窟内进行集会、朝拜、礼忏和供养,因而出现后广为传播,

[1] 这一节内容,主要依据笔者 *Chētiyagharas in Indian and Chinese Buddhist Caves: A Comparative Study* (Dissertation submitted to the University of Delhi for the Award of the Degree of Doctor of Philosophy, Delhi: University of Delhi, 1993) 和《中印佛教石窟寺比较研究:以塔庙窟为中心》(北京:北京大学出版社,2003 年)写就。

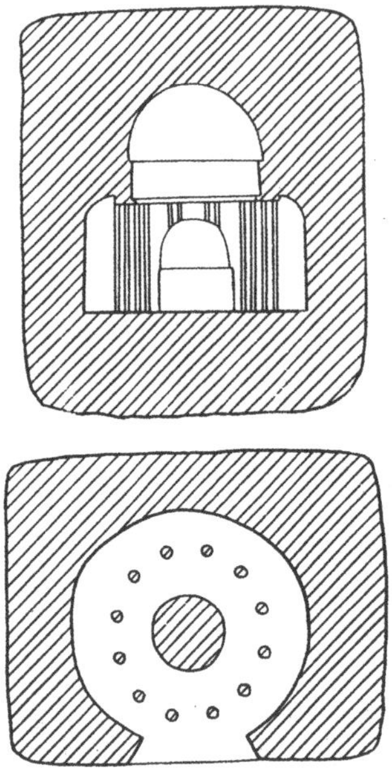

图 22　杜尔贾莱纳第 3 窟平面及横向垂直剖面图

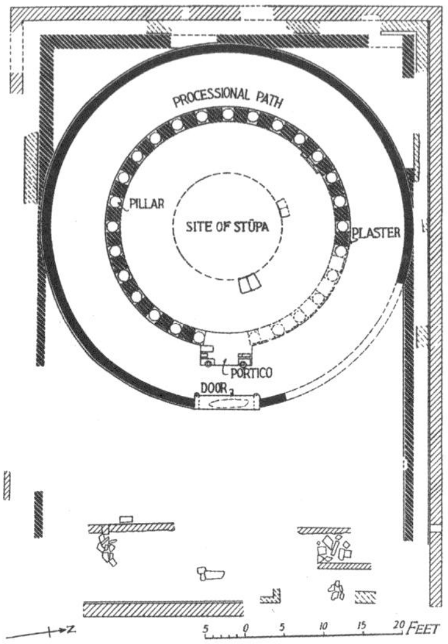

图 23　拜拉特（波里夜呾罗国）木构塔殿遗址平面图

图 24　珀贾第 12 窟外立面及窟内佛塔

并从第一阶段一直沿用到第三阶段（公元前 2 世纪到公元 1 世纪中叶），即从创始期延续到繁盛期。到了第四、五阶段（公元 1 世纪中叶到 3 世纪中叶），即功利主义时期，塔庙窟的平面改作长方形或方形，顶作平顶，塔刹与窟顶相连，窟内列柱消失，前壁大多不开明窗（图 25）。这显示出在总体设计上，它与倒 U 字形平面塔庙窟大

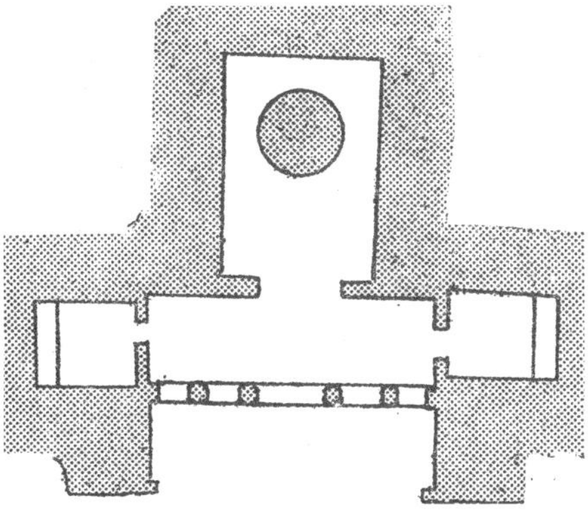

a　　b

图 25　古达第 15 窟平面图及窟内佛塔

为不同，更加适合实际需要。可以说，这是塔庙窟营造史上的一次变革。需要指出的是，摩诃剌侘地区塔庙窟营造的开端，几乎与定都普拉蒂什塔纳 (Pratishṭhāna)[1] 的沙多婆汉那 (Sātavāhanas/ 娑多婆诃) 王朝的崛起相吻合；而洞窟营造活动的起落，也与沙多婆汉那王朝的盛衰密切相关。

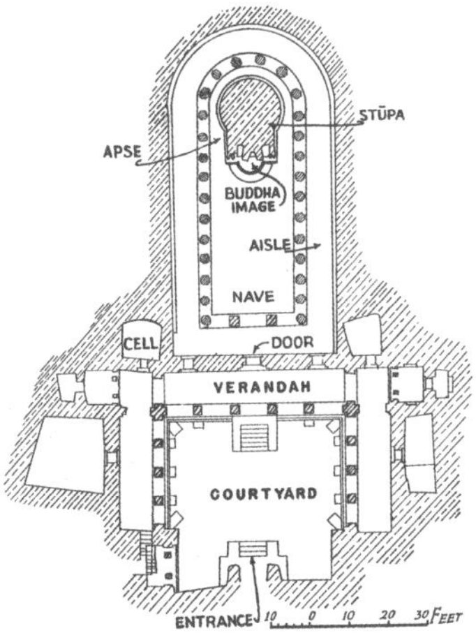

a　　b　　c

图 26　埃洛拉第 10 窟外立面、平面图及塔前主像

随着大乘佛教的传入，摩诃剌侘，尤其是阿旃陀、奥兰伽巴德、埃洛拉和根赫里等地的开窟造像活动，又重新活跃起来。在瓦加塔格 (Vākāṭakas) 王朝统治者的倡导和赞助下，从 5 世纪后半到 7 世纪前半 (大约 475-625 年)，这里又开凿了一批新洞

[1] 1) M. N. Deshpande, "The Rock-cut Caves of Pitalkhora in the Deccan", in: *Ancient India,* 15 (1959): 67-69; 2) M. N. Deshpande, "The (Ajanta) Caves: Their Historical Perspective", in: *Ajanta Murals,* ed. A. Ghose, New Delhi: Archaeological Survey of India, 1967: 15.

窟。这一时期开凿的塔庙窟，基本上保留了早期，特别是繁盛期塔庙的特点，只是木构部分完全为石雕替代，洞窟结构更加繁复（图 26）。因而，他们可以看作是繁盛期塔庙窟（公元前 1 世纪到公元 1 世纪中叶）的复兴。这一期洞窟最显著的特征，是大乘多佛思想的流行。除了刻在窟内及外立面上的小型佛像之外，大乘观念主要是通过雕在塔前的主像来表现的[1]。

(2) 龟兹中心柱窟：随着佛教传入新疆地区，石窟艺术也在那里扎根落户。新疆拜城克孜尔石窟现存中心柱窟 60 座，从考古学角度可以大体分作四期，其中现存最早的中心柱窟，可定在公元 4 世纪上半叶。不过从其成熟的形态判断，古龟兹中心柱窟的开凿，约始于公元 3 世纪后半叶或更早；到了 4、5 世纪，开窟造像活动达到高潮。克孜尔第一期中心柱窟的平面为长方形或方形，后部中央凿出蘑菇状佛塔；左右甬道及后甬道顶部较主室纵券顶偏低，但皆作券顶。主室正壁雕塑帝释窟场景，侧壁绘系列说法图，窟顶画本生或因缘故事，后甬道侧壁画涅槃及其相关情节，主室门道上方半圆形壁面为弥勒示现（图 27）。到了第二期（图 28），即 4 世纪中叶到 5 世纪，后甬道被加高、拓宽成后室，内置涅槃台，上塑涅槃像。这一变化，与当时天竺流行涅槃图像恰好相合。第三、四期中心柱窟，窟龛形制与画塑题材皆在此基础（图 29）上进一步演化。作为石窟的主要部分，龟兹中心柱窟后部中央凿出的蘑菇形实体，实际上是把龟兹地面上建造的“露塔”抽象化了。塔前开龛造像，表明龟兹中心柱窟主要具有了神龛性质，摩诃剌佗原型所含有的“陵墓”意义减少。这一变化，也暗示着佛陀正从一圣者向神转变[2]。

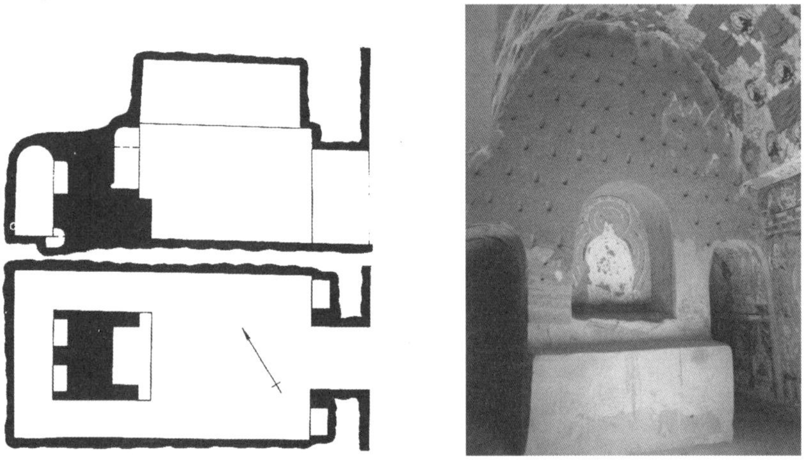

a　　　　b

图 27　克孜尔第 38 窟平面及水平剖面、纵向垂直剖面图及内景

[1] 1) Chongfeng Li, *opere citato:* 85-172; 2) 李崇峰，上引书，第 63-126 页。

[2] 1) Chongfeng Li, *opere citato:* 173-216; 2) 李崇峰，上引书，第 127-209 页。

图 28　克孜尔第 17 窟侧壁说法图

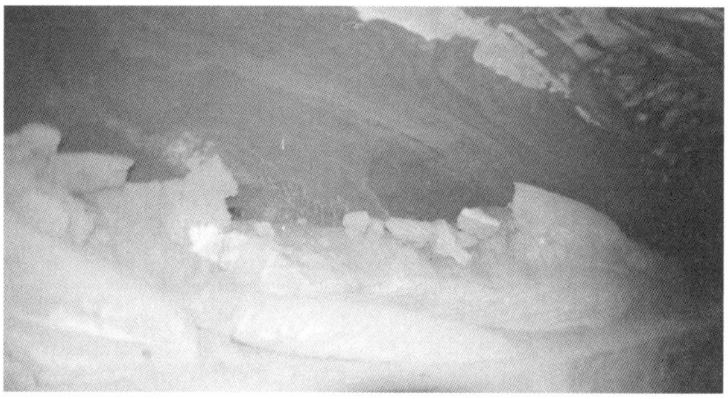

图 29　克孜尔新 1 窟后室后壁
涅槃台上涅槃残像

(3) 中原北方塔洞，是在摩诃剌佗塔庙窟和龟兹中心柱窟的基础上演化和发展的。以敦煌莫高窟为例，第一期塔洞大约开凿于 489-525 年左右，平面皆作长方形，每窟后部中央皆雕凿一座简化了的方形佛塔，塔四面开龛造像。窟顶前半部呈汉式人字披形，后半部为平顶 (图 30)。云冈石窟现存八座塔洞，其中第 1、2 窟可能为双窟，每窟后部中央雕造佛塔，塔基方形，塔身二或三层，每层每面开龛造像，饰斗拱与平座，塔顶雕出华盖与须弥山。这种佛塔，应模仿当时地面建造的楼阁型浮图雕造。窟后壁雕造大龛，侧壁分上、中、下三栏经营；上栏镌装饰图案与千佛，下栏雕供养人，中间部位开列龛并浮雕佛教故事 (图 31)。巩县石窟中的塔洞 (图 32)，堪称云冈塔庙窟的简化形式，尤其那里的石塔看起来确如方柱。

中原北方地区塔庙窟，是外来石窟艺术形式，如龟兹中心柱窟与本土传统汉文化结合的产物。这里，塔的陵墓含义进一步减弱甚至消失。塔柱四面开龛造像清楚地

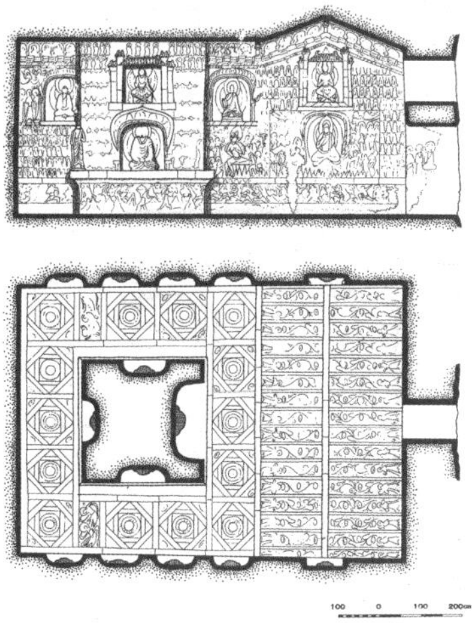

a

b

图 30　莫高窟第 254 窟平面及水平剖面、纵向垂直剖面及透视图和内景

图 31　云冈第 2 窟内景

a　　　　b

图 32　巩县石窟第 1 窟平面及水平剖面、纵向垂直剖面及透视图和内景

表明：佛陀已完成了从圣人转变为神的漫长旅程。此外，方塔顶部所雕须弥山，是凡人与神仙皆向往的妙境神宇。故此，这种塔柱就成了连接凡人与神仙，即尘世与天堂的升华之路[1]。

通过上述分析后再回到正题，我们清楚地看到：石窟寺院不是普通的建筑，它是一种附加精神价值——实际上是由它产生的特殊建筑。对于一位科学研究者来说，正确的态度应当是把这种石雕建筑看作是一种装满价值和出产价值的卓越文化。创

［1］1) Chongfeng Li, *opere citato:* 217-270; 2) 李崇峰，上引书，第 210-268 页。

造这种文化的古代摩诃剌佗人,既因其发明获此殊荣,又因这种文化在印度本土及域外的传播而青史留名。

我们认为,任何一个国家或地区的本民族思想体系或意识形态是不能原装输出的。任何外来思想,当被另一国家或地区的民族接纳并产生大批追随者之前,不得不首先改换面孔、格义附会,设法迎合接纳地的传统思想与意识形态,以便立足。当古代天竺抽象的佛教思想与其具象的表现形式于公元前后输入中国时,便经历了这样的过程。倘若当初龟兹和中原北方在此之前没有形成一种类似古代摩诃剌佗的社会文化环境,没有发达的本土寺院文化,摩诃剌佗就不可能向其输出石雕建筑技术及形式,中国也不会创造出具有摩诃剌佗石雕建筑特点的中国式石窟寺。塔庙、僧坊、方形窟以及地上寺塔从印度洋岸边远布于中国北方大同附近的云冈,则有力地说明了历史上强有力的佛教运动。中国的统治者、富商、乡绅以及被压迫的劳苦大众,就是在这种强大的佛教文化驱使下,创造出了具有天竺烙印的中国式佛教“天堂”。

本文简略勾画出了塔庙、僧坊、方形窟从南向北、自西而东的传布足迹,并强调了途中具有特殊历史价值和艺术价值的地上遗存。与此同时,笔者也用实例论证了文化上异体受精的潜在调和性。而塔庙窟,对这一问题的讨论提供了一个极好的例证。这个问题,如同钱币一样具有两面性。一方面,塔庙窟不论是在摩诃剌佗所见之原型,还是在古龟兹或内地所看到的中国化样式,都是塔庙窟;它不论在性质上,还是在形态上,总是天竺式的。即使在遥远的云冈,塔庙窟也毫无疑问地带有摩诃剌佗的标记。这显示出塔庙窟建筑中的普遍性。另一面,由于塔庙窟建筑形式创始于摩诃剌佗,因此一定是摩诃剌佗的环境才产生了塔庙窟;同样,中原北方所采用的塔庙窟形式,必须首先属于那里的社会文化背景与环境。这就使它必须放弃异己的摩诃剌佗特有样式,增补本土特征。

比如,摩诃剌佗塔庙窟内的佛塔,是一半圆坟冢形;在龟兹中心柱窟中,它演变为一高大的蘑菇状;到了中原北方开凿的塔洞里,它进一步演进为多层木构楼阁式。对此,我们不应把它视为形式上的简单变化,而应看到这种变化的深层含义。在古代天竺,“塔”意味着纪念高贵贤哲和文化豪杰——乔达摩佛的涅槃。因此,摩诃剌佗塔庙窟的佛塔被设计成一座圆冢,同“露塔”一致。在古龟兹,中心柱窟内的佛塔采用蘑菇形,塔前开龛造像。古代龟兹人之所以摒弃坟冢式样,是因为坟冢乃死者的屋舍,而佛是“神”。至此塔的社会功能已发生了重要变化,即它从纪念死者的象征变成了拜神的标志。塔主要具有了神龛的性质,摩诃剌佗原型所含有的陵墓意义减少。这一变化,也象征着佛陀正从一“圣者”向“神”转变。当这种石雕建筑通过西域传至中原北方时,面临礼拜全能佛的强大浪潮,早期纪念过去圣贤的天竺式旨趣到此渐渐消失，“佛”成为权力与命运“保护神”的象征。在中国信徒的脑海中，释迦牟尼是一位全能大神，人类的恩人。故而，中原北方塔庙窟内的中心塔采纳了楼阁型高塔型建筑，它是外来佛教艺术与中土传统文化相融合的产物，意味着对权利和命运的保护。此外，为了把这通天佛塔与人间区分开来，常在塔柱顶部加雕一座须弥山。须弥山乃凡人与神仙皆向往之妙境。因此，这种塔柱就成了连接凡人与神仙，即尘世与天堂的升华之路。需要指出的是，尽管由于佛教的影响，古代中国人也像天竺人一样珍重须弥天堂，但印度历代寺庙建筑上的天堂须弥，总是富于暗示性，经常使整个建筑产生一种崇高之感，就像我们在秣菟罗等地所看到的那种峰峦状的建筑形式；而中国的须弥山设计，更具描述性而非抽象性。不管怎么说，中国人在使用须弥象征中的自如和随意，是文化上异体受精辩证法的另一例证。一方面，起源于天竺的精神必须保留，使其可以辨识；另一方面，采纳地之中国精神则明显占据优势，以消除异己之感。

总之，虽然佛教艺术起源于古代天竺，但它后来不断向外传播。每传至一地，便与当地的文化相结合。结果，一种具有该民族特征的新风格或新样式便随之产生。这种现象明显地反映在石窟寺的演化上。不同文化圈内的石窟寺院，确实存在着较大的差异与地域性。简言之，摩诃剌侘的塔庙、僧坊及方形窟，为整个佛教石雕建筑的原型；龟兹境内的石窟，可以看作是摩诃剌侘与中原北方塔庙、僧坊及方形窟之间的媒介形式；而中原北方石窟寺，则是汉化了的天竺石雕建筑。由此我们不难得出这样的结论：上述三大文化圈内的塔庙、僧坊及方形窟，分别代表了摩诃剌侘、古代龟兹和中原北方三种不同的石窟寺模式；而这三大地域里石雕建筑的兴凿历史，在一定程度上，可以看作是佛教石窟寺发展史的缩影[1]。

（本文主要内容 2010 年 9 月 11 日曾在上海博物馆演讲过。）

---

[1] 1) Chongfeng Li, *opere citato:* 271-280; 2) 李崇峰，上引书，第 269-271 页。

The Sinicizing Process of the Cave-temples: The Evolution of the *Lēṇa, Maṭapa* and *Chētiyaghara*

The birth of Buddhism is an epic. So is the creation of an entire universe of Buddhist culture and art in India. Mahārāshṭra (present day Maharashtra) is the cradle of cave-temples, a story of great invention and creation. Today, this Buddhist monument is dotting the map of Asia, particularly China. A modern tourist can see as many monuments of Indian invention in China as an ancient visitor could in Hinduka (Present-day the South Asian Subcontinent)[1]. With *chētiyagharas, lēṇas, maṭapas,* as well as *saṃghārāmas, stūpas* and other architectural inventions of Hinduka now adorning the skyline of China, it amounts to the creation of a Buddhist landscape of Hinduka on Chinese soil. Such an extraordinary phenomenon speaks of the unprecedented socio-cultural transformations that have taken place in China. Hence, the spread of Buddhist art and architecture from Hinduka to China is equally a long story of epic dimensions.

As a scholar of Buddhist art and archaeology, I can say for sure that the number of remains of Buddhist monuments found in China is greater than those found in India. An even greater number of them have been destroyed in China than in India

[1] For the ancient Chinese names of Hinduka, *confer:* P. C. Bagchi, "Ancient Chinese Names of India", in: *India and China: Interactions through Buddhism and Diplomacy; A Collection of Essays by Professor Prabodh Chandra Bagchi,* compiled by Bangwei Wang and Tansen Sen, Delhi: Anthem Press India, 2011: 3-11, esp. 8-9. ; 2) Qian Wenzhong, "The Ancient Chinese Names of India and their Origins", in: *Land Routes of the Silk Roads and the Cultural Exchanges between the East and West before the 10th Century*; Desert Route Expedition International Seminar in Urumqi August 19-21, 1990, Beijing: New World Press, 1996: 601-611.

in the long course of historical vicissitudes. To confine it to the rock-cut temples, even here China has outstripped India in quantity as well. China has the world's largest Buddhist cave temple complex at Yungang, Longmen and Dunhuang. Quantitatively, the Buddhist caves of Ajaṇṭā and Ellorā/Ēlūra (excluding the Hindu and Jain caves there) have paled in comparison with these Chinese Buddhist sites.

Rock-cut temple building was a great engineering feat of the ancients considering the difficult terrain of the hills where such caves were located, and the primitive tools as well as transportation and elevation facilities to their builders. Without a high degree of religious devotion and dedication of a community for generations and centuries, such a feat would have impossible to accomplish. Building such cave-temples would have cost a lot of human and material resources. The entire local society, including the rulers, the rich merchants and landlords as well as the down-trodden masses, had to make great sacrifices.

There could not have been any great sacrifice without a mighty social justification. The rock-cut temple building must have generated a sacred cause in the minds of those who have their sacrifice in creating them. One could imagine the ecstasy created among the locals when the cave-temple complex and other rock-cut architectural edifices were completed. A hallowed shrine suddenly emerged from the sleepy jungle for the religious fancy to enjoy the heavenly bliss. Dead rocks were suddenly transformed into places of activity. The cave-temple complex is an abode not only for the devotees and pilgrims, but also for the Buddhas, Bodhisattvas, flying angels, and supernatural animals etc. You can imagine how the ancients felt. Shone upon by feeble candle or lamp light, the dark terrestrial cavity became so dreamlike, giving the effect of seeing the Buddha and his disciples in the paradise on earth. The ancient mortals would see rocks praying, preaching, smiling, flying; and their devoted ears would hear celestial music as if gently reverberating from the cave ceilings to the bottom of their hearts[1].

---

[1] Song Yu［宋昱，?-756 AD］wrote a poem on the Cave Temple Complex at Yungang, which has a similar words of praise. Song Yu, "*Ti shikusi ji weixiaowendi zhi suozhi*［题石窟寺即魏孝文帝之所置，The Cave Temples commissioned to be built by Emperor Xiaowen of the Northern Wei Dynasty］", in: *Wenyuan yinghua*［文苑英华，*The Best Works in the Literature and Art Circles* or *Corpus of the Literary World*］ed. Li Fang［李昉］et al, Facsimile edition, Beijing: Zhonghua Book Company, 1966: 1181.

The cave-temples are sophisticated and complicated pieces of art and architecture cut out for humanity to forget the striving and sufferings of the madding crowds, and to embrace the serenity and solemnity of a pure atmosphere of peace, compassion and other noble and lofty ideas and ideals of mind. There is always a magical quality in a rock-cut temple. The magnificent sculptures and murals have created the beauty and charm that cannot be matched by anything of the mundane world. They have even transformed the mundane cultural ecology into an imaginary celestial other world. So, when the famous Chinese pilgrim Xuanzang of the early 7th century reported *Azheluo qielan* (Ācārasaṃghārāma)—Ajaṇṭā Caves, he wrote "this is held in its place by the force of the vow of the Arhat. They also say it is by the force of his miraculous powers; others say by the virtue of some magical compound" [1].

1. Types of the Indian Caves

It is noteworthy that in India multipart and differently formed cave-temple settlements were not constructed all at once, but evolved with time. The first ones to be carved around the 3rd century BC expressed the necessity of supplying monk habitations and were called *bhikṣu-guhā,* but later on, *stūpa* cave, square cave (*maṭapa*) and cisterns were added, step by step, to this initial rock-cut settlement[2]. This reflects, of course, the situation during the founding period of the cave-temples. While such cave-temples were favored by most monastic communities and were widely accepted, their lay-out nevertheless evolved. Thus, a cave-temple complex or settlement came to be formed by habitable caves, *stūpa* caves and some other living facilities (fig.1).

On the basis of structural form and function or nature of rock-cut architecture, the Indian caves can be roughly divided into two categories or

[1] Samuel Beal, *Si-Yu-Ki—Buddhist Records of the Western World; Chinese Accounts of India,* translated from the Chinese of Hiuen Tsiang, London: Trubner, 1884: 451.

[2] M. C. Joshi, "Buddhist Rock-cut Architecture: A Survey" , in: *Proceedings of the International Seminar on Cave Art of India and China,* Theme I: Historical Perspective, New Delhi: Indira Gandhi National Centre for the Arts, November 25, 1991: 1-28, esp. 3-8.

kinds: one refers to caves built as monk quarters, the other refers to ritual spaces where monks could participate in a religious rites and worship. The former includes a cave to live in as a main component together with a square cave and a cistern. Moreover, in later periods, Buddhist images were also part of this kind of habitable cave. The latter is the *stūpa* cave. Based on textual evidence, four varieties of rock-cut caves or architecture are available[1].

(1) Habitable cave, commonly called *vihāra* in Sanskrit, and *lēṇa* according to the Prākṛta/Prākṛit/Prakrit inscriptions originally carved inside the caves of Mahārāshṭra[2], was a rock-cut architecture used as monk living quarter and place for *dhyāna* practice. The Pāli equivalent of this Prākṛta word is *leṇa* and the Sanskrit one is *layana,* both meaning "to hide"[3]. They are caves in a rock or mountain caves, which were used by *bhikṣus* or ascetics as a hermitage. According to the Prākṛta inscriptions, some of the habitable caves were designated as four-celled cave or five celled *lēṇa,* such as the one that carved on the back wall of the verandah of cave 6 at Nāsik. It reads: "*Sidhaṃ Viragahapatisa nyegamasa leṇa deyadhama kuṭuṁbiṇiya chasa Naṁdaśrīya ōvarako duhutuya chasa Purisadatâva ovarakâ eva leṇaṁ chatugabhaṁ ṇiyuta bhikusaṁghasa châtudisasa niyâchitaṁ*". H. Lüders translated it into English as follows: Gift of a four-celled *lēṇa* by the merchant, the householder Vira, one cell being the gift of his wife Naṁdasirī, and one that of his daughter Purisadatū, to the community of monks of the four quarters[4].

---

[1] Chongfeng Li [李崇峰], *Zhongyin fojiao shikusi bijiao yanjiu: Yi tamiaoku wei zhongxin* [中印佛教石窟寺比较研究：以塔庙窟为中心, *Chētiyagharas in Indian and Chinese Buddhist Cave-temples: A Comparative Study*], Beijing: Peking University Press, 2003: 4-5.

[2] H. Lüders, "*A List of Brāhmī Inscriptions from the Earliest Times to about* A.D. *400 with the Exception of those of Aśōka*", in: *Epigraphia Indica,* Volume X (1909-10), Appendix, Calcutta: Superintendent Government Printing, 1912: Nos. 998, 1000, 1001, 1006, 1007, 1012, 1014, 1016, 1020, 21, 1024, 1039-41, 1048, 1051, 1060, 1062, 1063, 1065, 1066, 1073, 1107, 1123-26, 1131-33, 1138, 1140, 1144, 1152, 1175, etc.

[3] 1) T. W. Rhys Davids and William Stede, *Pali-English Dictionary,* London: Pali Text Society, 1925: 586; 2) Monier Monier-Williams, *A Sanskrit-English Dictionary,* London: Oxford University Press, 1899: 903.

[4] 1) Jas. Burgess, *Report on the Buddhist Cave Temples and Their Inscriptions; Supplementary to the volume on "The Cave Temples of India"*, in: *Archaeological Survey of Western India,* Vol. IV, 1883: 116, Nâsik, No. 24, Plate LV; 2) H. Lüders, *opere citato:* No. 1127.

In addition, cave 21 at Manmodi, Junner, was designated by a Prākṛta inscription carved outside its hall as "a five-celled cave" (fig.2)[1], cave 5 at Ganesh Pahar, Junnar, was called as a seven-celled cave by another Prākṛta inscription over the left window outside, and cave 15 at Kārlē was known as a nine-celled hall[2], because it consists of a big hall and eight small cells.

The *lēṇas* in Mahārāshṭra, which are generally flat-roofed, can be divided into two types according to the plan and structure[3]. The first type is single cell or a few cells variety, with one to three cells (fig.3) or a cell and a recess (fig.4) set behind or on a side of a oblong or square hall, and a narrow verandah in front. This type of *lēṇa* was found mainly in the rock-cut temples at Junnar, Kaṇhēri, Kuḍā and Mahāḍ, occasionaly at Bhājā、Nāsik and Śailārwāḍi[4].

The second type is multiple cells variety. A big square or oblong hall (*kodhi/maḍapa*) was carved in the center, and a row of small cells were cut along the three sides of the central hall. Each of the small cells (*ōvaraka/gabha*)[5] has a doorway opening into the central hall, and one or two beds carved inside (fig.5). A shrine chamber is added at the centre of the back wall of the hall of the *lēṇa*

[1] 1) Jas. Burgess, *opere citato:* 98, No. 31, Plate LI; 2) H. Lüders, *opere citato:* No. 1157.

[2] 1) Jas. Burgess, *opere citato:* 113, 114, No. 21, Plate LIV; 2) H. Lüders, *opere citato:* No. 1106.

[3] S. Nagaraju, *Buddhist Architecture of Western India* (*C. 250* BC-*C.* AD *300*), Delhi: Agam Kala Prakashan, 1981: 69-70.

[4] For instance, those belonging to this type are cave Nos. 1, 2, 8, 11-13, 15, 17-19, 25-28 at Ganesh Pahar of Junnar, cave Nos. 1, 27, 28 at Manmodi of Junnar, cave Nos. 33-35, 57, 60 at Sivaneri of Junnar, cave Nos. 21, 22, 32, 42, 50, 53, 54, 56-59, 64, 65, 70, 73, 74, 78, 88, 91, 93-98 at Kaṇhēri, cave Nos. 2, 3, 5, 7, 10-12, 16-18, 23, 24 at Kuḍā, cave Nos. 4, 7, 9, 11, 13, 16, 19, 22-24, 26-28 at Mahāḍ as well as cave Nos. 15, 16 at Bhājā, cave 8 at Nāsik and cave Nos. 10-12 at Sailārwāḍi.

[5] The small cells cut in all the three sides of the square or oblong hall are called *ōvaraka* or *gabha* in the Prākṛta inscriptions. The Pāli equivalent of the Prākṛta *ōvaraka* is *ovaraka* which means an inner room, and the Sanskrit equivalent is *apavaraka* which appeared some centuries later, meaning a forbidden or secret room. The Prākṛta *gabha* derived from Vedic *garbha,* the Pāli equivalent of this Prākṛta word is *gabbha* which means interior, cavity, an inner room, private chamber, bedroom, and cell of a *vihāra.* The Chinese paraphrase is *sengfang*［僧房］which was called by Yijing, and the Sanskrit equivalent is *garbha* which means the womb, interior of anything, an inner apartment, sleeping room, any interior chamber, adytum or sanctuary of a temple. Therefore, the meaning of the Prākṛta *ōvaraka* and that of the *gabha* is almost same. *confer*：1)T. W. Rhys Davids and William Stede, *opere citato:* 171, 244; 2) Monier Monier-Williams, *opere citato:* 52, 349.

carved in the later period (fig.6). This type of *lēṇa* was chiefly used in the cave temple complexes at Ajaṇṭā, Beḍsā, Bhājā, Ēlūra, Kārlē, Junnar, Nāsik, Pitalkhōrā, and seldom at Kaṇhēri, Kondāṇē, Pawala and Śailārwāḍi[1]. The *lēṇas* of first type which appeared in the 3rd century BC, were popular from the middle of the 1st century AD to the middle of the 3rd century, and those of the second type were scattered in vast area and had been in use continuously from the middle of the 2nd century BC to the 7th century AD[2].

According to Yijing's records, Nālandā saṃghārāma(Nālandā Mahāvihāra) consists of eight *yuan* (courtyard) or *si* (monastery). Each *si* is square-built and made of bricks, with a long veranda around. It is a building of three storeys, and each storey is about ten feet high. There are nine *sengfang* (monk's cell) set on each side of the court, and each monk's cell is about 10 feet square. The quadrangular court is about 30 paces in its face, and the door of the *si* opens westward[3]. Here, the Chinese term *yuan* which was called by Yijing means a courtyard or yard. It is similar to the Chinese word *fang*[4], that is, *sengfang* (monks' block or/quarters?). *Sengfang* is the Chinese paraphrase of the Sanskrit

---

[1] For instance, those belonging to this type are cave Nos. 1, 2, 4, 6, 7, 11-13, 15A, 15-17, 20-24, 27 at Ajaṇṭā, cave No. 11 at Beḍsā, cave Nos. 5-11, 13, 14, 18, 22, 25 at Bhājā, cave Nos. 1-4 at Ēlāra, cave Nos. 5, 7, 32 at Ganesh Pahar of Junnar, cave Nos. 21, 38, 43, 45 at Manmodi of Junnar, cave Nos. 18, 36, 42, 52 at Sivaneri of Junnar, cave Nos. 2 and 4 at Tūljālēnā of Junnar, cave Nos. 4, 12-15 at Kārlē, in addition to cave No. 67 at Kaṇhēri, cave Nos. 2 and 3 at Kondāṇē, cave 1 at Pawala and cave 3 at Sailārwāḍi.

[2] As for a chronology and dating of the cave-temples of Mahārāshṭra, *confer*: 1)Chongfeng Li, *Chētiyagharas in Indian and Chinese Buddhist Caves: A Comparative Study* (Dissertation submitted to the University of Delhi for the Award of the Degree of Doctor of Philosophy), Delhi: University of Delhi, 1993: 85-172; 2) Chongfeng Li, *Zhongyin fojiao shikusi bijiao yanjiu: Yi tamiaoku wei zhongxin* (*Chētiyagharas in Indian and Chinese Buddhist Cave-temples: A Comparative Study*), Beijing: Peking University Press, 2003: 63-126.

[3] 1) Yijing, *Nanhai ji gui neifa zhuan*［南海寄归内法传, *Record of Buddhist Monastic Traditions of Southern Asia*］, emended and annotated by Wang Bangwei［王邦维］, Beijing: Zhonghua Book Company, 1995: 176-177; *confer*: *Taishō*, No. 2125, Vol. 54: 227a; 2) Yijing, *Datang xiyu qiufa gaoseng zhuan*［大唐西域求法高僧传, *Biographies of Eminent Priests of the Great Tang Dynasty Who Sought the Law in the Western Regions*］, emended and annotated by Wang Bangwei, Beijing: Zhonghua Book Company, 1988: 112-113; *confer*: *Taishō*, No. 2066, Vol. 51: 5b-c.

[4] Huilin［慧琳］, *Yiqiejing yinyi*［一切经音义, *The Pronunciation and Meaning of the Canon* or *The Pronunciation and Meaning in the Buddhist Scriptures*), in: *Taishō*, No. 2128, Vol. 54: 443c.

vihāra[1]. And, the Chinese term *si* used by Yijing is another Chinese paraphrase of the Sanskrit word *vihāra* on the basis of *Yiqiejing yinyi* (*The Pronunciation and Meaning in the Buddhist Scriptures* or *The Pronunciation and Meaning of the Canon*) by Xuanying[2].

"For about twenty years beginning with 1915-16, the Archaeological Survey of India excavated the site"[3] of Nālandā. As result, the ruins of a large number of structures have come to light, extending lengthwise from south to north with a range of monasteries (*vihāras*) along the east side and temples along the west of a seemingly approach-avenue. Among the ten *vihāras* uncovered, eight were set on one row facing west and two joined them at right angles on the southern side. The structure and plan of all the *vihāras* at Nālandā are similar (fig.7), which prove Yijing's records to be quite faithful.

According to *Da piluzhena chengfojing shu* (*Annotations on Mahā-vairocanā-sūtra or Annotations on the Mahā-vairocanābhisaṃbodhi-vikurvitādhiṣṭhāna-vaipulya-sūtrendra-vāja-nāma-dharmaparyāya*), which is notes made by Yixing (683-727 AD) of Śubhākarasiṃha (637-735 AD)'s preaching or lectures on the very *sūtra,* the Chinese characters *sengfang* is a paraphrase of Sanskrit *vihāra,* meaning a dwelling place. And, the Chinese character *si* is also a paraphrase of Sanskrit *vihāra.* A rock-cut cave, however, is a deep and quite place for those who practise the intensive *dhyāna*[4].

On the basis of historical records and archaeological excavations, we find the *lēṇa* in Mahārāshṭra was carved in imitation of the free-standing contemporary *vihāra.* In other words, the *lēṇa* was petrified version of the contemporary brick-and-timber or the humbler wattle mud-and thatch structure of the *vihāra.* The design of the interior of a *lēṇa* was fully modelled on that of a *vihāra,* the central *kodhi* or *maḍapa* in the *lēṇa* was a copy from a court of the *vihāra,* and the

[1] *Taishō,* Vol. 39: 615c.

[2] Xuanying, *Yiqiejing yinyi* (*The Pronunciation and Meaning of the Canon* or *Pronunciation and Meaning in the Buddhist Scriptures*), emended by Sun Xingyan[孙 星 衍]et al, Shanghai: The Commercial Press, 1936: 291, 1113.

[3] A Ghosh, *Nālandā,* 6th ed., New Delhi: Archaeological Survey of India, 1986: 16.

[4] *Taishō,* Vol. 39: 615c, 695a-b.

ōvarakas or *gabhas* along the three sides of the central *maḍapa* in the *lēṇa* were totally replicas of the garbha (cells) in the *vihāra* (fig.8a, b). In other words, the *leṇa* was a petrified verson of the contemporary brick-and-timber *vihāra*, as a result, such a rock-cut cave (*lēṇa*) was commonly called *vihāra*[1]. Although the term *vihāra* appears in the Prākṛta inscriptions carved inside the caves in Mahārāshṭra, however, it does refer in particular to the free-standing *vihāra* not a rock-cut cave[2].

(2) *Stūpa* cave, commonly called *chaityagriha/caityagṛha* in Sanskrit or *cetiyaghāra* in Pālī, was desingnated as *chētiyaghara* in the Prākṛta inscriptions originally carved inside the caves of Mahārāshṭra[3]. It was translated into English as *chaitya* building and Chinese scholars call it *caitya* cave or *stūpa* cave. According to the Buddhist *vinaya* text in Chinese, *caityagṛha* (*chētiyaghara*) is one of the three kinds of the *stūpa* allowed to be built by the Buddha and its function is identical to that of the open-air *stūpa*[4]. As to the ground plan, a typical *chētiyaghara* is generally divided by two colonnades into three parts—the central nave (being wide and high) and two side aisles (narrow and low). The front of the nave has an entrance while the back part of the nave forms an apse in whose center a *stūpa* was carved out. The two colonnades meet

---

[1] That this kind of cave was called by some scholars as *sengfangku*［僧房窟，monk's room cave］is sometimes not entirely proper, because *sengfang* (monk's room) should be a single room. Yang Xuanzhi records that Yongning "Monastery［永宁寺，in Luoyang］had over one thousand cloisters and rooms for the monks, both single cloisters and multilevel ones［僧房楼观一千余间］"; and "five hundred or more rooms in the nuns' quarters and lecture halls［讲殿尼房五百余间］presented a spectacular view of an unbroken line of carved window panes" at Yaoguang Monastery［瑶光寺］in Luoyang. With regard to the small rooms set on each side of the court of a *vihāra,* Yijing recorded clearly that they are *sengfang*［僧房 monk's cells］. *Sengfang*［僧坊，*vihāra,* monks' block］, however, was originally a hall where the monks met or walked about; afterwards the hall was used as a temple. *Vihāra* is a larger building for housing *bhikṣus* or a cluster of several rooms set around a central quadrangle courtyard. Therefore, 僧房 cannot be equated with 僧坊. *confer*: 1) Yi-t'ung Wang, tr., *A Record of Buddhist Monasteries in Lo-yang* by Yang Hsüan-chih, Princeton: Princeton University Press, 1984: 16, 48. 2) Yijing, *opere citato* (*Datang xiyu qiufa gaoseng zhuan*): 112-113; 3) Monier Monier-Williams, *opere citato:* 1003; 4) T. W. Rhys Davids and William Stede, *opere citato:* 642.

[2] H. Lüders, *opere citato:* Nos. 988, 998, 1037.

[3] H. Lüders, *opere citato:* Nos. 1050, 1058, 1072, 1141, 1153, 1178, 1179, 1183, etc.

[4] Chongfeng Li, *opere citato* (*chētiyagharas in Indian...*)：72-74.

and end in the back of the *stūpa* (*caitya*). The nave ceiling is barrel vaulted, while the aisle ceilings are half barrel vaulted. The cave's façade decoration is very complicated: the *chaitya* arch above the doorway was cut in imitation of the original façade of a free-standing *caityagṛha.* The cave's main focus is the *stūpa* standing in the center of the apse. Buddhist monks and laymen could circumambulate the *stūpa,* recite Buddhist *sūtras* and participate in religious functions (fig.9). According to Benjamin Rowland, the U-shaped plan of *stūpa* caves, which is similar to that of a basilica, "was specially evolved to provide for the rite of circumambulation around the symbol of the Buddha's Nirvāṇa and to provide space for services within the main body of the church" . The resemblance is no more than accidental[1]. As for the *chētiyaghara* plan, round, square and rectangular plans besides the U-shaped one are available. However, the U-shaped ground plan was widespread and lingered on for quite a long time in India[2].

(3) Square cave, called *maṇḍapa* in Sanskrit, was also designated as *maṭapa* in the Prākṛta inscriptions originally carved inside the caves of Mahārāshṭra[3], meaning a hall, shed, hut, house, pavilion, temple, and so on. The cave, as the term suggests, was square in plan, with a flat roof. Some of the square caves had an ante-chamber, some had a bench carved against the back wall or side walls (fig.10a, b). As for the function and nature of this type of cave, some of them were used for monks' living or dining[4], and some were storeroom. In later periods, a few square caves had niches and images carved on the main wall and sidewalls.

(4) Cistern, which was designated as *pōḍhī* in the Prākṛta inscriptions carved

---

[1] B. Rowland, *The Pelican History of Art; The Art and Architecture of India: Buddhist/Hindu/ Jain,* reprinted with revisions and updated bibliography by J. C. Harle, New York: Penguin Books, 1977: 114.

[2] D. Mitra, *Buddhist Monuments,* Calcutta: Sahitya Samsad, 1971: 41.

[3] H. Lüders, *opere citato:* Nos. 1174, 1182.

[4] According to a Prākṛta inscription carved on the left wall, cave 64 at Sivaneri of Junnar was a refectory (*bhōjaṇamaṭapa*). *confer*: 1) Jas. Burgess, *opere citato:* 94, No. 8, Plate XLIX; 2) H. Lüders, *opere citato:* No. 1182.

inside the caves[1], is in fact a small underground stone pond with sufficient volume or capacity to store water. Usually a cistern had a small square opening connected to a stone channel through which rain water poured during the rainy season (fig.11). This kind of cistern was normally used for drinking water (*pāṇīapōḍhī/pāṇīyapōḍhī*)[2] but a few of them were used for bathing, in this case they were called *sanānapōḍhī*[3].

2. Sinicization of the *Lēṇas* and *Maṭapas*

The Buddhist cave-temples in Mahārāshṭra, in a sense, are the epitome of all the Buddhist rock-cut architecture of Hinduka. Hence, the rock-cut architecture is famous and celebrated for its great numbers in quantity, manifold varieties in type and its long uninterrupted history. With the development of trade between Hinduka and foreign countries and the widespread dissemination of Buddhism, the rock-cut architecture of Hinduka, along with the other artistic forms such as Buddhist sculptures and paintings, all crossed the borders and began to spread and diffuse gradually in the Orient, because the Buddhist monks found such secluded spots were very beneficial to the wholesome monastic life. It fully proves the fact that the rock-cut architecture is one of the most effective ways and means to spread Buddhism.

The Buddhist art of Hinduka was gradually disseminated into China along with Buddhism spreading into its boundary decades before the Christian era[4]. "The general rule that governed the construction of *gongta* (*grihya-chaitya/caityagṛha* or

---

[1] H. Lüders, *opere citato:* Nos. 995, 996, 1000, 1007, 1013, 1014, 1039, 1041, 1061, 1064, 1072, 1079, 1107, 1119, 1131, 1140, 1148-50, 1152, 1154, 1155, 1173, 1176, 1177, 1180, etc.

[2] H. Lüders, *opere citato:* Nos. 998, 1006, 1016, 1020.

[3] H. Lüders, *opere citato:* No. 1056.

[4] Tang Yongtong [汤用彤], *Han wei liang jin nanbeichao fojiao shi* [汉魏两晋南北朝佛教史, *A History of Buddhism from the Han down to the Southern and Northern Dynasties* (1st to 6th century AD), Shanghai: The Commercial Press, 1938; 2nd ed., Beijing: Zhonghua Book Company, 1982: 34-36.

gṛha-stūpa)[1] at that time was still based on the prototype or form of Hinduka, the *stūpas* were built with from one to three, five, seven or nine stories"[2]. As one of the component parts of the Buddhist art, the rock-cut architecture had also spread into China following the eastward dissemination of Buddhism. It entered the Western Regions (present day Xinjiang) at first, then gradually spread eastward, and finally scattered all over China.

It is interesting that the four varieties of Mahārāshṭran caves were transmitted to China along with the eastward dissemination of the Mahārāshṭran rock-cut architecture. The constitution of the cave-temples in China, in general, followed the tradition of the rock-cut architecture of Mahārāshṭra. Like the other visual forms of the Buddhist art, however, the rock-cut architecture of Mahārāshṭran origin had no choice but to integrate with the local culture of the tradition and the aesthetic standards due to the struggle for its existence and development as well as some limitation of natural elements. Thus, varied kinds of Buddhist cave-forms with distinctively local features had taken shape in different regions. For instance, the form of the *stūpa* caves in Kucīna (Kucha)[3] is not similar to the prototype of Mahārāshṭra, nor is it identical with that of the *chētiyagharas* of north China. In terms of the square caves (*maṭapas*), while a few kept their original nature after spreading into China, most of them were

---

[1] The Chinese term *gongta* [宫塔], which is composed of two characters, should be probably a derivative of the Sanskrit compound word *gṛihya-chaitya/caityagṛihā. gong* [宫] was derived from *gṛihā* (house) or *grihya* that means belonging to a house, and *ta* [塔] was derived from *chaitya/caitya. confer*: 1) M. C. Joshi, *opere citato:* 7-8; 2)Monier Monier-Williams, *opere citato:* 361-363; 3)Unrai Ogiwara[荻原雲來], *Bon-wa Daijiten* [漢訳対照梵和大辭典, *A Sanskrit-Chinese-Japanese Dictionary*], Tōkyō: Kōdansha, 1974: 432b.

[2] Wei Shou [魏收, 506-572 AD], *Weishu: Shilaozhi*[魏书·释老志, *History of the Wei Dynasties: Treatise on Buddhism and Taoism*], punctuated edition, Beijing: Zhonghua Book Company, 1974: 3025-3062, esp. 3029. *confer*: 1) James R. Ware, "Wei Shou on Buddhism", in: *T'oung Pao* 30 (1930): 100-181, esp. 122; 2) Leon Hurvitz, tr., *Treatise on Buddhism and Taoism* by Wei Shou, in: *Yun-kang; The Buddhist Cave-temples of the Fifth Century* AD *in North China; detailed report of the archaeological survey carried out by the mission of the Tōhōbunka Kenkyūsho 1938-45* by S. Mizuno and T. Nagahiro, Vol. XVI, Supplement and Index, Kyoto: Jimbunkagaku Kenkyūshō, Kyoto University, 1956: 23-103, esp. 47.

[3] *confer*: 1) Li Yan [礼言], *Fanyu zaming* [梵语杂名, *Sundry Names in Sanskrit]*, in: *Taishō*, No. 2135, Vol. 54: 1236a; 2) Unrai Ogiwara, *opera citato*: 352b.

altered and became Buddha-hall caves, namely they were used for Buddhist activities instead of living quarters. The second type of *lēṇa* which was most popular in the cave-temple complexes of Mahārāshṭra was seldom seen in China with the exception of a few found in Kucha and western part of Gansu Province. Moreover, the colossal Buddha-image-cave, which cannot be found in Mahārāshṭra, used to be in vogue both in Kucha as well as in China proper[1].

As for the Mahārāshṭran *lēṇa,* those built in the fourth period (mid-5th century to the mid-7th century AD), with complex facilities and spaces, were built sumptuously and were embellished with major and minor niches and sculptures. The niche built in the back wall became a place of Buddha worship (fig.12). Thus, such a complex acquired a double nature: not only was it a special locus of the highest worship, but also a place for monks to reside in. This arrangement was considerably influenced by the *chētiyaghara*-cum-*lēṇa* (fig.13) of the third period (mid-1st century to mid-3rd century AD).

Compared with the *chētiyaghara,* the typical *lēṇa* found in China is very rare, being sparsely available in Xinjiang and in western part of Gansu and dating from the 4th to 6th century. According to my reconnaissance, there are 4 *lēṇas* (caves 1, 2, 3 and 5) at Subashi site, Kucha (fig.14), 1 *lēṇa* (Cave 12) at Šorčuq, Karashahr, 2 *lēṇas* (caves 1 and 42) at Tuyok and 1 at Yarhu(cave 4), Turfan, 3 *lēṇas* (caves 268, 285 and 487) at Mogao, Dunhuang (fig.15) and 1 at Wenshushan, Jiuquan.

With regard to the *lēṇas* at Mogao, cave Nos. 268 and 285 are fully covered with murals besides the main image-niche carved against the back wall of each cave. As one of the earliest extant caves at Mogao, cave 268 combined originally with caves 272 and 275 and formed a religious group. Cave 285 was constructed during a period when Prince Dongyang was a governor of Dunhuang Prefecture,

[1] Su Bai［宿白］, "*Xinjiang baicheng kezi'er shiku bufen dongku de leixing yu niandai*［新疆拜城克孜尔石窟部分洞窟的类型与年代, Types and Dating of Some Caves at Kizil in Baicheng, Xinjiang］", in: *Zhongguo shikusi yanjiu*［中国石窟寺研究, *Studies of the Cave-temples of China*］, Beijing: Cultural Relics Press, 1996: 21-38, esp. 22.

from about 525 to 540 AD[1], and cave 288 was built simultaneously with that of cave 285. These two caves stand side by side and both have same design of the murals at the front chamber. Cave 288 is a *chētiyaghara,* while cave 285 is a *lēṇa*. It appears that they are twin caves and constitute a group[2], which was a popular design of the rock-cut architecture in Mahārāshṭra[3]. On the back wall of cave 285 is a large niche occupied by a Buddha with legs pendant, while on either side are smaller niches containing a monk in *dhyāna mudrā.* The rest of this wall is covered by strange figures, such as Candradevī (the moon goddess), Sūrya (the sun god), Viṣṇu, Maheśvara, Kumāra, Rishi Vāsu as well as the elephant-headed Vināyaka, i. e., Gaṇeśa (fig.16)[4]. The motif is charged with a strong foreign meaning and feeling, which should be the result of a closely cultural exchange between China proper and Hinduka at that time[5]. Cave 487, which was unearthed during an archaeological excavartion carried out in the mid 1960s, has a similar design with that of cave 285 and used to be covered with murals[6]. All these caves, which resemble the design of Mahārāshṭran *lēṇa* and have corresponding sculptures and murals inside, acquire a double nature: not

---

[1] 1) Su Bai, "*Dongyangwang yu jianpinggong*［东阳王与建平公, Prince Dongyang and Duke Jianping］", in: *Zhongguo shikusi yanjiu* (*Studies of the Cave-temples of China*), Beijing: Cultural Relics Press, 1996: 244-259, esp. 246-249; 2) Su Bai, "*Canguan dunhuang mogaoku di 285 hao ku zhaji*［参观敦煌莫高窟第 285 号窟札记, Notes on Cave 285 of the Mogao Caves, Dunhuang］", in: *Zhongguo shikusi yanjiu* (*Studies of the Cave-temples of China*), Beijing: Cultural Relics Press, 1996: 206-213, esp. 211.

[2] Su Bai, *opere citato* (*Canguan dunhuang mogaoku*...): 206-213, esp. 213.

[3] For instance, caves 3 (*chētiyaghara*) and 4 (*lēṇa*) at Pitalkhōrā may be assigned to the second century BC. "That they are contemporary with each other is also indicated by their sharing a common forecourt, which shows that their excavation was designed simultaneously." M. N. Deshpande, "The Rock-cut Caves of Pitalkhora in the Deccan", in: *Ancient India,* No. 15 (1959): 66-93, esp. 70.

[4] Basil Gray, *Buddhist Cave Paintings at Tun-huang,* photography by J. B. Vincent, with a preface by Arthur Waley, London: Faber and Faber Limited, 1959: 43.

[5] 1) Su Bai, *opere citato* (*Canguan dunhuang mogaoku*...): 206-213, esp. 213; 2) Su Bai, *Zhongguo fojiao shikusi yiji*［中国佛教石窟寺遗迹——3 至 8 世纪中国佛教考古学, *The Buddhist Cave-temples of China*］, Beijing: Cultural Relics Press, 2010: 66.

[6] Pan Yushan［潘玉闪］and Ma Shichang［马世长］, *Mogaoku kuqian diantang yizhi*［莫高窟窟前殿堂遗址, *Ruins of Frontal Buildings added to the Mogao Caves*］, Beijing: Cultural Relics Press, 1985: 93-94.

only were they a special locus for Buddhists to carry out the highest worship, but also a place for monks to practise *dhyāna* and to reside in.

In addition, nine more *lēṇas* were rediscovered at the northern part or block of Mogao during an archaeological excavation carried out from 1988 to 1995 by archaeologists of the Dunhuang Academy[1]. Such a kind of cave, however, can not be found in the cave temple complex in the east of Jiuquan, Gansu.

The limited number of *lēṇas* built from the 4th to 6th century in China might be explained as follows:

(1) On the basis of Sengcun's record, 4th century, the monks who resided in the Kingdom of Kucīna (Kucha), had to move house or cell after they lived in a room or occupied a bed or stayed in a temple for three months; those who had not spent five years as monks were required to live together with a master monk and could not sleep alone according to the *Prātimokṣa*. The nuns of Kucīna who were ordered to follow the same *Prātimokṣa* or monastic discipline could not go out of the monastery or temple without other two escorts unless the nun was a master nun[2]. According to our reconnaissance, a large number of rock-cut monk-rooms were constructed at Kizil in the early period, but some of them were transformed into a special locus of worship after using for some time, such as cave 80, a *chētiyaghara.* Therefore, the said monastic discipline that monks who resided in the Kingdom of Kucīna had to move house or cell after they lived in a room or occupied a bed or stayed in a temple for three months seem to be followed strictly by the Buddhists there, and the large number of rock-cut monk-rooms constructed at Kizil in the early period are the result of the above *Prātimokṣa,* because the monks had to change the dwelling place very often[3].

---

[1] Peng Jinzhang [彭金章] and Wang Jianjun [王建军], *Dunhuang mogaoku beiqu shiku* [敦煌莫高窟北区石窟, *The Rock-cut Architectures at the Northern Part of Mogao, Dunhuang*], Vol. I, Beijing: Cultural Relics Press, 2000: 343.

[2] Sengyou [僧佑 445-518 AD], *Chu sanzang ji ji* [出三藏记集, *A Collection of Records concerning the Tripiṭaka* or *A Collection of Records of Translations of the Tripiṭaka*], emended and annotated by Su Jinren [苏晋仁] and Xiao Lianzi [萧鍊子], Beijing: Zhonghua Book Company, 1995: 46, 410-411; *confer*: *Taishō*, No. 2145, Vol. 55: 10a, 79c.

[3] Su Bai, *opere citato* (*Xinjiang baicheng kezi'er shiku*...): 21-38, esp. 36.

The Mahārāshṭran *lēṇa* was not only a large, labor costly cave and not easily built, but also a permanent residence for the monks. It was a deep and quite cave for those who practise intensive *dhyāna* as explained by Śubhākarasiṃha[1]. Therefore, such a cave could not suit the living regulations imposed on monks and nuns of Kucīna. Since the cost of building such complexes was relevant, it was not acceptable to abandon it and rebuild another after monks had occupied it only for a short time. The most suitable way is to draw some useful part or essential factor of the Mahārāshṭran *lēṇa* and to transform it into a simple dwelling cave. The Buddhism of north China had a close relation with that of Kucīna, so the regulation of rock-cut architecture in north China was much influenced by that of Kucīna.

(2) Xinjiang and north China are located in the northern temperate zone; most people living in this region use stove and *kang* (a heating bed made of bricks or stones and warmed by fire), especially in the cold winter, these being the most suitable and convenient facilities for keeping warm. Indian *lēṇa,* however, was not only a dwelling place, but also "a deep and quite cave for those who practise intensive *dhyāna*" . They were especially popular in Mahārāshṭra because this region is very hot in the summer season and cool, as well as comfortable, in winter. Therefore, there is no need to think about warming a *lēṇa*'s interior. When Buddhist cave-temple spread into Xinjiang, the typical Mahārāshṭran *lēṇa* had to be transformed in response to local habit and circumstances, because a heating stove or a kang warmed by fire could not be easy to put in the right place of the typical *lēṇa*. As a result, in the Kingdom of Kucīna a residence cave or monk-room-cave with local characteristics was created (fig.17), which is similar to local free-standing house, in other words, the rock-cut monk-room of Kucīna was remade after a cell in the Mahārāshṭran *lēṇa*. It was an enlarged and transformed Mahārāshṭran *ōvaraka,* but supplemented with a corridor, window and foyer of Kuchean characteristics. This kind of a residence cave in Kucīna, which might also derive some elements of the habitable caves appeared in the third period in

[1] *Taishō,* Vol. 39: 615c, 695a-b.

India such as those at Ganesh Pahar(fig.18)[1] and Kudā, became a dominant type of the habitable cave and had an influence on the residence caves built in Dunhuang and Datong in the early period of the rock-cut temple building, such as cave 11 at Jiaoshan, Datong. At first appearance, the rock-cut monk-room or habitable cave of Kucīna seem to be a simple "transplanting" of the first type of Mahārāshṭran *lēṇa,* it should be, in substance, a fundamental change or evolution from *lēṇa* (*vihāra*) to *ōvaraka* (cell).

(3) On the basis of our reconnaissance, the rock-cut caves for worship and those for monks living in China appear to be constructed in different block or part according to their function. This phenomenon is very prominent in the cave temple complex in the east of Xinjiang. For instance, the cave-temples built in the early period at Mogao follow the design of rock-cut architecture of Mahārāshṭra, with a *chētiyaghara* or a Buddha-hall cave as a centre of the highest worship and a *lēṇa* as a place for monks living and practising *dhyāna,* thus making up a religious group, such as cave Nos. 268, 272 and 275 as well as cave Nos. 288 and 285, while the caves constructed later were separated or classified according to their actual use or function. After an archaeological excavation carried out at the northern part of Mogao, it demonstrates that the rock-cut architectures at the southern part were chiefly functioned as locus of worship, while those carved at the northern part, where contains various kinds of caves for meditation, living, burial and storage[2], were places for monks living and practising *dhyāna.* This phenomenon seems to be a localization of the design of Mahārāshṭran cave-temples after they spread into north China.

(4) According to the available records, most rock-cut temples in China proper, which became places of worship and religious rites, were responding to the intention of acquiring merit to benefit the ruler, ministers, dignitaries, monks as well as common believers[3]. In the early period, however, the idea

---

[1] S. Nagaraju, *opere citato:* 168, fig.35.

[2] Peng Jinzhang and Wang Jianjun, *opere citato:* 343-350.

[3] Li Yukun[李玉昆], *Longmen beike jiqi shiliao jiazhi*[龙门碑刻及其史料价值, Inscriptions at Longmen and Their Historical Value]", in: *Longmenshiku beike tiji huilu*[龙门石窟碑刻题记汇录, *Inscriptions of the Longmen Cave Temples*], Beijing: Chinese Encyclopedia Press, 1998, Vol. II: 20-22.

that "to carve a celestial cave in the rock is to supply a place for a monk sitting in meditation"[1] was popular in north China. Monks, pilgrims and Buddhist devotees, after finishing their religious activities at the cave sites, would go back to the free-standing monasteries or temples built nearby, where various facilities were provided. For instance, there used to be ten free-standing monasteries near the cave-temple complex at Longmen, which were built by order of the imperial house, aristocrats as well as rich merchants during the Tang Dynasty (618 to 907 AD). Each of the monasteries had a large number of living quarters for monks and Buddhists devotees[2]. This situation greatly differs from Hinduka. In Mahārāshṭra *bhikṣus* or monks usually lived in the *lēṇas* near the *chētiyagharas* which formed together a complex cave-temple settlement.

The cave-temples constructed in north China, however, adopted a mixed architectural structure. The practice of *dhyāna* and worship might take place in the rock-cut caves, while the living quarters for the daily life of monks and Buddhist devotees were built in timber structure on the ground, thus forming an integrated Buddhist monastery. This kind of monastery was first created in the Great Cave Temple Complex at Wuzhou by the ruling family of the Northern Wei Dynasty[3], and was imitated in vast areas and continued in use for quite a long time.

While the *maṭapas* of Hinduka—which were simply cut in the 2nd century BC but deployed carved niches and became *Buddha-bimba-gṛha* (Buddha-image-cave) in the 5th or 6th century AD (fig.19)—were limited in number, in China, instead, they were very popular especially in the northern part and became the major caves for worship. Although the structure is very similar to

---

[1] Gao Yun [高允], "*Luyuan fu* [鹿苑赋, Rhapsody on the Deer-park]", in: *Guang hongmingji* [广弘明集, *Further Anthology of the Propagation of Light*] by Daoxuan, *confer*: *Taishō*, Vol. 52: 339b.

[2] Wen Yucheng [温玉成], "*Tangdai longmen shisi kaocha* [唐代龙门十寺考察, A Reconnaissance on the Ten Monasteries of the Tang Dynasty at Longmen, Luoyang]", in: *Zhongguo shiku: Longmen shiku* [中国石窟·龙门石窟, *The Cave-temples of China: Longmen Caves*], II, Beijing: Cultural Relics Press, 1992: 217-232.

[3] Chongfeng Li, "From Gandhāra to Yungang: Design of a Free-standing Buddhist Monastery", in: *Ancient Pakistan*, Vol. XXIII: 13-54.

the Mahārāshṭran *maṭapa,* square in plan, it was adapted and transformed into the cave for religious activity, a Chinese Buddha-hall-cave, with a main image occupying the back wall. This kind of Buddha-hall-cave was first created at Yungang, Datong, in the 470s AD (fig.20) and became afterward widespread in north China[1], gradually replacing the early *chētiyaghara*'s function and remaining in use as locus of worship for quite a long time (fig.21). It was an imitation of Buddha hall in a monastery or temple constructed in timber.

With regard to the rock-cut cisterns, which were built in large number in Mahārāshṭra, they are seldom seen in China, and a few remains have been found in the cave temple complex at Xumishan, Guyuan and at Longmen, Luoyang.

3. Evolution of the *Chētiyaghara*[2]

As mentioned above, the Buddhist rock-cut architecture of India can be divided into two categories. The first category comprises the caves for monks' daily life and *dhyāya* practice; the second was chiefly used by the Buddhist devotees for the activity of religious rites and worship. As a Buddhist monastery and temple, the latter played a leading role while the former was subordinate to it. The former was a cave for habitation, a *lēṇa;* while the latter was a *stūpa* cave—*chētiyaghara.* A rock-cut temple usually consisted of one *chētiyaghara* and several *lēṇas;* a number of rock-cut caves were linked with each other to form a complex Buddhist cave-temple settlement. As the focus of worship, the *chētiyaghara* evolved in accordance with the development of Buddhism. For

---

[1] Su Bai [宿白], "*Yungangshiku fenqi shilun* [云冈石窟分期试论, Perodization of Yungang Cave-temples]", in: *Zhongguo shikusi yanjiu* (*Studies of the Cave-temples of China*), Beijing: Cultural Relics Press, 1996: 76-88.

[2] This part was rewritten on the basis of my works, that is, *Chētiyagharas in Indian and Chinese Buddhist Caves: A Comparative Study* (Dissertation submitted to the University of Delhi for the Award of the Degree of Doctor of Philosophy, Delhi: University of Delhi, 1993) and its Chinese version, *Zhongyin fojiao shikusi bijiao yanjiu: Yi tamiaoku wei zhongxin* (*Chētiyagharas in Indian and Chinese Buddhist Cave-temples: A Comparative Study,* Beijing: Peking University Press, 2003).

instance, no image was found on the *stūpa* of the early *chētiyagharas;* but Buddhist niches and images were part of later *chētiyagharas* in response to the rise of Mahāyāna Buddhism; likewise, the *stūpa* became more complicated. Therefore, *chētiyagharas* evolved through time much more so than *lēṇas.*

The *chētiyagharas,* moreover, are also representative of rock-cut architecture whether executed in Indian or in Chinese cave-temples. For instance, there are 30 caves in Ajaṇṭā, five of which (Caves 9, 10, 19, 26 and 29) are *chētiyagharas.* And, there are 60 central-pillar-caves (*chētiyagharas*) at Kizil, which account for a quarter of the entire available caves. Moreover, of the 36 caves belonging to the Northern Dynasties' period (about 489 to 581 AD), 15 are *stūpa* caves (*chētiyagharas*). Therefore, *chētiyagharas* were one of the most important rock-cut architectures both in India and in China.

(1) *Chētiyagharas* in Mahārāshṭra: Fifty-five *chētiyagharas* are found in Mahārāshṭra, the cradle of Indian cave-temples. For each of the caves, six elements with chronological implications have been taken into account: ground plan, façade, *chaitya* arch, roof, column and *stūpa.* The typological analysis of such elements with respect to their identities and similarities allows for a classification of these *chētiyagharas* into six stages or four periods. The earliest *chētiyagharas* ascribed to mid-2nd century BC (fig.22) appear to be a rendition in stone of similar free-standing *caityagṛha* which possesses a circular ground plan (fig.23). Later, a vault-roofed apsidal *chētiyaghara* came into being and found favor among monks and laymen who needed to congregate, to worship and to perform rituals in a covered space. This kind of *chētiyaghara* was widely diffused and lasted from the first to the third stage, i. e., from the initial to the flourishing periods (2nd century BC to mid-1st century AD). In its typical form it has a central nave separated from the lateral aisles by two rows of columns and leading to a semicircular apse in which the main symbol of worship, a rock-cut *stūpa,* is located (fig.24). During the fourth and fifth stages, i. e. the utilitarian period (mid-1st century to the mid-3rd century AD) the *chētiyaghara* had a rectangular ground plan and flat roof; it did not have a colonnade at all, and the *stūpa* summit was connected to the ceiling (fig.25).

The different design indicates a more functional approach to the rock-cut architecture and marks a turning point in the architectural history of *chētiyagharas*. In addition, we must take into consideration the historically significant fact that the beginning of rock-cut architecture in Mahārāshṭra coincided with the rise of the Sātavāhana rulers, whose capital was Pratishṭhāna (present day Paithan). The rise and fall of the Sātavāhana Kingdom was responsible for the rise and fall of the construction of these cave-temples[1].

Because of the increased importance of Mahāyāna around the 4th century AD, the sites of western India, especially Ajaṇṭā, Aurangābād and Ēlūra, were humming with renewed architectural activity. As a result, a number of *chētiyagharas* were completed between 475 and 625 AD under the patronage of the Vākāṭaka rulers. The *chētiyagharas* of this period retain the basic features of the earlier ones, especially those built during the flourishing period (1st century BC to mid-1st century AD), with timber-imitation décor rendered totally in stone and relatively complex structural forms. In this sense, they are considered a revival or a transient renaissance of the earliest *chētiyagharas.* The most striking Mahāyāna characteristic reflected in the *chētiyagharas* of this period is the human representation of the Buddha carved in front of the *stūpa* (fig.26), as well as additional smaller Buddhist figures placed on the façade and inner walls of the cave. The *stūpa* reminiscent of the dead master and worshipped by the pilgrims and Buddhist followers, however, has become a sitting for the living Buddha, thus slightly changing its primitive nature[2].

(2) Central pillar caves in Kucīna: Following the penetration of Buddhism into Xinjiang, Buddhist cave art also gained a foothold in that region. There are 60 central-pillar caves (*chētiyagharas*) extant in Kizil, which can be classified into four chronological stages. The dating of the earliest central-pillar-caves at Kizil is usually assigned to the first half of the 4th century AD. However, considering the development of its more mature form, the construction of the central-pillar

---

[1] 1) M. N. Deshpande, "The Rock-cut Caves of Pitalkhora in the Deccan", in: *Ancient India,* 15 (1959): 67-69; 2) M. N. Deshpande, "The (Ajanta) Caves: Their Historical Perspective", in: *Ajanta Murals,* ed. A. Ghose, New Delhi: Archaeological Survey of India, 1967: 15.

[2] 1) Chongfeng Li, *opere citato* (1993): 85-172; 2) Chongfeng Li, *opere citato* (2003): 63-126.

caves in Kucīna may well have begun earlier, around the second half of the 3rd century AD, while the climax of architectural activity was reached during the 4th and 5th centuries. In the first stage, the ground plan of central-pillar caves at Kizil is rectangular. The ceiling of the main chamber and that of the ambulatory path enclosing the central *stūpa* are barrel-vaulted, with the ceiling of the ambulatory path being lower than that of the main chamber. As a result, the façade of the central *stūpa* acquires a mushroom-like profile (fig.27), with the Indraśālaguhā scene (Indra's visit to the Buddha) shown to us. Mural portraying a line of celestial beings such as the sungod, moongod, windgod, *garuḍa,* and standing Buddha can be seen in the middle of the vault and on its both sides are murals of *jātaka* and *avadāna* stories. A series of scenes of Buddha delivering his sermon were depicted on the lateral walls and the Buddha in *Parinirvāṇa* as well as related events on the sidewalls of the *pradakṣiṇāpatha* (circumambulatory path). The Bodhisattva Maitreya preaching in Tuṣita, moreover, was portrayed in the lunette above the entrance.

During the second stage (fig.28) of development (mid-4th century to 5th century), the back passage was made taller and wider to form a rear chamber, with an image couch cut against the rear wall and a Buddha in *Parinirvāṇa* sculpted on it. This change in design parallels the increase in popularity of the *Parinirvāṇa*-image in Hinduka during that same period. In addition, the central pillar caves built in the 3rd and 4th stages developed on the basis of these caves (fig.29).

The most important element, the mushroom-shaped *stūpa* here, is indeed a three-dimensional representation of the open-air *stūpa* of Kucīna or to be precisely, an ideal representation of a local *stūpa,* and bears a Buddha-image-niche cut out in the façade. This demonstrates that the *stūpa* in the central pillar cave of Kucīna was conceived as a god-shrine, a derivation from the original concept of "tomb" that the *stūpa* maintained in most of the Mahārāshṭran *chētiyagharas.* This same fact suggests that an evolution from a sage to a god had already occurred in regard to how Buddha was viewed as a person [1].

---

[1] 1) Chongfeng Li, *opere citato* (1993): 173-216; 2) Chongfeng Li, *opere citato* (2003): 127-209.

(3) *Stūpa* caves in north China: Through a comparative study, here I will endeavor to show how the *stūpa*-cave of north China evolved from the Mahārāshṭran and Kuchean *chētiyagharas,* both having acted as models for its creation. All the *chētiyagharas* (Cave Nos. 259, 254, 251, 257, 263, 260, 265) of the first period, dating from about 489 to 525 AD, at Mogao, Dunhuang, have a rectangular ground plan and a simplified square pillar (*stūpa*) cut in the centre of the rear area of the cave, with image-niches carved into its four faces. The ceiling around the *stūpa* pillar is flat, whereas the section in front of the *stūpa* is provided with a gabled roof (fig.30).

There are eight *chētiyagharas* (Cave Nos. 1, 2, 4, 6, 11, 39, 5:28, 13:13) at Yungang, Datong. Of which, cave Nos. 1 and 2 were probably designed as twin caves, with rectangular ground plan and flat roof. Each of them has a *stūpa* chiselled in the rear, which is surmounted with a decorative canopy and Sumerū. The *stūpa* which has a low square base consists of two or three storeys, with image-niches cut into its four faces and decorative *dougong* brackets attached on each storey. It should be abstractly an imitation of the towering *stūpa* constructed in timber. A large niche was built into the back wall, while the lateral walls were mostly divided into three friezes or levels, with decorative motifs and *Buddhāsahasa* (Thousand Buddhas) carved on the upper frieze and donors' figures in the lower. A row of image-niches and the storied sequences in low relief, which are arranged in continuous order along horizontal strips, occupy the middle (fig.31). As for the *stūpa*-caves at Gongxian, they are the simplified form of the Yungang *chētiyagharas,* especially the *stūpa* carved out there looking like a square pillar (fig.32).

Despite these differences, one can still observe how the square pillar in the *chētiyaghara* of north China inherited features of the Kuchean model while further developing it by absorbing elements of the Han Chinese tradition and culture. Here, the *stūpa*'s original meaning of "tomb" is absent. The four images in each face of the *stūpa* which show Lord Buddha's enlightenment and preaching the Law clearly indicate that the Buddha had completed his long journey and attained the status of deity abandoning that of a holy person. Moreover, the Sumerū mountain carved atop the *stūpa* is a wonderful place that both mortals and immortals yearn to be in. Therefore, this *stūpa* becomes a special path connecting mortals and immortals or the human and heavenly realms[1].

Through the above analyses, we have seen clearly that cave-temples are not ordinary architecture *per se*. It is a special architecture with a spiritual value attached to it—in fact, created by it. Thus, the correct attitude for a researcher is to view this type of rock-cut architecture as an extraordinary value-laden and value-yielding culture. The ancient Mahārashtrans who invented this culture deserve kudos for their invention. They should also get the credit for spreading this culture not only within, but also beyond the boundaries of Hinduka.

We say that an ideology cannot be exported because any alien thinking has to take root in the recipient country first and cease to appear to be alien before it can gather mass following in the country of its adoption. Similarly, India could not have exported the rock-cut temple architecture to Central Asia and China without the latter's first developing and indigenous temple culture. In other words, the cave-temples would not have been created in China if a socio-cultural milieu similar to that of Mahārāshṭra had not been created there. That *chētiyagharas, lēṇas, maṭapas* as well as free-standing *saṃghārāmas* have spread from the coast of Indian Ocean to as far as Yungang near Datong city, speaks volumes about the powerful movement of Buddhism through history. The Chinese rulers, rich merchants, landlords, and down-trodden masses were driven by a powerful culture to make sacrifices to create the extrordinary celestial surroundings on earth.

In this paper the author not only has mapped out the trail of this powerful movement of the Eastward Ho of *chētiyagharas, lēṇas, maṭapas* and highlighted the important landmarks en route, but also has demonstrated the underlying rhythm of cultural cross-fertilization. The *chētiyagharas,* however, have provided a good example for discussion. There are always two sides to the coin in question. First, a *chētiyaghara* is always a *chētiyaghara,* whether seen in Mahārāshṭra or Kucīna or north China. A *chētiyaghara* is always Mahārāshṭran. Even in the remote Yungang the *chētiyaghara* bears the Mahārāshṭran label for sure. We can

---

[1] 1) Chongfeng Li, *opere citato* (1993): 217-270; 2) Chongfeng Li, *opere citato* (2003): 210-268.

immediately establish a direct linkage between the *chētiyagharas* at Ajaṇṭā and their counterparts at Yungang or Dunhuang. This brings out the universality in the architecture of *chētiyagharas.*

There is also the other side of the coin. As the *chētiyaghara* genre of architecture was born in Mahārāshṭra, it has to be Mahārāshṭran to become a *chētiyaghara.* So also, the adopted form of *chētiyaghara* in north China must first belong to the social-cultural milieu of north China to be there. This makes it necessary to shed some of its alien Mahārāshṭran idiosyncrasies, and supplement them with indigenous characteristics.

For instance, the *stūpa* inside a Mahārāshṭran *chētiyaghara* is a tomb-shaped hemisphere, which is transformed into the shape of a mushroom inside a Kuchean *chētiyaghara,* and further transformed into the shape of a multi-storeyed wooden-like tower inside a north China *chētiyaghara.* We should not treat all this as varying minute details void of larger social significance. In Hinduka the *stūpa* is meant to commemorate the *Nirvāṇa* of Gautama Buddha—the noble sage and culture hero—hence the Mahārāshṭran *chētiyaghara* has it designed like a tomb which is similar to that in the open. In Kucīna, the *stūpa* assumes the shape of a mushroom with a Buddha-image-niche chiselled on its façade. The ancestors of the people of Kucīna discarded the tomb design because a tomb was the house of a dead person while the Buddha was a deity. The social function of the *stūpa* has already undergone a significant change from the symbol of commemoration of the dead sage into that of God-worshipping. When the rock-cut architecture came to north China through Central Asia, the earlier Hinduka significance of commemorating the dead sage further faded in the face of strong wave of worshipping the almighty Buddha—a symbol of power and fortune, a benefactor to mankind in the minds of his Chinese devotees. Hence, the *stūpa* inside a north China *chētiyaghara* has assumed the shape of a towering building signifying the preserve of fortune and power. In order to distinguish this celestial tower from those of the mankind, a design of Mount Sumerū usually crowns the tower-like *stūpa* of a north China *chētiyaghara.* Because of the influence of Buddhism, Chinese, too, have been cherishing the paradise of Meru like Indians. The symbol of paradise Meru has been commonly used in Hinduka temple architecture in all times, but always used suggestively, often creating a sense of admirable loftiness of the entire building, like the peak-like shape of temples you see at Mathurā. The Chinese designs of Mount Meru have, however, been more descriptive than abstract. Anyway, the Chinese freedom in employing the Meru symbol is an added example of the dialectics of cultural cross-fertilization. On the one hand, the Indianness of the origin must be preserved to make it recognizable. On the other hand, the Chineseness of the land of adoption clearly prevails to eliminate an alien feeling[1].

Buddhist art, which originated in Hinduka, was disseminated later in all directions and underwent a process of integration with the cultures of the regions and countries it had reached. As a result, new local styles were created. This phenomenon can be clearly seen in the evolution of the rock-cut architectures as the regional characteristics of each cultural area are most evident in their structure. Indeed, the *chētiyagharas, lēṇas* and *maṭapas* in Mahārāshṭra appear as the Hinduka prototype, while those in Kucīna can be interpreted as the intermediate form between the *chētiyagharas, lēṇas* and *maṭapas* of Mahārāshṭra and those of north China which, in turn, represent the Hanized[2] interpretations. We may conclude that the *chētiyagharas, lēṇas* and *maṭapas* in the above three cultural areas represent three different types of *chētiyaghara, lēṇa* and *maṭapa*: the Indian, the Kuchean and the northern Chinese. The history of the rock-cut architectures in these three regions can also be considered, in some respect, to be the epitome of the history of development of Buddhist cave-temples in general.

(This paper was presented to "*Exploring Buddhist Cave Temple*: *International Conference in honor of Walter M. Spink*", May 24, 2008 Seoul)

---

[1] 1) Chongfeng Li, *opere citato* (1993): 271-280; 2) Chongfeng Li, *opere citato* (2003): 269-271.

[2] The term Hanized and the idea of Hanization may sound to be utterly new, but to the author it appears a preferable term to the usual ones such as Sinicization. The reason for this is that the term Hanization possesses an extensive meaning and so do the term like Khotanization and Kucheanization, whereas here I want to be specific towards our reference to the culture of the Han nationality proper in China.

陕西周至大秦寺塔记

陕西周至（盩厔）大秦寺，因与唐代传入中国的景教（即基督教）关系密切，一直受到学术界的关注。1933年4月25-26日，向达先生曾专程考察了大秦寺，并刊布《盩厔大秦寺略记》[1]，详细记录了当时大秦寺的状况。2001年10月22-24日，笔者再访大秦寺，发现20世纪30年代向达先生记述的大秦寺殿堂已经毁坏，寺内有关文物，如明正统九年铁钟、清乾隆五十七年寺僧墓碣和咸丰九年大秦寺残碑已佚失，惟大秦寺塔尚存。故笔者在前贤调查研究基础上，草就此文。

一、寺塔概况

大秦寺位于陕西省周至县城东南20. 5公里处的塔峪村南，从周至县城出发，沿西（安）宝（鸡）公路东行9公里到终台路口，后南行9公里至楼观台林场路口，再西行2. 5公里即抵大秦寺塔下。塔的方位为北纬34° 03’ 44”，东经108° 18’ 48”。塔全部砖砌，立于五峰邱木山北麓一底长约75米，左边宽76米，右边宽33米的梯形台地上，俯瞰山下塔峪村。

大秦寺塔基座[2]和塔身平面皆作八角形，基座高约0.8米。基座上共立塔身七层，自第二层塔身以上外部仿楼阁式；每层平面向上递减、收进，顶作八角攒尖式，上立椭圆形相轮及铁刹（图1)。

第一层八角形塔身外壁多为1999年加固时重新垒砌，其平面边长4.3米、宽

---

［1］该文以附录形式发表在1933年10月出版的《燕京学报》专号之二《唐代长安与西域文明》上，后收入向达先生论文集《唐代长安与西域文明》，北京：生活·读书·新知三联书店，1957年，第110-116页。

［2］现存基座系1999年春季加固大秦寺塔时在原基座上以砖块砌筑，外包石边。据时任大秦寺文物保管所所长关应见告，原始基座也为砖垒砌。又，笔者在大秦寺考察时承蒙关应、袁渊及该所同仁大力协助，谨此致谢。

10.7米,塔壁厚约4米。北面(正面)辟圆拱形门道,宽1.38米、高2.25米;东、南、西三面各作一圆拱形假门;四偶面素面无饰。现存四正面及四偶面顶部无斗拱,仅有明代沿顶端贴壁砌置的陶质花瓣。塔檐采用叠涩砖挑出和收进的办法,第一、三层砖用菱角牙子挑出,以上到第十三层皆逐层挑出,然后又逐层收进;挑出的檐砖逐层加大,使叠涩呈现出向内拯曲的弧形曲线。

图1　周至大秦寺塔

第二至七层外壁尚存原貌,其中,第二至六层每层正面,即东、南、西、北面对开圆拱形门道两个(图2),交错而上[1];第七层则前后左右对开四门(图3)。第二至七层塔身,每层皆有平座施于下层的塔檐之上,塔檐处理方式同第一层,唯层数向上递减为九至十层。每层门道两侧靠角柱处,残存竖向排列圆孔二或三个;其余正面及四偶面,即东南、西南、东北、西北皆有布局相似的圆

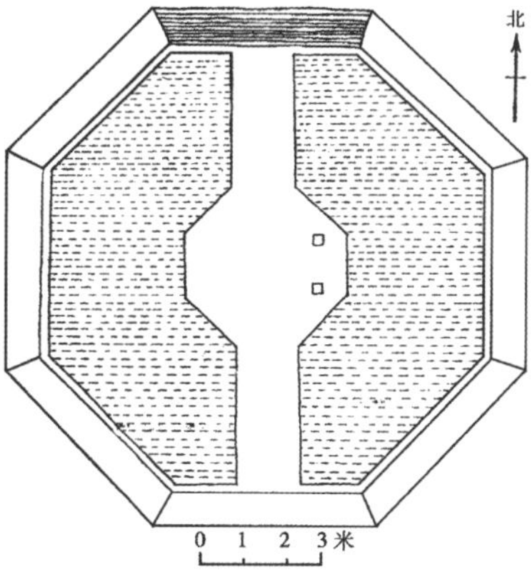

图2　大秦寺塔第二层平面

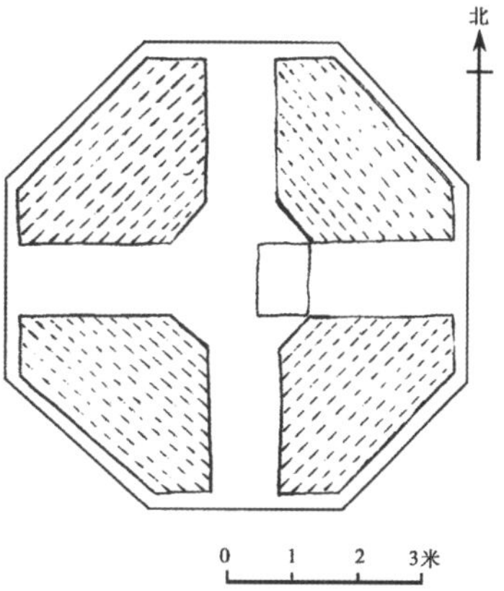

图3　大秦寺塔第七层平面

[1] 第二层门道南北走向,第三层门道东西向,第四层门道南北向,第五层门道东西向,第六层门道南北向。

孔。每层角柱高度均有缩减，各层柱头之间皆施阑额。阑额与柱头相交处，并不出头。柱头直接承托栌斗，不设普拍方。每层角柱间施补间铺作一朵。补间直接施于阑额之上。第二、三、六、七层的柱头铺作及补间铺作皆为一斗三升出耍头的简单作法（把头绞项造），第四、五层的柱头及柱头之间的补间仅用一栌斗（图4）。

图4　大秦寺塔阑额及斗拱

第一层八角形小室左右后三壁环高坛，坛上有清末民国初塑像一铺。小室顶部中央偏西有一圆孔[1]遗迹，原应有木梯通向上层。第二至六层塔内辟八边形小室，无塔心柱之设，但皆有木构楼梯通向上层。其中，第二层楼梯向西，三层向南，四层向东，五层向北，六层向东。

塔内第二、三两层正壁现各存残悬塑一铺。其中，第二层西壁（正壁）悬塑，残高2.83米，宽1.52米。上部是峰峦起伏的嶙峋山石，中部为滴水岩谷造就的石天宫。天宫中央残存一像，作斜倚姿（图5）。该像上半身已毁，右膝弯曲，小腿直立；左膝微曲，大腿及小腿平放座上；左手放置大腿左侧山岩座。

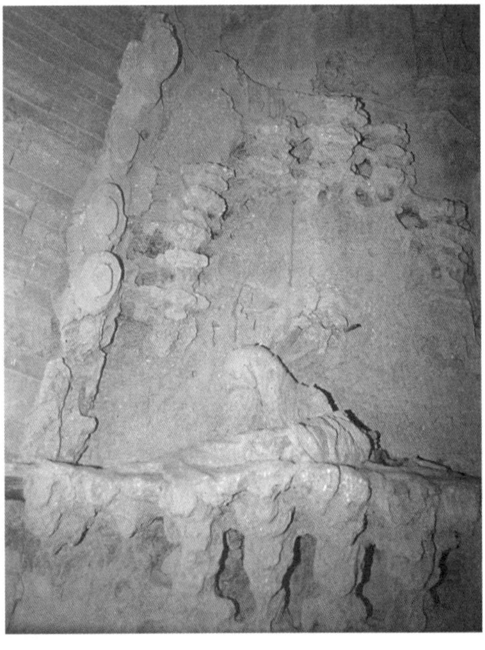

图5　大秦寺塔第二层西壁雕塑

[1] 该孔在1933年4月向达先生游访时已被封堵，封堵时间及原因待考。

斜倚像所着长裙摆边覆于岩座之上（图6）。第三层南壁（正壁）悬塑，残存面积与第二层的大体接近，布局亦基本相似，唯上半部雕塑出三座楼阁型建筑，下半部也作石天宫。宫内主人原侧倚岩壁而坐，现仅存下半身（图7），双腿处理同前者。

图6　大秦寺塔第二层西壁雕塑局部

图7　大秦寺塔第三层南壁雕塑

此外，第四层北侧门道右壁一砖侧面残存一非汉文题刻，第七层南侧门道及西侧门道左壁均阴刻藏文六字真言。

二、营造年代

关于大秦寺塔的建造年代，没有可靠的文字记录。现从建筑、雕塑和有关文献方面做一推测。

建筑　1. 大秦寺塔外观作楼阁式，平面为八角形。据鲍鼎研究[1]，楼阁型佛塔

[1] 关于唐宋时期佛塔的研究，迄今为止仍以20世纪30年代中期鲍鼎于《中国营造学社汇刊》第六卷第四期发表的《唐宋塔之初步分析》最为系统，观点亦中肯。本文关于大秦寺塔建筑方面的论述，主要采自鲍鼎的观点。下文中未注明出处者，皆引自该文。参见《中国营造学社汇刊》，第六卷第四期(1937年)，第1-29页。

平面，“最先概为方形，如唐西安大雁塔等，宋辽时代几尽变作八边形”。这种八边形佛塔，现知年代明确的最早实例，是苏州罗汉院双塔（图 8），建造年代为宋太平兴国七年（982 年）。2. 作为木建筑中的主要结构，柱额在楼阁型佛塔中皆有表现。如唐代楼阁型佛塔均于砖砌墙壁上隐出柱额，柱子或为方形或作八角状；“至于额枋，则仅有阑额无普拍方，宋初诸塔犹多与此相合”。此外，宋代砖石塔中，以角隅隐出圆柱者较多。大秦寺塔于角隅置角柱，阑额之上无普拍方。3. 大雁塔与香积寺塔柱头上仅用斗而无拱，玄奘塔才用简单的一斗三升（图 9）。“终唐之世，塔上所表现的斗拱结构，均非常简单”，“宋辽金时代塔上斗拱的结构，日趋复杂”。大秦寺塔第四、五层柱头及补间皆有斗无拱，第二、三、六、七层铺作皆为简单的一斗三升，似表明其时代较早。4. 唐代楼阁型砖塔“各层门窗，皆设于东、西、南、北四面，遂至塔身重量，集中于其余四面，而门窗下，复无反券补助”[1]，“致空虚部位集中于一垂线，往往全塔自各层门中心线裂开，如大雁塔、香积寺塔等均所不免。宋塔中始有逐层转移门窗之方位者”，如苏州罗汉院双塔和泉州开元寺双塔等。这种新型佛塔，“不但外观参差错落，富于变化，且令壁体重量之分布，较

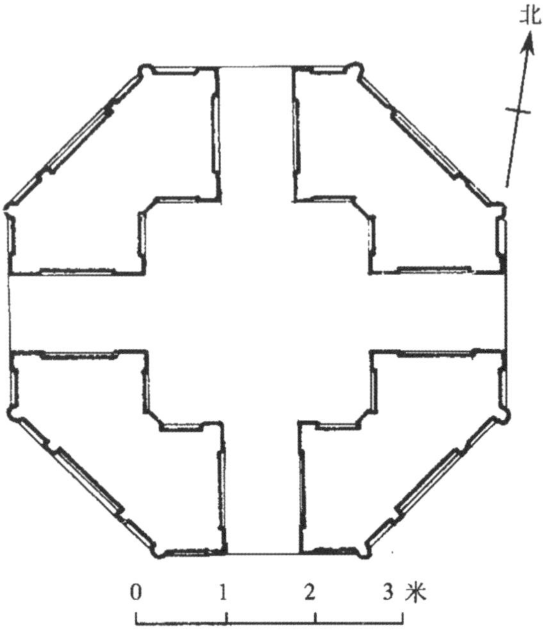

图 8　苏州罗汉院西塔第一层平面图

图 9　西安玄奘塔外景

[1] 刘敦桢《苏州古建筑调查记》，见《刘敦桢文集》二，北京：中国建筑工业出版社，1984 年，第 297 页。

为平均，足证创建当时，经营考案，极费匠心”[1]。大秦寺塔第二至六层对开双门，交错而上，即为宋代造塔的惯常手法。

雕塑　1. 尽管大多数唐宋砖塔外表朴素，但也有施逾量之雕饰者；而石塔则通常于拱门两侧雕造佛像，“塔内壁面亦多满琢佛像，宗教色彩较为浓厚”。大秦寺塔身表面残存的竖向规则圆孔，原来应为固定佛教造像之用。这种布局，应是受到当时砖石塔内外雕造佛像的影响。2. 大秦寺塔内第二层西壁和第三层南壁残存的造像，应是水月观音。1933 年 4 月向达先生考察周至大秦寺时，曾明确记述该塔“第二级第三级西壁[2]俱塑有观自在像作斜倚势，彩饰全然剥落，只余泥胎，然其姿态之幽静，身段之优美，令人见而起肃静之感。疑为古塑，即非李唐，亦当为宋元高手之作，近代工匠不能企及也”[3]。向先生虽然没有进一步说明他们是水月观音，但对观音像姿态的描写是非常准确的。因此，向达先生《盩厔大秦寺略记》，应是这两铺造像现存的最早文字记录。据画史记载，堪称佛像画“模范”四家之一的周昉，所绘“菩萨端严，妙创水月之体”[4]。周昉为唐代中期杰出的画家，主要活动似在 8 世纪下半叶[5]。《历代名画记》卷三《记两京外州寺观画壁》明载长安胜光寺“塔东南院，周昉画水月观自在菩萨掩障，菩萨圆光及竹，并是刘整成色”[6]。《太平广记》卷二百十三引《画断》“周昉条”，亦记“今上都有观自在菩萨，时人云：水月”[7]。作为唐代绘画“神品”第二人，周昉创作的水月观音像，颇为时人喜好。《文苑英华》卷七百八十三辑录唐代诗人白居易《画水月菩萨赞》一首：“画水月菩萨赞周助[8]画：净渌水上，虚白光中，一睹其相，万缘皆空。弟子居易，誓心皈依，生生劫劫，长为我师”[9]。这既表达了白居易对水月观音的信仰，也道出了水月观音像所映现出的宗教神秘境界。由于这个独创的主题及其美妙的图像极富艺术性与宗教性，于是在绘画界迅速流行开来，而且遍及京师及周边各地[10]。《益州名画录》卷上记载成都大慈

---

[1] 同前注。

[2] 第三层雕塑在南壁。此言西壁，疑向先生笔误。

[3] 向达《盩厔大秦寺略记》，见向达《唐代长安与西域文明》，北京：三联书店，1957 年，第 114 页。

[4] 张彦远《历代名画记》，秦仲文、黄苗子点校，北京：人民美术出版社，1963 年，第 201 页。

[5] 金维诺《〈纨扇仕女图〉与周昉》，见金维诺《中国美术史论集》，北京：人民美术出版社，1981 年，第 181 页。

[6] 张彦远，上引书，第 62 页。

[7] 李昉等编《太平广记》，点校本，北京：中华书局，1961 年，第 1632 页。

[8] “助”应为“昉”字之讹。

[9] 李昉等《文苑英华》，影印本，北京：中华书局，1966 年，第 4137 页。

[10] 史岩《杭州南山区雕刻史迹初步调查》，见《文物参考资料》，1956 年第 1 期，第 14 页。

寺“文殊阁东畔水月观音”，系“声驰阙下”的左全在宝历(825-827年)中完成[1]；而被誉为“神格”第二人的范琼，自唐宣宗大中至僖宗乾符年间(847-880年)，与陈皓、彭坚于圣寿寺、圣兴寺、净众寺和中兴寺“图画二百余间墙壁”，其中圣寿寺就画有水月观音像[2]。五代以后，这一题材更加盛行[3]，见于文献的如王霭[4]、武宗元[5]、黄居宷[6]、吴元瑜[7]等都曾画过水月观音。现存最早的有明确纪年的水月观音图像，应是法国巴黎集美博物馆收藏的一幅绘于五代后晋天福八年(943年)的绢画[8]。该画系伯希和1907年从敦煌藏经洞劫掠。画面中，水月观音头戴宝冠，面相方圆，袒上身，下着裙；挂项饰，佩臂钏，戴手镯，璎珞环身。观音游戏坐于山岩座上，左手托钵，右手持柳枝；右膝弯曲，腿脚平放座上，左腿压覆右踝，左脚自然垂下，跣足踏于水中莲花。观音周围环以圆光，身后绘出翠竹和塔形植物，山岩座下画出流水。值得注意的是，观音右前方白色榜题框内明确书写“水月观音菩萨”字样[9]。此外，原北平日本山中商会也曾收藏一幅宋乾德六年(968年)“南无大悲救苦水月观音菩萨”绢画[10]。除纸、绢画外，这一形象屡见于五代、宋、西夏和蒙元的包括莫高窟、榆林窟、东千佛洞和五个庙在内的敦煌石窟壁画中和延安、杭州[11]、大足[12]等地的五代、宋、金和元代石窟雕刻里。其中，敦煌石窟水月观音壁画现存31幅[13]，

---

[1] 黄休复《益州名画录》，秦岭云点校，北京：人民美术出版社，1964年，第12页。

[2] 黄休复，上引书，第3-4页。

[3] 据[宋]刘道醇《圣朝名画评》卷一记载，作为宋代“人物门”神品画家，“(武)宗元亦不常奋笔，虽贵人名臣日走于门，求之甚勤，未尝肯诺。京师富商高生，今安远门中茶铺者是也，有画癖，常刺拜于庭下迨十余年，欲得《水月观音》一轴。宗元许之，又三年方成。携诣高生，生已殂矣。焚画垂泣而去”(据泰东图书局民国十一年景印王世贞编《王氏画苑》本叶五)。这从另一方面说明当时人们对水月观音图像的喜好。此外，五代时期简短易颂的伪经——《佛说水月观音菩萨经》的流传，可能进一步促进了水月观音信仰的流布。参见王惠民《敦煌写本水月观音经研究》，见《敦煌研究》，1992年第3期，第93-97页。

[4] 刘道醇，上引书，叶二。

[5] 刘道醇，上引书，叶五。

[6] 《宣和画谱》，俞剑华标点注译，北京：人民美术出版社，1964年，第270页。

[7] 同上书，第296页。

[8] 画面正中绘千手眼大悲像，右下方画水月观音(画幅仅为55×55厘米)，左下方绘一女供养人及侍女，正下方书写长篇纪年题记。

[9] ジャック・ジエス編，秋山光和監修《西域美術：ギメ美術館ペリオ・コレクション；ジャン・フランソワ・ジャリージエ》，東京：講談社，1994年，図86。

[10] 松本榮一《燉煌畫の研究：圖像篇・附圖》，東京：東方文化學院東京研究所，1937年，图222b。

[11] 浙江省文物考古研究所编《西湖石窟》，杭州：浙江人民出版社，1986年，第56、57、126、156、168、190页。

[12] 李永翘、胡文和《大足石刻内容总录》，载刘长久等编《大足石刻研究》，成都：四川省社会科学院出版社，1985年，第386、391、393、437、542、558、566-567页。

[13] 敦煌研究院编《敦煌石窟内容总录》，北京：文物出版社，1996年，第278页。

延安石窟水月观音雕像现存至少 80 余壁[1],由此可见其盛。至于中国石窟中现存有明确纪年、最早的水月观音像,是史岩先生 1955 年在杭州西湖石屋洞发现的五代后汉乾祐二年 (950 年) 雕造的水月观音[2]。据史岩先生调查,该观音像虽经后代恶劣重装,但"像的姿态极为自然舒适,作坐于岩石上休息的样子,左脚下垂踏于莲花,右脚上屈踏于岩上,左手按着岩石,支撑着微倒的身体,右臂置于膝头,背光以月亮的光圆代替,作大圆形。毫无疑问,这是以'水月观音'为主题的典型的构图"[3]。敦煌五代、宋时期的水月观音壁画现存 14 幅,主要集中在莫高窟,少数在榆林窟[4]。这一时期的水月观音,全部画在洞窟前室或甬道。水月观音通常坐在上大下小的山岩座上,一腿弯曲横置座上,另一腿压覆其上并自然下垂,脚踏水中莲台; 菩萨一手持净瓶,一手拈柳枝。画面中没有出现月亮[5]。大足宋代石窟中的水月观音像,造型与此基本接近[6],此不赘。至于敦煌石窟中沙州回鹘、西夏[7]和蒙元时期的水月观音壁画,现存达 17 幅之多,分布在莫

[1] 2000 年 9-11 月,北京大学考古系佛教考古方向研究生何利群对延安地区 20 多处宋金时期开凿的佛教石窟进行了较为详细的踏查。这次调查,主要是为他撰写硕士学位论文收集资料。回京后,何利群先整理出《延安地区佛教石窟调查报告》(现存北京大学考古系资料室),后完成学位论文《延安地区宋金石窟分期研究》。据该调查报告并承何利群见告,延安地区钟山第 3、5 窟,万佛洞第 1、2、4 窟,石泓寺第 2 窟,马渠寺第 2 窟,柳园石窟,招安第 3、7 窟,樊庄第 2 窟,城台石窟,孟家坬第 5 窟,黄陵万佛寺等都有这一题材。有的一座洞窟之内重复雕镌十几幅水月观音像,如钟山第 3 窟雕出 12 幅,石泓寺第 2 窟雕 10 幅。参见延安地区群众艺术馆编《延安宋代石窟艺术》,西安: 陕西人民美术出版社,1983 年,第 26、28、44、58、71-73、75、87-89、91-93、100 页。

[2] 尽管该像右侧题铭在史岩先生调查时"文字已剥落难辨",但[清]丁敬《武林金石记》卷五和阮元《两浙金石志》卷四皆有录文,文多残缺,后者录之较详。参见清光绪十六年 (1890 年) 浙江书局刊本《两浙金石志》卷四叶二十七。从铭文和阮元按语知道,朱知家所镌观自在菩萨的确是一躯"水月观音",地点就在杭州西湖石屋洞。据新近检出资料,四川绵阳圣水寺第 3 龛的水月观音像,系"唐中和五年 (885 年) 敬造",应为中国石窟中现存最早的水月观音纪年像。参见: 文齐国《绵阳唐代佛教造像初探》,刊《四川文物》,1991 年第 5 期,第 47-53 页。

[3] 史岩,上引书,第 14 页,图十。

[4] 莫高窟第 6、124、176、203、294、331、427、431 窟和榆林窟第 20、38 窟都有这一题材,有些洞窟,如莫高窟第 294、431 窟和榆林窟第 20、38 窟则成对出现。参见: 敦煌研究院编,上引书,第 6、47、70、80、120、135、173、176、211、219 页。

[5] 王惠民《敦煌水月观音像》,见《敦煌研究》,1987 年第 1 期,第 33-34 页。

[6] 大足北山佛湾第 113、128、133 窟,北塔第 10 窟,石门山第 4 窟,妙高山第 5 窟,佛安桥第 6 窟都雕有这一题材。其中,石门山第 4 窟有宋绍圣元年 (1094 年)、佛安桥第 6 窟有宋绍兴十年 (1140 年)、妙高山第 5 窟有宋绍兴二十五年 (1155 年) 的题记。参见: 李永翘,胡文和,上引书,第 542、566-567、558 页。

[7] 沙州回鹘在瓜、沙主要活动于 976-1050 年前后的七十余年,而西夏于北宋仁宗景祐三年 (1036 年) 占领瓜、沙二州,至南宋理宗宝庆三年 (1227 年) 被蒙古所灭,统治瓜沙近两个世纪。参见: 1) 刘玉权《敦煌莫高窟、安西榆林窟西夏洞窟分期》,载敦煌文物研究所编《敦煌研究文集》,兰州: 甘肃人民出版社,1982 年,第 273-318 页; 2) 刘玉权《关于沙州回鹘洞窟的划分》,见《1987 敦煌石窟研究国际讨论会文集: 石窟考古》,沈阳: 辽宁美术出版社,1990 年,第 3 页; 3) 王静如《敦煌莫高窟和安西榆林窟中的西夏壁画》,见《王静如民族研究文集》,北京: 民族出版社,1998 年,第 347-355 页。

高窟、榆林窟、东千佛洞和五个庙等四处[1]。沙州回鹘和西夏时期的水月观音，大部分画在洞窟主室，画幅较前期增大，有的俨然鸿篇巨制。这说明，水月观音题材此时颇为流行。其中，榆林第2窟前壁门道两侧的水月观音，堪称这一时期的杰作。该窟门北侧那铺，画面中表现茫茫南海和寥廓景色(图10)。在透明的巨大圆光里，

图10　安西榆林窟第2窟前壁北侧壁画水月观音

观音于石天宫[2]内斜倚岩壁而坐，头戴宝冠，长发披肩，佩项饰、臂钏和手镯。袒上身，下着红蓝双色长裙，披绿色长巾。右膝微曲，腿平放山岩座之上；左膝微抬，双脚并放。右手曲至胸前托钵，左手自然放置左膝之上，仪态闲适。披巾及裙摆覆于座上。座前水中有莲花两朵，左侧岩石上放置柳枝净瓶。观音所倚岩壁矗立云中，石缝间可见修竹。座下水面平静，上方彩云浮动。左上方一轮弯月高悬，与观音周

[1] 具体洞窟有莫高窟第95、164、237窟，榆林窟第2、21、29窟，东千佛洞第2、5窟，五个庙第1、4窟。其中，除莫高窟第95窟和东千佛第5窟外，其余洞窟皆绘双铺。参见：敦煌研究院编，上引书，第37、65、93、204、212、215、222、223、225、226页。

[2] 石天宫在印度布呾落迦山(Potalaka)，唐玄奘《大唐西域记》卷十一“秣罗矩吒国”条曾记述此山。我国浙江普陀山由此得名。下文注释所述《华严经》中善财童子“五十三参”的第二十五参就有普陀洛迦山的描述。唐代周昉“妙创水月之体”，也许依据了这样的记载，抑或在普陀落迦观音图像的基础上创作而成。参见：1) 玄奘《大唐西域记》，季羡林等校注，北京：中华书局，1985年，第861-862页；2) 王惠民《敦煌水月观音像》，上引书，第35页；3) 李玉珉《中国观音的信仰与图像》，见台北故宫博物院编辑委员会编《观音特展》，台北：故宫博物院，2000年，第27页。

围巨大的透明圆光交相辉映；左前方一童子乘云而来，向观音合掌行礼[1]；左下方画面，为“唐僧取经”[2]。该窟门南侧的水月观音，与北侧的对称布局，构图亦基本相似[3]。值得注意的是，榆林第 2 窟前壁的两幅水月观音，都把双腿放置在山岩座上[4]。这种姿态，与大秦寺塔内的两铺水月观音相同。此外，敦煌石窟中沙州回鹘和西夏时期的水月观音像绝大多数成双出现，大秦寺塔二、三层正壁的经营应与之有关，只是限于空间改为上下层而已。延安地区宋代石窟中的水月观音像[5]，保存数量极多，以钟山、万佛洞和石泓寺等处最具代表性。除上述通常特征[6]之外，延安石窟水月观音像最值得注意者有两点：A. 水月观音像不但镌于窟壁表面，也雕于佛坛上塔柱之内，如钟山第 3 窟和石泓寺第 2 窟[7]。B. 水月观音周围除镌刻流水、山石、树木、莲花以及童子、龙女及行者外，观音身后还雕出了木构亭阁，如万佛洞第 4 窟右壁。故而，大秦寺塔内雕造水月观音、观音身后出现木构楼阁也就不是孤例了。

文献　关于周至大秦寺塔的文献资料，现存最早者是北宋苏东坡于仁宗嘉祐七年（1062 年）二月朝谒大秦寺所做的记述[8]及英宗治平元年（1064 年）元月重游故地时所作《大秦寺》诗：“晃荡平川尽，坡陁翠麓横；忽逢孤塔迥，独向乱山明；信足幽寻远，临风却立惊；原田浩如海，滚滚尽东倾”[9]。这表明苏东坡游历此地时，大秦寺似完好。此前塔寺，无明文记载。经检乾隆《重修盩厔县志》卷五《祠祀》，“大

---

[1] 这个场景，一般认为是善财童子在洛迦山寻拜观音。传说善财童子在文殊处发心，而后南行“五十三参”；拜观音是其中的第二十七参。

[2] 王静如先生早在 1973 年就完成了这一题材的考释，但直到 1980 年才在《文物》第 9 期上发表了他的研究成果。参见：王静如，上引书，第 353-354 页。

[3] 参见《中国石窟·安西榆林窟》，北京：文物出版社，1997 年，图版 137。

[4] 榆林窟第 21 窟的水月观音，双腿处理也是如此。此外，大足北山第 133 窟的水月观音和杭州飞来峰青林洞顶部、玉皇山南麓宋代雕造的水月观音像都是这种姿态。参见：1) 王惠民《敦煌水月观音像》，上引书，第 35 页；2) 浙江省文物考古研究所编，上引书，第 56、57 页。

[5] 据何利群调查，延安地区石窟中的水月观音像最早出现在北宋庆历二年（1042 年）开凿的柳园石窟，大量雕造于 11 世纪后期至 12 世纪初的北宋石窟中。参见何利群《延安地区宋金石窟分期研究》（硕士学位论文），北京：北京大学，2001 年，第 17-19 页。

[6] 参见：何利群，上引书，第 9、23 页。

[7] 延安地区群众艺术馆编，上引书，第 26、72、73 页。

[8] 据苏东坡《南山纪行诗》自序：“壬寅（1062 年）二月，有诏令郡吏分往属县减决囚禁。自十三日受命出府，至宝鸡、虢、郿、盩厔四县。既毕事，因朝谒太平宫，而宿于南溪溪堂，遂并南山而西，至楼观、大秦寺、延生观、仙游潭。十九日乃归。作诗五百言，以记凡所经历者寄子由。”参见[清]王文诰辑注《苏轼诗集》，孔凡礼点校，北京：中华书局，1982 年，第 122 页。

[9] [清]王文诰辑注，上引书，第 194 页。

秦寺在黑水谷东”[1]；而民国《盩厔县志》卷一《地理》条则详记“五峰邱木山在县东三十五里塔谷，山腰有大秦寺。旧碣[2]记宋建隆四年重修，寺内有镇仙宝塔（详见古迹）。塔侧一井，土人名曰御井……镇仙宝塔在县东南塔峪，高约七八丈，八稜形，相传为唐太宗敕建”[3]。据此记载，大秦塔相传最初为唐太宗(627-649年在位）敕建，大秦寺及镇仙宝塔[4]曾在宋太祖建隆四年(963年）重修。

以上我们从建筑、雕塑和相关文献三个方面对大秦寺塔进行了初步整理。从建筑方面看，大秦寺塔既有唐、五代佛塔之因素，如简朴的斗拱和无普拍方的额枋，又有宋代流行的成分，如八角形平面和逐层交错辟门，因此，塔的年代似当五代末至宋初。从雕塑方面来讲，水月观音系宋和西夏流行的题材，敦煌石窟从五代、宋开始流行每窟对称画水月观音的做法，这点在大秦寺塔第二、三层均有反映；而延安宋代石窟中水月观音像盛行以及观音雕于塔柱之内及其身后出现木构亭阁的设计，或与大秦寺塔内的悬塑有关。考虑到新样式传到边区会有一段时间，故将大秦寺塔内水月观音像定为宋代前期比较合适。基于上述两个方面，我们认为民国《盩厔县志》所言大秦寺有宋建隆四年重修碑碣是可信的。

三、宗教属性

周至大秦寺之名始于何时，文献无证。据前引苏东坡《南山纪行诗》及自注[5]，至少在北宋嘉祐七年该寺已称大秦寺。不过，从苏东坡所记，大秦寺“在宋时亦寻常伽蓝耳，无胡僧，无十字架，无称述景教碑碣，足招东坡注意也”[6]。此前之大秦寺，是否为唐时景教寺院，似可做些推测。据《大秦景教流行中国碑》(下文文献未注明出处者皆引

---

[1] 杨仪修、王开沃纂《(乾隆）盩厔县志》，清乾隆五十年刻本。

[2] 向达先生1933年4月25-26日游访周至大秦寺时曾记述过这块旧碣，但明确指出“今已无存”。参见：向达，上引书，第113页。

[3] 庞文中修，任肇新、路孝愉纂《(民国）盩厔县志》，铅印本，西安：艺林印书社，1925年，第5、47页。

[4] 金代俗称此塔为白塔。杨云翼于金承安四年至泰和元年(1199-1221年）任陕西东路兵马都总管判官时曾参谒过大秦寺，有诗为证：“寺废基空在，人归地自闲。绿苔昏碧瓦，白塔映青山。暗谷行云度，苍烟独鸟还。唤回尘土梦，聊此弄澄湾。”参见：1) 脱脱等《金史》，点校本，北京：中华书局，1975年，第2421页；2) 元好问编《中州集》卷四，影印明毛晋刊本，台北：台湾商务印书馆，1973年，第69页。

[5] 苏东坡记述到：“是日（二月十八日）游崇圣观，俗所谓楼观也。乃尹喜旧宅。山脚有授经台，尚在。遂与张杲之同至大秦寺，早食而别。有太平观道士赵宗有，抱琴见送，至寺，作鹿鸣之引，乃去。”参见：[清]王文诰辑注，上引书，第128页。

[6] 洪业《驳景教碑出土于盩厔说》，见《洪业论学集》，北京：中华书局，1981年，第62页。

自此碑),以景教大德阿罗本 (Alopen) 为团长的大秦景教宣教师团于“贞观九祀 (635 年) 至于长安。帝使宰臣房公玄龄,惣仗西郊,宾迎入内”。至贞观十二年 (638 年) 七月诏敕,景教乃为唐朝公认;太宗更动用国库[1],“即于京(长安)义宁坊造大秦寺一所,度僧二十一人”。这应是景教正式流行中国之始。高宗 (650-683 年在位) 时,“于诸州各置景寺,仍崇阿罗本为镇国大法主,法流十道[2],国富无休;寺满百城,家殷景福……肃宗文明皇帝 (756-762 年在位) 于灵武等五郡重立景寺”。至代宗 (763-779 年在位) 时,“每于降诞之辰,锡天香以告成功,颁御馔以光景众”。时景教信奉达到高潮。780 年即位的德宗皇帝更“阐九畴,以惟新景命”。在这种情况下,景教僧人于建中二年 (781 年) 竖立《景教碑》。当时“术高三代、艺博十全”的金紫光禄大夫、同朔方节度副使、试殿中监、赐紫袈裟僧伊斯,更于“每岁集四寺僧徒,虔事精供,备诸五旬”。此“四寺”,英人理雅各 (James Legge) 译作四方各堂或四寺[3],日人佐伯好郎推定为长安义宁坊、洛阳修善坊、灵武和周至四座大秦寺[4],朱谦之先生在同意佐伯好郎说的同时,认为它“亦可指长安附近之四寺,即包括周至之大秦寺”[5]。若然,周至大

---

[1] 有人认为唐代大部分景教寺院,都是官方出资建造的。参见杨森富《唐元两代基督教兴废原因之研究》,见林治平主编《基督教入华百七十年纪念集》,台北:宇宙光出版社,1984 年,第 52 页。

[2]“十道”中的关内、剑南和河南道确曾设立大秦寺。其中:1)《景教碑》明确记载关内道的长安义宁坊和灵武均建有大秦寺;2) 剑南道的成都也建有大秦寺,位于西门外石笥街。[宋]吴曾《能改斋漫录》卷七《杜石笥行》引赵清献《蜀郡故事》云:“石笥在衙西门外,二株双蹲。云真珠楼基也。昔有胡人,于此立寺,为大秦寺。其门楼十间……此寺,大秦国人所建也”;3) 作为东都,河南道洛阳的大秦寺详见于《唐会要》卷四十九“大秦寺”条:“贞观十二年七月,诏曰:‘道无常名,圣无常体,随方设教,密济群生。波斯僧阿罗本,远将经教,来献上京,详其教旨,元妙无为,生成立要,济物利人,宜行天下。所司即于义宁坊建寺一所,度僧廿一人。’天宝四载九月,诏曰:‘波斯经教,出自大秦,传习而来,久行中国。爰初建寺,因以为名,将欲示人,必修其本。其两京波斯寺,宜改为大秦寺;天下诸府郡置者,亦准此。’”参见:1) 吴曾《能改斋漫录》,点校本,上海:上海古籍出版社,1979 年,第 190 页;2) 王溥《唐会要》,影印本,北京:中华书局,1955 年,第 864 页。

此外,有些学者根据日人佐伯好郎刊布的《小岛文书》认为,陇右道沙洲,唐代开元前后也有大秦寺。不过,林悟殊和荣新江两先生认为《小岛文书》可能是古董商在李盛铎去世后伪造而成的。为谨慎起见,笔者暂不列入沙州大秦寺。参见:1) 佐伯好郎《清朝基督教の研究:附録》,東京:春秋社,1949 年,第 1-24 页;2) 林悟殊、荣新江《所谓李氏旧藏敦煌景教文献二种辩伪》,见《九州学刊》,1992 年第 4 卷第 4 期,第 19-34 页。

[3] 原文为 all the monasteries。不过,理雅各于该页脚注中又写作 four monasteries, or the monasteries of the four quarters。参见 James Legge, *The Nestorian Monument of Hsi-An Fu in Shen-hsi, China*, London: Trübner & Co., 1888: 25.

[4] P. Y. Saeki, *The Nestorian Documents and Relics in China*, Tokyo: The Academy of Oriental Culture, Tokyo Institute, 1937: 99-100.

[5] 朱谦之《中国景教:唐景教碑新探》,铅印本,北京:中国社会科学院世界宗教研究所,1982 年,第 108 页。

秦寺在唐朝建中年间已成为著名的景教寺院了[1]。至于大秦寺的废弃,应与唐武宗会昌法难有关。《旧唐书·武宗本纪》云:"[会昌五年(845年)秋七月]大秦穆护等祠,释教已厘革,邪法不可独存。其人并勒还俗,递归本贯充税户。如外国人,送还本处收管"[2]。僧徒被收管,景寺遭破坏,该地佛事的再次复兴,可能就是北宋初年的佛教重修了。或许将来的考古发掘,可为此提供确切的证据。

最后要说的是,关于《景教碑》的出土地点,学者论述颇多,归纳起来有四种,即长安说、盩厔说、三原说和长安盩厔之间说[3],且以长安、盩厔两说较为流行[4]。洪业1932年4月20日于《史学年报》第四期发表长文《驳景教碑出土于盩厔说》。该文从十个方面论证景教碑所立原地必在长安,出土处即长安大秦寺旧址[5]。洪业先生之说,较为可信。

(本文原刊《文物》2002年第6期第84-93页,此次重刊调换插图三张并改正了印刷错误。)

[1] 方豪及杨森富先生也认为周至唐代建有大秦寺。参见:1)方豪《中西交通史》,影印本,长沙:岳麓书社,1987年,第419页;2)杨森富《唐元两代基督教兴废原因之研究》,上引书,第35页。

[2] 刘昫等《旧唐书》,点校本,北京:中华书局,1975年,第605页。

[3] 参见:1)向达,上引书,第110页;2)朱谦之,上引书,第37-39页。

[4] 林悟殊《西安景教碑研究述评》,见刘东主编《中国学术》第四辑,北京:商务印书馆,2000年,第253-256页。

[5] 参见:洪业,上引书,第56-63页。

四、川滇窟龛：

汉化余韵

安岳圆觉洞调查记

圆觉洞窟群,位于安岳县城东南2公里的云居山上,分为前山(北崖)和后山(南崖)两处,1961年被公布为四川省文物保护单位。云居山,在北宋太平兴国年间(976-984年)乐史纂辑的《太平寰宇记》卷八十七《安岳县》作"灵居山",南宋宁宗嘉定和理宗宝庆年间(1208-1227年)王象之完成的《舆地纪胜》卷一百五十八《普州》仍作"灵居山",唯在南宋理宗嘉熙年间(1237-1240年)刻印的祝穆《方舆胜览》卷六十三《普州》作"云居山"。元《圣朝混一方舆胜览》卷中关于"普州"资料,系摘抄自《方舆胜览》,亦作"云居山"。《明一统志》卷七十一《潼川州・山川》及嘉庆《四川通志》卷十八《舆地・山川》皆从"云居山"。现通称云居山[1]。

一、现存最早的纪年龛像

第71号龛位于云居山后山西端,平面凸字形,右侧龛壁及顶部现残。造像组合原为一铺七身,现存五身。主尊结跏趺坐于束腰八角座上,头戴莲花冠,面相方圆,双眼微睁,两腮略鼓,双唇微闭;内着交领衣,外穿对襟"绛衣",且于胸前系带,下摆垂覆座上;双手均残。主尊右侧存立像一身,头残,外穿交领道服,脚穿云头履。双手屈置胸前,手已残,似合十。主尊左侧存立像两身,其中,内侧立像与主尊右侧的相似。外侧立像头残损,头两侧各有一飘带垂至上臂;内着交领衣,外穿对襟道衣且于胸前系带,脚穿云头履;双臂前伸,手已残,戴项饰、臂钏和璎珞。龛外左侧现存力

[1] 圆觉洞窟群,原称千佛院,北宋徽宗大观二年(1108年)前后改称真相院,南宋高宗绍兴二十八年(1158年)前后作真相寺。参见:1)王象之《舆地纪胜》,影印本,北京:中华书局,1992年,第4289-4292页;2)祝穆撰、祝洙增订《方舆胜览》,施和金点校,北京:中华书局,2003年,第1110页;3)圆觉洞第10、14窟内题铭。

图 1　安岳云居山圆觉洞第 71 号龛

士一身，头已毁，宽肩厚胸，臀部向左扭曲；右臂略外张，小臂及手残毁；左臂屈举握拳，手已残；袒裸上身，下着短裙，腰中束带。双脚残损（图 1）。

龛前左侧壁上方有楷书题铭五行[1]，行 12 字，行间有阴刻方格：“大唐开元廿四年岁次丙子□/月十五日前州仓督安岳县录/事骑都尉勋官五品黎令宾愿/平安敬造天尊像一龛永为供/养栖岩寺上座释沙门玄应书。”（图 2）

图 2　云居山圆觉洞第 71 号龛左侧题铭

据现存造像并结合题记，第 71 号龛像是唐开元廿四年（736 年）前普州仓督、安岳县录事、骑都尉勋官五品黎令宾祈愿平安所造，主像为道教“天尊”[2]。值得注意的是，安岳县千佛崖（栖岩寺）第 37、38 号龛，亦系黎令宾所造，但题材内容与前述龛像迥然不同。其中，第 37 号为三世佛；第 38 号是三立观音（图 3）。两龛之间阴刻造像记：“开元廿年岁次壬申十二月庚午朔十八日丁亥（733 年 1 月 8 日）/前安岳县录事骑都尉勋官五品黎令宾愿平/安造东面三世诸佛一龛又为亡父亡母及亡妻/敬造西面救苦观世音菩萨一龛三身并永为供/养前安居县市令普慈县助教笈恪男前州

[1] 题记第一行全部及第四行中间三字早年被人故意凿损，余行文字清晰。经现场仔细辨识残迹，缺损文字大部可恢复，现书于框内。

[2] 从纪年题记及龛像所在位置推断，这是云居山现存最早的一铺造像。换言之，云居山最早的宗教遗迹并非佛教，而是属于道教。考虑到《舆地纪胜》卷一百五十八《普州》“灵居山……其上为真相寺，有千佛龛、葛仙洞”，灵居山（云居山）最初可能仅为道教场所，晚唐以后佛教在此逐渐盛行，且于五代、宋达到高潮。道、佛二教在云居山共处，各有自己的礼拜场所，甚至出现了若干佛道合龛像。参见：王象之，上引书，第 4291 页。

图 3　安岳千佛崖第 38 号龛三观音

市令/县尉勋官七品虔运亦永供养寺上座玄应书。"[1] 显然,这是一处佛教遗迹。

黎令宾开元二十年 (732 年) 在千佛岩敬造三世佛与观世音,四年后 (736 年) 又在云居山大造天尊像,疑与唐朝皇帝兼崇释老的政策有关。

据汤用彤研究,唐玄宗 "酖嗜神秘,初不信佛,而好道术"[2]。开元三年 (715 年) 作《玄元皇帝赞》,称 "万教之祖,号曰玄元,东训尼父,西化金仙"[3]; 而天宝改元诏文明言,"朕粤自君临,载弘道教,崇清静之化,畅玄元之风,庶乎泽及苍生"[4]。玄宗即位之初,实施崇道抑佛策略,一方面继续打着老子旗号神化大唐,另一方面也为了消除武则天崇佛以来的政治影响[5]。尽管如此,他后来还是采用了释老兼崇之举措[6]。开元十二年闰十二月十一日 (725 年 1 月 29 日),就青城山常道观和飞赴寺佛道相争事,下敕区分道佛,使毋争夺[7]。开元十八年 (730 年),玄宗召沙门和道士于花萼楼,"御定二教优劣"。沙门道氤与道士尹谦对辩论议,玄宗 "再三叹羡,诏赐绢五佰匹,用充法施。别集《对御论衡》一本,盛传于代"[8]。"开元二十六年正月丁

[1] 此题记书体及款式,与云居山第 71 号龛题铭相同; 惜岩石风化,有些字迹已泯灭不清。参见: 1) 王家佑《安岳石窟造像》,见《敦煌研究》,1989 年第 1 期,第 46 页; 2) 傅成金《安岳石刻之玄应考》,见《四川文物》,1991 年第 3 期,第 48 页。

[2] 汤用彤《隋唐佛教史稿》,北京: 中华书局,1982 年,第 27 页。

[3] 谢守灏《混元圣纪》卷八,见《正统道藏》第 30 册,台北: 艺文印书馆,1977 年,第 23827 页。

[4] 谢守灏,同上书,第 23834 页。

[5] 任继愈主编《中国道教史》(修订本),北京: 中国社会科学出版社,2001 年,第 291 页。

[6] 汤用彤,上引书,第 26-27 页。

[7] 文作 "使佛道两所,各有区分"。参见陆增祥《八琼室金石补正》卷五十三《青城山常道观敕》,影印本,北京: 文物出版社,1985 年,第 360 页。

[8] 赞宁《宋高僧传 · 道氤传》,范祥雍点校,北京: 中华书局,1987 年,第 98 页。

酉(738年2月21日)制曰：道释二门,皆为圣教；义归弘济,理在尊崇。其天下观、寺,大小各度一十七人。简择灼然有经业、戒行为乡间所推,仍先取年高者。"[1]开元二十六年六月一日(738年6月22日),"敕每州各以郭下定形胜观、寺,改以开元为额"[2]。"二十七年(739年)二月制：天下观、寺,每于斋日,宜转读经典,愍恶劝善,以阐文教。"[3]。天宝三载(744年)三月,"两京及天下诸郡于开元观、开元寺以金铜铸帝等身、天尊及佛各一"[4]。具体在佛教方面,开元七年(719年),玄宗召见远游天竺而归的沙门慧日,赐号慈愍三藏[5]。开元前后,印度僧人善无畏、金刚智、不空相继来华,"俱住长安,结坛灌顶,祷雨禳灾"[6]。玄宗除"敕迎就慈恩寺……使一行禅师谨密候之(金刚智)"外,开元十一年(723年)敕金刚智于资圣寺翻译密教经《瑜伽念诵法》等[7]。玄宗尤敬重"能役百神"之不空[8],曾"诏入内立坛,为帝灌顶"[9]。开元十五年(727年),一行禅师卒。玄宗"为一行制碑文,亲书于石,出内库钱五十万,为起塔"[10]。开元二十四年(736年),因"僧徒固请、欲以兴教",玄宗把他"心有所得、辄复疏之"的《御注金刚般若经》颁行天下[11]。至于在道教方面,玄宗曾遣使迎请道士司马承祯"入京,亲受法箓,前后赏赐甚厚……玄宗从其言,因敕五岳各置真君祠一所,其形象制度,皆令承祯推按道经,创意为之。承祯颇善篆隶书,玄宗令以三体写《老子经》,因刊正文句,定著五千三百八十言为真本以奏上之……(承祯卒后)玄宗深叹之……仍为亲制碑文"[12]。"开元十年正月己丑(722年2月13日?),诏两京及诸州各置玄元皇帝庙一所[13],并置崇玄学,其僧徒令习《道德经》及《庄》、《列》、《文》

---

[1]《册府元龟》卷五十一《帝王部·崇释氏》,影印本,北京：中华书局,1960年,第575页。

[2]《唐会要》卷五十《尊崇道教》,北京：中华书局,1955年,第879页。

[3]《册府元龟》卷五十一《帝王部·崇释氏》,上引书,第575页。

[4]《册府元龟》卷五十三《帝王部·尚黄老》,上引书,第599页。

[5]《宋高僧传·慧日传》,上引书,第722-723页。

[6]汤用彤,上引书,第27页。

[7]《宋高僧传·金刚智传》,上引书,第5-6页。

[8]段成式《酉阳杂俎》卷三《贝编》,北京：中华书局,1981年,第39页。

[9]《宋高僧传·不空传》,上引书,第8页。

[10]《旧唐书·一行传》,点校本,北京：中华书局,1975年,第5113页。

[11]参见《全唐文》卷三十《答张九龄等贺御注〈金刚经〉手诏》,影印本,北京：中华书局,1983年,第343页。

[12]《旧唐书·司马承祯传》,点校本,北京：中华书局,1975年,第5128-5129页。

[13]据[明]曹学佺《蜀中名胜记》卷三十引[宋]欧阳修《集古录》,普州曾建玄元皇帝庙："《唐紫极宫碑》,乐阐撰,贾岛书,乐彦融篆额,玄元皇帝祠也。碑以会昌元年(841年)立,在普州。"曹学佺《蜀中名胜记》,刘知渐点校,重庆：重庆出版社,1984年,第445页。

子等。”[1]开元十四年(726年)九月制曰:“玄元皇帝,先圣宗师,国家本系……十八年(730年)十月命集贤院学士陈希烈等于三殿讲《道德经》……开元二十年(732年)正月制曰:老子《道德经》宜令士庶家藏一本。”[2]开元二十三年三月癸未(735年4月24日),玄宗“亲注《老子》并修疏义八卷及至《开元文字音义》三十卷,颁示公卿庶及道释二门,听直言可否”[3]。开元二十五年(737年)正月,“置崇玄学于玄元皇帝庙”[4]。

“不依国主,则法事难立”[5];“必假时君,弘传声略”[6]。这是历代僧俗奉行的法度。上有信者,下必甚焉。受当朝皇帝兼容佛道政策的影响[7],普州地方官先后雕造佛道二教形象。作为栖岩寺上座,玄应于开元二十年为黎令宾所造佛像题铭;四年后,受玄宗亲注《金刚经》与《老子》并为僧人、道士御制碑文、“亲书于石”精神的鼓舞,再次为老施主所造道教“天尊”等像书丹,只是为防止内、外误会,末尾特加一“释”字。

关于栖岩寺上座玄应,有人怀疑他是唐初撰写《一切经音义》的玄应[8]。实际上,《一切经音义》作者玄应,乃唐初高僧,早年隶属“(西)京大总持寺”[9]。“(玄)应博学字书,统通林苑;周涉古今,括究儒释”[10];贞观十九年(645年)六月,奉召参与玄奘译场[11]。玄应生卒年不详。据道宣《大唐内典录》卷五:“昔高齐沙门释道慧,为《一切经》音,不显名目,但明字类,及至临机,搜访多惑。应愤斯事,遂作此音;征核本据,务存实录,即万代之师宗,亦当朝之难偶也。恨叙缀才了,未及覆疏,遂从物故。惜哉!”[12]《大唐内典录》撰于“麟德元年甲子岁(664年)”[13],则玄应当卒于

---

[1]《册府元龟》卷五十三《帝王部·尚黄老》,上引书,第589页。

[2]同上书,第590页。

[3]同上书,第592页。

[4]《新唐书·百官志》,点校本,北京:中华书局,1975年,第1252-1253页。

[5]僧佑《出三藏记集》卷十五《道安法师传》,苏晋仁、萧錬子点校,北京:中华书局,1995年,第562页。

[6]道宣《大唐内典录》序,见《大正藏》第55卷,第219b页。

[7]据张彦远《历代名画记》卷三《记两京外州寺观画壁》,主要活跃于唐玄宗时期的韩干,曾在长安佛教大寺千福寺内塔院西廊画过“天师真”。而千福寺塔院北廊堂内当时画有“法华七祖及弟子影”、绕塔板上绘“传法二十四弟子”等。这说明佛道混于一地的情况在京都也有反映。张彦远《历代名画记》,俞剑华注释,上海:上海人民美术出版社,1964年,第66页。

[8]参见:王家佑《安岳石窟造像》,上引书,第46-47页。

[9]慧立、彦悰著《大慈恩寺三藏法师传》,孙毓棠、谢方点校,北京:中华书局,1983年,第131页。

[10]道宣《大唐内典录》卷五,参见《大正藏》第55卷,第283b页。

[11]慧立、彦悰,上引书,第131页。

[12]《大正藏》第55卷,第283b页。

[13]据智昇《开元释教录》卷十,“《大唐内典录》十卷,麟德元年甲子西明寺沙门释道宣撰”。见《大正藏》第55卷,第577a页。

麟德元年道宣书成之前[1]。因此，撰写《一切经音义》，即《大唐众经音义》的玄应，乃西京大慈恩寺沙门[2]，与安岳石窟中题铭的普州栖岩寺上座玄应不是同一人[3]。

二、聂 公 像

图 4　云居山圆觉洞第 58 号龛

第 58 号龛位于云居山后山中部上层，左与第 59 号相邻，龛敞口，平面长方形，后壁略弧，龛顶残塌，残高 2.75 米，宽 2.65 米，现右壁及龛前底部皆用条石修补。龛内造立像一身，高 2.06 米；头戴翘脚幞头，高颧厚唇，浓眉大眼，体躯健硕；身着圆领宽袖衣，腰围玉带，右侧挂一紫金鱼袋，双手于胸前持笏（已残毁，图 4)。像左侧（龛后壁）有榜题框，唯阴刻铭记上下皆勒出框外：“□□□第二指挥使金紫光禄大夫检校司徒使持节普州诸军事守刺使河东县开国男食邑三百户聂”；龛前左侧壁有题刻八行，经仔细辨识，抄录如下：“……间□皇之润声摇天地爰自出身鬼菟立事龟城而值……/……义□侯□能□大……/……思三度□虎符……暮梁□而咸有志思　公此政以才及临人迁因□/……不闻三马□□□积万家之□军州官吏等希延　异政列状闻……/……之间虑有□□□命请留　真彩以慰人情　公向此灵山成为胜地选□峰于西埵凿……/……濬□□迴分野□□洞府于岩扃透出烟光写仪形于天半亭亭　异相完若净□濬濬……于……/□正月初四年岁次辛丑三月二十七丁亥毕工壮丽伽蓝永立至坚之……篡□张……/……消……

[1] 陈垣《中国佛教史籍概论》，北京：中华书局，1962 年，第 66-68 页。

[2] 参见：1) 道宣《大唐内典录》卷五，见《大正藏》第 55 卷，第 283b 页；2) 道世《法苑珠林》卷一百，周叔迦、苏晋仁校注，北京：中华书局，2003 年，第 2884 页。

[3] 参见：傅成金《安岳石刻之玄应考》，上引书，第 48-50 页。

图 5　云居山圆觉洞第 58 号龛前左侧碑记

图 6　云居山圆觉洞第 59 号龛

灵□□庶……绝……耽华远敬兵伤……”(图 5)。此长篇铭记[1],从所处位置及内容推断,应是《舆地纪胜》卷一百五十八所记《聂公真龛记》。“《聂公真龛记》,在灵居山,军事判官何光远撰,广政四年建。”[2]

据上述两铭记,聂公出生鬼菀,立事于龟城(成都),官至第二指挥使、金紫光禄大夫、检校司徒、使持节普州诸军事、守刺使,受到普州官吏及百姓爱戴,拟“留真彩以慰人情”。故于灵居山胜地兴建伽蓝、雕凿佛像(图 6)[3],并“写仪形于天半”。全部工程于后蜀辛丑年(即广政四年)三月二十七日(941 年 4 月 26 日)告竣,并请军事判官何光远[4]撰碑记之。

[1] 此铭记由于苔蚀、风化,现存字迹多泯灭不清,难以释读。

[2] 王象之《舆地纪胜》,影印本,北京:中华书局,1992 年,第 4303 页。

[3] 聂公像右侧佛龛,现编为第 59 号,龛敞口,平面呈椭圆形,龛顶近于平顶。龛残高 2.00 米,宽 2.70 米,进深 1.49 米。龛正壁雕造一铺五身像,中央阿弥陀,左侧为迦叶与大势至,右侧为阿难与观世音。阿弥陀佛结跏趺坐于高莲座之上,大势至与观世音皆倚坐,两弟子作立姿(图 6)。此龛与第 58 号处于同一平面上,且共用一前庭,造像技法亦基本相同,疑为聂公所造。

[4] 据[清]吴任臣考述,“何光远,字辉夫,东海人也。好学嗜古。广政初,官普州军事判官。撰《聂公真龛记》。又曾著《鉴戒录》十卷,纂辑唐以来君臣事迹可为世法者。又有《广政杂录》三卷,皆行于世”。吴任臣《十国春秋·何光远传》,徐敏霞、周莹点校,北京:中华书局,1983 年,第 817 页。

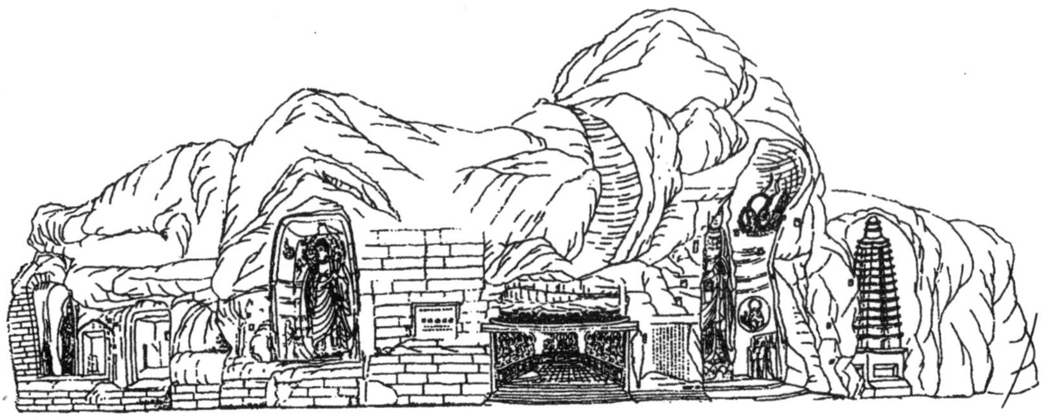

图 7　云居山圆觉洞前山（北崖）窟龛示意图

三、金峰长老真身宝龛

第 12 窟位于云居山前山东部（图 7），右邻第 13 窟。窟口为长方形，高 2.10 米，宽 1.72 米；门楣呈低平弧形，中央偏右竖刻题记两行，行 4 字，为“金峰长老 / 真身宝龛”。窟平顶，现存平面呈不规整方形，最宽处 2.95 米，高 2.20 米，正壁与右壁连接成钝角，与左壁呈弧形。正壁右上方现存一长 1.20 米、高 0.45 米、深 0.60 米的长方形浅龛。从现存遗迹推断，两侧壁后来向外扩凿，并非原始壁面，显得粗糙不平。窟地面微呈倾斜状，里高外低；地面中央有一长 0.53 米、深 0.25 米的凹槽。第 12 窟门楣上方的题铭，说明该窟系安置金峰长老真身之所，即真身宝龛。正壁之浅龛，疑为藏纳骨灰之处。

金峰长老，僧传中无传[1]。据《舆地纪胜》卷一百五十八《普州 · 仙释神》，“金峰长老，开山灵居寺，后赐额真相寺。长老曾作棋歌，以寓其禅机”[2]。据此可知，金峰长老乃灵居寺开山祖师、德长年老之禅宗高僧。

与第 12 窟毗邻的第 13 窟，亦为平顶方形窟，窟口宽 1.60 米、高 2.10 米。两龛

---

[1]《祖堂集》卷十一、《景德传灯录》卷二十一及《五灯会元》卷十三皆记载一位“金峰和尚”。据《祖堂集》：“金峰和尚嗣曹山，在抚州。师讳从志，抚州古田县人也。自离闽越，便造漕源。顿契玄猷，更不他往。初住金峰山，后往报恩寺。师号玄明禅师矣。”《景德传灯录》则作“（玄明大）师后住金陵报恩院，入灭谥号圆广禅师，塔曰归寂”。参见：1)［南唐］静、筠二禅师编撰《祖堂集》，张华点校，郑州：中州古籍出版社，2001 年，第 401 页；2) 道原纂《景德传灯录》，参见《大正藏》第 51 卷，第 364b 页。此金峰和尚，似与云居山金峰长老无关。

[2] 王象之，上引书，第 4301-4302 页。

图 8　云居山圆觉洞第 13 号龛

图 9　云居山圆觉洞第 13、14 号龛外景

外形结构颇为相似,可能为一组双窟。第 13 窟内造像分上下两层,上层正壁雕造三佛;下层正壁中央雕造明王像。明王三头六臂,前两手合于腹前,后四手各持长剑等武器,六臂皆缠绕黑蛇;其左右各雕七身面目各异的人物形象,七身人物之下各有一坐像(图8);窟两侧壁雕出力士、文官、武将、供养人等[1]。第13窟外立面人字形窟檐右端二梁孔,早年被第 14 窟(俗称"莲花手观音窟")左壁打破(图 9),说明第 14 窟开凿时间应晚于第 13 窟。第 14 窟的年代,据原立于该窟正壁左侧的《普州真相寺石观音记》[2],为北宋"大观丁亥(1107 年)告毕"。因此,第 13 窟应早于 1107 年完工。至于其具体时间,在缺乏明确纪年材料的前提下,我们依据造像内容暂时把它定在唐末五代[3];而"金峰长老真身宝龛"(第 12 窟),也应开凿于这一时期。倘若这一推断不误,金峰长老应是活跃于五代的一位禅宗高僧。

[1] 第 13 窟表现的题材与第 12 窟到底是何关系,目前尚难以作出判断。

[2] 此石碑现存安岳县文物局照相室。录文参见嘉庆《四川通志》卷四十二《舆地 · 寺观》,影印本,成都:巴蜀书社,1984 年,第 1651 页。

[3] 据王家佑调查,这种六臂缠绕黑蛇的明王像,又见于四川省眉山县广济水库大佛寺岩。大佛寺岩明王像,"是僧令珰于明德四年(937 年)敬造的揭谛明王神"。因此,云居山这种明王像似"为唐末、五代(后蜀)所造"。王家佑《安岳石窟造像》,上引书,第 51 页。

四、圜觉洞的开凿年代

第 9 号窟，俗称圆觉洞[1]，位于云居山前山西部第 7 号（俗称"净瓶观音窟"）与第 10 号窟（俗称"释迦牟尼佛窟"）之间（参见图 7）。窟外立面上部已残；窟口右侧早年塌毁，现存窟壁为后代以条石补砌而成；窟口外左侧有摩崖碑记。窟平面纵长方形、平顶；窟内正壁和左右侧壁起坛，高 0.60-0.75 米；正壁坛上造三坐佛，左右侧壁坛上各造六身结跏趺坐菩萨，皆圆雕而成。窟内所有造像在 20 世纪 60 年代遭到较大破坏，现存头部及部分躯干、手臂和佛座的残损部分系 1988 年补塑和重妆[2]。

图 10　云居山圆觉洞第 9 号窟前左侧碑记

[1] 圆觉洞之名，因窟内左右侧壁雕造 12 身圆觉菩萨而得。不过，依据窟外左侧的开窟题记，应作"圜觉洞"。

[2] 1982 年 7 月 14 日，大足县文物保管所赴安岳考察组调查了云居山遗迹，郭相颖曾对该窟做过简要记述。现抄录如下："圆觉洞，宽 5.3 米，深 9.4 米，高 4.3 米。正壁列坐三佛，身高 1.5 米，座高 1.2 米；两壁高台上对称列坐十二菩萨。头部尽毁，身躯亦多残缺。唯佛之莲台花瓣、托台石狮，菩萨方形宝座与宝顶圆觉洞相应部分较为相似。但衣纹远不如宝顶者柔和流畅。佛顶有宝盖痕迹，壁间无山石楼阁与宝顶相异。"郭相颖《安岳石刻考察纪实》，见重庆大足石刻艺术博物馆、大足县文物保管所编《大足石刻研究文集》，重庆：重庆出版社，1993 年，第 308-338 页。关于重修时间，参见傅成金《再识安岳圜觉洞摩崖造像》，见《四川文物》，1991 年第 6 期，第 37-38 页。

窟外左侧摩崖碑记，镌刻于高 284 厘米、宽 226 厘米的磨平石壁上，包括题名共 18 行，正文 17 行，满行 22 字，面积为 238×195 厘米，字径 8×9 厘米，楷书。碑铭保存尚完好，现抄录全文如下：

普州真相寺新建圜觉洞记 /
普州真相佛宫，林壑邃深，荫木森古，吾祖太师太傅经行 /
之地。邦君喻迪孺留诗，固知其为一州之佳处也。其主僧 /
了月等，穴石为洞，镌刻佛像，名之曰圜觉。幻化凡俗，警动 /
人意，使人慧月肃清，照耀心境，断诸邪见，乐由正道。维此 /
因幻而识真，缘物而明我，使由佛氏之圆觉，而知自已之 /
圜觉。夫所谓圜觉者，始于爱身，终则明道，初非难事。然吾 /
身之所急求圜觉者，曰：父子仁，兄弟睦，朋友信，夫妇恩；利 /
则思义，气则思和，酒则思柔，色则思节。且士务学，农力穑，/
工尽事，商勤志；专致好修，跬步不舍。传说曰："允怀于道，道 /
积于阙躬。"又曰："阙修乃来，阙德修罔觉。"夫尝以善念著予 /
怀，道行积予已。其修也，自然而来；其德也，自然而觉。如是，/
一性不昧，百行充实，天福毕至矣。昔伊君，天民之先觉，以 /
斯道觉斯民者，其亦以是欤？岂必曰：永断迷妄，轮转生死，/
圜则无相，而后为道也。芶凡具耳目识精一之真，去执著 /
之幻，明自性之我，转肢扰之物，则夫圜觉洞者，独非幻与 /
物也哉！余于道无见，姑以诵闻记予壁，尚待学子里中之 /
见道者。庆历四年中秋日，元士冯佽记，景一之书（图 10）。

碑文中框字者，原碑已缺，系据道光《安岳县志》补。倘若县志所记不误，碑文应撰于北宋仁宗庆历四年，即公元 1044 年[1]；至于主持"穴石为洞，镌刻佛像"之人，则为真相寺主僧了月。

据现场实地考察，笔者认为第 9 号窟是在第 7 号龛（窟）完工之后开凿的，理由如下：A. 第 9 号窟所在崖面不好，它是在第 7 号龛（窟）和第 10 号龛（窟）已占

[1]《巴蜀佛教碑文集成》所录该碑，系据道光《安岳县志》卷七。该录文与原碑文字有出入，如碑文作者冯佽在录文中误作冯俊。又，校订者认为：该"碑文撰于宋仁宗庆历四年(1044 年)"。参见龙显昭主编《巴蜀佛教碑文集成》，成都：巴蜀书社，2004 年，第 103 页。

据较好崖面后开工雕凿，属于石窟寺营造时崖面使用程序中的“见缝插针”之作；B. 第9号窟左侧开窟碑记，打破第7号龛（窟）右侧龛口并磨光而成，致使第7号龛（窟）右壁前部下方供养人所在龛边与窟口之间仅剩4厘米宽岩体；又，第7号龛（窟）现存左侧龛口边尚存一列七身小坐佛，而右侧龛口没有这样的形象，左右两边显得不对称（图11）。鉴于第9号窟内造像多为现代重妆，无法与其他材料进行对比，故学界通常以道光《安岳县志》所录碑文纪年，比定为第9号窟的开凿年代，把它定在北宋仁宗庆历四年，即1044年[1]。

图11　云居山圆觉洞第7号龛

2002年11月28日，笔者在考察云居山后山东端《福寿》碑右上方之《吠云》题铭时，仔细辨识了《吠云》文字。现依题铭原行款抄录如下（改直书为横书）：

庆元己未岁中秋
吠　云
邑令资中李圻书
葛仙祠在山后相传金狗
僧了月开石
伏此山下拄手即应声云

题铭字体皆为楷书，“吠云”字径为80×100厘米，“邑令”一行字径20×25厘米，其余字径10×25厘米。题铭中的“庆元己未岁”，应为南宋宁宗庆元五年，即公元1199年；题铭中的“僧了月”，我们推测应是主持开凿前山圜觉洞（第9号

[1] 参见：1）負安志《安岳石窟寺调查记要》，见《考古与文物》，1986年第6期，第48页；2）王家佑《安岳石窟造像》，上引书，第51页；3）傅成金《再识安岳圜觉洞摩崖造像》，上引书，第37-38页；4）郭相颖《安岳石刻考察纪实》，上引书，第319页。

龕）的真相寺主僧了月。若然，第9号窟外左侧碑文中残毁的年号应为庆元四年[1]，即公元1198年。换言之，第9号窟当完成南宋宁宗庆元四年中秋（1198年9月17日）之前[2]。两铭文皆选中秋“开石”，或许为真相寺主僧了月个人喜好而已。

又，第9号窟左侧碑文撰写者冯俣，正史及现存方志中无传。冯俣为川东绅耆，曾记述过铜梁县“东岩罗堠丘”[3]。据曹彦约南宋嘉定丁丑（1217年）二月所作《普州四贤院记》：“……四贤堂，则自今嘉定乙亥（1215年），贡士黄盈进之，请寓公冯俣之助，使君虞方简之力也……”[4]据此，南宋宁宗嘉定乙亥（1215年）时，冯俣仍活跃于当地文化界。这从另一方面证实，上述推断是正确的。

图12　云居山圆觉洞第7号龛右侧壁榜题

圜觉洞完工不久，遂成为“近城游览佳处”[5]灵居山一景，致使稍后不久王象之撰写《舆地纪胜》[6]，在记述普州千佛院（真相寺）时首先提到圆龟（觉）洞[7]。

---

［1］道光《安岳县志》为何把庆元四年抄作庆历四年，我们推测有两种可能：一是抄写人当时笔误，把“庆元”抄成“庆历”；二是碑文本身当时已有残损，“元”字可能不够清楚所致。

［2］前文提到第9号窟晚于第7号龛开凿。第7号龛右壁前数第一身供养人榜题为“僧□□僧□□□孙□／系使州都孔目官历职满，舍／俗陈乞剃度为僧，癸酉绍兴／二十三年九月二十二日（1153年10月11日）工毕”（图12），表明该窟至少在南宋高宗绍兴二十三年前已完工。这与现存第9、7号窟龛之间的打破关系吻合，它从另一方面证明了我们上述对庆元年号的推断。

［3］曹学佺，上引书，第257页。

［4］曹彦约《昌谷集》卷十五，《四库全书》本。

［5］王象之，上引书，第4291页。

［6］王象之《舆地纪胜》自序作于南宋嘉定辛巳（1221年）孟夏，但书中有宝庆（1225-1227年）以后沿革，故付梓或在绍定（1228-1233年）初年。参见邹逸麟《〈舆地纪胜〉的流传及其价值》，见王象之《舆地纪胜》，影印本前言，北京：中华书局，1992年，第3页。

［7］王象之，上引书，第4289页。

2002 年秋冬之际，为了辅导北京大学佛教考古研究生课程班学员进行考古实习，与全体学员一道在安岳县云居山圆觉洞窟群做了近一个月的考察学习。鉴于系统的调查报告正在撰写之中，因此借 2005 年中国重庆大足石刻国际学术讨论会之机，先就有关问题做初步梳理，以求正于海内外同好。

[本文原刊(北京)文物出版社 2007 年出版的《2005 年重庆大足石刻国际学术研讨会论文集》第 565-577 页，此次重刊仅改正了印制错误。]

剑川石窟：1999年考古调查简报

剑川石窟位于剑川县城西南30.4公里的石宝山（直线距离20.5公里），依据地理位置的差异，可分作沙登箐、石钟寺和狮子关三区。其中，沙登箐区现存窟龛5处，石钟寺区9处，狮子关区3处（图1）。由于石窟主要分布在石钟山，所以通称石钟山石窟。

剑川石窟由于位置偏僻、交通不便，20世纪40年代以前鲜为人知。1939年李霖灿踏查石钟山，应是近代学人对这处石窟寺所做的第一次学术考察[1]。1951年宋伯胤受中央人民政府文化部文物局委派，对剑川石窟进行了全面调查。这次调查结果先以简报形式刊布，后以专书发行[2]。两先生大作皆依据历代记录并参考当地传说，对石钟山现存遗迹做了较详的论述，后者应是剑川石窟研究中的第

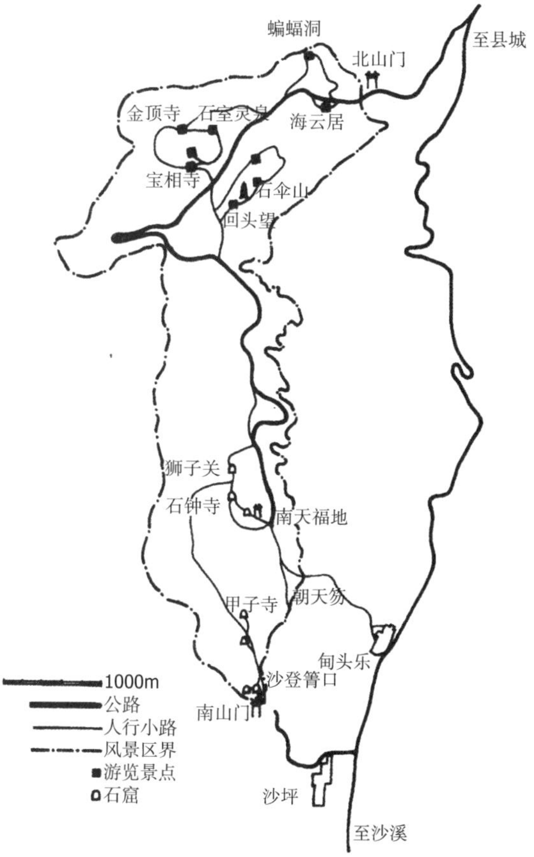

图1 剑川石宝山石窟位置示意图

---

［1］1）李霖灿《剑川石宝山石刻考察记》，见李霖灿《中国名画研究》上，台北：艺文印书馆，1971年，第119-151页；2）李霖灿《南诏大理国新资料的综合研究》，台北：故宫博物院，1982年。

［2］宋伯胤不但详细记述了剑川石窟当时的遗存，而且拍摄黑白照片115帧，墨拓铭刻19张。同时重新发现了狮子关"全家福"雕刻（现编狮子关区第3号）。参见：1）宋伯胤《记剑川石窟》，见《文物参考资料》，1957年第4期，第46-55页；2）宋伯胤《剑川石窟》，北京：文物出版社，1958年。

一座里程碑。近年来，国内外学者在此基础上做了多次报道和论述[1]，但真正从考古学角度研究剑川石窟的文章寥若晨星。

为了向学界提供一套比较完整的资料，根据云南省人民政府与北京大学加强省校合作、科教兴滇之精神，云南大学与北京大学商定联合申请"云南省省院省校教育合作项目——云南剑川石钟山石窟的调查与研究"。依据两校签订的合作协议，北京大学与云南大学共同组成"云南省剑川石窟联合考古队"，对剑川石窟进行了为期两个月的考古调查。考古队在队长马世长教授带领下[2]，按计划完成了第一阶段预定的石窟文字记录、龛像实测图、照相和墨拓工作。

我们这次考察特别注意了窟龛的各种遗迹现象及造像题记资料，拾遗补阙，辨伪存真，对剑川石窟有了一些新的认识。目前详细的考古报告正在整理中，仅将这次考古调查情况简述如下。为免重复，对前人论述较多的各区窟龛不再逐一介绍。

一、主要窟龛介绍

1. 沙登箐区第 1 号

沙登箐区第 1 号，位于石宝山支脉金鸡栖山南坡一座小山的西侧。摩崖造像分上下两列，上列为浅浮雕龛，下列为深龛。上列自右向左共开五龛（图 2）。其中：

第 1-1 龛，呈长方形，龛内雕造一铺三身像。

---

[1] 参见：1) 陈兆复《剑川石窟》，昆明：云南人民出版社，1980 年；2) 黄如英《石钟山石窟》，刊：《文物》，1981 年第 8 期，第 80-84 页；3) 张楠《南诏大理的石刻艺术》，载云南省文物管理委员会编《南诏大理文物》，北京：文物出版社，1992 年，第 140-149 页；4) Angela F. Howard, Li Kunsheng & Qiu Xuanchong, "Nanzhao and Dali Buddhist Sculpture in Yunnan" , in: *Orientations,* 23 (2): 51-60; 5) Angela F. Howard, "The Development of Buddhist Sculpture in Yunnan: Syncretic Art of A Frontier Kingdom" , in: *The Flowering of A Foreign Faith: New Studies in Chinese Buddhist Art,* ed. Janet Baker, Mumbai: Marg Publications, 1998: 134-145; 6) 云南省剑川县文化体育局编《南天瑰宝——剑川石钟山石窟》，昆明：云南美术出版社，1998 年。

[2] 当时北京大学方面参与调查的师生有北京大学考古系教师马世长、李崇峰，佛教考古研究生魏正中、姚崇新、何利群、达微佳，并邀中国社会科学院考古研究所李裕群、郭物和中国社会科学院世界宗教研究所张总一道前往；云南大学方面的有云南大学科研处李东红、历史系教师赵美、民族史研究生王东忻和立石谦次，以及云南省大理白族自治州博物馆田怀清、大理白族自治州文物管理所李学龙和剑川石窟文物保管所董增旭。此外，本项目领导小组组长林超民、常务副组长唐敏、副组长徐康明也多次与有关方面协调，并亲临现场指导；大理白族自治州文化局、中共剑川县委、剑川县人民政府、剑川县文体局以及剑川石窟文物保管所给予考古队大量无私的帮助，使第一阶段考古工作得以圆满结束。谨此致谢。

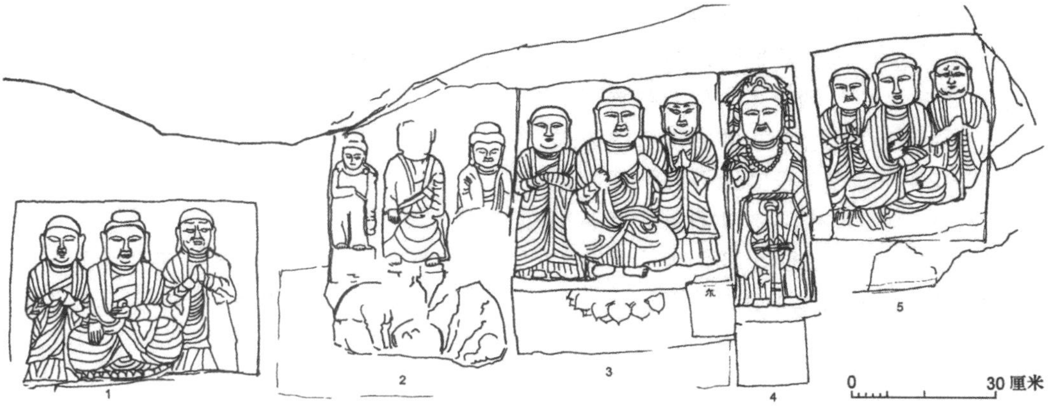

a

b

图 2a　沙登箐区 1 号龛上排浮雕
b　沙登箐区 1 号龛上排浮雕局部

中央坐佛，通高 31 厘米。顶为磨光高肉髻，面相方圆，双眸微睁，直鼻，小嘴，两耳细长垂肩，下颏宽肥，颈部刻出两道肉纹线。双肩较宽，胸腹扁平。内着僧祇支，外着双领下垂式袈裟[1]，褶襞为阴刻式。袈裟下摆覆盖双足，摆边覆于座上。左手横置腹前，手上刻出袈裟右衣边；右手抚于左腿之上，五指并拢作触地印。佛结跏趺坐于莲座之上。

[1] 据笔者近年研究，沙登箐区第 1-1 龛内佛及弟子这种"内着僧祇支、外着双领下垂式袈裟"的法衣或法服，似内着上衣、大衣作"右袒式"披覆；但第 1-2 龛中袈裟"衣边由左向右下方压覆右衣领"和"右衣边向上折转后为左衣边覆压"，又与"大衣作'右袒式'披覆"矛盾。因为原始遗迹过小，现存图像不十分清晰，加之暂时不能去实地核查，故未改存疑。下文此类法衣或法服披覆方式皆如此。鉴于南诏佛教受中原北方影响颇深，关于其佛像法服，可参考本书《龙门石窟唐代窟龛分期试论》(三)造像特征中的"佛像"部分。特此补注。

佛右侧为一年轻比丘像，通高 31 厘米。光头，面相方圆，眉眼细长，鼻较直，嘴较小，下颏刻一道弧线。内着僧祇支，外穿双领下垂式袈裟。双手交搭于胸前，双足露出下衣摆之外。

佛左侧为一年长比丘像，通高 30.5 厘米。面相方圆，额部高突，有皱纹，眉骨隆起，深目高鼻，两腮部各刻线两条，呈年老体态。法服同右侧弟子像。双手合十于胸前，右脚外露，左腿及左足均毁。

第 1-2 龛，在第 1-1 龛左侧偏上，近方形，龛内雕出三身像。

中央坐佛，头部已残，仅见痕迹，通高 31 厘米。佛内着僧祇支，外穿双领下垂式袈裟，唯袈裟衣边由左向右下方压覆右衣领。双腿间衣摆呈波状垂下，褶襞为阴刻式。佛倚坐，双足下踏莲花。右手抚于右膝之上，五指并拢作触地印；左手置于左膝之上，托一钵状物。

佛左侧雕另一坐佛，残高 16 厘米。磨光肉髻，面相方正，眉眼细长，双眸微睁，鼻翼较宽，双唇紧闭，下颏残损，大耳垂肩。着双领下垂式袈裟，唯右衣边向上折转后为左衣边覆压。双手已残，手印似同中央佛像。腿以下部分残毁。

右侧菩萨像，通高 24 厘米，形体略有扭动之感。头戴高冠，饰宝缯。面相方正，眉眼细长，颈戴项饰。袒上身，下着裙；裙褶稀疏，作阴刻式。右手屈至胸腹间，持柳枝；左手自然下垂至膝，持净瓶。双足踏莲座。

三身像下，另有一长 33 厘米、高 16 厘米的浅龛，龛内浮雕一瓶状物和两只狮子。中央瓶状物之颈，伸出两枝莲花，其顶部分别被上方中央主像两脚所踏。花瓶两侧各雕一蹲狮。左侧的狮子，头部已残，前腿直立，后腿蹲踞，雕刻极为写实；右侧的狮子，头部及后腿均残，其前腿的处理，同左侧的狮子。

此外，第 1-3 龛内，雕刻一佛二弟子三身像；第 1-4 龛内，雕造立菩萨像一身；第 1-5 龛内，亦浮雕出一佛二弟子三身像；龛像样式与上述相似。

第 1-7 龛，位于上层第 1-2 龛下方，龛内雕造两身佛像，右为善跏趺坐，左为结跏趺坐。其中，结跏坐佛像下存阴刻楷书榜题一方，共 11 行，行 5 字，全文如下：

> 沙追附尚邑 / 三赕甸张傍 / 龙妻盛梦和 / 男龙庆龙君 / 龙世龙家龙 / 千等有善因 / 缘敬造弥勒 / 佛阿弥陀佛 / 国王天启十 / 一年七月廿 / 五日 (850 年 9 月 4 日) 题记

2. 沙登箐区第 2 号

第 2 号龛位于第 1 号龛东侧山坡上方约 80 米处，崖面中心仅有一观音龛，龛两

a

b

图 3a　沙登箐区 2 号龛立面图
　　b　沙登箐区 2 号龛主像

侧各有四个浅浮雕小塔。此外，在左端塔左上方还有一个小龛（图 3a）。

观音龛（图 3b）作尖拱形，无龛楣，龛内雕一阿嵯耶观音像（真身观世音）[1]，通高 60. 5 厘米。头束高髻，发髻下端有发圈夹，头两侧饰有下垂及肩的宝缯，发际中心分叉，面相长圆，面部扁平，似经后代改凿。双耳戴环，颈下饰圆环形项圈。宽肩细腰，身体呈直筒状。上身袒露，腹部束革带，下着紧身贴体长裙，裙腰外翻，腰带打结后自腹部沿双腿间下垂。披巾横于腹下一道后于腰两侧打结，再沿身侧下垂及地。双臂戴臂钏，左手下垂，右手上举，持柳枝。双足叉立于三层叠涩方座之上。观音身后有头光和身光。

观音龛两侧的八座浅浮雕佛塔，依结构可分为多层密檐式、单层覆钵式和单层或多层方形亭阁式。其中第 2-6 号是八座塔中保存最好的一座，位于崖面转折处，为七层方形密檐式。塔由塔基、塔身和塔刹组成，通高 96 厘米，宽 25 厘米。塔基为方形叠涩束腰须弥座式，束腰处雕出壸门。塔身每层均有收分和叠涩出檐。最下层塔身较高，正中开一圆拱形龛，龛内雕一坐佛；其上各层塔身均阴刻出圆拱形塔门。第七层塔檐上有叠涩平座，上承覆钵和仰莲，仰莲上有相轮三重，再上为露盘、山花和宝瓶，并垂有铃铎。此外，第 2-1 号为单层方形亭阁式，第 2-2 号为四层方形密檐式，第 2-3、2-4 号为二层方塔，第 2-5、2-7、2-8 号为单层覆钵式。从八座佛塔位置经营上判断，它们并非一次完成。

第 2-8 号塔左侧上方小龛，作圆拱形，龛内雕一骑象普贤菩萨，造像表面略有风化。菩萨头束高发髻，头后有桃形头光，面相方圆，披巾从头后向前绕双臂后再上扬，双手合十，服饰不清。正面坐于大象身上。

在观音像左侧有一后代墨线勾勒的琉璃光佛（药师佛），佛像螺发，肉髻低平，面相浑圆，双肩略宽，身着通肩袈裟。左手持药钵；右手持禅杖。双足踩莲座。座下有云气纹。佛头后有圆形头光，头光顶上有一火焰纹。头光之上两侧有云气纹衬托的日轮和月轮，正中有墨书题记一行："南无琉璃光佛。"

第 2 号摩崖现存题记四则。其中，观音龛左侧龛边阴刻题记一行，共 12 字，楷书："奉为施主药（?）师祥妇观音得（似菩字）雕。"第 7、8 号塔之间阴刻题记二行，行 10 字，楷书："大理囶造像药师祥妇人 / 观音姑爱□□□等敬雕。"上述题刻应是开窟时原始榜题。

[1]"阿嵯耶观音（真身观世音）"和下文的"梵僧观世音"，系据日本京都有邻馆藏《南诏图传》和台北故宫博物院藏《张胜温画大理国梵像卷》附以汉文榜题的图像比定。

3. 狮子关区第 1 号

第 1 号，位于石钟寺东北方一座山岩上，隔一深箐（山谷）与石钟寺相连。龛立面作圆拱形，平面呈半圆形。

龛内正中雕一立像（图 4），残高 93 厘米。立像头部已残，仅在头两侧残存少数发卷（虬发？），另于左侧残存两冠带。形体粗壮，胸部较高。上身服饰残毁不清。下着窄口裤，腰束膝裙。腰右侧有一锁状物，以粗带斜挂左肩，唯左胸前之粗带已残，仅存痕迹。脚穿高鞠靴。双手屈至胸腹间，皆残。从遗迹看，双手似拄一宝杖，杖头着地作回卷状。像旁竖刻“波斯国人”四个大字。

a

b

图 4　狮子关 1 号龛主像

4. 狮子关区第 2 号

第 2 号，位于第 1 号北面约 130 米处的山腰间，在岩体风蚀形成的内凹部位浮雕一梵僧像，梵僧左侧浮雕一狗（图 5）。

梵僧像通高 168 厘米。头后有圆形光头，头部突出崖面 15 厘米，面朝东南。头部

a　　　　　　　　b

图 5　狮子关 10 号龛主像

上宽下窄，面相近长方形，头上盖二块方巾，额际有白毫，眉呈弯月，眉骨凸起，眼睛细长，眼珠雕成内凹的小圆孔。鼻宽且塌，颧骨突出，双唇微闭，双耳垂肩。颈短，双肩宽平。内着交领衫，大衣作“右袒式”披覆。躯体处衣纹阴线刻，手臂处则为阶梯式。左臂曲伸至胸前，手提一带盖净瓶；右臂曲伸向上，中指、食指伸直，似作上指状。双足叉立，足穿短靴。

狗居梵僧像左侧，高 68 厘米，长 62 厘米，作止步回首反顾状，眼睛注视着梵僧。宽耳下耷，闭嘴，露出二犬牙。颈戴一圆环圈。躯体壮实，前身下倾，后身弓起。

梵僧头像右侧镌刻纪年榜题，榜题高 42 厘米，宽 21 厘米。分上下二栏，上栏竖刻二行，行 4 字，楷书：“信境兰若 / 紫石云中。”下栏为落款，竖刻四行，行 4-6 字不等，楷书：“盛德四年 / 六月七日（1179 年 7 月 13 日）造像 / 施主工匠金榜 / 杨天王秀琍。”

崖底近地面处有明代李元阳游览石钟山时所留题记，阴刻三行，行 7-8 字，大字楷书：“嘉靖壬戌（1562 年）翰林庶 / 吉士中溪李元阳 / 同游五人过狮子关。”

5. 石钟寺区第 2 号

第 2 号，位于石钟寺上层崖面最西侧，正中雕一帐形龛。龛楣浮雕莲花、联珠纹和人字形垂幔；龛边雕饰一道联珠纹；龛下为一束腰龛台。龛内雕一平座，平座中部有半圆形凹槽，平座上部共雕 16 身人物（图 6）。正中雕一王者坐像，王者右侧前后簇拥七身人像，左侧雕六身人物，龛左右壁各雕一清平官。

王者头戴莲花宝珠塔形头囊[1]，头囊两展脚上翘呈 S 形，末端作尖状，头囊带系于颏下，两宝缯垂至肩上。面相长圆，眉骨隆起，双眼半睁，鼻、嘴及左半面颊已残毁，但残存的右嘴角微陷，双耳较小。胸部微凸，两肩宽厚，内着圆领衫，外穿圆领左衽偏襟大袖长袍，袖手盘坐于高方椅之上；大袖覆盖双足后垂覆于椅座上半部，腿两侧及大袖底下露出长袍摆边。

高方椅“搭脑”两端挑出部分各雕一回首龙头，皆口含流苏；椅背搭覆一厚锦。椅后有一长方形背屏，背屏凸缘中央雕一圈联珠纹；背屏上方卷云纹中雕一龙，作回首反顾状；背屏两侧偏上，雕出祥云烘托日月；日月之下可见两已相背之黻文。椅上铺座垫，座垫下雕出两只相向的蹲狮，双狮之下雕出椅座。座正面刻出三壸门，内雕火焰宝珠。

王者右侧所雕三排立像，有的环颈系虎头披膊（波罗皮），斜挂卷柄长剑；有的环颈系云头纹护膊，手握书卷状物；有的双手前伸，托举一高颈瓶；有的手握羽扇

图 6　石钟寺区 2 号龛测绘图

[1] 此名及下文的“波罗皮”，系据［唐］樊绰《蛮书》卷八《蛮夷风俗》拟定。参见樊绰《蛮书》，向达校注，北京：中华书局，1962 年，第 207-209 页。

柄；有的手持旌旗。

值得注意的是王者右侧盘坐于高椅上的高僧像。该像头部已残，仅存左耳。内着交领衣，外披袈裟；袈裟大袖和下摆以及内衣摆边垂覆于高椅之上。左臂屈至胸前，手持一串珠，拇指与食指似作数珠状；右手托串珠下部。其椅背"搭脑"呈弧形，两端挑出部分作卷云头饰，椅背右侧伸出一曲柄圆伞。

王者左侧所雕三排立像，有的手持曲柄长剑；有的手举旌旗，肩背一圆顶盾牌；有的紧握扇柄。

龛两侧各雕一清平官。其中右侧清平官头已残，残高 49.5 厘米；原似戴幞头，两短脚下垂至肩。着圆领左衽偏襟大袖长袍，倚坐高椅之上；大袖垂至膝下，袖手，双足着履。椅座上似铺锦皮，椅背"搭脑"呈弧形，两端挑出部分作方头；椅下部为一倒"凸"字形高座垫。左侧清平官与右侧的大体相似。

6. 石钟寺区第 8 号

位于石钟寺区上层崖面最东侧，龛像分作上下两列。

上列正中开一圆拱形龛（图 7）。龛顶上方有一榜题框，框内残存墨书题记九行，楷书："古以圣主自在灵台筏？道兰 / 若观世音者法法无相渡四生 / 而方便法师忙忙无形祥□情 / 而□□□□其造像主□坐 / 上士布□□□天王员者善言 / 维于相如功能□于□万 / 代次名□□□中福田无穷 / 子孙世世□□□果生生无尽后 / 盛德四年作□己亥岁八月三日 (1179 年 9 月 5 日）记。"（图 8)

在榜题框左右和上方雕莲花、荷叶及流苏等，框下雕刻云纹三朵，整体形成一个半圆形龛楣。由此推测：榜题与龛像系同时雕作而成；框内的墨书纪年，应是龛像毕工的年代。

龛内正中现存一高浮雕锥形物，锥形物中央刻一凹槽。即民间所谓的"阿姎白"（女性生殖器）；从整体造型看，锥形物雕凿粗糙。锥形物下为一仰莲台，莲台正面已经残损，莲台下为一束腰方座。

龛左右侧壁各存减地平钑结跏坐佛造像一铺（图 9)。

龛外两侧各有一天王（神王？）龛。二天王像样式大体相似，头及面部早年残毁，现存头冠及面部为 1953 年重雕[1]。以主龛右侧的天王像为例，天王头后雕出火焰

[1] 据剑川石窟文物保管所董增旭见告：1952 年 9 月中央曾拨专款维修剑川石窟，维修工程于 1953 年年初开始，年底竣工。除搬迁玉皇阁和搭建木构窟檐外，也补雕和新刻了少量造像，其中就包括此像。

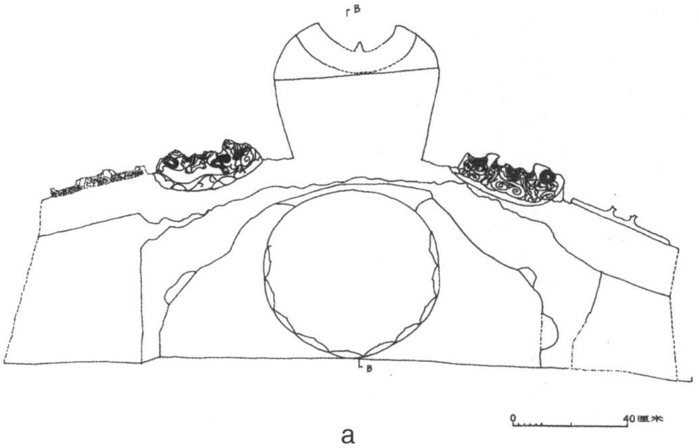

a

b

图 7a　石钟寺区 8 号龛平面图
b　石钟寺区 8 号龛外立面图

图 8　石钟寺区 8 号龛外“盛德四年”题记

a　　　　　　　　　　　　　　　　b

图 9a　石钟寺区 8 号龛内左侧壁坐佛
　　b　石钟寺区 8 号龛内右侧壁坐佛

头光，颈有项护，甲前身分左右两片，每片中心做一小圆护，胸背甲在两肩上用带前后扣联；腰带下战袍垂及踝骨处，两肩披膊作虎头状；兽面形脐护被压覆于腰带之下。右手置于腰部，手残；从残存的剑鞘遗迹来看，应握一剑。左手外扬前伸，手亦残，从残迹看，原应持琵琶颈。下缚吊腿，足着战靴。天王双脚各踏一小鬼（药叉）。小鬼均袒上身，下穿三角形牛鼻褌（禅裙），戴手镯、脚镯，腰饰串珠，趴跪于起伏的山峦之上。

左天王龛外侧，存一尖楣圆拱龛，龛内上半部雕一坐佛，胸部以上部分残毁，现存佛头及胸部为 1953 年重刻。佛结跏趺坐，袈裟衣摆垂覆莲座之上，双足不外露。右手手势不清；左手自然下垂，五指并拢抚膝。佛右下角，雕一三头六臂菩萨坐像；佛左下角，存一身单头四臂菩萨坐像。佛座下方，雕一高僧坐像[1]。

7. 石钟寺区第 9 号

第 9 号，位于石钟寺大殿西南 5 米处，这里正是有名的“石钟”所在；石钟为一

[1] 此龛像与主龛内左侧壁减地平钑造像的构图和造型相同。

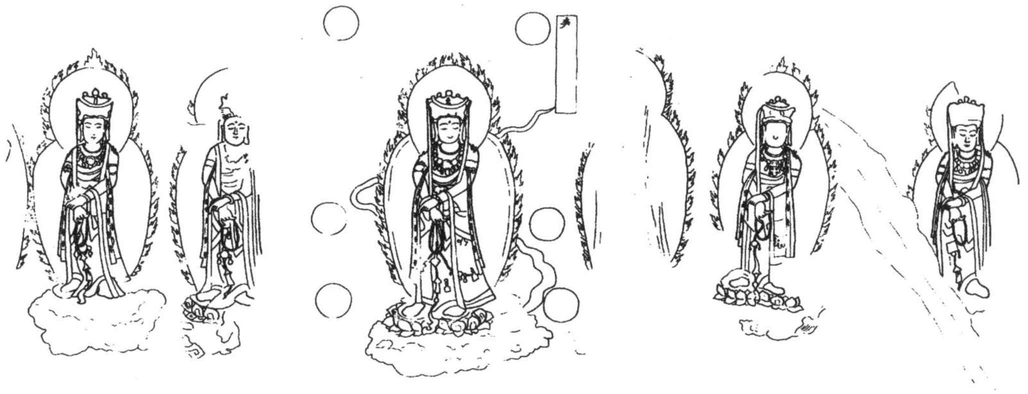

图 10　石钟寺区 9 号龛摩崖壁画

圆形小山，表面呈龟背状裂纹，以外形似钟，故得名。在其西侧下部高 130 厘米，长 400 厘米的内凹崖面上，共绘制一列 7 身菩萨立像（图 10），是石宝山石窟中唯一的一处摩崖壁画。绘制方式均以赭色勾勒轮廓，细部如发髻等用墨线勾勒，再施以彩绘，颜色主要有乳白、绿、赭和土红色；背光多着绿色，面部与裸露的肌体着乳白色，头饰以白线勾勒，内涂赭色；披巾和掩腋衣赭、绿相间，并饰有云纹；下裙着土红色；仰莲座着绿色，祥云着白色。

菩萨形象、服饰、身姿相同。其中，保存较好的第 9-4 号，菩萨通高 110 厘米、身高 77 厘米。头戴高花蔓宝冠，冠两侧垂长饰带，在腹部打结后垂至双膝，再上搭双手腕后下垂于地；面相浑圆，眉眼细长，窄鼻小嘴，双耳垂肩，下颌丰满圆润；颈下饰双重项圈，垂饰珠玉，装饰繁缛华丽；双肩圆润且下溜，披巾从双肩垂下，沿手臂外侧飘然下垂及地；菩萨含胸挺腹，臀部微向左侧扭动，身体丰满；上身斜披络腋，下身着裙，腹饰裙腰，腹下垂有复杂的缨络；双臂自然下垂，戴花形臂钏和手镯，双手置于腹部，左手握住右手腕，右手下垂，持一串念珠；赤足立于仰莲座上，莲座下有祥云烘托。菩萨身后有火焰形头光和身光，左右两侧各有三日轮。从整体看，第 9-4 号菩萨像居中间位置，形体略大，且有日轮和榜题，应是这铺像的主尊。

二、小　　结

这次调查所获全部文字、测图、照片和拓片资料正在整理之中。据上述资料，我们有以下几点初步认识：

1. 关于剑川石窟的分期问题。剑川石窟三区之间的造像题材和造像样式存在着明显的差异，沙登箐区流行弥勒佛和阿弥陀佛题材；造像面相方圆、身着“双领下垂式”袈裟，造像特点显示年代上应较早。石钟寺区和狮子关区则流行观音像、八大明王、毗沙门天王、大黑天像[1]和以南诏王及其眷属为主像的窟龛；造像样式多丰满圆润，与前者差别明显。据此暂将剑川石窟造像分为三期。

第一期：沙登箐区第 1 号，多为组合不规范的小型窟龛，雕造手法略显稚拙，可能是小型佛教邑社或民间信徒捐资开凿；造像题材比较单纯，主要是弥勒佛和阿弥陀佛。第 1 号下层 1-7 龛内造像题记“国王天启十一年”中的“天启”，是南诏第十世王劝丰佑的年号，天启十一年即公元 850 年。该题记是剑川石窟中现存最早的纪年造像题记，题记所在龛像较上列第 1-1 至 1-5 龛造像年代要晚。

第二期：大理国时期开凿的石钟寺区和狮子关区龛像及沙登箐区部分造像，雕造手法较为成熟，造像题材多样化，宗教成分趋于复杂，如石钟寺区第 6 号的八大明王、第 3 号的地藏、第 4 号的华严三圣以及与当地本主信仰有关的第 1、2 号和狮子关第 3 号王者窟等。根据两处有大理国“盛德”纪年造像题记判断，“盛德”年间 (1176-1180 年) 应是剑川石窟的开窟高峰[2]。

第三期：作为佛教圣地，尽管蒙元时期剑川大型开窟工程终止，但小型造像活动并未停歇。沙登箐区第 2 号的 2-5、2-7、2-8 浮雕佛塔和石钟寺区第 8 号主龛两侧的藏传佛教造像，应是这一时期的作品。

2. 关于剑川石窟的渊源问题。南诏时期沙登箐区流行弥勒佛和阿弥陀佛，且弥勒与阿弥陀佛成组合关系。这种题材源远流长，在汉地佛教造像中流传较广；沙登箐区佛面相方圆、身宽体壮、着“双领下垂式袈裟”的造像样式，颇与隋末唐初四川和陕西地区造像特点相似。因此，南诏时期的造像题材与样式应来自汉地佛教造像系统[3]。考虑到唐与南诏之关系主要是通过四川成都的大都督府及以后的节度使府相联系，使臣之往来也大多路经四川。加之唐朝与南诏的几次战争，南诏军队几乎攻占

---

［1］石钟寺区第 6 号雕出八大明王及大黑天和毗沙门天像，第 7 号主像为倚坐观音。

［2］剑川石窟现存三方纪年造像题记中，有两方为“盛德”，且均为盛德四年 (1179 年)，值得注意。

［3］关于佛教传入大理的时间，较可信的最早文献当推［明］陶宗仪《说郛》卷三十六所收［元］李京《云南志略》：“晟罗皮立，是为太宗王……开元二年 (714 年)，遣其相张建成入朝，玄宗厚礼之，赐浮屠像，云南始有佛书。”［元］张道宗《记古滇说集》，进一步记载张建成朝唐“入觐，过成都大慈寺……学佛书，归授滇人。成至京朝唐，时玄宗在位，厚礼待之，赐以浮屠像而归，王崇事佛教，自兹而启。”此外，［元］郭松年《大理行记》详载：“蒙昭成王保和九年 (832 年)，有高将军者即此地建遍知寺，其殿像壁绘于今罕见，意非汉匠名笔，不能造也。”参见：1) 郭松年《大理行记》，王叔武校注；李京《云南志略》，王叔武辑校，昆明：云南民族出版社，1986 年，第 14、73 页；2) 张道宗《记古滇说集》，《云南备征志》本。

这些文献，既说明南诏像教系唐代由内地传入，也为推测大理地区画塑与中原北方佛教艺术之关系提供了旁证。

成都，又俘虏汉人入滇。因此，南诏受到邻近的四川佛教造像的影响应是合理的[1]。

大理国时期开凿的石钟寺区龛像，如八大明王、地藏菩萨和华严三圣，也与四川地区的佛教造像有密切关系[2]。观音的信仰本是江南佛教的特色，成都地区亦同样如此；观音崇拜在南诏、大理时期盛极一时，疑与四川佛教有关。不过到大理国时期，观音的信仰逐渐占据主导地位，且演化出具有当地特色的观音菩萨，如狮子关区第2号及沙登箐区第5号的“梵僧观世音”和沙登箐区第2号的“真身观世音（阿嵯耶观音）”，成为云南大理地区特有的佛教造像。另外，石钟寺区第1、2号和狮子关区第3号以南诏王及其眷属为主像的窟龛，颇具地方特色。总之，大理国时期除了受汉地佛教造像影响之外，本地因素明显增加，构成了这一时期石窟造像的独特风貌。

世祖平定云南以后，元朝“崇尚释氏”[3]和“造寺、造塔”以修“福荫大千”[4]之风南来，大理地区的佛教有元一代更趋发展[5]。沙登箐区第2号的三座喇嘛塔，不闻元以前云南佛塔有此类型，且亦无直接传自印度或尼泊尔之证据，应为蒙元时期输入的新样式[6]。石钟寺区第8号的藏式龛像[7]，总体布局与某些较早的唐卡颇有关联，

---

[1] 唐大和三年（829年），南诏入寇成都，驱掠蜀中寻常百姓、伎巧、僧道乃至唐官与士大夫之家数万人至大理。两年后，时任检校兵部尚书、成都尹、剑南西川节度副大使、知节度事、管内观察处置、西山八国云南招抚等使的李德裕，因“西川承蛮寇剽虏之后，郭钊抚理无术，人不聊生。德裕乃复葺关防，缮完兵守。又遣人入南诏，求其所俘工匠，得僧道工巧四千余人复归成都”。关于这次战役对南诏产生的影响，向达先生在1962年中华书局出版的《蛮书校注》第175-178页中写到：“大和三年之役，对于南诏后来物质文化发展有极大关系……南诏后来工艺之盛，颇有赖于此役。”向先生所言极是。如［唐］樊绰《蛮书》卷七：“（南诏）俗不解织绫罗，自大和三年蛮贼寇西川，虏掠巧儿及女工非少，如今悉解织绫罗也。”《新唐书 · 南诏传》更有“南诏自是工文织，与中国埒”之语。因而，剑川石窟佛教造像与四川佛像颇为相似，亦情理中事。参见：1)《旧唐书 · 李德裕传》，点校本，北京：中华书局，1975年，第4519页；2) 樊绰《蛮书》，向达校注，北京：中华书局，1962年，第174页；3)《新唐书 · 南诏传》，点校本，北京：中华书局，1975年，第6282页。

[2] 如重庆大足北山第37、227、231、242、276等窟的地藏像，宝顶山第22窟的十大明王，北山第106窟和宝顶山第5窟的华严三圣像。

[3]《元史 · 释老传》，点校本，北京：中华书局，1976年，第4517页。

[4]《佛祖统记》卷三十六，见《大正藏》第49卷，第435a页。

[5] 元世祖笃信佛教，《佛祖统记》卷四十八记载忽必烈于“万机之暇，自持数珠，课诵、施食”。而郭松年《大理行记》，则有“（大理）其俗多尚浮屠法，家无贫富皆有佛堂，人不以老壮手不释数珠……沿山寺宇极多，不可殚记”。这既说明上行下效之理，也反映出大理佛教之盛。参见：1)《大正藏》第49卷，第435a页；2) 郭松年，上引书，第22-23页。

[6] 参见刘敦桢《云南古建筑调查记》，载《刘敦桢文集》三，北京：中国建筑工业出版社，1987年，第376-377页。

[7] 据不完全统计，剑川石窟现存后代纪年明确的游人题记42条。其中，元代就有21条（包括北元“宣光”纪年题记3条），足见元代剑川在这一地区佛教信徒心中的地位。值得注意的是，第8号窟现存9条纪年题记都是元代的，因此元代藏传佛教龛像较集中地出现在该处也就不是偶然的了。

应是受藏传佛教图像影响所致[1]。

3. 关于造像题材问题。对于石钟寺区第8号龛内椎形物，一些学者认为是生殖崇拜，有“阿姎白”之说；也有学者认为“阿姎白”系后人附会，时在窟内主像释迦牟尼被毁之后。这次考察时，我们仔细辨认了残存的墨书造像题记，释读出以前未被认出的“兰若观世音……造像主”等题字。题记既称造像主，则窟内原应雕造佛像，而非所谓的“阿姎白”，结合“观世音”题名，我们认为原来主像，即现存莲座之上有可能是救苦救难的观世音。因此，我们同意“阿姎白”应是主像残毁后才出现的看法[2]。

（本文受“云南剑川石钟山石窟的调查与研究”课题组委托撰写，原刊《文物》2000年第7期第71-84页。此次重刊增补了一条注释。）

[1] 中原藏式龛像影响云南佛教造型艺术，除剑川石窟外，云南晋宁县上蒜乡观音洞所存元代藏式佛像及喇嘛塔壁画，有些与杭州飞来峰造像在构图和造型上颇为相似。这进一步证实，云南佛教受到了元代藏地佛教的影响。参见李昆声《云南艺术史》，昆明：云南教育出版社，1995年，第305-306页，图版32。

[2] 宋伯胤《剑川石窟》，北京：文物出版社，1958年，第9页。

五、史料遗迹：

透视交流

Jibin and China as seen from Chinese Documents

1. Jibin in Chinese Literature

The meaning of the Chinese word Jibin［罽宾］[1], a geographical term, varies with different contexts in a discussion of the history of Central Asia. Although it generally covers the area of present-day Kashmir, it did involve or comprise Uḍḍiyāna/Udyāna, Takṣaśilā, Gandhāra, and Kāpiśa, at least from the 4th to early

［1］According to Xuanzang［玄奘, *ca.* 602-664 AD］, Jiashimiluo［迦湿弥罗, Kāśmīra］was "formerly written Ki-pin (Jibin) by mistake", it other words, Jibin "was an old and incorrect name for the country". We are told also by Daoxuan［道宣, 595-667 AD］that "Jiashimiluo (Kāśmīra) was called Jibin by the Chinese, a popular name handed down from ancient times, we do not know the origin of Jibin". However, Seishi Karashima［辛嶋静志］infers that Jibin was probably a transliteration of the Prākrit term Kaśpīr, and Kaśmīra was a corresponding Sanskrit term or homologue of Prākrit Kaśpīr. 1) Xuanzang, *Datang xiyu ji*［大唐西域记, *Record of the Western Regions of the Great Tang Dynasty*］, emended and annotated by Ji Xianlin［季羡林］et al, Beijing: Zhonghua Book Company, 1985: 320; 2) Samuel Beal, *Si-Yu-Ki-Buddhist Records of the Western World; Chinese Accounts of India,* translated from the Chinese of Hiuen Tsiang, London: Trubner, 1884: 188, note 86; 3)Thomas Watters, *On Yuan Chwang's Travels in India,* Vol. I, London: Royal Asiatic Society, 1904: 259; 4) Daoxuan, *Xü gaoseng zhuan*［续高僧传, *Continued Biographies of Eminent Priests* or *The Tang Dynasty Biographies of Eminent Priests* or *A Continuation of the Memoirs of Eminent Monks*］, in: *Taishō*, Vol. 50: 449a; 5) Seishi Karashima, "*Hanyi fodian de yuyan yanjiu*［汉译佛典的语言研究, On the Linguistic Form of the Chinese Translated Versions of *Tripiṭaka*］", in: *Fojiao hanyu yanjiu*［佛教汉语研究, *Studies of the Buddhist-Chinese*］, ed. Zhu Qingzhi［朱庆之］, Beijing: The Commercial Press, 2009: 33-74, esp. 56-57.

6th century AD[1]. As to the exact identification of Jibin, there has been a dispute in academic circles[2]. In the Han Dynasties [汉代, 206 BC -220 AD], Jibin is said to lie to the west of the Indus River and also to the south of the Hindukush Mountains, covering an area corresponding to the plains of the river valleys of the middle and lower reaches of the Kabul River and its tributaries. Kāpiśa, Gandhāra, Takṣaśilā, Uḍḍiyāna and some other kingdoms were included in this area; after the Jin Dynasties [晋, 265-420 AD], geographically, the term seems to refer to present day Kashmir[3].

It is well-known that the Chinese have provided an abundance of data for the study of the civilization of Central Asia. According to *Waiguo Shi* [外国事, *An Account of Foreign Countries*] by monk Zhi Sengzai [支僧载], about the 4th century AD[4], Jibin lies to the west of Śrāvastī [舍卫], the king of Jibin and the

---

[1] 1) S. Lèvi and É. Chavannes, "L'Itinéraire d'Ou-k'oung", in: *Journal Asiatique,* Octobre (1895): 371-384; 2) Edouard Chavannes, *Documents sur Les Tou-kiue (Turcs) Occidentaux: Recueillis et commentés,* St-Pétersbourg: Académie Impériale des Sciences de St-Pétersbourg, 1903: 130-132; 3) Kurakichi Shiratori [白鳥庫吉], "Keihinkou ku [罽賓國考, On the Jibin kingdom]", in: *Seiiki shi kenkyu* [西域史研究, *Collected Papers On the History of the Western Regions*], Vol. 1, Tokyo: Iwanami Shoten, 1944: 377-462, esp. 460-462; 4) Cen Zongmian [岑仲勉], *Hanshu xiyuzhuan dili jiaoshi* [汉书西域传地理校释, *Collation and Annotation to the Monograph on the Western Regions in the History of the Western Han Dynasty*], Beijing: Zhonghua Book Company, 1981: 150-164; 5) Fumio Enomoto [榎本文雄], "Keihin-Indo Bukkyō no Ichichūshinchi no Shozai [罽賓一インド仏教の一中心地の所在, Ji-bin: A Central Area of Indian Buddhism]", in: *Chi no Kaikō-Bukkyō to Kagaku* [知の邂逅——仏教と科学]; Tsukamoto Keishō Kyōju Kanreki Kinen Ronbunshū Kankōkai [塚本啓祥教授還暦紀念論文集刊行會], Tōkyō: Kōsei Publishing, 1993: 265-266; 6) Chongfeng Li, "The Geography of Transmission: The 'Jibin' Route and Propagation of Buddhism in China", in: *Kizil on the Silk Road: Crossroads of Commerce & Meeting of Minds,* ed. Rajeshwari Ghose, Mumbai: Marg Publications, 2008: 24-31.

[2] 1) S. Lèvi and É. Chavannes, *ibidem*; 2) Kurakichi Shiratori, *ibidem*; 3) Cen Zongmian, *ibidem*; 4) W. W. Tarn, *The Greeks in Bactria and India,* Cambridge: Cambridge University Press, 1951: 469-473.

[3] 1) Kurakichi Shiratori, *opere citato*: 377-462, esp. 379-403; 2) L. Petech, *Northern India According to the Shui-jing-chu,* Rome: IsMEO, 1950: 79; 3) Cen Zongmian, *opere citato*: 150-164, esp. 155-160; 4) Ma Yong, "The Chinese Inscription of the 'Da Wei' Envoy of the 'Sacred Rock of Hunza'", in *Antiquities of Northern Pakistan: Reports and Studies,* Vol. 1, *Rock Inscriptions in the Indus Valley,* ed. Karl Jettmar et al, Mainz: Verlag Philipp von Zabern, 1989: 139-157, esp. 153, Note 3.

[4] This book was lost after the 10th century AD, but some materials were preserved in the Chinese *leishu* [类书, a class of works combining to some extent the characteristics of encyclopedias and concordances, embracing the whole field of literature, methodically arranged according to subjects, and each heading giving extracts from other former works on the subject in question], such as *Taiping yulan* [太平御览, *The Taiping Reign-Period Imperial Encyclopedia*]. *confer*: Xiang Da [向达], *Tangdai chang'an yu xiyu wenming* [唐代长安与西域文明, *The Tang Dynasty Chang'an and the Civilization of Central Asia*], Beijing: SDX Joint Publishing Company, 1957: 565-578, esp. 570-572.

people in the country all believed in the way and doctrine of Buddhism. In the winter, men and monks would drink a little fruit wine before noon, and they could not eat anything after noon" [1]. This account seems to be the earliest extant Chinese record of Jibin.

In 402 AD, Faxian [法显,?-423 AD] went to India to search for monastic rules of discipline. While he made his pilgrimage to various sacred sites in this region, Faxian gave a clear account of Tuoli [陀历国], Uḍḍiyāna/Udyāna [乌苌国], Swastene/Swāt [宿呵多国], Gandhavatī/Gandhāra [犍陀卫国], Takṣaśilā [竺刹尸罗国], Puruṣapura [弗楼沙国] and Nagarahāra [那竭国]. Before mentioning these kingdoms, Faxian emphasized that he and his followers had gone to Čukupa/Kargalik [子合国], but Bhikṣu Sengshao [僧韶 / 僧绍], one of his followers in the group, went to Jibin with a monk from Xiyu [西域, the Western Regions] where they saw a ceremony of the image-procession [行像] in Khotan [2].

When we turn our attention from Faxian's account to *Chu Sanzang ji ji* [出三藏记集, *A Collection of Records concerning the Tripiṭaka*] [3] compiled by Sengyou [僧佑, 445-518 AD] [4], and move on to *Mingseng zhuan* [名僧传,

---

[1] Ouyang Xun [欧阳询, 557-641 AD], *Yiwen leijun* [艺文类聚, *Encyclopedia of Art and Literature in Dynastic Histories*] in 624 AD, emended and annotated by Wang Shaoying [汪绍楹], Shanghai: Shanghai Chinese Classics Publishing House, 1965: 1294.

[2] Faxian, *Faxian zhuan* [法显传, *The Travels of Faxian*], emended and annotated by Zhang Xun [章巽], Shanghai: Shanghai Chinese Classics Publishing House, 1985: 18-51. confer: Max Deeg, *Das Gaoseng-Faxian-Zhuan als religionsgeschichtliche Quelle; Der älteste Bericht eines Chinesischen buddhistischen Pilgermönchs über seine Reise nach Indien mit Übersetzung des Textes,* Wiesbaden: Harrassowitz Verlag, 2005: 219-267, Karte Nr. 4 Gandhāra und NW-Indien.

[3] For the Chinese literature or documents, I will first write down its name in *pinyin* system, then put the Chinese characters and its English translation in brackets. Whenever the literature or document is again cited or quoted afterwards, I use the *pinyin* system alone, but occasionally put the English translation in bracket.

[4] Sengyou, *Chu sanzang ji ji* (*A Collection of Records concerning the Tripiṭaka or A Collection of Records of Translations of the Tripiṭaka*), emended and annotated by Su Jinren [苏晋仁] and Xiao Lianzi [萧錬子], Beijing: Zhonghua Book Company, 1995; *confer*: *Taishō*, No. 2145, Vol. 55: 1-114.

According to Fei Zhangfang [费长房], *Chu sangzang ji ji* was compiled by Sengyou in the Jianwu period [建武, 494-497 AD] of the Southern Qi Dynasty [南齐, 479-502 AD]. *confer*: Fei Zhangfang, *Lidai sanbo ji* [历代三宝记, *Record of the Triratna through the Ages* or *Record concerning the Triratna under Successive Dynasties*] in 597 AD, in: *Taishō*, Vol. 49: 125c.

The Biographies of Famous Monks] composed by Baochang [宝唱][1] in 514 AD and *Gaoseng zhuan* [高僧传, *The Biographies of Eminent Priests*] compiled by Huijiao [慧皎, c. 495-554 AD][2] in 519 AD, we find that the territory of Jibin recorded in these texts extends far beyond the geographical boundaries of present-day Kashmir. Particular emphasis is placed on the fact that neither the name of Uḍḍiyāna/Udyāna nor that of Gandhavatī/Gandhāra are mentioned as a separate entity in *Chu sanzang ji ji, Mingseng zhuan* and *Gaoseng zhuan,* they were all grouped under a common name of Jibin by monks or literati of China[3] and those of the West Regions when these records were compiled. Furthermore, there was no separate record for Takṣaśilā in both *Weishu* [魏书, *History of the Wei Dynasties*] by Wei Shou [魏收, 507-572 AD] and *Bei shi* [北史, *History of the Northern Dynasties*] by Li Yanshou [李延寿, 570-628 AD] which indicates that Jibin is "on the southwest of Bolor". It seems that Takṣaśilā

---

[1] Baochang, *Mingseng Zhuan* (*Biographies of Famous Monks* or *Lives of Famous Bhikṣus*), partly preserved in the Japanese *Meisōden-shō* [名僧传抄, *A Transcript of Biographies of Famous Monks*] by Shü-shō [宗性] in 1235 AD, in: *Dainihon Zoku Zōkyō* [大日本續藏经, *Continued Tripiṭaka of Japan*], Vol. 7, No. 1: 1-17.

[2] Huijiao, *Gaoseng zhuan* (*Biographies of Eminent Priests* or *The Liang Dynasty Biographies of Eminent Priests* or *Biographies of Eminent Monks* or *Memoirs of Eminent Monks*), emended and annotated by Tang Yongtong [汤用彤], Beijing: Zhonghua Book Company, 1992; *confer*: *Taishō,* No. 2059, Vol. 50: 322-424.

[3] These three books were all written before 519 AD by the learned monks living in southern China. The records of the Buddhist mission of Song Yun [宋云] and Huisheng [惠生] of the Northern Wei Dynasty [北魏, 386-534 AD] to the west provide much information for this region. In 518 AD, the empress dowager née Hu dispatched Huisheng of the Chongli Monastery [崇立寺] to go to the Western Regions in search of Buddhist *sūtras*. And Song Yun went with him as the Northern Wei envoy to Uḍḍiyāna and Gandhāra besides other kingdoms. Huisheng even stayed in Uḍḍiyāna for two more years, and it was not until the second year of the Zhengguang period (521 AD) of the Northern Wei Dynasty that he returned to the national capital (Luoyang). Although Huisheng and Song Yun acquired one hundred seventy titles or texts, all the best of Mahāyāna classics, they left us quite a detailed account of the Western Regions, such as *Huisheng's Traveling Account* and *Private Record of Song Yun,* of which, some were quoted by Yang Xuanzhi [杨衒之] in his *Luoyang qielan ji* [洛阳伽蓝记, *A Record of Saṃghārāmas in Luoyang*]. *confer*: 1) Yang Xuanzhi, *Luoyang qielan ji* (*A Record of Saṃghārāmas in Luo-yang*), emended and annotated by Zhou Zumo [周祖谟], Beijing: Zhonghua Book Company, 1963:182-227; 2) Yi-t'ung Wang, tr., *A Record of Buddhist Monasteries in Lo-yang* by Yang Hsüan-chih, Princeton: Princeton University Press, 1984: 215-246.

was already incorporated in Jibin by this time[1]. From the *Jātaka* stories, moreover, it appears that Kāsmīra once formed a part of the Gandhāra[2]. Therefore, the Jibin region, for a period of time, "was northwestern India, of which Kaśmīra was an important part, but not the only part"[3]. In other words, Jibin in Chinese ancient literatures basically corresponds to the Greater Gandhāra (fig.1)[4] or Gandhāran cultural area[5], two modern terms used in academic circles.

From the Wei [魏, 220-265 AD] to the Southern-and-Northern Dynasties [南北朝, 420-589 AD], "Jibin abounds with saints and wise men"[6]. There

---

[1] 1) Chongfeng Li [李崇峰] "*Xixing qiufa yu jibindao* [西行求法与罽宾道, Jibin Route and Propagation of Buddhism into China]", in: *Yenching Journal of Chinese Studies* [燕京学报], New No. 21 (2006): 175-188; 2) Chongfeng Li, "The Geography of Transmission: The 'Jibin' Route and Propagation of Buddhism in China", in: *opere citato*: 24-31.

[2] *The Jātaka or Stories of the Buddha's Former Births*; translated from the Pāli by various hands, 6 volumes, Nos. 406, 408, ed. E. B. Cowell, Cambridge: Cambridge University Press, Vol. III, 1895: 221-224, 228-232.

[3] According to Charles Willemen, Jibin "is not necessarily a phonetic rendering, but it may indicate the region of foreigners, guests [bin, 宾], who use ji [罽], a kind of cloth, very appreciated by the Han. Udyāna, the Gilgit area, may have been the original area, but it gradually developed to encompass the whole northwestern area, certainly in the 4th century". Charles Willemen, "Sarvāstivāda Developments in Northwestern India and in China", in: *The Indian International Journal of Buddhist Studies* (New Series in continuation of the *Indian Journal of Buddhist Studies,* Vol. X, Varanasi: B. J. K. Institute of Buddhist and Asian Studies), No. 2 (2001): 163-169, esp. 167. *confer*: Chongfeng Li, "The Geography of Transmission: The 'Jibin' Route and the Propagation of Buddhism in China", in: *opere citato*: 24-31, esp. 25.

[4] Richard Salomon, *Ancient Buddhist Scrolls from Gandhāra: The British Library Kharoṣṭhī Fragments,* Seattle: University of Washington Press, 1999: 3.

[5] Charles Willemen believes that "the Gandhāran cultural area of Gandhāra and Bactria was known as Jibin 罽宾 in Chinese", "Gandhāran cultural area, i. e. non-Kāśmīra Jibin 罽宾". 1) Charles Willemen, "Kumārajīva's 'Explanatory Discourse' about Abhidharmic Literature", in: *Kokusai Bukkyōgaku Daigaku-in Daigaku Kenkyū Kiyō* [国際仏教大学院大学研究紀要第12号(平成20年)/ *Journal of the International College for Postgraduate Buddhist Studies*], Vol. XII (2008): 37-83 (156-110), esp. 39 (154), 69 (124); 2) Charles Willemen, *Outlining the Way to Reflect* [思维略要法] (T. XV 617), Mumbai: Somaiya Publications Pvt Ltd, 2012: 16; 3) Charles Willemen, "Kaniṣka and the Sarvāstivāda Synod", in: *Glory of the Kushans: Recent Discoveries and Interpretations,* ed. Vidula Jayaswal, New Delhi: Aryan Books International, 2012: 218-222, esp. 218.

[6] Sengyou, *opere citato*: 545; *confer*: *Taishō,* Vol. 55: 105a.

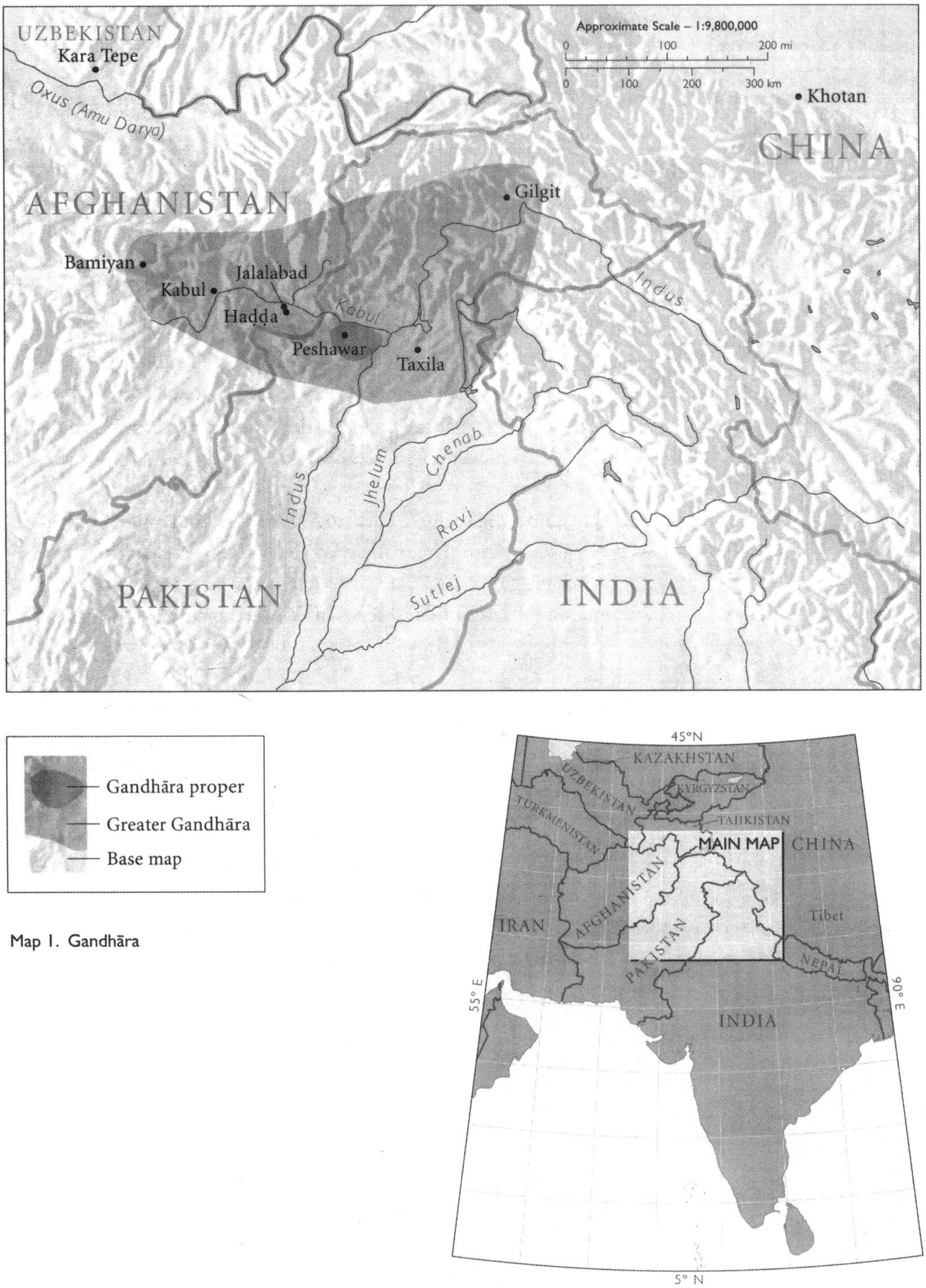

Map 1. Gandhāra

fig.1 A Map of Greater Gandhāra

were frequent exchanges between Jibin and China during this period[1]. Those who came from Jibin to recite or translate Buddhist texts and to propagate the doctrines in China, such as Buddhabhadra, Buddhajīva, Buddhayaśas, Dharmamitra, Dharmanandi, Dharmapriya, Dharmayaśas, Guṇavarman, Puṇyatāra, Saṃghabhadra, Saṃghadeva, Saṃgharakṣa and Vimalākṣa, were clearly recorded in the *Chu sanzang ji ji* by Sengyou, which is the earliest extant descriptive catalogue of the Chinese translations of the Buddhist canon that contains prefaces and postscripts to the translation of the *Tripiṭaka* as well as biographies of some eminent priests or master monks.

Moreover, Kumārajīva [鸠摩罗什 /Jiumoluoshi, 究摩罗 /Jiumoluo, 鸠摩耆婆 / Jiumoqipo, 鸠摩罗耆婆 /Jiumoluoqipo, 童寿 /Tongshou, 344-413 AD] traveled back and forth between Jibin and Kucīna [龟兹, Kucha] several times early in life[2]. Later on, the śramaṇa Shixian [师贤, Siṃhabhadra?, ?-460 AD], who was a relative of the King of Jibin and entered the Buddhist order at a young age, came east to Liangzhou [凉州], a Buddhist center of then north China. After Liangzhou was subdued by the Northern Wei Dynasty in 439 AD, Siṃhabhadra went on to its capital Pingcheng [平城, present-day Datong]. While Buddhism was forbidden by Emperor Taiwu [太武帝, 424-452 AD] of the Northern Wei in 444 AD, Siṃhabhadra, who disguised himself as a medical practitioner, reverted to the lay life but observed the doctrine without alteration. On the very day of the restoration of Buddhism by Emperor Wencheng [文成帝, 452-465 AD] of the Northern Wei Dynasty in 452 AD, Siṃhabhadra became a *śramaṇa* again. The

---

[1] According to *Zhongguo wenwu bao* [中国文物报, *China Cultural Relics News*] dated October 26, 2005, a tomb that belongs to the Northern Zhou Dynasty [北周, 557-581 AD] was discovered at Nankang [南康] village in northern Xi'an. In the light of the epitaph unearthed from the tomb, the deceased was Li Dan [李诞] of the brāhmaṇa race [婆罗门种], who came to China from Jibin during the Zhengguang period [正光, 520-525 AD] of the Northern Wei Dynasty and died at age of 59 at Wannianli [万年里] in 564 AD. He was buried in his home village and conferred posthumous honor on Hanzhou *cishi* [邯州刺史, Regional Inspector of Hanzhou] by the Northern Zhou Dynasty. This is not only the first tomb that bears the name of a brāhmaṇa but also a tomb that records a foreigner who came from Jibin and lived in China. It further indicates that Jibin and China had a close contact besides the Buddhist relationship.

[2] Sengyou, *opere citato*: 234, 530-535; *confer*: *Taishō,* Vol. 55: 41b, 100a-102a.

a

b

fig.2a A gilded bronze image of Buddha, from site of Shifo Monastery at Huangliang, Chang'an

b A Kharoṣṭhī inscription carved on the back of the pedestal of the above image

emperor personally performed the hair-cutting ceremony for Siṃhabhadra and his associates, altogether five men; the *Śramaṇa* Siṃhabhadra was appointed Chief of the Clerics［道人统, In Control of the Religious］by the emperor in the same year[1].

On the other hand, those who went to Jibin from China to seek for Buddhist texts and images or just to make pilgrimages to famous sacred sites include

[1] Wei Shou, *Weishu: Shilaozhi*［魏书·释老志, *History of the Wei Dynasties*: *Treatise on Buddhism and Taoism*］, punctuated edition, Beijing: Zhonghua Book Company, 1974: 3025-3062, esp. 3036-37. *confer*: 1) James R. Ware, "Wei Shou on Buddhism", in: *T'oung Pao,* 30 (1930): 100-181, esp. 145-146; 2) Wei Shou, *Treatise on Buddhism and Taoism,* tr. by Leon Hurvitz, in: *Yun-kang: The Buddhist Cave-temples of the Fifth Century* AD *in North China; detailed report of the archaeological survey carried out by the mission of the Tōhōbunka Kenkyūsho 1938-1945* by S. Mizuno and T. Nagahiro, Vol. XVI, Supplement and Index, Kyoto: Jimbunkagaku Kenkyūshō, Kyoto University, 1956: 23-103, esp. 71-72.

Zhiyan [智严][1], Zhimeng [智猛][2], Fayong [法勇, Dharmodgata][3] and some other monks besides Faxian during the 4th and 5th centuries AD.

2. Chinese Translation of Buddhist Texts

Now, I take *Chu sanzang ji ji* by Sengyou as a case study and refer also to the *Mingseng zhuan* by Baochang and *Gaoseng zhuan* by Huijiao; if needed, I will also rely on *Lidai sanbo ji* by Fei Zhangfang[4], *Datang neidian lu* [大唐内典录, *The Great Tang Dynasty Catalogue of Buddhist Scriptures*] by Daoxuan[5] dated to 664 AD. and *Kaiyuan shijiao lu* [开元释教录, *The Kaiyuan Era Catalogue of the Buddhist Canon*] by Zhisheng [智昇][6] dated to 730 AD. These catalogues, which record the presence of many foreigners on Chinese soil and in particular the Buddhist activities of the master monks from Jibin, will reveal valuable information on Buddhism in Jibin and supply fresh evidence on the relationship between Jibin Buddhism and that of China.

In fascicle 2 of *Chu sanzang ji ji*[7], Sengyou discussed the earlier records and sources with great care and gave a detailed account of nine eminent priests or great master-monks, who came to China from Jibin and recited or translated Buddhist texts

---

[1] Sengyou, *opere citato*: 576-578; *confer*: *Taishō,* Vol. 55: 112b-113a.

[2] Sengyou, *opere citato*: 579-580; *confer*: *Taishō,* Vol. 55: 113b-c. In addition, a gilded bronze image of Buddha (fig.2a) was discovered from a site of the Shifo Monastery [石佛寺] at Huangliang Town [黄良], Chang'an County [长安县], Shaanxi in 1979. The image looks quite foreign and has a Kharoṣṭhī inscription carved on the back of the pedestal, which records the image was donated by or made for Monk Zhimeng (fig.2b). This image seems to be brought back from the Greater Gandhāra by the Monk Zhimeng. Sun Fuxi [孙福喜] ed., *Xi'an wenwu jinghua: Fojiao zaoxiang* [西安文物精华：佛教造像, *Masterworks of the Antiquities from Xi'an: Buddhist Images*], Xi'an: World Publishing Corporation, 2010: 2, 202.

[3] Sengyou, *opere citato*: 581-582; *confer*: *Taishō,* Vol. 55: 113c-114a.

[4] Fei Zhangfang, *Lidai sanbo ji* (*Record of the Triratna through the Ages* or *Record concerning the Triratna under Successive Dynasties*), in: *Taishō,* Vol. 49: 22-128.

[5] Daoxuan, *Datang neidian lu* (*The Great Tang Dynasty Catalogue of Buddhist Scriptures* or *A Catalogue of the Buddhist Canon compiled under the Tang Dynasty*), in: *Taishō,* Vol. 55: 219-341.

[6] Zhisheng, *Kaiyuan shijiao lu* (*The Kaiyuan Era Catalogue of the Buddhist Canon* or *A Catalogue of the Buddhist Canon compiled in the Kaiyuan Period*), in: *Taishō,* Vol. 55: 477-723.

[7] Sengyou, *opere citato*: 22-90; *confer*: *Taishō,* Vol. 55: 5-15.

into Chinese before the early 6th century AD. Their sequential order is as follows.

(1) Dharmapriya, a *śramaṇa* from Jibin[1], whose name was transliterated as Tanmopi［昙摩蜱］[2]/Tanmobei［昙摩卑］[3] or paraphrased as Fa'ai［法爱］[4], is recorded as having recited or transmitted orally the two following Buddhist texts:

1) *Mohe boluore boluomi jing chao*［摩诃钵罗若波罗蜜经抄, *Daśasāhasrikā-prajñāpāramitā*］[5], 5 *juan*［卷, fascicle］, was also called *Chang'an pin jing*［长安品经］or went by the name of *Mohe bore boluomi jing*［摩诃般若波罗蜜经］. It was recited or translated in the 18th year of the Jianyuan period［建元］(of Fu Jian［符坚, 357-384 AD］, ruler of the Former Qin state［前秦, 351-394 AD］), i. e. in 383 AD[6].

This text has 5 fascicles. During the reign period of Emperor Jianwen［简文帝, 371-372 AD］[7] of the Eastern Jin Dynasty［东晋, 317-424 AD］, Dharmapriya, a

---

［1］Sengyou, *opere citato*: 381; *confer*: *Taishō,* Vol. 55: 73b.

［2］Sengyou, *opere citato*: 46, 66, 290; *confer*: *Taishō,* Vol. 55: 10b, 14a, 52b.

［3］Sengyou, *opere citato*: 381; *confer*: *Taishō,* Vol. 55: 73b.

［4］Fei Zhangfang, *ibidem,* in: *Taishō,* Vol. 49: 75c.

［5］For the Chinese version of the Buddhist texts, I will first write down its name in *pinyin* system, then put the Chinese characters and its Sanskrit name or English translation in brackets. Whenever the Chinese version of the Buddhist texts is again cited or quoted afterwards, I just use the *pinyin* system first, with Prākṛta/Prakrit or Sanskrit name or English translation in bracket, because "the earliest Buddhist texts transmitted to China were written not in the classical Sanskrit used by later Indian Buddhist scholiasts but instead in one or another of the regional Prakrit languages-especially the northwestern Prakrit dialect, Gāndhārī", either oral or textual during this period. *confer*: 1) Robert E. Buswell, Jr., "Prakritic Phonological Elements in Chinese Buddhist Transcriptions: Data from Xuanying's *Yiqiejing Yinyi*", in: *Collection of Essays 1993: Buddhism Across Boundaries-Chinese Buddhism and Western Religions* by Erik Zürcher, Lore Sander and others, ed. John R. McRae, Jan Nattier, Taipei: Foguang Cultural Enterprise Co., Ltd, 1999: 187-217, esp. 189 and footnote 2; 2) Charles Willemen, "Kaniṣka and the Sarvāstivāda Synod", in: *opere citato*: 219.

This version was included in *Taishō,* No. 226, Vol. 8: 508-535.

［6］Sengyou, *opere citato*: 46; *confer*: *Taishō,* Vol. 55: 10b. According to *Mohe boluore boluomi jing chao xü*［摩诃钵罗若波罗蜜经抄序, Preface to the Chinese version of *Daśasāhasrikā-prajñāpāramitā*］by Dao'an［道安, 312-385 AD］, Dharmapriya held or recited the original text, Fohu［佛护, Buddharakṣa］, not Fonian, checked it and had it translated, Huijin［慧进］took down what was dictated. Sengyou, *opere citato*: 289-291; *confer*: *Taishō,* Vol. 55: 52b-c. See: Tang Yongtong［汤用彤］, *Han wei liang jin nanbeichao fojiao shi*［汉魏两晋南北朝佛教史, *A History of Buddhism from the Han down to the Southern and Northern Dynasties*］, Beijing: Zhonghua Book Company, 1982: 160.

［7］Here, the mention of Emperor Jianwen was an error. It should be Emperor Xiaowu［孝武帝, 372-396 AD］of the Eastern Jin Dynasty.

śramaṇa of Hinduka [天竺, present-day the South Asian Subcontinent][1] who held the *Huben* [胡本, Kharoṣṭhī or Brāhmī script][2] original, acted as an informant to recite or write out the text first, then Zhu Fonian [竺佛念, Buddhānusmṛti ?] had it translated into Chinese[3].

2) Dharmapriya, a *śramaṇa* from Jibin, was familiar with *Bajiandu apitan* [八犍度阿毗昙, *Abhidharmāṣṭagrantha*]. Thus, he recited *Bajiandu apitan genjiandu* [八犍度阿毗昙根犍度, *Abhidharmāṣṭagrantha-mula-khaṇḍa*?] and Saṃghadeva had it translated into Chinese[4].

(2) Saṃghabhadra[5], whose name was transliterated or transcribed as Sengqiebadeng [僧伽跋澄][6] or paraphrased as Zhongxian [众现][7], is

---

[1] For the ancient Chinese names of Hinduka, *see* D. P. C. Bagchi, "Ancient Chinese Names of India", in: *India and China: Interactions through Buddhism and Diplomacy; A Collection of Essays by Professor Prabodh Chandra Bagchi,* compiled by Bangwei Wang and Tansen Sen, Delhi: Anthem Press India, 2011: 3-11, esp. 8-9; 2) Qian Wenzhong, "The Ancient Chinese Names of India and their Origins", in: *Land Routes of the Silk Roads and the Cultural Exchanges between the East and West before the 10th Century*; Desert Route Expedition International Seminar in Urumqi August 19-21, 1990, Beijing: New World Press, 1996: 601-611.

[2] Charles Willemen, "Kaniṣka and the Sarvāstivāda Synod", in: *opere citato*: 219.

[3] Sengyou, *opere citato*: 46; *confer*: *Taishō,* Vol. 55: 10b.

[4] See *Bajiandu apitan genjiandu hou bieji* [八犍度阿毗昙根犍度后别记, Postscript of the Chinese version of *Abhidharmāṣṭagrantha-mula-khaṇḍa*?] by unknown author. Sengyou, *opere citato*: 381; *confer*: *Taishō,* Vol. 55: 73b.

[5] For the restitution of 僧伽跋澄, it used to be restored to Saṃghabhūti, but both Paul Demiéville and Erik Zürcher prefer to Saṅghabhadra. *confer*: 1) Paul Demiéville, "La *Yogācārabhūmi* de Saṅgharakṣa" in: *Bulletin de l'Ēcole française d'Extrême-Orient,* XLIV (1954): 339-436, esp. 364, note 8; 2) Erik Zürcher, *The Buddhist Conquest of China: The Spread and Adaptation of Buddhism in Early Medieval China,* Leiden: E. J. Brill, 1972: 393, note 105.

I was told by Professor Charles Willemen in an email dated March 20, 2012 as follows: "Saṃghabhūti is indeed Saṃghabhadra (Zhong, Saṃgha; xian, bhadra). He is the translator of the *Vibhāṣā* in 383 ... *Ba jiandu lun* is *Aṣṭagrantha,* written in Gandhāra, and it has many *Vibhāṣās,* e. g. Samghabhadra's *Jñānaprasthāna, Fazhi lun,* is a rewritten *Aṣṭagrantha,* rewritten in Sanskrit in Kaśmir. Its new *Vibhāṣā* is the *Mahāvibhāṣā*. *Za apitan xin lun,* Dharmatrāta's work, is *Miśrakābhidharmahṛdaya* ... The *Hṛdaya* is the oldest, then follows the *Miśraka*, and finally the *Abhidharmakośa*. This lineage is different from the *Vaibhāṣikas* in Kaśmir. *Shi song lü* is *Daśabhaṇavāra* in Sanskrit". In the evening of April 4, 2012, moreover, he also gave me some good suggestion and comments on my paper during our meeting in Beijing. Here, I want to express my sincere thanks to Professor Charles Willemen.

[6] Sengyou, *opere citato*: 46-47, 374-375, 382, 522-523, 524, 565, 572; *confer*: *Taishō,* Vol. 55: 10b, 71b-c, 73c, 99a-b, 99c, 109a, 111b.

[7] Huijiao, *opere citato*: 33; *confer*: *Taishō,* Vol. 50: 328a-b.

recorded as having recited or transmitted orally the three following Buddhist texts:

1) *Za apitan piposha*［杂阿毗昙毗婆沙[1]，*Saṁyuktābhidharma-vibhāṣā*］[2], 14 fascicles, was recited or translated in the 4th month of the 19th year of the Jianyuan period (May 18-June 16, 383 AD) of the Former Qin state and completed on the 29th day of the 8th month of the same lunar year (October 11, 383 AD)[3]. The text could also be called *Za apitanxin*［杂阿毗昙心］[4].

---

[1] It was later called *Apitan piposha*［阿毗昙毗婆沙］by Fei Zhangfang in *Lidai sanbao ji;confer*: *Taishō,* Vol. 49: 76a.

[2] This version was later called *Piposha lun*［鞞婆沙论，*Vibhāṣā-śāstra*］by Zhi Sheng in *Kaiyuan shijiao lu* and included in *Taishō,* No. 1547, Vol. 28: 416-524. *confer*: *Taishō,* Vol. 55: 510c.

[3] According to "*Piposha xü*［鞞婆沙序，Preface to the Chinese version of *Vibhāṣā*］" by Monk Dao'an, this *Piposha* (*Vibhāṣā*) recited by Saṃghabhadra was composed by Shituopanni［尸陀槃尼，Sitapāṇi or Śītapāṇi］. Tanmonanti［昙无难提，Dharmanandi］wrote down the text in Brāhmī script［梵语］, Buddharakṣa had it translated, Minzhi［敏智］took down what was dictated in Chinese and Zhao Lang［赵郎，i. e. Zhao Zheng/Zhao Wenye］rectified the interpretation. Sengyou, *opere citato*: 381-382; *confer*: *Taishō,* Vol. 55: 73b-c.

According to Charles Willemen, "the Chinese term *fanwen,* actually meaning Brāhmī-script, text, and not Sanskrit as a language, is a term used when the majority of texts in China used Brāhmī, not e. g. the earlier Kharoṣṭhī, a writing system of the Gandhāran cultural area". Charles Willemen, "Kaniṣka and the Sarvāstivāda Synod", in: *opere citato*: 219.

[4] It was later called *Za apitanxin lun*［杂阿毗昙心论］by both Fajing in *Zhongjing mulu* and Fei Zhangfang in *Lidai sanbao ji*; *confer*: *Taishō,* Vol. 55: 142b, 49: 71b.

I have a doubt about this *Za Apitanxin*. According to *Zhongjing mulu*［众经目录 *A Catalogue of Tripiṭaka*) by Fajing［法经］in 594 AD, *Za apitan piposha* (*Saṁyuktābhidharma-vibhāṣā*) translated by Sengqiebadeng (Saṃghabhadra) and Fotuluocha (Buddharakṣa) in 383 AD, *Za apitan xin lun*［杂阿毗昙心论，*Miśrakābhidharmahṛdaya* or *Saṁyaktābhidharmahṛdaya*］translated by Sengqiebamo［僧伽跋摩/Saṃghavarman］and Baoyun［宝云］in 433 or 434 AD, *Za apitan xin lun* (*Miśrakābhidharmahṛdaya* or *Saṁyaktābhidharmahṛdaya*) translated by Fotuobatuoluo［佛陀跋陀罗/Buddhabhadra］and Faxian in *ca*. 417 AD, and *Za apitan xin lun* (*Miśrakābhidharmahṛdaya* or *Saṁyaktābhidharmahṛdaya*) translated by Yiyeboluo (伊叶波罗/Īśvara) and Qiunabamo (求那跋摩/Guṇavarman) in 431 AD all belong to the same original, in other words, the above four Chinese versions were all translated from the same original text by different translators at different times and places. On the basis of Zhisheng's catalogue, *Za apitan xin lun* (*Miśrakābhidharmahṛdaya* or *Saṁyaktābhidharmahṛdaya*) was also called *Za apitan piposha* (*Saṁyuktābhidharma-vibhāṣā*) which was composed by Fajiu［法救，Dharmatrāta］. In the light of "*Piposha xü* (Preface to *Vibhāṣā*)" by Monk Dao'an, however, *Piposha* (*Vibhāṣā*), i. e., *Za apitan piposha* (*Saṁyuktābhidharma-vibhāṣā*) was compiled indeed by Shituopanni (Sitapāṇi or Śītapāṇi). See 1) Fajing, *Zhongjing mulu*, in: *Taishō,* Vol. 55: 15-150, esp. 142b; 2) Zhisheng, *ibidem*, *Taishō,* Vol. 55: 621a; 3) Sengyou, *opere citato*: 381-382; *confer*: *Taishō,* Vol. 55: 73b-c.

Therefore, if it were called *Za apitanxin*, it should be *Miśrakābhidharmahṛdaya* composed by Fajiu［Dharmatrāta, 达摩多罗/Damoduoluo］, which is an exegesis of *Abhidharmahṛdaya* (*The Heart of the Abhidharma*) by Fasheng［法胜，Dharmaśreṣthin/达磨失梨帝/Damoshilidi］. See 1) Sengyou, *opere citato*: 384-385; *confer*: *Taishō,* Vol. 55: 74b-c; 2) Lü Cheng［吕澂］, *Xinbian hanwen dazangjing mulu*［新编汉文大藏经目录，*A New Catalogue of the Chinese Versions of the Buddhist Tripiṭaka*］, Ji'nan: Qilu Publishing House, 1980: 87, Nos. 1044, 1047.

2) *Poxumi ji* [婆须蜜集, *Vasumitra-śāstra*][1], 10 fascicles, was recited or translated on the 15th day of the 3rd month of the 20th year of the Jianyuan period (April 21, 384 AD) and completed on the 13th day of the 7th month of the same lunar year (August 15, 384 AD)[2].

3) *Sengqieluocha ji jing* [僧伽罗刹集经, *Saṃgharakṣa-sañcaya-buddhacarita-sūtra* or *Saṅgharakṣa's Yogācārabhūmi*][3], 3 fascicles, was recited or translated on the 30th day of the 11th month of the 20th year of the Jianyuan period (December 28, 384 AD) of the Former Qin[4].

There were altogether 27 fascicles of the above three texts. Saṃghabhadra,

---

[1] This version, which was later called *Zun poxumi suo ji lun* [尊婆须蜜所集论] in *Zhongjing mulu* [众经目录, *A Catalogue of the Tripiṭaka*] by Jingtai [静泰] in 664 AD, goes by the name of *Zun poxumi pusa suoji lun* [尊婆须蜜菩萨所集论, *Āryavasumitrabodhisattvasaṃgīti-śāstra*] in *Kaiyuan shijiao lu* by Zhi Sheng and was included in *Taishō*, No. 1549, Vol. 28: 721-808. *Taishō*, Vol. 55: 188c, 510c.

[2] According to *Poxumi ji xü* [婆须蜜集序, Preface to the Chinese version of *Vasumitra-śāstra*] by unknown author, the original text was brought to Chang'an by Saṃghabhadra in the 20th year of the Jianyuan period (384 AD). The original was held or checked up together by Saṃghabhadra, Dharmanandi and Saṃghadeva, Zhu Fonian had it translated into Chinese and Huisong [慧嵩] took down what was dictated. The work started on the 5th day of the 3rd month and was finished on the 13th day of the 7th month of the same lunar year (April 11 to August 15, 384 AD). 1) Sengyou, *opere citato*: 375-376; *confer*: *Taishō*, Vol. 55: 71c-72a; 2) Tang Yongtong, *opere citato*: 159.

[3] This version was later called *Sengqieluocha suo ji jing* [僧伽罗刹所集经] by Daoxuan in *Datang neidian lu* and included in *Taishō*, No. 194, Vol. 4: 115-145. *Taishō*, Vol. 55: 312b.

[4] According to *Sengqieluochajing xü* [僧伽罗刹经序, Preface to the Chinese version of *Saṅgharakṣa's Yogācārabhūmi* or *Saṃgharakṣa-sañcaya-buddhacarita-sūtra*] by Dao'an, the original text was brought to Chang'an by Saṃghabhadra in the 20th year of the Jianyuan period (384 AD), Zhu Fonian had it translated into Chinese and Huisong took down what was dictated. Murong [慕容] happened to lead a rebellion in the outskirts of the city when the translation was carried out, which hampered the translation. Fahe [法和] and I (Dao'an) checked the translation against the original and made the corrections, then finalized the Chinese version on the 30th day of the 11th month (December 28, 384 AD). On the basis of *Sengqieluocha jijing houji* [僧伽罗刹集经后记, Postcript to the Chinese version of *Saṅgharakṣa's Yogācārabhūmi* or *Saṃgharakṣa-sañcaya-buddhacarita-sūtra*] by unknown author, moreover, on the 30th day of the 11th month of the Jianyuan period (December 28, 384 AD) of the Great Qin (Former Qin state), Saṃghabhadra recited this text at the Shiyang Monastery [石羊寺] in Chang'an and Fotuoluocha (Buddharakṣa) had it translated into Chinese. Because the Chinese version was not of fine quality, Dao'an and Zhao Wenye [赵文业] rectified the translation and finalized its version on the 9th day of the 2nd month of 21st year of the Jianyuan period (March 6, 385 AD). Sengyou, *opere citato*: 373-375; *confer*: *Taishō*, Vol. 55: 71b-c.

a *śramaṇa* from Jibin, came to Chang'an［长安，present-day Xi'an］during the reign period of Fu Jian, which corresponds to the reign period of Emperor Xiaowu of the Eastern Jin Dynasty. Saṃghabhadra transmitted orally *Piposha*［毗婆沙，*Vibhāṣā*］first and then Buddharakṣa had it translated into Chinese. The original *Huben* (Kharoṣṭhī or Brāhmī script) text of *Poxumi* (*Vasumitra-śāstra*), however, was also brought here by Saṃghabhadra and Zhu Fonian had it translated into Chinese[1].

Saṃghabhadra often called on master monks and pursued his studies earlier on while he was in Jibin. After having extensively read Buddhist texts, Saṃghabhadra, who had expertise in several texts, especially recited the *Abhidharma-vibhāṣā* secretly and was well versed in its intent and main idea. Not long after arriving in Chang'an by the end of Fu Jian's reign period, Saṃghabhadra who recited and translated some texts was called by his believers *fajiang*［法匠，Dharma-master］, a teacher able to mould his pupils[2]. Among all the versions that he had recited or translated into Chinese, *Za apitan piposha* (*Saṁyuktābhidharma-vibhāṣā*) compiled by Shituopanni (Sitapāṅi or Śītapāṇi)[3] and others is an exegesis of *Apitan sishisipin*［阿毗昙四十四品，*Abhidharmajñānaprasthāna*］by Kātyāyanīputra［迦旃延子］who is often regarded as the founder of the Sarvāstivāda school[4]. *Poxumi ji* (*Vasumitra-śāstra*) or *Zun poxumi pusa suoji lun* (*Āryavasumitrabodhisattvasaṃgīti-śāstra*) is a text based on the doctrine of the Sarvāstivāda school in which Poxumi［婆须蜜 Vasumitra/ 世友 Shiyou］[5] explains the nature of various *dharmas*

---

［1］Sengyou, *opere citato*: 46-47; *confer*: *Taishō*, Vol. 55: 10b.

［2］Sengyou, *Chu sanzang ji ji: Sengqiebadeng zhuan*［出三藏记集：僧伽跋澄传，*A Collection of Records concerning the Tripiṭaka: Hagiography of Saṃghabhadra*］, Sengyou, *opere citato*: 522-523; *confer*: *Taishō*, Vol. 55: 99a-b.

［3］Lü Cheng, *opere citato*: 87, No. 1044.

［4］Sengyou, *opere citato*: 381-382; *confer*: *Taishō*, Vol. 55: 73b-c.

［5］Vasumitra is said to have led the 4th Buddhist Council in Jibin around the 2nd century AD and to help compile *Apidamo dapiposha lun*［阿毗达磨大毗婆沙论，*Abhidharmamahāvibhāṣā-śāstra* or *Mahāvibhāṣā, The Great Commentary on the Abhidharma*］, and *Yibu zonglun lun*［异部宗轮论，*Samayabhedoparacana-cakra, The Doctrines of the Different Schools*］seems to have been also compiled by him.

and their phenomenal expression respectively[1]. *Sengqieluocha ji jing* or *Sengqieluocha suoji jing* (*Saṃgharakṣa's Yogācārabhūmi*/*Saṃgharakṣa-sañcaya-buddhacarita-sūtra*) is a text written by Sengqieluocha [Saṃgharakṣa / 众护 /Zhonghu], whose detailed accounts about Buddha's forty-five-year tranquil dwelling and preaching after his enlightenment cannot be found in other Buddhist texts[2].

(3) Saṃghadeva, whose name was transliterated as Sengqietipo [僧伽提婆][3]/Sengqietihe [僧伽提和][4]/Sengjiadipo [僧迦禘婆]/Sengqiedipo [僧伽禘婆][5] or paraphrased as Zhongtian [众天][6], came to Chang'an around 383 AD. Then he moved to Luoyang [洛阳] and Mount Lu [庐山], and finally arrived in Jiankang [建康, present-day Nanjing], capital of the Eastern Jin Dynasty. Saṃghadeva is recorded as having recited or translated six following Buddhist texts into Chinese:

1) *Zhong ahanjing* [中阿经, *Madhyamāgama, Medium-Length Āgama Sūtra*][7], 60 fascicles, was recited and translated on the 10th day of the 11th month of the 1st year of the Long'an [隆安] period (December 15, 397 AD) of the Eastern Jin Dynasty at the Dongting Monastery [东亭寺] (in Jiankang), the translation work was completed on the 25th day of the 6th month of 2nd year of the same period (July 25, 398 AD)[8]. It is different from the version translated by Tanmonanti (Dharmanandi);

2) *Apitan bajiandu* [阿毗昙八揵度, *Abhidharmāṣṭagrantha* or *Aṣṭagrantha, Treatise on the Source of Wisdom in Eight Compositions*][9], 20 fascicles, also called *Jiazhanyan apitan* [迦旃延阿毗昙, *Kātyāyanīputra's Abhidharma*], was

---

[1] Sengyou, *opere citato*: 375-376; *confer*: *Taishō,* Vol. 55: 71c-72a.

[2] Sengyou, *opere citato*: 373-375; *confer*: *Taishō,* Vol. 55: 71b-c.

[3] Sengyou, *opere citato*: 49, 71, 79, 377-378, 379, 380, 523, 524, 565, 568; *confer*: *Taishō,* Vol. 55: 10c, 14b, 15a, 72b, 72c-73a, 73a-b, 99b, 109a, 110a.

[4] Sengyou, *opere citato*: 337-338; *confer*: *Taishō,* Vol. 55: 63c.

[5] Sengyou, *opere citato*: 376-377; *confer*: *Taishō,* Vol. 55: 72a-b.

[6] Huijiao, *opere citato*: 37-39; *confer*: *Taishō,* Vol. 50: 328c-329a.

[7] This version was included in *Taishō,* No. 26, Vol. 1: 421-809.

[8] Sengyou, *opere citato*: 337-338; *confer*: *Taishō,* Vol. 55: 63c-64a.

[9] This version was included in *Taishō,* No. 1543, Vol. 26: 771-917.

recited or translated in the 19th year of the Jianyuan period (383 AD)[1];

3) *Apitan xin*［阿毗昙心, *Abhidharmahṛdaya*］[2], 16 or 13 fascicles, was recited or translated in Luoyang at the end of the Jianyuan period (365-384 AD) of Emperor Fu Jian;

4) *Piposha apitan*［鞞婆沙阿毗昙, *Vibhāṣābhidharma*］[3], 14 fascicles, which was also called *Guangshuo*［广说, *Vibhāṣā*］, was recited or translated into Chinese at the same time with *Apitan xin* (*Abhidharmahṛdaya*) in Luoyang;

5) *Apitan xin*［阿毗昙心, *Abhidharmahṛdaya, The Heart of the Abhidharma*］[4], 4 fascicles, was recited or translated into Chinese at the request of Monk Huiyuan［慧远, 334-416 AD］at Mount Lu in the 16th year of the Taiyuan［太元］period of

---

［1］Acccording to *Apitan xü*［阿毗昙序, Preface to the Chinese version of *Abhidharmāṣṭagrantha*］by Dao'an, Saṃghadeva, who recited this text very fluently and smoothly, arrived in Chang'an in the 19th year of the Jianyuan period (383 AD). *Bhikṣu* Fahe requested him to recite or write out this text, Zhu Fonian had it translated into Chinese, Huili［慧力］and Sengmao［僧茂］took down what was dictated. The translation began on the 20th day of the 4th month of the same lunar year (June 6, 383 AD) and completed on the 23rd day of the 10th month of the same year (December 3, 383 AD). Because Dao'an and Fahe were not satisfied with the translation, corrections were made to this version for over 46 days and it was then finalized. Sengyou, *opere citato*: 376-377; *confer*: *Taishō,* Vol. 55: 72a-72b.

［2］According to *Zhongjing mulu* (*A Catalogue of Tripiṭaka*) by Fajing in 594 AD, Saṃghadeva recited and translated the original text of *Apitanxin* (*Abhidharmahṛdaya*) into Chinese twice. The first translated version, 5 fascicles or 16 fascicles, was completed either in Chang'an or Luoyang during the Jianyuan period (365-384 AD) of the Former Qin State; while the second version, 4 fascicles, was finished at Mt. Lu during the Taiyuan period (376-396 AD) of the Eastern Jin Dynasty. Fajing, *Zhongjing mulu*, in: *Taishō,* Vol. 55: 142b.

On the basis of *Erqin lü*［二秦录, *The Former Qin and Later Qin States' Catalogue of the Buddhist Scriptures*］by Sengrui［僧叡］, Fei Zhangfang records this version had 16 fascicles in *Lidai sanbao ji*; *confer*: *Taishō,* Vol. 49: 76a.

［3］translator's name of this version was labeled as Saṃghabhadra later by Sengyou, on the basis of "*Piposha xü*［鞞婆沙序, Preface to the Chinese version of *Vibhāṣā*］" by Monk Dao'an, in *Chu sanzang ji ji*; and the name of the version was slightly changed to *Piposha lun*［鞞婆沙论, *Vibhāṣā-ṣāstra*］in *Kaiyuan shijiao lu* by Zhisheng. 1) Sengyou, *opere citato*:381-382; *confer*: *Taishō,* Vol. 55: 73b-73c; 2) Zhisheng, *ibidem,* in：*Taishō,* Vol. 55: 510c.

Presently, most scholars believe this *Vibhāṣā* was recited and translated by Saṃghabhadra. 1) Tang Yongtong, *opere citato*: 158-159; 2) Lü Cheng, *Zhongguo foxue yuanliu luejiang*［中国佛学源流略讲, *A Survey of Chinese Buddhism*］, Beijing: Zhonghua Book Company, 1979: 66.

The version is included in *Taishō,* No. 1547, Vol. 28: 416-524.

［4］This text was included in *Taishō,* No. 1550, Vol. 28: 809-832.

the Eastern Jin Dynasty, i. e., 391 AD[1];

6) *San fadu* [三法度, *Tri-dharmika-śāstra* or *Tridharmakhaṇḍa, Treatise on the Three Dharmaskandhas*][2], 2 fascicles, was recited or translated into Chinese at Mount Lu in the 16th year of the Taiyuan period, i. e., 391 AD[3].

The above six texts, 116 fascicles in all, were recited or translated by Saṃghadeva, a monk from Jibin, during the reign period of Emperor Xiaowu and Emperor An [安帝, 396-418 AD] of the Eastern Jin Dynasty.[4]

Saṃghadeva was a specialist of *Apitanxin* (*Abhidharmahṛdaya*); he was considered to be well versed in the *Tripiṭaka,* by reciting always *Sanfadu* (*Tri-dharmika-śāstra* or *Tridharmakhaṇḍa*)[5]. Saṃghadeva is credited with the translation of 6 *sūtras* and treatises. Among them, *Zhong ahanjing* (*Madhyamāgama*), one of the four Chinese *Āgama sūtras*, consists of 222 *sūtras* of medium length and explains such basic doctrines as the four noble truths and the twelve-linked chain of causation[6]. Because of this renowned translation, Saṃghadeva became a famous teacher and eminent scholar in Jiankang at the end of the 4th century AD. *Apitan bajiandu* (*Abhidharmāṣṭagrantha*) or

---

[1] According to "*Apitanxin xü* [阿毗昙心序, Preface to the Chinese version of *Abhidharmahṛdaya*)" by an unknown author and "*Apitanxin xü* (Preface to the Chinese version of *Abhidharmahṛdaya*)" by Monk Huiyuan, this *Apitanxin* (*Abhidharmahṛdaya*), which was compiled by Fasheng (Dharmaśreṣṭhin) on the basis of *Apitan jing* [阿毗昙经, *Abhidharmamahāvibhāṣā-śāstra*], was recited and translated into Chinese by Saṃghabhadra at the Nanshan Monastery [南山精舍] in Xunyang [浔阳, present-day Jiujiang/ 九江]. Daoci [道慈] took down what was dictated. In the autumn of the next year, Saṃghabhadra and Daoci rectified the translation and finalized the Chinese version. Sengyou, *opere citato*: 377-379; *confer*: *Taishō*, Vol. 55: 72b-73a.

[2] This version was included in *Taishō,* No. 1506, Vol. 25: 15-29. The original of this text was compiled by Posubatuo [婆素跋陀/Vasubhadra, 世贤/Shixian] who was regarded as the master or founder of Xianzhoubu [贤胄部 Bhadrayānīyāḥ/Bhadrayānika] school. Lü Cheng, *opere citato* (*Zhongguo Foxue...*) : 73-74.

[3] see: "*Sanfadujing xü* [三法度经序, the Preface to Chinese version of *Tri-dharmika-śāstra*]" by Huiyuan and "*Sanfadujing ji* [三法度经记, Postscript to the Chinese version of *Tri-dharmika-śāstra*]" by an unknown author, in: Sengyou, *opere citato*: 379-380; *confer*: *Taishō,* Vol. 55: 73a-b.

[4] Sengyou, *opere citato*: 48-49; *confer*: *Taishō,* Vol. 55: 10c.

[5] Sengyou, *Chu sanzang ji ji: Sengqietipo zhuan* [出三藏记集：僧伽提婆传, *A Collection of Records concerning the Tripiṭaka: Hagiography of Saṃghadeva*], in: Sengyou, *opere citato*: 524-525; *confer*: *Taishō,* Vol. 55: 99b-100a.

[6] Sengyou, *opere citato*: 337-338; *confer*: *Taishō,* Vol. 55: 63c-64a.

Jiazhanyan apitan (*Kātyāyanīputra's Abhidharma*), another version of *Apitan sishisipin* (*Abhidharmajñānaprasthāna* or *Jñānaprasthāna-sūtra*)[1] written by Kātyāyanīputra, is a major work of the Sarvāstivāda or a fundamental *śāstra* of the Sarvāstivāda school. It contributes greatly to the systematization of the school's doctrine[2]. *Apitan xin* (*Abhidharmahṛdaya*) was compiled by Dharmaśresthin, with materials drawn from *Apitan jing* [阿毗昙经, *Abhidharmamahāvibhāṣā, The Great Commentary on the Abhidharma*] which is a detailed commentary on Kātyāyanīputra's *Abhidharmāṣṭagrantha* or *Jñānapraṣṭhāna-sūtra,* because *Apitan jing* (*Abhidharmamahāvibhāṣā*) was too extensive and profound for ordinary believers[3]. *Apitanxin* (*Abhidharmahṛdaya*) is the basic canon of the Sarvāstivāda school and was extremely popular for a time in Hinduka. As for *Piposha apitan* (*Vibhāṣābhidharma*) or *Guangshuo* (*Vibhāṣā*), the original text might be Sitapāṇi or Śītapāṇi's abridged copy of the *Mahāvibhāṣā*[4]. *Sanfadu* (*Tri-dharmika-śāstra* or *Tridharmakhaṇḍa*), which was originally compiled by Posubatuo (Vasubhadra) on the basis of the four *āgamas,* is an explanation of three *dharmas,* in other words, it is a commentary on the four *āgamas*; later, Sengqiexian [僧伽先, Saṃghasena] made an exegesis of it, for which monk Huiyuan wrote a preface[5].

(4) Buddhayaśas, whose name was transliterated as Fotuoyeshe [佛陀耶舍[6]/佛驮耶舍[7]] or paraphrased as Jueming [觉明[8]/觉名[9]]/Juecheng [觉称][10], is recorded as having recited or translated the following four texts into Chinese:

---

[1] This text is called as *Apitan* [阿毗昙], or *Fazhilun* [发智论] or *Bajiandulun* [八犍度论] in Chinese. Lü Cheng, *opere citato*: 66.

[2] Sengyou, *opere citato*: 376-377; *confer*: *Taishō,* Vol. 55: 72a-b.

[3] Sengyou, *opere citato*: 376-379; *confer*: *Taishō,* Vol. 55: 72a-73a.

[4] 1) Sengyou, *opere citato*: 381-382; *confer*: *Taishō,* Vol. 55: 73b-73c. 2) Kao Kuan-ju, "*Abhidharma-mahāvibhāṣā*", in: *Encyclopaedia of Buddhism,* Vol. I: 80-84.

[5] Sengyou, *opere citato*: 379-380; *confer*: *Taishō,* Vol. 55: 73a-b.

[6] Sengyou, *opere citato*: 77, 117-118, 336-337, 531, 536-538; *confer*: *Taishō,* Vol. 55: 14c, 20b-c, 63b-c, 100c, 102a-b.

[7] Sengyou, *opere citato*: 49, 51-52, 78, 81; *confer*: *Taishō,* Vol. 55: 10c, 11b, 14c, 15a.

[8] Sengyou, *opere citato*: 536; *confer*: *Taishō,* Vol. 55: 102a.

[9] Fei Zhangfang, *ibidem,* in: *Taishō,* Vol. 49: 79c.

[10] Zhi Sheng, *ibidem,* in: *Taishō,* Vol. 55: 516c.

1) *Chang ahanjing* [长阿含经, *Dīrghāgama, The Long Āgama Sūtra*][1] has 22 fascicles. The original was recited or wrote down by Buddhayaśas and Zhu Fonian had it translated into Chinese in the 15th year of the Hongshi period [弘始, 399-415 AD] of the Later Qin state [后秦], i. e., 413 AD[2];

2) *Tanwude lü* [昙无德律, *Dharmaguptaka-vinaya*][3], 45 fascicles, was put into *Lülu* [律录, *A Catalogue of the Vinaya-piṭaka*][4];

3) *Xukongzang jing* [虚空藏经, *Ākāśagarbha-sūtra*], 1 fascicle, was also called *Xukongzang pusa jing* [虚空藏菩萨经, *Ākāṣagarbhabodhisattva-sūtra,* The (*Bodhisattva*) *Space Treasury Sūtra*][5]. After Buddhayaśas returned to a foreign land, he found this *sūtra* in Jibin and asked a merchant to carry the version to

---

[1] This version was included in *Taishō,* No. 1, Vol. 1: 1-149.

[2] According to "*Chang ahanjing xü* [长阿含经序, Preface to the Chinese version of *Dīrghāgama*]" by Monk Sengzhao [僧肇, 384-414 AD], this *Chang ahanjing* (*Dīrghāgama*) was recited or written down by Buddhayaśas in the 15th year of the Hongshi period (413 AD); Zhu Fonian had it translated into Chinese, Daohan [道含] took down what was dictated, and some eminent monks living in Chang'an rectified the interpretation or translation. Sengyou, *opere citato*: 336-337; *confer*: *Taishō,* Vol. 55: 63b-c.

[3] This version was also called *Tanwude sifen lü* [昙无德四分律, *The Fourfold Rules of Discipline of the Dharmaguptakas* or *Dharmagupta-caturvarga-vinaya-piṭaka*] by Sengyou, or later simplified as *Sifen lü* [四分律, *The Fourfold Rules of Discipline* or *Caturvarga-vinaya-piṭaka*] by Fei Zhangfang in *Lidai sanbao ji*. It was divided into 60 fascicles and included in *Taishō,* No. 1428, Vol. 22: 567-1014. *confer*: 1) Sengyou, *opere citato*: 117-118, or *Taishō,* Vol. 55: 20b-c; 2) *Taishō,* Vol. 49: 79c-80b.

"*Fourfold*" in the title refers to the fact that the work consists of four *vargas* or divisions.

[4] According to *Chang ahanjing xü* (Preface to the Chinese version of *Dīrghāgama*) by Sengzhao and *Xinji lü lai handi sibu jilu* [新集律来汉地四部记录, *A Record of newly collected Four Vinayas spread to China*] by Sengyou, Buddhayaśas began to recite or write down the original text of *Lüzang sifen* [律藏四分, *The Fourfold Rules of Discipline* or *Caturvarga-vinaya-piṭaka*] in the 12th year of the Hongshi period (410 AD) and completed the work in the 14th year (412 AD) of the same period, then, he completed the task of reciting or writing down the original of *Chang ahanjing* (*Dīrghāgama*) in the 15th year of the Hongshi period (413 AD); Zhu Fonian had them translated into Chinese, Daohan took down what was dictated and eminent monks living in Chang'an rectified the interpretation or translation. *Sifen lü xü* [四分律序, Preface to the Chinese version of *The Fourfold Rules of Discipline*] by an unknown author, however, records this *vinaya* was recited by Buddhayaśas in the 10th year of the Hongshi period (408 AD) and Huibian [慧辩] had it translated into Chinese. 1) Sengyou, *opere citato*: 117-118, 336-337, 536-538; *confer*: *Taishō,* Vol. 55: 20b-c, 63b-c, 102a-c; 2) *Taishō,* Vol. 22: 567a-b.

[5] This version stands alone originally from the *Mahāsaṃnipāta-sūtra* [大集经] on the basis of *Kaiyuan shijiao lu* by Zhiseng and was included in *Taishō,* No. 405, Vol. 13: 647-655. *confer*: *Taishō,* Vol. 55: 516b.

Liangzhou.

4) The *Tanwude jieben* [昙无德戒本, *Dharmaguptaka-prātimokṣa or Prātimokṣa of the Dharmaguptaka-nikāya*][1], 1 fascicle.

The above four texts, 69 fascicles in all, were recited or translated by Buddhayaśas, a *dharma-bhāṇaka* or *tripiṭakācārya* (a master of three *piṭakas*) from Jibin, in Chang'an in the middle of the Hongshi period of Yao Xing [姚兴], ruler of the Later Qin state, which corresponds to the reign period of Emperor An of the Eastern Jin Dynasty[2].

It is alleged that Buddhayaśas could recite 2 million words of both Hīnayāna and Mahāyāna texts when he was 19 years old. He went to Chang'an at the invitation of Kumārajīva and assisted him in the translation of *Shizhujing* [十住经, *Daśabhūmika*][3]. Because Buddhayaśas was an expert in *Vibhāṣā,* he was known as the Red-beard *Vibhāṣā*[4]. Buddhayaśas recited and translated the *Dharmaguptaka-vinaya* in 412 AD, and then the Chinese version of *Dīrghāgama* was also recited and completed by him along with his colleagues in 413 AD.[5] According to *Sifenlü xü* [四分律序, *Preface to the Chinese version of the Fourfold Rules of Discipline*][6], Buddhayaśas, who embodied Mahāyāna Buddhism, was a scholar of Hīnayāna, a master monk of the *Dharmaguptaka*. Among his translations, *Chang ahanjing* (*Dīrghāgama*), one of the four Chinese *Āgama sūtras,* is a collection of 30 comparatively long *sūtras*[7]. It is generally believed

[1] This version was later called *Sifenlü biqiu jieben* [四分律比丘戒本, *Caturvarga vinaya-bhikṣu-pratimokṣa*] by Daoxuan in *Datang neidian lu* or *Sifenseng jieben* [四分僧戒本, *Caturvarga-Saṃgha-pratimokṣa* or *Dharmagupta-bhikṣu-pratimokṣa*] by Zhiseng in *Kaiyuan shijiao lu* and was included in *Taishō,* No. 1429 and 1430, Vol. 22: 1015-1023 or 1023-1030; *confer*: *Taishō,* Vol. 55: 324a, 516b.

[2] Sengyou, *opere citato*: 51-52; *confer*: *Taishō,* Vol. 55: 11b.

[3] Sengyou, *opere citato*: 49; *confer: Taishō,* Vol. 55: 10c.

[4] Sengyou, *Chu sanzang ji ji: Fotuoyeshe zhuan* [出三藏记集·佛陀耶舍传, *A Collection of Records concerning the Tripiṭaka: Hagiography of Buddhayaśas*], in: Sengyou, *opere citato*: 536-538; *confer*: *Taishō,* Vol. 55: 102a-c.

[5] Sengzhao, "*Chang ahanjing xü* (Preface to the Chinese version of *Dīrghāgama*)", in: Sengyou, *opere citato*: 336-337;*confer*: *Taishō,* Vol. 55: 63b-c.

[6] The author of the "*Preface to the Chinese version of the Fourfold Rules of Discipline*" is unknown. *Confer*: *Taishō,* Vol. 22: 567a.

[7] Sengyou, *opere citato*: 336-337; *confer*: *Taishō,* Vol. 55: 63b-c.

that the prototype of the Chinese *Dīrghāgama* was preserved and transmitted by the Dharmaguptakas[1]. *Tanwude lü* (*Dharmaguptaka-vinaya*), which is a text of the *Dharamaguptaka* on the rules of monastic discipline, had a great influence on the Chinese Buddhism. *Xukongzang jing* (*Ākāśagarbha-sūtra*) or *Xukongzang pusa jing* (*Ākāśagarbhabodhisattva-sūtra*) is a text on a bodhisattva, whose wisdom and good fortune is as vast and boundless as the universe. *Tanwude jieben* (*Dharmaguptaka-prātimokṣa*) is a text on commandments for monks that belong to the *Dharmaguptaka* school.

(5) The Dharmayaśas, whose name was transliterated as Tanmoyeshe [昙摩耶舍][2]/ Damoyeshe [达摩耶舍][3] or paraphrased as Faming [法明][4]/ Facheng [法称][5], had a sobriquet "*Dapiposha* [大毗婆沙 /*Mahā-vaibhāṣika,* a great master of *Vibhāṣā*]", of which, the abbreviated form is *Piposha* (毗婆沙 , *vaibhāṣika*)[6].

Shelifu apitan [舍利弗阿毗昙 , *Śāriputrābhidharma-śāstra, The Treatise on Śāriputrā's Abhidharma*] consists of 22 or 20 fascicles[7].

The above text, 22 fascicles in all, was recited or translated by the foreign

[1] Chongfeng Li, "Representation of the Buddha's *Parinirvāṇa* in the *Chetiyagharas* at Kizil, Kucha", in: *Buddhist Narrative in Asia and Beyond,* Vol. I, eds. Peter Skilling and Justin McDaniel, Bangkok: Institute of Thai Studies, Chulalongkorn University, 2012: 59-81, esp. 69-74.

[2] Sengyou, *opere citato*: 232, 373; *confer*: *Taishō,* Vol. 55: 40c, 71a.

[3] Sengyou, *opere citato*: 538; *confer*: *Taishō,* Vol. 55: 102c.

[4] 1) Sengyou, *opere citato*: 538; *confer*: *Taishō,* Vol. 55: 102c; 2) Huijiao, *opere citato*: 41; *confer*: *Taishō,* Vol. 50: 329b.

[5] Daoxuan, *ibidem,* in: *Taishō,* Vol. 55: 252b.

[6] Here, *piposha* (毗婆沙 , *Vaibhāṣika*) means a master of *Vibhāṣā* or an exegete of *Vibhāṣā*. Sengyou, *opere citato*: 52, 80, 118; *confer*: *Taishō,* Vol. 55: 11b, 15a, 20c.

[7] According to *Shelifu apitan xü* [舍利弗阿毗昙序 , Preface to the Chinese version of *Śāriputrābhidharma-śāstra*] by Daobiao [道标], when *śramaṇa* Tanmojueduo [昙摩崛多 , Dharmagupta] and Tanmoyeshe (Dharmayaśas) of Hinduka came to Chang' an, the king of the Later Qin state [秦王] made an imperial edict to translate *Śāriputrābhidharma-śāstra*. The *dharma-bhāṇakas* [经师 , masters of the *Tripiṭaka*] were ordered to recite and to write down the *Huben* (Kharoṣṭhī or Brāhmī script) text in the 9th year of the Hongshi period (407 AD) of the Later Qin state. After they had become progressively familiar with the Chinese language, the *dharma-bhāṇakas* had it translated in the 16th year (414 AD) and the crown prince took down what was dictated. With the help of literati and learned monks, the version was rectified and finalized in the 17th year of the Hongshi period (415 AD). Sengyou, *opere citato*: 372-373; *confer*: *Taishō,* Vol. 55: 70c-71b.

śramaṇa Piposha (*vaibhāṣika*) for Yao Xing at Shiyang Monastery [石羊寺] in Chang'an during the reign period of Emperor An of the Eastern Jin Dynasty[1].

According to *Gaoseng zhuan* by Huijiao, Dharmayaśas, a *vyākhyātṛ* [义学, an exegete of Buddhist text] or *dharma-bhāṇaka* (a master of the *Tripiṭaka*)[2] from Jibin, who was known by Puṇyatāra when he was fourteen years old, was well versed in the *sūtras* and *vinayas* and was extremely outstanding in comprehension. It is said that Dharmayaśas, when he was about thirty, was told by a *deva* that he should go to different places to observe and to propagate Buddha's teaching. Then, he roamed all around the world, embarking on a series of journeys to other lands and countries. In the middle of the Long'an period (397-401 AD) of the Eastern Jin Dynasty, Dharmayaśas arrived in Guangzhou [广州] and stayed at the Baisha Monastery [白沙寺]. Because Dharmayaśas was an expert in *Vibhāṣā* or *Samantapāsādikā* [毗婆沙律], he was known by the name of *Dapiposha* [大毗婆沙, the great *vaibhāṣika*]. He was eighty-five years old by that time, with followers numbering to eighty-five. In the middle of the Yixi period [义熙, 405-418 AD], Dharmayaśas arrived in Chang'an, where Yao Xing had a deep respect for him. In the meanwhile, Tanmojueduo (Dharmagupta) happened to be in Chang'an, as like attracts like, Dharmayaśas and Dharmagupta together translated the *Śāriputrābhidharma-śāstra* into Chinese. Later, Dharmayaśas went southward to Jiangling [江陵] and stayed at the Xin Monastery [辛寺], where he carried forward *dhyāna* and widely disseminated meditative practice, with more than three hundred followers gathering around him. In the middle of the Yuanjia period (424-453 AD), he travelled west to Central Asia and nobody knew about his remaining years or his full span of life[3].

(6) Buddhabhadra, whose name was transliterated as Fotuobatuo [佛驮跋

---

[1] Sengyou, *opere citato*: 52; *confer*: *Taishō,* Vol. 55: 11b.

[2] Sengyou, *opere citato*: 373; *confer*: *Taishō,* Vol. 55: 71a.

[3] Huijiao, *opere citato*: 41-43; *confer*: *Taishō,* Vol. 50: 329b-c.

陀][1]/Fotuobatuoluo[佛驮跋陀罗[2]/佛陀跋陀罗[3]]/Fodabatuo[佛大跋陀][4]/Fodabatuoluo[佛大跋陀罗][5]/Fodubatuoluo[佛度跋陀罗][6] or paraphrased as Foxian[佛贤][7] or Juexian[觉贤][8], is recorded as having recited or translated the following 11 texts into Chinese:

1) *Dafangguangfo huayan jing* [大方广佛华严经, *Buddhāvataṃsaka-nāmamahāvaipulya-sūtra or Avataṃsaka-sūtra, The Flower Garland Sūtra*] has 50 fascicles[9]. The original *Huben* (Kharoṣṭhī or Brāhmī script) text was brought back from Khotan by *śramaṇa* Zhi Faling [支法领] and was translated at the Daochang Monastery [道场寺] on the 10th day of the 3rd month of the 14th year of the Yixi period of the Eastern Jin Dynasty, i. e, April 30, 418 AD. The translation work was completed on the 28th day of the 12th month of the 2nd year of the Yongchu period [永初] of the Song Dynasty [宋, 420-479 AD], i. e. February 5, 422 AD[10].

---

[1] Sengyou, *opere citato*: 54, 55, 71, 72, 76, 119, 541-543; *confer*: *Taishō,* Vol. 55: 11c, 12a, 14b-c, 21a, 112c.

[2] Sengyou, *opere citato*: 576, 578; *confer*: *Taishō,* Vol. 55: 112c, 113a.

[3] Fajing, *Zhongjing mulu*, in: *Taishō,* Vol. 55: 115a, 116b, 119b-c, 130b, 140a-b.

[4] Sengyou, *opere citato*: 316; *confer*: *Taishō,* Vol. 55: 60b.

[5] Sengyou, *opere citato*: 474; *confer*: *Taishō,* Vol. 55: 89c.

[6] Sengyou, *opere citato*: 326; *confer*: *Taishō,* Vol. 55: 61a.

[7] 1) Sengyou, *opere citato*: 541-43; *confer*: *Taishō,* Vol. 55: 103b-104a; 2) Huijiao, *opera citato*: 142; *confer*: *Taishō,* Vol. 50: 345c.

[8] Huijiao, *opere citato*: 69-75; *confer*: *Taishō,* Vol. 50: 334b-335c.

[9] Later, this version was redivided into 60 fascicles and called *Sixty Huayan,* it was included in *Taishō,* No. 278, Vol. 9: 395-788.

[10] Sengyou, *opere citato*: 53-54; *confer*: *Taishō,* Vol. 55: 11c. According to *Huayanjing ji* [华严经记, Preface to the Chinese version of *Avataṃsaka-sūtra*], the original *Huben* (Kharoṣṭhī or Brāhmī script) text of the *Huayan jing* (*Avataṃsaka-sūtra*) consisted of 100, 000 *ślokas,* but that brought back by *śramaṇa* Zhi Faling from Khotan and left untranslated contained 36, 000 *ślokas*. The latter was translated on the 10th day of the 3rd month of the 14th year of the Yixi period of the Eastern Jin Dynasty, i. e, April 30, 418 AD, at the Daochang Monastery which was set up at Yangzhou [扬州] by Xieshi [谢石]. Buddhabhadra, a master of *dhyāna* from Hinduka, was invited to check up the original *Fanwen* (Brhāmī-script) text and to translate it into Chinese, Shi Faye [释法业] personally took down what was dictated. The translation work, which was supported by two donors, Mengyi [孟顗] and Chu Shudu [褚叔度], was completed on the 10th day of the 6th month of the 2nd year of Yuanxi [元熙] period of the Eastern Jin Dynasty, i. e., July 6, 420 AD, but the final revision was completed on the 28th day of the 12th month of the 2nd year of the Yongchu period of the Song Dynasty , i. e. February 5, 422 AD. Sengyou, *opere citato*: 326; *confer*: *Taishō,* Vol. 55: 61a.

2) *Guanfo sanmei jing* [观佛三昧经, *Buddhadhyāna-samādhisāgara-sūtra,* Contemplation of the Buddha], 8 fascicles[1];

3) *Xin wuliangshou jing* [新无量寿经, *New Amitābhavyūha*], 2 fascicles, was translated at the Daochang Monastery in the 2nd year of the Yongchu period (422 AD);

4) *Chanjing xiuxing fangbian* [禅经修行方便, *Yogacaryā-bhūmi-sūtra* or *Yogācārabhūmi*], 2 fascicles, which was also called *Yuqiezheluofumi* [庾伽遮罗浮迷] and paraphrased as *Xiuxing daodi* [修行道地] or *Bujingguan jing* [不净观经][2], consists of 17 *vargas* [品][3];

5) *Dafangdeng rulaizang jing* [大方等如来藏经, *Tathāgatagarbha-sūtra*], 1 fascicle, was also designated as *Rulaizang* [如来藏], presently missing[4].

6) *Pusa shizhu jing* [菩萨十住经], 1 fascicle;

7) *Chusheng wuliangmen chijing* [出生无量门持经, *Anantamukhanīhāra-dhāraṇī*][5], 1 fascicle;

8) *Xin weimi chijing* [新微密持经][6], 1 fascicle, presently missing;

9) *Benye jing* [本业经], 1 fascicle, presently missing;

10) *Jing liu boluomi jing* [净六波罗蜜经, *The Pure Six Pāramitā Sūtra*], 1 fascicle, presently missing;

11) *Wenshushili fayuan jing* [文殊师利发愿经, *Samantabhadrapraṇidhāna* or *Samantabhadra-caryā-praṇidhāna-rāja*][7], 1 fascicle, was translated at Daochang[8] Monastery in the 2nd year of the Yuanxi period of the Eastern Jin

---

[1] It was later divided into 10 fascicles and included in *Taishō,* No. 643, Vol. 15: 645-697.

[2] Huiyuan and Huiguan [慧观] wrote a preface to this text, respectively. According to their prefaces, this text was derived and translated from the works of both Dharmatrāta and Buddhasena on the methods of *dhyāna*. Sengyou, *opere citato*: 343-345, 346-348; *confer*: *Taishō,* Vol. 55: 65b-66a, 66b-67a.

[3] It is often called *Damoduoluo chan jing* [达摩多罗禅经, *Dharmatrāta's Dhyāna-sūtra*] and was included in *Taishō,* No. 618, Vol. 15: 300-325.

[4] It was included in *Taishō,* No. 666, Vol. 16: 457-460.

[5] It was included in *Taishō,* No. 1012, Vol. 19: 682-685.

[6] It seems to be another version of the above *Chusheng wuliangmenchijing* (*Anantamukhanīhāra-dhāraṇī*).

[7] It was included in *Taishō,* No. 296, Vol. 10: 878-879.

[8] Daochang was often written as Douchang [斗场]. Sengyou, *opere citato*: 350; *confer*: *Taishō,* Vol. 55: 67c.

Dynasty, i. e. 420 AD.

The above 10 or 11 texts, 67 or 69 fascicles in all, were recited and translated by Buddhabhadra, a master of *dhyāna* from Hinduka, at Mount Lu or in the capital (Jiankang), in the earlier Song Dynasty. Buddhabhadra came to Jiangdong [江东, a region lying to the east of the Yangzi river, i. e., Jiankang] during the reign period of Emperor An of the Eastern Jin Dynasty[1].

Buddhabhadra, a native of North Hinduka, became a monk at age 17 and showed extraordinary skills and aptitude in reciting the scriptures, often finishing one month's lessons in a single day. He had a comprehensive understanding of canonical texts and was particularly famous for his cultivation of *dhyāna* and *vinaya*. Later, he went to Jibin and applied more strenuous efforts under the instruction of Buddhasena, a great *dhyāna* master at that time. It was there that he met the Chinese monk Zhiyan who invited him to go to China to propagate Buddha's teaching; as this was just what Buddhabhadra had long wished for, he immediately complied. After arriving in Chang'an, Buddhabhadra and Kumārajīva were on very friendly terms at first, the former had assisted the latter in the translation of the Buddhist scriptures, and they often had discussions together and mutually explored some of the abstruse implications of canonical texts. Nevertheless, their intellectual approach differed because in matters of doctrine they belonged to different schools. Kumārajīva devoted himself to disseminating the teachings of *sūtras,* particularly the Mahāyāna doctrine of Nāgārjuna, and was favourably recognized by Yao Xing, ruler of the Later Qin state. Moreover, Kumārajīva and his disciples, more than three thousands in number, could freely go in and out of the palace and court. Buddhabhadra, instead, strictly adhered to the modes of teaching of the Sthaviravāda of the Śrāvakayāna, cultivating meditation and concentration, living a plain and simple life without any display or show. Owing to such divergences, gradually discord arose between the disciples of the two masters. In the 17th year of the Yixi period (411 AD) of the Eastern Jin Dynasty, some disciples of Kumārajīva blamed Buddhabhadra of being guilty of telling a lie—thus breaking a fundamental commandment—and relying upon

[1] Sengyou, *opere citato*: 53-54; *confer*: *Taishō,* Vol. 55: 11c.

popular support. This situation compelled Buddhabhadra to leave Chang'an; he went southward to Mt. Lu where he was welcomed by Huiyuan, who had heard of Buddhabhadra's fame. During his residence at Mt Lu, Buddhabhadra, at the request of Huiyuan, lectured on the doctrine of meditation and translated a special *dhyāna* work—the *Yogacaryā-bhūmi-sūtra*—which greatly helped him in his meditation. It is generally believed that the monk's wish of Hinduka was to go to different places to propagate Buddha's teaching. Later on, Buddhabhadra left Mt. Lu and went westward to Jingzhou［荆州］and finally arrived in the capital (Jiankang). He lived at the Daochang Monastery where he translated a number of Buddhist scriptures into Chinese[1].

After his arrival in Jiankang, Buddhabhadra still taught his *dhyana* method; his residence, the Daochang monastery, became known as "the cave of masters of *dhyāna*". "Not long after, Faxian came back from his travels in India. Then they began to cooperate in doing translation work". From the 12th to the 14th year of the Yixi period (416-18 AD), Buddhabhadra and Faxian translated into Chinese the *Huben* (Kharoṣṭhī or Brāhmī script) manuscripts brought back by the latter, namely the *Dabonihuan jing*［大般泥洹经, *Mahāparinirvāṇa-sūtra*］[2], *Mohesengqi lü*［摩诃僧祇律, *Mahāsaṃghika-vinaya, The Great Canon of*

［1］1) Sengyou, *Chu sanzang ji ji: Fotuobatuo zhuan*［出三藏记集：佛陀跋陀传, *A Collection of Records concerning the Tripiṭaka: Hagiography of Buddhabhadra*］, Sengyou, *opere citato*: 541-543; *confer*: *Taishō*, Vol. 55: 103b-104a; 2) Huijiao, *opere citato*: 69-75; *confer*: *Taishō*, Vol. 50: 334b-335c; 3) Lü Chêng, "Buddhabhadra", in: *Encyclopaedia of Buddhism*, Vol. III: 382-384.

［2］The original text of the *Dabonihuan jing* (*Mahāparinirvāṇa-sūtra*) was brought back to China by Faxian from the Tianwang Monastery (Heavenly King Vihāra) in Pāṭaliputra, Magadha.

According to *Liujuan nihuanjing ji*［六卷泥洹经记, Postcript to the Chinese version of *Six-volume Mahāparinirvāṇa-sūtra*］, this *Fangdeng dabonihuan jing*［方等大般泥洹经, *Vaipulya-Mahāparinirvāṇa-sūtra* or *Mahāparinirvāṇa-sūtra*］began to be translated on the 1st day of the 10th month or 11th month of the 13th year of the Yixi period (October 26, 417 AD or November 25, 417 AD) at the Daochang Monastery. Buddhabhadra, a master of *dhyāna*, checked up the original *Huben* (Kharoṣṭhī or Brāhmī script) text, Baoyun had it translated into Chinese, with 250 followers gathering to listen. The Chinese revision was finalized on the 1st day of the 1st month of the 14th year of the same period (February 21, 418 AD). Sengyou, *opere citato*: 55, 316; *confer*: *Taishō*, Vol. 55: 11c, 60b.

Monastic Rules][1], *Sengqi biqiu jieben* [僧祇比丘戒本, *Mahāsaṃghika-bhikṣu-prātimokṣa*] and *Zazang jing* [杂藏经, *Kṣudraka-sūtra*][2]. Having accumulated a great deal of experience in translation, Buddhabhadra accepted a request from both Meng Yi and Chu Shudu in 418 AD and worked together with more than one hundred *śramaṇas* to translate the *Buddhāvataṃsaka-nāmamahāvaipulya-sūtra.* In the course of more than three years, he completed the translation and made the version faithfully reflect the original; this work later greatly influenced the development of Buddhist teaching in China and greatly contributed to it. Buddhabhadra died in the 6th year of the Yuanjia period (429 AD), at the age of seventy-one[3].

According to the study by Lü Cheng, although Buddhabhadra's translations touched upon different aspects of Buddhism, his special attention was concentrated on the methods of meditative contemplation. Buddhabhadra had translated the works of both Dharmatrāta and Buddhasena on the methods of *dhyāna*. Of course, Kumārajīva also taught meditation, but he recommended only some essentials of *dhyāna* of the old masters of the Sthaviravāda of the Śrāvakayāna without giving them an orderly and systematic formulation. Buddhabhadra's methods, however, were those handed down from master to disciples for generations and therefore kept their purity intact or the original version. Thus, Buddhabhadra's translations have unexpectedly become the precursor of the eastern flowering of the *Yogācāra* doctrines of Mahāyāna, which has implication on the history of Chinese Buddhism[4].

---

[1] According to *Mohesengqilü siji* [摩诃僧祇律私记, A Private Note of *Mahāsaṃghika-vinaya*] by Faxian, he wrote down the *Fanben* (Brāhmi script) text of *Mahāsaṃghika-vinaya* at the Tianwang Monastery [天王精舍, Heavenly King's Vihāra] in Pāṭaliputra, Magadha and brought it back to Yangzhou [扬州, i. e., Jiankang]. It began to be translated at the Douchang Monastery in the 11th month of the 12th year of the Yixi period (December 5, 416 AD to January 3, 417 AD) of the Eastern Jin Dynasty, but the translation work was completed at the end of the 2nd month of the 14th year of the same period (March 23-April 20, 418 AD). The master of *dhyāna* (Buddhabhadra) and I had the *Brāhmi* script text translated into Chinese. *Taishō,* Vol. 22: 548a-b.

[2] Sengyou, *opere citato*: 54-55; *confer*: *Taishō,* Vol. 55: 11c-12a.

[3] Sengyou, *opere citato*: 54-55, 542-543, 576; *confer*: *Taishō,* Vol. 55: 11c-12a, 104a, 112b.

[4] Lu Chêng, "Buddhabhadra", in: *Encyclopaedia of Buddhism,* Vol. III: 382-384.

(7) Buddhajīva, whose name was transliterated as Fodashi [佛大什][1]/ Fotuoshi [佛驮什[2]/佛陀什[3]] or paraphrased as Jueshou [觉寿][4], is recorded as having recited or translated the following three texts into Chinese:

1) *Mishasai lü* [弥沙塞律, *Mahīśāsaka-vinaya*][5] has 34 fascicles. The original of this text, brought back to China by Faxian, was written in *Huben* (Kharoṣṭhī or Brāhmī script) and was translated in the 7th month of the 1st year of the Jingping period [景平] of the Song Dynasty, i. e., August 23-September 20, 423 AD.[6] It had been already placed into *Lülu* (*A Catalogue of the Vinaya-piṭaka*);

2) *Mishasai biqiu jieben* [弥沙塞比丘戒本, *Mahīśāsaka-bhikṣu-prātimokṣa*][7], 1 fascicle, was translated into Chinese along with *Mishasai lü* (*Mahīśāsaka-vinaya*)

---

[1] Sengyou, *opere citato*: 119-120, 572; *confer*: *Taishō,* Vol. 55: 21a-b, 111b.

[2] Sengyou, *opere citato*: 57, 78; *confer*: *Taishō,* Vol. 55: 12b, 14c.

[3] Fei Zhangfang, *ibidem,* in: *Taishō,* Vol. 49: 89b.

[4] Huijiao, *opere citato*: 96; *confer*: *Taishō,* Vol. 50: 339a.

[5] The original text of *Mishasai lü* (*Mahīśāsaka-vinaya*) was brought back to China by Faxian from Siṃhala (present day Sri-Lanka). Because it consists of five divisions, this text was also called *Wufen lü* [五分律, *The Fivefold Rules of Discipline*] by Sengyou, or *Mishasai wufenlü* [弥沙塞五分律, *The Fivefold Rules of Discipline of the Mahīśāsaka* or *Mahīśasaka-nikāya-pañcavarga-vinaya*] by Daoxuan in *Datang neidian lu*. It was divided into 30 fascicles and included in *Taishō,* No. 1421, Vol. 22: 1-194. Sengyou, *opere citato*: 119-120; *confer*: *Taishō,* Vol. 55: 21a-b; *Taishō,* Vol. 55: 300a.

[6] According to *Xinji lü lai handi sibu jilu* (*Record of the newly collected Four Vinayas spread to China*) by Sengyou and *Lidai sanbao ji* by Fei Zhangfang, the original *Fanben* [梵本, Brāhmī script] text of *Mishasai lü* (*Mahīśāsaka-vinaya*) was brought back to China by Faxian in the 2nd year of the Yixi period of the Eastern Jin Dynasty, i. e., 406 AD. In the 7th month of the 1st year of the Jingping period of the Song Dynasty (August 23-September 20, 423 AD), Buddhajīva, a master of *vinaya* from Jibin, arrived in the capital (Jiankang). At the request of *śramaṇa* Shi Huiyan [释慧严] from the Dong'an Monastery [东安寺] and Zhu Daosheng [竺道生] from the Longguang Monastery [龙光寺], Buddhajīva recited or translated the text in the 11th month of the same lunar year (December 19, 423 AD to January 16, 424 AD) at the Longguang Monastery in the capital. During that period, Buddhajīva checked up the *Huwen* [胡文, Kharoṣṭhī or Brāhmī script] or *Fanben* (Brāhmī script) text, Zhisheng [智胜], a *śramaṇa* from Khotan, had it translated into Chinese, Zhu Daosheng and Huiyan took down what was dictated. The translation work was completed in the 12th month of the next year, i. e., January 6-Febrary 3, 425 AD. 1) Sengyou, *opere citato*: 119-120; *confer*: *Taishō,* Vol. 55: 21a-b; 2) Fei Zhangfang, *ibidem, Taishō,* Vol. 49: 89b.

[7] This version was later called *Mishasai wufen jieben* [弥沙塞五分戒本, *Mahīśāsaka-nikāya-pañcavarga-vinaya-pratimokṣa*] by Daoxuan in *Datang neidian lu* and was included in *Taishō,* No. 1422, Vol. 22: 194-206. *confer*: *Taishō,* Vol. 55: 324b.

at the same time;

3) *Mishasai jiemo* [弥沙塞羯磨, *Mahīśāsaka-karmavākya/karmavācana*][1], 1 fascicle, was translated into Chinese along with the *Mishasai lü* (*Mahīśāsaka-vinaya*) at the same time.

The above three texts, 36 fascicles in all, were recited or translated by Buddhajīva, a *vainayika* or specialist of the Buddhist *vinaya* from Jibin, at the request of *śramaṇa* Zhu Daosheng and Shi Huiyan at Longguang Monastery in the capital (Jiankang) during the reign period of Prince Yingyang [营阳王], i. e, Emperor Shao [少帝, 422-424 AD] of the Song Dynasty.[2]

According to Huijiao and Fei Zhangfang, Buddhajīva initially received instruction from the Mahīśāsakas. Not only was he familiar with the *vinaya* works, but also proficient in the *dhyāna* discipline[3]. Buddhajīva nearly had all the rules of the monastic discipline of the Mahīśāsaka school translated into Chinese. Among them, *Mishasai lü* (*Mahīśāsaka-vinaya*) is the basic *vinaya* text of the Mahīśāsaka school, while *Mishasai biqiu jieben* (*Mahīśāsaka-bhikṣu-prātimokṣa*) is an extract from the *Mahīśāsaka-vinaya. Mishasai jiemo* (*Mahīśāsaka-karmavākya*), which was also extracted from the *Mahīśāsaka-vinaya,* was a text of Official Acts that are read at the ecclesiastical formal meetings of *bhikṣus* in which matters of vital importance to the monastic order are discussed and decisions taken[4].

(8) Guṇavarman, whose name was transliterated as Qiunabamo [求那跋摩][5] or paraphrased as Gongdekai [功德铠, 367-431 AD][6], is recorded as having recited or translated four texts into Chinese:

1) *Pusa shanjie* [菩萨善戒, *Bodhisattvacaryā-nirdeśa* or *Bodhisattva-bhadraśīla-*

[1] This version was already lost when Zhisheng compiled *Kaiyuan shijiao lu* in 730 AD. Zhiseng, *ibidem,* in: *Taishō,* Vol. 55: 523c.

[2] Sengyou, *opere citato*: 57; *confer*: *Taishō,* Vol. 55: 12b.

[3] 1) Huijiao, *opere citato*: 96; *confer*: *Taishō,* Vol. 50: 339a; 2) Fei Zhangfang, *ibidem,* in: *Taishō,* Vol. 49: 22-128, esp. 89b.

[4] T. Ariyadhamma "Kammavācā", in: *Encyclopaedia of Buddhism,* Vol. VI: 124-125.

[5] Sengyou, *opere citato*: 57-58, 78, 333-334, 384, 543-544; *confer*: *Taishō,* Vol. 55: 12b, 14c, 62c, 74b, 104b-c.

[6] Sengyou, *opere citato*: 543; *confer*: *Taishō,* Vol. 55: 104b.

sūtra], 10 fascicles, was also called *Pusa di*［菩萨地，*Bodhisattvabhūmi*], 10 fascicles[1];

2) *Youposai wujie luelun*［优婆塞五戒略论，*Upāsaka-pañca-śīlāni-sūtra*], 1 fascicle, was also designated as *Youposai wujie xiang*［优婆塞五戒相］[2];

3) *Sangui ji youposai ershi'er jie*［三归及优婆塞二十二戒，*Tri-śaraṇa and Upāsaka-śīlās*][3], 1 fascicle, was also called *Youposai jie*［优婆塞戒］;

4) *Tanwude jiemo*［昙无德羯磨，*Dharamagupta-karmavākya* or *Dharamagupta-karmavācana*][4], 1 fascicle, was also called *Za jiemo*［杂羯磨，*Saṃyukta-karmavākya* or *Kṣudraka-karmavācana*].

The above four texts, 13 fascicles in all, were recited or translated by Guṇavarman, a *tripiṭakācārya* or master of *Tripiṭaka* from Jibin, in the capital during the reign period of Emperor Wen［文帝，424-453 AD］of the Song

---

[1] Sengyou, *opere citato*: 333-334; *confer*: *Taishō,* Vol. 55: 62c-63a. This version was later divided into two parts, a nine-fascicle *Bodhisattvacaryā-nirdeśa* and a one-fascicle *Bodhisattvacaryā-nirdeśa,* and included in *Taishō,* No. 1582 and No. 1583, Vol. 30: 960-1018.

According to *Dazhou kanding zhongjing mulu*［大周刊定众经目录，*A Catalogue of the Buddhist Canon compiled during the Reign Period of Empress Wu Zetian*］by Mingquan［明佺］in 695 AD, the original of this text was translated by Guṇavarman at the request of monk Huiyi［慧义］from the Qihuan Monastery［祇洹寺，Jetavana-ārāma］on the 21st day of the 2nd month of the 8th year of the Yuanjia period (March 20, 431 AD), and the latter took down what was dictated. When Guṇavarman moved to the Dinglin Monastery for *vārṣika* or *varṣa,* with two fascicles of the original text left unfinished, Sengqiebamo［僧伽跋摩，Saṃghavarman］, a brother of Guṇavarman, had the rest translated for him. *Taishō,* Vol. 55: 404a.

Here, it is worth noting that if Saṃghavarman was really the brother of Guṇavarman, consequently Saṃghavarman was a native of Jibin. What Saṃghavarman recited or translated seems to originate from Jibin. See Sengyou, *opere citato*: 58; *confer*: *Taishō,* Vol. 55: 12b.

[2] According to Fei Zhangfang's catalogue, the original of this text was translated into Chinese at the Qihuan Monastery in Jiankang in 431 AD. It was included in *Taishō,* No. 1476, Vol. 24: 939-944. *confer*: *Taishō,* Vol. 49: 90a.

[3] This version was already lost when Zhisheng compiled *Kaiyuan shijiao lu* in 730 AD. Zhisheng, *ibidem,* in: *Taishō,* Vol. 55: 526a.

[4] This version was called *Sifenjiemo*［四分羯磨，*Caturvarga-karmavākya/karmavācana*］by Fajing in *Zhongjing mulu* (*A Catalogue of Tripiṭaka*) in 594 AD or *Sifenni jiemo*［四分尼羯磨，*Caturvarga-vinaya-bhikṣuṇī-karmavākya/karmavācana* or *Dharmagupta-bhikṣuṇī-karmavākya/karmavācana*］by Daoxuan in *Datang neidian lu* or *Sifen biqiuni jiemo fa*［四分比丘尼羯磨法，*Caturvarga-vinaya-bhikṣuṇi-karmavākya/karmavācana* or *Dharmagupta-bhikṣuṇī-karman*］by Zhisheng in *Kaiyuan shijiao lu* and was included in *Taishō,* No. 1434, Vol. 22: 1065-1072. *confer*: *Taishō,* Vol. 55: 140b, 324b, 526a.

Dynasty[1].

Guṇavarman was an offspring [支胤] of the Jibin king, thus a member of the royal family of Jibin. He entered the Buddhist Order as a *śrāmaṇerika* at the age of 15 and mastered three divisions of the Buddhist texts. As a result, he became a specialist of *vinaya* works. At the age of 30, upon the death of the Jibin king, he was expected to become a king. Guṇavarman was afraid to mount the throne, so he went away to Siṃhala (present-day Sri Lanka) and then to Java to propagate Buddha's teaching, where he played a very important role in establishing Buddhism. Guṇavarman arrived in Jiankang in the 1st month of the 8th year of the Yuanjia period of the Song Dynasty, i. e., January 29-Febrary 27, 431 AD, and stayed at the Qihuan Monastery (Jetavana-ārāma). Later, he had the above-mentioned texts translated into Chinese at the same monastery before he died on the 28th day of the 9th month of the same lunar year (November 18, 431 AD), at the age of 65. In accordance with a foreign custom and way of *jhāpita* (cremation), he was cremated with sandalwood, and then a white *stūpa* was set up on the cremation[2].

As for his translations, the first chapter of *Pusa shanjie* (*Bodhisattvacaryā-nirdeśa* or *Bodhisattva-bhadraśīla-sūtra*) or *Pusa di* (*Bodhisattvabhūmi*) is similar to *Jueding pini jing* [决定毗尼经, *Vinaya-viniścaya-upāli-paripricchā*?], and the rest of *Pusa shanjie* (*Bodhisattvacaryā-nirdeśa*) is similar to the 15th part of *Pusa di* [菩萨地, *Bodhisattva-bhūmi*] in the first division of *Yuqie shidi lun* [瑜伽师地论, *Yogacārabhūmi*]. Not only does it give a minute description of a bodhisattva's seed nature, his bestowing the commandments on a disciple, his conducting and obtaining the fruit of deeds as well as his original seed and new seed, but also the ways of receiving the commandments or rules of a bodhisattva[3]. *Youposai wujie luelun*/*Youposai wujie xiang* (*Upāsaka-pañca-śīlāni-sūtra*) is a text preached

---

[1] Sengyou, *opere citato*: 57-58; *confer*: *Taishō*, Vol. 55: 12b.

[2] Sengyou, *Chu sanzang ji ji: Qiunabamo zhuan* [出三藏记集：求那跋摩传, *A Collection of Records concerning the Tripiṭaka: Hagiography of Guṇavarman*], in: Sengyou, *opere citato*: 543-544;*confer*: *Taishō*, Vol. 55: 104b-c.

[3] Sengyou, *opere citato*: 333-334; *confer*: *Taishō*, Vol. 55: 62c-63a.

by Śākyamuni Buddha at the request of King Suddhodana on the degree of seriousness of the *pañca-śīlāni* (five errors or sins) with examples. According to Fajing's catalogue, *Sifen jiemo* (*Caturvarga-karmavākya/karmavācana*) or *Tanwude jiemo* (*Dharamagupta-vinaya-karmavākya/karmavācana*) is a re-translation of *Jiemo* [羯磨, *Dharamagupta-vinaya-vinaya-karmavākya/karmavācana*] which was translated into Chinese by Tandi [昙谛, Dharmasatya], a Pathian [安息] monk, in Luoyang in the 1st year of the Zhengyuan period [正元] of Gaoguixianggong [高贵乡公] of the Wei Kingdom, i. e., 254 AD [1]. *Tanwude jiemo* (*Dharamagupta-vinaya-karmavākya/karmavācana*) is an extract from The *Dharmagupta-vinaya,* showing the ways of how to be rewarded with good and not with evil.

(9) Dharmamitra, whose name was transliterated as Tanmomiduo [昙摩蜜多[2]/ 昙摩密多[3]] or paraphrased as Faxiu [法秀][4], is recorded as having recited or translated the following four texts into Chinese:

1) *Guan puxian pusa xingfa jing* [观普贤菩萨行法经, *Samantabhadra-bodhisattva-dhyāna-caryādharma-sūtra, Sūtra on How to Practice Meditation on the Bodhisattva Universal Worthy*][5], which was also called *Puxian guan jing* [普贤观经, *Meditation on Universal Worthy Sūtra*], 1 fascicle, was produced or came from *Shen gongde jing* [深功德经] by its attached note;

2) *Xukongzang guan jing* [虚空藏观经, *Ākāśagarbha-sūtra* or *Ākāśagarbhabodhisattvadhāraṇī-sūtra*], 1 fascicle, was also called *Guan xukongzang pusa jing* [观虚空藏菩萨经, *Meditation on Bodhisattva Space Treasury Sūtra*][6];

3) *Chan miyao* [禅秘要, *Sūtra about the Secret Essence of Dhyāna*][7], 3 fascicles, was recited or translated in the 18th year of the Yuanjia period (441 AD).

---

[1] Fei Zhangfang, *ibidem,* in: *Taishō,* Vol. 49: 37a, 56c.

[2] Sengyou, *opere citato*: 58, 76, 545-547; *confer*: *Taishō,* Vol. 55: 12b-c, 14c, 105a-b.

[3] Huijiao, *opere citato*: 120-122; *confer*: *Taishō,* Vol. 50: 342c-343a.

[4] Sengyou, *opere citato*: 545; *confer*: *Taishō,* Vol. 55: 105a.

[5] This version was included in *Taishō,* No. 277, Vol. 9: 389-394.

[6] This version was included in *Taishō,* No. 409, Vol. 13: 677-680.

[7] According to Zhisheng, this version had been already lost when Zhisheng compiled *Kaiyuan shijiao lu* in 730 AD. *confer*: *Taishō,* Vol. 55: 664c.

It was also called *Chan fayao* [禅法要, *Sūtra on the Hidden and Important Law of the Meditation*], or 5 fascicles;

4) *Wumenchan jing yaoyong fa* [五门禅经要用法, *Pañcadvara-dhyāna-sūtra-mahāratha-dharma, Basic Ways in Sūtras about Five Gates Dhyāna* or *Essentials of Fivefold Meditation*][1], 1 fascicle.

The above four texts, 6 fascicles in all, were recited or translated by Dharmamitra, a *dhyātṛ* or master of *dhyāna* from Jibin, at Qihuan Monastery in the middle of the Yuanjia period (424-453 AD) of Emperor Wen of the Song Dynasty[2].

Dharmamitra entered the Buddhist Order in his very young days. He travelled through various lands and countries to pursue his study of the Buddhist texts before he visited Kucīna (Kucha) and stayed there for several years. Then, he went to Dunhuang [敦煌] and set up a *vihāra* planted with *āmra* trees in the wilderness. Later, he went to Liangzhou where he had many disciples who practiced *dhyāna* with him. Dharmamitra dedicated himself to the practice of meditation as a *dhyātṛ,* and went to Sichuan [蜀] and Jingzhou before he finally arrived in Jiankang, capital of southern China, where he converted Empress Yuan of Emperor Wen [宋文袁皇后] as well as crown princes and princesses of the Song Dynasty. While staying at the Qihuan Monastery, he recited or translated the above texts into Chinese and exhorted followers to practice meditation. Therefore he was called a great master of *dhyāna*. Dharmamitra had a peaceful and an understated character and was very fond of natural surroundings with hills and waters. He asked that a *stūpa* be built at a mountain near Maoxian [鄮县] and founded the famous Dinglin Shangsi [定林上寺, Upper Dinglin Monastery] at Mount Zhong [钟山], where he lived until he died, at the age of 87, on the 6th day of the 7th month of the 19th year of the Yuanjia period of the Song Dynasty, i.

[1] According to Zhisheng, this is the second version or a re-translation of the original; the first translation was completed by An Shigao [安世高]; in other words, the original of this text was compiled by Fotuomiduo [佛陀密多, Buddhamitra], a work identified with that of An Shigao's translation. Zhisheng, *ibidem,* in: *Taishō,* Vol. 55: 524a, 622c, 641b.

This version was included in *Taishō,* No. 619, Vol. 15: 325-333.

[2] Sengyou, *opere citato*: 58; *confer*: *Taishō,* Vol. 55: 12b-c.

e., August 27, 442 AD. [1] According to Fei Zhangfang, Dharmamitra devoted his life to the translation of *dhyāna* and *dhāraṇī* works[2]. Thus, seemingly he was extremely good in the matters of *dhāraṇī* besides *dhyāna*[3].

Among his translations, *Guan puxian pusa xingfa jing* (*Samantabhadra-bodhisattva-dhyāna-caryādharma-sūtra, Sūtra on How to Practice Meditation on the Bodhisattva Universal Worthy*) or *Puxian guan jing* (*Meditation on Universal Worthy Sūtra*) is a one-volume text that describes the beneficent power of the Bodhisattva Universal Worthy (Samantabhadra) and how to meditate on him. According to the *sūtra,* Śākyamuni Buddha says that the believers would attain Buddhahood by practicing meditation on the Bodhisattva Samantabhadra, carrying out repentance, and embracing the teaching of the Great Vehicle. *Xukongzang guan jing* (*Ākāśagarbha-sūtra*) or *Guan xukongzang pusa jing* (*Ākāśagarbhabodhisattvadhāraṇī-sūtra, Meditation on Bodhisattva Space Treasury Sūtra*) is another version of the *Ākāśagarbha-sūtra* translated by Buddhayaśas. *Chan miyao* (*Sūtra about the Secret Essence of Dhyāna*) or *Chan fayao* (*Sūtra on the Hidden and Important Law of the Meditation*), as the term suggests, is a text that describes the true nature and essential factors or elements of meditation, and *Wumenchan jing yaoyong fa* (*Pañcadvara-dhyāna-sūtra-mahāratha-dharma, Basic Ways in the Sūtra about Five Gates Dhyāna* or *Essentials of Fivefold Meditation*) compiled by Fotuomiduo (Buddhamitra)[4], a great master of *dhyāna,* is a text that describes the essentials of the fivefold meditation on impermanence, suffering, void, nonego, and *nirvāṇa*.

Besides the aforementioned nine eminent priests or great masters, there are

---

[1] Sengyou, *Chu sanzang ji ji: Tanmomiduo zhuan* [出三藏记集：昙摩蜜多传, *A Collection of Records concerning the Tripiṭaka: Hagiography of Dharmamitra*], in: Sengyou, *opere citato*: 545-547; *confer*: *Taishō,* Vol. 55: 105a-b.

[2] Fei Zhangfang, *ibidem,* in: *Taishō,* Vol. 49: 22-128, esp. 92c.

[3] Jingmai [静迈], *Gujin yijing tuji* [古今译经图纪, *Illustrated Record of Ancient and Modern Translations of Sūtras or Record of Illustration of Translating Buddhist Tripiṭaka through the Ages*] in mid-7th century AD. *confer*: *Taishō,* Vol. 55: 348-367, esp. 361b.

[4] Some scholars believe that this text was compiled by Dharmamitra between 424 and 442 AD in south China. Charles Willemen, *Outlining the Way to Reflect* [思维略要法] (T. XV 617), Mumbai: Somaiya Publications Pvt Ltd, 2012: 6-7.

four more master-monks from Jibin recorded in *Chu sanzang ji ji* by Sengyou.

(10) Saṃgharakṣa[1], whose name was transliterated as Sengqieluocha [僧伽罗叉], helped Saṃghadeva translate *Madhyamāgama* into Chinese.

According to *Zhong ahanjing xü* [中阿含经序, Preface to the Chinese version of *Madhyamāgama*] by Daoci, *Zhong ahanjing* (*Madhyamāgama*) was translated on the 10th day of the 11th month of the 1st Year of the Long'an era (December 15, 397 AD) of the Eastern Jin Dynasty at a monastery set up by Wang Yuanlin [王元琳] in Jiankang, Sengqieluocha (Saṃgharakṣa), a *śramaṇa* from Jibin, recited and checked up the original *Huben* (Kharoṣṭhī or Brāhmī script) text and Saṃghadeva had it translated into Chinese, Daoci took down what was dictated, Li Bao [李宝] and Tang Hua [唐化] copied the translation. A preliminary draft of the translation was completed on the 25th day of the 6th month of the 2nd year of the same period (July 24, 398 AD), and the final Chinese version was rectified and circulated in the 5th year of the Long'an period (401 AD)[2].

(11) Puṇyatāra, whose name was transliterated as Furuoduoluo [弗若多罗][3]/ Buruoduoluo [不若多罗][4] or paraphrased as Gongdehua [功德华][5], was a *vinaya* specialist and came to western Shaanxi early in the 5th century AD. On the 17th day of the 10th month of the 6th year of Hongshi period of the Later Qin state, i. e., December 4, 404 AD, Puṇyatāra began to recite or transmitted orally the original *Fanben* (Brāhmī script) text of *Shisong lü* [十诵律, *Daśābhāṇavāra-vinaya, The Ten Divisions of Monastic Rules*][6]. Kumārajīva, with the help of three thousand monks, had it translated into Chinese at the Xiaoyao Garden [逍遥园] in Chang' an. Puṇyatāra died before completing the translation, therefore the translation work had to be suspended for a while. Upon the request of Monk Huiyuan as well as the ruler Yao Xing of the Later Qin state, Kumārajīva finished the rest of *Shisong lü* (*Daśābhāṇavāra-vinaya*) along with Tanmoliuzhi

[1] Huijiao, *opere citato*: 37-38; *confer*: *Taishō,* Vol. 50: 329a.

[2] Sengyou, *opere citato*: 337-338, 525; *confer*: *Taishō,* Vol. 55: 63c-64a, 99c-100a.

[3] Sengyou, *opere citato*: 116-117, 474, 568; *confer*: *Taishō,* Vol. 55: 20a-b, 90a, 110a.

[4] Sengyou, *opere citato*: 473; *confer*: *Taishō,* Vol. 55: 89b.

[5] Huijiao, *opere citato*: 60-61; *confer*: *Taishō,* Vol. 50: 333a.

[6] Huijiao, *ibidem*.

[昙摩流支, Dharmaruci], whose name was paraphrased as Fale [法乐] or Faxi [法希][1].

(12) Vimalākṣa[2], whose name was transliterated as Beimoluocha [卑摩罗叉][3] or paraphrased as Wugouyan [无垢眼][4], was a specialist of *vinaya* from Jibin. Vimalākṣa was also known by the sobriquet "*Qingmulüshi* [青目律师, Green-eye *vainayika* or specialist of *vinaya*]", because he had green eyes. [5] It is said that Kumārajīva learned *Shisong lü* (*Daśābhāṇavāra-vinaya*) from Vimalākṣa while he was in Kucīna (Kucha) or the Western Regions[6]. Vimalākṣa arrived in the central Shaanxi plain or Chang'an in the 8th year of the Hongshi period (406 AD) and Kumārajīva treated him respectfully as a disciple. Later, he went eastward and stayed at the Shijian Monastery [石涧寺] in Shouchun [寿春, present-day Shouxian], where he emended or checked the work against the authoritative version of *Shisong lü* (*Daśābhāṇavāra-vinaya*) and divided the Chinese version into 61 fascicles[7].

(13) The last monk likely from Jibin was Dharmanandi. According to the records of both Sengyou and Huijiao[8], Dharmanandi, whose name was transliterated as Tanmonanti [昙摩难提][9]/ Tanwunanti [昙无难提][10] or paraphrased as Faxi [法喜][11], was a native of Douqule kingdom [兜佉勒国, Tukhāra/Tuḥkhāra][12]. On the basis of *Piposha xu* (Preface to the Chinese version

---

[1] Sengyou, *opere citato*: 116-117, 568; *confer*: *Taishō,* Vol. 55: 20a-b, 110a.

[2] Huijiao, *opere citato*: 63-64; *confer*: *Taishō,* Vol. 50: 333b-c.

[3] Sengyou, *opere citato*: 117, 474, 535; *confer*: *Taishō,* Vol. 55: 20b, 90a, 101c-102a.

[4] Huijiao, *opere citato*: 63-64; *confer*: *Taishō,* Vol. 50: 333b-c.

[5] Jingmai, *ibidem,* in: *Taishō,* Vol. 55: 348-367, esp. 357a-b.

[6] Huijiao, *opere citato*: 48; *confer*: *Taishō,* Vol. 50: 331a.

[7] Sengyou, *opere citato*: 117; *confer*: *Taishō,* Vol. 55: 20b.

[8] 1) *Chu sanzang ji ji: Tanmonanti zhuan* [出三藏记集：昙摩难提传, *A Collection of Records concerning the Tripiṭaka: Hagiography of Dharmanandi*], in: Sengyou, *opere citato*: 523-524; *confer*: *Taishō,* Vol. 55: 99b; 2) Huijiao, *opere citato*: 34-36; *confer*: *Taishō,* Vol. 50: 328b-c.

[9] Sengyou, *opere citato*: 522-524, 572-573; *confer*: *Taishō,* Vol. 55: 99a-b, 111b.

[10] Sengyou, *opere citato*: 382; *confer*: *Taishō,* Vol. 55: 73c.

[11] Huijiao, *opere citato*: 34; *confer*: *Taishō,* Vol. 50: 328b.

[12] 1) Sengyou, *opere citato*: 523; *confer*: *Taishō,* Vol. 55: 99b; 2) Huijiao, *opere citato*: 34; *confer*: *Taishō,* Vol. 50: 328b.

of *Vibhāṣā*) by Dao'an, Dharmanandi was a fellow countryman of Saṃghabhadra and assisted him in the translation of *Za apitan piposha* (*Saṁyuktābhidharma-vibhāṣā*) in 383 AD[1]. According to *Chu sanzang ji ji: Sengqiebadeng zhuan* (*A Collection of Records concerning the Tripiṭaka: Hagiography of Saṃghabhadra*), moreover, Saṃghabhadra recited the original text of *Apitan piposha* (*Abhidharma-vibhāṣā*), Dharmanandi wrote it out in *Fanwen* (Brhāmī script), Buddharakṣa had it translated and Minzhi took down what was dictated in Chinese. As for the translation of *Poxumi ji* (*Vasumitra-śāstra*), Saṃghabhadra, Dharmananti and Saṃghadeva together checked up the original *Fanben* (Brhāmī script) text, Zhu Fonian had it translated, and Huisong took down what was dictated, while Dao'an and Fahe rectified the translation and finalized the Chinese version. It appears that the three master-monks came to Chang'an one after the other and worked together for a while[2]. Since Saṃghabhadra and Saṃghadeva were both natives of Jibin, Dharmanandi who was a fellow countryman of Saṃghabhadra should be a native of Jibin, because Douqule (Tukhāra/Tuḥkhāra), i. e. Bactria, used to be part of Jibin at one time.

3. Jibin Buddhism

Although the Chinese translated versions of the above texts consist of *sūtra* (the Buddha's doctrinal teachings), *vinaya* (rules of the monastic discipline) and *śāstra* or *abhidharma* (commentaries on the *sūtra*), all being a reflection of the Buddhist *Tripiṭaka* in Jibin, there is the suspicion that we look at the sky through a bamboo tube and measure the sea with a calabash. The texts recited or translated by the master-monks from Jibin, however, do provide a faithful picture of the origin and the development of Buddhism in Jibin up to the 6th century AD.

The Chinese translated versions belonging to the *Sūtra-piṭaka* include *Mohe boluore boluomi jing chao* (*Daśasāhasrikā-prajñāpāramitā*) recited or

---

[1] Sengyou, *opere citato*: 381-382; *confer*: *Taishō,* Vol. 55: 73b-c.

[2] Sengyou, *opere citato*: 572-573, 565, 522-524; *confer*: *Taishō,* Vol. 55: 111b, 109a, 99a-c.

translated by Dharmapriya, *Zhong ahanjing* (*Madhyamāgama*) by Saṃghadeva, *Chang ahanjing* (*Dīrghāgama*) and *Xukongzang jing* (*Ākāśagarbha-sūtra*) by Buddhayaśas, *Dafangguangfo huayan jing* (*Buddhāvataṃsaka-nāmamahāvaipulya-sūtra*), *Xin wuliangshou jing* (*New Amitābhavyūha*), *Dafangdeng rulaizang jing* (*Tathāgatagarbha-sūtra*), *Pusa shizhu jing*, *Chusheng wuliangmen chijing* (*Anantamukhanīhāra-dhāraṇī*), *Xin weimi chijing*, *Benye jing*, *Jing liu boluomi jing* (*The Pure Six Pāramitā Sūtra*) and *Wenshushili fayuan jing* (*Samantabhadrapraṇidhāna* or *Samantabhadra-caryā-praṇidhāna-rāja*) by Buddhabhadra as well as *Dabonihuan jing* (*Mahāparinirvāṇa-sūtra*) and *Zazang jing* (*Kṣudraka-sūtra*) translated by Buddhabhadra and Faxian, *Guan puxian pusa xingfa jing* (*Samantabhadra-bodhisattva-dhyāna-caryādharma-sūtra*) and *Xukongzang guan jing* (*Ākāśagarbhabodhisattvadhāraṇī-sūtra*) by Dharmamitra.

The Chinese translated versions belonging to the *Vinaya-piṭaka* are *Tanwude lü* (*Dharmaguptaka-vinaya*) and *Tanwude jieben* (*Dharmaguptaka-prātimokṣa*) recited or translated by Buddhayaśas, *Mohesengqi Lü* (*Mahāsaṃghika-vinaya*) and *Sengqi biqiu jieben* (*Mahāsaṃghika-bhikṣu-prātimokṣa*) translated by Buddhabhadra and Faxian, *Mishasai lü* (*Mahīśāsaka-vinaya*), *Mishasai biqiu jieben* (*Mahīśāsaka-bhikṣu-pratimokṣa*) and *Mishasai jiemo* (*Mahīśāsaka-karmavākya*) recited or translated by Buddhajīva, *Pusa shanjie* (*Bodhisattvacaryā-nirdeśa*), *Youposai wujie luelun* (*Upāsaka-pañca-śīlāni-sūtra*), *Sangui ji youposai ershi'er jie* (*Tri-śaraṇa and Upāsaka-śīlās*) and *Tanwude jiemo* (*Dharamagupta-karmavākya*) by Guṇavarman, *Shisong lü* (*Daśābhāṇavāra-vinaya*) recited by Puṇyatāra, translated by Kumārajīva and emended by Vimalākṣa.

The Chinese translated versions belonging to the *Abhidharma-piṭaka* comprise *Bajiandu apitan genjiandu* (*Abhidharmāṣṭagrantha-mula-khaṇḍa*?) recited by Dharmapriya, *Za apitan piposha* (*Saṁyuktābhidharma-Vibhāṣā*), *Poxumi ji* (*Vasumitra-śāstra*), *Sengqieluocha ji jing* (*Saṃgharakṣa-sañcaya-buddhacarita-sūtra*) and *Piposha apitan* (*Vibhāṣābhidharma*) recited or translated by Saṃghabhadra, *Apitan bajiandu* (*Abhidharmāṣṭagrantha*), *Apitanxin* (*Abhidharmahṛdaya*) and *San fadu* (*Tri-dharmika-śāstra*) by Saṃghadeva, *Shelifu apitan* (*Śāriputrābhidharma-śāstra*) by Dharmayaśas, *Guanfo sanmei jing* (*Buddhadhyāna-samādhisāgara-sūtra*) and *Chanjing xiuxing fangbian* (*Yogacaryā-bhūmi-sūtra*) recited or translated by Buddhabhadra, *Chan miyao* (*Sūtra about the Secret Essence of Dhyāna*) and *Wumenchan jing yaoyong fa* (*Pañcadvara-dhyāna-sūtra-mahāratha-dharma*) translated or compiled by Dharmamitra[1].

On the basis of an investigation in India, Yijing [义净, 635-713 AD] emphasized the following fact:

> On examining carefully the distinctions between these schools and the differences of their discipline, we see that they present very many points of disagreement; that which is important in one school is not so in another, and that which is allowed by one is prohibited by another. But priests should follow the customs of their respective schools, and not inter exchange the strict rules of their doctrine for the more lenient teaching of another. At the same time, they should not despise others' prohibitions, because they themselves are unrestricted in their own schools; otherwise the differences between the schools will be indistinct, and the regulations as to permission and prohibition will become obscure. How can a single person practice the precepts of the four schools together? The parable of a torn garment and a gold stick shows how we (who practice according to the different schools) may equally gain the goal of *Nirvāṇa*. Therefore those who practice in accordance with the Laws should follow the customs of their own schools[2].

In other words, each Buddhist school had its own *sūtras, vinayas* and *śāstras*; each did things in its own way and stuck to its own view[3].

---

[1] The classification and affiliation of the above Buddhist texts are sorted out on the basis of *Xinbian hanwen dazangjing mulu* (*A New Catalogue of the Chinese Versions of the Buddhist Tripiṭāka*) by Lü Cheng, Ji'nan: Qilu Publishing House, 1980.

[2] I-Tsing, *A Record of the Buddhist Religion as Practiced in India and the Malay Archipelago (AD 671-695)*, tr. by J. Takakusu, London: Clarendon Press, 1896: 13. *Confer*: Yijing, *Nanhai ji gui neifa zhuan* [南海寄归内法传, *A Record of Buddhist Monastic Traditions of Southern Asia*], emended and annotated by Wang Bangwei [王邦维], Beijing: Zhonghua Book Company, 1995: 19.

[3] Lü Cheng, *opere citato* (*Zhongguo Foxue...*): 68.

Regarding the school affiliation of the above Chinese translated versions, *Zhong ahanjing* (*Madhyamāgama*) belongs to the Sarvāstivāda[1], and *Chang ahanjing* (*Dīrghāgama*) belongs to the Dharmaguptaka[2]. *Dabonihuan jing* (*Mahāparinirvāṇa-sūtra*) seems to be related to the Mahāsaṃghika[3]. *Tanwude lü* (*Dharmaguptaka-vinaya*), i. e., *The Fourfold Rules of Discipline*, "is a *vinaya* text of the Dharmaguptaka"[4], while *Tanwude jieben* (*Dharmaguptaka-prātimokṣa*) and *Tanwude jiemo* (*Dharamagupta-karmavākya*) or *Za jiemo* (*Saṃyukta-karmavākya*) belong also to the same school. *Mohesengqi Lü* (*Mahāsaṃghika-vinaya*) and *Sengqi biqiu jieben* (*Mahāsaṃghika-bhikṣu-prātimokṣa*) belong to Mahāsaṃghika. *Mishasai lü* (*Mahīśāsaka-vinaya*), i. e., *The Fivefold Rules of Discipline,* is linked to the Mahīśāsaka[5], while *Mishasai biqiu jieben* (*Mahīśāsaka-bhikṣu-prātimokṣa*) and *Mishasai jiemo* (*Mahīśāsaka-karmavākya*) also belong to the same school. *Shisong lü* (*Daśābhāṇavāra-vinaya*), i. e., *The Ten Divisions of the Monastic Rules,* belongs to the Sarvāstivāda[6]. Moreover, the "Sarvāstivāda *Abhidharma* in the first century BC consisted mainly of the *Abhidharmahṛdaya* and *Aṣṭagrantha*"[7]. Among

---

[1] Lü Chêng, "Āgama", in: *Encyclopedia of Buddhism*, Vol. I: 241-244.

[2] 1) A. Bareau, *Les sectes bouddhiques du Petit Véhicule,* Paris: Publications de l'École française d'Extrême-Orient 38, 1955: 191; 2) É. Lamotte, *Histoire du Bouddhisme Indien: des origines à l'ére Šaka,* Bibliothèque du Muséon 43, Louvain: Institut Orientaliste de Louvain, 1958: 629-630; 3) Lü Chêng, "Āgama", *opere citato,* Vol. I: 241-244; 4) Ernst Waldschmidt, "Central Asian Sūtra Fragments and their Relation to the Chinese Āgamas", in: *Die Sprache der ältesten buddhistischen Überlieferung; The Language of the Earliest Buddhist Tradition* (Symposien zur Buddhismusforschung II), Abhandlungen der Akademie der Wissenschaften in Göttingen: Philologisch-historische Klasse, Ser. 3, Vol. 117, Heinz. Bechert, hrsg, Göttingen: Vandenhoeck & Ruprecht, 1980: 136-174, esp. 136-137.

[3] Chen Yinke [陈寅恪], *Chen Yinke ji: Dushu zhaji san ji* [陈寅恪集：读书札记三集, *Collected Works of Chen Yinke: Reading Notes III*], Beijing: SDX Joint Publishing House, 2001: 81, 83.

[4] 1) Sengyou, *opere citato*: 117-118; *confer*: *Taishō,* Vol. 55: 20b-c; 2) Kuiji [窥基, 632-682 AD], *Miaofa lianhuajing xuanzan* [妙法莲华经玄赞, In Praise of *the Lotus Sūtra*], *Taishō,* Vol. 34: 651-854, esp. 657a.

[5] *Sengyou, opere citato:* 119-120; *confer*: *Taishō,* Vol. 55: 21a-b.

[6] Sengyou, *opere citato*: 116-117; *confer*: *Taishō,* Vol. 55: 20a-b.

[7] Charles Willemen, "Kaniṣka and the Sarvāstivāda Synod", in: *opere citato*: 218-222, esp. 218.

the Chinese versions of the above-mentioned *śāstras* or *abhidharmas, Apitan bajiandu* (*Abhidharmāṣṭagrantha*) compiled by Kātyāyanīputra, along with *Za apitan piposha* (*Saṁyuktābhidharma-vibhāṣā*) compiled by Sitapāṇi, *Apitanxin* (*Abhidharmahṛdaya*) compiled by Dharmaśresthin, *Za apitan xin* (*Miśrakabhidharmahṛdaya*) compiled by Dharmatrāta, all of them belong to the Sarvāstivāda school, because Kātyāyanīputra was considered as the first exegete of the Buddhist texts[1] or regarded as the 7th or 5th *guru* or *śāstṛ* (teacher or master) of the Sarvāstivādins, Dharmaśresthin the 33rd or 30th *guru* or *śāstṛ* and Dharmatrāta the 53rd or 50th *guru* or *śāstṛ,* respectively[2]. *Poxumi* (*Vasumitra-śāstra*) compiled by Vasumitra and *Sengqieluocha ji jing* (*Saṃgharakṣa-sañcaya-buddhacarita-sūtra*) compiled by Saṃgharakṣa also belong to the Sarvāstivāda school, because Vasumitra was regarded as the 8th or 6th *guru* or *śāstṛ* of the Sarvāstivādins and Saṃgharakṣa the 29th or 26th *guru* or *śāstṛ*[3]. *Chanjing xiuxing fangbian* (*Yogacaryā-bhūmi-sūtra*) by Buddhabhadra is thought to belong to the Sarvāstivāda school, because it was extracted from the works of both Buddhasena and Dharmatrāta on the methods of *dhyāna,* who were regarded respectively as the 52nd or 49th and 53rd or 50th *guru* or *śāstṛ* of the Sarvāstivādins[4]. Buddhabhara, moreover, was also one of the most important monks recorded in *Chang'an chengnei qigongsi sapoduobu fodabatuoluo shizong xiangcheng zhuanlue* [长安城内齐公寺萨婆多部佛大跋陀罗师宗相承传略, *A Genealogy of Buddabhadra's Predecessors of the Sarvāstivāda School at the Qigong Monastery in Chang'an*][5]. Although the affiliation of *Shelifu apitan* (*Śāriputrābhidharma-śāstra*) is not very clear, the Chinese version translated by Dharmayaśas seems to be derived from a system of the Mahīśāsaka and

[1] Dao'an, "*Apitan xü* [阿毗昙序, Preface to the Chinese version of *Abhidharmāṣṭagrantha*]", in: Sengyou, *opere citato*: 376-377, esp. 376; *confer*: *Taishō*, Vol. 55: 72a-72b, esp. 72a.

[2] Sengyou, "*Sapoduobu shizi ji mulu xü* [萨婆多部师资记目录序, Preface to *Record of the Teachers and Masters of the Sarvāstivāda School*]", in: Sengyou, *opere citato*: 466-476, esp. 467-473;*confer*: *Taishō,* Vol. 55: 88c-90b, esp. 89a-90a.

[3] Sengyou, *opere citato*: 466-476, esp. 467-472; *confer*: *Taishō,* Vol. 55: 88c-90b, esp. 89a-c.

[4] Sengyou, *opere citato*: 466-476, esp. 470, 473; *confer*: *Taishō,* Vol. 55: 88c-90b, esp. 89b, 90a.

[5] Sengyou, *opere citato*: 470-476; *confer*: *Taishō,* Vol. 55: 89c-90b.

Dharmaguptaka schools[1].

After Śākyamuni Buddha's *Parinirvāṇa,* the Buddhist Order experienced several schisms and eventually split into eighteen or twenty schools[2]. According to *Yibu zonglun lun* (*Samayabhedoparacanacakra, The Doctrines of the Different Schools*) translated by Xuanzang[3] and *Xinji lü lai handi sibu jilu* (*A Record of the newly collected Four Vinayas spread to China*) compiled by Sengyou[4], there were two schools formed by the first split in the Buddhist Order about a century after the Buddha's *Parinirvāṇa,* i. e, *Dazhongbu* [大众部, Mahāsaṃghikāḥ or Mahāsaṃghika, 摩诃僧祇部 / *Mohesengqibu*] and *Shangzuobu* [上座部, Sthaviravāda or ārya-sthavira-nikāya]. Afterwards, *Shuoyiqieyoubu* [说一切有部, Sarvāstivādāḥ or Sarvāstivāda, 萨婆多部 / *Sapoduobu*, 说因部 / *Shuoyinbu*] school broke away from *Shangzuobu* (Sthaviravāda) early in the third one-hundred-year period after the Buddha's *Parinirvāṇa*. *Duzibu* [犊子部, Vātsī-putrīyāḥ][5] and *Huadibu* [化地部, Mahīśāsakāḥ or Mahīśāsaka, 弥沙塞部 / *Mishasaibu*] derived respectively from *Shuoyiqieyoubu* (Sarvāstivāda) school in the third one-hundred-year period after the Buddha's *Parinirvāṇa*. During this very period, however, *Facangbu* [法藏部, Dharmaguptakāḥ or Dharmaguptaka, 昙无德部 / *Tanwudebu*, 昙摩毱多部 / *Tanmojuduobu*, 法镜部 / *Fajingbu*] eventually branched away from *Huadibu* (Mahīśāsaka) school, and *Yin'guangbu* [饮光部, Kāśyapīyāḥ or Kāśyapīya, 善岁部 / *Shansuibu*, 迦叶维部 / *Jiayeweibu*, 迦叶毗部 / *Jiayepibu*] was

---

[1] 1) Lü Cheng, *opere citato* (*Zhongguo Foxue...*): 301; 2) Lü Cheng, *Yindu foxue yuanliu luejiang* [印度佛学源流略讲, *A Survey of Indian Buddhism*], Shanghai: Shanghai People's Publishing House, 1979: 41.

[2] Lü Cheng, "*Lun lüxue yu shibabu fenpai zhi guanxi* [论律学与十八部分派之关系, On the Relationship between Studies of the Discipline and Schism of Eighteen Hīnayāna Schools]", in: *Lü Cheng foxue lunzhu xuanji* [吕澂佛学论著选集, *Collected Works of Lü Cheng on Buddhism*], Ji'nan: Qilu Publishing House, Vol. I, 1991: 131-143.

[3] It was translated into Chinese by Xuanzang in 662 AD and included in *Taishō,* No. 2031, Vol. 49：15a-17b.

[4] Sengyou, *opere citato*: 116-122; *confer*: *Taishō,* Vol. 55：20a-21b.

[5] Duzibu [犊子部, Vātsī-putrīyāḥ] was transcribed as *Pocufuluo* [婆麁富罗部], but Sengyou mistook *Pocufuluo* (Vātsī-putrīyāḥ) school for *Mohesengqibu* (Mahāsaṃghikāḥ or Mahāsaṃghika) school. Sengyou, *opere citato*: 116-122, esp. 118-119; *confer*: *Taishō,* Vol. 55：20c-21a.

formed out of *Shuoyiqieyoubu* (Sarvāstivāda) school at the end of the third one-hundred-year period after the Buddha's *Parinirvāṇa*[1].

The "Sthāvirīya, i. e., Sarvāstivāda and Dharmaguptaka, but also Mahāsaṃghika" seem to have been the major doctrinal schools present in Jibin or the Gandhāran cultural area[2]. According to Sengyou's accounts, not only the Sarvāstivāda, Dharmaguptaka, Mahāsaṃghika and Mahīśāsaka were very popular in Jibin, but also *Chanfa* [禅法, *Dhyāna* discipline] exercised a particular influence in that region. The Buddhist texts recited or translated by the master monks from Jibin, Dharmapriya, Saṃghabhadra, Saṃghadeva, Saṃgharakṣa, Puṇyatāra, Vimalākṣa and Dharmanandi point to the Sarvāstivāda school as their source, while the texts recited by Buddhayaśas and Guṇavarman belong to the Dharmagupta school. Dharmayaśa's association with the Dharmaguptaka and the Mahīśāsaka school is backed by the fact that the Chinese version of *Shelifu apitan* (*Śāriputrābhidharma-śāstra*), recited or translated by him, was probably derived from these two schools. The school affiliation of Buddhabhadra is difficult to ascertain, since he translated not only the works of both Dharmatrāta and Buddhasena on the methods of *dhyāna,* but also *Mohesengqi lü* (*Mahāsaṃghika-vinaya*) and *Sengqi biqiu jieben* (*Mahāsṃghika-bhikṣu-prātimokṣa*). Buddhajīva belonged to the Mahīśāsaka[3]. Dharmamitra, who was a great master of *dhyāna* besides Buddhajīva and Kumārajīva, probably belonged to the Dharmagupta school, because *Xukongzang guan jing* (*Ākāśagarbhabodhisattvadhāraṇī-sūtra*) translated by Dharmamitra and *Xukongzang jing* (*Ākāśagarbha-sūtra*) translated first by Buddhayaśas belong to the same original text[4], but the latter was

---

[1] 1) *Yibu zonglun lun* (*Samayabhedoparacanacakra*), *Taishō,* Vol. 49: 15a-b; 2) Sengyou, *Xinji lü lai handi sibu jilu* (*A Record of newly collected Four Vinayas spread to China*), Sengyou, *opere citato*: 116-122; *confer*: *Taishō,* Vol. 55: 20a-21b.

[2] Charles Willemen, "Kaniṣka and the Sarvāstivāda Synod" , in: *opere citato*: 218.

[3] As for the Mahīśāsaka school, *see* Charles Willemen, "*Yindu bupai fojiao 'huadibu' de xin yanjiu* [印度部派佛教'化地部'的新研究, Some New Ideas on Mahīśāsaka of Indian Buddhism]" , in: *Renwen zongjiao yanjiu* [人文宗教研究, *Journal of Humanistic Religion*], Vol. I, ed. Li Silong [李四龙], Beijing: Religious Culture Press, 2011: 126-140.

[4] 1) Fajing, *ibidem, Taishō,* Vol. 55: 118c; 2) Fei Zhangfang, *ibidem, Taishō,* Vol. 49: 111c.

absolutely a master monk of the Dharmagupta school. Among the additional four Buddhist schools popular in Jibin, the Sarvāstivāda school was the main one and the Dharmagupta school came second.

4. Early Buddhist Schools in China

Buddhism was formally disseminated in China proper in the middle of the Yongping period [永平, 58-75 AD] of Emperor Ming [明帝] of the Eastern Han Dynasty [东汉, 25-220 AD], and strongly influenced the Chinese culture and ideology from the 3rd century onwards[1].

After the fall of the Western Jin Dynasty [西晋, 266-316 AD) in 316 AD, a large number of northern literati migrated to south China and brought *Xuanxue* [玄学, metaphysics] school[2] to the South. Later, it flourished in south China, especially in the area around Jiankang, the capital of south China. The southern style of Buddhism was inspired by *Xuanxue* and took on a strong philosophical aspect, which emphasized discourse, theory and exegesis of the Buddhist texts. Thus, Buddhism in south China became very different from north China's Buddhism, which emphasized Buddhist practice[3]. The Buddhist monks in north China not only built free-standing monasteries to carry out worship and repentance [礼忏], but also hewed caves out of the rock where monks practiced meditation. In the South, however, Buddhist followers tended to emphasize monastery ceremonies, to discuss theory and to make exegesis of the Buddhist texts[4].

According to *Gaoseng Zhuan* and *Weishu* (*History of the Wei Dynasties*),

---

[1] Tang Yongtong, *opere citato*: 1-21.

[2] *Xuanxue* is a mystical school in the realm of philosophy, which developed in the 3rd and 4th centuries AD, characterized by metaphysical speculations seeking to adapt Daoist theories to a Confucian subject. Bai Shouyi [白寿彝], ed., *An Outline History of China,* Beijing: Foreign Languages Press, 1982: 177-178.

[3] Tang Yongtong, *opere citato*: 350-394.

[4] 1) Shenqing [神清], *Beishan lu* [北山录, *Buddhism recorded at the Northern Mountain*] in 806 AD, in: *Taishō,* Vol. 52: 573-636, esp. 596c; 2) Tang Yongtong, *opere citato*: 297-394.

a monk named Dharmakāla [昙摩迦罗] from Hinduka arrived in Luoyang some time during the Jiaping [嘉平, 249-253 AD] period of the Wei Kingdom, translating and spreading *Sengqi jiexin* [僧祇戒心, *Prātimokṣa of the Mahāsaṃghika*][1], generally acknowledged as the origin of *śīla* in China[2]. In the light of *Xinji lü lai handi sibu jilu* (*A Record of newly collected Four Vinayas spread to China*) by Sengyou, moreover, the *sūtra* doctrines were the first to be heard in China and *vinaya* or discipline second. The *vinaya* spread far and wide from the end of the Eastern Jin dynasty onwards. The texts on the monastic rules of discipline produced by five of the eighteen or twenty Hīnayāna schools in Hinduka are as follows: *Sapoduobu shisonglü* [萨婆多部十诵律, *the Ten Divisions of Monastic Rules of the Sarvāstivāda school*], *Tanwudebu sifenlü* [昙无德四分律, *the Fourfold Rules of Discipline of the Dharmagupta school*], *Pocufuluo lü* [婆麁富罗律, *Vātsīputrīyāḥ-vinaya*] which was later renamed *Mohesengqi lü* [摩诃僧祇律, *Mahāsaṃghika-vinaya, the Great Canon of Rules of Discipline of the Mahāsaṃghika school*][3], *Mishasai lü* [弥沙塞律, *Mahīśāsaka-vinaya* or *the Fivefold Rules of Discipline of the Mahīśāsaka school*] and *Jiayewei lü* [迦叶维律, *the Monastic Rules for Emancipation of the Kāśyapīya school*]. Among these five *vinayas,* the *Kāśyapiya-vinaya* was not spread to China proper.[4]

The Sarvāstivāda, which was a major early Buddhist school that broke away from the Sthaviravāda or Ārya-sthavira-nikāya, whose followers are called Sarvāstivādins, was one of the most influential Hīnayāna schools in Jibin, and had

---

[1] This text was not recorded in chapter 2 of *Chu sanzang ji ji* by Sengyou, but it was recorded as *Sengqi jieben* [僧祇戒本, *Prātimokṣa of the Mahāsaṃghika*] in fascicle 5 of *Lidai sanbao ji* by Fei Zhangfang who, on the basis of *Weishi lü* [魏世录, *The Caowei Kingdom's Catalogue of the Buddhist Scriptures*] by Zhu Daozu [竺道祖], recorded that the *Prātimokṣa of the Mahāsaṃghika* was translated in 250 AD. *confer*: *Taishō,* Vol. 49: 56b.

[2] 1) Huijiao, *opere citato*: 12-14; *confer*: *Taishō,* Vol. 50: 324c-325a; 2) Wei Shou, *Weishu: Shilaozhi* (*History of the Wei Dynasties: Treatise on Buddhism and Taoism*), punctuated edition, Beijing: Zhonghua Book Company, 1974: 3025-3062, esp. 3029. *confer*: James R. Ware, "Wei Shou on Buddhism", in: *opere citato*: 122; Wei Shou, *Treatise on Buddhism and Taoism,* tr. by Leon Hurvitz, in: *opere citato*: 46-47; 3) Chen Yinke, *opere citato*: 24.

[3] *Pocufuluo lü* (*Vātsīputrīyāḥ-vinaya*) is not identified with *Mohesengqi lü* (*Mahāsaṃghika-vinaya*). What Sengyou recorded here seems to be an error.

[4] Sengyou, *opere citato*: 116-120; *confer*: *Taishō,* Vol. 55: 20a-21b.

an important influence on Mahāyāna thought, along with the Dharmagupta as well. The Sarvāstivādins, who set forth the view that everything has an existence of its own, holds that since living beings are formed by a temporary union of the five components there is no real or permanent self, but elements of existence that form the living being are real and have their own existence throughout the past, present, and future. The Sarvāstivādins developed the *Abhidharma* to an extent surpassing that of any other Hīnayāna schools, therefore the Sarvāstivāda was famous for the vast scholastic systematizations in the field of *Abhidharma*. An Shigao [安世高, Ashkani] [1], a monk from Parthia who was active in China as a translator in the later part of the 2nd century AD, recited or translated a few parts of the *Abhidharma* works, but few had studied them at that time. Therefore, Saṃghabhadra and Saṃghadeva were the very first foreign specialists to make available to the Chinese *Abhidharama* literature [2].

According to *Pimoluojietijing yishu xü* [毗摩罗诘提经义疏序, A Preface to *Exegesis of Vimalakīrti-nirdeśa*] by Sengrui [僧叡, 355-439 AD], who was one of Dao'an's disciples and later became an assistant of Kumārajīva, "there were no monks from Hinduka who devoted themselves to *yixue* [义学, *vyākhyāna,* exegetics or exegesis of the Buddhist texts] in China before Saṃghadeva. Nowadays we began to hear their informed opinion and their talking glibly about the texts" [3], in other words, Saṃghadeva was the first Buddhist *vyākhyātṛ* (exegete) who came to China. While at Chang'an, Saṃghadeva recited or translated *Apitan bajiantu lun* (*Abhidharmāṣṭagrantha*) into Chinese and made the Chinese followers acquainted with the great scholastic literature of the Sarvāstivādins; this translation work was probably affected by the war between the Former Qin state and Eastern Jin Dynasty as well as that between the Former Qin and Xiyan [西燕, Western Yan state]. Before long, the central Shaanxi plain was in chaos. As a result, detailed corrections were not made to the rushed

[1] Charles Willemen, *opere citato* (Kumārajīva's 'Explanatory Discourse' ...): 51-52 (142-141), esp. 39 (154); 2) Charles Willemen, *opere citato* (*Outlining the Way...*): 5.

[2] Erik Zürcher, *opere citato*: 202.

[3] Sengyou, *opere citato*: 311-312, esp. 312; *confer*: *Taishō*, Vol. 55: 58c-59a, esp. 59a.

translations, because monks, reciters or translators had to leave and the teaching of the Dharma could not be extended or pushed forward[1]. Therefore, few of the Chinese followers were concerned with what Saṃghadeva had translated and were not deeply engrossed in the study of *Abhidharma* works[2]. After the fall of Fu Jian in 384 AD, Saṃghadeva had to move to Luoyang and stayed there for a few years, then he crossed the Yangzi river and arrived at Mount Lu in 391 AD, where he was requested by Monk Huiyuan to translate *Apitanxin* (*Abhidharmahṛdaya*) and *San fadu* (*Tri-dharmika-śāstra* or *Tridharmakhaṇḍa*) into Chinese again. The *bhikṣus* or monks at Mount Lu had energetically encouraged the practice of studying *Abhidharma* after the arrival of the great *Abhidharma*-master Saṃghadeva. It was the first sign in the field of *Abhidharma* exegesis. When Saṃghadeva came to the capital (Jiankang) in 397 AD, princes and dukes of the Eastern Jin Dynasty as well as brave young scholars and personages with literary reputation in the capital all of them called at his residence and paid their hearty respects to him. Saṃghadeva stayed in the monastery built by Wang Xun [王珣, 349-400 AD], a famous scholar in south China, where he was requested to expound *Apitanxin* (*Abhidharmahṛdaya*), while many famous *bhikṣus* gathered to listen. Later, he translated *Zhong ahanjing* (*Madhyamāgama*) into Chinese at the request of Wang Xun at the same monastery[3]. Although the Sarvāstivādins' texts on *Abhidharma* were first recited or translated in north China, some of them were not finished in the North but completed in the South. The educational or cultural level of the Buddhist followers in south China was higher than that in north China, so exegesis of the *Abhidharma* works did begin to appear in the South, and this research was popular for a while[4]. It appears that Saṃghadeva's works and teachings had been very influential at that time among monks, laymen and even literati, with many *bhikṣus* skilled in the study

---

[1] Sengyou, *opere citato*: 337, 374, 524; *confer*: *Taishō*, Vol. 55: 63c, 71b, 99c.

[2] 1) Tang Yongtong, *opere citato*: 252; 2) Lü Cheng, *opere citato* (*Zhongguo foxue...*): 67.

[3] 1) Sengyou, *opere citato*: 524-525; *confer*: *Taishō*, Vol. 55: 99b-100a; 2) Tang Yongtong, *opere citato*: 251-253.

[4] Lü Cheng, *opere citato*: 127.

of *Abhidharma* during the Song and Qi dynasties[1]. According to Daoxuan, *Sapoduobu shisonglü* (*The Ten Divisions of Monastic Rules of the Sarvāstivāda*) was carried far and wide in the early days when the Buddhist *vinaya* spread in China. The main ideas of monastic discipline were indeed elaborated and disseminated by Vimalākṣa during the Eastern Jin Dynasty, and became a school because of Huiyuan highly praising and applauding it. Later, it was spread or made known by Sengqu [僧璩] of the Song Dynasty and Faying [法颖, 415-482 AD] of the Southern Qi Dynasty and then further promoted by Sengyou of the Liang Dynasty[2]. Therefore, the Buddhist believers in the territory of the Southern Qi Dynasty and even of the Liang Dynasty were particularly fond of the *Sarvāstivāda-vinaya*[3], in other words, from the Song Dynasty to Qi and Liang dynasties (420-557 AD), the *Sarvāstivāda-vinaya* became almost the only monastic rule of discipline in south China, with a few studying *Sifenlü* (*The Fourfold Rules of Discipline*), *Wufenlü* (*The Fivefold Rules of Discipline*) and *Mohesengqi lü* (*Mahāsaṃghika-vinaya*)[4]. In this case, south China seems to be the stronghold of the Sarvāstivāda during the period from end of the 4th century to middle of the 6th century AD[5].

In north China, however, study of *The Fourfold Rules of the Discipline of the Dharmagupta* took precedence over that of *The Ten Divisions of the Monastic Rules of the Sarvāstivāda school*. According to Yijing's record, "in China, Buddhists practice mostly according to the Dharmagupta school [法护], but in many places in Shaanxi [关中] some belong, from olden times, to the Mahāsaṃghika school [僧祇] as well as to the above. In olden times in Jiangnan [江南] and Lingbiao [岭表], i. e., south China, the Sarvāstivāda school has first flourished. When

---

[1] Tang Yongtong, *opere citato*: 251-253, 606-609.

[2] Daoxuan, *Xü gaoseng zhuan* (*Continued Biographies of Eminent Priests*), fascicle 22, *Comments on the Vinaya*, in: *Taishō*, Vol. 50: 620b.

[3] Sengyou, "*Sapoduobu shizi ji mulu xü* (Preface to *the Record of the Teachers and Masters of the Sarvāstivāda School*)", in: Sengyou, *opere citato*: 466-476, esp. 466; *confer*: *Taishō,* Vol. 55: 88c-90b, esp. 89a.

[4] Tang Yongtong, *opere citato*: 593-594.

[5] Daoxuan, *ibidem,* in: *Taishō,* Vol. 50: 620b.

we speak of the *vinaya* as being divided into *Ten Divisions of the Monastic Rules* or into *Fourfold Rules of the Discipline,* these names are chiefly taken from the divisions or bundles of the texts adopted by those schools" [1].

The Dharmaguptas attached greater importance to making offerings to the Buddha himself rather than to the Buddhist Order. They asserted that the building of *stūpa* would result in great reward. [2] On the basis of *Yibu zonglun lun* (*Samayabhedoparacanacakra*), the Dharmaguptakas did pay special attention to the merit acquired through *stūpa* worship. Whoever took the cult of the *stūpa* seriously would obtain great profit and a good retribution [3]. And, according to the *Dharmaguptaka-prātimokṣa* translated by Buddhayaśas, more than 24 items of *śila* concerning the *stūpa* were stipulated in the rules of the monastic discipline for the monks of the Dharmaguptaka [4]. This particular rule or the items cannot be found in any other versions of the *prātimokṣas* or *vinayas* of any schools in existence. It demonstrates that the *stūpa* played a very important role in the life of the Dharmaguptakas; in other words, the Dharmaguptakas laid a particular stress on the *stūpa* cult [5]. An immense construction of Buddhist monasteries and a great number of rock-cut temples, especially the *chētiyaghara* (*stūpa*-cave) in north China might have a close relation with the popularity of the Dharmagupta school, which was formally opened up in China by Facong [法聪] during the reign period of Emperor Xiaowen [孝文帝, 471-499 AD] of the Northern Wei Dynasty at the Northern Capital [北台, present-day Datong] and then carried forward by Daofu [道覆] [6]. Later, it was enhanced by a master monk named Huiguang [慧

---

[1] I-Tsing, *opere citato* (*A Record of the Buddhist Religion*...) : 13; *confer*: Yijing, *opere citato* (*Nanhai ji gui neifa zhuan*...): 19.

[2] Chongfeng Li, "*Kezi'er bufen zhongxinzhuku yu Chang'ahanjing deng fodian* [克孜尔部分中心柱窟与《长阿含经》等佛典, *The Dīrghāgama* Texts and the *Chētiyagharas* of Kizil, Kucha]", in: *Xu Pingfang xiansheng ji'nian wenji* [徐苹芳先生纪念文集, *Papers in Commemoration of Professor Xu Pingfang*], Shanghai: Shanghai Chinese Classics Publishing House, 2012: 419-465, esp. 441-442.

[3] *Taishō,* Vol. 49: 17a.

[4] *Taishō,* Vol. 22: 1029b-c.

[5] Lü Cheng, *opere citato* (*Lun lüxue yu shibabu*...): 131-143, esp. 142.

[6] 1) Daoxuan, *Xü gaoseng zhuan* (*Continued Biographies of Eminent Priests*), fascicle 22, *Comments on the Vinaya,* in: *Taishō,* Vol. 50: 620c; 2) Gyōnen [凝然], *Risshü kōyō* [律宗纲要, *The Essentials of the Vinaya School*], in: *Taishō,* Vol. 74: 16a.

光] of the Northern Qi Dynasty [北齐, 550-577 AD], and then widely spread and studied from the early Tang Dynasty [唐代, 618-907 AD] onwards[1].

(It will be published in the *Archaeology of Buddhism in Asia,* edited by B. Mani, New Delhi: Archaeological Survey of India.)

[1] 1) Tang Yongtong, *opere citato*: 595-596; 2) Ann Heirman, "Can we trace the early Dharmaguptakas?" in: *T'oung Pao* (通报), Vol. LXXXVIII (2002). Fasc. 4-5: 396-429.

西行求法与罽宾道

“佛教为异域宗教，根据自在传译。故印度中国之交通道路，其通塞改易，均与我国佛教有关系。”[1]据法人沙畹研究，“印度佛教圣地有二：一在辛头河（印度河）流域，一在恒河流域。中夏巡礼之僧俗多先历辛头，后赴恒河；盖中印通道中，直达中印度之尼泊尔 (Népal) 一道，在唐代以前似尚不知有之。常循之路，盖为葱岭 (Pamirs)，南达克什米尔 (Cachemire) 与乌苌之路。有不少巡礼之人，如宋云、惠生之徒者，且不远赴中印度，而以弗楼沙国或呾叉尸罗 (Taksaçila) 为终点也。乾陀罗在佛教传播中夏中任务重大之理，盖不难知之矣”[2]。

一、罽　　宾

克什米尔及乌苌等地，即中国史书所称之罽宾[3]。据欧阳询《艺文类聚》卷七十六《内典部》征引支僧载《外国事》：“罽宾国在舍卫之西，国王民人悉奉佛；道人及沙门，到冬，未中前饮少酒，过中不复饭。”[4]关于罽宾国的地域范围，学术界争议颇大[5]。其中汉代的罽宾，主要指今印度河以西、兴都库什以南，以喀布尔河中下

[1] 汤用彤《汉魏两晋南北朝佛教史》，长沙：商务印书馆，1938 年，第 374 页。

[2] 沙畹《宋云行纪笺注》，冯承钧译，见冯承钧《西域南海史地考证译丛》第二卷《西域南海史地考证译丛六编》，北京：商务印书馆，1995 年，第 7 页。

[3] 参见：1) 列维、沙畹《罽宾考》，冯承钧译，见冯承钧《西域南海史地考证译丛》第二卷《西域南海史地考证译丛七编》，北京：商务印书馆，1995 年，第 58 页；2) 羽溪了谛《西域之佛教》，贺昌群译，上海：商务印书馆，1933 年，第 313-318 页。

[4] 欧阳询《艺文类聚》，汪绍楹校，上海：上海古籍出版社，1965 年，第 1294 页。

[5] 参见：1) 列维、沙畹《罽宾考》，上引书，第 58-61 页；2) 羽溪了谛，上引书，第 313-318 页；3) 足立喜六《法顯傳：中亞、印度、南海紀行の研究》第二《法顯の蔥嶺通過の研究》第二節《罽賓考》，東京：法藏館，1940 年，第 275-283 页；4) 白鳥庫吉《罽宾国考》，见白鳥庫吉《西域史研究》上，東京：岩波書店，1944 年，第 377-462 页；5) W. W. Tarn, *The Greeks in Bactria and India,* Cambridge: Cambridge University Press, 1951: 469-473.

游及其各支流河谷平原为中心的地区，包括迦毕试、犍陀罗、呾叉始罗、乌苌等地在内[1]。至于晋以后之罽宾，岑仲勉认为“即支僧载《外国事》之罽密，《西域记》之迦湿弥罗，今之克什米尔”[2]。

为了确定罽宾国的方位，现以《北史》卷九十七《西域传》为准[3]，将罽宾及有关西域小国罗列如下：

波路国，在阿钩羌西北，去代一万三千九百里。其地湿热[4]。

小月氏国，都富楼沙城……在波路西南，去代一万六千六百里……其城东十里有佛塔，周三百五十步，高八十丈。自佛塔初建计至武定八年(550年)，八百四十二年，所谓“百丈佛图”也[5]。

罽宾国，都善见城，在波路西南[6]，去代一万四千二百里。居在四山中，其地东西八百里，南北三百里。地平，温和[7]。

钵和国，在渴槃陁西……有两道，一道西行向嚈哒，一道西南趣乌苌，亦为嚈哒所统[8]。

波知国，在钵和西南。土狭人贫，依託山谷，其主不能总摄[9]。

赊弥国，在波知之南。山居，不信佛法，专事诸神……东有钵卢勒(波路)国，路险，缘铁锁而度，下不见底。熙平中，宋云等竟不能达[10]。

乌苌国，在赊弥南。北有葱岭，南至天竺……事佛，多诸寺塔，极华丽……西

---

[1] 参见：1) 岑仲勉《汉书西域传地理校释》，北京：中华书局，1981年，第155-160页；2) 马雍《巴基斯坦北部所见“大魏”使者的岩刻题记》，见马雍《西域史地文物丛考》，北京：文物出版社，1990年，第136-137页。

[2] 岑仲勉，上引书，第151页。参见：1) 白鳥庫吉，上引书，第379-403页；2) L. Petech (伯戴克)，*Northern India According to the Shui-Ching-Chu*, Rome: IsMEO, 1950: 79.

[3] 今本《魏书》在北宋中期以前已散佚，其《西域传》乃据《北史·西域记》补作而成。中华书局1974年出版的唐长孺点校的《魏书》，有详细校勘记，可参看。

[4]《北史》，点校本，北京：中华书局，1974年，第3228页。

[5] 同上书，第3228-3229页。

[6] 据《旧唐书》卷一百九十八《西戎传》，“勃律国在罽宾、吐蕃之间”(点校本，北京：中华书局，1975年，第5310页)；而《新唐书》卷二百二十一《西域传》，“大勃律，或曰布露，直吐蕃西，与小勃律接，西邻北天竺乌苌”(点校本，北京：中华书局，1975年，第6251页)。由此可知，五代修《旧唐书》时，罽宾也常常包括乌苌。

[7]《北史》，点校本，北京：中华书局，1974年，第3229页。

[8] 同上书，第3232页。

[9] 同上。

[10] 同上。

南有檀特山,山上立寺[1]。

乾陁国,在乌苌西……其王本是敕勒,临国已二世矣。好征战,与罽宾斗,三年不罢,人怨苦之……都城东南七里有佛塔,高七十丈,周三百步,即所谓"雀离佛图"也[2]。

根据以上记述,罽宾在波路西南,小月氏在罽宾西南,两者相距约二千四百里;赊弥、乌苌皆在波路之西,亦即罽宾之西;乌苌之西的乾陀和波路西南的小月氏乃一国之不同称谓。换言之,信奉佛教的罽宾、乌苌和乾陀是自东向西分布的。

魏晋南北朝时期,"罽宾多出圣达"[3]。中国与罽宾在佛教方面的交往非常频繁[4]。当时到中土译经传法的罽宾高僧,以见于《出三藏记集》者次第为例,有僧伽提婆[5]、佛驮耶舍[6]、佛驮什[7]、求那跋摩[8]、昙摩密多[9]、弗若多罗[10]、卑摩罗叉[11]、僧伽罗叉[12]、僧伽跋澄[13]、昙摩卑[14]等十余人,而赴罽宾求法或瞻礼游历的中土大德,则有智严[15]、智猛[16]、法勇[17]等,著名高僧鸠摩罗什更是几进罽宾[18],由

[1]《北史》,点校本,北京:中华书局,1974年,第3233页。

[2] 同上。

[3] 僧佑《出三藏记集》,苏晋仁,萧錬子点校,北京:中华书局,1995年,第545页。

[4] 据2005年10月26日《中国文物报》,2005年9月,西安市北郊南康村村民在基建工程中,发现一座北周墓,墓主李诞,婆罗门种,北魏正光年间(520-525年)自罽宾归到中土,保定四年(564年)薨于万年里,春秋五十九,死后被授为邯州刺史,葬中乡里。该墓既是目前国内第一座有明确记载的婆罗门后裔墓葬,也是中土明确记载的第一座罽宾人坟冢,这进一步说明当时罽宾和中国除佛教外在其他方面也有着极为密切的往来。

[5] 僧佑,上引书,第49、337、377、379、380、524、568页。

[6] 僧佑,上引书,第52、117、118、336、536页。

[7] 僧佑,上引书,第57、120、572页。

[8] 僧佑,上引书,第58、543页。

[9] 僧佑,上引书,第58、545页。

[10] 僧佑,上引书,第116、117页。

[11] 僧佑,上引书,第117页。

[12] 僧佑,上引书,第338、525页。

[13] 僧佑,上引书,第374、382、522页。

[14] 僧佑,上引书,第381页。

[15] 僧佑,上引书,第576、577页。

[16] 僧佑,上引书,第579页。

[17] 僧佑,上引书,第581页。

[18] 僧佑,上引书,第234、530页。

此可见两国佛教关系之密切。

经检《出三藏记集》、《名僧传》及《高僧传》，发现经录和僧传中所记述的罽宾，涵盖范围远远超出今克什米尔地区。如法勇（昙无竭）等“进至罽宾国，礼拜佛钵。停岁余，学胡书竟，便解胡语。求得《观世音受记经》梵语一部。无竭同行沙门余十三人，西行到新头那提河，汉言狮子口。缘河西入月氏国，礼拜佛肉髻骨，及睹自沸水船。后至檀特山南石留寺，住僧三百人，杂三乘学。无竭便停此寺，受具足戒”[1]。法勇所记佛钵，乃法显在弗楼沙国所见之佛钵[2]；檀特山，即前述《北史・西域传》所记乌苌国之檀特山；而藏纳佛肉髻骨的月氏国，乃《法显传》所载建有佛顶骨精舍的那竭国[3]。值得注意的是，乌苌、乾陀或小月氏在上述三书中无任何记载。这或许暗示出：当时往来中土和西域的高僧，常常把乌苌、乾陀和迦湿弥罗统称罽宾[4]。

---

[1] 僧佑，上引书，第 581 页。

[2] 法显《法显传》，章巽校注，上海：上海古籍出版社，1985 年，第 39 页。该书记载“宝云、僧景只供养佛钵便还（秦土）”。足见佛钵在佛教信徒心中的地位。此外智猛“既至罽宾城，恒有五百罗汉住此国中……又于此国见佛钵，光色紫绀，四边燦然”（僧佑，上引书，第 580 页）。高僧惠榄“与玄高俱以寂观见崇于西土，遂远游外国，供养罗汉，礼敬佛钵，习禅于罽宾达摩达。以元嘉四年（427 年）于树上得菩萨戒”（宝唱《名僧传》第二十，见宗性《名僧传抄》，载《大日本續藏經》，第壹辑第贰編乙第七套第壹册，第十叶）。凉州人僧表“闻弗楼沙国有佛钵。钵今在罽宾台寺，恒有五百罗汉供养钵。钵经腾空至凉州，有十二罗汉随钵停六年后还罽宾。僧表恨不及见，乃至西逾葱岭，欲致诚礼。并至于宾（阗）国。值罽宾路梗……还凉州”（宝唱《名僧传》第二十六，上引书，第十三叶）。

[3] 法显，上引书，第 46 页。

[4]《魏书・西域传》与《北史・西域传》没有单独为竺沙尸罗立传；上述两书中的《西域传》皆言罽宾国在“波路西南”，疑当时竺沙尸罗已并入罽宾。又，巴利语《本生经》第 406 号《犍陀罗本生》和第 408 号《陶师本生》暗示迦湿弥罗曾是犍陀罗国的一部分。此外，比利时学者魏查理认为：“罽宾”二字之“罽”，应源自罽，“宾”为外国人或客人；“罽宾”是指使用“罽”的外国人。又，罽宾当时指西北印度，迦湿弥罗只是罽宾的一个重要组成部分；而乌苌系罽宾的最初范围，以后扩大至整个西北印度。马雍推测“汉代罽宾国主要是指印度河以西、兴都库什山以南，以喀布尔河中下游及其各支流河谷平原为中心的地区，包括迦毕试、健陀罗、呾叉始罗、乌苌（斯瓦特）等地在内”。桑山正进认为：隋代之罽宾，并非指迦毕试，而是指迦湿弥罗，自 4 世纪至 5 世纪则指犍陀罗。

参见：1) *The Jātaka or Stories of the Buddha's Former Births*; translated from the Pāli by various hands, 6 volumes, ed. E. B. Cowell, Cambridge: Cambridge University Press, Vol. III, 1895: 221-224, 228-232; 2) Charles Willemen, “Sarvāstivāda Developments in Northwestern India and in China”, in: *The Indian International Journal of Buddhist Studies* (New Series in continuation of the *Indian Journal of Buddhist Studies*, Vol. X, Varanasi: B. J. K. Institute of Buddhist and Asian Studies), No. 2 (2001): 163-169, esp. 167; 3) 马雍，上引书，第 136-137 页注释 10; 4) 桑山正進《罽賓と佛》，见《展望アジアの考古學——樋口隆康教授退官記念論集》，東京：新潮社，1983 年，第 598-607 页。

二、罽 宾 道

关于汉唐时期中土通往印度的陆路通道，道宣(596-667年)在《释迦方志》卷上《遗迹篇》中详细记述了东、中、北三道[1]。其中：东道从河州经鄯城、吐谷浑、吐蕃、末上加三鼻关，东南行抵北印度尼波罗国[2]。此道在《大唐西域记》、《旧唐书》、《新唐书》及同时代其他史籍中均未提及，唐以前似不为世人所知，但对于研究唐代中外交通史非常重要[3]，唐代王玄策等人多循此道赴尼波罗和中天竺[4]。北道从瓜州经伊州、西州(高昌)、阿耆尼国、屈支国(丘慈)、跋禄迦国(姑墨)、大清池、素叶水城、呾逻私城、笯赤建国、赭时国(石国)、飒秣建国(康国)、羯霜那国(史国)，后东南山行至铁门关，“即汉塞之西门也。出铁门关便至睹货逻国(古云吐火罗也)之故地”，“自分二十七国”，如呾密国、忽露摩国、鞠和衍那国、拘谜陀国、忽懔国、缚喝国、揭职国、达摩悉铁帝国、屈浪拏国、钵铎创那国、呬摩呾罗国、瞢健国、活国、阔悉多国、安呾罗缚国等。“出睹货逻故地，又至梵衍那国”，后历迦毕试国、那揭罗曷国、健驮逻国、乌仗那国、呾叉始罗国、迦湿弥罗国后南下中印度[5]。玄奘西行求法之路(图1)，即取北道[6]，现通称丝绸之路新疆段北道。中道从鄯州经凉州、沙洲、纳缚波故国(楼兰/鄯善)、折摩陀那故国(沮沫)、尼壤城、瞿萨旦那国(于阗)、皮山、斫句迦国、佉沙(疏勒)、乌鎩国、葱岭、朅盘陁国和商弥国，“又南越山河至达摩悉铁帝国(护密国)，即睹货逻之故地也”。后经迦毕试国、弗栗恃萨傥那国、漕矩吒国，“至西印度

---

[1] 道宣《释迦方志》，范祥雍点校，北京：中华书局，1983年，第14页。

[2] 东道经过的重要地点有：河州、大河、漫天岭、鄯城镇、承风戍、清海、吐谷浑、白兰羌、苏毗国、敢国、吐蕃国、小羊同国、呾仓法关、末上加三鼻关、十三飞梯、十九栈道、北印度尼波罗国。道宣，上引书，第14-15页。参见：1) 严耕望《唐代交通图考》第二卷《河陇碛西区》，台北：中研院历史语言研究所，1985年，图八；2) 范祥雍《唐代中印交通吐蕃一道考》，原刊《中华文史论丛》1982年第四期，后收入范祥雍著《范祥雍文史论文集》，上海：上海古籍出版社，2014年，第143-181页。

[3] 参见：1) 沙畹《宋云行纪笺注》，上引书，第7页；2) 范祥雍点校《释迦方志》前言，见道宣，上引书，第2页。

[4] 1) 冯承钧《王玄策事辑》，见冯承钧《西域南海史地考证论著汇辑》，北京：中华书局，1957年，第102-128页；2) 黄盛璋《关于古代中国与尼泊尔的文化交流》，见黄盛璋《中外交通与交流史研究》，合肥：安徽教育出版社，2002年，第36-66页；3) 范祥雍《唐代中印交通吐蕃一道考》，载：范祥雍著，前引书，第143-181页；4) 西藏自治区文管会文物普查队《西藏吉隆县发现唐显庆三年〈大唐天竺使出铭〉》，刊《考古》1994年第7期，第619-623页。

[5] 道宣，上引书，第15-20页。参见：严耕望，上引书，图八、九。

[6] 参见：玄奘《大唐西域记》，季羡林等校注，北京：中华书局，1985年，第29-349页。

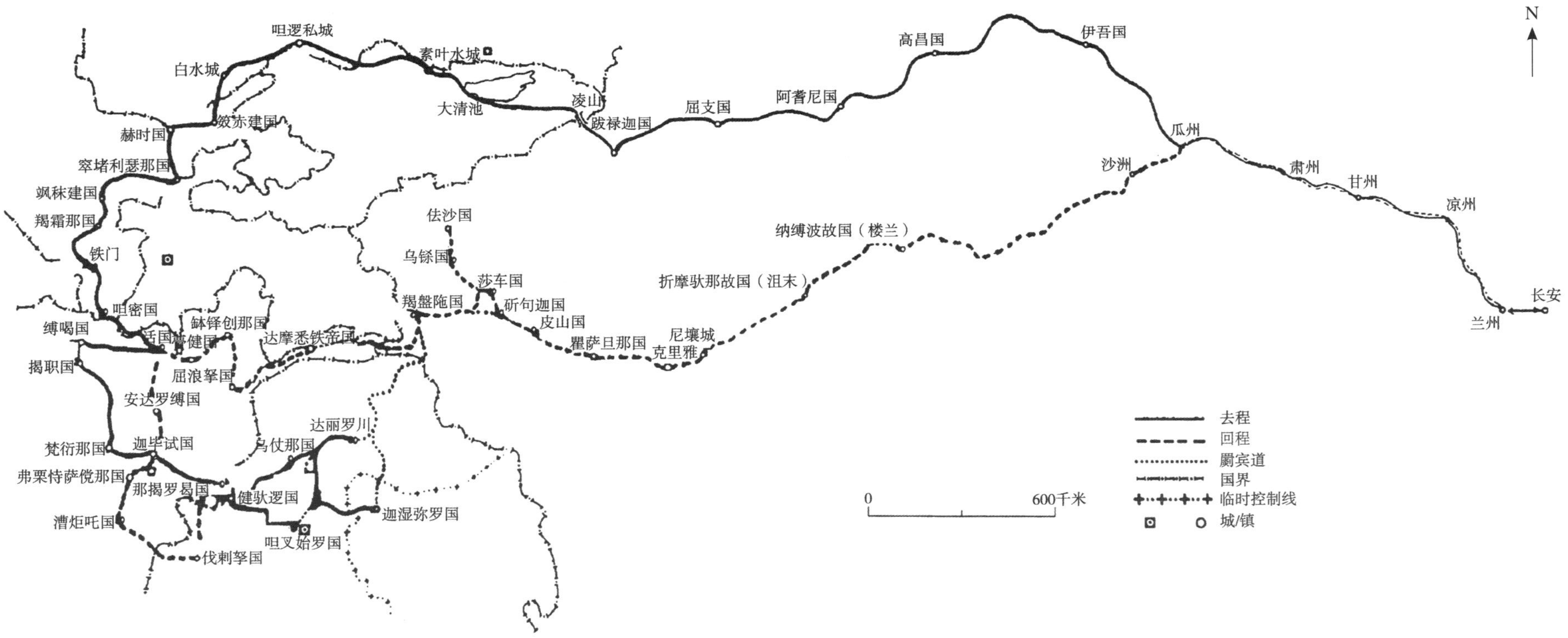

图1　玄奘西行求法路线示意图（前半）

伐刺拏国，方合北道，南趣佛国”[1]。玄奘法师东归之路(图1)，即此中道[2]，现通称丝绸之路新疆段南道。

道宣所记述的中道与北道，主要依据玄奘《大唐西域记》[3]。值得注意的是，后两道自中土进入北印度，皆通过初唐陇右道安西都护府所辖区域[4]，中土使节、僧侣及朝圣者据此或可获得都护府的保护及供给。

除上述三道之外，道宣还在同书卷下《游履篇》中提及了陀历道：“后燕建兴(386-395年)末，沙门昙猛者从大秦路入，达王舍城。及返之日，从陀历道而还东夏”[5]。此陀历，即《法显传》中所记的陀历国，《大唐西域记》卷三中的达丽罗川地区，故址在今克什米尔西北部印度河北岸的达丽尔(Darel)[6]。陀历国是古代自中土度葱岭后进入北印度的必经之地[7]。此“陀历道”，亦即汉代以来的罽宾道[8]。

罽宾道是古代丝绸之路(新疆段)南道上的一条支线[9]，前半段与道宣所述中道大体接近，唯从朅盘陁向南直抵罽宾，开通年代应在汉武帝(前140-前87年在位)

---

[1] 道宣，上引书，第15-20页。

[2] 参见：玄奘，上引书，第948-1036页。

[3] 据《隋书》征引裴矩《西域图记》自序，当时中原通往西域之道路，“发自敦煌，至于西海，凡为三道，各有襟带。北道从伊吾，经蒲类海铁勒部、突厥可汗庭，度北流河水，至拂菻国，达于西海；其中道从高昌、焉耆、龟兹、疏勒，度葱岭，又经钹汗、苏对萨那国、康国、曹国、何国、大小安国、穆国，至波斯，达于西海；其南道从鄯善、于阗、朱俱波、喝槃陀，度葱岭，又经护密、吐火罗、挹怛、忛延、漕国，至北婆罗门，达于西海。其三道诸国，亦各自有路，南北交通。其东女国、南婆罗门国等，并随其所往，诸处得达。故知伊吾、高昌、鄯善，并西域之门户也。总凑敦煌，是其咽喉之地。”《隋书》卷六十七《裴矩传》，标点本，北京：中华书局，1973年，第1579-1580页。裴矩(547？-627年)所记隋代中原通往西域之三道，系对汉、魏以降“丝绸之路”的总结与发展。其南道、中道与《汉书·西域传》所载南、北二道和《释迦方志》所述中、北二道大体相同，其北道即由敦煌、伊吾沿天山山脉以北和伊犁河之间的道路西行，可能相当于《魏略·西戎传》所谓的“北新道”。参见：陈寿撰《三国志·魏书·乌丸鲜卑东夷传》裴松之注引《魏略·西戎传》，点校本，北京：中华书局，第858-863页。

[4] 参见谭其骧主编《中国历史地图集》第五册，上海：地图出版社，1982年，图32-33、63-64。

[5] 道宣，上引书，第97页。

[6] 1) 法显，上引书，第26-27页；2) 玄奘，上引书，第295-297页；3)A. H. Dani, *Chilas: The City of Nanga Parvat*, Islamabad; Quaid-i-Azam University, 1983: 50-52, Map No. 1, Karakorum Region.

[7] 与法显同行的宝云，“于陀历国见金薄(箔)弥勒成佛像，整高八丈。云于像下算诚启忏五十日，夜见神光照烛，皎然如曙。观者盈路，彼诸宿德沙门，并云灵辉数见”。参见：宝唱《名僧传》第二十六，上引书，第十三叶。

[8]《汉书》卷九十六《西域传》下“皮山国”条明确记载了罽宾道：“皮山国，王治皮山城，去长安万五十里……西南至乌秅国千三百四十里，南与天笃接，北至姑墨千四百五十里，西南当罽宾、乌弋山离道，西北通莎车三百八十里。”班固《汉书》，颜师古注，点校本，北京：中华书局，1962年，第3881-3882页。

[9] 豪普特曼《巴基斯坦北部印度河上游古代文物研究：兼论丝绸之路南线岩画走廊的威胁与保护》，见李崇峰主编《犍陀罗与中国》，北京：文物出版社，2019年，第421-474页。

始通罽宾之时[1]。据《汉书·西域传》引杜钦语：汉成帝（前33年–前7年在位）时，这条支线“起皮山南，更不属汉之国四五，斥候士百余人，五分夜击刀斗自守，尚时为所侵盗。驴畜负粮，须诸国禀食，得以自赡。国或贫小不能食，或桀黠不肯给，拥疆汉之节，馁山谷之间，乞丐无所得，离一二旬则人畜弃捐旷野而不反。又历大头痛、小头痛之山，赤土、身热之阪，令人身热无色，头痛呕吐，驴畜尽然。又有三池、盘石阪，道狭者尺六七寸，长者径三十里。临峥嵘不测之深，行者骑步相持，绳索相引，二千余里乃到县度。畜队，未半坑谷尽靡碎；人堕，势不得相收视。险阻危害，不可胜言”[2]。《后汉书·西域传》所述路线，与此基本相同：“自皮山西南经乌秅，涉悬度，历罽宾，六十余日行至乌弋山离国。”[3]由此看出，两汉时期通往罽宾的丝路南道支线从今新疆皮山县开始，不经过莎车，直接转向西南，经过红其拉甫山口或明达盖山口或星峡尔山口等南下至今洪扎（Hunza）河谷[4]。过洪扎河谷之后，罽宾道（县度道、悬度道）向南沿吉尔吉特（Gilgit）河和印度河上游河谷至今本吉（Bunji）地区。此后，一路顺印度河延伸至北天竺，其路线与20世纪60、70年代修筑的中巴公路“大致相符”，但附有若干支线[5]；另一路南下至今印控克什米尔首府斯利那伽（Srīnagar）[6]，进而通往中印度[7]。

“汉明帝永平年中，遣使往西域求法，是为我国向所公认佛教入中国之始。”[8]迄今所知永平求法事，最早见于《牟子理惑论》：“昔孝明皇帝，梦见神人，身有日光，飞在殿前，欣然悦之。明日，博问群臣：‘此为何神？’有通人傅毅曰：‘臣闻天竺有得道者，号之曰佛，飞行虚空，身有日光，殆将其神也。’于是上悟，遣使者张骞、羽林郎中秦景、博士弟子王遵等十二人，于大月支写佛经四十二章。”[9]关于这次求法之路，道宣《释迦方志·游履篇》明确记载他们“从雪山南头悬度道入，到天竺，图其形像，寻访佛法。将沙门迦叶摩腾、竺法兰等还，寻旧路而届雒阳”[10]。

---

[1] 参见《汉书》卷九十六上《西域传·罽宾国》，上引书，第3885-3886页。

[2] 同上书，第3886-3887页。

[3]《后汉书》卷八十八《西域传》，点校本，北京：中华书局，1965年，第2917页。

[4] 马雍认为今洪扎（Hunza，一作罕萨）河谷应为汉代的乌秅国。马雍，上引书，第135-137页。

[5] 1) A. H. Dani, *opere citato*: Map No. 1；2) 马雍，上引书，第129-137页。

[6] 此Srīnagar，即文献所载罽宾都城善见城。参见：白鳥庫吉，上引书，第403-407页。

[7] 参见：1) A. H. Dani, *opere citato*: Map No. 1；2) *Reader's Digest Atlas of the World*, London: The Reader's Digest Association Limited, 1987: 114.

[8] 汤用彤，上引书，第16页。

[9] 僧佑《弘明集》卷一《牟子理惑》，见《大正藏》第52卷，第4c-5a页。

[10] 道宣，上引书，第96页。四川绵阳梓潼卧龙山唐贞观八年（634年）《阿弥陀佛并五十二菩萨传》记载：“至后汉，明帝使郎中蔡愔从雪山南悬度道而入天竺，请三藏法师迦叶摩腾至此洛州，为立精舍。”这条碑刻，较道宣麟德元年（664年）撰《集神州三宝感通录》早三十年，较《释迦方志》的编撰年代也要早许多年。

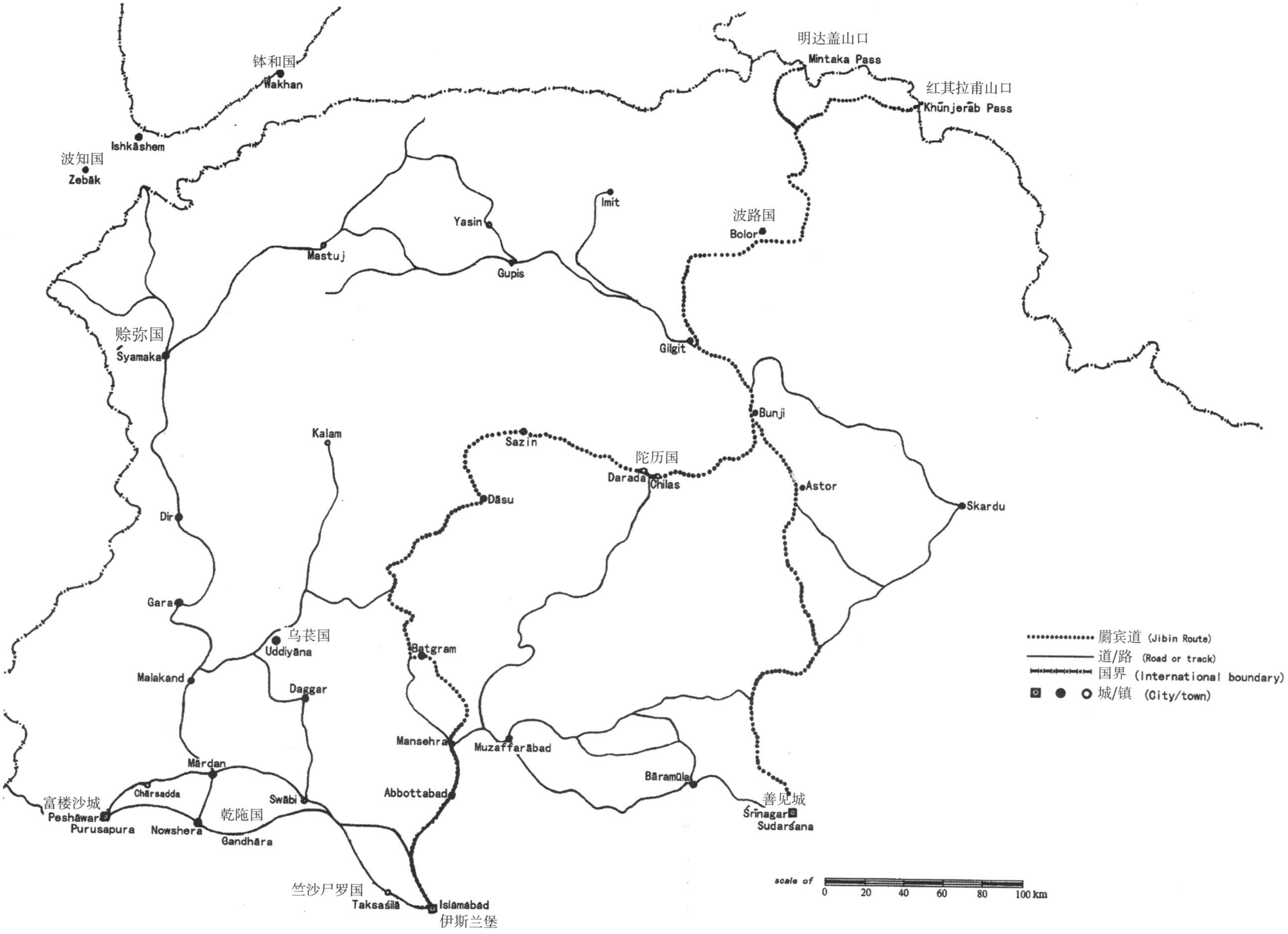
明达盖山口
Mintaka Pass
红其拉甫山口
Khūnjerāb Pass
钵和国
Wakhan
Ishkāshem
波知国
Zebāk
波路国
Bolor
Imit
Yasin
Mastuj
Gupis
赊弥国
Śyamaka
Gilgit
Bunji
Kalam
Sazin
陀历国
Darada
Chilas
Astor
Skardu
Dāsu
Dir
Gara
乌苌国
Uddiyāna
Batgram
Malakand
Daggar
Mansehra
Muzaffarābad
Bāramūla
Mārdan
Chārsadda
Swābi
Abbottabad
善见城
Śrīnagar
Sudarśana
富楼沙城
Peshāwar
Purusapura
Nowshera
乾陁国
Gandhāra
竺沙尸罗国
Taksaśilā
Islāmabād
伊斯兰堡
罽宾道 (Jibin Route)
道/路 (Road or track)
国界 (International boundary)
城/镇 (City/town)
scale of
0
20
40
60
80
100 km

图 2　罽宾道示意图

秦景等人西行求法往还皆取悬度道，反映出佛教传入中国之始即重罽宾道。到了魏晋南北朝时期，罽宾道仍是通往南亚的重要陆路。当时中外使节及传译、求法之高僧多选此道（图 2）。

后秦弘始元年（399 年），法显从长安出发，沿河南道经乾归国[1]、耨檀国[2]、张掖、敦煌、鄯善国、焉夷国[3]沙行至于阗。后历子合国[4]、於麾国[5]、竭叉国[6]，"度（葱）岭已，到北天竺。始入其境，有一小国名陀历……于此顺岭西南行十五日。其道艰岨，崖岸险绝，其山唯石，壁立千仞，临之目眩，欲进则投足无所。下有水，名新头河。昔人有凿石通路施傍梯者，凡度七百，度梯已，蹑悬緪过河。河两岸相去减八十步。九译所绝，汉之张骞、甘英皆不至……古老相传：自（此）立弥勒菩萨像后，便有天竺沙门赍经、律过此河者"[7]。后度河到乌苌国[8]夏坐。之后南下到宿呵多国[9]、犍陀卫国[10]、竺刹尸罗国[11]和弗楼沙国[12]。接下来游访西天竺、中天竺、东天

[1] 乾归，指十六国时期西秦统治者乞伏乾归（388-400 年在位）的都城——金城，故址在今甘肃省兰州市西。

[2] 耨檀，指十六国时期南凉统治者都城乐都（今乐都）或西平（今青海省西宁市）。参见：法显，上引书，第 4 页。

[3] 焉夷，今新疆焉耆回族自治县。

[4] 子合国，《洛阳伽蓝记》卷五引《宋云家记》等作朱驹波；《北史·西域传》作朱俱波（一作朱驹波、朱句、悉居半），《魏书·世宗纪》作朱句槃；《大唐西域记》作斫句迦。《文献通考》卷三百三十七"疏勒"条云："（疏勒）南去莎车五六百里，去朱俱波八九百里。"这说明：朱俱波应在莎车稍南，其地当今新疆叶城县。

[5] 於麾国址未确。章巽先生认为该国故址可能在今新疆叶城库拉玛特山口西南之叶尔羌河中上游一带。参见：法显，上引书，第 20 页。

[6] 竭叉国，《洛阳伽蓝记》卷五引《宋云家记》等作汉盘陁，《北史·西域传》作渴槃陁，《大唐西域记》作朅盘陁国。《梁书》卷五十四《诸夷传·西北诸戎》云："渴槃陁国，于阗西小国也。西邻滑国，南接罽宾国，北连沙勒国，所治在山谷中。城周回四十余里，国有十二城。风俗与于阗相类。"（《梁书》，点校本，北京：中华书局，1973 年，第 814 页）由此可见竭叉与罽宾、疏勒和于阗在地理位置上之关系。其地当在今新疆塔什库尔干县。

[7] 法显，上引书，第 26 页。

[8] 乌苌国，《洛阳伽蓝记》卷五引《宋云家记》等作乌场国，《北史·西域传》作乌苌国，《大唐西域记》卷三作乌仗那国。其地当今巴基斯坦北部斯瓦特河上中游流域，都城故址在今 Mingora。

[9] 宿呵多国故地应在今巴基斯坦西北部斯瓦特河中下游两岸地区。

[10] 犍陀卫国，《洛阳伽蓝记》卷五引《宋云家记》等作乾陀罗国，《北史·西域传》作乾陁国，《魏书·西域传》作乾陀国，《大唐西域记》作健驮罗国。其地应在今斯瓦特河流入喀布尔河之附近一带。

[11] 竺沙尸罗国，《大唐西域记》作呾叉始罗国，其地在今巴基斯坦拉瓦尔品第的塔克西拉地区。

[12] 弗楼沙国，即《洛阳伽蓝记》卷五引《宋云家记》等所载乾陀罗国之乾陀罗城，《魏书·西域传》作富楼沙城，《大唐西域记》作健驮罗国布路沙布罗（Puruṣapura）城，故址在今巴基斯坦白沙瓦（Peshāwar）。

竺和狮子国。412 年从海上返回北青州长广郡牢山 (今山东省青岛市崂山)[1]。

智猛于后秦弘始六年 (404 年) 招结同志沙门十有五人西行求法，疑走同一路线。智猛“发迹长安，渡河顺谷三十六渡，至凉州城。既而西出阳关，入流沙……遂历鄯善、龟兹、于阗诸国，备观风俗。从于阗西南行二千里，始登葱岭，而同侣九人退还。猛遂与余伴进行千七百余里，至波沦国[2]。三度雪山，冰崖皓然，百千余仞，飞絙为桥，乘虚而过，窥不见底，仰不见天，寒气惨酷，影站魂慄。汉之张骞、甘英所不至也。复南行千里，至罽宾国，再渡辛头河，雪山壁立，转甚于前。下多瘴气，恶鬼断路，行者多死。猛诚心冥彻，履险能济。既至罽宾城，恒有五百罗汉住此国中，而常往反阿耨达池”[3]。

至于寓于高昌的法盛，“年造十九，遇沙门智猛从外国还，述诸神迹，因有志焉。辞二亲，率师友，与二十九人远诣天竺。经历诸国，寻觅遗灵及诸应瑞，礼拜供养，以申三业。口憂长国[4]东北，见牛头旃檀弥勒像，身高八寻”[5]。既受智猛西行影响，法盛所选游履之路，应与智猛的大体相近。

刘宋永初元年 (420 年) 西行的法勇 (昙无竭)，更详述了罽宾道。法勇“招集同志沙门僧猛、昙郎之徒二十有五人，共赍幡盖供养之具，发迹北土，远适西方。初至河南国，仍出海西郡，进入流沙，到高昌郡。经历龟兹、沙勒[6]诸国，前登葱岭雪山。栈路险恶，驴驼不通，层冰峩峩，绝无草木，山多障气，下有大江，浚急如箭。于东西两山之肋，系索为桥，相去五里。十人一过，到彼岸已，举烟为帜，后人见烟，知前已度，方得更进。若久不见烟，则知暴风吹索，人堕江中。行葱岭三日方过。复上雪山，悬崖壁立，无安足处，石壁皆有故杙孔，处处相对。人各执四杙，先拔下杙，手攀上杙，展转相代。三日方过，乃到平地相待，料检同侣，失十二人。进至罽宾国，礼拜佛钵”[7]。

20 世纪六七十年代修筑中巴公路时，沿途发现了许多古代行旅在岩石上所刻画的题记及大量不同时代的岩画。“洪扎灵岩二号”，即著名的“大魏使谷巍龙今向迷密使去”题刻 (图 3)，就是极为重要的发现[8]。关于古巍龙出使迷密的时间，马雍定在

[1] 法显，上引书，第 2-177 页。参见：汤用彤，上引书，第 380-385 页。

[2] 波沦国，《洛阳伽蓝记》卷五引《宋云家记》等作钵卢勒，《北史·西域传》作波路国，《大唐西域记》作波露罗国。其地约当克什米尔西北部巴勒提斯坦 (Baltistan)。

[3] 僧佑，上引书，第 579 页。参见慧皎《高僧传》，汤用彤校注，北京：中华书局，1992 年，第 125 页。

[4] 此憂长国，疑乌苌国之讹。

[5] 宝唱《名僧传》第二十六，上引书，第十三叶。

[6]《汉书》以下正史均作疏勒，《大唐西域记》作佉沙，《悟空入竺记》作沙勒，《慧超往五天竺国传》作伽师祇离，当今新疆喀什地区。

[7] 僧佑，上引书，第 581 页。参见：慧皎，上引书，第 93 页。

[8] A. H. Dani, *Human Records on Karakorum Highway*, Lohore: Sang-E-Meel Publications, 1995: 95.

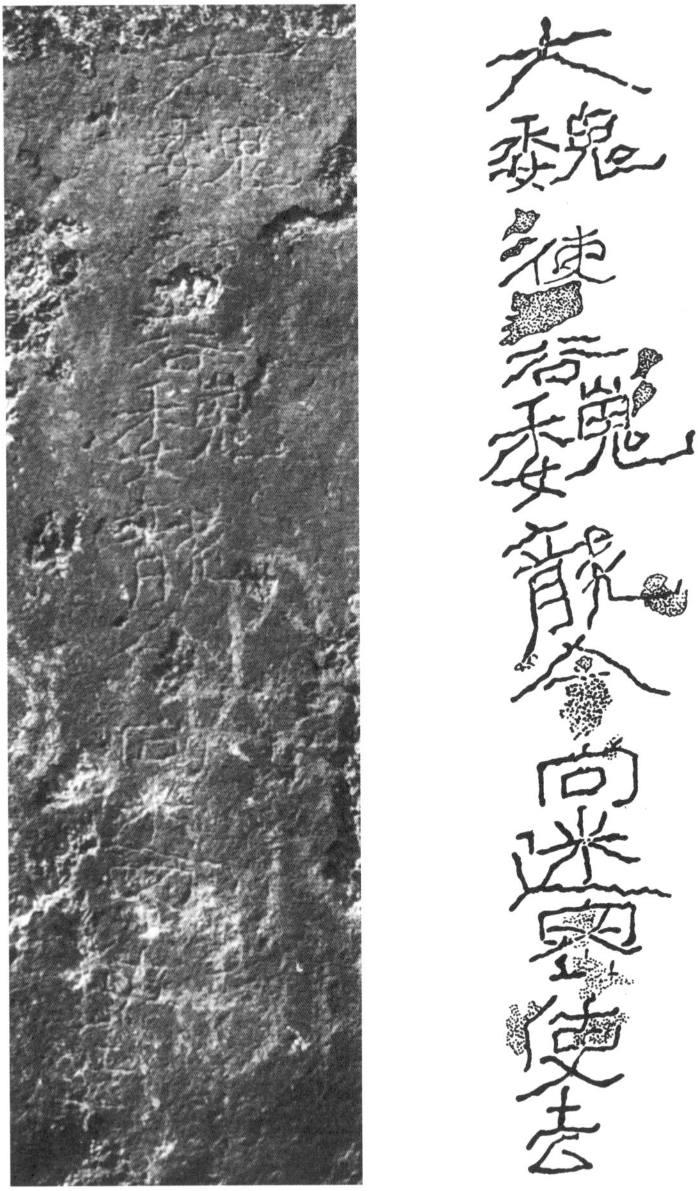

a　　　　　　　　　　　　　　　　b

图 3　中巴公路“洪扎灵岩二号”题铭及摹本

444-453 年之间，并“推测：其所取的路线很可能是从新疆的皮山开始分道向西南，溯塔斯洪河而上，经吐孜拉克达坂，转向西，至阿喀孜达坂，再沿今天的公路线，溯哈拉斯坦河，直至麻扎。由麻扎顺叶尔羌河向西北，经阿拉萨勒，转向西南，越过中巴边境，至星峡尔，再沿星峡尔河往西，即至‘洪扎灵岩’。这一段路程应即汉代通往罽宾、乌弋山离的旧道”[1]。

北魏神龟元年（518 年）十一月冬，灵太后遣宋云、惠生西域取经。二人过赤岭[2]、渡流沙、历吐谷浑、鄯善[3]、左末[4]，经捍麽城[5]到于阗。后入朱驹波国、汉盘陀、钵盂城[6]。“自此以西，山路欹侧，长坂千里，悬崖万仞，极天之阻，实在于斯。太行孟门，匹兹非险，崤关陇坂，方此则夷。自发葱岭，步步渐高，如此四日，乃得至岭……葱岭高峻，不生草木。是时八月，天气已冷，北风驱雁，飞雪千里。”[7]九月中旬入钵和国[8]，十月初抵嚈哒[9]，十一月初入波知国[10]、中旬入赊弥国[11]。“此国渐

[1] 马雍，上引书，第 132-134 页。

[2] 赤岭，北魏“国之西疆也”，在今青海省西宁之西。参见《新唐书》卷四十《地理志》“鄯州鄯城”条，点校本，北京，中华书局，1975 年，第 1041 页。

[3] 鄯善本名楼兰，汉昭帝元凤四年（前 77 年）更名为鄯善。其地当今新疆若羌县。

[4] 左末，《北史·西域传》作且末，《大唐西域记》作沮末，《释迦方志》作沮末。其地当今新疆且末县。

[5] 捍嫲城即扞弥城，约在今和田县东北 90 公里处。据《洛阳伽蓝记》卷五引《宋云家记》等，“城南十五里有一大寺，三百余僧众。有金像一躯，举高丈六，仪容超绝，相好炳然，面恒东立，不肯西顾。父老传云：此像本从南方腾空而来，于阗国王亲见礼拜，载像归。中路夜宿，忽然不见，遣人寻之，还来本处。王即起塔，封四百户以供洒扫。户人有患，以金箔贴像所患处，即得阴愈。后人于此像边造丈六像及诸像塔，乃至数千，悬彩幡盖，亦有万计。魏国之幡过半矣。幡上隶书，多云太和十九年（495 年）、景明二年（501 年）、延昌二年（513 年）。唯有一幡，观其年号是姚兴（394-415 年在位）时幡”。由此可见，此乃十六国到北魏时中土入西域之重要孔道。

[6] 钵盂其地未详，周祖谟认为“在今之 Onkul 等地”。参见杨衒之《洛阳伽蓝记》，周祖谟校释，北京：中华书局，1963 年，第 192 页。

[7] 杨衒之，上引书，第 193-194 页。周祖谟认为“宋云当自 Neza-tash 山口入葱岭，经 Taghdumbash 区域，由 Palik Pass 出 Wakhjir Pass 而抵钵和国”。参见：上引书，第 194 页。

[8] 钵和国当今瓦罕（Wakhan）南山间一带，其都城当今阿富汗伊什卡什姆（Ishkashem）。参见：1）沙畹《宋云行纪笺注》，上引书，第 25 页；2）杨衒之，上引书，第 194-195 页。

[9] 据《北史》卷九十七《西域传》，“嚈哒国，大月氏之种类也，亦曰高车之种。其原出于塞北。自金山而南，在于阗之西，都乌浒水南二百余里，去长安一万一百里。其王都拔底延城”。《北史》，点校本，北京，中华书局，1974 年，第 3230 页。

[10] 波知国其地当今阿富汗 Zébak 与巴基斯坦 Chitral 之间地区。参见：沙畹《宋云行纪笺注》，上引书，第 30 页。

[11] 赊弥国，沙畹认为其地在今巴基斯坦的 Chitral 或 Mastuj，以前者可能性较大。参见：1）沙畹《宋云行纪笺注》，上引书，第 31 页；2）沙畹《西突厥史料》，冯承钧译，北京：中华书局，1958 年，第 146、308 页。

出葱岭，土田峣峭，民多贫困。峻路危道，人马仅通。一直一道，从钵卢勒国向乌场国，铁索为桥，悬虚而度，下不见底，旁无挽捉，倏忽之间，投躯万仞，是以行者望风谢路耳。十二月初入乌场国。北接葱岭，南连天竺。”[1]宋云、惠生出使西域路线，可分前、中、后三段。前段路线与法显游履大体相当，即从京师出发后，先走河南道，然后抵于阗、过葱岭；过葱岭后先至钵和国，后访嚈哒王大毡帐，然后经波知国、赊弥国抵钵卢勒（波路）国，此段（中段）与大魏使谷巍龙过洪扎河谷西行的路线接近；后段循罽宾道从波路经悬度、今 Bunji 和 Chilas 到乌苌国及乾陀国等地。

由此可见，从东汉明帝永平年间遣使秦景等 12 人“从雪山南头悬度道入，到天竺图其形象、寻访佛法”迄北魏神龟元年灵太后遣宋云、惠生到西域取经，这 450 多年间，西行求法者多选罽宾道。考虑到西汉杜钦关于罽宾道之记述、洪扎灵岩之“古巍龙”题刻及道宣所记西汉迄唐 16 则“寻经”游履[2]，我们认为罽宾道是汉唐之间中国通往南亚乃至中亚和西亚的一条交通要道。罽宾道开通的重要原因之一，是罽宾和中国两地具有紧密结合着的佛教背景与环境。如，佛塔既是犍陀罗和乌苌地区佛寺的中心，也是新疆和田地区古代寺院的核心，更是龟兹地区中心柱窟的主体。两地重视佛塔，抑或法藏部派当时流行罽宾和龟兹地区的一个真实反映[3]。不过随着僧侣志趣的演进和唐初政治局势的变化，唐代中印交通主要采纳道宣所记述的东、中、北三道，故自唐中叶 (8-9 世纪）以后，罽宾道随逐渐衰落[4]。

［本文原刊《燕京学报》，新 21 期 (2006 年）第 175-188 页，此次重刊略有修订。］

［1］杨衒之，上引书，第 198-199 页。

［2］道宣，上引书，第 96-100 页。

［3］李崇峰《克孜尔部分中心柱窟与〈长阿含经〉等佛典》，见《徐苹芳先生纪念文集》，上海：上海古籍出版社，2012 年，第 419-465 页。

［4］参见：马雍，上引书，第 129 页。

The Geography of Transmission: The "Jibin" Route and the Propagation of Buddhism in China

Buddhism, a proselytizing faith, was introduced to China at a very early date by zealous missionaries. Acquiring and translating the canon was an important aspect of this process. This is the main reason why the communication route linking India to China in ancient times is of great importance for the study of the transmission of Indian Buddhism via Central Asia to China. The route was not a fixed one nor always accessible: sometimes a route was open, at other times it was blocked; sometimes it changed direction, and other times a new route had to be opened[1].

1. Jibin

In Hinduka (present-day the South Asian Subcontinent)[2], there were two regions which could be considered as sacred for Buddhism in a broad sense: the reaches of the Sindhu (Indus) River and of the Ganga River. Buddhist monks and

---

[1] Tang Yongtong [汤用彤], *Han wei liang jin nanbeichao fojiao shi* [汉魏两晋南北朝佛教史, *A History of Buddhism from the Han down to the Southern and Northern Dynasties* (1st to 6th century AD], Changsha: The Commercial Press, 1938: 374.

[2] 1) P. C. Bagchi, "Ancient Chinese Names of India", in: *India and China: Interactions through Buddhism and Diplomacy; A Collection of Essays by Professor Prabodh Chandra Bagchi*, compiled by Bangwei Wang and Tansen Sen, Delhi: Anthem Press India, 2011: 3-11, esp. 8-9; 2) Qian Wenzhong, "The Ancient Chinese Names of India and their Origins", in: *Land Routes of the Silk Roads and the Cultural Exchanges between the East and West before the 10th Century*; Desert Route Expedition International Seminar in Urumqi August 19-21, 1990, Beijing: New World Press, 1996: 601-611.

laymen from China proper in most cases first visited the Sindhu, closest to the Silk Roads, and then the Ganga. Till the Tang Dynasty (618-907 AD) the more direct route to central Hinduka via Nepal was not well known. Before Tang times, among all the communication routes between ancient China and Hinduka, the most frequently taken was the "Jibin route" because that was the only link from the Pamirs to Kāśmīra and Uḍḍiyāna/Udyāna (present day Swāt valley). Some Buddhist monks and pilgrims like Song Yun and Huisheng never went to central Hinduka but stopped at Puruṣapura (present day Peshawar) or Takṣaśila (Taxila). That is why the region of Gandhāra is considered to have played a vital role in the early dissemination of Buddhism in China[1].

Kāśmīra and Uḍḍiyāna were both referred to as Jibin in some ancient Chinese documents[2]. According to *Waiguo Shi* (*An Account of Foreign Countries*), by monk Zhi Sengzai, about the 4th century AD[3], "Jibin lies to the west of Śrāvastī, the king of Jibin and the people in the kingdom all believed in the way and doctrine of Buddhism. In the winter, men and monks would drink a little wine before noon, and they could not eat anything after noon"[4]. This account seems to be the earliest extant Chinese record of Jibin. As to the exact boundaries of Jibin, however, the identification "is not yet finally settled, because

---

[1] Édouard Chavannes, "Voyage de Song Yun dans l'Udyāna et le Gandhāra (518-22)", in: *Bulletin de l' Ecole française d' Extrēme-Orient,* III (1903): 379-441.

[2] 1) S. Lèvi and É. Chavannes, "L'Itinéraire d'Ou-k'oung", in: *Journal Asiatique,* Octobre (1895): 371-84; 2) É. Chavannes, *Documents sur Les Tou-kiue (Turcs) Occidentaux: Recueillis et commentés,* St-Pétersbourg: Académie Impériale des Sciences de St-Pétersbourg, 1903: 130-132; 3) Kurakichi Shiratori [白鳥庫吉], "Keihinkou ku [罽賓國考, On the Jibin Kingdom]", in: *Seiiki shi kenkyu* [西域史研究, *Collected Papers On the History of the Western Regions*], Vol. 1, Tokyo: Iwanami Shoten, 1944: 377-462, esp. 460-462; 4) Cen Zongmian [岑仲勉], *Hanshu xiyuzhuan dili jiaoshi* [汉书西域传地理校释, *Collation and Annotation to the Monograph on the Western Regions in the History of the Western Han Dynasty*], Beijing: Zhonghua Book Company, 1981: 150-164.

[3] This book was lost after the 10th century AD, but some materials were preserved in the Chinese *leishu* [类书, a class of works combining to some extent the characteristics of encyclopedias and concordances, embracing the whole field of literature, methodically arranged according to subjects, and each heading giving extracts from other former works on the subject in question], such as *Taiping yulan* [太平御览, *The Taiping Reign-Period Imperial Encyclopedia*]. *confer*: Xiang Da [向达], *Tangdai chang'an yu xiyu wenming* [唐代长安与西域文明, *The Tang Dynasty Chang'an and the Civilization of Central Asia*], Beijing: SDX Joint Publishing Company, 1957: 565-578, esp. 570-572.

[4] Ouyang Xun [欧阳询, 557-641 AD], *Yiwen leijun* [艺文类聚, *Encyclopedia of Art and Literature in Dynastic Histories*] in 624 AD, emended and annotated by Wang Shaoying [汪绍楹], Shanghai: Shanghai Chinese Classics Publishing House, 1965: 1294.

in the different periods of Chinese history the term denoted different regions, though all these regions were contiguous to each other" [1] . In the Han Dynasties (206 BC-220 AD) records, Jibin is said to lie to the west of the Sindhu and to the south of the Hindukush mountains, covering an area in the plains of the valleys of the middle and lower reaches of the Kabul River and its tributaries. Kapiṣa, Gandhāra, Takṣaśila, Uḍḍiyāna, and some other states were included under this designation [2]. The term Jibin after the Jin Dynasties (265-420 AD), according to the late Professor Cen Zhongmian, refers to present-day Kashmir, used in the geographical sense [3]. Jibin was called Kāśmīra by Xuanzang (602-664 AD) in his *Datang xiyu ji* (*Record of the Western Regions of the Great Tang Dynasty*) [4].

During the period of the Wei (220-265 AD), Jin (265-420 AD), and Southern-and-Northern dynasties (420-589 AD), according to Sengyou (445-518 AD): "Jibin abounded with saints and wise men." [5] At this time, there were frequent exchanges between Jibin and China, many having to do with the spread of Buddhism. The names of those who came from Jibin to China proper to recite or translate Buddhist *sūtras* and to propagate the doctrines of Buddhism were recorded in *Chu sanzang ji ji* (*A Collection of Records concerning the Tripiṭaka*) by Sengyou. They contain many eminent monks from Jibin including people like Buddhabhadra, Buddhajīva, Buddhayaśas, Dharmamitra, Dharmanandi, Dharmapriya, Dharmayaśas, Guṇavarman, Puṇyatāra, Saṃghabhadra, Saṃghadeva, Saṃgharakṣa and

---

[1] A. K. Narain, *The Indo-Greeks,* Oxford: The Clarendon Press, 1957: 135. *confer*: 1) S. Lèvi and É. Chavannes, *ibidem*; 2) Kurakichi Shiratori, *ibidem*; 3) Cen Zongmian, *ibidem*; 4) W. W. Tarn, *The Greeks in Bactria and India,* Cambridge: Cambridge University Press, 1951: 469-473.

[2] 1) Cen Zongmian, *opere citato*: 155-160; 2) Ma Yong, "The Chinese Inscription of the 'Da Wei' Envoy of the 'Sacred Rock of Hunza'", in: *Antiquities of Northern Pakistan: Reports and Studies,* Vol. 1, *Rock Inscriptions in the Indus Valley,* ed. Karl Jettmar et al, Mainz: Verlag Philipp von Zabern, 1989: 139-157, esp. 153 footnote.

[3] Cen Zongmian, *opere citato*: 151.

[4] Samuel Beal, tr., *Si-Yu-Ki-Buddhist Records of the Western World; Chinese Accounts of India,* translated from the Chinese of Hiuen Tsiang, London: Trubner, 1884: 188.

[5] Sengyou [僧佑], *Chu sanzang ji ji* [出三藏记集, *A Collection of Records concerning the Tripiṭaka* or *A Collection of Records of Translations of the Tripiṭaka*], emended and annotated by Su Jinren [苏晋仁] and Xiao Lianzi [萧錬子], Beijing: Zhonghua Book Company, 1995: 545; *confer*: *Taishō,* No. 2145, Vol. 55: 1-114, esp. 105a.

Vimalākṣa[1]. On the other hand, those who went to Jibin from China proper during the 4th and 5th centuries AD, either in quest of Buddhist *sūtras* and images or simply on pilgrimages, included Fayong (Dharmodgata), Zhimeng, Zhiyan, among many others[2]. Kumārajīva, the great Kuchean translator, is recorded as having travelled back and forth between Jibin and Kucīna (Kucha) several times[3]. Thus it can be seen that a close relationship existed between Jibin and China[4] as far as the Buddhist cultural exchange was concerned.

When we turn our attention to *Chu sanzang ji ji* by Sengyou, *Mingseng zhuan* (*Biographies of the Famous Monks*) by Baochang[5] in 514 AD and *Gaoseng zhuan* (*Biographies of Eminent Priests*) by Huijiao[6] in 519 AD, we find that the territory of Jibin recorded in these books extends far beyond the present-day geographical boundaries of Kashmir. For instance, in these texts it is stated that Fayong (Dharmodgata) and his fellow pilgrims "came to Jibin and

[1] Sengyou, *opere citato*: 46-58, 522-537, 541-546; *confer*: *Taishō,* Vol. 55: 10-12, 100-102, 103-105.

[2] Sengyou, *opere citato*: 576-582; *confer*: *Taishō,* Vol. 55: 112-114. Zhiyan is said to have led a group of about 4 monks, Zhimeng led 15, and Fayong 25 monks from China to Jibin. There are other lists of monks in other documents as well. Their number, thus, was considerable.

[3] Sengyou, *opere citato*: 234, 530-535; *confer*: *Taishō,* Vol. 55: 41b, 100a-102a.

[4] According to *Zhongguo wenwu bao* [中国文物报, *China Cultural Relics News*] dated October 26, 2005, a tomb that belongs to the Northern Zhou Dynasty [北周, 557-581 AD] was discovered at Nankang [南康] village in northern Xi'an in September 2005. In the light of the epitaph unearthed from the tomb, the deceased was Li Dan [李诞]of the brāhmaṇa race [婆罗门种], who came to China from Jibin during the Zhengguang period [正光, 520-525 AD] of the Northern Wei Dynasty and died at age of 59 at Wannianli [万年里] in 564 AD. He was buried in his home village and conferred posthumous honors on Hanzhou *cishi* [邯州刺史, Regional Inspector of Hanzhou] by the Northern Zhou Dynasty. This is not only the first tomb that bears the name of a brāhmaṇa but also a tomb that records a foreigner who came from Jibin and lived in China. It further indicates that Jibin and China had a close contact besides the Buddhist relationship.

[5] Baochang [宝唱], *Mingseng Zhuan* [名僧传, *Biographies of Famous Monks* or *Lives of Famous Bhikṣus*], partly preserved in the Japanese *Meisōden-shō* [名僧传抄, *A Transcript of Biographies of Famous Monks*] by Shū-shō [宗性] in 1235 AD, in: *Dainihon Zoku Zōkyō* [大日本續藏經, *Continued Tripiṭaka of Japan*], Vol. 7, No. 1: 1-17.

[6] Huijiao [慧皎 ca. 495-554 AD], *Gaoseng zhuan* [高僧传, *Biographies of Eminent Priests* or *The Liang Dynasty Biographies of Eminent Priests* or *Biographies of Eminent Monks* or *Memoirs of Eminent Monks*], emended and annotated by Tang Yongtong [汤用彤], Beijing: Zhonghua Book Company, 1992; *confer*: *Taishō,* No. 2059, Vol. 50: 322-424.

then worshipped the holy alms bowl of the Buddha". They are said to have stayed there for more than a year and could, we are told, understand the *Hu* language, a general term for all foreign languages in ancient Chinese records. They are said to have studied the local language initially in its written form. They entreated the local ecclesiastics and received copies of a set of *Guanshiyin shouji jing* (*Avalokiteśvara-mahāsthamapraptav-yākarana-sūtra*) in *fanwen* (Brāhmī-script)[1].

Furthermore, we are told that Dharmodgata, together with 13 fellow pilgrims[2], went westwards to Xintounatihe (the Sindhu River) which was referred to as the "Lion's Mouth" in Chinese. They then crossed river and arrived in the state of Yuezhi (Indoscythe/Gandhāra)[3], which was on the west side of the river, and there they worshipped the holy skull bone of the Buddha[4]. Then they proceeded to a Buddhist temple named Shiliusi (Dāndima-vihāra), to the south of the Dandaloka mountain, where 300 monks practised *trīṇi-yānāni* (the three vehicles), i. e. *śrāvaka-yāna, pratyeka-buddha-yāna* and *bodhisattva-yāna* or *mahā-yāna*. Dharmodgata stayed in this temple and obtained the complete rules or commandments[5].

The above-mentioned Buddha's alms bowl in Jibin was also referred to

---

[1] Sengyou, *opere citato*: 581; *confer*: *Taishō,* Vol. 55: 114a.

According to Charles Willemen , "the Chinese term *fanwen,* actually meaning Brāhmī-script, text, and not Sanskrit as a language, is a term used when the majority of texts in China used Brāhmī, not e. g. the earlier Kharoṣṭhī, a writing system of the Gandhāran cultural area". Charles Willemen, "Kaniṣka and the Sarvāstivāda Synod", in: *Glory of the Kushans: Recent Discoveries and Interpretations,* ed. Vidula Jayaswal, New Delhi: Aryan Books International, 2012: 218-222, esp. 219.

[2] According to *Chu sanzang ji ji,* it took Fayong (Dharmodgata) and his fellow pilgrims "three days to get over the Congling Range and another snowy mountain was lying ahead. The cliff was like walls with no place to put one's foot. There were many small holes aligned on the face of the cliff. Each one of the people had four wooden sticks and when they tried to go ahead, they had to insert the sticks into the upper holes for hand and lower holes for foot and when they went one step further, they drew out the sticks and inserted them into the holes ahead of them. They spent three days to cross the snowy mountain. When they counted the survivors after they came to the flat ground, they found that twelve of them were lost". Sengyou, *opere citato*: 581; *confer*: *Taishō,* Vol. 55: 113c-114a.

[3] The term Yuezhi is equivalent to Tukhāra/ Tokharians. *confer*: A. K. Narain, *The Tokharians: A History without Nation-State Boundaries,* RGF-NERC-ICSSR Lecture-Series, Shillong: North-Eastern Hill University Publications, 2000: 6-7, 21.

[4] This is the place where the skull bone of the Buddha was enshrined.

[5] Sengyou, *opere citato*: 581; *confer*: *Taishō,* Vol. 55: 114a.

by Faxian who had seen it in the state of Fulousha (Puruṣapura)[1], and the Dandaloka mountain in Uḍḍiyāna is also mentioned in *Beishi* (*History of the Northern Dynasties*) by Li Yanshou in 659 AD[2]. The state of Yuezhi, in which was enshrined the skull bone of the Buddha, was called the state of Najie (Nagarahāra) by Faxian, who also mentions that a *vihāra* by that name existed in this state[3]. We should particularly note that the names of Wuchang (Uḍḍiyāna) and Qiantuo (Gandhāra) or Xiao Yuezhi (Small Yuezhi/Gandhāra)[4] are not mentioned as separate entities in *Chu sanzang ji ji, Mingseng zhuan* nor *Gaoseng zhuan*. It seems that the monks of China and of the Western Regions grouped them all under the common name of Jibin at the time that these records were compiled or emended[5].

---

[1] Faxian［法显，?-423 AD］, *Faxian zhuan*［法显传，*The Travels of Faxian*］, emended and annotated by Zhang Xun［章巽］, Shanghai: Shanghai Chinese Classics Publishing House, 1985: 39; *confer*: *Taishō,* No. 2085, Vol. 51: 858b.

[2] Li Yanshou［李延寿］, *Beishi*［北史，*History of the Northern Dynasties*］in 659 AD, punctuated edition, Beijing: Zhonghua Book Company, 1974: 3233.

[3] Faxian, *opere citato*: 46; *confer*: *Taishō,* Vol. 51: 858c.

[4] Wuchang and Qiantuo appear in Chinese records as early as the 4th century AD and were popularly quoted in Chinese texts in the 5th century.

With regard to Xiao Yuezhi or Little Yüeh-chi, *confer*: John Marshall, *Taxila: An illustrated account of archaeological excavations carried out at Taxila under the orders of the government of India between the years 1913 and 1934,* London: Cambridge University Press, 1951, Vol. I: 74-75.

[5] These three books were all written before 519 AD by the learned monks living in south China. And, the records of the Buddhist mission of Song Yun［宋云］and Huisheng［惠生］of the Northern Wei Dynasty［北魏，386-534 AD］to the Western Regions provide much information for this region. In 518 AD, the Empress Dowager Ling, née Hu, dispatched Huisheng to go to the Western Regions in search of Buddhist *sūtras*. And Song Yun went with him as the Northern Wei envoy to Uḍḍiyāna and Gandhāra besides other states. Huisheng even stayed in Uḍḍiyāna for two more years, and it was not until the second year of the Zhengguang period (521 AD) of the Northern Wei Dynasty that he returned to the national capital (Luoyang). Huisheng and Song Yun left us quite a detailed account of the Western Regions, such as *Huisheng's Traveling Account* and *Private Record of Song Yun*, of which, some were quoted by Yang Xuanzhi［杨衒之］in his book. Yang Xuanzhi, *Luoyang qielan ji*［洛阳伽蓝记，*A Record of Saṃghārāmas in Luo-yang*］, emended and annotated by Zhou Zumo［周祖谟］, Beijing: Zhonghua Book Company, 1963:182-227; 2) Yi-t'ung Wang, tr., *A Record of Buddhist Monasteries in Lo-yang* by Yang Hsüan-chih, Princeton: Princeton University Press, 1984: 215-228.

confer: Charles Willemen, "Sarvāstivāda Developments in Northwestern India and in China", in: *The Indian International Journal of Buddhist Studies* (New Series in continuation of the *Indian Journal of Buddhist Studies*, Vol. X, Varanasi: B. J. K. Institute of Buddhist and Asian Studies), No. 2 (2001): 163-169, esp. 167.

2. Jibin Route

There were three main routes of communication between India and China in the Tang time, as recorded in *Shijia fangzhi* (*A Geographical Record of Buddhist World*) by Daoxuan (?-667 AD)[1]. These were the eastern, the middle, and the northern routes. The eastern route started from Hezhou, went through Shanzhou, Qinghai, Tu-yu-hun (Aza), Tubo (Tibet), the Marsyangbi Pass and then southeastwards, reaching Nepāla and central India[2]. This route, however, is not mentioned in *Datang xiyu ji* (*Record of the Western Regions of the Great Tang Dynasty*) by Xuanzang in 646 AD nor pointed out clearly in *Jiu Tangshu* (*The Old Book of the History of the Tang Dynasty*) by Liu Xu and other in 945 AD, nor even in *Xin Tangshu* (*The New Book of the History of the Tang Dynasty*) by Ouyang Xiu and Song Qi in 1060 AD[3]. The route, which does not seem to have been known to the people before the Tang Dynasty, has become very important from Tang times even down to the present day and is called *Tangbo gudao* (Sino-Tibetan Route) by scholars. Wang Xuance, a famous diplomatic envoy of the Tang Dynasty chose this route to Nepal and from there to central India three times between 643 and 660 AD[4].

The northern route started from Guazhou and passed through Yizhou (Hami), Xizhou (Turfan/Qoco), Aqini (Agni/Karashahr), Quzhi (Kucīna/Kucha), Balujia (Bālukā/Aksu), Daqingchi (Issyk-kul), Suyeshui (Sūyāb/Ak-Beshim), Daluosi (Tarāz/Talas, Aulia-Ata), Nuchijian (Nujakath/Nejkend), Heshi (Shash/Binkath, Taškent), Fengmojian (Samarkand, Afrasiab), Jieshuangna (Kasanna, Shahri-śabz), Tiemen (Dar-i Āhanīn/Tämir Qapïγ). After passing the Dar-i

---

[1] Daoxuan [道宣], *Shijia fangzhi* [释迦方志, *A Geographical Record of Buddhist World*], emended and annotated by Fan Xiangyong [范祥雍], Beijing: Zhonghua Book Company, 1983: 14; *confer*: *Taishō,* Vol. 51: 950c.

[2] Daoxuan, *opere citato*: 14-15; *confer*: *Taishō,* Vol. 51: 950c.

[3] Fan Xiangyong, "Introduction to *Shijia fangzhi* (*A Geographical Record of Buddhist World*) by Daoxuan", in: Daoxuan, *opere citato*: 2.

[4] Feng Chengjun [冯承钧], "*Wang Xuance shiji* [王玄策事辑, Collection of Wang Xuance's Events and Deeds]", in: *Xiyu nanhai shidi kaozheng lunzhu huiji* [西域南海史地考证论著汇辑, *Collected Works on the History and Historical Geography of the Western Regions and Southeast Asia*] by Feng Chengjun, Beijing: Zhonghua Book Company, 1957: 102-128.

Āhanīn one arrived in the old territory of the Tokharians (Tukhāra)[1], which comprised 27 more states such as Dami (Tirmidh/Termid), Hulumo (Kharün), Juheyanna (Kuvāyāna/Quwādhiyān), Jumituo (Kumedh/Komidai), Hulin (Khulm/ Tāshkurghān), Fuhe (Bactra/Balkh, Mazār-i-Sharīf), Jiezhi (Gachi/Karčik), Damoxitiedi (Dar-i Mastit, Wakhan), Qulangna (Kurān), Boduochuangna (Badakshan/Badakhshān), Ximodaluo (Himatala), Mengjian (Mundzān/Munjān), Huoguo (Warwālīz/Valvālig, Qunduz), Kuoxiduo (Khost), Andaluofu (Andarāb), etc. Coming out of the old territory of the Tokharians, one arrived at Fanyanna (Bāmīyān) and then started eastwards for Jiabishi (Kapiṣa/Kapiṣaya, Begram), Najieluohe (Nagarahāra, Jalālābād), Jiantuoluo (Gandhāra), Wuzhangna (Uḍḍiyāna/Udyāna), Dachashiluo (Takṣaśilā, Taxila), Jiashimiluo (Kāśmīra, Kashmir], and finally went southwards to central India[2]. This was the very route that Xuanzang took on his way to India (fig.1)[3]. It is now known as the northern route of the Silk Road in the Xinjiang region.

The middle route started from Shanzhou and went through Liangzhou (Wu wei), Shazhou (Dunhuang), Loulan (Charklik), Jumo (Charchan/Calmadana), Nirang (Niya), Qusadanna (Gostana, Khotan), Pishan (Guma), Zhuojujia (Čukupa, Karghalik), Qusha (Kashgar), Wusha (Yarkand), Congling Range, Jiepantuo (Kavanta, Tashkurghan), Shangmi (Śyamaka), the old territory of Tokharians, Kapiṣa, Fulishisatangna (Vrjisthana/ Vardasthana), Caojuzha (Jāguḍa, Zabulistan), and then it joined the northern route[4]. This was the very route taken by Xuanzang on his return journey to China (see fig.1)[5], and is now known as the southern route of the Silk Road in the Xinjiang region.

The middle and northern routes elaborated by Daoxuan here were based mainly on *Datang xiyu ji* (*Record of the Western Regions of the Great Tang Dynasty*) by Xuanzang. It should be stressed that the northern and middle routes from China proper to northern India had to pass through vast areas, which were

---

[1] With regard to the Tokharisans, *confer*: A. K. Narain, *opere citato* (*The Tokharians...*) : 6-7.

[2] Daoxuan, *opere citato*: 20-33; *confer*: *Taishō,* Vol. 51: 952b-956b.

[3] Xuanzang [玄奘], *Datang xiyu ji* [大唐西域记, *Record of the Western Regions of the Great Tang Dynasty*] in 646 AD, emended and annotated by Ji Xianlin [季羡林] et al., Beijing: Zhonghua Book Company, 1985: 46-347, 961-978; *confer: Taishō,* No. 2087, Vol. 51: 870a-888a, 939c-941a.

[4] Daoxuan, *opere citato*: 15-20; *confer*: *Taishō,* Vol. 51: 950c-952b.

[5] Xuanzang, *opere citato*: 948-1033; *confer: Taishō,* Vol. 51: 938c-945c.

under the control of the Anxi Protectorate of the Longyou Administration in the early Tang Dynasty. Diplomatic envoys, monks, pilgrims, and merchant travelers, who often took these two routes, could seek probably some protection, offerings, and supplies from the Anxi Protectorate.

In addition to the above three routes[1], Daoxuan also mentioned a route called "Tuolidao (Daraḍa route)" in the book referred to earlier: "Towards the end of the Jianxing period (386-395 AD) of the Late Yan state, the monk Tanmeng (Dharmotikśṇa) who went along the Daqin route reached Rājagṛha, but when he returned, he took the Daraḍa route to go back home. "[2] This "Daraḍa" was the very Daraḍa mentioned by Faxian and corresponded to the place with the similar name Daliluo (Daraḍa) recorded by Xuanzang, which is located on the northern side of the Sindhu River, northwest of present-day Kashmir[3]. Daraḍa (present-day Dardistān) was the place one had to pass through on the way from the great snow mountains to Hinduka in ancient times. The "Daraḍa route" here, however, is just another name of the "Jibin route" known since the days of the Han dynasties.

The Jibin route was a branch line of the southern route of the Silk Roads in Xinjing, in ancient time. The first half of the Jibin route was more or less similar to the central route elaborated by Daoxuan in his book. But the second half started from Tashkurghan and then went southwards directly to Uḍḍiyāna and Kāśmīra. The Jibin route seems to be opened somewhere between 141 and 88 BC, corresponding to the reign of the Emperor Wudi (141-87 BC) of the Han Dynasty, when the communication between China proper and Jibin had just been established. A clearer picture may be had from Du Qin's description cited under the heading of "Ji-bin Kingdom" in *Hanshu: xiyuzhuan* (*History of the Western*

---

[1] Pei Ju [裴矩 547?-627 A.D.] also records three routes that connect China proper and the West, i.e., the Northern Route, the Middle Route and the Southern Route. Among which, the Southern Route and the Middle Route are similar to, or almost coincided with, the Middle Route and Northern Route mentioned by Daoxuan. *confer*: Wei Zheng [魏徵] and Zhangsun Wuji [长孙无忌], *Suishu* [隋书, *History of the Sui Dynasty*], punctuated and emended ed., Beijing: Zhonghua Book Company, 1973: 1579-1580.

[2] Daoxuan, *opere citato*: 97; *confer*: *Taishō,* Vol. 51: 969b.

[3] A. H. Dani, *Chilas: The City of Nanga Parvat,* Islamabad; Quaid-i-Azam University, 1983: 2-4, Map No. 1.

Han Dynasty: *Monograph on the Western Regions*) by Ban Gu (31-92 AD), which occurs as the account of the routes that the Han envoys' took when escorting tribute carriers from Ji-bin back home. It states:

Starting in the area south of Pishan (Guma), one passes through some four to five sates or kingdoms along the route which are not subject to the Han. Envoys, travelers and merchants, who used asses or donkeys to transport grains, had to live on charity. While some small and poor states could not afford to give much in charity others were just unwilling to offer any. Most of the travelers died and the animals too would die within ten to twenty days. In addition, they had to pass over the ranges known as the hills of the Greater and the Lesser Headache, and the slopes of the Red Earth and the Fever of the Body. These cause a man to suffer fever; he has no color, his head aches and he vomits; asses and stock animals all suffer in this way. Furthermore there are the Three Pools and Great Rock Slopes, with a path that is one Chinese foot and six or seven inches wide, but leads forward for a length of thirty Chinese *li*, overlooking a precipice whose depth is unfathomed. Travelers passing on horse or foot hold on to one another and pull each other along with ropes; and only after a journey of more than two thousand *li* do they reached the Xuandu (Suspended Crossing/Chain Bridge). Several asses and draught animals slipped into the valley and were lost, and even when a man fell down into the valley the others could not look for him for fear of slipping too. Dangers defy enumeration[1]. In *Hou Hanshu: xiyuzhuan* (*History of the Eastern Han Dynasty: Monograph on the Western Regions*) by Fan Ye, moreover, we are told that "one starts in the southwest of Pishan (Guma), passes through Wucha, crosses the Suspended Crossing, passes through Jibin and then arrives in Wuyishanli (Alexandria/Herāt) after traveling for over sixty days"[2].

Thus it proves that the branch of the southern route of the Silk Roads to Jibin started from Guma. It did not go through Yarkand, but instead turned immediately to the southwest and extended over today's Sino-Pakistan boundary

---

[1] Ban Gu [班固, 31-92 AD], *Hanshu* [汉书, *History of the Western Han Dynasty*], punctuated edition, Beijing: Zhonghua Book Company, 1962: 3886-87.

[2] Fan Ye [范晔, 398-445 AD], *Hou Hanshu* [后汉书, *History of the Eastern Han Dynasty*], punctuated edition, Beijing: Zhonghua Book Company, 1965: 2917.

through the Mintaka pass or Khūnjerāba pass or Shimshal Pass. Then, it went southwards to the present-day Hunza valley[1]. After going through the Hunza valley, the Jibin route went southwards along the Gilgit River and then along the upper reaches of the Sindhu River, and finally arrived at present-day Bunji. From here the route, with several branch lines[2], went all the way along the Sindhu River to northern India, which approximately corresponds to the present-day Karakorum Highway[3]. Another route went southwards to Sudarśana (Śrīnagar), the capital of today's Indian Kashmir, and then to central India.

According to *Weishu: Shilaozhi* (*History of the Wei Dynasties: Treatise on Buddhism and Taoism*) by Wei Shou in 554 AD, "in the first year of the Yuanshou period (2 BC) of Emperor Ai of the Western Han Dynasty (206 BC-25 AD), a scholar named Qin Jingxian received oral instruction on the Buddhist scriptures from Yichun, envoy of the King of the Da Yuezhi (Greater Yuezhi), but while China had heard of the scriptures, they were not yet part of their beliefs. Later, Emperor Ming (57-75 AD) of the Eastern Han Dynasty (25-220 AD) dreamed one night of a golden man, sunlight issuing form the nape of his neck, flying in mid-air towards the palace courtyard. Thereupon the Emperor inquired from the assembled ministers. Fu Yi was the first to answer that it was the Buddha. The Emperor then dispatched Cai Yin and Qin Jing with a party on a mission to Hinduka in *ca.* 64 AD[4], to seek out or to copy the canon left behind by the Buddha. Cai Yin then returned eastward to Luoyang, capital of China at that time, with the monks Kāśyapa Mātaṅga and Zhu Falan[5]. The route that they took to Hinduka was

[1] Ma Yong gave a hypothesis that Hunza should be the Wucha state mentioned during the Han period. Ma Yong, *opere citato*: 153.

[2] A. H. Dani, *opere citato*: Map No. 1.

[3] Ma Yong, *opere citato*: 140.

[4] Tang Yongtong, *opere citato*: 11-21.

[5] Wei Shou [魏收, 506-572 AD], *Weishu: Shilaozhi* [魏书·释老志, *History of the Wei Dynasties: Treatise on Buddhism and Taoism*], punctuated edition, Beijing: Zhonghua Book Company, 1974: 3025-3062, esp. 3025-26. *confer*: 1) James R. Ware, "Wei Shou on Buddhism", in: *T'oung Pao* 30 (1930): 100-181, esp. 110-12; 2) Leon Hurvitz, tr., *Treatise on Buddhism and Taoism* by Wei Shou, in: S. Mizuno [水野清一] and T. Nagahiro [長廣敏雄], *Yun-kang; The Buddhist Cave-temples of the Fifth Century AD. in North China; detailed report of the archaeological survey carried out by the mission of the Tōhōbunka Kenkyūsho 1938-45* [雲岡石窟：西暦五世紀における中國北部佛教窟院の考古學的調查報告；東方文化研究所調查，昭和十三年——昭和二十年], Kyoto: Jimbunkagaku Kenkyūshō, Kyoto University, Vol. XVI supplement (1956): 23-103, esp. 28-29.

the Jibin Route, in other words, they ascended the snow-mountain and "entered Hinduka through the Xuandudao (the Suspended Crossing Route/Chain-bridge Route)" . When they planned to return home, they chose the same old route and reached Luoyang finally[1].

Up until the Wei, Jin, and Southern-and-Northern dynasties i.e. from the 3rd to 6th century AD, the Jibin route was still an important land route to South Asia. Buddhist pilgrims and diplomats such as Baoyun, Faxian, Zhiyan, Zhimeng, Tanmeng (Dharmotikśṇa?), Fasheng, Fayong (Dharmodgata), Daorong/Daoyao, Song Yun and Huisheng[2] as well as Gu Weilong generally chose this route (fig.2)[3].

In 399 AD, Faxian and his fellow pilgrims left Chang'an, capital of the Late Qin state, and then went, along the Henan route, through the states of Qiangui, Noutan, Zhangye, Dunhuang, Shanshan (Charklik), Yanyi (Karashahr) and then they reached Yutian (Khotan) after crossing the desert. They continued and passed the states of Zihe (Karghalik), Yuhui and Jiecha (Tashkurghan). Upon crossing the Congling Range, they arrived in northern Hinduka. We are told that just at the frontier there is a small state called Tuoli (Daraḍa/Darada). Keeping to the range, the party journeyed in a southwestern direction for 15 days over a difficult, precipitous and dangerous route, the side of the mountain being "like a stone wall thousand *ren*" (more than 2, 000 meters) in height. "On nearing the edge, the eye becomes confused; and wishing to advance, the foot finds no resting-place." Below was the Sindhu River. The men of former times had cut away the rock to make a way down and had placed ladders along the side of the rock. There are 700 rock-cut steps in all; and once one had successfully come down the steps and ladders, the river was crossed by a suspension bridge or chain bridge. The two banks of the river are somewhat less than 80 *bu* (about 118 meters) apart. The route was dangerous and difficult, so there were not any tracks of human beings to be seen. Neither Zhang Qian nor Gan Ying of the

---

[1] Daoxuan, *opere citato*: 96; *confer: Taishō,* Vol. 51: 969a.

[2] Daoxuan, *opere citato*: 96-100; *confer: Taishō,* Vol. 51: 968c-969c.

[3] H. Hauptmann, "Ancient Heritage along the Upper Indus in Northern Pakistan: Threat and Protection of the Rock Art Galleries along the Southern Branch of the Silk Road" , in: *Gandhāra and China,* ed. Chongfeng Li, Beijing: Cultural Relics Press, 2019: 421-474.

Han Dynasty reached this place. According to an old tradition, the monks from Hinduka began to bring the *sūtras* and *vinayas* across this river from the date of setting up an image of Maitreya Bodhisattva (in Daraḍa)[1]. Faxian and his fellow pilgrims crossed the river and stopped in Uḍḍiyāna for the *varṣa* (rainy season). They continued southwards after the rains and went through Śuvastu, Gandhāra, Takṣaśila, and Puruṣapura. Then Faxian, parting with his companions, travelled and visited western, central, and eastern Hinduka and finally moved to Siṃhala (Sri Lanka). In 412 AD, Faxian returned to China via the sea route.

Zhimeng, Fasheng, Fayong and others, moreover, all took the Jibin route while they made their pilgrimages to Hinduka respectively[2].

When the Karakorum Highway was being built during the 1960s and 1970s, many rock carvings and inscriptions left by travelers from different time periods were found all along the highway[3]. On the so-called Sacred Rock II of Hunza was inscribed in Chinese characters: "Gu Weilong, envoy of the great Wei, is dispatched to Mi-mi now" (fig.3). According to Ma Yong, "it seems a reasonable conclusion that Gu Wei-long went to Mi-mi within the period 444-453 AD" . "In the light of Gu Wei-long's inscription we may suppose that it was likely for Gu Wei-long to have turned to the south-west at Pi-shan in Xinjiang, and then to have traveled upstream along the Tasihong River. After passing Tuzlak Daban, he would have turned westward to Aghzi Daban, where he took the line of today's highway. Thence he would follow the Harastan River upstream to Mazar, going north-west again at Arasal and crossing today's Sino-Pakistan border to Shimshal. There he traveled westwards along the Shimshal River until reaching the 'Sacred Rock of Hunza' . The course he took is indeed the old route from China to Ji-bin and Wu-i-shan-li in the Han period." [4]

According to *Song Yun jiaji* (*Private Records of Song Yun*) and *Huisheng*

---

[1] Faxian, *opere citato*: 26.

[2] 1) Sengyou, *opere citato*: 579, 581; *confer*: *Taishō,* Vol. 55: 113b, 114a. 2) Huijiao, *opere citato*: 125; *confer*: *Taishō,* Vol. 50: 343b, 339c-340a. 3) Baochang, *opere citato*: 13.

[3] A. H. Dani, *Human Records on Karakorum Highway,* Lahore: Sang-e-Meel Publications, 1995: 95.

[4] Ma Yong, *opere citato*: 147, 150-151.

xingji (*Hui-sheng's Traveling Account*) cited in *Luoyang qielan ji* (*A Record of Saṃghārāmas in Luo-yang*) by Yang Xuanzhi, Song Yun, "a native of Dun-huang, went with Hui-sheng as [Wei] envoys to the Western Regions. In the winter, that is, the eleventh month, of the first year of Shen-gui period (December AD 518 to January AD 519), the Empress Dowager (née Hu) dispatched Hui-sheng of the Chong-li Temple (Temple of Respect for the Efficacious) to go to the Western Regions in search of *sūtras*. Altogether they acquired one hundred seventy titles, all the best of Mahāyāna classics. After leaving the capital and traveling westward for forty days, they reached the Chi-ling (Bare Mountain Range), the western boundary of the state and the location of frontier passes" . Leaving Chi-ling, they crossed the Liu-sha (Shifting sands) area, went through the states of Tu-yu-hun (Aza/Kokonor), Shan-shan (Charklik/Loulan), Zuomo (Charchan), Han-mo (Uzun-tati), Yu-tian (Khotan), and later on, Zhu-ju-bo (Cokkuka, Karghalik). "Early in the eighth month (early September), they entered Han-pan-tuo (modern Tashkurghan). Traveling westward for six days, they ascended the Cong-ling Range. Traveling westward again for three days, they arrived at the city of Bo-yu (Onkul). Traveling three more days they reached the Bu-ke-yi Mountain (Unreliable Mountain), where it was very cold. The mountain was snow-clad in winter and summer alike... Westward from this point, the mountain path was steep and sloping. [There were] banks one thousand *li* long, and a precipice rising eighty thousand Chinese feet above ground. Here indeed were great obstacles [to be faced by] travelers. By comparison, the Tai-hang and Meng-men ranges were really not impassable, and the Yao Pass and Long-ban were simply flatlands. After setting out from the Cong-ling Range, [they found] the altitude increasing with every step, and it took four days before they were able to reach the summit. Once there it looked like low land, but actually it was already halfway to heaven. Here at the top of the mountain was the country of Han-pan-tuo ... In the high steep parts of the Cong-ling Range there was no vegetation. It was eight month (September) [when they were there], and it was already cold. The north wind forced the wild geese [to fly southward], and snow scudded over one thousand *li*. In the middle of the ninth month (late October), they entered the state of Bo-he (Parvata, in modern Wakhan)" ... In the early part of the tenth month (mid-November), they reached the state of Ye-da (Russian Turkestan, Ephthal or Hephthalitai) ... Early in the eleventh month (early to mid-December), they arrived at the state of Bo-zhi (modern Zebāk) ... "In the middle of the eleventh month (mid-to late December), they entered the state of She-mi (Sambhi), which was located at a short remove from the Cong-ling Range. The land was barren, and the people by and large poor and distressed. The path was steep and dangerous, barely passable for a single person or a horse. A straight road connected the state of Bo-lu-le (Bolora) and state of Wu-chang, where an iron-chain bridge served as a suspended passageway. Beneath was bottomless spaces; on the sides, there was nothing to hold on to, and in an instant, one might fall eighty thousand Chinese feet [to one's death]. As a result, travelers refused to go by this route when they heard about it. In the early twelfth month (January to February AD 520), they entered the state of Wu-chang, which bordered on the Cong-ling Range to the north and India to the south" [1].

The route that Song Yun and Huisheng took could be divided into three sections. The first section almost coincided with the route taken by Faxian. It started from Chang'an, and went along Henan road to Khotan and then climbed over the Congling Range. Song Yun and his men arrived at Wakhan after crossing the mountains, and then they visited the Grand Tent of the Ephthal or Hephthalitai and arrived at Bolor/Bolora via Zebāk and Sambhi or Śyamaka. The second section was similar to the route taken by Gu Weilong, the envoy of the great Wei, when he passed through the valley of the Hunza River. And the last section corresponded to the Jibin route which started from Bolor and passed Xuandu (present Bunji?) as well as Chilas and reached Uḍḍiyāna and Gandhāra.

Thus the Jibin route appears to have been the main route taken by Buddhist monks and pilgrims who went westward in search of Buddhist *sūtras* or made their pilgrimages to Hinduka at least from *ca*. 64 AD to 518 AD. Moreover, Du Qin's description about the Jibin route, Gu Weilong's inscription at Hunza, and

---

[1] Yi-t'ung Wang, tr., *A Record of Buddhist Monasteries in Lo-yang* by Yang Hsüan-chih, Princeton: Princeton University Press, 1984: 215-228. *confer*: Yang Xuanzhi, *opere citato*: 182-199.

Daoxuan's record about 16 Buddhist journeys[1] all corroborates directly the importance of the Jibin route as one of the main land roads connecting China, South Asia, Central Asia, and West Asia from the 2nd century BC to the 6th century AD[2].

The Buddhist art of Central Asia and Jibin shared some common traits. A *stūpa* was generally placed in the centre of a Buddhist temple or monastery in Uḍḍiyāna and Gandhāra, forming a focal point, and such an architectural layout can be seen in the *chētiyagharas* in Kizil. This lay-out could reflect the popularity of Buddhist schools like the Dharmaguptaka in both these areas, as this school laid strong emphasis on *stūpa* worship and was very popular in both Jibin and Kucha[3]. However, with the shifting interest of Buddhist monks and the political changes of the early Tang Dynasty, the three major routes recorded by Daoxuan became the main passageways in the communication between China and India. Hence, from the middle of the Tang Dynasty, the Jibin route was declining and gradually fell into disuse[4], which may have affected the fortunes of Kucha as well as Kizil.

(This paper was published first in the *Proceedings of ICOMOS 15th General Assembly and Scientific Symposium,* edited by Organizational Office of the ICOMOS 15th General Assembly, Xi'an: World Publishing Corporation, 2005: 985-990, and then in the *Kizil on the Silk Road*: *Crossroads of Commerce & Meeting of Minds*, edited by R. Ghose, Mumbai: Marg Publications, 2008: 24-31)

---

[1] Daoxuan, *opere citato*: 96-100; *confer: Taishō,* Vol. 51: 968c-969c.

[2] 1) A. H. Dani, *opere citato* (*Chilas...*): 233-243; 2) A. H. Dani, *opere citato* (*Human Records on...*): 13-21.

[3] Chongfeng Li, "*Kezi'er bufen zhongxinzhuku yu Chang'ahanjing deng fodian* (*The Dīrghāgama Text* and the *Chētiyagharas* of Kizil, Kucha)" , in: *Xu Pingfang xiansheng ji'nian wenji* (*Papers in Commemoration of Professor Xu Pingfang*), Shanghai: Shanghai Chinese Classics Publishing House, 2012: 419-465.

[4] Ma Yong, *opere citato*: 139.

犍陀罗、秣菟罗与中土早期佛像

在研究佛教造像时，犍陀罗艺术（Gandhāran art）和秣菟罗艺术（Mathurā art）是我们常常遇到的两个术语。它们既是两种不同的艺术流派（school），又代表了两种截然不同的艺术模式（style），皆因地而名。

一、犍陀罗流派

犍陀罗是亚洲古代历史上的一个大国。它位于印度与西亚交界处，自公元前6世纪以来就成为各强国之间的拉锯地带，曾先后被波斯的阿黑美尼德（Achaemenids）王朝、马其顿的亚力山大大帝（Alexander the Great）和孔雀（Maurya）王朝的旃陀罗笈多（Chandragupta）征服或控制。公元前3世纪中叶，当时新皈依佛教的阿育王（Aśoka）派末阐提（Madhyāntika）到犍陀罗传教，这或许为佛教正式传入犍陀罗之始。孔雀王朝瓦解后，希腊人和塞种人（Scythians）又各自主宰犍陀罗达一个多世纪。故而，犍陀罗的文化与艺术曾受到了波斯、希腊、印度和中亚文化的多重影响。公元1世纪中叶，贵霜（Kushān）帝国兴起。贵霜帝国鼎盛时期的疆域，西起伊朗东部，东至恒河（Ganga River）中游，北自咸海（Aral Sea）、锡尔河（Sir Daria）至葱岭，南到德干地区纳尔马达河（Narmada River），从而成为拥有中亚和南亚次大陆北部大部分地区的一个庞大帝国，国都富楼沙（Puruṣapura）。

贵霜帝国诸王[1]对所统区域内各种不同的文化及宗教信仰，采取了兼容并包

[1] 1993年3月，在阿富汗海巴克的拉巴塔克（Rabatak）地区的卡法尔斯（Kafirs）城堡发现了一通宽90厘米、高50厘米、厚25厘米的铭刻，质地为微白色石灰岩，依据出土地点，学界称之为拉巴塔克铭刻。铭文中详细列出迦腻色迦之前贵霜诸王顺序，即丘就却（Kujula Kadphises），阎膏珍（Vima I Taktu），Vima II Kadphises（此前考定为阎膏珍）和迦腻色迦（Kanishka）。尽管铭文中并无贵霜诸王具体的在位年代，但研究者依据其他资料考订拉巴塔克铭刻所记贵霜诸王具体年代如下：丘就却在位时间大约为公元30-80年，阎膏珍大约为公元80-90年或80-110年，Vima II Kadphises大约为公元90-100年或110-120年，迦腻色迦大约为公元100-126年或120-146年。参见Nicholas Sims-Willams and Joe Cribb, “A New Bactrian Inscription of Kanishka the Great”, in: *Silk Road Art and Archaeology*, Kamakura: Journal of the Institute of Silk Road Studies, Vol. 4 (1995/96): 75-142.

和保护鼓励的政策。在宗教上,从其钱币上的铸像可以看出：印度的湿婆和佛,伊朗袄教和希腊的神祇,早期都受到了重视；到了迦腻色迦 (Kaniṣka) 和胡维色迦 (Huviṣka) 统治时期,佛教在犍陀罗和贵霜帝国的大部分地区有了长足发展。在艺术上,东西文化的交融现象非常明显；犍陀罗出土的建筑遗迹和雕刻,大多是希腊艺术形式与佛教主题相结合,呈现出贵霜文化特有的韵味。从考古学角度,犍陀罗佛教艺术可以大体分作如下四期[1]。

第一期：公元 1 世纪,是犍陀罗佛教艺术的形成阶段。造像多为石浮雕,通常用来装饰"还愿塔" (votive stūpa) 的塔基,题材主要为佛传故事；本期后段开始出现圆雕佛像[2]。浮雕像与圆雕之间关系密切,人物造型承袭古希腊传统艺术形式,人物姿态和服饰的处理也是希腊式的。佛与其他人物具有相同的身高及外貌,只比常人多了头光和肉髻 (图 1)。佛肉髻偏大,双目圆睁,上唇留髭。大衣通肩披,边缘多从腕部垂下,衣褶僵直,衣料质感厚重。浮雕佛像与圆雕像略有差异：浮雕佛像头光大小适中,唯顶上肉髻过大,显得头重脚轻；圆雕佛像的头光过大,与主像不协调,顶上肉髻低平；浮雕佛像的衣褶处理粗糙,圆雕像大衣褶襞处理细腻并很好地表现出大衣之下的肉体曲线。

第二期：公元 1 世纪末或 2 世纪初,下迄 2 世纪中叶[3],主要当在迦腻色迦统治时期。从本期开始,犍陀罗工匠开始广泛使用千枚岩 (phyllite) 石料,逐渐替代了此前使用的各种片岩 (schist)。本期仍以浮雕为主,浮雕佛像与圆雕佛像肉髻扁平,大多眉间刻白毫,双眸微闭,上唇蓄髭。佛大衣通肩披,大衣类似古希腊罗马元老或哲人所披之长方形外衣 (himation)。衣褶采用正规的希腊式方法雕刻,褶襞在大衣表面呈凸起状 (图 2)。浮雕的故事画,有些仿效希腊神庙的雕刻手法,让连续情节中

---

[1] 参见：1) John Marshall, *Taxila: An illustrated account of archaeological excavations carried out at Taxila under the orders of the government of India between the years 1913 and 1934,* London: Cambridge University Press, 1951, Vol. I: 75-76, II: 514-516; 2) John Marshall, *Buddhist Art of Gandhara: The Story of the Early School; its birth, growth and decline,* London: Cambridge University Press, 1960: 51ff; 3) W. Zwalf, *A Catalogue of the Gandhāra Sculpture in the British Museum,* London: British Museum Press, 1996, Vol. I: 69-72.

[2] 所谓犍陀罗"圆雕佛像",严格意义上说是高浮雕,因为大多石雕像的背部没有进一步处理,佛像原来贴壁安置于寺塔之中。为了行文方便,故采用这一传统说法。

[3] 英国考古学家马歇尔 (John Marshall),20 世纪二三十年代利用春、秋两季在呾叉始罗进行考古发掘工作,前后持续了 21 年 (1913-1934 年)。根据发掘成果,他后来撰写了《犍陀罗佛教艺术》一书,认为早期犍陀罗派佛教艺术可分为萌芽期、成熟期前段和成熟期后段三个时期。其中,成熟期前段含盖的时间为公元 1 世纪末至 140 年前后,后段自 140 年迄贵霜帝国灭亡,即迦腻色迦、胡维色迦和波薮提婆统治时期。参见 John Marshall, *opere citato* (*Buddhist Art of Gandhara...*): 67.

图 1　布施祇园，出自 Guides Mess，Mardan，现藏卡拉奇国家博物馆
a. 全景；　b. 局部

的人物成横列一字展开，并非严格按照故事情节的先后顺序排列。有些浮雕甚至违反透视规律，出现后排人物身躯较前排高大的情形（图 3）。装饰性题材“花环和小爱神”(garland bearing erotes)，本期开始流行。

图 2　立佛，出土于 Mamāne Dheṛi，现藏白沙瓦考古博物馆

第三期：公元 2 世纪中叶至 3 世纪前半，主要当在胡迦色迦和波薮提婆 (Vāsudeva)[1]统治时期，是犍陀罗艺术史上最著名、最多产的一个阶段。迄今世界各地公私博物馆收藏的犍陀罗遗物，大多属于这个时期。本期浮雕故事继续流行，浮雕故事中的佛像大多具有圆雕效果。圆雕佛像的雕造成上升趋势，佛像已逐渐从佛传浮雕中独立出来，开始单独设龛。大多数佛像的头部呈典型的希腊阿波罗式美男子面相，脸型椭圆，五官端正。额部较高，正中发际线前伸，头发向后梳理，呈一绺绺波状。眉毛细长、弯曲，眉间雕作白毫，眼角较深，双眸微闭，强调沉思和内省之精神因素。鼻高直，鼻梁与额头连成直线。双唇较薄，嘴角

[1] 波薮提婆 (Vāsudeva) 应为汉文史籍中的波调。据《三国志》卷三《魏书·明帝纪》记载，“[魏明帝太和三年十二月]癸卯（公元 230 年 1 月 25 日），大月氏王波调遣使奉献，以调为亲魏大月氏王”。见《三国志》，点校本，北京：中华书局，1959 年，第 97 页。

图 3　乘公羊车上学，出土于 Chārsada，现藏伦敦 Victoria and Albert Museum

深陷，大多无髭。佛大衣多“通肩被服”，少数作“右袒式”披覆，大衣襞褶交迭、厚重，衣纹开始采用“双线式”刻划，毛料质感清晰。佛像的全身比例，一般为六位首甚至五位首，显得短粗低矮。头后圆光简朴。佛像分作立像与坐像两类。立佛头部微前倾，双脚分开，重心多置于左脚，手势通常为“施无畏印 (abhayamudrā)”（图 4）；坐佛结跏趺坐 (padmāsana)，手势多为“禅定印 (dhyānamudrā)”和“转法轮印 (dharmacakrapravartanamudrā)”。菩萨像数量增多，弥勒 (Maitreya) 像流行。菩萨大多戴宝冠，面相与佛像类似，双眸微闭，上唇多有波髭。袒上身，披披巾，下着裙。有的斜披络腋，佩戴缨络、臂钏和手镯，裙摆多呈扇形。佛或菩萨像座上多雕出其他人物形象，像座表面的人物有的与主像有关（图 5）。在浮雕整体构图上，有些过分强调建筑物作为故事背景，建筑构件越来越繁复。在雕刻技法上，除了菩萨像的裙摆呈锐角或扇形外，有些像的衣褶在转折处不是竖直垂下，而是沿肢体走向刻出，不符合自然规律。此外，财神般遮迦 (Pāñcika) 和繁殖女神鬼子母 (Hāritī) 是本期流行的另一种题材。

第四期：公元 4 世纪后半至 5 世纪末，主要当在寄多罗 (Kidārite) 统治时期。这一期被学术界称作“后犍陀罗派”(Post-Gandhāra school) 或“印度–阿富汗流派”(Indu-Afghan school)，流行范围从印度河西岸的呾叉始罗 (Taxila) 向西北延伸至古代大夏 (Bactria) 和妫水 (Oxus)，即阿姆河 (Amu Daria，乌浒水）西岸，较前三

图 4　立佛，出土地不详，现藏新德里国家博物馆

图 5　树下观耕，出土于 Sahri Bahlol，现藏白沙瓦考古博物馆

期限于白沙瓦 (Peshāwār) 谷地及印度河以西地区要广泛得多。第四期较前三期最大的不同，是绝大多数造像采用犍陀罗传统造型，用灰泥 (stucco) 或黏土雕塑而成，表面赋色，如黑色波发，洁白面部，柳叶黑眉，红色白毫，上眼睑勾红弧，鼻翼饰红线，两薄唇涂红 (图 6)。本期佛像除延续前期固有样式之外，还较多吸收了印度本土即秣菟罗艺术因素，脸形趋圆，表情富于活力；服饰变薄，人物形体把握娴熟 (图 7)。

二、秣菟罗流派

秣菟罗是公元前 6 世纪印度十六国之一苏罗森那 (Sūrasena) 的首府，曾先后被并入摩揭陀 (Magadha) 帝国、孔雀王朝、巽伽 (Śuṇga) 王朝的版图之内，再后来又一度落入希腊人和塞种—安息人之手。大约在阎膏珍统治期间，秣菟罗地区被贵霜帝国吞并，并一度成为贵霜帝国的陪都。如胡维色迦曾用许多纪念性建筑来美化这座城市，就像其前王迦腻色迦美化首都富楼沙一样。贵霜帝国最后一位国君波调的碑铭，大部分也是在秣菟罗及其附近发现的，这进一步表明秣菟罗的重要性。此外，贵霜帝国诸王雕像 (图 8、9) 在秣菟罗的出土，也从另一方面证明它的确是贵霜帝国一

图 6　佛头像，出土于 Tapa Kalān，哈达 (Haḍḍa)，原藏喀布尔博物馆

图 7　坐佛，*Stūpa* 11，哈达 Tapa Shotor 遗址

图 8　阎膏珍雕像，出土于 Māṭ，现藏秣菟罗博物馆

图 9　迦腻色迦雕像，出土于 Māṭ，现藏秣菟罗博物馆

处举足轻重的中心[1]。大约在4世纪中叶,秣菟罗被纳入笈多帝国(Gupta Empire)的版图。笈多帝国被称作印度历史上的黄金时代,不仅在德政方面取得了巨大成就,而且文学和艺术亦达到全盛,造型艺术臻于完善。秣菟罗的佛教艺术也可以大体分作四期[2]:

第一期:公元前1世纪迄公元1世纪末,是秣菟罗佛教艺术的形成期,主要包括象征物表现(symbolic representation)和前迦腻色迦(Pre-Kaniṣka)两个阶段。

佛陀以人格化形式(anthropomorphic representation)出现之前,他的存在通过一个或更多的象征物表现。如摩耶夫人梦见大象表示乘象入胎,摩耶夫人站在娑罗树下表示树下诞生,无人骑驭之马或头巾表示出家,菩提树表示觉悟成道,鹿苑或狮驮法轮表示初转法轮,阶梯表示佛从忉利天降下,三宝标(triratna)表示佛(Buddha)、法(dharma)、僧(saṃgha),塔表示涅槃等。

象征物在迦腻色迦即位之前已转变为人格化形象并逐渐形成了最初的萌芽偶像(rudimentary icons)。佛坐像,与耆那教供施板(āyāgapaṭṭas)上的主像(图10)极为相似;佛立像,则受到了早期药叉(yakṣa)像的影响。其显著特征如下:佛像头光素面,多具贝壳形结发(kaparda),双眼凸出,外眼角刻短线,耳垂较小。胸部发达,肚脐深陷。右手施无畏印,手背与肩之间雕出叶枕(cushion)图案;左手置大腿上。除左肩褶襞外,轻薄透体的袒右大衣多无衣纹(图11)。佛座为叠涩须弥式,有的两侧刻出狮子。

图10 耆那教供施板,出土于秣菟罗Kankālī,现藏勒克瑙博物馆

第二期:公元1世纪末或2世纪

[1] 1) J. Ph. Vogel "Explorations at Mathurā", in: *Archaeological Survey of India: Annual Report 1911-12*: 120-133, esp. 120-127, Figs. 3, 4; 2) R. C. Sharma, *Buddhist Art: Mathura School,* New Delhi: Wiley Eastern Limited & New Age International Limited, 1995: 27, 29.

[2] 参见:1) J. Ph. Vogel "The Mathurā School of Sculpture", in: *Archaeological Survey of India: Annual Report 1906-07*: 137-160 and *Archaeological Survey of India: Annual Report 1909-10*: 63-79; 2) R. C. Sharma, *opere citato*: 161-219.

图 11　佛与净饭王，出土于秣菟罗 Kankālī，现藏勒克瑙博物馆

初，下迄 2 世纪中叶，主要当在迦腻色迦统治时期。佛像造型完美，称作正典佛或结发佛 (Canonized or Kapardin Buddha)，为印度中部和北部地区造像的楷模。坐佛多为高浮雕，发髻形如贝壳。白毫多浮雕而成，双眼呈杏仁状，表情略带微笑；耳垂较小。胸部突出，肚脐深陷。右手施无畏印，手后有叶枕图案；左手放置大腿或膝上。双腿相交结跏趺坐，脚掌刻有法轮、三宝标等吉祥图案。佛大衣作"右袒式"披覆，唯左肩衣褶厚重，下摆覆于座上。头光中央素面，边缘刻连弧纹。佛座为叠涩须弥式，表面多雕三狮 (图 12)。立佛特征与坐像相似，唯体态僵直；右手施无谓印，左手叉腰。大衣轻纱透体，下摆垂至膝下，衣边遮覆左手；腰带束下衣后于右侧打结，双腿间常有一串花饰。造像多刻铭文，记述造像名称、时间或统治君王 (图 13)。

第三期：公元 2 世纪中叶至 3 世纪前半，主要当在胡迦色迦和波调统治时期，可细分前、后两个阶段。

前段佛发髻渐高，已具螺发雏形。眼角刻线加深，颈部肉褶一道。体形拉长，唯药叉影响尚存，佛与菩萨之间在图像志上的差异开始出现。头光中央多雕出莲花，边缘除连弧纹外，有时加一圈连珠纹。大衣轻纱透体，作"右袒式"披覆，唯左上臂衣褶繁复 (图 14)。由于受犍陀罗艺术影响，有的佛像大衣通肩披，下缘覆盖双脚，摆边呈半圆形垂下；褶襞多作阴线式，少数为阶梯式。右手上举施无畏印，左手上举持衣边，双手几乎持平。佛两侧多有胁侍，身着北方服饰的金刚手 (Vajrapāṇi) 开始出现。

后段佛像多作螺发，个别为波发。大衣通肩披，质地厚重，褶襞作阶梯式或棱线式；衣褶自双肩下垂后向右上方聚集，颈下 V 形衣边渐圆，覆于座上的衣摆形如软垫 (图 15)；稍晚直接雕出吉祥草垫 (kuśāgrass)。除施无畏印外，禅定印、转法轮印和

图 12　坐佛，出土于 Kaṭrā，现藏秣菟罗博物馆

图 13　菩萨 / 佛立像，出土于萨尔那特，现藏萨尔那特考古博物馆

图 14　坐佛，出土于 Maholī，现藏秣菟罗博物馆

图 15　坐佛，出土于 Govindnagar（戈温德纳格尔），现藏秣菟罗博物馆

触地印 (bhūmisparśamudrā) 也开始出现。造像多无胁侍，佛传情节流行。

第四期：公元 3 世纪后半至 6 世纪，主要当在笈多时期。笈多艺术最重要的贡献，是发展了佛教和婆罗门教两种宗教神祇的完美形式。笈多雕刻，是高度发展的和谐美与崇高的理想主义相融合的产物；设计与表现手法颇具气魄，制作极为精致。秣菟罗艺术家和工匠所创造出的佛教艺术，在 4 至 6 世纪的笈多时期达到了峰巅[1]。造像强调表情，通过面部显示人物内在情感，达到肉体与精神上的高度和谐。佛“身端严”[2]，头光繁复，“顶有肉髻”，“螺发绀青”。面相椭圆，“额广平正”，“眉纤而长”，“目如青莲”，眼睑低垂；“鼻高修直”，鼻翼舒张，嘴角自然，下唇较厚，耳垂拉长。颈部三折，形同海螺 (图 16)。佛像造型健硕，形体优美，富有朝气。以立像为例，身躯颀长，“两肩齐亭，充满圆好”；一腿微屈，表示动感。佛大衣通肩披，质地轻薄贴体，如水浸般呈半透明状态，隐约显现身体轮廓；从双肩垂下的一道道平行的 U 字形衣褶，形如水波。“手足网缦”，右手上举施无畏印；左手持大衣边，自手下垂的衣边，呈两条平行的波状延至膝下 (图 17)。这种半透体法服，进一步暗示出佛像的庄严，与贵霜时期流行的厚重大衣形成对照。与高大佛像相比，在佛足两侧出现的供养人，显得极为渺小，这是本期佛像的重要特征，暗示出佛与凡人的区别。

秣菟罗与犍陀罗之间很早就有密切的政治和文化交往，并在贵霜时期达到高潮。尤为重要的是，两地自成体系的造型艺术，在贵霜时期臻于完善，声誉登峰造极。公元 1 至 5 世纪，秣菟罗是北印度佛教造像的中心。秣菟罗创造的佛像，曾被安置在印度各地并极大地激发了当地工匠的创作灵感，致使其所造佛像多受秣菟罗影响。秣菟罗佛教艺术在胡维色迦统治之初，由于帝国政治中心南移，经历了第一次犍陀罗艺术的冲击。其后，这种冲击与影响迅速发展并扩大。到了波调继位时，秣菟罗好像是犍陀罗雕刻的一个分号，不过这种外来影响并未持续很久；到了波调统治后期，外来潮流开始衰落。又过了一个世纪，犍陀罗成分在秣菟罗造像中已属罕见。归纳起来，秣菟罗佛教艺术中融入的犍陀罗因素主要有：大衣通肩披，佛传故事、波发、多种手印、金刚手、般遮迦与鬼子母、斯基泰式服饰、上唇之髭、吉祥草垫、花环与小爱神及科林斯式圆柱等。另一方面，犍陀罗艺术也羼入了若干秣菟罗成分，如本生故事、螺发、

---

[1] 虽然笈多王朝在政治上的霸权只延续到 5 世纪末叶不久，但他们所倡导的艺术风格和样式却一直保持到公元 600 年甚至更晚一些。所以“笈多王朝”在艺术意义上所包含的时间，比它在政治上所认可的期限要长久得多。R. C. Majumdar et al, *An Advanced History of India*, 4th ed., London: Macmillan & Company Limited, 1978: 233; *confer*: A. K. Coomaraswamy, *History of Indian and Indonesian Art*, New York: E. Weyhe, London: E. Goldston, 1927: 71.

[2] 文中描述佛像的文字，系采自不同佛经，恕不一一注明出处。下同，谨此说明。

图 16　佛头像，出土于 Chāmuṇḍā，现藏秣菟罗博物馆

图 17　立佛，出土于 Jamalpur，现藏秣菟罗博物馆

莲花座、狮子座、大衣作“右袒式”披覆、施无畏手印、象征物表现、栏楯图案、禅裙与披帛等[1]。就整个艺术体系而言，尽管犍陀罗与秣菟罗在佛教艺术的相互交流中有了一定发展，但彼此既未在对方产生持久影响，又没有真正控制对方；彼此受到影响的某些样式 (manner) 及主题 (motif)，很快就地方化了。

三、鹿野苑及其他造像

除秣菟罗和犍陀罗流派外，笈多时期另一佛教艺术中心——萨尔那特佛像需要我们特别注意。萨尔那特 (Sārnāth) 即文献记载的鹿野苑，位于恒河中游波罗奈 (今瓦拉纳西市) 东北 8 公里，传说为释迦牟尼初转法轮之处[2]。在后孔雀 (Post-Mauya) 和前笈多 (Pre-Gupta) 时期，萨尔那特没有任何艺术流派。萨尔那特的佛像样式，系建立在秣菟罗深厚的艺术传统之上。换言之，萨尔那特的佛教艺术，主要从秣菟罗衍生

[1] 1) R. C. Sharma, *opere citato*: 221-228; 2) R. C. Sharma, “Mathurā and Gandhāra: The Two Great Styles” , in: *Buddhism and Gandhāra Art,* ed. R. C. Sharma and Pranati Ghosal, Shimla: Indian Institute of Advanced Study, Varanasi: Jñāna-Pravāha and New Delhi: Aryan Books International, 2004: 66-72.

[2] U. R. Tiwari, *Sculptures of Mathura and Sarnath, A Comparative Study* (*Up to Gupta Period*), Delhi: Sundeep Prakashan, 1998: 11-14.

而来[1]。笈多盛世,使萨尔那特成为天竺诸多佛教艺术中心之一[2]并创造出了许多重要佛像,尤以鹿野苑初转法轮(图 18)著称于世。佛像庄严而神圣的表情,是秣菟罗艺术的典型特征,这在后贵霜时期已凸显出来并成为笈多时期雕造佛像的终极目标。萨尔那特风格因循了这种表情,可以视为秣菟罗佛像的进一步完善,并最终形成了自己独特式样[3]。萨尔那特佛像最具特色之处,是那种轻纱透体的无褶式大衣,即雕造时舍弃衣纹,除颈下边缘及下摆外,造像表面不见任何褶襞。不过根据戈温德讷格尔(Govindnagar)出土的造像(图 19),我们认为这种特有的造型形式也是秣菟罗创造的,只是后者较前者更为精致并发扬光大而已[4]。这种无褶式大衣,遂成为 5、6 世纪印度各地佛像竞相模仿的式样[5]。兹以阿旃陀(Ajaṇṭā)石窟为例,说明这一时期佛教造像的情形。阿旃陀第 1 窟佛殿内的主像,螺发、杏仁眼、直鼻,嘴角微陷,两耳垂肩,结跏趺坐,双手转法轮印。佛具头光及背屏式身光,座前雕出法轮、双鹿及若干弟子[6]。这尊佛像的最大特征,是大衣作"右袒式"披覆,质地轻纱透体,全身几乎没有褶襞,仅在胸前、脚腕处可见衣边,大衣下摆压于腿下并覆于座上少许(图 20)。根据佛像表面的彩绘遗迹,并与阿旃陀其他洞窟的同类造像对比,我们发现这种所谓的无褶贴体式大衣,褶襞当初大多系彩绘而成。具体做法为：在已完成的石像表面,先薄涂一层白灰泥,稍后于灰泥表层彩绘衣纹。阿旃陀石窟中现存的大多数石雕佛像,如第 2 窟佛殿主尊、第 4 窟佛殿主尊坐像和前室立像、第 6 窟上、下层佛殿内主尊坐佛及各种坐、立佛像、第 19 窟外立面坐佛与塔前立佛,大衣的处理都是如此。有些立佛双脚外侧所雕小型供养人,与秣菟罗笈多时期立佛两侧的供养人,采用相同的布局与设计。另外,阿旃陀第 16 窟佛殿内主尊倚坐,大衣作"右袒式"披覆,左腿内侧连通手腕和脚腕的 Z 字形摆边,是通过覆盖左小臂后下垂形成的。这种 Z 字形摆边,在纳西克(Nāsik)石窟的造像中多有使用,疑为笈多艺术地方化之结果。虽然阿旃陀所在地域当时为瓦加塔

---

[1] J. C. Harle, *Gupta Sculpture: Indian Sculpture of the Fourth to Sixth Century* AD, Oxford: Clarendon Press, 1974: 18.

[2] 这一时期,印度各地都有地方性的雕塑作坊(ateliers)负责用各种材料制作佛像,如萨尔那特的 Chunār 砂岩石像、秣菟罗的 Sikrī 砂岩石像、阿旃陀的 Trap 岩石佛像等。这些地方造像,可统称笈多艺术,显然都是从秣菟罗类型派生而出的。A. K. Coomaraswamy, *opere citato*: 74; *confer*: D. Mitra, *Buddhist Monuments,* Calcutta: Sahitya Samsad, 1971: 15, 67.

[3] David L. Snellgrove, ed., *The Image of the Buddha,* New Delhi: Vikas Publishing House Pvt Ltd/UNESCO, 1978: 99-101.

[4] R. C. Sharma, *opere citato* (*Buddhist Art ...*): 208, 230.

[5] 笔者以为,笈多艺术中的石雕佛像主要采用两种表现形式：一种是我们通常所见的典型秣菟罗佛像,包括褶襞在内的所有细部皆雕刻而成,后适量涂色,贴金箔或涂金粉；一种是雕绘结合,即首先雕出五官清晰的头部及躯体,然后以彩绘形式对全身各个部位敷色,并贴金箔或涂金粉。

[6] 这一时期的阿旃陀石窟造像,坐佛手印大多为初转法轮,或许与萨尔那特同一题材的坐像有某种联系。

图 18　坐佛，出土于萨尔那特，现藏萨尔那特考古博物馆

图 19　立佛，出土于戈温德讷格尔，现藏秣菟罗博物馆

图 20　坐佛，阿旃陀第 1 窟佛殿

图 21　立佛，出土于加德满都 Cā-bāhī，现藏勒克瑙博物馆

格 (Vākāṭaka) 王朝统治，未纳入笈多帝国版图，但笈多的超日王 (旃陀罗 · 笈多二世 / Chandragupta II) 把普拉巴瓦蒂 · 笈多 (Prabhāvatīguptā) 公主嫁给瓦加塔格王子鲁陀罗犀那二世(Rudrasēna II)，使笈多与德干地区强大的瓦加塔格王朝联姻结盟[1]，因此两地艺术形式的相似是顺理成章的。此外，桑吉 (Sāñcī) 大塔四门内的坐佛，也采用这种轻纱透体式大衣[2]。甚至远在尼泊尔的5、6世纪的石雕佛像，如Cā-bālī立佛也具同样类型 (图 21)[3]。由此可见，笈多艺术的影响是深远而广泛的。

四、中土早期佛像

中国与南亚次大陆的文化交流，源远流长，史无绝书。东晋南北朝以降，随着佛教在中土的发展，建寺起塔，开窟造像的风气逐渐盛行[4]。两地人民之间在造型艺术领域内的接触，文献记载比比皆是。如汉明帝 (58-75 年) "[遣使天竺] 问其道术，遂于中国而图其形象焉"[5]。法显412年从天竺返国时，亦带回不少佛教 "经像"[6]。6 世纪初，宋云、惠生出使西域，曾于犍陀罗 "以铜摹写雀离浮图仪一躯及释迦四塔变"[7]。随着中国与南亚文化交流的扩大与加深，南亚僧人持经像来华者增多。如 "太安 (455-459 年) 初，有狮子国胡沙门耶奢遗多、浮陀难提等五人，奉佛像三，到京都 (平城)"[8]。姚最《续画品录》明确记述有三位外国僧人画家到了中国，其中的释迦佛陀，就是天竺人，约北魏时入华[9]。天竺与狮子国僧人和画家来华，一定会把南亚当时的佛教雕刻与绘画技艺同时带入中土。由于佛教传自域外，所以其造像从题材到技法都必然受到浓厚的外来文化影响。梁代画家张僧繇接受退晕式 "天竺

[1] V. V. Mirashi, ed., *Inscriptions of the Vākāṭakas: Corpus Inscriptionum Indicarum* V, Ootacamund: Government Epigraphist for India, 1963: XXIII.

[2] John Marshall & Alfred Foucher, *The Monuments of Sāñchī,* Calcutta: Archaeological Survey of India, 1940: Plate LXX.

[3] David L. Snellgrove ed., *opere citato*: Plates 71-74, 125.

[4] 李崇峰《中印佛教石窟寺比较研究：以塔庙窟为中心》(修订版), 北京：北京大学出版社, 2003 年。

[5] 袁宏《后汉纪 · 孝明皇帝纪》, 北京：中华书局, 2002 年, 第 187 页。

[6] 僧佑《出三藏记集》, 苏晋仁、萧鍊子点校, 北京：中华书局, 1995 年, 第 575 页。

[7] 杨衒之《洛阳伽蓝记》, 周祖谟校释, 北京：中华书局, 1963 年, 第 220 页。

[8]《魏书 · 释老志》, 点校本, 北京：中华书局, 1974 年, 第 3036 页。

[9] 1) 姚最《续画品录》。明王世贞万历初年郧阳初刻《王氏画苑》本；2) 张彦远《历代名画记》卷七, 叶八。明王世贞万历初年郧阳初刻《王氏画苑》本；3) 伯希和《六朝同唐代的几个艺术家》, 冯承钧译, 载冯承钧《西域南海史地考证译丛》第二卷《西域南海史地考证译丛八编》, 北京：商务印书馆, 1995 年, 第 120-167 页。

遗法”[1]，“善图塔庙，超越群工”[2]，“(梁)武帝崇饰佛寺，多命僧繇画之”[3]，创立了佛像绘画及雕塑中有名的“张家样”[4]。以画“梵像”著称的北齐画家曹仲达，“本曹国人，善于丹青，妙尽梵迹，传模西瑞，京师所推”[5]；所“创佛事画”之“曹家样”，具有独特的艺术风格，“外国佛像，亡兢于时”[6]，被后人概括为“曹衣出水”。“曹之笔，其体稠叠，而衣服紧窄”[7]。“其体稠迭”，系形容曹画人物衣褶重迭垂下；“衣服紧窄”，则指衣服质料轻薄，紧贴躯体[8]。这种“曹衣出水”式样，显然是受到了秣菟罗佛像类型的启发，并吸收和糅进了笈多时期各地造像因素。

迄今为止，中国“南方最早的佛像似皆出于以四川为中心的东汉—蜀汉墓葬中……(佛结跏趺坐)，着通肩衣，右手施无畏印，左手握衣端”[9]。这种坐像，在中原北方发现的最早实例，见录于松原三郎编著的《中国佛教雕刻史论》，乃鎏金铜像(图22)，年代拟定在3世纪末或4世纪初，唯现藏地不详[10]。这种佛像在造型上，与秣菟罗第三期佛像颇为相似。两地坐佛皆“通肩披衣”，双手平行屈举至胸侧，右手施无畏印，左手持衣边，应具有某种联系。

图22　鎏金铜佛，出土地不详

中原北方现存早期的佛教雕塑，年代明确、数量

[1] 张僧繇曾在建康(今南京)一乘寺画“凹凸花”。“其花乃天竺遗法，朱及青绿所成。远望眼晕如凹凸，就视即平，世咸异之，乃名凹凸寺。”参见：1) 许嵩《建康实录》，北京：中华书局，1986年，第686页；2) 王逊《中国美术史》，上海：上海人民美术出版社，1985年，第112页。

[2] 姚最《续画品录》。明王世贞万历初年郧阳初刻《王氏画苑》本。

[3] 张彦远《历代名画记》卷七，叶五。明王世贞万历初年郧阳初刻《王氏画苑》本。

[4] 张彦远《历代名画记》卷二《叙师资传授南北时代》阐述了萧梁张僧繇、北齐曹仲达及唐吴道子所创作的佛像式样，明确记载“曹创佛事画，佛有曹家样、张家样及吴家样”。张彦远《历代名画记》卷二，叶二。明王世贞万历初年郧阳初刻《王氏画苑》本。

[5] 道宣《集神州三宝感通录》卷中，见《大正藏》第52卷，第421b页。

[6] 张彦远《历代名画记》卷八，叶三引僧悰(彦悰)《后画录》。明王世贞万历初年郧阳初刻《王氏画苑》本。

[7] 郭若虚《图画见闻志》卷一《论曹吴体法》，《四部丛刊续编》本(宋刻配元钞本)。

[8] 宿白《青州龙兴寺窖藏所出佛像的几个问题》，见宿白《魏晋南北朝唐宋考古文稿辑丛》，北京：文物出版社，2011年，第343页。

[9] 宿白《四川钱树和长江中下游部分器物上的佛像》，见宿白《魏晋南北朝唐宋考古文稿辑丛》，北京：文物出版社，2011年，第211页。

[10] 松原三郎《中国仏教彫刻史論》，東京：吉川弘文館，1995年，《本文編》第243頁，《図版編》第5a。

图 23　立佛，炳灵寺第 169 窟

较大的两处是炳灵寺第 169 窟和云冈的昙曜五窟。炳灵寺第 169 窟因甘肃省文物工作队 1963 年首次登临并发现了迄今为止中国石窟寺中最早的汉文纪年——西秦“建弘元年(420 年)”题记[1]，从而为研究中国早期石窟寺提供了珍贵的年代学标尺。其中，第 169 窟北壁中间第 7 龛内的一躯造像，应完成于 420 年前后。佛“身渐纤直”，面相方圆，“眉端渐细”，“双目修广”，厚唇赤红，鼻梁高直。形体健硕，“两肩平正”。佛大衣通肩披，全身衣纹作下垂之重环迭襞，表现轻纱透体，显露出肌体的变化。右腿微屈，似展示“行道”之步履；双手皆残，自左手垂下的大衣边，呈规整的对称波状(图 23)。这些特征，与秣菟罗第四期的佛像极为相似。此外，第 169 窟内其他完成于 420 年前后的佛像，也大多具有类似特征。立佛姿态、贴体大衣表面的平行褶襞以及摆边呈喇叭状外张之形式，都是秣菟罗而非犍陀罗佛像之风格。

以“雕饰奇伟、冠于一世”[2]著称的云冈昙曜五窟，开凿于北魏和平年间(460-465 年)。五窟中的佛像，融外来造型艺术精华与中国传统文化于一体，在许多方面本土化了[3]。第 18 窟北、东、西三壁雕刻的巨大佛像，大衣质地轻薄，襞褶紧密平行(图 24)。这种特征，无疑受到了秣陀罗第四期造像的影响；而第 19 窟南壁的立佛，无论从形体上，还是在法衣上，皆显示出极为清晰的秣菟罗第三、四期佛像“体法”。第 16 窟的大立佛，系昙曜五窟佛像的特例；其波发造型与犍陀罗第三、四期佛像不无关系，但所穿汉式褒衣博带大衣系北魏“门才术艺”所创造(图 25)。第 20 窟主尊大衣褶襞厚重凸起，令我们不由想起犍陀罗佛像所著“毛质”大衣；但其右肩偏覆式样(图 26)，似为平城艺术家及工匠所发明。喜龙仁(O. Siren)曾指出：当时云冈的工匠，虽然不大可能熟悉真正的犍陀罗造像，但他们一定多少知晓那些类型[4]。

[1] 甘肃省文化局文物工作队《调查炳灵寺石窟的新收获》，见《文物》，1963 年第 10 期，第 1 页。

[2]《魏书·释老志》，点校本，北京：中华书局，1974，第 3037 页。

[3] 宿白《平城实力的集聚和“云冈模式”的形成与发展》，见宿白《中国石窟寺研究》，北京：文物出版社，1996 年，第 125-126 页。

[4] O. Siren, *Chinese Sculpture from the fifth to the fourteenth century,* London:E. Benn, 1925: XLIII.

a

b

图 24　云冈第 18 窟立佛
a. 西壁；b. 东壁

图 25　立佛，云冈第 16 窟正壁

图 26　坐佛，云冈第 20 窟正壁

在此基础上，加以模仿、改造和创新。总之，在昙曜五窟佛像上，我们没有发现早期犍陀罗流派的直接影响，但秣菟罗或犍陀罗第四期佛像的间接或混合影响还是清晰可见的；两者之中，云冈造像在样式上更接近秣菟罗而非犍陀罗[1]。受到上述影响的佛像，不仅在昙曜五窟中可以看到，而且在稍晚的第 9、10 窟中也多有发现，如两窟前室立佛所著质地轻薄的大衣。

除上述两处年代明确的石窟群外，20 世纪在四川成都和山东青州发现的佛像窖藏[2]，值得我们特别关注。

成都的佛教造像，以万佛寺和西安路两处出土的最为著名。西安路出土有梁"太清五年 (551 年) 九月卅日佛弟子杜僧逸为亡儿李佛施敬造育王像"(图 27)[3]，万佛寺曾出土"(益) 州总管柱国赵国公招敬造阿育王像一躯"及其他同类造像[4]。上述石像造型几乎完全相同，皆作螺发，大衣通肩披覆，颈下衣边偏右侧略有折转。衣料质地轻薄，全身衣纹自胸前呈水波状垂下。这种轻薄大衣，尤其是腰部以下衣纹的处理，与秣菟罗出土的立佛颇相似；自胸部平行下垂的褶襞，是笈多时期秣菟罗造像的流行样式。据《广弘明集》卷十五《佛德篇》记载："荆州长沙寺瑞像者……金像也……光上有梵书云：育王所造。梁武闻，迎至都，大放光明。"[5]因此，似可推测益州这种新型佛像的图样可能源自建康。建康地区自刘宋开始与天竺往来密切，宋元嘉五年 (428 年)，天竺国王月爱曾致宋文帝国书一封，明帝泰始二年 (466 年)，宋朝授予天竺使者竺扶大、竺阿弥"建威将军"封号[6]，可见两国关系之密切。萧梁时，天竺国多次遣使入梁，"天监初 (503-504 年)，其王屈多遣长史竺罗达 (或竺达多) 奉表"，再致国书[7]。因此，建康佛像粉本源自天竺应为情理中事[8]。遗憾的是，

---

[1] 参见：1) O. Siren, *opere citato*: XLII-XLIII；2) 水野清一、長廣敏雄《雲岡雕刻の西方様式》，見《雲岡石窟》，第 12 卷，京都：雲岡刊行會，1954 年，第 1-16 页；3) 宿白《中国石窟寺研究》，北京：文物出版社，1996 年，第 37 页及[注]23、第 125 页及[注]26。

[2] 工布查布《造像量度经续补 · 妄造诫》记述："所有旧像木偶者，净绵或净布缠绕，以净香油合密渍之，以火然化，而沈其灰于清渊。石泥等胎者，旷野净处，掘地仞许深窖，而谨藏之。若系金银铜铁等像，则可镕化，仍复合用于新像胚质。"《大正藏》No. 1419，第 21 卷，第 950b 页。

[3] 成都市文物考古工作队《成都市西安路南朝石刻造像清理简报》，见《文物》，1998 年第 11 期，第 7-8 页、图 11、图 14、彩页贰：1。

[4] 刘志远、刘廷壁《成都万佛寺石刻艺术》，北京：中国古典艺术出版社，1955 年，图版 9。

[5]《大正藏》第 52 卷，第 202b 页。

[6]《宋书 · 夷蛮列传》，点校本，北京：中华书局，1974 年，第 2384-2386 页。

[7]《梁书 · 诸夷列传》，点校本，北京：中华书局，1973 年，第 799 页。

[8] 宿白《青州龙兴寺窖藏所出佛像的几个问题》，上引书，第 340-342 页。

a　　b

图 27　育王像，成都西安路出土
a. 正面；b. 背面

a　　b　　c　　d

图 28　立佛像，青州龙兴寺出土，现藏山东青州博物馆

这种轻纱透体式佛像，除南京栖霞山造像外，在以南朝都城建康为中心的长江下游地区迄今未发现。

青州龙兴寺窖藏以北朝，尤其是北齐时期造像数量最多，形体最大。北齐造像不仅造型多姿，服饰也极富变化，而且越晚越突出。北齐佛像的基本特征是：大衣质薄透体，褶襞舒迭下垂(图28)，衣纹多用双线[1]。北齐后期雕造的单体立佛，更流行贴身薄衣、隐现肌体、不雕饰衣纹的作法。佛像外施彩绘，有的百衲衣表面绘画人物。除此之外，其他地区的北齐造像全身自头到脚，各部皆以管形为基本单位，头大，胸高，肩阔，体无曲线，似上下垂直[2]。梁思成认为：北齐这种“新影响者，殆来自西域，或用印度取回样本，或用西域工匠，其主要像（本尊）则用新式，而胁侍菩萨则依中原原样，此所以使本尊与菩萨异其形制也”[3]。实际上，北齐佛像造型的新趋势，应与5、6世纪天竺佛像一再直接东传和北齐王朝西胡化有关[4]。“西胡化”一词，系陈寅恪所拟。“所谓‘西胡化’，是指那些鲜卑或鲜卑化的贵族，沉溺于西域的歌舞、游戏与玩物中，甚至想做‘龟兹王子’。北齐起用了大批西域胡人，专门从事游乐。按照‘化’的原则，如果那些鲜卑贵族继续沈溺下去，将会为西胡所同化，变成西胡人或西胡化人”[5]。当时，“西域丑胡、龟兹杂伎，封王者接武，开府者比肩”。[6]可知北齐朝廷西域胡人之多。致使胡小儿能以工于歌舞封王，鲜卑贵人包括武成帝皇后胡氏在内都喜爱西域游戏，更有波斯狗也被“齐主”封为仪同、郡君[7]。可见北齐鲜卑贵人爱好西胡习俗程度之深。在西胡化潮流影响下，佛教在北齐得到了长足的发展。自天竺东来中原的沙门、信士逐年增多。他们除了参与译经之外，有些还被授予掌管佛教事务、与中央诸卿寺并列的昭玄寺官员——昭玄都（都维那），如中天竺的优

---

[1] 这种双线衣纹，在犍陀罗第三期雕刻中大量使用，参见栗田功編著《ガンダーラ美術》，I 佛伝，東京：二玄社，1988，図 219、223、229、238、387、390-392、425、450、468。

[2] 北齐造像倾向，自头至脚上大下小；而北魏则上小下大，肩窄头小。参见梁思成《中国雕塑史》，载《梁思成文集》(三)，北京：中国建筑工业出版社，1985 年，第 332 页。

[3] 梁思成，上引书，第 332-336 页。

喜龙仁甚至认为：天龙山第 16 窟佛像，是依据外国粉本或由外国人直接雕造的。该窟佛像形神两方面皆为印度式，在样式上与 5、6 世纪秣菟罗的某些佛像密切相关。因此他推测：某位对秣菟罗流派造像相当熟悉的印度雕塑高手曾在天龙山工作了一段时间。参见：O. Siren, *opere citato*: LXVI.

[4] 1) 陈寅恪《陈寅恪集：讲义及杂稿》，北京：生活·读书·新知三联书店，2002 年，第 187-189 页；2) 陈寅恪《魏晋南北朝讲演录》，万绳楠整理，合肥：黄山书社，1987 年，第 297-300 页。

[5] 陈寅恪《魏晋南北朝讲演录》，上引书，第 298 页。

[6]《北齐书·恩倖传》，点校本，北京：中华书局，1972 年，第 685 页。

[7] 同上书，第 685-686、693-694 页。

婆塞达摩般若(Dharmaprajñā)[1]；还有的甚至升任更高一级的昭玄统[2]，如北天竺那连提黎耶舍(Narendrayaśas)[3]。他们受到如此重用，应与北齐崇尚“西胡”有关。此外，创造佛像画“曹家样”之曹仲达，与深受北齐文宣帝高洋(550-559年在位)器重、封王开府的琵琶高手曹妙达“当亦一家”[4]，后“官至朝散大夫”[5]。因此，北齐出现秣菟罗类型或笈多样式佛像，应与他们有某种必然的关系。换言之，北齐盛行的秣菟罗式及犍陀罗式佛像，应是北齐“西胡化”的必然结果。

需要指出的是，佛教造像在中国的产生与发展，绝非外来艺术形式在中土的简单移植或机械模仿，而应是在吸收外来优秀造型艺术精髓之后，在中国传统文化基础上的再创造。这点，与犍陀罗和秣菟罗佛教艺术的交互影响颇为相似。这种再创造或称本土化，自始至终贯穿于中国佛教造型艺术之中。

---

[1] 据道宣《续高僧传·阇那崛多传附达磨般若传》，达磨般若，“隋言法智……智本中天国人，流滞东川，遂乡华俗……高齐之季为昭玄都。齐国既平，佛法同毁，智因僧职转任俗官，再授洋州洋川郡守。隋氏受禅，梵牒即来，有敕召还，使掌翻译”。参见《大正藏》第50卷，第434c页。

[2] 据道宣《续高僧传·法上传》，北齐“天保之中，国置十统，有司闻奏，事需甄异。文宣(帝)乃手注状云：‘(法)上法师可为大统，余为通统’”。见《大正藏》第50卷，第485a页。关于北齐沙门统与都维那，参见谢重光、白文固《中国僧官制度史》，西宁：青海人民出版社，1990年，第71-73页。

[3] 据道宣《续高僧传·那连提黎耶舍传》，那连提黎耶舍，“隋言尊称，北天竺乌场国人……天保七年(556年)届于京邺……文宣礼遇隆重，安置天平寺中，请为翻经三藏。殿内梵本千有余夹，敕送于寺，处以上房。为建道场，供穷珍妙，别立厨库，以表尊崇。又敕昭玄大统沙门法上等二十余人，监掌翻译……耶舍每于宣译之暇，时陈神咒，冥救显著，立功多矣。未几，授昭玄都，俄转为统”。见《大正藏》第50卷，第432a-c页。

这里的乌场国，相当于今天巴基斯坦西北部的斯瓦特(Swāt)地区，属古代罽宾国范畴之内。那连提黎耶舍从乌场国来到此土，或许把罽宾当时流行的佛教及佛教艺术也带到了中原。如此，两地佛教关系之密切，则乃情理中事。

[4] 向达《唐代长安与西域文明》，北京：生活·读书·新知三联书店，1957年，第19页。

[5] 张彦远，上引书，第158页。

Gandhāra, Mathurā and Buddha Images of Medieval China

Gandhāran art and Mathurā art, two terms frequently mentioned in the study of Buddhist images, indicate not only two distinctive art schools, but also two entirely different art styles. These schools or styles are named after their respective birth places — Gandhāra and Mathurā.

1. Gandhāra School

Gandhāra, situated at the juncture of western Asia and India — an area which frequently changed the hands of the great powers since the 6th century BC-was a big country in ancient Asia. It was conquered and controlled successively by the Achaemenids of Persia, Alexander the Great of the Macedonian Empire and by Chandragupta Maurya I. In mid-3rd century BC, Aśoka, who was just converted to Buddhism, sent Madhyāntika as a missionary to Gandhāra, thus starting the spread of Buddhism in this area. After the collapse of the Maurya, Greeks and Scythians each separately ruled Gandhāra for more than one century, consequently, Gandhāran culture and art were influenced simultaneously by the cultures of Persia, Greece, India, as well as Central Asia. In mid-1st century AD, a powerful Kushān Empire was established. At the height of its power and splendor, the Kushān Empire had expanded to the eastern part of Iran in the west, to the middle reaches of the Gaṅgā (Ganges) in the east, the Aral, Sir Daria (Yaxartes) and the Pamirs in the north and to the Narmada River in the south. It was, consequently, a great power, covering Central Asia and almost the northern part of the South Asian Subcontinent, with Puruṣapura (Peshāwār) as its capital.

The Kushān kings[1] adopted a lenient and liberal policy to protect, encourage, as well as to incorporate the variety of the cultures and religious beliefs in their vast empire. This pluralism of beliefs is visible in Kushān coins as they include Buddha and Śiva of India, the Persian gods of Zoroastrianism and the Greek gods and goddesses, an eloquent proof of Kushān tolerance at this early stage. While under King Kaniṣka and King Huviṣka, Buddhism was popularized in Gandhāra and in most part of the Kushān territory, in the field of art, the cultures of East and West merged. The unearthed architectural remains and sculptures show the combination of Hellenistic art form with Buddhist motif, a unique characteristic of Kushān art. In respect to archaeology, Gandhāran art can be classified into four periods[2]:

The first period, about the 1st century AD, represents the formative period of the Buddhist art of Gandhāra. In this period, relief sculpture was the main form with representation of Buddhist stories as its subject; sculpture was used basically in the *methī* (drum) decoration of the *stūpa*. Round sculpture emerged in the later part of this period and became interrelated in countless ways with relief sculpture. Figure modeling followed the Hellenistic style in the rendering

---

[1] A rectangular piece of a whitish limestone, 90 cm wide, 50 cm high and 25 cm thick, was found in a hill known locally as the Kafirs' Castle in a region called Rabatak, Haibak, Afghanistan in March 1993. All over one face of the stone was an inscription written in Greek letters, twenty three lines each containing more than fifty letters. The inscription, called by scholars as Rabatak Inscription, gives a sequence of four Kushān kings down to Kaniṣka I. They are Kujula Kadphises, Vima I Taktu, Vima II Kadphises and Kaniṣka I. Although there is no date given in the Rabatak Inscription, Nicholas Sims-Willams and Joe Cribb proposed, on the basis of other inscriptions and coins as well as the Chinese source, an approximate dates as follows: Kujula Kadphises, 30-80 AD; Vima I Taktu, 80-90 AD or 80-110 AD; Vima II Kadphises, 90-100 AD or 110-120 AD and Kaniṣka I, 100-126 AD or 120-146 AD. *confer*: Nicholas Sims-Willams and Joe Cribb, "A New Bactrian Inscription of Kanishka the Great", in: *Silk Road Art and Archaeology,* Kamakura: Journal of the Institute of Silk Road Studies, Vol. 4 (1995/96): 75-142.

[2] 1) John Marshall, *Taxila: An illustrated account of archaeological excavations carried out at Taxila under the orders of the government of India between the years 1913 and 1934,* London: Cambridge University Press, 1951, Vol. I: 75-76, Vol. II: 514-516; 2) John Marshall, *Buddhist Art of Gandhara: The Story of the Early School; its birth, growth and decline*, London: Cambridge University Press, 1960: 51ff; 3) W. Zwalf, *A Catalogue of the Gandhāra Sculpture in the British Museum,* London: British Museum Press, 1996, Vol. I: 69-72.

of postures and drapery. Buddha was represented with the height and physical appearance of a human being but with the addition of a halo and *uṣṇīṣa* (cranial protuberance). The oversized *uṣṇīṣa*, the widely open eyes and delicate mustache as well as the stiff drapery folds of the robe display Greek artistic influence (fig.1). Furthermore, a slight difference between reliefs and round sculptures was evident. Firstly, the halo of Buddha reliefs was of proportionate size, but the *uṣṇīṣa* was oversized, a trait which made the statue to appear top-heavy. Secondly, the halo of Buddha sculpture in the round was oversized, thus failing to harmonize with the image. In this case the *uṣṇīṣa* was low and flat. Thirdly, the drapery folds used in relief sculptures were roughly cut while those used in round sculptures were delicately arranged and fully displayed the body modeling under the robe.

The second period corresponds mainly to King Kaniṣka's rule, from *circa* end of the 1st century AD or the beginning of the 2nd century AD to mid-2nd century[1]. Relief sculpture was still the major production. Phyllite stone was widely used in relief sculpture by the carvers instead of the previously used schist. At this time, Buddha images were rendered with a flat *uṣṇīṣa* in both relief and round sculpture, together with the *ūrṇa* or dot in between the eyebrows, half-closed eyes and moustache. Most of the Buddha images wore a monk robe, covering both shoulders, similar to the *himation* worn by men and women in ancient Greece. The drapery folds, cut in standard Greek way, were convex (fig.2). Imitating the arrangement of Greek temples, figures were arranged into a single line in relief instead of being made according to proper position in space. The laws of perspective were defied as in some reliefs exaggerated size figures placed in the back row were more noticeable than those placed in the front (fig.3). The decoration of garland bearing *erotes* came into fashion during this period.

The third period lasted from mid-2nd century AD to the first half of the 3rd

---

[1] John Marshall, a British archaeologist, carried out excavations at Taxila for 21 years from 1913 to 1934, mainly in the spring and autumn seasons. He wrote, based on his excavation work, *The Buddhist art of Gandhāra.* In this work, he proposed that the Buddhist art of Gandhāra could be divided into three periods: the adolescence period, the early maturity period and the later maturity period. The early-maturity period covered the time from the end of the 1st century AD to *ca*. AD 140 and the late maturity period from AD 140 to the downfall of the Kushān Empire, during the rule of Kaniṣka, Huviṣka and Vāsudeva. John Marshall, *opere citato* (*Buddhist Art* ...): 67.

century AD, chiefly during the reigns of King Huviṣka and King Vāsudeva[1]. During this particular time, Gandhāran art was at its height regarding both quality of execution and quantity. In fact, most of the Gandhāran sculptures kept in museums or in private collections were made during this very period. Buddhist stories were still popular and the majority of Buddha reliefs had some traits of the sculpture in the round. The latter started to prevail over the other form. Furthermore, the sculpted image of Buddha was gradually separated from the relief of Buddhist stories and an independent shrine for the Buddha emerged. Most of Buddha sculptures presented a typical Apollo-looking Greek male with oval face and well-arranged facial features. The forehead was somewhat higher, the central hair-line was pushed back, the hair was brushed backward with wavy locks, the eyebrows were fine and curved with the *ūrṇa* carved in between, the *canthus* were deep and the eyes half-closed suggesting the spiritual state of meditation and introspection. The nose was high and the bridge of the nose was connected to the forehead in a straight line, the lips were thinner, the corners of the mouth sank deeply and most of these images had no moustache. Both shoulders were covered with a robe in Greek style with massive drapery folds which indicated their woolen quality. The standing statue was designed and executed out of proportion with six, sometimes even five heads in height, making the Buddha look short and stout. The halo was simple. The statues were classified into two groups of standing Buddha and seated Buddha. The head of the standing Buddha bent forward slightly while he stood with feet apart, the gravity laying mostly on the left foot. Buddha's hands performed the *abhayamudrā* or Fear not gesture. The seated Buddha was shown in *padmāsana* (full lotus posture), performing the *dhyānamudrā* (meditation) or *dharmacakrapravartanamudrā* (turning of the wheel) mostly (fig.4). At this

[1] Vāsudeva is supposed to be Bo Diao in the Chinese documents: "In 24th day of the 12th month of the 3rd year (January 25, 230 AD) of Taihe period of Emperor Ming of the Wei Dynasty, Bo Diao (Vāsudeva), King of the Kushāns sent messengers to the Wei Kingdom and offered a tribute, for Bo Diao was close to and friendly with the Wei Kingdom." Chen Shou [陈寿, 233-297 AD], *Sanguo Zhi* [三国志, *History of the Wei, the Shu and the Wu Kingdoms*], punctuated edition, Beijing: Zhonghua Book Company, 1959: 97.

time, the number of Bodhisattva sculptures increased and the statue of Maitreya became popular. Most of the Bodhisattva sculptures wore a headdress, their facial appearance was most of the times marked by a wavy moustache and their eyes were half closed, which resembled Buddha's attitude. A Bodhisattva's torso was not covered by a formal dress but by a scarf-like cloth draped over the shoulders; the lower part of the body, below the waist, wore a skirt with a fan shaped hem. Some Bodhisattva images were embellished with ribbons, netted tassels, pearl and jade necklaces, armlets and bracelets. Human figures were carved on the pedestal of Buddha and Bodhisattva sculptures; some of these figures were related to the principal statue (fig.5). Looking at the composition as a whole, architectural structures used in the background of the narrative reliefs were over-stressed as more and more complicated structures were added. Regarding the carving method, with the exception of the lower hem of Bodhisattva's skirts rendered into a fan shape or in acute angle, the drapery folds of some of the sculptures were not carved hanging straight down but were made to fall along the lower limbs with no respect for realism. *Pāñcika* and *Hārītī* were another two prevailing subjects or motifs in this period.

The fourth period, covering the second half of the 4th century to the end of the 5th century AD, took place under the rule of the Kidārites or Kidāra Kushāns. The art of this period has been named by archaeologists or art-historians as Post Gandhāran or Indu-Afghan school. It spread its influence from Taxila, on the west bank of the Indus, to ancient Bactria as well as the west bank of the Oxus/ Amu Daria. In contrast, the art school of the three previous periods was bound only to the Peshāwār valley and its adjoining area on the west bank of the Indus. Post-Gandharan art is very dissimilar from that of the three previous periods. For instance, most of the sculptures were made with stucco or mortar. The surface of the stucco or terracotta statues was colored, the wavy hair were painted black, the face white, the eyebrows black, the *ūrṇa* red, the upper eyelids were marked with a red curve, the nose contour with red lines and the lips were reddened (fig.6). The making of Buddha sculptures not only followed the model of previous periods, but also absorbed some factors from the Mathurā art of India, notably a round face, vigorous expression, thin drapery and realistic rendering of the body (fig.7).

2. Mathurā School

Mathurā, the capital city of Sūrasena which was one of the sixteen Indian kingdoms in the 6th century BC, was successively merged into the Magadha, Maurya and Śuṇga empires and then conquered by the Greeks and Scythians-Persians. The Mathurā area, during the reign of Vima I Taktu or Vima II Kadphises, was occupied by the Kushāns and soon became the second capital of the Kushān Empire for a time. King Huviṣka built many memorial buildings to beautify the city of Mathurā just like his predecessor King Kaniṣka did in Puruṣapura. Most of the carved inscriptions of King Vāsudeva, the last emperor of the Kushāns, were found in and around Mathurā, a clear sign of the historical importance of Mathurā. In addition, some stone sculptures of the Kushān kings such as Wima (Vima II?) Kadphises and Kaniṣka (figs. 8, 9) excavated in Mathurā no doubt strengthen the fact that Mathurā played a prominent role in Kushān history[1]. Around mid-4th century AD, Mathurā became part of the Gupta Empire. The Gupta Empire was considered the golden age in the history of India, not only because of its benevolent rule, but also on account of the great flourishing of its literature and art. Figurative sculpture reached its peak at this time. The Buddhist art of Mathurā can be also divided into four periods[2]:

The first period, from the 1st century BC to the end of the 1st century AD, is considered the formative period of the Buddhist art of Mathurā. In turn, it can be further subdivided in two stages—that of symbolic or aniconic representation and of pre-Kaniṣka.

Prior to the anthropomorphic rendering of Buddha, his presence was indicated through one or more symbols. For instance, Buddha's conception was

---

[1] 1) J. Ph. Vogel, "Explorations at Mathurā", in: *Archaeological Survey of India: Annual Report 1911-12*: 120-133, esp. 120-127, Figs. 3, 4; 2) R. C. Sharma, *Buddhist Art: Mathura School,* New Delhi: Wiley Eastern Limited & New Age International Limited, 1995: 27, 29.

[2] 1) J. Ph. Vogel, "The Mathurā School of Sculpture", in: *Archaeological Survey of India: Annual Report 1906-7*: 137-160 and *Archaeological Survey of India: Annual Report 1909-10*: 63-79; 2) R. C. Sharma, *opere citato*: 161-219.

indicated by Māyādevī's dream in which a white elephant was seen entering her womb, Māyādevī's standing under a Śāla tree indicated the birth of the Buddha, a riderless horse or a turban alluded to the event of the renunciation, the *Bodhi* tree referred to Buddha's Enlightenment, the Deer park and the wheel symbolized his first sermon, the stairways or steps stood for Buddha's descent from Trāyastriṃśa, the *triratna* or triple jewel represented the Buddha, the *dharma* and the *Saṃgha* or monastic community and the last event, the *Mahāparinīrvaṇa* (the great demise) was indicated by a *stūpa*.

The passage from symbolic representation to anthropomorphic representation emerged before Kaniṣka came to power and it coincided with the gradual use or making of rudimentary icons. The seated Buddha closely resembled the Jina figures carved on the *āyāgapaṭṭas* (gift-tablet given at a sacrifice, fig.10) and the standing Buddha was evidently influenced by the early statues of *yakṣa* or tectonic forces from which obvious characteristics were derived. While the small Buddha images are devoid of the *uṣṇīṣa* the others are shown with a snail-like hairdo and with a plain halo behind his head. The eyes are protruding with a short line carved on the outer corner and the earlobes are smaller than the upper part of the ear. Furthermore, the chest is well developed and the navel is sunken. The right hand performs the *abhaya* gesture while the left rests on Buddha's lap. The space between the back of the hand and shoulder was not cut but a chunk of stone linked the two. With the exception of the folded drape on the left shoulder, the Buddha's robe or *saṃghāṭī* had no fold and was transparent; it was worn leaving the right shoulder uncovered (fig.11). The seat of the statue showed a few tiers one over the other looking like an altar and sometimes two lions flanked the seat.

The second period, from the end of the 1st century AD or the beginning of the 2nd century AD to mid-2nd century AD, corresponded to the reign of King Kaniṣka. During this time, the Buddha image, known as Canonized or *Kapardin* Buddha, reached perfection and was considered the most representative icon in the northern area of India. Most of the seated Buddha images were carved in high relief with clear and expressive traits. The top hair knot of the Buddha was shaped like a snail shell, *kaparda,* hence the Buddha images were known as *Kapardin*. Most of the *ūrṇa* were also rendered in relief; the almond-shaped eyes were wide open. The expression of the face was faintly smiling. The earlobes were small. The chest was prominent and the navel was sunk in. The right hand was up-raised in *abhaya* and reached slightly above the shoulder in the protection pose, with cushion decoration between the back of the hand and shoulder. The left hand resting on the thigh or knee was sometimes clenched suggesting the commanding attitude of a prince or *Cakravartin* (Universal King). The legs crossed each other in the *padmāsana* pose and the upturned soles of the feet were marked with the wheel, or the *triratna* or other auspicious motifs. The left part of the body was covered by a thin and light drapery, with thick and heavy pleats shown on the upper arm and the hem of the drapery falling on the seat. The large halo, when intact, emerges from the shoulders and bears a scalloped border, while the remaining surface is left blank. The seat was shaped as an altar with ridges and was complemented by three lions (fig.12). The characteristics of the standing Buddha resembled those of the seated Buddha. The body is straight and stiff, with the right hand in *abhaya* and the left hand hanging alongside the body. The lower drapery reaches below the knees, its hem rests on the left hand. The thinness and fine quality of the transparent drapery is indicated by the fact that the body is clearly visible underneath, in other words the body appears semi-nude. The lower drapery or *dhoti* was tied with a knot. A bunch of flowers is usually visible between the two legs. The sculptures generally carried an inscription which sometimes recorded the name of the sculpture, date of installation and name of the reigning king (fig.13).

The third period dates from mid-2nd century to the first half of the 3rd century AD, falling under the rule of King Huviṣka and King Vāsudeva. This period can be subdivided into two phases. In the earlier phase, the hair top knot is more conspicuously tall and has more than one twist. The eyes were sharpened at the ends and a line could be seen on the neck. The figure is elongated although the similarity with the *yakṣa* figure continues and the iconographic distinction between Buddha and Bodhisattva emerges. A full-blown lotus was frequently carved in the centre of the halo while the perimeter was carved with a scalloped pattern. Sometimes a beaded line is used. The thin and light *saṃghāṭī,* worn leaving the right shoulder bare, has no folds and is transparent, but bunched, thick pleats are present on the upper left arm (fig.14). Traces of Gandhāran influence can be felt for the first time in the Buddhist sculptures of Mathurā. For instance, a semicircular or V-shaped pattern of the *saṃghāṭī* is carved on Buddha's neck; the hem of the *saṃghāṭī* hangs down in a semicircular form and covers the feet. The folds or pleats were often incised while stepped lines were rarely used. The upraised right hand was in the *abhayamudrā* and the left hand was lifted up holding the hem of the *saṃghāṭī*. Attendants could be found frequently on both sides of the Buddha as well as *Vajrapāṇi,* clad in the northern style, a newly introduced trait.

In the later phase, the hair becomes curly with a topknot and sometimes is wavy. The drapery becomes thicker and stiffer but the broader folds show a rib effect. The folds hang from the left shoulder and are gathered up to the right side. The usual V shaped space below the neck is roundish and the hem of the drapery on the seat assumes the shape of a cushion. Later, a cushion of *kuśa* grass is seen on the seat (fig.15). Besides the *abhayamudrā,* other gestures such as *dhyānamudrā, bhūmisparśamudrā* and *dharmacakrapravartanamudrā* are used. The attendants were rarely found but the Buddha's life-cycle becomes more popular.

The fourth period, from the second half of the 3rd century to the 6th century AD, fell mostly under Gupta rule. The most important contribution of Gupta art is the achievement of perfect types of divinities, both Buddhist and Brāhmanical. In general, a sublime idealism, combined with a highly-developed sense of rhythm and beauty, characterizes Gupta sculptures; their design and execution show vigour and refinement. The Buddhist art, created by the artists and craftsman of Mathurā from the 4th to the 6th century AD reached its zenith during the Gupta period[1]. More attention was paid to the facial expression and a constant effort

[1] "Although the political supremacy of the Imperial Guptas did not last much beyond AD 495, the style of art ushered in by them continued until AD 600 or even somewhat later. Hence the title 'Gupta period' in relation to art covers a much longer period than what would be understood in political history." R. C. Majumdar et al, *An Advanced History of India,* 4th ed., London: Macmillan & Company Limited, 1978: 233. *confer*: A. K. Coomaraswamy, *History of Indian and Indonesian Art,* New York: E. Weyhe and London: E. Goldston, 1927: 71.

was made to achieve a harmonious combination of the physical form and the spiritual; inner feelings are especially evident in the facial expression of the image[1]. Buddha is now rendered slim and elegant. The halo carried intricate ornaments, the *uṣṇīṣa* topped the head and the hair was executed with snail curls painted dark blue. The face was oval, the forehead was broad and well proportioned, and the eyebrows slim and long. The eyes were carved horizontally and made large, lotus-bud or sinuously shaped and half-open, suggesting a state of inward vision and meditation. The nose bridge was high and straight while the sides were smoothed out. The corners of the mouth were relaxed with a somewhat prominent and thicker lower lip, the earlobes were quite elongated. The beauty mark of three lines on the neck achieved the *kambugrīva* (conch-like neck) effect (fig.16). The high quality carving that marked Buddha's body stressed the qualities of vigour and strength. Taking the standing Buddha as an example, one notices that the figure is more straight and static and at the same time relaxed. The shoulders are round and strong and one leg is slightly bent to impart a sense of movement. The *saṃghāṭī* had no pleats giving the impression of a soaked robe tightly adhering to the body; the flowing curves of the body were faintly visible beneath the robe. The parallel U-shaped folds, descending from the shoulders, were like the rippling waves of water, producing a graceful appearance. The Buddha has webbed hands and webbed feet. The right hand was raised in *abhayamudrā* and the left hand held the hem of the *saṃghāṭī*. Two parallel waved hems hanging from the left hand extended below the knees (fig.17). The expression of wet, translucent drapery folds, what is referred to as 'soaking method carving' , further suggested the beauty and refinement of Buddhist sculpture at that time. It stood in sharp contrast with the heavy drapery of the Kushān period. The two attendants or donors placed on each side of the Buddha were extremely small compared with the huge and high stature of the main image.

Gandhāra and Mathurā started a close political intercourse very early, and cultural exchanges reached the climax at the time of the Kushān period.

---

[1] Descriptions of the Buddha's features below are derived from various Buddhist *sūtras* which are here as well as afterward omitted.

Gupta sculpture established a distinctive aesthetic that attained a degree of perfection never reached before. From the 1st to the 5th century AD, Mathurā was a prominent center of Buddhist art in northern India; its sculpture became a model all over the country and its impact is apparent in the creativity of local sculptors. The Buddhist art of Mathurā, in turn, came under Gandhāran influence at the start of King Huviṣka's rule on account of the political center having moved to the South. By the time of King Vāsudeva, Mathurā seemed to have become a branch-workshop of the Buddhist art of Gandhāra. But this did not last long and the influence from Gandhāra began to decline by the end of Vāsudeva's reign. A century later, this influence could barely be detected ... The last or concluding stage of Gandhāra influence on Mathurā sculpture can be summarized by the following traits: a robe covering both shoulders, wavy hair, variety of *mudrās*, events of the Buddha's life, presence of *Vajrapāṇi, Pāñcika* and *Hārītī,* Scythian costume, moustache, *kuśā*-grass cushion on a lion throne, garland bearing *erotes*, round pillars with Corinthian capital. Conversely, Gandhāran Buddhist sculptures were also affected by Mathurā—*Jātaka* stories, curly hair, lotus seat, lion throne, drapery covering the left shoulder alone, *abhayamudrā,* iconic symbols, railing pattern, monks wearing *dhoti* and shawl[1]. Considering the aesthetic as a whole, the mutual influence did not last very long and none of these elements really controlled the opposite side. In short, both schools progressed through mutual influence and exchanges. The reason is that some manners and motifs from the opposite side had been rapidly assimilated and transformed.

3. Sculptures from Sārnāth and other Sites

In addition to the art schools of Gandhāra and Mathurā, special attention should be paid to Sārnāth which was another art centre of Buddhist sculptures during the Gupta rule. Sārnāth, known as *Mṛgadāva* (Deer park) in the historical documents, is situated in the middle reaches of the Ganges, 8 km north-east

[1] 1) R. C. Sharma, *opere citato*: 221-228; 2) R. C. Sharma, "Mathurā and Gandhāra: The Two Great Styles", in: *Buddhism and Gandhāra Art,* ed. R. C. Sharma and Pranati Ghosal, Shimla: Indian Institute of Advanced Study, Varanasi: Jñāna-Pravāha and New Delhi: Aryan Books International, 2004: 66-72.

of Benares (present day Varanasi). It is the place where Gautama Buddha gave his first sermon[1]. However, in post-Maurya and pre-Gupta times there was no art school in Sārnāth. The Buddhist art of Sārnāth was totally derived from the Buddhist art of Mathurā[2]. During the Gupta period, Sārnāth became one of the centers of Buddhist art[3] and many notable sculptures were made there at that time. The sculpture representing the First Sermon was the most profound masterpiece ever made in Sārnāth (fig.18). The sacred and relaxed expression of the Buddha was a typical characteristic of Mathurā art, which emerged during the post-Kushān period and became one of the ultimate achievements of Guptan Buddhist sculpture. The Sārnāth artists and craftsmen not only adopted as a model the Mathurā image that was available to them, but also gradually evolved their own form and style[4]. The most remarkable and distinguishing feature of Sārnāth style is the light and transparent wet drapery with practically no folds. The presence of a robe was indicated by using a few pleated lines around the neck and along the hem of the robe. Judging from the sculptures unearthed at Govindnagar (fig.19), this particular feature was also invented by the Mathurā school, but Sārnāth artists promoted it and made it more delicate[5]. This 'foldless' style, thus, became a new fashion imitated by carvers in India during the 5th and 6th centuries AD[6]. I consider now the Ajaṇṭā caves as the embodiment of this

[1] U. R. Tiwari, *Sculptures of Mathura and Sarnath, A Comparative Study* (*Up to Gupta Period*), Delhi: Sundeep Prakashan, 1998: 11-14.

[2] J. C. Harle, *Gupta Sculpture: Indian Sculpture of the Fourth to Sixth Century* AD, Oxford: Clarendon Press, 1974: 18.

[3] During this period, many local ateliers which were separately located in all Buddhist centers of India managed to make Buddha images with various materials, such as Chunār sandstone in Sārnāth, Sikrī sandstone in Mathurā, Trap in Ajaṇṭā and so on. All these local plastic arts were collectively called "Gupta art" which were all obviously derived from style of the Mathurā art. A. K. Coomaraswamy, *opere citato*: 74; *confer*: D. Mitra, *Buddhist Monuments,* Calcutta: Sahitya Samsad, 1971: 15, 67.

[4] David L. Snellgrove, ed., *The Image of the Buddha,* New Delhi: Vikas Publishing House Pvt Ltd/ UNESCO, 1978: 99-101.

[5] R. C. Sharma, *opere citato* (*Buddhist Art...*): 208, 230.

[6] The author believes that there were two main approaches to stone-made Buddha in Gupta art. One was the typical Buddha of Mathurā, with all the details including the drapery folds carved. Another was the combination of carving and painting; in other words, face and body of Buddha were carved first and then colors were applied on every surface, face and body.

style during this period. The main Buddha in Cave 1, seated crossed legged and performing the *dharmacakrapravartanamudrā,* has curly hair, almond-shaped eyes, straight nose, slightly sinking mouth corners and long earlobes stretching to the shoulders. The image has a halo and huge nimbus; on the front pedestal, a wheel and two deer as well as disciples were carved[1]. A remarkable feature is the drapery which was carved with almost no folds except a suggestion of it on the upper chest and at the ankles. The lower hem of the robe is visible under the legs and covers the seat. Judging by the traces of color and comparing them with Buddhist sculptures of the same kind in other Ajaṇṭā caves, we conclude that the drapery folds or pleats were originally painted. The painter first applied a thin layer of white plaster on the surface of the sculpture and proceeded to paint the drapery folds on the dried surface (fig.20). The drapery folds or pleats on most of the extant Buddhist sculptures of Ajaṇṭā — the main figure in Cave 2, the seated Buddha in the main hall as well as the standing Buddha in the ante-hall of Cave 4, the main seated Buddha and other seated or standing Buddha in the halls of both upper and lower stories of Cave 6, and the seated Buddha on the façade and standing Buddha in the nave of cave 19 — were all made and painted in the same way. Moreover, some small devotees carved at the feet of the standing Buddha resemble those in the standing Buddha sculpture of Mathurā of the Gupta period. Furthermore, the main Buddha of Cave 16 wears a *saṃghāṭī* with the right shoulder bare, but the left wrist was covered with one layer of drapery while the lower hem of the drapery displays two layers. The hem of the drapery from the inner side of the left wrist leading to the ankle forms a "zigzag" pattern. This zigzag motif was used frequently in the making of Buddha images in the Nāsik caves; it might be a distinguishing feature of Gupta art. The Ajaṇṭā area was not brought into the realm of the Gupta Empire but was ruled by the Vākāṭakas. King Chandragupta II of the Gupta "sought to cement the political alliance with the Vākāṭakas by giving his daughter Prabhāvatīguptā in marriage to the Vākāṭaka

[1] In this period, the hand gestures of the seated Buddha in Ajaṇṭā caves were mainly *dharmacakrapravartanamudrā,* which perhaps had some relations with the typical seated Buddha of Sārnāth or Mathurā.

prince Rudrasēna II"[1]. This can explain the similarity of the art form. Moreover, four images of the Buddha seated under canopies against the berm of *Stūpa* I facing the four entrances at Sāñcī also adopted this "foldless" transparent style[2]. Even the Buddhist sculpture of Nepal such as the standing Buddha in Cā-bālī (fig.21), far away from India, carries this same art form[3]. Thus, the influence of Gupta art had a wide-ranging and far-reaching impact.

4. Early Buddha Images of China

China had long cultural exchanges and interactions with the countries in the South Asian subcontinent. Early on from the Eastern Han Dynasty (25-220 AD) and after, around the early 2nd century AD, the building of Buddhist temples or monasteries and the making of Buddhist sculptures gradually took shape and flourished especially after the widespread of Buddhism in China[4]. The interaction between the artists and sculptors of ancient Hinduka (present-day the South Asian Subcontinent and part of Pakistan) and those of ancient China can be found in many historical records. To give a few examples: Emperor Ming (58-75 AD) of the Han Dynasty once ordered to "send envoys to Hinduka to gather Buddhist doctrines and images with the purpose of imitating them in China"[5]. When the monk Faxian came back from Hinduka in 412 AD, he brought with him some Buddhist sculptures and *sūtras*[6]. And at the beginning

---

[1] V. V. Mirashi, ed., *Inscriptions of the Vākāṭakas: Corpus Inscriptionum Indicarum* V, Ootacamund: Government Epigraphist for India, 1963: XXIII.

[2] John Marshall & Alfred Foucher, *The Monuments of Sāñchī,* Calcutta: Archaeological Survey of India, 1940: Plate LXX.

[3] David L. Snellgrove ed., *opere citato*: Plates 71-74, 125.

[4] Chongfeng Li, *Zhongyin fojiao shikusi bijiao yanjiu: Yi tamiaoku wei zhongxin* [中印佛教石窟寺比较研究：以塔庙窟为中心, *Chētiyagharas in Indian and Chinese Buddhist Cave-temples: A Comparative Study*], Beijing: Peking University Press, 2003.

[5] Yuan Hong [袁宏 328-376 AD], *Houhanji: Xiaominghuangdiji* [后汉纪·孝明皇帝纪, *History of the Eastern Han Dynasty: Memoir of Emperor Xiaoming*], Beijing: Zhonghua Book Company, 2002: 187.

[6] Sengyou [僧佑, 445-518 AD], *Chu sanzang ji ji* [出三藏记集, *A Collection of Records concerning the Tripiṭaka* or *A Collection of Records of Translations of the Tripiṭaka*], emended and annotated by Su Jinren [苏晋仁] and Xiao Lianzi [萧鍊子], Beijing: Zhonghua Book Company, 1995：575; *confer Taishō,* No. 2145, Vol. 55: 112a.

of the 6th century, Song Yun and the monk Huisheng were dispatched to the Western Regions on a Buddhist mission. While in Gandhāra, "Song Yun, [on his part], gave two slaves—one male and one female — to serve for life the Que-li Stūpa, sweeping the ground and sprinkling water. Huisheng, too, by saving from his travel allowance, was able to select a skilled artisan to copy in bronze (the following pictures): one Que-li Stūpa, and four other *stūpas* depicting the transformation of Śākya (muni)[1]. The number of monks from South Asia who brought Buddhist *sūtras* and sculptures to China increased with the expansion of cultural exchanges between China and South Asian subcontinent. Early in the Tai'an period (455-459 AD) of Emperor Wencheng (452-465 AD) of the Northern Wei Dynasty, the *śramaṇas* Yaśagupta, Buddhanandi and other three from Siṃhala (Sri Lanka), who brought three Buddha images with them, arrived in the capital (Pingcheng, present day Datong)"[2]. In the book *Xu huapin* (*Continuation of the Classification of Painters*) written by Yao Zui, we read that three foreign monk-artists came to China: Śākyabuddha, one of the three, a native of Hinduka, arrived in China approximately at the time of the Northern Wei Dynasty (386-534 AD)[3]. The monks and artists of Hinduka who came to China no doubt brought their Buddhist sculptures and paintings along as models of their skills in three-dimensional and two-dimensional arts. Because Buddhism was propagated from Hinduka and Western Regions, Chinese Buddhist art was accordingly greatly influenced by the foreign art and culture. Zhang Sengyou, a leading painter of

---

[1] Yi-t'ung Wang, tr., *A Record of Buddhist Monasteries in Lo-yang* by Yang Hsüan-chih, Princeton: Princeton University Press, 1984: 242-243. *confer*: Yang Xuanzhi [杨衒之], *Luoyang qielan ji* [洛阳伽蓝记, *A Record of Saṃghārāmas in Luoyang*] in 547 AD, emended and annotated by Zhou Zumo [周祖谟], Beijing: Zhonghua Book Company, 1963: 220.

[2] Wei Shou [魏收, 506-572 AD], *Weishu: Shilaozhi* [魏书 · 释老志, *History of the Wei Dynasties: Treatise on Buddhism and Taoism*] in 554 AD, punctuated and emended, Beijing: Zhonghua Book Company, 1974: 3025-3062, esp. 3036.

[3] 1) Xie He [谢赫, active ca. 500-535 AD], *Gu hua pin lu* [古画品录, *Classification of Painters*]; Yao Zui [姚最, 535-602 AD], *Xu hua pin lu* [续画品录, *Continuation of the Classification of Painters*], emended, annotated and translated by Wang Bomin [王伯敏], Beijing: People's Fine Arts Publishing House, 1962: 17-18; 2) Zhang Yanyuan[张彦远, 815-877 A.D.], *Lidai minghua ji* [历代名画记, *Record of Famous Painters of All the Dynasties/ On Chinese Paintings through the Ages*], emended and annotated by Yu Jianhua [俞剑华], Shanghai: Shanghai People's Fine Arts Publishing House, 1964: 154.

the Liang Dynasty who adopted the Hinduka painting method named *Tianzhu yifa* (Shading and High-lighting Techniques of Hinduka or Hinduka technique of painting, i. e., three-dimensional method)[1], "did excel in making pictures or paintings for Buddhist temples or monasteries and surpassed in ability the multitude of artisans"[2]. "Since Emperor Wu (502-549 AD) of the Liang Dynasty deeply venerated Buddhism, he often sent for Zhang to make paintings for Buddhist temples or monasteries."[3] Zhang was so famous for his unique ability both in Buddhist painting and sculpture that his superb technique was named "Zhang Style" in regard to Buddhist imagery. Cao Zhongda, a noted painter of the Northern Qi Dynasty (550-577 AD), was by origin a native of the kingdom of Cao (Kebud/ Kapūtānā); he was highly esteemed for his skill in painting Buddhist icons[4]. Cao Zhongda created a new interpretation of the Buddha image and his Buddhist painting; both were the pinnacle of his time. Thus, he was admired as the best painter in the capital city of the Northern Qi Dynasty[5]. He not only adopted painting skills from Hinduka, but also developed a characteristic

---

[1] Zhang Sengyou painted the wall of the Yicheng Monastery in Jiankang (present day Nanjing). The technique or method that he used was called "*Tianzhu yifa* (Shading and High-lighting Techniques of Hinduka or Hinduka technique of painting or Hinduka technique of chiaroscuro)". He painted the walls with red, blue and green colors. The painting was convexo-concave likeness or had chiaroscuro effect when looking from the distance, but flat in from closer. People were all amazed about this receding and protruding painting at that time. Hence, Yicheng Monastery was known as *Aotusi* (the Convexo-concave Monastery)". Xu Song [许嵩], *Jiankang shilu* [建康实录, *True Records of Jiankang*] in 756 AD, emended and annotated by Zhang Chenshi [张忱石], Beijing: Zhonghua Book Company, 1986: 686.

[2] Xie He/ Yao Zui, *opere citato*: 13. *confer*: Acker's translation: "He excelled in making pictures for pagodas and temples, and was far and away superior to the general run of artisans." William Reynolds Beal Acker, *Some T'ang and Pre-T'ang Texts on Chinese Painting*, translated and annotated, Vol. I, Leiden: E. J. Brill, 1954: 49.

[3] Zhang Yanyuan *opere citato*: 150. *confer*: Acker's translation: "The Emperor Wu Ti (regn. 502-550) in his reverent adornment of Buddhist temples often ordered Seng-yu to do paintings for them." William R. B. Acker, *Some T'ang and Pre-T'ang Texts on Chinese Painting*, translated and annotated, Vol. II, Leiden: E. J. Brill, 1974: 174.

[4] Zhang Yanyuan, *opere citato*: 158. *confer*: Acker's translation: "Ts'ao Chung-ta was originally a man of the country of Ts'ao, and during the Northern Ch'i dynasty he was very well known for his skill in painting Indian icons." Acker, *opera citato*, Vol. II: 193.

[5] Daoxuan, *Ji shenzhou sanbao gantong lu* [集神州三宝感通录, *Collection of the Strange and Extraordinary Events and Deeds of the Buddhist Triratna in China*], in: *Taishō*, No. 2106, Vol. 52: 421b.

style of his own which was named "Cao Style". Monk Yancong said: Cao's Buddhist paintings were so inspiring that the Buddhist paintings made by other contemporary artists were quite inferior to his[1]. Cao Style was called "Soaked drapery" by later generations[2], in recognition of Cao's contribution to the making of Buddhist images. "The figures in Cao's paintings were rendered with layered drapery folds hanging down from the upper body but the drapery was so thin and light that it looked as if it were closely adhering to the skin."[3] Cao's style, evidently, must have drawn inspiration from the transparent robe worn by the Buddha in the sculptures of Mathurā; his style further absorbed stylistic elements from those of the Gupta period.

The earliest Buddha images in south China seem to have been discovered from tombs of Sichuan, dated from the mid-2nd century to the mid-3rd century AD. The seated Buddha wears a *saṃghāṭī* with both shoulders covered, his upraised right hand is in *abhayamudrā* and left hand is lifted up holding the hem of the *saṃghāṭī*[4]. And, the earliest Buddha image extant in north China appears to be a gilt bronze seated Buddha (fig.22), datable to end of the 3rd century or the early 4th century AD, whose provenance is unknown[5], with posture, *saṃghāṭī* and *mudrā* similar to those of Sichuan. These Buddha images, in visual form and

[1] Zhang Yanyuan, *opere citato*: 158. *confer*: Acker's translation: The Monk Yancong says: "At the time there was none who could compete with him in (painting) foreign Buddha icons." Acker, *opera citato*, Vol. II: 193.

[2] Guo Ruoxu [郭若虚], *Tuhua jianwen zhi* [图画见闻志, *An Account of My Experiences in Painting* or *Continuation of Record of Famous Painters of All the Dynasties*] in 1074 AD, emended and annotated by Yu Jianhua [俞剑华], Shanghai: Shanghai People's Fine Arts Publishing House, 1964: 20.

[3] Su Bai [宿白], "*Qingzhou longxingsi jiaocang suo chu foxiang de jige wenti* [青州龙兴寺窖藏所出佛像的几个问题, Some Questions Concerning the Buddhist Sculptures Unearthed from a Hoard at Longxing Monastery, Qingzhou]", in : *Wei jin nanbeichao tang song kaogu wengao jicong* [魏晋南北朝唐宋考古文稿辑丛, *Collected Papers on the Chinese Archaeology from the Wei down to the Song Dynasties* (3rd *to* 13th *century AD*)] by Su Bai, Beijing: Cultural Relics Press, 2011: 333-350, esp. 343.

[4] Su Bai [宿白], "*Sichuan qianshu he changjiang zhongxiayou bufen qiwu shang de foxiang* [四川钱树和长江中下游部分器物上的佛像, The Buddha Images on the Money-trees and Figured Jars unearthed from the Tombs of South China]", in: *Wei jin nanbeichao tang song kaogu wengao ji cong* (*Collected Papers on the Chinese Archaeology from the Wei down to the Song Dynasties*) by Su Bai, Beijing: Cultural Relics Press, 2011: 211-223, esp. 211.

[5] Saburō Matsubara [松原三郎], *A History of Chinese Buddhist Sculpture* [中国仏教彫刻史論], Tokyo: Yoshikawa Kōbunkan, 1995: 243, Plate 5a.

modeling, are similar to or identical with the Buddha images of Mathurā of the 3rd and 4th periods (fig.15).

The extant Buddha sculptures in Cave 169 at Binglingsi, Gansu, and in the Caves 16-20 at Yunkang, moreover, represent the early stage of Buddhist sculpture in China. They are of good quality and carry a precise dating. The inscription of "the first year of the Jianhong period (420 AD) of the Western Qin state (385-431 AD)" in niche 6 of Cave 169 at Binglingsi, discovered by Gansu archaeologists in 1963[1], is the earliest dated record in the cave temple complexes of China. It can provide a chronological template for the study of China's Buddhist cave art. A standing Buddha image below niche 6 of Cave 169 might have been completed around 420 AD, for the image has characteristics similar to those of Mathurā sculptures in the 4th period, with elegant expression, round face, thin and lined eyebrows, long and big eyes, thick and reddened lips, straight and high nose-bridge. The Buddha image also has a robust and strong body with well-proportioned shoulders covered by drapery. The overlapping drapery folds are hanging down from the shoulders, revealing the body contours and a sense of movement. The slightly bended right leg looks as if the Buddha were walking. Both hands are damaged but the drapery folds falling down from the left hand were carved with zigzag symmetric ripples (fig.23). Astonishing parallels are available in the Buddha sculptures of the 4th period of Mathurā. The other Buddha sculptures in Cave 169, made around 420 AD, carry similar characteristics. Here, the gesture of the standing Buddha, the drapery with symmetric ripple folds and slightly expanding hem of the drapery present the style of Mathurā art instead of that of Gandhāran art.

The Caves 16 to 20 at Yungang, which were built for the ruling family of the northern Wei by monk Tanyao between 460 and 465 AD, ranked first for their unique workmanship[2]. The Buddha sculptures in the caves show the

---

[1] Gansusheng wenhuaju wenwu gongzuodui [甘肃省文化局文物工作队, Archaeological Team of Gansu Cultural Heritage Bureau], "*Diaocha binglingsi shiku de xin shouhuo* [调查炳灵寺石窟的新收获, New Discoveries on the Buddhist Cave-temple Complex at Binglingsi]", in: *Cultural Relics,* 10 (1963): 1-6, 10, esp. 1.

[2] Wei Shou, *opere citato*: 3037.

compromise between the essential qualities of foreign sculptural art and Chinese tradition. The domestication of this art is noticeable in many aspects[1]. The giant Buddha sculptures on the northern, eastern and western walls of Cave 18 at Yungang wear a light and thin *saṃghāṭī* whose folds are compact and parallel (fig.24), no doubt revealing the influence of the Mathurā art of the 4th period. The modeling and the drapery of the standing Buddha images on the southern wall of Cave 19 at Yungang also distinctly show the style of the Mathurā art of the 4th period. A special feature was found in Cave 16 where the giant standing Buddha wore a wavy hair related to the Gandhāran style, but the drapery was of Chinese style (fig.25), an invention of Chinese artists and carvers. The heavy and protruding drapery pleats and folds on the main Buddha in Cave 20 at Yungang, however, make us think of the woolen drapery on the Buddha sculptures of Gandhāra; the unique *saṃghāṭī* worn with the right shoulder slightly covered was perhaps invented by the artists and craftsmen of Pingcheng (fig.26). "It is hardly possible that the artisans who worked at Yün Kang were acquainted with real Gandhāra sculptures; they must have known those types in rather free translations, and their artistic culture was, on the whole, not of a very high degree."[2] Chinese carvers imitated, changed and finally brought forth new ideas based on their understanding of Gandhāran art. Generally speaking, we do not find direct influence of earlier Gandhāran art on the sculpture of the five Yungang caves, but indirect or mixed influence from Gandhāran and Mathurā art of the 4th period is obviously clear. "As a matter of fact, some of these Yün Kang figures are more closely related in style to statues made at Mathurā than to the proper Gandhāra sculptures."[3] However, the Buddha sculptures presenting the

[1] Su Bai［宿白］, "*Pingcheng shili de jiju he yungang moshi de xingcheng yu fazhan*［平城实力的集聚和"云冈模式"的形成与发展, Gathering of Manpower and Material Resources in Pingcheng and the Creation as well as Development of the 'Yungang Style'］", in: *Zhongguo shikusi yanjiu*［中国石窟寺研究, *Studies of the Cave-temples of China*］by Su Bai, Beijing: Cultural Relics Press, 1996: 114-144, esp. 125-126.

[2] O. Siren, *Chinese Sculpture from the fifth to the fourteenth century,* London: E. Benn, 1925: XLIII.

[3] O. Siren, *ibidem*.

above-mentioned influence were found not only in the above five caves, but as well in Caves 9 and 10 which were built later. The standing Buddha images in the antechambers of these two caves are good examples as they all wear thin and transparent *saṃghāṭī*.

In addition to the above-mentioned cave-temple complexes, furthermore, the discoveries of pit storages or hoards in Chengdu and Qingzhou in the middle and late 20th century respectively have attracted our special attention.

In Chengdu, Sichuan Province, the discovery of Buddhist sculptures in 1953 from the former site of the Wanfo Monastery and that of the pit storage in Xi'an Road in May 1995 are most notable. A standing stone sculpture excavated from Xi'an Road is dated by inscription, namely "on the 30th day of the 9th month (the Chinese lunar calendar) of the 5th year (November 13, 551 AD) of the Taiqing period of Emperor Wu of the Liang Dynasty, a Buddhist layman named Zhu Sengyi reverentially commissioned this Aśoka image in memory of his dead son Li Foshi" (fig.27)[1]. Another stone sculpture of Aśoka from the Wanfo Monastery is also dated by an inscription. It was reverentially commissioned by Yuwen Zhao, Commander in Chief of Yizhou Prefecture (Sichuan) and dated to "Baoding period (562-565 AD) of Emperor Wu (560-578 AD) of the Northern Zhou Dynasty (557-581 AD)"[2]. These two sculptures are very similar; in fact, they reflect the same typology with curved hair and the *saṃghāṭī* covering both shoulders[3]. The *saṃghāṭī* was draped to form a V-shaped cowl around the neck, the rim of

---

[1] Chengdushi wenwu kaogu gongzuodui [成都市文物考古工作队, Archaeological Team of Chengdu], "*Chengduoshi xi'anlu nanchao shike zaoxiang qingli jianbao* [成都市西安路南朝石刻造像清理简报, A Report on the Excavation of the Buddhist Stone Sculptures of the Southern Dynasties Period from a Hoard at Xi'an Road, Chengdu]", in: *Cultural Relics,* 11 (1998): 4-20, esp. 7-8, color plate 2-1, Figs. 11, 14.

[2] Liu Zhiyuan [刘志远] and Liu Tingbi [刘廷壁], *Chengdu wanfosi shike yishu* [成都万佛寺石刻艺术, *Stone Sculptures from Site of the Wanfo Monastery, Chengdu*], Beijing: China Ancient Arts Publishing House, 1955: Figure 9.

[3] Angela. F. Howard named this type of statue as "Ashoka-type Buddha". Angela F. Howard, "Standing Ashoka-type Buddha", in: *China Dawn of a Golden Age, 200-750 AD,* ed. James C. Y. Watt et al, New York: The Metropolitan Museum of Art, New Haven and London: Yale University Press, 2004: 227-229.

the drapery turns to the right and forms a cowl. The drapery seems to be light and thin with all the folds falling down in the form of water waves. The thin and transparent *saṃghāṭī,* especially the handling of the drapery folds below the waist, has a striking similarity with the standing Buddha images from Mathurā. This type of parallel drapery folds falling down from the chest was a fashion popular in Mathurā during the 4th period. The sculptures of Aśoka, to be precise, Aśoka-type Buddha image, excavated in Chengdu might have some relations with the Buddha statue made by Aśoka and enshrined by Emperor Wu of the Liang Dynasty in Jiankang (present day Nanjing), which may have originated from Hinduka. According to fascicle 15 of *Guang Hongmingji* (*Further Anthology of the Propagation of Light*), compiled by Daoxuan in the early 7th century, "the Buddha statue in the Changsha Monastery of Jingzhou was made of gold and some words in Brāhmī-script were engraved on the halo, to the effect that 'this statue was commissioned to be made by King Aśoka' . On hearing this, Emperor Wu of the Liang Dynasty had it send to the capital (Jiankang) and the statue shined with light thereafter"[1]. We could, therefore, infer that the model used in making the statue by the artists or craftsmen of Yizhou was a copy of the statue from Jiankang, because there had been a close intercourse between Jiankang and Hinduka ever since the Song Dynasty (424-479 AD). In the 5th year (428 AD) of Yuanjia period of Emperor Wen of the Song Dynasty, Yue Ai［月爱，Chandra Gupta II］[2], the King of Hinduka, sent a letter of credence to Emperor Wen. Moreover, in the 2nd year (466 AD) of the Taishi period of Emperor Ming of the Song Dynasty, two envoys or messengers from Hinduka, whose names were transliterated as Zhu Fuda and Zhu Ami, were conferred separately the title "Jianwei General" by Emperor Ming of the Song Dynasty[3]. These records

［1］Daoxuan, *Guang Hongmingji*［广弘明集，*Further Anthology of the Propagation of Light*］, in: *Taishō,* No. 2103, Vol. 52: 202b.

［2］Zhang Xinglang/ Chang Hsing-lang［张星烺］, *Zhongxi jiaotong shiliao huibian*［中西交通史料汇编 *The Materials for a History of Sino-Foreign Relations*], 6 volumes, Peking: The Catholic University of Peking, 1930; Vol. 6, Beijing: Zhonghua Book Company, 1979: 31 note 2.

［3］Shen Yue［沈约，441-513 AD］, *Songshu*［宋书，*History of the Song Dynasty*］in 488 AD, punctuated and emended ed, Beijing: Zhonghua Book Company, 1974: 2384-2386.

speak of the close relation between the two countries. During the Liang Dynasty, furthemore, Hinduka sent envoys to south China several times. In the 2nd year (503 AD) of Tianjian period of Emperor Wu of the Liang Dynasty, "King Gupta of Hinduka sent a messenger whose name was transliterated as Zhu Luoda or Zhu Daduo to deliver a letter again"[1]. Therefore, it stands to reason that the model of the Buddha images carved around Jiankang, the capital during the Southern Dynasties period (420-589 AD), originated in Hinduka[2]. Regretably however, no Buddha statue wearing a thin and transparent *saṃghāṭī*, besides the Buddha images carved in the Cave Temple Complex at Qixiashan, Nanjing, has ever been found in present day Nanjing.

The pit storage from the former site of the Longxing Monastery in Qingzhou, Shandong Province, included chiefly sculptures of the Northern Dynasties period (386-581 AD). Among them, the Buddhist sculptures made during the Northern Qi Dynasty (550-577 AD) were greater in number and bigger in size. They are characterized by a variety of postures, patterns and drapery designs. It is clear that the later the sculptures were made, the greater is the variety of their features. The main characteristic of the Northern Qi Buddha sculptures was their wearing a transparent robe without folds which fell naturally along the body (fig.28) or hang with parallel double pleats[3]. The thin and light weight *saṃghāṭī,* with no folds which reveals the body underneath, was chiefly used in making independent standing Buddha images. This type was especially fashionable in the later part of the Northern Qi Dynasty. The sculptures discovered at Qingzhou were painted and in some cases figure paintings even adorned the robe. The Buddha statues made in other areas of the Northern Qi Dynasty, for

[1] Wang Qinruo [王钦若, 962-1025 AD] and Yang Yi [杨亿, 974-1020 AD], *Cefu yuangui* [册府元龟, *The Imperial Encyclopaedia on the Monarch and his Subjects of the Past Dynasties*], Fascicle 968, Facsimile edition, Beijing: Zhonghua Book Company, 1989: 3834.

[2] Su Bai, *opere citato* (*Qingzhou longxingsi*...): 340-342.

[3] This kind of double pleats was widely used in the Buddhist sculptures of Gandhāra of the 3rd period *confer*: Isao Kurita [栗田 功], *Gandhāra bijutsu* [ガンダーラ美術, *Gandhāran Art*], I: 佛伝 [Vol. I *The Buddha's Life Story*], Tokyo: Nigensha, 1988: Plates 219, 223, 229, 238, 387, 390-92, 425, 450 and 468.

instance in Hebei, at Xiangtangshan, were carved to suggest a cylinder shape from head to foot, with the feature of an off-sized head, protruding chest, broad shoulders and a stiff, vertical body, with no anatomic detail[1]. Therefore, the late Professor Liang Sicheng (Liang Ssu-ch'eng) stressed in 1930s that "the new impact or influence on the images of the Northern Qi Dynasty came from Central Asia, or the typology was brought from India, or craftsmen from Central Asia were employed. The main Buddha was made in a new style while the attendant Bodhisattvas were carved in the old pattern of traditional Chinese Buddhist art, which was the reason of the difference of the styles between the main Buddha and its attendant Bodhisattvas"[2]. In fact, the new fashion or trend of the Northern Qi Dynasty was related to the continuous, direct diffusion of the Indian style to China in the 6th century AD and the "westernization" or, more precisely, "*xihuhua* [西胡化 Western *Hunization* or Western Barbarization]" of the Northern Qi Dynasty. The term "*xihuhua* (Western *Hunization* or Western Barbarization)", invented by the late Professor Chen Yinke, refers to Sienpi (Xianbi) nobles who indulged in sensual pleasures, games and other amusements originally from Central Asia, as some of these nobles claimed to be "Prince of Kucha". Numerous non-Han nationalities from Central Asia were employed by the Northern Qi Dynasty in the field of entertainment. According to the principle of transformation or conversion, if the Sienpi nobles went on indulging in pleasure, they would have been assimilated and became non-Han nationalities of

[1] Buddha images made during the Northern Qi Dynasty, from head to foot, were wider on the top and narrower on the lower part; in contrast those made during the Northern Wei Dynasty were narrower on the top and wider on the lower part, with narrow shoulders and a smaller head.

[2] Liang Sicheng [梁思成], *Zhongguo diaosushi* [中国雕塑史, *History of the Chinese Sculpture*], in: *Liang Sicheng wenji* [梁思成文集, *Collected Works of Liang Sicheng*], III, Beijing: China Building Industry Press, 1985: 332-336.

Osvald Siren believed that the Buddha sculptures in Cave 16 at Tianlongshan were made after foreign models or by foreign artists. The Buddha sculptures are altogether quite Indian in spirit and form, and are stylistically closely related to certain sculptures at Mathurā from the 5th to 6th century. Therefore, he was "inclined to suppose that some Indian artist who was well acquainted with the products of the great Mathurā school worked for some time at T'ien Lung shan". O. Siren, *opere citato*: LXVI.

the Central Asia[1]. There were numerous and varied non-Han nationalities from Central Asia at the imperial court of the Northern Qi. For instance, even a commoner named Hu Xiao'er was conferred the title of "duke" only because he was adept at dancing and singing. The Sienpi nobility, including Emperor Wucheng's consort, were all fond of Central Asian games. It was recorded that even a Persian dog had been conferred the title of "*yitong/junjun* (director/daughter of an imperial prince)"[2]. These instances indicate the deep influence of Central Asian *mores* on the Northern Qi nobles. Under the impact of Central Asia, Buddhism and Buddhist art made considerable progress during the Northern Qi Dynasty. Moreover, the number of monks and laymen from Hinduka who came to China increased year by year. They were engaged in the translation of Buddhist *sūtras* and some of them were appointed officials of the *Zhaoxuansi* (Ministry/Bureau of Buddhist Affairs), one of the central administrations of the Northern Qi Dynasty. For examples, Dharmaprajñā who came from central Hinduka was conferred the title of "*Zhaoxuandu* (Director of the Ministry of Buddhist Affairs)"[3]. Narendrayaśas who came from northern Hinduka, Uḍḍiyāna, was conferred the title of "*Zhaoxuantong*" , one of ten ministers in the Ministry of Buddhist Affairs of the Northern Qi Dynasty[4]. The reason that they were placed in such important posts was the "*xihuhua* (Western *Hunization* or Western Barbarization)" of the Northern Qi Dynasty which upheld and advocated the cultures of non-Han nationalities of Central Asia. Cao Zhongda, inventor of Cao's style used in the making of Buddhist images, must be from the same family of Cao Miaoda, who

---

[1] Chen Yinke [陈寅恪], *Wei jin nanbeichao shi jiangyan lu* [魏晋南北朝史讲演录, *Lectures on the History of the Wei, Jin and the Southern-and-Northern Dynasties*], ed. Wan Shengnan [万绳楠], Hefei: Huangshan Publishing House, 1987: 297-300, esp. 297; *confer*: Chen Yinke, *Chen Yinke ji*: *Jiangyi ji zagao* [陈寅恪集：讲义及杂稿, *Collected Works of Chen Yinke*: *Teaching Materials and Essays*], Beijing: SDX Joint Publishing House, 2002: 187-189.

[2] Li Baiyao [李百药, 565-648 AD], *Beiqishu* [北齐书, *History of the Northern Qi Dynasty*], punctuated and emended edition, Beijing: Zhonghua Book Company, 1972: 685-686、693-694.

[3] Daoxuan [道宣], *Xü gaoseng zhuan* [续高僧传, *Continued Biographies of Eminent Priests* or *The Tang Dynasty Biographies of Eminent Priests* or *A Continuation of the Memoirs of Eminent Monks*], in: *Taishō*, No. 2060, Vol. 50: 434c.

[4] Daoxuan, *opere citato*: 432a-c.

was highly regarded by Emperor Wenxuan of the Northern Qi Dynasty and used to be a master *pipa*[1] or lute player at the imperial court[2]. Cao Zhongda was finally conferred the title of "*Chaosandafu* (Grand Master for Closing Court)"[3]. Therefore, the diffusion of the Mathurā school to Buddha images during the Northern Qi Dynasty was definitely connected with the people mentioned above. In other words, the prevalence of Buddha images in the Mathurā or Gandhāran styles was the inevitable result of the Northern Qi Dynasty's conversion to Central Asian *mores* or "*xihuhua* (Western *Hunization* or Western Barbarization)".

I once more emphasize that the emergence and dissemination of Buddha images in China was by no means the outcome of a mechanical imitation of foreign art forms, but a re-creation of the best foreign models that the Chinese had assimilated and transformed according to their own tradition. This process was rather similar to the reciprocal influence that had intervened between Gandhāran and Mathurā art. This process of recreating a foreign model can also be called a process of domestication. The latter, indeed, took place in China in regard to the making of Buddha images.

(This paper was published in the *Glory of the Kushans*: *Recent Discoveries and Interpretations*, edited by Vidula Jayaswal, New Delhi: Aryan Books International, 2012: 378-391).

[1] *Pipa* is a plucked Chinese string instrument with a fretted fingerboard.

[2] Xiang Da [向达], *Tangdai chang'an yu xiyu wenming* [唐代长安与西域文明, *The Tang Dynasty Chang'an and the Civilization of Central Asia*], Beijing: SDX Joint Publishing Company, 1957: 19.

[3] Zhang Yanyuan, *opere citato*: 158.

The Aśoka-type Buddha Images found in China

There are, as far as I know, two types of Aśoka images associated with Aśoka that are found in China. The first type consists of Buddha images reputedly made by King Aśoka[1] or by his daughter[2], and the second type consists of portrait-images of King Aśoka commissioned by Buddhist monks and laymen, which are meant to honor his contribution to Buddhism. Of these, scholars call the first type the Aśoka-type Buddha image[3].

In Chengdu, Sichuan Province, there were major discoveries of Buddhist sculptures from site of the Wanfo Monastery in 1953[4] and from a hoard at Xi'an Road in 1995[5]. A standing image excavated from the Xi'an Road

---

[1] 1) Huijiao [慧皎, *ca*. 495-554 AD], *Gaoseng zhuan* [高僧传, *Biographies of Eminent Priests* or *The Liang Dynasty Biographies of Eminent Priests*], in 519 AD, emended and annotated by Tang Yongtong [汤用彤], Beijing: Zhonghua Book Company, 1992: 199; *confer Taishō*, No. 2059, Vol. 50: 355c-356a; 2) Daoxuan [道宣], *Guang hongmingji* [广弘明集, *Further Anthology of the Propagation of Light*], in: *Taishō,* No. 2103, Vol. 52: 202b.

[2] 1) Huijiao, *opera citato*: 478; 2) Fei Zhangfang [费长房], *Lidai sanbo ji* [历代三宝记, *Record of the Triratna through the Ages* or *Record concerning the Triratna under Successive Dynasties*], in: *Taishō* No. 2034, Vol. 49: 38a; 3) Daoshi [道世 ? -668? AD], *Fayuan zhulin* [法苑珠林, *Forest of Gems in the Garden of the Law/ A Grove of Pearls in the Garden of the Dharma*], in: *Taishō* No. 2122, Vol. 53: 384a.

[3] Angela F. Howard, "Standing Ashoka-type Buddha", in: *China Dawn of a Golden Age, 200-750 AD*, ed. James C. Y. Watt et al, New York: The Metropolitan Museum of Art, New Haven and London: Yale University Press, 2004: 227-229.

[4] Yuan Shuguang [袁曙光], "*Sichuansheng bowuguan cang wanfosi shike zaoxiang zhengli jianbao* [四川省博物馆藏万佛寺石刻造像整理简报] (The Buddhist Sculptures from Site of the Wanfo Monastery in the Collection of Sichuan Museum)", *Cultural Relics*, 10 (2001): 19-38.

[5] Chengdushi wenwu kaogu gongzuodui [成都市文物考古工作队, Archaeological Team of Chengdu], "*Chengduoshi xi'anlu nanchao shike zaoxiang qingli jianbao* [成都市西安路南朝石刻造像清理简报, A Report on the Excavation of the Buddhist Stone Sculptures of the Southern Dynasties Period from a Hoard at Xi'an Road, Chengdu]", in: *Cultural Relics*, 11 (1998): 4-20, color Plates 1-4 and Plates inside the front cover.

is made of sandstone with gilding and pigments and dated by an inscription (fig.1)［1］, which informs us that “on the 30th day of the 9th month (of the Chinese lunar calendar) of the 5th year of the Taiqing period (November 13, 551 AD)［2］, the Buddhist layman named Zhu Sengyi［柱僧逸］［3］ reverentially commissioned this Aśoka image in memory of his dead son Li Foshi, who aspired to have all his family dependents, living or dead, to be reborn to meet the Buddha and hear Buddha's preaching of the Law and awake to the truth of *Nirvāṇa*, with the hope that seven generations of predestined relationship as well as animate beings of the six states of reincarnation fulfill the pledge” . The inscription was carved atypically on the tablet affixed to the lower back of the image［4］ (fig.2). Another stone sculpture of Aśoka image from the site of the Wanfo Monastery is also dated by its inscription. The text records that it was reverentially commissioned by Yuwen Zhao［宇文招］, commander-in-chief of Yizhou Prefecture (present-day Sichuan), during the Baoding period (562-565 AD)［5］ of Emperor Wu of the Northern Zhou Dynasty［6］. These two sculptures are very similar to each other in typology; in fact, they were commissioned to have the

［1］The inscription in Chinese reads: “太清五年 / 九月卅日 / 佛弟子柱僧逸为亡儿李 / 仏施敬造育王像供养 / 愿存亡眷属在所生处 / 值仏闻法早悟无生七 / 世囙缘及六道含令（灵）普 / 同斯誓谨□.” *confer: Cultural Relics*, 11 (1998): 14, fig.14.

［2］Emperor Wu of the Liang Dynasty died in 549 AD. The 5th year of the Taiqing period is, in fact, the 1st year of the Tianzheng period of Prince Yuzhang, corresponding to 551 AD.

［3］The Chinese characters 柱僧逸 (Zhu Sengyi) should be 竺僧逸 (Zhu Sengyi), the carver seems to make an error by confusing similar sound but a different character, because most monks and laymen in medieval China liked to have their secular family name to be changed to 竺, meaning Hinduka, after they converted to Buddhism.

［4］Chengdushi wenwu kaogu gongzuodui (Archaeological Team of Chengdu), *opere citato*: 7-8, Figs. 11, 14, color plate 2.

［5］This inscription reads: “益州摠管柱国 / 赵国公招敬造 / 阿育王像一躯”。Here, “招 (Zhao)” is the abbreviation for Yuwen Zhao who was granted the title “Duke Zhaoguo” and was later appointed the governor of Yizhou Prefecture by Emperor Wu of the Northern Zhou Dynasty in 562 AD. *confer*: Linghu Defen［令狐德棻, 583-666 AD］, *Zhoushu*［周书, *History of the Northern Zhou Dynasty*］, punctuated edition, Beijing: Zhonghua Book Company, 1971: 67, 77.

［6］1) Liu Zhiyuan［刘志远］and Liu Tingbi［刘廷壁］, *Chengdu wanfosi shike yishu*［成都万佛寺石刻艺术, *Stone Sculptures from Site of the Wanfo Monastery in Chengdu*］, Beijing: China Ancient Arts Publishing House, 1955: Fig.9; 2) Yuan Shuguang, *opere citato*: 21-23, Fig.2.

a

b

fig.1 Aśoka-type Buddha image, 48 cm height, from a hoard at Xi'an Road, Chengdu; a. front of the image; b. back of the image

fig.2 Rubbing copy of the inscription carved at the back of the image

same iconography or in imitation of the same model. According to the report by Yuan Shuguang, there are five Aśoka-type images and two pieces of the head of Aśoka image excavated from the site of the Wanfo Monastery in Chengdu, Sichuan. All extant sculptures of the Aśoka-type image have the same traits (figs.3-4), which suggest that they apply exclusively to the same iconography[1].

The images are shown standing firmly on lotus pedestals, with feet apart. The tied hair-curls for the *uṣnīṣa* (cranial protuberance) are larger and unusual, and the face is marked with almond eyes, high-bridged nose and handlebar mustache. Outlines of the body are clearly visible under his robe (*saṃghāṭī*). Both hands are missing and the arms are broken, but originally, the right hand should have been in the *abhayamudrā* (fear-not-*mudrā*) posture, and the left hand should have held the robe in place. The outer robe, or *saṃghāṭī*, was draped to form a wide U-shaped cowl around the neck; in other words, the rim of the drapery turns to the right and forms a cowl. The robe is light and thin with all the

[1] Yuan Shuguang, *opere citato*: 21-23, Figs. 7, 8.

fig.3 Head of an Aśoka-type Buddha image, from the site of Wanfo Monastery in Chengdu, Sichuan

fig.4 A headless Aśoka-type Buddha image, from the same site

pleats falling down in the form of water waves, an unusual system of pleats. "Wide catenaries mark the body's central axis, contrasting with the rigid vertical folds falling from the arms. The under robe forms catenaries over the legs and rigid folds in between"[1].

The images, especially in the treatment of the head, facial features, and attire "reveal a determined effort to distinguish this image from conventional likenesses of the Buddha"[2]. The face reveals foreign features. The thin and transparent *saṃghāṭī* that covers both shoulders, particularly the handling of the drapery folds below the waist, has a striking similarity, in a broad manner, with the standing Buddha images from Mathurā. In other words, this type of parallel drapery folds falling down from the chest was a fashion popular in Mathurā during the Kushān and the Gupta periods (figs.5-6).

The self-appellation in the inscriptions makes reference to the miraculous appearance of an Aśoka image that emerged from the sea along the coastal

[1] Description of the images here are from Angela. F. Howard, who named this type of the image, in English, as Aśoka-type Buddha. Angela F. Howard, *opere citato*: 227-229.

[2] Angela F. Howard, *opere citato*: 228.

fig.5 Standing Buddha in *abhaya-mudrā*, from Govindnagar, Archaeological Survey of India

fig.6 Torso of a Buddha image, from Govindnagar, Mathurā Museum

areas of China during the Eastern Jin Dynasty (317-420 AD). It was believed that this image originated with King Aśoka.

According to accounts given by both Daoshi and Daoxuan[1], who were eminent monks in the 7th century AD, during the Xianhe period (326-334 AD) of Emperor Chengdi of the Eastern Jin Dynasty, Gao Kui［高悝］, governor of Danyang Prefecture (another name of Jiankang, present-day Nanjing), went back and forth between his home and the city. It was he who saw an extraordinary light in the river by chance while he passed through the Zhanghouqiaopu［张候桥浦］riverside every time. He asked somebody to search the area and finally a golden image was discovered, which was made in a foreign style or a style of

［1］1) Daoshi［道世］, *Fayuan zhulin*［法苑珠林, *Forest of Gems in the Garden of the Law/ Encyclopaedia of the Buddhist World*］in 668 AD, emended and annotated by Zhou Shujia［周叔迦］and Su Jinren［苏晋仁］, Beijing: Zhonghua Book Company, 2003: 455-457; *confer*: *Taishō,* No. 2122, Vol. 53: 383c-384b; 2) Daoxuan［道宣, 596-667 AD］, *Ji shenzhou sanbao gantong lu*［集神州三宝感通录, *Collection of the Strange and Extraordinary Events and Deeds of the Buddhist Triratna in China/ Records of Spiritual Response of the Three Jewels in China*］, in: *Taishō,* No. 2106, Vol. 52: 414a-c.

the Western Regions, with the halo and pedestal missing. Gao Kui got off his cart and asked somebody to load the image onto it. When the cart reached the Chang'gan Alley, the driver failed to get the ox to move forward any further. Gao Kui stopped the driver and let the ox go anywhere it wanted to go. The ox drew the cart directly to the Changgan Monastery [长干寺][1], and the image was finally enshrined there. The news greatly surprised men and women in the city, and most of them became awakened and enlightened. The image shone resplendently every midnight. A year later, Zhang Xishi [张系世], a fisherman of Linhai, found a bronze lotus pedestal in the sea and had it sent to an official. The Emperor ordered that it be fixed to the image, and they fitted perfectly. Later, five monks from the Western Regions called on Gao Kui and told him that they had obtained an Aśoka-type image when they visited Hinduka [天竺, present-day the South Asian Subcontinent][2]. While they came to central China, they had it buried by the bank of a river because of the chaos in the Capital Ye. After the chaos was over, they were looking for the image and recently had a dream that it was found by Gao Kui and enshrined at the Aśoka Monastery (another name of the Changgan Monastery). They came here from afar and only wanted to worship the image. Then, Gao Kui led them into the monastery. When the five monks saw the image, they all began to sob and the image shone for them with unusual light reflected in the hall and around the monks. The monks added that there used to be a round halo belonging to the image, which was left far away, and that one should search for it. Then they resided in the monastery and made offerings to the image. In the first year of Xian'an period (371 AD) of Emperor

---

[1] Incidentally, an Aśoka-type *stūpa* made around the 4th year of Dazhongxiangfu period (1011 AD) of Emperor Zhenzong of the Northern Song Dynasty was unearthed from site of the Changgan Monastery, Nanjing in 2008. It is the most exquisite and the biggest one of such Aśoka-type *stūpas* ever found in China.

[2] 1) P. C. Bagchi, "Ancient Chinese Names of India", in: *India and China: Interactions through Buddhism and Diplomacy; A Collection of Essays by Professor Prabodh Chandra Bagchi*, compiled by Bangwei Wang and Tansen Sen, Delhi: Anthem Press India, 2011: 3-11, esp. 8-9; 2) Qian Wenzhong, "The Ancient Chinese Names of India and their Origins", in: *Land Routes of the Silk Roads and the Cultural Exchanges between the East and West before the 10th Century*; Desert Route Expedition International Seminar in Urumqi August 19-21, 1990, Beijing: New World Press, 1996: 601-611.

Jianwen of the Eastern Jin Dynasty, Dong Zongzhi［董宗之］, a pearl diver from Hepu, Cochi［交州 , present day Vietnam］, saw a light reflected from the seabed of the South China Sea and found a halo of the Buddha image. He reported to a higher body and the Emperor Jianwen gave an imperial edict that an attempt should be made to fix it to the image. The tenon of the image and the mortise of the halo, and even the colors of both, were completely identical. It is paranormal that the pedestal and halo were lost and recovered in different areas during a period of over forty years. It is a spiritual response that they in the end matched. The pedestal of the image had an inscription in a foreign language, which nobody could decipher. It is Guṇavarman［求那跋摩 , 367-431 AD］who said that it was written in ancient Brāhmi script［梵书］, and that it recorded the image was made or commissioned by the fourth daughter of King Aśoka[1].

At that time, Huisui［慧邃］, a monk from the Waguan Monastery［瓦官寺］in Jiankang, wanted to make a copy of it, but the abbot of the Changgan Monastery, who was afraid of losing its golden color after it was copied, told Huisui that if he could let the Buddha image shine, turn its face to the west and spare no effort on his part, he would be allowed to make a copy of it. Monk Huisui prayed reverentially; he heard an extraordinary sound at midnight and, when he opened the door of the hall, found the image sitting facing west and shining. Then, Huisui was allowed to have someone make a copy of it, and several dozen replicas of the image were made and circulated.

During the reign of Emperor Wu of the Liang Dynasty (502-549 AD), seven

---

［1］According to *Xijing ji* [西京记 , *Record of the Western Capital*] cited in *Taiping yulan* [太平御览 , *The Taiping Reign-Period Imperial Encyclopedia*], a stone image, 5 *chi* (about 150 cm) high, is installed at Chongjiao Monastery in Xijing (Western Capital, present-day Xi'an). Though the image was of poor workmanship, it is highly efficacious. It is said that the image was carved by the fourth daughter of King Aśoka. As an ugly lady, she always heaved a sign of regret and swore to make more Buddha images. At first, the images that she carved look like her in appearance. After a thousand images were accomplished and her prayers were said regularly and reverentially, she found the images she carved were like the Buddha. Thus, she had more statues to be made, which were qualified for the facial features and appearance of the Buddha. As a result, her father, King Aśoka, sent spirits and supernatural beings to spread the Buddha images in the whole world and the stone image kept at Chongjiao Monastery is one of the images carved by her.

Li Fang[李昉], *Taiping yulan* (*The Taiping Reign-Period Imperial Encyclopedia*), Fascicle 657, Facsimile edition, Beijing: Zhonghua Book Company, 1960: 2937. *confer*: Daoxuan [道宣], *Lüxiang gantong zhuan* [律相感通传 , *Responses to Dreamlike Dialogues with Devas*], in: *Taishō*, No. 1898, Vol. 45: 879a.

flying *deva* or celestial figures were fixed on the halo and two Bodhisattva figures added on both sides. In the middle of the Tianjia period (560-565 AD) of Emperor Wen of the Chen Dynasty, some people rose up in arms in the southeast regions, and the Emperor prayed in front of the image that the assailants should withdraw. As soon as his supplication was over, the hall and the steps where the image was enshrined were illuminated, and the southeast regions such as Dongyang and Fujian were reunited peacefully. During a persistent drought, the image was brought into the palace by the Emperor's carriage, and a monk became a rain doctor. This was done to ensure that there was heavy rain. The image was said to be always efficacious. In the first year of the Zhide period (583 AD) of Emperor Houzhu of the Chen Dynasty, a square pedestal was added to the image.

From the Eastern Jin to the Chen Dynasties (317-589 AD), the Emperors and ministers of the five dynasties, i. e., Eastern Jin, Song, Qi, Liang and Chen, all worshipped the image and converted to Buddhism. As soon as Emperor Wen of the Sui Dynasty (589-604 AD) heard this story, he issued an edict that the image should be sent to the imperial court and should be enshrined there. The Emperor always stood beside the image personally, attending and worshipping. Devotional activity of making copies of this image, moreover, had been flourishing even in the early Tang Dynasty when Daoshi and Daoxuan compiled and wrote the aforesaid books[1].

These records clearly inform us that the image made or commissioned by the fourth daughter of King Aśoka is the Buddha image with its own features.

fig.7 Mural on the western section of the south wall of Cave 323 at Mogao, Dunhuang

[1] 1) Daoshi, *opere citato*: 455-457; *confer*: *Taishō*, Vol. 53: 383c-384b; 2) Daoxuan, *opere citato* (*Ji shenzhou sanbao*...): 414a-c. Besides, other documents also carry several records of such miraculous occurrences.

a

b

c

fig.8 Detail of the aforesaid mural

a. Welcoming the Buddha image; b. The Aśoka-type Buddha image shining in the river; c. The halo of the Buddha image shining in the sea.

Further, the mural on the western section of the south wall of cave 323 at Mogao, Dunhuang, which was built in the early Tang Dynasty, has a simple depiction of this miraculous story (figs.7-8); only the names of the place and the monastery differ from the aforesaid records[1]. This story spread far and wide among all the legends about Aśoka-type Buddha images recorded in China[2].

In addition, an Aśoka-type Buddha image found in a niche (figs.9a,9b) on the west wall of the Tangzi Cave at Longmen was carved in the early Tang Dynasty. The image was commissioned by Jingming [净命], a *bhikṣuṇī* or nun from the Jingfu Monastery [景福寺], who transferred the merit to a dead monk[3].

a b

fig.9 Aśoka-type Buddha image carved on the west wall of Tangzi Cave at Longmen, Luoyang; a. photo *in situ;* b. line-drawing of the same image

[1] Ma Shichang [马世长], "*Mogaoku di 323 ku fojiao ganying gushihua* [莫高窟第323窟佛教感应故事画, Illustration of 'Received Grace' Stories in Cave 323 at Mogaoku]", *Zhongguo fojiao shiku kaogu wenji* [中国佛教石窟考古文集, *Essays on the Buddhist Cave Temples of China*], by Ma Shichang, Taipei/Hsinchu: Chueh Feng Buddhist Art & Culture Foundation, 2001: 241-263.

[2] Wang Jianping [王剑平] and Lei Yuhua [雷玉华], "*Ayuwangxiang de chubu kaocha* [阿育王像的初步考察, A Preliminary Investigation on the Aśoka-type Buddha Images]", *Xi'nan minzu daxue xuebao* [西南民族大学学报, *Bulletin of Southwest University for Ethnics*], Vol. 28, No. 9 (2007): 65-69.

[3] The inscription about this image in Chinese reads: "景福寺尼/净命为亡/和上敬造/阿育王像记". *confer*: Zhang Naizhu [张乃翥] et al. 2000. "*Luelun longmen shiku xin faxian de ayuwang xiang* [略论龙门石窟新发现的阿育王像, An Aśoka-type Buddha Image found at Longmen Caves, Luoyang]", in: *Dunhuang Yanjiu* [敦煌研究, *Dunhuang Research*], No. 4 (2000): 21-26.

The style of the Aśoka-type Buddha images found at both Dunhuang and Longmen, however, is slightly different from those excavated in Chengdu.

On the basis of Chinese literary records, many such images made or commissioned either by Aśoka or by his fourth daughter had traveled all the way to China in extraordinary circumstances, alighting in particular along the coast areas[1].

In the nineteenth year of the Taiyuan period (394 AD) of Emperor Xiaowu of the Eastern Jin Dynasty, an image miraculously landed in Jiangling. It was received and enshrined at the Changsha Monastery[长沙寺]by the Monk Tanyi[昙翼]. Later, it was recognized by Saṃghānanda[僧伽难陀], who came from Jibin (Greater Gandhāra), as a Buddha image commissioned by King Aśoka according to the inscription in Brāhmi script on the halo[2]. The Emperor Yuan of the Liang Dynasty (552-554 AD), furthermore, used to write an inscription on a tablet in praise of an Aśoka-type Buudha image enshrined at the Changsha Monastery, extolling this famous Buddha statue[3].

The Aśoka-type Buddha image enshrined in the Hanxi Monastery[寒溪寺] in Wuchang was originally discovered in the South China Sea by a fisherman and sent there by Tao Kan[陶侃], who was the Governor of Guangzhou when the image was found. After the monastery was burned down later by fire, only the hall that enshrined the image commissioned by Aśoka survived. It was said that the hall was protected by a dragon-god while the monastery was burning. When the Monk Huiyuan[慧远, 334-416 AD] set up a monastery in the Lushan Mountains, he reverentially prayed for an image, and the image enshrined at the Hanxi Monastery traveled freely back and forth between the two monasteries[4].

---

[1] Angela F. Howard, "Buddhist Art in China", in: *China Dawn of a Golden Age, 200-750 AD*, ed. James C. Y. Watt et al, New York: The Metropolitan Museum of Art, New Haven and London: Yale University Press, 2004: 94.

[2] Huijiao, *opere citato*: 199; *confer*: *Taishō*, Vol. 50: 355c-356a.

[3] Ouyang Xun[欧阳询, 557-641 AD], *Yiwen leijun*[艺文类聚, *Encyclopedia of Art and Literature in Dynastic Histories/Collected Descriptive Accounts of Books in Category*], in 624 AD, emended and annotated by Wang Shaoying[汪绍楹], Shanghai: Shanghai Chinese Classics Publishing House, 1965: 1301-1302.

[4] Huijiao, *opere citato*: 213-214; *confer*: *Taishō*, Vol. 50: 358c.

In terms of the pictorial realm, Wei Xie [卫协] who was a famous painter during the reign period of Emperor Ming (323-325 AD) of the Eastern Jin Dynasty, Dai Kui [戴逵, 326?-396 AD] and his son (grandson?) Dai Yong [戴颙, 377-441 AD] seem all to make paintings of the Aśoka-type Buddha icons[1].

During the Sui Dynasty, Zheng Fashi [郑法士], a famous painter of the time, also drew a fine painting of an Aśoka-type Buddha icon[2].

The Aśoka-type Buddha images, under the patronage of influential members of society and with the backing of distinguished prelates, became widespread in China during the reign of Emperor Wu of the Liang Dynasty, who strove in his devotion to emulate his Indian predecessor, the Mauryan emperor Aśoka. Meanwhile, monks from Hinduka and southeast Asia came to China one after another along the Silk Roads and Marine Rutes, and translations of Buddhist *tripiṭaka,* as well as constructions of the Buddhist *stūpas* and monasteries in the style of the Hinduka originals, expanded greatly, showing the support given to art and culture of Hinduka by the ruling elite. For example, Saṃghapāla [僧伽婆罗, 460-524 AD], a monk from Banam [扶南] and a disciple of monk Guṇabhadra [求那跋陀, 394-468 AD] from Hinduka, came to Jiankang, the capital of the Southern Qi Dynasty (479-502 AD), by the Marine Rutes. He was ordered by Emperor Wu of the Liang Dynasty in 512 AD to translate *Ayuwang zhuan* [阿育王传, *Biography of King Aśoka*] into Chinese. The Emperor became his attendant and wrote down his translations[3]. In the 3rd year of the Putong period (522 AD) of Emperor Wu of the Liang Dynasty, the Emperor ordered the building of a *stūpa* and a monastery after the original of Hinduka on the ruined site of Maoshan *Stūpa* in Maoxian [鄮县, present day Yinxian], which was later named Aśoka Monastery by the imperial

[1] Zhang Yanyuan [张彦远, 815-877 AD], *Lidai minghua ji* [历代名画记, *Record of Famous Painters of All the Dynasties/On Chinese Paintings through the Ages*)] in 847 AD, emended and annotated by Yu Jianhua [俞剑华], Shanghai: Shanghai People's Fine Arts Publishing House, 1964: 125.

[2] Zhang Yanyuan, *opere citato*: 161.

[3] Fei Zhangfang [费长房], *Lidai sanbo ji* [历代三宝记, *Record of the Triratna through the Ages* or *Record concerning the Triratna under Successive Dynasties*] in 597 AD, in: *Taishō,* No. 2034, Vol. 49: 98b.

order[1]. Furthermore, features of the Buddha image were standardized according to the original of Hinduka by Emperor Wu of the Liang Dynasty, with *kaparda* (snail-shell)-like hair curls to be modeled carefully and the palms of the hands or soles of the feet to be marked with the auspicious motif of the wheel[2]. Thus, links to the style of Hinduka and portrayal of icons rooted in the tradition of Hinduka were intrinsic components of the Buddhist art of the Liang Dynasty. In other words, "legitimacy was conferred on Chinese Buddhist art by its link to India, the holy land, while the patronage of local elites placed it in a Chinese locale. Very likely, the iconography of Aśoka-type Buddha icons originated in Jiankang, the capital of the Southern Dynasties"[3]. Since Sichuan became an integral part of the South after being annexed in 347 AD by the Eastern Jin Dynasty, especially during the period of the Song, Qi and Liang dynasties[4], "Sichuan Buddhist art to some degree reflected the doctrinal choices and aesthetic taste of the southern capital"[5]. To be precise, "Chengdu Buddhist art was transmitted from Jiankang along the lower Yangzi River"[6].

The Aśoka-type Buddha images excavated from Chengdu, however, might have some connection to the Buddha images commissioned by King Aśoka or by his fourth daughter and enshrined by Emperor Wu of the Liang Dynasty in Jiankang, the images that may have originated from Hinduka. According to

---

[1] Daoxuan, *opere citato* (*Ji shenzhou...*): 405a.

[2] Ouyang Xun, *opere citato*: 1317.

[3] Angela F. Howard, "Standing Ashoka-type Buddha", in: *opere citato*: 227-228.

[4] Meng Mo [蒙默] et al., *Sichuan gudaishi gao* [四川古代史稿, *A History of Ancient Sichuan*], Chengdu: Sichuan People's Publishing House, 1988: 140-149.

[5] Angela F. Howard, "Buddhist Art in China", in: *opere citato*: 93-94. According to an inscription on an image of Śakyāmuni Buddha dated to 529 AD, excavated at the site of the Wanfo Monastery, attendants and servants of Xiao Fan, the eldest son of Pince Poyang and nephew of Emperor Wu of the Liang Dynasty, came to Chengdu along with their master and commissioned a Buddha image there. Since the attendants and servants came from Jiankang, the origin of their image type should also be from Jiankang. See Su Bai [宿白], "*Qingzhou longxingsi jiaocang suo chu foxiang de jige wenti* [青州龙兴寺窖藏所出佛像的几个问题, Some Questions Concerning the Buddhist Sculptures Unearthed from a Hoard of the Longxing Monastery at Qingzhou]", in: *Wei jin nanbeichao tang song kaogu wengao jicong* [魏晋南北朝唐宋考古文稿辑丛, *Collected Papers on the Chinese Archaeology from the Wei down to the Song Dynasty* (3rd *to* 13th *century* AD), Beijing: Cultural Relics Press, 2011: 333-350, esp. 341-342, 350.

[6] Su Bai, "Buddha Images of the Northern Plain, 4th-6th century", in: *China Dawn of a Golden Age, 200-750 AD*, ed. James C. Y. Watt et al, New York: The Metropolitan Museum of Art, New Haven and London: Yale University Press, 2004: 84.

records in fascicle 15 of *Guang Hongmingji* (*Further Anthology of the Propagation of Light*), by Daoxuan in the early 7th century, "the Buddha image in the Changsha Monastery of Jingzhou was made of gold and some words in Brāhmi script were engraved on the halo, to the effect that 'this image was made by King Aśoka'. On hearing this, Emperor Wu of the Liang Dynasty had it sent to the capital (Jiankang), and the image shone with light thereafter"[1].

If we accept the above information, we can hypothesize that the model used in making the image by artists or carvers of Yizhou Prefecture was a replica of the image from Jiankang or of a prototype of Hinduka[2]. In other words, the Aśoka-type Buddha image privileged in Sichuan might be modeled on the original commissioned by King Aśoka or his fourth daughter, because there had been a close political intercourse, besides Buddhist exchanges, between South China and Hinduka ever since the Song Dynasty (424-479 AD).

In the 5th year (428 AD) of the Yuanjia period of Emperor Wen of the Song Dynasty, Yue Ai [月爱, Chandra Gupta II][3], the King of Hinduka, sent a diplomatic envoy to present his credentials to Emperor Wen. Moreover, in the 2nd year (466 AD) of the Taishi period of Emperor Ming of the Song Dynasty, two envoys or messengers from Hinduka, whose names were transliterated as Zhu Fuda [竺扶大] and Zhu Ami [竺阿弥], were conferred separately the title "Jianwei General [建威将军]" by Emperor Ming of the Song Dynasty[4]. These records reveal a close relationship between the two countries. During the Liang Dynasty, moreover, Hinduka sent envoys to south China several times. In the 2nd year (503 AD) of Tianjian period of Emperor Wu of the Liang Dynasty, "King Gupta of Hinduka [天竺国王屈多] again sent a messenger, whose name was transliterated as Zhu Luoda [竺罗达] or Zhu Daduo [竺达多], to deliver a letter"[5]. Therefore, it

---

[1] *Taishō*, Vol. 52: 202b.

[2] Su Bai, *opere citato* (*Qingzhou longxingsi...)*: 347-348 note [31].

[3] Zhang Xinglang/ Chang Hsing-lang [张星烺], *Zhongxi jiaotong shiliao huibian* [中西交通史料汇编, *The Materials for a History of Sino-Foreign Relations*], 6 volumes, Peking: The Catholic University of Peking, 1930; Vol. 6, Beijing: Zhonghua Book Company, 1979: 31 note [2].

[4] Shen Yue [沈约, 441-513 AD], *Songshu* [宋书, *History of the Song Dynasty*] in 488 AD, punctuated and emended ed., Beijing: Zhonghua Book Company, 1974: 2384-2386.

[5] Wang Qinruo [王钦若, 962-1025 AD] and Yang Yi [杨亿, 974-1020 AD], *Cefu yuangui* [宋本册府元龟, *The Imperial Encyclopaedia on the Monarch and his Subjects of the Past Dynasties/Corpus of Historical Data on the Monarch and his Subjects of the Past Dynasties*], facsimile edition, Beijing: Zhonghua Book Company, 1989: 3834.

stands to reason that the model of the Buddhist images made around Jiankang, the capital during the Southern Dynasties period (317-589 AD), originated in Hinduka. Regrettably, however, no Buddha image wearing a thin and transparent *saṃghāṭī*, besides the Buddha images carved in the Cave Temple Complex at Qixiashan, Nanjing, has ever been found in Jiankang, although there are meticulous records of dynastic histories and Buddhist literature[1]. The reason is that Jiankang city was completely razed, even ploughed under, by troops of the Sui Dynasty (581-618 AD) in order to destroy the imperial spirit and atmosphere after it was conquered in 589 AD[2].

As for the second type of the Aśoka image, there is a sculpture of an Aśoka portrait in the Aśoka Monastery at Yinxian County, Zhejiang Province. The monastery was rebuilt in 1680 on the site of the former Aśoka Monastery named by Emperor Wu of the Liang Dynasty and the sculpture therein might have been carved or made in the same year (figs.10-11).

fig.10 Aśoka Temple at Yinxian, Zhejiang

fig.11 A Sculpture of King Aśoka's portrait in the same temple

(This paper was published in the *Reimagining Aśoka*: *Memory and History*, edited by Patrick Olivelle et al, New Delhi: Oxford University Press, 2012: 380-393)

[1] Su Bai, *opere citato* (*Qingzhou longxingsi*...): 340-342.

[2] Wei Zheng [魏徵, 580-643 AD] and Zhangsun Wuji [长孙无忌, 597-659 AD] et al., *Suishu* [隋书, *History of the Sui Dynasty*], emended and punctuated ed., Beijing: Zhonghua Book Company, 1973: 876.

金刚力士钩稽

金刚力士[1]，通常对称雕造于石窟寺前庭正壁门道两侧(图1)，应源于印度地面佛寺(包括石窟寺)的执杖药叉，即门神。《根本说一切有部毗奈耶杂事》卷十七：

图1 龙门奉南洞前庭正壁金刚力士

给孤长者施园之后，作如是念：若不彩画，便不端严；佛若许者，我欲庄饰。即往白佛，佛言：随意当画。闻佛听已，集诸彩色并唤画工。报言：此是彩色可画寺中。答曰：从何处作？欲画何物？报言：我亦未知，当往问佛。佛言：长者，于门两颊应作执杖药叉。[2]

---

[1] 关于中国石窟中的金刚力士像，中国学者阎文儒、日本学者八木春生和韩国学者林玲爱分别就云冈、龙门和克孜尔石窟中的金刚力士做过论述。参见：1) 阎文儒《云冈石窟研究》附录《密迹金刚力士与地夜叉》，桂林：广西师范大学出版社，2003年，第291-304页；2) 八木春生《中国北魏时期的金刚力士像》，见《宿白先生八秩华诞纪念文集》，北京：文物出版社，2002年，第353-369页；3) 林玲爱《克孜尔石窟金刚力士的特征及其意义》，见中山大学艺术史研究中心编《艺术史研究》第八辑，中山大学出版社，2006年，第251-268页。

[2]《大正藏》第24卷，第283a-b页。

执杖药叉，在印度早期地上寺院及佛教石窟中多有表现，如桑吉 (Sāñcī) 大塔四座塔门 (toraṇa) 内侧，皆对称雕出两身护法神 (genii)，担当门神 (dvāra-pālas 娜缚罗钵逻)，被赋予阻止鬼神及异教徒入内之责。dvāra-pāla 系诸药叉之名[1]，他们戴头巾，挂耳珰，配项饰，套手镯；上身袒裸，下系禅裙 (dhotī)，腰束带，衣 (uttarīya) 下垂，跣足而立；左手叉腰或置于体侧，右手多持花卉；个别手持长矛，如西门南柱内侧之药叉 (图 2c)。桑吉大塔四门所雕门神，没有显现文献所言东方乾闼婆 (Gandharvas)、南方鸠槃荼 (Kumbhāṇḍas)、西方那伽 (Nāgas) 或北方药 (夜) 叉 (Yakshas) 之属性，与其他诸神形貌相似。因此，难于从图像志上给予合理解释[2]。至于石窟寺中出现的这种形象，现存最早者应是比德尔科拉 (Pitalkhora) 第 4 窟门道两侧的门神 (dvārapāla)，雕凿年代为公元前 2 世纪后半，较桑吉大塔四座塔门略早。比德尔科拉石窟，系印度考古工作者 20 世纪 50 年代中期清理后重新发现。第 4 窟门神缠头巾，挂耳珰，戴项饰，配臂钏、手镯；上着紧身战袍 (tunic)，下系禅裙，跣足而立。门神一手持标枪 (javelin)，一手握长方形盾牌；右侧门神宽大的剑鞘中插一短剑 (dagger)，左侧门神覆勇囊 (chhanna-vīra) 上佩刀 (sword)，刀柄位于腰与左手间[3] (图 3)。两门神俨然武士形象。

a　　　　　　　　　　b　　　　　　　　　　c

图 2　桑吉大塔塔门门柱浮雕门神像

a. 北塔门西柱下部内侧；b. 北塔门东柱下部内侧；c. 西塔门南柱下部内侧

[1] 1) Monier Monier-Williams, *A Sanskrit-English Dictionary,* Oxford: Oxford University Press, 1899: 504; 2) 荻原雲来《漢訳対照梵和大辭典》，東京：鈴木学術財団，1974 年，第 623a 页。

[2] John Marshall and Alfred Foucher, *The Monuments of Sāñchī,* Calcutta: Manager of Publications, 1940: 243, Pl. XXXVI a/b, Pl. La, Pl. LIIIb, Pl. LXVIa.

[3] M. N. Deshpande, "The Rock-cut Caves of Pitalkhora in the Deccan", in: *Ancient India* (Bulletin of the Archaeological Survey of India), No. 15 (1959): 66-93, esp. 74-75, Pl. LI.

图 3　印度比德尔科拉第 4 窟门道两侧门神

这种执杖药叉或门神，后来演变为佛之“左辅”、“右弼”，通常置于寺门两侧，守护伽蓝。据法琳《破邪论》卷下：

唯我大师，体斯妙觉，二边顿遣，万德俱融。不喧不寂，安能以境智求；非爽非昧，明可以形名取。为小则小而无内，处大则大而无垠。故能量法界而兴悲，揆虚空而立誓。所以，现生秽土，诞圣王宫。示金色之身，吐玉毫之相。布慈云于鹫岭，则火宅炎销；扇慧风于鸡峰，则幽途雾卷。行则金莲捧足，坐则宝座承躯，出则帝释居前，入则梵王从后。左辅密迹，以灭恶为功；右弼金刚，以长善为务。声闻、菩萨，俨若侍臣；八部、万神，森然翊卫。演涅槃，则地现六动；说般若，则天雨四华。百福庄严，状满月之临苍海；千光照曜，犹聚日之映宝山。师子一吼，则外道摧锋；法鼓暂鸣，则天魔稽首。是故，号佛为法王也。[1]

其中左辅密迹，据《大宝积经》卷八，“金刚力士，名曰密迹，住世尊右，手执金刚……密迹所云有二，事业近于如来，慧仁能乐住宣，于如来秘密之业，非诸声闻、缘觉之地所能及逮”[2]。《入楞伽经》卷八《化品》：“世尊复说诸识，念念差别不住，金刚密迹常随侍卫”[3]。唐初玄应《一切经音义》卷一《大方广佛华严经音义》曰：

[1]《大正藏》第 52 卷，第 487a 页。
[2]《大正藏》第 11 卷，第 43b 页。
[3]《大正藏》第 16 卷，第 560b 页。

“密迹，梵言散那 (saṇḍa)，此译云密主。密是名，以知佛三密功德故也。主者夜叉主也。案：梵本都无迹义，当以示迹为神，故译经者义立名耳”[1]，即守护佛法之夜叉主，或法云《翻译名义集》卷二所记“密迹金刚神”[2]。密迹金刚，亦名执金刚神，梵语作 vajradhara/vajrapāṇi/vajrapāṇi-yakṣa/vajrapāṇirmahā-yakṣaḥ[3]，或称执金刚神密迹力士 (guhyapāda-vajra)[4]。据慧琳《一切经音义》卷十八《大乘大集地藏十轮经》，“卢至如来 (Rucika)，梵语佛名，古译楼至，唐云爱乐，即此贤劫中第一千佛劫末后成佛，即今之执金刚神是也，亦名密迹金刚”[5]。玄应《一切经音义》卷三《放光般若经》：“和夷罗洹阅叉 (vajrapāṇi-yakṣa)，即执金刚神也，谓手执金刚杵，因以名焉。”[6]法云《翻译名义集》卷二则进一步说明：“跋阇罗波腻(vajrapāṇi)，梁云金刚。应法师云：跋阇罗此云金刚，波腻此云手，谓手执金刚杵，以立名。”[7]

右弼金刚，有人认为即那罗延 (nārāyaṇa)。据《佛说法集经》卷三，“那罗延，身金刚力士；为教化众生，降伏憍慢”[8]。玄应《一切经音义》卷二十四《阿毗达磨俱舍论》：“那罗延，那罗 (nārā)，此翻为人；延那 (yaṇa)，此云生本。谓人生本，即是大梵王也。外道谓一切人皆从梵王生，故名人生本也。”[9]慧琳《一切经音义》卷二十六《大般涅槃经音义》：“那罗延，此云力士，或云天中，或云人中力士，或云金刚力士也，或云坚固力士。”[10]据此，那罗延似为右弼金刚。

不过，依据道宣《关中创立戒坛图经》：

> 凡诸鬼神，各有依住，故依地之神，名曰坚牢。乃至寺塔、山林、河海、风雨，如《长阿含经》，并依止所往而守卫之……今前列护佛塔神名，多出《华严》、《灌顶》、《孔雀王》、《贤愚》、《大集》、《大智论》等，以繁文故，于此总而叙之。神名

---

[1] 玄应《一切经音义》，见《一切经音义：三种校本合刊》，徐时仪校注，上海：上海古籍出版社，2008 年，第 11 页。

[2]《大正藏》第 54 卷，第 1078a 页。

[3] 参见：荻原雲來，上引书，第 1165b-1166a 页。

[4] 玄奘《大唐西域记》卷六“拘尸那揭罗国”条，季羡林等校注，北京：中华书局，1985 年，第 546-547 页。

[5]《大正藏》第 54 卷，第 421c 页。

[6] 玄应，上引书，第 65 页。

[7]《大正藏》第 54 卷，第 1078a 页。

[8]《大正藏》第 17 卷，第 626a-b 页。

[9] 玄应，上引书，第 497 页。

[10]《大正藏》第 54 卷，第 472b 页。

跋闍罗波尼(vajrapāṇi),梁言金刚；神名婆里旱[河但反](balin)[1],梁言力士；初坚固光曜神、二日光曜神、三须弥华神、四净云音神、五阿修罗王神(取修罗为名,非修罗也)、六胜光明神、七树音声神、八师子王神(如上,已解)、九淳厚光藏神、十珠髻华光神。右十二金刚、力士、神王,依《杂阿含经》:金刚神,持金刚杵,猛火炽然……《华严经》:"诸金刚神与微尘数力士[2],俱久发誓愿,侍卫如来,住持遗法。"[3]

故而,金刚、力士位居十二大神之首,地位显要;萧梁至唐初,金刚、力士似各有所指。

据《觉禅钞》卷一百二十二:金刚力士,名号有"一身二像"与"二身二像"之别。"一身成二像……《宝积经》云:'法王太子,今金刚力士是也。'云:二身变二尊。注《梵网经》云:'其二子誓护佛性,金刚力士二像是也,此力士也'……注《梵网经》云:'菩萨有千二王子,时千子发心成佛,其二子誓护佛性,今诸寺门金刚力士二像是也。'"[4]这一记载,或为金刚力士之原意[5]。

另据《大方广佛华严经》卷四十七《入法界品》:"有众生能行善者,及众贤圣、诸菩萨等,若向正道,若得果证,皆悉防卫而守护之,或作金刚力士,守护诸佛及佛住处。"[6]又,《大宝积经》卷八:"金刚力士,侍佛而自显耀;众人恐怖。自归作礼。"[7]

---

[1] 据法云《翻译名义集》卷二,"婆里旱,梁云力士。又梵云末罗,此云力。言力士者,梵本无文,译人义立。"参见:《大正藏》No.2131,第54卷,第1086b页。

梵语balin,汉译婆里旱、强力、福力、兵士、力士等,意为强者、大力士、英雄等。梵语malla,汉译末罗、力、力士、壮士、勇力等,意为强健之人、非常有力的人、职业角力者等。若依据法云记述,梵语似无"力士"一词。参见:1) Monier Monier-Williams, *opere citato*: 723, 793; 2) William Edward Soothill & Lewis Hodous, *A Dictionary of Chinese Buddhist Terms*, London: Kegan Paul, Trench, Trubner & Co. Ltd, 1937: 347; 3) 荻原雲来《漢訳対照梵和辭典》,東京:鈴木学術財团 / 講談社,1974年,第914a、1010a页。

[2] 这种力士,或许包括诺健那(nagna)。据玄应《一切经音义》卷二十四《阿毗达磨俱舍论音义》,"诺健那,此谓露形有,大力神名也"。玄应,上引书,第491页。

[3]《大正藏》第45卷,第809a-b页。

[4]《大正新修大藏经·图像》第5卷,第562c-563b页。

[5] 西晋竺法护译《大宝积经》卷九《密迹金刚力士会》对此有较详细地记载:"时有转轮圣王,名曰勇郡王……王有千子……其二正夫人,一名不行步,二名无虚损,从宫中出,洗身沐浴,适还去已,以香熏衣,坐莲华台妙胜床席。有二孩童自然来,上夫人膝上结加趺坐,端正殊好非世所见,有二十八大人之相……是二孩童则法神圣,一名法意,二名法念……其后二子各心念言,汝等正士,所志云何?法意太子曰:吾自要誓,诸人成得佛时,当作金刚力士,常亲近佛,在外威仪,省诸如来,一切秘要,常委托依,普闻一切诸佛秘要、密迹之事,信乐受憙不怀疑结。法念太子曰:诸正士,听吾心自誓言,诸仁成佛道身,当劝助使转法轮……其时诸子,此贤劫中千佛兴者是也。从拘留孙为始作佛,至楼由竟千佛也。其法意太子,则今金刚力士名密迹是也;其法念太子者,今识其梵天是也。"《大正藏》第11卷,第49b-53a页。

[6]《大正藏》第9卷,第696a页。

[7]《大正藏》第11卷,第44b页。

道宣《关中创立戒坛图经》表述诸神位置时，特别指出“下层四角大神，所谓金刚、力士、金毗罗、散脂，并护佛塔，故峙列四隅，以护持本也；东南角神，名跋阇罗波尼，又领般支分大军主神；西南角神，名婆里旱，又领般遮罗遮驮大军主神；西北角，神王名金毗罗，又领婆多祁利大军主神；东北角神将，名散脂，又领酰摩跋多大军主神”[1]。依据南山宗祖师道宣所制，金刚、力士、金毗罗、散脂，护持四维。其中，金刚和力士位居戒坛或塔寺之前，分列左右，即左侧（东侧）金刚，右侧（西侧）力士；金毗罗和散脂紧随其后，与力士、金刚对应设置。据此，疑唐初以前置于地上寺塔正门两侧的守护神应为金刚和力士。

又，南宋嘉熙元年（1237年）沙门宗鉴所集《释门正统》卷三记载：

> 于门两颊，应画执仗药叉是也。今殿中设释迦、文殊、普贤、阿难、迦叶、梵王、金刚者，此土之像也。阿难合掌，是佛堂弟，理非异仪。迦叶擎拳，本外道种，且附本习，以威来象；盖若以声闻入辅，则迦叶居左，阿难居右。若以菩萨入辅，则文殊居左，普贤居右。今四大弟子俱列者，乃见大、小乘各有二焉耳。梵王执炉，请转法轮。金刚挥杵，卫护教法也。[2]

这种造像组合形式，包括佛、弟子、菩萨、神王、金刚、力士等，应是中土所创。如北齐河清二年（563年）阿鹿交村七十人等“敬造石室一区，纵旷、东西、南北、上下五尺，□有一佛六菩萨、阿难、迦叶、八部、神王、金刚、力士”[3]，符合当时此土僧俗之观念，因为“伽蓝土地，护戒神王；金刚、力士，幽显灵祇。唯愿不违本誓”[4]。

受佛教影响，金刚、力士也成为当时南亚、东南亚及中土俗界流行的守护神，通常分置城门两侧。

古代东南亚之赤土，王“居僧祇城，有门三重，相去各百许步。每门图画飞仙、仙人、菩萨之像，县金花铃毦，妇女数十人，或奏乐，或捧金花。又饰四妇人，容饰如佛塔边金刚、力士之状，夹门而立，门外者持兵仗”[5]。

北魏“什翼珪始都平城……大筑郭邑，截平城西为宫城，四角起楼……自佛狸至

[1]《大正藏》第45卷，第809b页。

[2]《卍新纂大日本續藏經》（共90卷），東京：日本國書刊行會，1980-1989年，第75卷，第298a页。

[3] 参见胡聘之《山右石刻丛编》卷二，载《石刻史料新编》第一辑第20册，台北：新文丰出版公司，1979年，第14973-14974页。

[4] 怀海集编《百丈丛林清规》，仪润证义，载《卍新纂大日本续藏经》第63卷，第464a页。

[5]《隋书》卷八十二《南蛮·赤土》，点校本，北京：中华书局，1973年，第1833页。

万民，世增雕饰。正殿西筑土台，谓之白楼。万民禅位后，常游观其上。台南又有伺星楼。正殿西又有祠屋，琉璃为瓦。宫门稍覆以屋，犹不知为重楼，并设削泥采，画金刚、力士”[1]。

这种形象，后来甚至演化为南方世俗神灵，驱邪消灾。据《太平御览》引萧梁宗懔《荆楚岁时记》：“十二月八日，沐浴转除罪障”；“谚云：腊鼓鸣，春草生。村人并系细腰鼓，戴胡头，及作金刚、力士以逐大疫”[2]。

石窟寺乃地面佛寺的石化形式。中国佛教石窟寺所见最早的金刚力士，可能是云冈第7、8窟拱门两侧的“门神(dvārapāla)”。第9、10窟前室后壁门道两侧雕造的门神，水野清一和长广敏雄认为是第7、8窟外来护法立像的进一步汉化形式[3]。现存较为规制的金刚、力士，应是云冈北魏第三期洞窟外壁门道两侧的造像[4]。据不完全统计，云冈第5A、5B、26、30、31I、32F、35、35B、36A、36B、37、38、39、42等窟的窟门两侧皆雕造金刚力士，唯大多风化严重，细部不易辨识(图4)。水野清一与长广敏雄认为：这种“门神”，是手执金刚杵(vajra)、护持佛陀的金刚力士(vajrapāṇi)[5]。由于《云冈石窟》采用日、英双语刊行，因此他们把这种对称雕刻的门神，日文版直接迻录汉字“金刚力士”或“力士”，英文表述时则多用vajrapāṇi或vajrapāṇi guardian god，少数作guardian deity[6]。

我们认为云冈石窟门道两侧雕造的金刚力士，可能是平城佛教信徒与工匠在印度塔寺门前“执杖药叉”或“门神”的基础上，借鉴“什翼珪始都平城、(宫门)画金刚、力士”之传统形式，结合金刚力士“誓护佛性”、“守护诸佛及佛住处”之理念的一种汉化布局或再创造，即当时碑铭所言“金刚力士，在户之旁”[7]。

北魏迁洛后，虽然洛阳地区开始兴建石窟主要参考云冈，但龙门北魏洞窟前庭布

---

[1]《南齐书》卷五十七《魏虏》，点校本，北京：中华书局，1972年，第984-986页。

[2]《太平御览》卷二十七《时序部·冬》、卷三十三《时序部·寒》，影印宋本，北京：中华书局，1960年，第128、157页。

[3] 1)水野清一、長廣敏雄《雲岡石窟：西曆五世紀における中國北部佛教窟院の考古學的調查報告》，東方文化研究所調查，昭和十三年—昭和二十年，京都：京都大學人文科學研究所，第四卷(1952年)第19、81页，第五卷(1951年)第10、74页，第六卷(1951年)第18、95页，第七卷(1952年)第17、85页；2)阎文儒，上引书，第297页；3)八木春生，上引书，第357-359页。

[4] 宿白《云冈石窟分期试论》，见宿白《中国石窟寺研究》，北京：文物出版社，1996年，第85页。

[5] 水野清一、長廣敏雄，上引书，第二卷(1955年)第20、68页，第八/九卷(1953年)第18、86页。

[6] 水野清一、長廣敏雄，上引书，第二卷(1955年)第20、21、68、69页，Plan VIII；第十五卷(1955年)第44、47、49、51、52、53、55、57、59、145、147、148、149、151、152、153、155页，圖版68、82。

[7] 语出“刘碑寺造像碑”。参见：1)王景荃编《河南佛教石刻造像》，郑州：大象出版社，2008年，第206页；2)林玲爱，上引书，第261页。

局规律、外壁窟口两侧对称雕凿金刚、力士则在云冈石窟的基础上为当地所创造[1]。其中，正始二年(505)起工的宾阳中洞，前庭正壁门道两侧雕造金刚、力士。左侧(北侧)金刚保存较好(图5)，上身侧向窟门，造型孔武有力；头戴冠，双目圆睁，唇薄露齿，颈部较短，后具头光；上身袒裸，下身着裙，腰间束带，披帛交叉于腹前；左手贴腰紧握

图4　云冈第39窟门道两侧金刚、力士

图5　龙门宾阳中洞门道两侧金刚、力士

[1] 宿白《中国佛教石窟寺遗迹——3至8世纪中国佛教考古学》，北京：文物出版社，2010年，第38-39页。

金刚杵，右手于胸前展掌，跣足而立。右侧力士残损较甚，原貌不清。不过，略早于宾阳中洞开凿的莲花洞，尽管左侧金刚不存，但右侧力士保存尚好，力士上身侧向窟门，后有头光；上身袒裸，下身着裙，披帛交叉于胸前；左手于胸前展掌，右臂残，似无持物。北朝晚期开凿的路洞，左侧金刚亦毁，右侧力士头残，上身侧向窟门，袒上身，下着裙；左手展掌至胸前，右手似抚膝，跣足而立。莲花洞与路洞窟门右侧的护法像，表明力士手无持物。

此外，这一时期的造像碑，有些对我们探讨这种护法形象的名号颇具价值。1976 年在河南荥阳大海寺遗址出土的道晗造像碑，系北魏孝昌元年 (525 年) 雕造，现藏河南博物院。依据题铭，该碑正面龛内为“弥勒大像”，两侧各一弟子一菩萨，龛外两侧护法形象为“金刚”[1]。日本京都国立博物馆收藏的一件北魏神龟三年 (520 年) 造像碑，主尊亦作交脚弥勒，两侧各雕一身立菩萨；主尊双脚外侧对称雕出蹲狮与护法形象。两护法像皆一膝着地，一腿弓起，其中左侧持金刚杵者，榜题为“金钢力士”，右侧握拳者作“护塔善神”(图 6)[2]。这说明当时人们对金刚力士的理解，似与正统经典已有一定偏差，疑为供养人或工匠随意而为，或与“右弼金刚，以长善为务”有关。

图 6　北魏神龟三年 (520 年) 造像碑，日本京都国立博物馆收藏

唐“永徽元年 (650 年) 十月五日，汝州刺史、驸马都尉、渝国公刘玄意，敬造金刚力士”于宾阳南洞前壁门道左侧[3]。该像高 2.7 米，左半身残，面部右半尚存；上身袒裸，下身着裙，腿间可见如绅大带，披巾横于

[1] 王景荃，上引书，第 92-104 页。

[2] 大阪市立美術館编集《中国の石仏：莊厳なる祈り》/*Chinese Buddhist Stone Sculpture: Veneration of the Sublime*, 大阪市立美術館，1995 年，第 87、148 页。

[3] 该造像铭记，镌刻于金刚力士像左肩上部。参见：1) 李文生《龙门石窟的新发现及其他》，见李文生《龙门石窟与洛阳历史文化》，上海：上海人民美术出版社，1993 年，第 16-29 页；2) 刘景龙、李玉昆主编《龙门石窟碑刻题记汇录》，北京：中国大百科全书出版社，1998 年，第 49-50 页。

图 7　龙门宾阳南洞主室前壁示意图

胸腹间两道；右手握拳上举至肩，似立于山岩座上（图 7）。从前壁现存遗迹推断，该窟前壁门道右则无类似的护法形象。虽然刘玄意当时仅造一身护法像，但题名“金刚力士”，这或许说明萧梁时期的“金刚”与“力士”，自北魏迄唐初已混为一谈。故而，法云《翻译名义集》卷二《八部篇》引智圆《索隐记》云：“据经唯一人，今状于伽蓝之门，而为二像，夫应变无方，多亦无咎。”[1]尽管如此，龙门唐代洞窟外壁门道两侧雕造的金刚力士[2]，或与道宣所制戒坛、塔寺前左金刚、右力士有关。

（本文原为《龙门石窟唐代窟龛分期试论》中的一个附录，现抽出单行。）

[1]《大正藏》第 54 卷，第 1078a 页。

[2] 龙门石窟大卢舍那像龛造像为一铺九身，即一佛二弟子二菩萨二神王和金刚力士，系“大唐高宗天皇大帝之所建也，佛身通光座高八十五尺，二菩萨七十尺，迦叶、阿难、金刚、神王各高五十尺……”参见：刘景龙、李玉昆主编，上引书，第 379-381 页。

菩提像初探

一、引　言

图 1　龙门石窟擂鼓台北洞主尊

龙门石窟东山擂鼓台北洞主室正壁和左右侧壁各雕一坐佛,坐佛之间雕游戏坐菩萨像,前壁门道两侧各造一多臂菩萨立像。正壁主尊,结跏趺坐,五官漫漶,颈部三道,宽肩、挺胸、细腰、收腹,珠璎宝冠,奇珍交饰,项严繁复,臂钏精致,偏袒右肩；右臂与左小臂残损,左手似内敛置放腹前,双腿已残毁,东面而坐；下为方形束腰叠涩须弥座(图 1)。

迄今为止,学界对北洞正壁主像争议较大。多数学者认为,他是密教的大日如来[1]；也有学者认为是密教的释迦佛顶佛[2],有的认为是“释迦成道像”[3],有

[1] 参见：1) 李文生《龙门唐代密宗造像》,见李文生《龙门石窟与洛阳历史文化》,上海：上海人民美术出版社,1993 年,第 38-46 页；2) 温玉成《中国石窟与文化艺术》,上海：上海人民美术出版社,1993 年,第 349-350 页；3) 常青《初唐宝冠佛像的定名问题》,见《佛学研究》第 6 期(1997 年),第 91-97 页。

[2] 吕建福《中国密教史》,北京：中国社会科学出版社,1995 年,第 193 页。

“佛顶佛”之概念,现存汉译佛典中,似仅见于《陀罗尼集经》卷十二《佛说诸佛大陀罗尼都会道场印品》:“释迦如来顶上化佛,号佛顶佛。”参见《大正藏》第 18 卷,第 888b 页。又,梵语中有 uṣṇi(顶高、佛顶)或 uṣṇīṣa(顶、髻、佛顶、尊胜、最胜顶相)之名,似无“佛顶佛”之号。

[3] 肥田路美《唐代における仏陀伽耶金剛座真容像の流行について》,見町田甲一先生古稀紀念會編《論叢仏教美術史》,東京：吉川弘文館,1986 年,第 157-186 頁。

的认为是菩提瑞像[1]，还有学者推测"是'当今'的皇帝，即中宗的造像"[2]。

值得注意的是，擂鼓台北洞外立面窟门上方的一圆拱龛（原编 2071 号，现编擂鼓台区 5-32 龛），内造一佛、二弟子、二菩萨及金刚力士，主尊头部已残，结跏趺坐，偏袒右肩，左小臂内屈，手已残失，右小臂前伸，似垂手指地（图 2）。龛下题记作："佛弟子阎 / 门冬奉为 / 圣神皇帝 / 陛下及太 / 子诸王师 / 僧父母七 / 世先亡法 / 界一切众 / 生敬造菩 / 提像□龛 / 及诸菩萨 / 以此造像 / 功德普及 / 法界苍生 / 俱出爱河 / 咸升佛果 / 大足元年 / 三月八日 (701 年 4 月 20 日)/ 庄严成就 /。"[3]此龛应为北洞完工后开凿，龛内主像与北洞主尊样式相似，疑仿洞内主尊雕造[4]。倘若此推断不误，北洞主像应为菩提像。

图 2　龙门擂鼓台区第 5-32 龛（原编 2071 号）

[1] 1) 李玉珉《试论唐代降魔成道式装饰佛》，刊《故宫学术季刊》第二十三卷第三期 (2006 年)，第 39-90 页； 2) 李玉珉《四川菩提瑞像窟龛研究》，见重庆大足石刻艺术博物馆编《2005 年重庆大足石刻国际学术研讨会论文集》，北京：文物出版社，2007 年，第 548-561 页。

[2] 古正美《龙门擂鼓台三洞的开凿性质与定年》，见《龙门石窟一千五百周年国际学术讨论会论文集》，北京：文物出版社，1996 年，第 179 页。

[3] 参见：1) 陆增祥《八琼室金石补证》卷三十二《阎门冬题记》，影印本，北京：文物出版社，1985 年，第 211 页； 2) 刘景龙、李玉昆主编《龙门石窟碑刻题记汇录》，北京：中国大百科全书出版社，1998 年，第 631 页。

[4] 北洞外立面编号 2063 龛（现编第 5-9 号）外侧小龛、2064 龛（现编第 5-3 号）、2070 龛（现编第 5-31 号）、2072 龛（现编第 5-12 号）均晚于北洞开凿，尽管其主尊头部皆残，但均结跏趺坐，偏袒右肩，右手垂作触地印，或为同一题材。参见刘景龙、杨超杰编《龙门石窟总录》第拾贰卷，北京：中国大百科全书出版社，1999 年，第 38-40 页，图版 199、200、206、208。

二、菩 提 像

菩提像,汉文史料中有不同名称,既称“菩提像”[1]、“菩提树像”[2]或“摩诃菩提树像”[3],也叫“慈氏菩萨所作成道时像”[4],还作“真容像”[5]、“真容”[6]或“金刚座真容像”[7],表现的是“如来初成佛像”[8]。它的原创地,应是古代摩揭陀国的伽耶(Gayā)。

据冯承钧研究,“中国同印度交际最活动的时间,从来无及唐初百年者。这个时代出了一位玄奘大师,又出了一位建功异域的外交使臣王玄策”[9]。玄奘唐贞观元年(627年)西行求法,贞观十九年正月七日(645年2月8日)返抵长安,三月住弘福寺,奉敕撰《大唐西域记》[10],“记其所历诸国风俗”[11]。王玄策于唐贞观十七年(643年)、二十一年(647年)和显庆二年(657年)“前后三度”[12]奉使天竺,所著《中天竺行记》,亦作《王玄策行传》,成为当时中土了解印度的重要资料[13],如麟德三年(666年)百官奉敕撰写的《西国志》,文字六十卷,图画四十卷,合成一百卷,主要“依《(玄)奘法师行传》、《王玄策传》及西域道俗、任土所宜”[14]完成,惜早已亡佚。

《大唐西域记》卷八“摩揭陀国”条记述摩揭陀国伽耶菩提树东有精舍。

> 精舍故地,无忧王先建小精舍,后有婆罗门更广建焉……精舍既成,招募工人,欲图如来初成佛像。旷以岁月,无人应召。久之,有婆罗门来告众曰:“我善图写如来妙相。”众曰:“今将造像,夫何所须?”曰:“香泥耳。宜置精舍之中,并一灯照我,入已,坚闭其户,六月后乃可开门。”时诸僧众皆如其命。尚余四日,未满六月,众咸骇异,开以观之。见精舍内佛像俨然,结加趺坐,右足居上,左手

[1] 义净《大唐西域求法高僧传》,王邦维校注,北京:中华书局,1988年,第154页。
[2] 慧立、彦悰《大慈恩寺三藏法师传》,孙毓棠、谢方点校,北京:中华书局,2000年,第37页。
[3] 道世《法苑珠林》,周叔迦、苏晋仁校注,北京:中华书局,2003年,第906页。
[4] 慧立、彦悰,上引书,第66页。
[5] 义净,上引书,第153-154页。
[6] 义净,上引书,第10页。
[7] 智昇《续古今译经图纪》,见《大正藏》第55卷,第370a页。
[8] 玄奘《大唐西域记》,季羡林等校注,北京:中华书局,1985年,第675页。
[9] 冯承钧《王玄策事辑》,见冯承钧《西域南海史地考证论著汇辑》,北京:中华书局,1957年,第102页。
[10] 慧立、彦悰,上引书,第4-145页。
[11] 晁公武《郡斋读书志》,孙猛校证,上海:上海古籍出版社,1990年,第290页。
[12] 道世,上引书,第1661页。
[13] 冯承钧,上引书,第102-128页。
[14] 道世,上引书,第888页。

> 斂，右手垂，东面而坐，肃然如在。座高四尺二寸，广丈二尺五寸；像高丈一尺五寸，两膝相去八尺八寸，两肩六尺二寸。相好具足，慈颜若真，唯右乳上图莹未周。既不见人，方验神鉴。众咸悲叹，殷勤请知。有一沙门，宿心淳质，乃感梦见往婆罗门而告曰："我是慈氏菩萨，恐工人之思不测圣容，故我躬来图写佛像。垂右手者，昔如来之将证佛果，天魔来娆，地神告至，其一先出，助佛降魔。如来告曰：汝勿忧怖，吾以忍力，降彼必矣。魔王曰：谁为明证？如来乃垂手指地言：此有证。是时第二地神踊出作证。故今像手仿昔下垂。"众知灵鉴，莫不悲感。于是乳上未周，填厕众宝，珠璎宝冠，奇珍交饰……像今尚在，神工不亏。[1]

关于这身造像，唐道世《法苑珠林》卷二十九《感通篇·圣迹部》特别征引王玄策记载。

> 依《王玄策行传》云：西国瑞像无穷。且录摩诃菩提树像云：昔师子国王名尸迷佉拔摩[唐云功德云]梵王，遣二比丘来诣此寺。大者名摩诃諵[此云大名]，小者优波[此云授记]。其二比丘礼菩提树、金刚座讫，此寺不安置，其二比丘乃还其本国。王问比丘："往彼礼拜圣所来，灵瑞云何？"比丘报云："阎浮大地，无安身处。"王闻此语，遂多与珠宝，使送与此国王三谟陀罗崛多。因此以来，即是师子国比丘。又金刚座上尊像，元造之时，有一外客来告大众云："我闻慕好工匠造像，我巧能作此像。"大众语云："所须何物？"其人云："唯须香及水及料灯油艾料。"既足，语寺僧云："吾须闭门营造，限至六月，慎莫开门，亦不劳饮食。"其人一入，即不重出，唯少四日，不满六月。大众评章不和，各云："此塔中狭窄，复是漏身，因何累月不开见出？"疑其所为，遂开塔门。乃不见匠人，其像已成，唯右乳上有少许未竟。后有空神，惊诫大众云："我是弥勒菩萨。"像身东西坐，身高一丈一尺五寸，肩阔六尺二寸，两膝相去八尺八寸；金刚座高四尺三寸[2]，阔一丈二尺五寸。其塔本阿育王造，石钩栏塔。后有婆罗门兄弟二人，兄名王主，弟名梵主；兄造其塔高百肘，弟造其寺。其像自弥勒造成已来，一切道俗规模图写，圣变难定，未有写得。王使至彼，请诸僧众及此诸使人至诚殷请，累日行道、忏悔，兼申来意，方得图画，仿佛周尽。直为此像出其经本，向有十卷，将传此地。其匠宋法智等巧穷圣容，图写圣颜；来到京都，道俗竞摸。[3]

故而，玄奘所记"如来初成佛像"，依《王玄策行传》，亦作"摩诃菩提树像"或"金

---

[1] 玄奘，上引书，第 675 页。
[2]《大唐西域记》卷八"摩揭陀国"条作"四尺二寸"。
[3] 道世，上引书，第 906-907 页。

刚座上尊像”。

王玄策所记菩提树像，尤其像的尺寸，与玄奘所录几乎相同，盖因王玄策拜谒天竺圣迹时，常有“以笏量之”习惯[1]。此外，王玄策特别记述弥勒所造尊像置金刚座(Vajrāsana)上，故后来有“金刚座真容”之称。

> 又依《王玄策传》云：此汉使奉敕往摩伽陀国摩诃菩提寺立碑，至贞观十九年二月十一日(645年3月13日)，于菩提树下塔西建立，使典司门令史魏才书：昔汉魏君临，穷兵用武，兴师十万，日费千金，犹尚北勒阗颜，东封不到。大唐牢笼六合，道冠百王，文德所加，溥天同附。是故身毒诸国，道俗归诚。皇帝愍其忠款，遐轸圣虑，乃命使人朝散大夫行卫尉寺丞上护军李义表、副使前融州黄水县令王玄策等二十二人，巡抚其国，遂至摩诃菩提寺。其寺所菩提树下金刚之座，贤劫千佛，并于中成道。观严饰相好，具若真容；灵塔净地，巧穷天外。此乃旷代所未见，史籍所未详。皇帝远振鸿风，光华道树，爰命使人，届斯瞻仰。此绝代之盛事，不朽之神功。如何寝默詠歌、不传金石者也！乃为铭曰：“大唐抚运，膺图寿昌。化行六合，威棱八荒。身毒稽颡，道俗来王。爰发明使，瞻斯道场。金刚之座，千佛代居。尊容相好，弥勒规摹。灵塔壮丽，道树扶疏。历劫不朽，神力焉如。”[2]

王玄策等使臣奉敕立《身毒国摩诃菩提寺碑》于摩诃菩提寺，实修敬于菩提树下金刚座及弥勒所规摹之“真容”像。

摩诃菩提寺(图3)，玄奘称摩诃菩提僧伽蓝[3]，系梵语Mahābodhi-saṃghārāma之汉译[4]。《法苑珠林》征引《王玄策行传》所载摩诃菩提寺，与玄奘《大唐西域记》所记摩诃菩提僧伽蓝大同小异；两文皆记该寺系锡兰国王所造，只是王玄策所载国王及其派遣之比丘，较玄奘所记更为具体。据王玄策记载，狮子国(僧伽罗国 Siṃhala)王，名尸迷佉拔摩，唐云功德云，梵语称Śrīmeghavarṇa，巴利语作Sirimeghavaṇṇa，亦称吉祥云色王；在位时间应为公元362-390年，共二十八年。尸

---

[1] 据道宣《释迦方志》卷上《遗迹篇》：“(吠舍厘国)宫城西北六里寺塔，是说净名(Vimalakīrti，维摩诘，意译净名)处……寺东北四里许塔，是净名故宅基，尚多灵神。其舍叠砖，传云积石，即说法现疾处也。近使者王玄策以笏量之，止有一丈，故方丈之名因而生焉。”道宣《释迦方志》，范祥雍点校，北京：中华书局，1983年，第48-49页。

[2] 道世，上引书，第908-909页。参见《全唐文》卷九百九十《阙名·身毒国摩诃菩提寺碑》，影印本，北京：中华书局，1983年，第10248-10249页。

[3] 玄奘对该寺有详细记载，参见：玄奘，上引书，第693-698页。

[4] 义净674年前后游历此地时，称之为金刚大觉寺(Vajra-mahābodhisaṃghārāma？)。参见：义净，上引书，第103页。

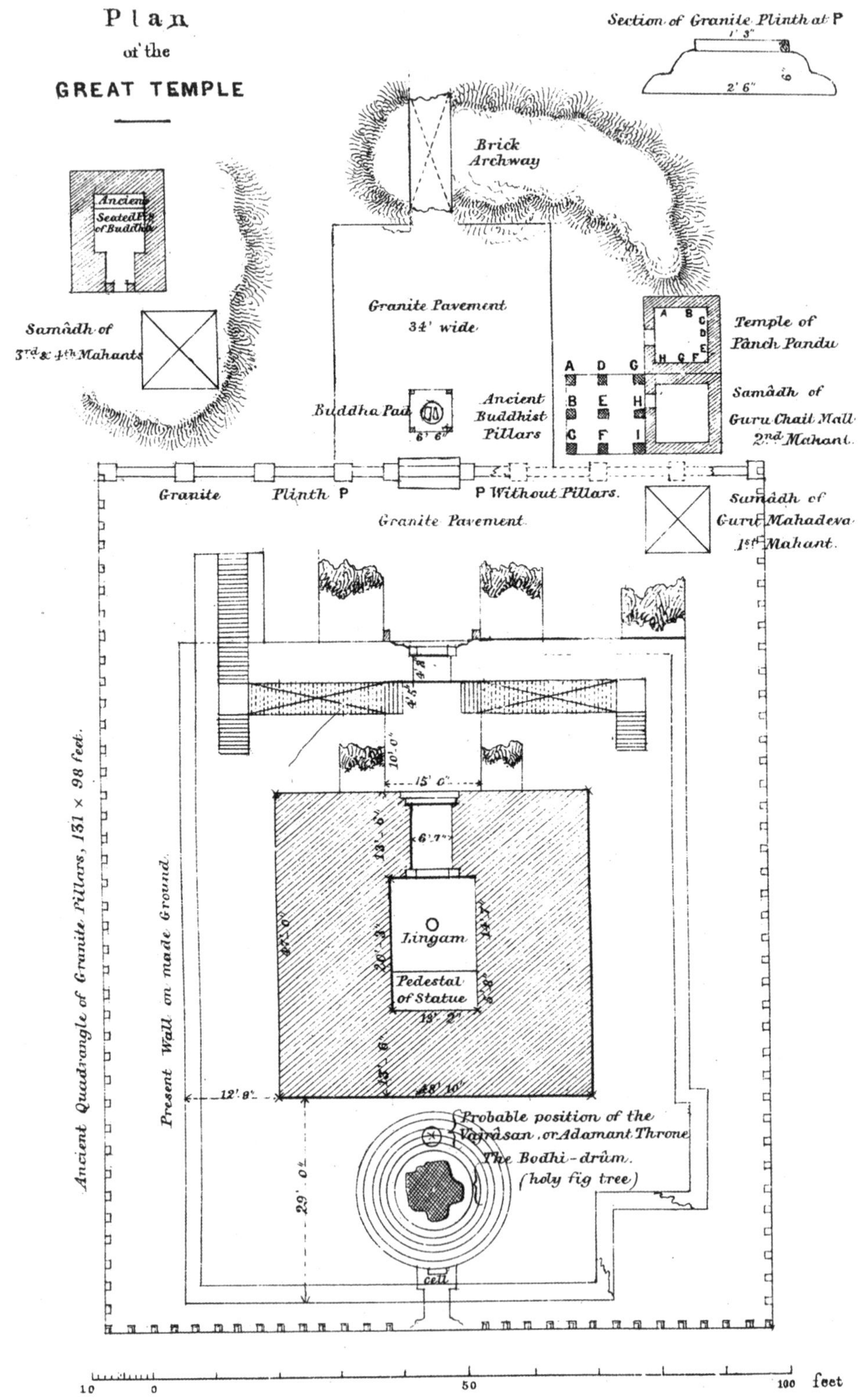

图 3　印度伽耶摩诃菩提寺平面图

迷佉拔摩登基之后，曾修复大寺 (Mahāvihāra)，重集僧众，在狮子国佛教史上占有重要地位[1]。身毒国王，名三谟陀罗崛多，亦作三谟陀罗笈多，梵语作Samudra Gupta，意译海护，约公元 320 年以后即位，380 年之前驾崩[2]。据此，摩诃菩提寺建造的时间，应为公元 4 世纪后半叶[3]。实际上，依据摩诃菩提寺出土之碑铭，狮子国僧俗从公元前 150 年到公元 800 年不断拜谒菩提树及金刚座，多渴望"向正道、得果证"[4]。

大约从公元 600 年到 1200 年，摩诃菩提寺经历了多次重修[5]。尽管玄奘和王玄策所瞻仰并详细记述的菩提树像早已不存，但摩诃菩提寺僧众迄今仍保持着崇奉菩提树及金刚座之传统，菩提树下成道像一直是摩诃菩提寺的主流朝拜形象，如现存大塔面向金刚座的那身(图4)[6]。又，该寺现存较早的一件触地印成道像，系用黑色玄武岩雕造，藏于摩诃菩提寺内一小院中。像高 5.5 呎 (1.68 米)，结跏趺坐，螺发，偏袒右肩，左手内敛置于腹前，右手垂作触地印。像座铭文为 Kuṭila 体，雕造年代应为 9-10 世纪

图 4　摩诃菩提寺金刚座及大塔西侧面成道像

[1] Wilhelm Geiger, ed. & tr., *Cūḷavaṃsa being the more recent part of the Mahāvaṃsa,* translated from the German into English by C. Mabel Rickmers, London: Pali Text Society, 1929, Part I: 1-8, 351; Part II: X.

[2] R. C. Majumdar et al, *An Advanced History of India,* 4th ed., Madras: Macmillan India Limited, 1978: 138-141.

[3] 参照玄奘记载，菩提像的塑造应在寺院建造完工之后；而王玄策命宋法智等人图写之圣容，应是摩诃菩提寺的菩提树像。

[4] T. Bloch, "Notes on Bōdh Gayā" , in: *Archaeological Survey of India: Annual Report 1908-09*: 139-158, esp. 156-157.

[5] T. Bloch, *opere citato*: 153-155.

[6] T. Bloch, *opere citato*: 139-158, Pl. L.

图 5　摩诃菩提寺藏成道像

(图 5)。这身造像之规模、材质及像座细部，与摩诃菩提寺第一层佛殿内像座相似，故有学者推测原为摩诃菩提寺主殿之像，但缺乏可靠证据。尽管如此，这件造像的姿态是典型的“如来初成佛像”，类似形象在印度佛教造型艺术中多有发现[1]。

印度北方邦勒克瑙博物馆收藏的一件浮雕 (No. B208)，出土于秣菟罗 Jamālpur 遗址，可能原置贵霜时期修造的胡维色迦 (Huviṣka) 大寺。该浮雕表现多幅佛传场景 (图 6)，包括成道像[2]。秣菟罗博物馆收藏的另一件同期佛传浮雕 (No. H. 1)，出土于秣菟罗 Rājghāt 遗址，也表现了成道像[3]。不过，秣菟罗出土的两件浮雕佛传中的成道像，皆作螺发，通肩披衣，左手敛，右手垂作触地印，结跏趺坐。萨尔纳特 (Sārnāth) 的佛传雕刻，多以造像碑形式表现，通常采用四相或八相图表现。当地艺术家或工匠对成道题材给予很大关注，同时加入了若干新因素，可以分作两种类型：

[1] R. Mitra, *Bodh Gayā: The Great Buddhist Temple, the Hermitage of Śakyamuni,* Calcutta: Bengal Secretariat Press, 1878: 132-133, Pl. XI.

[2] J. Ph. Vogel, “The Mathurā School of Sculpture”, in: *Archaeological Survey of India: Annual Report 1909-10*: 63-79, esp. 69-70, Pl. XXVa.

[3] R. C. Sharma, *Buddhist Art: Mathura School,* New Delhi: Wiley Eastern Limited/New Age International Limited, 1995: Pl. 168.

图 6　勒克瑙博物馆藏佛传浮雕

一种作为四相图或八相图之一相，另一种则系单幅成道场景[1]。在四相图或八相图中，佛螺发，大多偏袒右肩，个别通肩披衣，左手内敛置于腹前，右手垂作触地印，结跏趺坐，如萨尔纳特遗址寺院区出土的一件八相图造像碑，大约雕造于 5 世纪，表现了这一题材[2]。单幅场景的触地印成道像，现仅存一件，1905 年出土于同一遗址（图 7)。佛头已毁，双臂残损，偏袒右肩，左手内敛置于腹前，右手垂作触地印，结跏趺坐于须弥座上；佛座表面雕出二地神，座上沿铭文作："佛教高僧般豆笈多 (Bandhugupta) 奉施"，铭文字体可定在 6-7 世纪[3]。这是迄今所知印度现存最早的单幅触地印成道像。加尔各答印度博物馆收藏的另一件八相图，出土于那烂陀 (Nālandā)，系波罗王朝 (Pāla) 时期 (8-12 世纪) 雕造，中央主像结跏趺坐，螺发，偏袒右肩，左手内敛置于腹前，右手垂作触地印[4]。加尔各答印度博物馆收藏的另一件造像碑（图 8)，则出土于比哈尔 (Bihār)，大约雕造于波罗王朝后期，主尊珠璎宝冠，奇珍交饰，佩饰项严，偏袒右肩，左手内敛置于腹前，右手垂作触地印，结跏趺坐于莲座上，表现了菩提树下成道场景[5]。

上述遗物表明：菩提树下成道像，在印度有两种表现形式。一种螺发，偏袒右肩，结跏趺坐，左手内敛置于腹前，右手垂作触地印，通称触地印佛像 (Buddha in *bhūmisparśamudrā*)，象征悉达多太子在伽耶菩提树下降魔成道。另一种"珠璎宝冠，奇珍交饰"，佩项严及臂钏，余同前者，通称宝冠佛 (Crowned Buddha)，表现悉达多太子指名地神作证、行将成道前之光彩形象。这位穿着华贵的太子，结跏趺

[1] Usha Rani Tiwari, *Sculptures of Mathura and Sarnath: A Comparative Study* (*Upto Gupta Period*), Delhi: Sundeep Prakashan, 1998: 127-130, Pl. 72-79.

[2] John. H. Marshall and S. Konow, "Sārnāth", in: *Archaeological Survey of India: Annual Report 1906-07*: 68-101, esp. 92-93, Pl. XXVIII4.

[3] F. O. Oertel, "Excavations at Sārnāth", in: *Archaeological Survey of India: Annual Report 1904-05*: 50-104, esp. 80-81, Pl. XXVIIIa.

[4] Debala Mitra, *Buddhist Monuments,* Calcutta: Sahitya Samsad, 1971: 259, Pl. 20.

[5] Debala Mitra, *opere citato*: 262, Pl. 32.

图 7　萨尔纳特遗址出土造像碑

图 8　加尔各答印度博物馆藏菩提像

坐 (paryaṅka-banddha)，偏袒右肩 (ekāṃsam uttarāsaṅgaṃ kṛtvā)，璎珞庄严 (ābharaṇa)，珠瓔宝冠 (mukuṭa)、项严 (kaṇṭhābharaṇa) 宽大、臂钏 (keyūra) 精致。在印度早期佛教雕塑中，太子辞别车匿后从未发现佩戴任何饰物[1]。故而，我们可以揣度玄奘和王玄策等人昔日在印度所见菩提像之形貌。

远在东南亚的缅甸，与佛成道地伽耶曾有密切交往，惟现存早期雕塑中似不见宝冠佛像[2]。钦巴 (Khin Ba) 遗址曾出土一件镏金银舍利盒 (图 9)，现藏摩萨博物馆 (Hmawza Museum)。舍利盒周围雕刻四佛，皆螺发，偏袒右肩，左手内敛置于腹前，右手垂作触地印。依据铭刻，这四身佛像分别表现的是释迦佛及其前三佛，即 Kassapa（迦叶佛），Kakusandha（拘留孙佛），

图 9　缅甸摩萨博物馆藏银质舍利盒

[1] Debala Mitra, *opere citato*: 259-262, Pls. 20, 32.

[2] David L. Snellgrove, *The Image of the Buddha,* New Delhi: Vikas Publishing House Pvt Ltd/ UNESCO, 1978: 145-147, 311-313.

Koṅgāmana（拘那含佛），雕造时间应为5、6世纪[1]。此外，蒲甘地区金洛(Kyinlo)佛塔和敏蒲甘(Myinpagan)佛塔也出土了若干触地印成道像，大多为11世纪雕造。其中的一件许愿碑上表现百身"如来集会"，均结跏趺坐，螺发，偏袒右肩，作触地印[2]。至于1090年完工的蒲甘阿难寺(Ānanda Temple)，保存了大量造像碑。其中的三件，皆螺发，偏袒右肩，左手内敛置于腹前，右手垂作触地印，结跏趺坐，分别表现了悉达多树下落座、魔军战扰和魔女诱惑三个连续场景[3]。

三、那烂陀寺与摩诃菩提寺

魏晋南北朝迄隋唐时期，中土高僧西行求法留学之处，主要是摩揭陀的那烂陀寺和摩诃菩提寺。那烂陀寺在恒河右岸，古王舍城之北，其名不见法显记载。该寺系笈多国王铄迦罗阿迭多(Śakrāditya，帝日王)[4]于5世纪上半始造，后"历代君王继世兴建"[5]，至唐蔚为印度最大寺院，被誉为"像法之泉源，众圣之都会也"[6]。至于摩诃菩提寺，位于王舍城西南，乃释迦成道之地，因有佛之真容像，故为求法者必礼之处[7]。实际上，那烂陀寺也有菩提像。据《大慈恩寺三藏法师传》卷三："那烂陀寺西北有大精舍，高三百余尺，婆罗阿迭多王(Bālāditya，幼日王)[8]之所建也，庄严甚丽，其中佛像同菩提树像。"[9]

现存汉文史料中，以法显最早亲历并记述伽耶城及菩提树，时间大约在东晋元兴二、三年(404-405年)间。不过，法显仅记"后人皆于中起塔立像，今皆在……佛得道处有三僧伽蓝，皆有僧住，众僧民户供给饶足，无所乏少。戒律严峻，威仪、坐起、入众之法，佛在世时圣众所行，以至于今"[10]。故而，法显似乎没有注意到该地有弥勒所造菩提树像。智猛于后秦弘始六年(404年)自长安西行求法。"至迦维罗卫国，见佛

[1] David L. Snellgrove, *opere citato*: 147, Fig.100.

[2] Taw Sein Ko, "Some Excavations at Pagan", in: *Archaeological Survey of India: Annual Report 1905-06*: 131-134.

[3] Charles Duroisell, "The Stone Sculptures in the Ānanda Temple at Pagan", in: *Archaeological Survey of India: Annual Report 1913-14*: 63-97, esp. 92-93, Pls. XXXVI 50, XXXVII 51-52.

[4] 一般认为铄迦罗阿迭多系印度笈多王朝第四代王鸠摩罗笈多一世(Kumāragupta I)，在位时间为公元415-455年。参见：玄奘，上引书，第754页注释（二）。

[5] 玄奘，上引书，第747-757页。参见：义净，上引书，第112-131页。

[6] 李华《大唐东都大圣善寺故中天竺国善无畏三藏和尚碑铭并序》，《大正藏》第50卷，第290c页。

[7] 参见汤用彤《隋唐佛教史稿》，北京：中华书局，1982年，第73-74页。

[8] 6世纪初在位。参见：1) 玄奘，上引书，第748页及756页［注释］五；2) 义净，上引书，第115页及128页［注释］四〇。

[9] 慧立、彦悰，上引书，第73页。

[10] 法显《法显传》，章巽校注，上海：上海古籍出版社，1985年，第122页。

发、佛牙，及肉髻骨、佛影、佛迹，炳然具在。又睹泥洹坚固之林（涅槃处），降魔菩提之树（成道处），猛喜心内充，设供一日，兼以宝盖大衣覆降魔像。”[1]智猛所覆“降魔像”，疑为后世所言“如来初成佛像”。不过，佛像是否珠璎宝冠，奇珍交饰，佩饰项严及臂钏？是否偏袒右肩，左手敛，右手垂作触地印？则不得而知。

上述珠璎宝冠、奇珍交饰、佩饰项严及臂钏、偏袒右肩、左手敛、右手垂作触地印之佛像，传为弥勒所造，或者说弥勒“图写佛像”、“弥勒规摹”真容之说，似与5世纪以降无著、世亲及护法、戒贤一派有关[2]。

“无著(Asaṅga)、世亲(Vasubhandu)是北印犍陀罗人，兄弟二人都在有部出家。无著先是修习小乘空观，感到不满足，后经弥勒的指点而改信大乘，所以他所传习的是弥勒学说。世亲对有部的阿毗达磨很有研究，著《俱舍论》，表示对小乘很有自信，所以那时他的立场是反对大乘的，后来得到无著的帮助改宗大乘，兄弟两人就共同弘扬弥勒的学说。弥勒的学说是以《瑜伽师地论》为根本”[3]。“《瑜伽师地论》之本地分，即弥勒所作之本母也”。此外，佛在菩萨藏（即大乘经典）中所说戒学要义，“原本散见于佛说契经中，由弥勒菩萨综集而成书”。约当中土东晋(317-420年)之前，“印土弥勒之学犹黯然未彰”[4]。吕澂认为：据《婆薮盘豆传》记载，世亲深得笈多朝正勤日王（铄迦罗阿迭多）和新日王（婆罗阿迭多）两代的信仰，两王曾捐助世亲建造寺庙，或系那烂陀寺一部分，因为玄奘曾看过世亲讲学的场所。无著、世亲的学说出自弥勒。弥勒并非实在的人，而是居住于兜率天、将要成佛的菩萨。无著、世亲所传，以弥勒署名的书有五部，即《瑜伽师地论》、《分别瑜伽论》、《分别中边论》、《大乘庄严经论》和《金刚般若论》。这五部书都是弥勒说，所以称为“弥勒五论”，其中《瑜伽师地论》是五论中主要的一部。无著、世亲学说的基本典据，就是《瑜伽师地论》。那烂陀寺建成后，以无著、世亲学说为中心，对各种佛学思想同时弘扬。这一派的学者，主要在那烂陀寺活动，著名者有护法、德慧、安慧、光友、戒贤等，都极为推崇弥勒。其中，护法(Dharmapāla)出家后，便去那烂陀寺，其后在该寺当主持，时年仅二十余岁。护法主持寺学时，主要是瑜伽行派。传说护法与人辩论时，曾说“释迦后应是弥勒成佛”乃弥勒的主张。护法门下最出色之高足，是戒贤

[1] 僧佑《出三藏记集》卷十五《智猛法师传》，苏晋仁、萧錬子点校，北京：中华书局，1995年，第579-580页。

[2] 王邦维在整理义净《大唐西域求法高僧传》时，对该书卷上“太州玄照法师”条中“仰慈氏所制真容”有较详细的注释，颇具启发。参见：义净，上引书，第20-21页[注释]二三。

[3] 吕澂《印度佛学源流略讲》，上海：上海人民出版社，1979年，第185页。

[4] 吕澂《瑜伽菩萨戒本羯磨讲要》，见《吕澂佛学论著选集》卷二，济南：齐鲁书社，1991年，第1005-1041页。

(Śīlabhadra 尸罗跋陀罗)。护法 29 岁时,即大约 543 年前后,离开那烂陀寺而赴佛成道地伽耶,在摩诃菩提寺住了三、四年,修习禅观并从事著述。玄奘和义净都曾翻译过护法的著作[1]。护法离职后,戒贤受命主持那烂陀寺讲座,到玄奘抵那烂陀时,他已 106 岁,是玄奘的老师。故“戒贤,法相之大师,传护法唯识之学”[2],“常愿生于尊 (兜率天) 宫”[3]。因此推崇弥勒,系那烂陀寺包括摩诃菩提寺僧众之传统[4]。

现存文献表明:摩诃菩提寺的菩提树像和那烂陀寺的同类造像,因其“具若真容”在中古时期受到了各地佛教徒,尤其瑜伽行学派的极大推重。这种佛像,应该是“珠瓔宝冠,奇珍交饰”,佩项严、臂钏,偏袒右肩,左手内敛置于腹前,右手垂作触地印,结跏趺坐的“宝冠佛”。如沉浸世亲《俱舍论》之高僧玄照,以贞观 (627-649 年) 中杖锡西迈,“渐次南上,到莫诃菩提,复经四夏。自恨生不遇圣,幸睹遗踪。仰慈氏所制真容,着精诚而无替。爰以翘敬之余,沈情《俱舍》,既解《对法》,清想律仪,两教斯明。后之那烂陀寺,留住三年。就胜光 (Jinaprabha) 法师学《中》、《百》等论,复就宝师子 (Ratnasiṃha) 大德受《瑜伽十七地》。禅门定潋,亟睹关涯。既尽宏纲,遂往弶[巨亮反]伽河北,受国王苫部供养”[5]。

王玄策三次奉使印度,其中两次游历摩诃菩提寺,瞻仰菩提树像,“观严饰相好,具若真容”。因感“此乃旷代所未见,史籍所未详”,故为此像出其经本,请工匠宋法智图写圣颜。后带回京都,“道俗竞摸”。

玄奘法师西行求法前,曾从长安大觉寺道岳法师学《俱舍论》。后“誓游西方,以问所惑,并取《十七地论》以释众疑,即今之《瑜伽师地论》也”[6],换言之,“大师去国,旨在取《瑜伽》大论”[7]。故而,虽在那揭罗曷国佛顶骨城时“印得菩提树像”[8],但玄奘仍远赴瑜伽行派重镇、摩揭陀国那烂陀寺和摩诃菩提寺,“欲礼菩提树像”[9]。

---

[1] 吕澂《印度佛学源流略讲》,第 165-167、184-217 页。据吕澂研究,“玄奘受护法之学,义理究密,远出古旧……能以究密之思,理解传本,以为宣译”。吕澂《佛典汎论》,上海:商务印书馆,1935 年,第 16 页。

[2] 汤用彤,上引书,第 142 页。

[3] 慧立、彦悰,上引书,第 67 页。

[4] 吕澂《印度佛学源流略讲》,第 163-170、184-217 页。

[5] 义净,上引书,第 9-10 页。

[6] 慧立、彦悰,上引书,第 9-10 页。

[7] 汤用彤,出处同上。

[8] 慧立、彦悰,上引书,第 37 页。

[9] 慧立、彦悰,上引书,第 55 页。

"法师至，礼菩提树及慈氏菩萨所作成道时像，至诚瞻仰讫，五体投地，悲哀懊恼，自伤叹言：'佛成道时，不知漂沦何趣。今于像季，方乃至斯缅惟业障一何深重，悲泪盈目。'时逢众僧解夏，远近辐凑数千人，观者无不呜噎。"[1]依据《大唐故三藏玄奘法师行状》："法师从少以来，常愿生弥勒佛所。及游西方，又闻无著菩萨兄弟，亦愿生睹史多天宫，奉事弥勒，并得如愿，俱有证验，益增克励。自至玉花，每因翻译及礼忏之际，恒发愿上生睹史多天，见弥勒佛。除翻经时以外，若昼若夜，心心相续，无暂倦废。从翻《大般若》讫后，即不复翻译，唯行道礼忏……至（麟德元年）正月三日（664年2月4日），法师又告门人：'吾恐无常，欲往辞佛。'遂与弟子等往，先造俱胝(koṭi)[2]像所，礼忏辞别。"[3]临终之际，玄奘又命塑工宋法智[4]于嘉寿殿竖菩提树像骨，"复口说偈教傍人云：'南无弥勒如来应正等觉，愿与含识速奉慈颜；南无弥勒如来所居内众，愿舍命已必生其中。'"[5]这既表明：玄奘毕生奉传无著、世亲瑜伽行派学说，创慈恩宗（法相宗/唯识宗），临终之际在菩提树像前礼忏，祈求往生兜率，值遇弥勒，证得佛果[6]；同时也暗示出：弥勒与菩提像乃一固定组合形式。又，高僧灵运"追寻圣迹，与僧哲同游。越南溟，达西国。极闲梵语，利物在怀。所在至处，君王礼敬。遂于那烂陀画慈氏真容、菩提树像，一同尺量，妙简工人。赍以归国，广兴佛事，翻译圣教，实有堪能矣"[7]。

---

[1] 慧立、彦悰，上引书，第66页。

[2] 玄应《一切经音义》卷二十四《阿毗达磨俱舍论音义》："俱胝，陟迟反。或言俱致，此当亿，谓千万也。或十万为亿，或万万为亿。西国俱胝或千万，或十亿，或百亿，而甚不同，故存本名耳。"玄应《一切经音义》，见《一切经音义：三种校本合刊》，徐时仪校注，上海：上海古籍出版社，2008年，第490页。

[3]《大正藏》第50卷，第219a-c页。

[4] 此塑工宋法智，应是随王玄策等到印度，在摩诃菩提寺巧穷圣容、图写圣颜的宋法智。参见：冯承钧，上引书，第112页。

[5] 麟德元年二月十七日（664年3月19日），法师"向寺主慧德具说前事。法师又云：'玄奘一生以来所修福慧，准斯相貌，欲似功不唐捐，信如佛教因果并不虚也。'遂命嘉尚法师具录所翻经、论，合七十四部，总一千三百三十八卷。又录：造俱胝画像、弥勒像各一千帧，又造塑像十俱胝……至二十三日，设斋嚫施。其日，又命塑工宋法智，于嘉寿殿竖菩提像骨已，因从寺众及翻经大德并门徒等乞欢喜辞别，云：'玄奘此毒身深可厌患，所作事毕，无宜久住，愿以所修福慧回施有情，共诸有情同生睹史多天、弥勒内眷属中，奉事慈尊；佛下生时，亦愿随下，广作佛事，乃至无上菩提'……复口说偈教傍人云：'南无弥勒如来应正等觉，愿与含识速奉慈颜；南无弥勒如来所居内众，愿舍命已，必生其中……'至（二十）五日（3月27日）夜半，弟子光等问云：'和尚决定得生弥勒内众不？'法师报云：'得生。'言讫，喘息渐微，少间神游"。慧立、彦悰，上引书，第219-222页。

[6] 在隋唐佛教各个宗派中，慈恩宗，亦作法相宗或唯识宗，被看作最接近于印度佛学，其学说基本上继承印度瑜伽行学派。参见：1) 吕澂《中国佛学源流略讲》，第183-191、335-352页；2) 汤用彤，上引书，第141-157页。

[7] 义净，上引书，第168页。

义净仰慕传承世亲律学之德光(Guṇaprabha),因“德光乃再弘律藏”[1]。674年前后,义净“往大觉寺,礼真容像。山东道俗所赠絁绢,持作如来等量袈裟,亲奉披服。濮州玄律师附罗盖数万,为持奉上。曹州安道禅师寄拜礼菩提像,亦为礼讫。于时,五体布地,一想虔诚。先为东夏四恩,普及法界含识。愿龙华初会,遇慈氏尊,并契真宗,获无生智”[2]。值得注意的是,在义净行将启程求法之前,竟有各地信徒托付义净代之拜谒、瞻礼,甚至供奉菩提树像。义净游历印度之后,“以天后证圣之元乙未(695年)仲夏还至河洛,将梵本经、律、论近四百部合五十万颂,金刚座真容一铺,舍利三百粒。天后敬法、重人,亲迎于上东门外”[3]。中土传统上称佛教为像教,即立像设教。唐李周翰注《文选》时明确指出:“‘象教’,谓为形象以教人也。”[4]故而,至迟迄开元初年,佛像仍为传法之主要媒介或手段之一。义净自印度返国时仅请“金刚座真容像”,由此可见它在当时佛教信徒心目中的崇高地位。

> 中天竺国三藏法师地婆诃罗(Divākara),唐言日照,婆罗门种。幼而出家,住摩诃菩提及那烂陀寺。三藏风仪温雅,神机朗俊。负笈从师,研精累岁,器成琱玉,学擅青蓝。承沙门玄奘传教东归,思慕玄门,留情振旦,既而占风圣代,杖锡来仪,载阐上乘,助光神化。爰以永隆初岁(680年),言届京师。高宗弘显释门,克隆遗寄,乃诏:缁徒龙象,帝邑英髦。道诚律师、薄尘法师十大德等,于魏国西寺翻译经论之次……更译《密严》等经论十有余部,合二十四卷,并皇太后御制序文,深加赞述,今见流行于代焉。三藏辞乡之日,其母尚存。无忘鞠育之恩,恒思顾复之报,遂诣神都,抗表天阙,乞还旧国。初未之许,再三固请,有敕从之。京师诸德,造绯罗珠宝袈裟,附供菩提树像[5]。

地婆诃罗来中土前长期居住摩诃菩提寺及那烂陀寺,浸透二寺宗旨,疑深受护法、戒贤一派影响,推崇弥勒规摹之菩提树像。又,地婆诃罗于两京东西太原寺及西京弘福寺译经时,沙门薄尘担当证义。咸亨(670-673年)年间奉诏入武则天家庙太

---

[1] 1) 义净《南海寄归内法传》,王邦维校注,北京:中华书局,1995年,第205页;2) 吕澂《印度佛学源流略讲》,第197-198页。

[2] 义净《大唐西域求法高僧传》,王邦维校注,北京:中华书局,1988年,第153-154页。

[3] 智昇《开元释教录》卷九《总括群经录》上“义净”条,见《大正藏》第55卷,第568b页。

[4]《六臣注文选》,影印日本足利学校藏宋刊明州本,北京:人民文学出版社,2008年,第891页。

[5] 法藏《华严经传记》,见《大正藏》第51卷,第154c页。

原寺之思恒，深为薄尘所重。思恒后来参与义净译场，亦作证义，或许目睹过义净所请“金刚座真容像”。据《唐大荐福寺故大德思恒律师志文并序》，思恒“陟方山、五台间”，“尝致舍利七粒，后自增多，移在新瓶，潜归旧所。有为之福，所以济群品也，造菩提像一铺”[1]。思恒所造菩提像，疑与地婆诃罗或义净有关。

宋叶廷珪《海录碎事》卷九下《圣贤人事部 · 奉佛仙门》引武周时期沈佺期（？-714 年）《菩提像文》：“欢喜园，沈佺期奉敕撰《菩提像文》：冕旒多暇，每寻欢喜之园；舆辇经行，即对醍醐之沼。”[2]又，据周一良研究：“‘道场’本来是用来翻译 bodhimaṇḍa 的词，指菩提树下释迦成佛之地，后来演变成举行佛教仪式的地方……武则天是一个虔诚的佛教徒，她在长安、洛阳的宫中都修建了寺院，改称‘内道场’……（尽管）内道场首创人不可确言，（但）武则天是一位导入新观念、新制度、创用新字的女皇，因此，她很可能赞同隋炀帝创造的新名词而放弃旧名‘寺’。”[3]这种改动是否有崇奉摩诃菩提寺，即菩提树像之意？

综上所述，菩提像既是 7 世纪天竺流行的佛教造像，也是当时中土信徒推崇至上的礼拜对象[4]，这种形象在武则天前后确为朝野所重。

四、中土遗存

中国现存最早的纪年菩提像遗迹，疑为四川浦江飞仙阁第 60 龛。该龛主尊头戴宝冠，双耳缀饰，佩臂钏，偏袒右肩；结跏趺坐，左手内敛置于腹前，右手垂作触地印。龛外左侧刻“永昌元年 (689 年) 五月为天皇天后敬造瑞像壹龛□□合家大小□通供养”[5]。此外，广元千佛崖第 366 号窟（菩提瑞像窟），主尊珠璎宝冠，奇珍交饰、颈饰项严，右臂佩钏，偏袒右肩；结跏趺坐，左手内敛置于腹前，右手垂作触地印（图 10）；窟口右壁碑额篆书“菩提像颂”，碑文题作“大唐利州刺史毕公柏堂寺菩提瑞像颂并序”，推测该窟开凿于唐睿宗景云、延和年间 (710-712 年)[6]。依据近年调查及刊布的资料，四川地区至少保存了十六龛此类造像，其中最晚纪年者为巴中南龛第 103 龛

[1] 王昶《金石萃编》卷七十七 · 叶一、二《唐大荐福寺故大德思恒律师志文并序》，影印本，北京：中国书店，1985 年。

[2] [宋] 叶廷珪《海录碎事》，李之亮校点，北京：中华书局，2002 年，第 457 页。

[3] 周一良《唐代密宗》附录三，钱文忠译，上海：上海远东出版社，1996 年，第 84-85 页。

[4] 据李玉珉统计，“初唐至盛唐是菩提瑞像制作的鼎盛时期”。李玉珉《试论唐代降魔成道式装饰佛》，上引书，第 65 页。

[5] 雷玉华、王建平《四川菩提瑞像研究》，见李正刚主编《2004 年龙门石窟国际学术研讨会文集》，郑州：河南人民出版社，2006 年，第 492-497 页。

[6] 罗世平《广元千佛崖菩提瑞像考》，见《故宫学术季刊》，第九卷二期 (1991 年)，第 117-138 页。

（乾符四年，即877年）[1]。四川石窟中的菩提像，主要有两种类型：一种结跏趺坐，珠瓔宝冠，奇珍交饰，偏袒右肩，左手内敛置于腹前，右手垂作触地印，如浦江飞仙阁第60龛和广元千佛崖第366窟主尊。这种类型占多数，且与龙门擂鼓台北洞主尊相同；另一种数量较少，造型与前一种基本相似，唯螺发，如广元千佛崖第535号窟（莲花洞）和巴中西龛第87号龛主尊。此外，四川石窟中还出现了菩提像与弥勒像成组开凿的现象，如广元千佛崖第366窟（菩提像）与365窟（弥勒），巴中西龛第87龛（菩提像）与第90龛（弥勒），浦江鸡公树山漏米石第15龛（菩提像）与第14龛（弥勒）；有的甚至把菩提像与弥勒像同置一龛之内，如巴中西龛第73龛（图11），巴中石门第12龛[2]。

图10　四川广元千佛崖第366窟菩提像

图11　四川巴中西龛第73号菩提像、弥勒像合龛

[1] 参见：1) 雷玉华、王建平《四川菩提瑞像研究》，上引书，第492-501页；2) 肥田路美《四川地区的触地印如来坐像的造像次第》，载李正刚主编《2004年龙门石窟国际学术研讨会文集》，郑州：河南人民出版社，2006年，第430-435页；3) 李玉珉《四川菩提瑞像窟龛研究》，上引书，548-561页。

[2] 参见：雷玉华、王建平《四川菩提瑞像研究》，上引书，第492-501页。

实际上，早在唐总章元年（668）之前，四川地区已经出现了菩提像[1]。段成式《酉阳杂俎前集》卷六《艺绝》更详载“成都宝相寺偏院小殿中有菩提像，其尘不集如新塑者。相传此像初造时，匠人依名堂先具五脏，次四肢百节。将百余年，纤尘不凝焉”[2]。段成式卒于唐咸通四年（863年）[3]，所记菩提像至迟应完工于8世纪中叶前后。

四川地区雕造菩提像之粉本或图样，应来自两京[4]。“盖益都多名画，富似他郡，谓唐二帝播越及诸侯作镇之秋，是时画艺之杰者，游从而来。故其标格楷模，无处不有。”[5]

西京长安“横街之北光宅寺，仪凤二年（677年）望气者言此坊有兴气，敕令掘得石函，函内有佛舍利骨万余粒，遂立光宅寺。武太后始置七宝台，因改寺额名”[6]。七宝台造像，据统计国内外现存9件同类龛像，约为武则天长安三、四年（703-704年）间雕造。其中，日本细川家旧藏六龛，日本原家藏一龛；另外二龛现存西安[7]。这批龛像之龛楣多雕菩提树或宝盖，龛内造一佛、二菩萨或一佛、二弟子、二菩萨；主尊结跏趺坐，多数螺髻，少数（二身）珠璎宝冠，多佩臂钏，皆偏袒右肩；左手内敛置于腹前，右手垂作触地印，身后多有高背屏（图12）。尽管诸龛题铭泯灭不清，但据姚元景长安四年（704年）“于光宅寺法堂石柱造像”“真容”[8]，这批龛像应与武周时期

[1]［唐］王勃（649/650-675/676年）668年出游巴蜀，记梓州玄武县福会寺有一菩提像：“紫宸有裕，苍旷胥悦。都人狎至，瞻雁塔而欢心；野老相趋，寻鹿园而顿颡。或至诚冥发，争知不尽之虚；或道恩旁流，竟委忘缘之施。乃于寺内造菩提塑像一座，实彭氏绝群之迹。洞参瑶铣，体备丹青。得埏范之奇模，尽陶甄之能事。功分实相，变入冥机。丹果长春，（青）莲不染。灵仪若动，以临王舍城中；神足疑行，即坐菩提树下。银床地涌，宝帐犹悬。珍木天成，金花下落”。王勃《梓州玄武县福会寺碑》，见《文苑英华》卷八百五十三，影印本，北京：中华书局，1966年，第4503页。

[2] 段成式《酉阳杂俎》，方南生点校，北京：中华书局，1981年，第61页。

[3] 参见：段成式，上引书，第1-4页《点校前言》。

[4] 参见：1）罗世平《巴中石窟三题》，见《文物》，1996年第3期，第64页；2）Henrik H. Sorensen, “The Buddhist Sculptures at Feixian Pavilion in Pujiang, Sichuan”, in: *Artibus Asiae*, Vol. 58, No. 1/2 (1998): 33-67, esp. 33-34; 3）雷玉华、王建平《四川菩提瑞像研究》，上引书，第497-498页。

[5] 李畋《益州名画录序》，载黄休复《益州名画录》，秦岭云点校，北京：人民美术出版社，1964年，第1-2页。

[6] 宋敏求《长安志》卷八《唐京城》，影印《丛书集成》本，北京：中华书局，1991年，第95页。

[7] 参见：1）Yen Chuan-ying, *The Sculptures from the Tower of Seven Jewels: The Style, Patronage and Iconography of the Tang Monument* [Ph. D Dissertation], Harvard University, May, 1986: 69-100; 2）颜娟英《武则天与长安七宝台石雕佛相》，见《艺术学》第1期（1987年），第56页；3）松原三郎《中國仏教雕刻史論》，図版編三，東京：吉川弘文館，1995年，第660a-b、661a-b、663a-b页；4）李玉珉《试论唐代降魔成道式装饰佛》，上引书，第44-45、70-71页。

[8] 王昶《金石萃编》卷六十五·叶六《姚元景造像铭》，影印本，北京：中国书店，1985年。

图 12　日本文化厅藏长安七宝台雕像

流行的“真容像”或“金刚座真容像”,如“信法寺真容像”[1]等有关系。其中,头戴宝冠者应为“菩提像”,即菩提树下降魔成道之像。据《太平广记》卷二百十一引《唐画断》:“光宅寺七宝台后面画降魔像,千怪万状,实奇踪也。然其画功德人物花草,皆是外国之象,无中华礼乐威仪之德。”[2]另据张彦远《历代名画记》卷三《记两京外州寺观画壁》,“光宅寺东菩提院内北壁东西偏,尉迟画降魔等变”[3]。据此,七宝台或在菩提院内。七宝台大量装饰菩提像,与菩提院北壁画巨幅降魔成道像彼此配合,相得益彰。此外,西安碑林博物馆所藏一束腰须弥像座,原为供奉菩提树像之用。依据像座上题铭,西崇福寺僧曾于神龙二年(706 年)雕造四尊玉石菩提树像,并供奉于西安

[1] 王昶《金石萃编》卷六十五·叶三–四《信法寺真容像之碑并序》,影印本,北京:中国书店,1985 年。信法寺舍利塔中真容像及夹侍菩萨像,乃柱国张黑刀等人于武周长寿二年(693 年)敬造。参见:1) 罗尔纲《金石萃编校补》,北京:中华书局,2004 年,第 117 页;2) 陆增祥《八琼室金石补正》卷十九,影印本,北京:文物出版社,1985 年,第 333-334 页。

[2] 1) 李昉等编《太平广记》,点校本,北京:中华书局,1961 年,第 1619 页;2) 朱景玄《唐朝名画录》,温肇桐注,成都:四川美术出版社,1985 年,第 9 页。

[3] 张彦远《历代名画记》,俞剑华注释,上海:上海人民美术出版社,1964 年,第 62 页。

近郊华严寺[1]。考虑到前述“沈佺期奉敕撰《菩提像文》”，疑供奉菩提树像乃武氏家庙一大传统。

需要补充的是，神龙三年（707 年）或稍后不久，苏常侍（杨思勖）所造泥质灰陶佛像，螺发，偏袒右肩，结跏趺坐，左手内敛置于腹前，右手垂作触地印；佛两侧各一胁侍菩萨。这种佛像，清光绪初年以来多出土于西安大慈恩寺遗址，疑为菩提像，唯像背铭文作“印度佛像”[2]。前述日本原家藏七宝台佛龛，有开元十二年（724 年）杨思勖等新妆龛像题记[3]。杨思勖选择重妆七宝台龛像，是否意味着这些陶制“印度佛像”与菩提像之关系呢？此外，清代王昶曾在西安城南隍中发现一件开元九年（721 年）前后的残造像碑，系“菩提像一铺，居士张爱造”[4]。

东都洛阳怀仁坊敬爱寺，系“显庆二年（657 年）孝敬在春宫为高宗、武太后立之，以敬爱寺为名，制度与西明寺同。天授二年（691 年），改为佛授记寺，其后又改为敬爱寺”[5]。敬爱寺改名佛授记寺，正值武则天声称得佛授记、改国号为大周之后[6]。此前的龙朔三年（663 年），高宗曾“敕令于敬爱道场写一切经典”[7]。这说明敬爱寺（佛授记寺）确为高宗、武则天时期一座举足轻重的大寺。张彦远《历代名画记》卷三《记两京外州寺观画壁》记载了敬爱寺，不过该书现存无善本[8]，鲁鱼亥豕现象甚多，现以北京大学图书馆藏王世贞明万历初年郧阳初刻《王氏画苑》本《历代名画记》卷三、叶十六为例抄录如下：敬爱寺“佛殿内菩萨树下弥勒菩萨塑像[9]，

---

[1] 参见裴珍达《龙门石窟擂鼓台南洞研究》，载《2004 年龙门石窟国际学术研讨会文集》，北京：文物出版社，2006 年，第 166-167 页。

这件像座铭记似表明华严宗信众也奉菩提像，因为法藏于唐先天元年“十一月二十四日（712 年 12 月 26 日）葬于神和原华严寺南”。又，吕澂认为：“华严宗思想的真正来源，一部分属于慈恩宗”，即该“宗因袭慈恩家理论”。参见：1) 阎朝隐撰《大唐大荐福寺故大德康藏法师之碑》，见《大正藏》第 50 卷，第 280b-c 页；2) 吕澂《中国佛学源流略讲》，第 353-368 页。

[2] 1) 陈直《西安出土隋唐泥佛像通考》，见陈直《文史考古论丛》，天津：天津古籍出版社，1988 年，第 502-512 页；2) 西安市文物保护考古所编著《西安文物精华：佛教造像》，西安：世界图书出版西安公司，2010 年，第 186 页。

[3] 参见：1) 颜娟英《唐长安七宝台石刻的再省思》，见陕西省考古研究所编《远望集：陕西省考古研究所华诞四十周年纪念文集》，西安：陕西人民美术出版社，1998 年，下册第 830 页；2) 李玉珉《试论唐代降魔成道式装饰佛》，上引书，第 44 页。

[4] 王昶《金石萃编》卷七十三 · 叶五、六，影印本，北京：中国书店，1985 年。

[5]《唐会要》卷四十八《寺》，影印《丛书集成》本，北京：中华书局，1955 年，第 848 页。

[6] 王邦维《义净与〈南海寄归内法传〉》，见义净《南海寄归内法传》，王邦维校注，北京：中华书局，1995 年，第 161 页注[32]。

[7] 静泰《大唐东京大敬爱寺一切经论目序》，见《大正藏》第 55 卷，第 181a 页。

[8] 参见宿白《张彦远和〈历代名画记〉》，北京：文物出版社，2008 年，第 15-21 页。

[9]“佛殿内菩萨树下弥勒菩萨塑像”这句话，疑张彦远原本为“佛殿内菩提树下弥勒造菩萨塑像”。

麟德二年(665年)自内出,王玄策取致西域所图菩萨像为样(巧儿、张寿、宋朝塑,王玄策指挥,李安贴金)。东间弥勒像(张智藏塑,即张寿之弟也,陈永承成),西间弥勒像(窦弘果塑。已上三处像光及化生等,并是刘爽刻)”[1]。倘若无传抄之误,敬爱寺佛殿内的这尊造像,应为弥勒规摹之菩提树像[2],与东、西间的弥勒像构成一种新型的造像题材组合。又,据《开元释教录》卷九《总括群经录》上,义净抵达神都时,女皇武则天亲自出城迎接,“敕于佛授记寺安置”[3]。据宋赵明诚记载,义净回国伊始为武则天称述符命,释读玉册,助其“受‘天册金轮圣神’之号,故大赫改元”[4];反之,武则天推重义净,把他称作“缁俗之纲维,绀坊之龙象”[5]。故而,义净偏重那烂陀及摩诃菩提寺一系之学问及所请金刚座真容像,势必对武则天的宗教志趣产生影响。除敬爱寺外,洛阳地区雕造的这种佛像主要集中在龙门东山,大型者如擂鼓台北洞主尊和原置擂鼓台南洞主室中央佛坛上的圆雕(图13)[6]。至于原藏擂鼓台院内碑廊下的另外二尊圆雕佛像,也具相同造型,据传从附近寺院移来,大约也是武周时期雕造。

目前在唐两京及四川地区发现的触地印佛像,可以大体分作两种类型:一种“珠璎宝冠”,一种螺发。从印度本土早已出现螺发、偏袒右肩、触地印造型之佛像考量,后者似不属“菩提像”之列[7]。当然,由于王玄策、义净和灵运等人分别带回的粉本有别[8],两件摹自摩诃菩提寺,一件画于那烂陀,因此不便断然否定螺发者非菩提像。

---

[1] 参见:1)张彦远《历代名画记》,秦仲文、黄苗子点校,北京:人民美术出版社,1963年,第67页;2)《历代名画记》,俞剑华注释,上海:上海人民美术出版社,1964年,第71页。

[2] 冯承钧认为:敬爱寺所塑菩提树像,其“图样必定是宋法智在摩诃菩提图写,而到京都道俗竞摸的那张图样,去年(664年)宋法智在嘉寿殿竖菩提像骨之时,大约也曾用过。此处的宋朝,不知同宋法智是否一人,我们知道王玄策的事迹,只能到665年”。冯承钧《王玄策事辑》,上引书,第121页。

[3]《大正藏》第55卷,第568b页。

[4] 赵明诚《金石录》,金文明校证,桂林:广西师范大学出版社,2005年,第434-435页。

[5] 唐则天皇后《三藏圣教序》,见《昭和法寶總目録》第三卷,第1425b页;另见《大正藏》第15卷,第706a页。

[6] 据1918年日人关野贞等拍摄的照片,擂鼓台南洞主室中央佛坛上置一“顶饰宝冠、身佩璎珞”、偏袒右肩、结跏趺坐、作触地印之佛像,后来因种种原因此像被移离南洞,现置龙门石窟研究院办公院内。笔者疑此像为南洞开窟时原始雕刻,其造型与南洞四壁及窟顶小型坐像相称。

[7] 广西桂林西山唐调露元年(679年)李实造像为一佛二菩萨,主尊肉髻低平,宽肩厚胸,结跏趺坐,大衣作“右袒式”披覆;左手内敛置于腹前,右手垂作触地印,佩臂钏,疑为菩提像。参见:罗香林《唐代桂林之摩崖佛像》,香港:中国学社,1958年。

[8] 李玉珉推测还有一种摹本,该本“可能是迦毗罗国的工匠根据摩诃菩提寺菩提瑞像为祖本所绘制”。李玉珉《试论唐代降魔成道式装饰佛》,上引书,第57页。

图 13　龙门擂鼓台南洞“主尊”

据唐湛然永泰元年（765 年）撰《止观辅行传弘决》，“唐请菩提像，使王（玄）策亲至其室，既致敬已，欲题壁记，壁乃目前，久行不至。息心欲出，近远如初。叹不思议踪，今尤未灭”[1]。

五、道俗竟礼

菩提像当时之所以备受信徒推崇，首先缘于高僧大德之夙愿。如玄奘临终之际，既命塑工宋法智于嘉寿殿竖菩提树像骨，又“愿与含识速奉慈颜”，“共诸有情同生睹史多天（Tuṣita）弥勒内眷属中，奉事慈尊”。义净“往大觉寺，礼真容像……愿龙华初会，遇慈氏尊，并契真宗，获无生智”。这种推崇弥勒，即弥勒与菩提像并重，除了说明菩提像系弥勒所造，信徒通过礼拜菩提像，既可追念现在佛释迦之功德，又祈望有缘知遇未来佛弥勒，于龙华三会中证得佛果[2]之外，疑与上述 5 世纪以降瑜伽行派或者说摩诃菩提寺及那烂陀推崇菩提像与弥勒有关。无著、世亲弘扬弥勒学说，后来护法学说在那烂陀及摩诃菩提寺的影响极大。据说在贤劫世界中，释迦前有三佛，释迦后应是弥勒成佛。关于这一点，护法曾说是弥勒的主张，由此可见瑜伽师推崇

[1]《大正藏》第 46 卷，第 282a-b 页。

[2] 参见：李玉珉《试论唐代降魔成道式装饰佛》，上引书，第 60、67 页。

弥勒[1]。玄奘所创慈恩宗,崇奉从弥勒、无著、世亲相承而下直到护法、戒贤的瑜伽一系学说,以《瑜伽师地论》为本;"后因弟子窥基建议,乃以护法论师之说为中心"[2]。据道世《法苑珠林》卷十六《弥勒部·赞叹》,玄奘曾有《赞弥勒四礼文》:"故我顶礼弥勒佛,唯愿慈尊度有情。愿共诸众生上生兜率天,奉见弥勒佛"[3]。窥基在《妙法莲华经玄赞》卷九《寿量品》更有"初释迦三敕,次弥勒四请"[4]之句。又,前述杨思勖所造泥质灰陶佛像之铭文"诸法从缘生如来说是因诸法从缘灭大沙门所说",似采自窥基所撰《妙法莲华经玄赞》卷八《法师品》"是以佛教造像、书(经)、法身舍利安于像中。云:'诸法从因生,如来说是因;彼法从缘灭,大沙门所说'。是为法身舍利"[5]。这既透视出菩提像及弥勒与玄奘、窥基一派之关系,也从另一方面说明杨思勖等人供奉菩提像。

其次,这种造像也同其他题材的佛教形象一样,被赋予功利主义色彩或杂密性质的现实利益效验,如除病、延寿、赐福等,且随佛教世俗化的不断深入而扩展。如据唐僧皎然《杼山集》卷八《唐石圯山故大禅师塔铭并序》记载,高僧神悟为求宿疾康复,被传"礼忏"、"事忏"二法,遂于菩提像前潜心忏悔,最后痊愈,身披缁服。"师讳神悟,字通性,陇西李氏之子。其先属西晋版荡,迁家于吴之长水。世袭儒素,幼为诸生。及冠,忽婴业疾,有不可救之状。咎心补行,力将何施?开元中,诣前溪光律师,请医王之方,执门人之礼。师示以遣业之教,一曰理忏、二曰事忏。此仁圣所授,行必有征。遂于菩提像前,秉不屈之心,爇难舍之指。异光如月,瞳朦绀宫,极苦可以感明神,至精可以动天地。盖菩萨之难事欤?洎天四中,受具足戒,身始披缁"[6]。此外,前述浦江飞仙阁第60龛是为天皇、天后敬造;擂鼓台北洞窟门上方原编2071号龛(现编擂鼓台区5-32龛),乃"阎门冬奉为圣神皇帝陛下及太子、诸王、师僧父母、七世先亡、法界一切众生敬造","以此造像功德,普及法界苍生,俱出爱河,咸升佛果"。

最后,僧俗信徒若"右绕菩提树像,诵咒满千万遍,即见菩萨为其说法。欲随菩萨,即得随从"[7]。据智昇《开元释教录》卷十二,"《佛顶尊胜陀罗尼经》一卷,大唐朝散郎杜行顗奉制译(出《大周录》,第一译);《佛顶最胜陀罗尼经》一卷,大唐中天

[1] 参见吕澂《印度佛学源流略讲》,第184-217页。

[2] 颜尚文《隋唐佛教宗派研究》,台北:新文丰出版公司,1980年,第161页。

[3] 道世,上引书,第534-535页。

[4]《大正藏》第34卷,第828c页。

[5]《大正藏》第34卷,第809c页。

[6] 皎然《杼山集》卷八《唐石圯山故大禅师塔铭并序》,《文渊阁四库全书》本。赞宁《宋高僧传》卷十七《神悟传》据此改写。参见:赞宁《宋高僧传》,范祥雍点校,北京:中华书局,1987年,第416-417页。

[7] 地婆诃罗译《佛说七俱胝佛母心大准提陀罗尼经》,参见《大正藏》第20卷,第186a页。

竺三藏地婆诃罗译（拾遗编入，第二译）;《佛顶尊胜陀罗尼经》一卷，大唐罽宾沙门佛陀波利译（出《大周录》，第三译）[1];《最胜佛顶陀罗尼净除业障[咒]经》一卷，大唐中天竺三藏地婆诃罗于东都再译（拾遗编入，第四译）;《佛顶尊胜陀罗尼经》一卷（或加咒字），大唐三藏义净译（新编入录，第五译）。右五经同本异译"[2]。

《佛顶尊胜陀罗尼经》是7世纪时中土极为流行的密宗陀罗尼[3]，传为消灾、延寿、"除病秘方，为世俗所特重"[4]。当时"汉地众生多造罪业，出家之辈亦多犯戒律。唯有《佛顶尊胜陀罗尼经》，能灭众生一切恶业……广利群生……此经救拔幽冥，最不可思议"[5]。智昇所记五种译本中，地婆诃罗便占了三译[6]。由于唐高宗"赏其(佛陀波利)精诚，崇斯秘典，遂诏鸿胪寺典客令杜行顗及日照三藏于内共译"[7]。不久，地婆诃罗"奉诏再译，名《佛顶最胜陀罗尼》"[8]，"沙门彦琮笔授，为正杜行顗所译经中隐讳不书之字所以重译"[9]。垂拱元年(685年)地婆诃罗三藏随驾，于神都武后家庙与沙门慧智再译，名《佛顶尊胜名净除业障经》或《最胜佛顶陀罗尼净除业障咒

[1] 佛陀波利译本《佛顶尊胜陀罗尼经》，武周时曾刻于北京房山（七洞七七号）。《房山石经题记汇编》没有录出该经尾题，虽然《房山石经·隋唐刻经》2目录中给出天授二年(691年)字样，但影印之拓本无法辨识。承罗炤函告，该题记之原拓确为天授二年。谨此致谢。

值得注意的是，洛阳地区现存最早的石本《佛顶尊胜陀罗尼》，都是佛陀波利译本，一件刻在龙门西山莲花洞，敬造者为史延福，镌刻时间为武周如意元年(692年)；另一件在擂鼓台中洞前壁门道右侧，残蚀严重，镌刻时间应为武周圣历二年(699年)之前。参见：1)北京图书馆金石组、中国佛教图书文物馆石经组编《房山石经题记汇编》，北京：书目文献出版社，1987年；2)中国佛教协会、中国佛教图书文物馆编《房山石经·隋唐刻经》2，北京：华夏出版社，2000年，第402页；3)刘景龙、李玉昆主编，上引书，第274-276页。

[2]《大正藏》第55卷，第600a页。又，据贞元十八年(802年)慧琳《一切经音义》卷三十五《记佛顶尊胜陀罗尼经翻译年代先后》，自北周武帝保定四年(564年)至唐代宗广德二年(764年)，"前后约二百余年，已经八度出本，经则五翻，念诵法即三种差别。唯有善无畏所译是《加句尊胜陀罗尼》，中加十一句、六十六字，仪轨法则乃是瑜伽，与前后所译不同，多于诸本。余七译陀罗尼，字数多少相似"。《大正藏》第54卷，第544b页。

[3] 周一良，上引书，第105-108页。

[4] 汤用彤，上引书，第27页。

[5] 志静《佛顶尊胜陀罗尼经序》，《大正藏》第19卷，第349b页。又，洛阳地区出土的《佛顶尊胜陀罗尼》经序皆采纳"志静序"，说明志静所言确为当时信徒所重。参见王振国《洛阳经幢研究》，见王振国《龙门石窟与洛阳佛教文化》，郑州：中州古籍出版社，2006年，第157页。

[6] 实际上，杜行顗所译，乃地婆诃罗与之"奉敕共译"。据志静《佛顶尊胜陀罗尼经序》，佛陀波利"永淳二年(683年)回至西京，具以上事闻奏大帝。大帝遂将其本入内，请日照三藏法师及敕司宾寺典客令杜行顗等，共译此经"。《大正藏》第19卷，第349b页。这也说明地婆诃罗重视此经。

[7] 智昇《续古今译经图记》，见《大正藏》第55卷，第369a页。

[8] 智昇《开元释教录》卷九《总括群经录》上"地婆诃罗"条，见《大正藏》第55卷，第564b页。

[9] 慧琳《记佛顶尊胜陀罗尼经翻译年代先后》，见《大正藏》第54卷，第544a页。

经》[1]，“具说善住天子往昔口业感果因缘，并说受持法则”[2]，即“前缘后法”[3]。

虽然智昇在《开元释教录》中标记“五经同本异译”，但日人大村西崖认为：“杜行顗译《佛顶尊胜陀罗尼经》二本，日照译《佛顶最胜陀罗尼经》、《最胜佛顶陀罗尼净除业障经》各一本（各一卷）。四本皆一咒一印，所说有多少出入，盖梵本不必一。后法崇撰其疏（后出）。《净除业障经》，事相最详，印名佛护身。其坛方圆四肘，三重界隅安四瓶，行人于坛西畔跪而祈念，是即尊胜佛顶法初出”[4]。地婆诃罗于神都武后家庙奉制重译本，即《最胜佛顶陀罗尼净除业障咒经》与前后所译不同，在内容上多于诸本，较其有所增益。其中的一些内容，如反复强调在菩提像前诵最胜佛顶陀罗尼，可净除诸罪、荡涤一切业障，为诸本所不见，疑为地婆诃罗自己增补，这或许受到了摩诃菩提寺及那烂陀寺弥勒与菩提像并重及“最胜佛顶法”之影响。

> 佛告护世及大梵王、阎摩罗等谛听，谛听吾为汝说。若有一切苦难众生，罪极重者，无救护者，当于白月十五日，洗浴清洁，着净衣裳，受八戒斋。于菩提像前正心右跪，诵此陀罗尼咒满一千八遍，是人所有诸罪业障，悉皆消灭。当得总持陀罗尼门，辩才无碍，清净解脱。[5]
>
> 佛告天帝，若人生来具造十恶、五逆，四重根本等罪，自惟乘此恶业，命终之后必定当堕阿鼻地狱，受诸大苦，经于多劫，劫尽更生；若堕畜生、杂类、禽兽、循环恶道，无复救护。是人应当白月十五日在菩提像前，以金银器可受一升，盛好净水安置坛内，受菩萨戒，持斋洁净，于坛西畔面东向像[6]，烧香礼拜，右跪系念，至诚启白，诵此陀罗尼咒满一千八遍。于其中间，不得间断，而以是水，散洒四方及以上下，愿令一切同得清净。作是法已，如上恶业应入地狱、畜生、饿鬼，

[1] 慧琳《记佛顶尊胜陀罗尼经翻译年代先后》，见《大正藏》第 54 卷，第 544a 页。参见：智昇《开元释教录》卷九《总括群经录》上“地婆诃罗”条，上引书，第 564a 页。

据王振国统计，在洛阳地区发现的 16 件唐代陀罗尼经幢中，有 10 件为地婆诃罗译本《最胜佛顶陀罗尼净除业障咒经》，其中四件标注“东都福先寺西律院勘定本”或“东都福先寺西律院玉石幢本”，这是因为福先寺乃地婆诃罗译经所在。至于地婆诃罗所译《最胜佛顶陀罗尼净除业障咒经》中之咒语，在洛阳石经幢中大多单刻流行。参见：王振国，上引书，第 163 页。

[2] 慧琳《记佛顶尊胜陀罗尼经翻译年代先后》，上引书，第 544a 页。

[3] 智昇《开元释教录》，上引书，第 564a 页。

[4] 大村西崖《密教發達志》，東京：佛書刊行會圖像部，1918 年，第 257-258 页。

[5] 地婆诃罗译《最胜佛顶陀罗尼净除业障咒经》，《大正藏》第 19 卷，第 360c 页。

[6] 擂鼓台北洞主尊“坐东朝西”，这既与《大唐西域记》所记如来初成佛像“东西而坐”相符，也与《王玄策行传》所载菩提树像“身东西坐”吻合，更与《最胜佛顶陀罗尼净除业障咒经》所制在菩提像前置坛、“于坛西畔面东向像”礼拜、诵咒一致。擂鼓台北洞的这种设计或许不是巧合。

便得解脱；一切罪报，悉皆消灭。阎罗放赦，司命欢喜；不生瞋责，反更心恭；合掌随喜，赞其功德；若舍其报，生诸佛国；十方净刹，欲往随愿。又十五日咒，其酥蜜及于荜茇（毕钵）一千八遍，与人食之。其人食已，所有十恶、五逆等罪，悉皆消灭，而复当得阿耨多罗三藐三菩提。[1]

至于诵咒时所用之菩提像，疑为王玄策等人请回的“弥勒规摹”之像，因为当时赴印求法之高僧，皆先赴摩诃菩提寺瞻仰菩提像，后抵“像法之泉源”那烂陀求法。作为像教，当时两寺寺学对中土影响巨大；这种佛像粉本被请回京都后，为“道俗竞摸”[2]。

（本文原刊《石窟寺研究》第三辑第 190-211 页。）

---

[1] 地婆诃罗译《最胜佛顶陀罗尼净除业障咒经》，上引书，第 361a 页。

[2] 近读罗炤《试论龙门石窟擂鼓台的宝冠–佩饰–降魔印佛像》，受益良多。罗炤文中对大日如来像、香王菩萨像、释迦成道像–菩提瑞像、释迦佛顶像、卢舍那佛以及释迦成道像、释迦佛顶像和毗卢遮那像三者之关系等问题做了系统阐述。尤为重要的是，罗炤从武周历史和造像组合关系考述擂鼓台洞窟诸问题，颇具启发。不过，考虑到北洞外立面上方闫门冬所造菩提像与北洞主尊之相似、北洞的三佛和两菩萨并未在《陀罗尼集经》中固定成组，地婆诃罗奉制再译《最胜佛顶陀罗尼净除业障咒经》仍作“菩提树像”以及现存这种“宝冠佛”造像之铭记似仅题“菩提像”，笔者仍持北洞主尊为“菩提像”。参见罗炤《试论龙门石窟擂鼓台的宝冠–佩饰–降魔印佛像》，见《徐苹芳先生纪念文集》，上海：上海古籍出版社，2012 年，第 466-501 页。

征引文献

（按著译者拉丁字母或拼音次第）

汉文部分

（包括汉译本及部分汉文论著的英文译名）

史料

A. 正史（按朝代顺序）

［西汉］司马迁《史记》，点校本，北京：中华书局，1959 年。

［东汉］班固《汉书》，点校本，北京：中华书局，1962 年。

Ban Gu (31-92 AD), *Hanshu*［*History of the Western Han Dynasty*］, punctuated and emended ed., Beijing: Zhonghua Book Company, 1962.

［宋］范晔《后汉书》，点校本，北京：中华书局，1965 年。

Fan Ye (398-445 AD), *Hou Hanshu*［*History of the Eastern Han Dynasty*］, punctuated and emended ed., Beijing: Zhonghua Book Company, 1965.

［晋］陈寿《三国志》，点校本，北京：中华书局，1959 年。

Chen Shou (233-297 AD), *Sanguozhi*［*History of the Wei, the Shu and the Wu Kingdoms*］, punctuated and emended ed. , Beijing: Zhonghua Book Company, 1959.

［唐］房玄龄等《晋书》，点校本，北京：中华书局，1974 年。

Fang Xuanling (579-648 AD) et al, *Jinshu*［*History of the Jin Dynasties*］, punctuated and emended ed., Beijing: Zhonghua Book Company, 1974.

［梁］沈约《宋书》，点校本，北京：中华书局，1974 年。

Shen Yue (441-513 AD), *Songshu*［*History of the Song Dynasty*］, punctuated and emended ed., Beijing: Zhonghua Book Company, 1974.

［南朝梁］萧子显《南齐书》,点校本,北京：中华书局,1972 年。

［唐］姚思廉《梁书》,点校本,北京：中华书局,1973 年。

［唐］姚思廉《陈书》,点校本,北京：中华书局,1972 年。

［北齐］魏收《魏书》,点校本,北京：中华书局,1974 年。

Wei Shou (506-572 AD), *Weishu* [*History of the Wei Dynasties*], punctuated and emended ed., Beijing: Zhonghua Book Company, 1974.

［唐］李百药《北齐书》,点校本,北京：中华书局,1972 年。

Li Baiyao (565-648 AD), *Beiqishu* [*History of the Northern Qi Dynasty*], punctuated and emended ed., Beijing: Zhonghua Book Company, 1972.

［唐］令狐德棻《周书》,点校本,北京：中华书局,1971 年。

Linghu Defen (583-666 AD), *Zhoushu* [*History of the Northern Zhou Dynasty*], punctuated and emended ed., Beijing: Zhonghua Book Company, 1971.

［唐］魏徵、长孙无忌《隋书》,点校本,北京：中华书局,1973 年。

Wei Zheng (580-643 AD) and Zhangsun Wuji (597-659 AD) et al., *Suishu* [*History of the Sui Dynasty*], punctuated and emended ed., Beijing: Zhonghua Book Company, 1973.

［唐］李延寿《南史》,点校本,北京：中华书局,1975 年。

［唐］李延寿《北史》,点校本,北京：中华书局,1974 年。

Li Yanshou, *Beishi* [*History of the Northern Dynasties*], punctuated and emended ed., Beijing: Zhonghua Book Company, 1974.

［后晋］刘昫《旧唐书》,点校本,北京：中华书局,1975 年。

Liu Xu (887-946 AD) et al., *Jiu Tangshu* [*The Old Book of the History of the Tang Dynasty*], punctuated and emended ed., Beijing: Zhonghua Book Company, 1975.

［北宋］欧阳修、宋祁《新唐书》,点校本,北京：中华书局,1975 年。

Ouyang Xiu (1007-1072 AD) and Song Qi (998-1061 AD), *Xin Tangshu* [*The New Book of the History of the Tang Dynasty*], punctuated and emended ed., Beijing: Zhonghua Book Company, 1975.

［元］脱脱等《金史》,点校本,北京：中华书局,1975 年。

［明］宋濂《元史》,点校本,北京：中华书局,1976 年。

B. 其他史料

曹学佺《蜀中名胜记》,刘知渐点校,重庆：重庆出版社,1984 年。

曹寅等编《全唐诗》,北京：中华书局,1960 年。

晁公武《郡斋读书志》,孙猛校证,上海：上海古籍出版社,1990 年。

陈耀文《天中记》。明隆庆三年 (1569 年) 刻本 (北京大学图书馆藏)。

陈振孙《直斋书录解题》,徐小蛮、顾美华点校,上海：上海古籍出版社,1987 年。

Cui Hong［崔鸿 , 478-525 AD］, *Shiliuguo chunqiu: Beiliang lu*［十六国春秋：北凉录 , *Annals of the Sixteen States: the Northern Liang*］, in: *Taiping yulan*［太平御览 , *The Taiping Reign-Period Imperial Encyclopedia*］compiled by Li Fang［李 昉］et al., facsimile edition, Beijing: Zhonghua Book Company, 1960.

邓名世《古今姓氏书辨证》,王力平点校,南昌：江西人民出版社,2006 年。

董诰等编《全唐文》,影印本,北京：中华书局,1983 年。

独孤及《毗陵集》。《四部丛刊》本。

杜佑《通典》,王文锦等点校,北京：中华书局,1988 年。

端方《匋斋藏石记》,载《石刻史料新编》第一辑,第 11 册,台北：新文丰出版公司,1977 年初版,1982 年再版。

段成式《酉阳杂俎》,方南生点校,北京：中华书局,1981 年。

樊绰《蛮书》,向达校注,北京：中华书局,1962 年。

龚松林修、汪坚纂《重修洛阳县志》。乾隆十年 (1745 年) 刻本。

顾野王《大广益会玉篇》,影印本,北京：中华书局,1987 年。

郭若虚《图画见闻志》。《四部丛刊续编》本。

郭若虚《图画见闻志》,俞剑华注释,上海：上海人民美术出版社,1964 年。

Guo Ruoxu, *Tuhua jianwen zhi*［*An Account of My Experiences in Painting* or *Continuation of Record of Famous Painters of All the Dynasties*］, emended and annotated by Yu Jianhua, Shanghai: Shanghai People's Fine Arts Publishing House, 1964.

郭松年《大理行记》,王叔武校注 / 李京《云南志略》,王叔武辑校,昆明：云南民族出版社,1986 年。

胡聘之《山右石刻丛编》四十卷,载《石刻史料新编》第一辑,第 20-21 册,台北：新文丰出版公司,1979 年。

黄休复《益州名画录》。明万历庚寅金陵“王氏淮南书院重刻”《王氏画苑》本。

黄休复《益州名画录》,秦岭云点校,北京：人民美术出版社,1964 年。

黄永武主编《敦煌宝藏》,全 140 册,台北：新文丰出版公司,1981-1986 年。

计有功《唐诗纪事》,北京：中华书局,1965 年。

嘉靖《漳德府志》,影印本,上海：中华书局上海编辑所,1964 年。

劳格、赵钺《唐尚书省郎官石柱题名考》，徐敏霞、王桂珍点校，北京：中华书局，1992 年。
乐史《太平寰宇记》，王文楚等点校，北京：中华书局，2007 年。
郦道元《水经注》，王先谦合校，北京：中华书局，2009 年。
Li Daoyuan (466 or 472-527 AD), *Shuijing zhu* [*Commentary on Waterways Classic*], sub-commentated by Yang Shoujing [杨守敬] and Xiong Huizhen [熊会贞], Nanjing: Jiangsu Chinese Classics Publishing House, 1989.
李昉等编《太平御览》，影印本，北京：中华书局，1960 年。
Li Fang (925-996 AD) et al., *Taiping yulan* [*The Taiping Reign-Period Imperial Encyclopedia*], facsimile edition, Beijing: Zhonghua Book Company, 1960.
李昉等编《太平广记》，点校本，北京：中华书局，1961 年。
李昉等编《文苑英华》，影印本，北京：中华书局，1966 年。
Li Fang et al., *Wenyuan yinghua* [*The Best Works in the Literature and Art Circles* or *Corpus of the Literary World*], facsimile edition, Beijing: Zhonghua Book Company, 1966.
李吉甫《元和郡县图志》，贺次君点校，北京：中华书局，1983 年。
李善等《六臣注文选》，影印《四部丛刊》本，北京：中华书局，1987 年。
Li Shan (630-689 AD) et al., *Liuchen zhu wenxuan* [*Annotations to Anthology Through the Ages*] compiled by Xiao Tong [萧统 , 501-531 AD], facsimile edition, Beijing: Zhonghua Book Company, 1987.
《六臣注文选》，影印日本足利学校藏宋刊明州本，北京：人民文学出版社，2008 年。
李焘《续资治通鉴长编》，全 20 册，点校本，第 2 版，北京：中华书局，2004 年。
李宗莲《怀岷精舍金石跋尾》，载《石刻史料新编》第二辑第十九册，台北：新文丰出版公司，1979 年。
刘道醇《圣朝名画评》。明万历庚寅金陵“王氏淮南书院重刻”《王氏画苑》本。
刘熙《释名》，毕沅疏证，王先谦补，北京：中华书局，2008 年。
路朝霖《洛阳龙门志》。光绪十三年 (1887 年) 刊本。
陆心源《唐文续拾》，《全唐文》附，影印本，北京：中华书局，1983 年。
陆增祥《八琼室金石补证》，影印本，北京：文物出版社，1985 年。
马端林《文献通考》，影印本，上海：商务印书馆，1936 年。
米芾《画史》。明万历庚寅金陵“王氏淮南书院重刻”《王氏画苑》本。
缪荃孙编《藕香零拾》，影印本，北京：中华书局，1999 年。
欧阳修《集古录跋尾》，载《欧阳修全集》，影印本，北京：中国书店，1986 年。

欧阳询《艺文类聚》,汪绍楹校,上海：上海古籍出版社,1965 年。

Ouyang Xun (557-641 AD), *Yiwen leijun* [*Encyclopedia of Art and Literature in Dynastic Histories/Collected Descriptive Accounts of Books in Category*], emended and annotated by Wang Shaoying, Shanghai: Shanghai Chinese Classics Publishing House, 1965.

阮元《两浙金石志》,杭州：浙江书局,清光绪十六年 (1890 年) 刻本。

邵伯温《邵氏闻见录》,李剑雄、刘德权点校,北京：中华书局,1983 年。

司马光《资治通鉴》,胡三省音注,标点本,北京：中华书局,1956 年。

司马光《资治通鉴目录》,《四部丛刊》初编缩印本,上海：商务印书馆,1936 年。

司马贞《史记索隐》。汲古阁本。

嘉庆《四川通志》,影印本,成都：巴蜀书社,1984 年。

宋敏求《唐大诏令集》,点校本,北京：商务印书馆,1959 年。

宋敏求《长安志》,影印本,北京：中华书局,1991 年。

苏过《斜川集》。《四部备要》本。

王昶《金石萃编》,影印本,北京：中国书店,1985 年。

王溥《唐会要》,影印本,北京：中华书局,1955 年。

王钦若等编《册府元龟》,影印本,北京：中华书局,1960 年。

《宋本册府元龟》,影印本,北京：中华书局,1989 年。

Wang Qinruo [王钦若, 962-1025 AD] and Yang Yi [杨亿, 974-1020 AD], *Cefu yuangui* [*The Imperial Encyclopaedia on the Monarch and his Subjects of the Past Dynasties/Corpus of Historical Data on the Monarch and his Subjects of the Past Dynasties*], facsimile edition, Beijing: Zhonghua Book Company, 1989.

王文诰辑注《苏轼诗集》,孔凡礼点校,北京：中华书局,1982 年。

王象之《舆地纪胜》,影印本,北京：中华书局,1992 年。

韦述《两京新记》,辛德勇辑校,西安：三秦出版社,2006 年。

吴兢《贞观政要》,点校本,上海：上海古籍出版社,1978 年。

吴任臣《十国春秋》,徐敏霞、周莹点校,北京：中华书局,1983 年。

吴曾《能改斋漫录》,点校本,上海：上海古籍出版社,1979 年。

谢守灏《混元圣纪》,载《正统道藏》第 30 册,台北：艺文印书馆,1977 年。

解缙等编《永乐大典》,“寺”字韵,影印本,北京：中华书局,1986 年。

谢赫《古画品录》。明王世贞万历初年郧阳初刻《王氏画苑》本。

谢赫《古画品录》/ 姚最《续画品录》,王伯敏标点注译,北京：人民美术出版社,1962 年。

Xie He (active ca. 500-535 AD), *Guhuapinlu* [*Classification of Painters*]; Yao Zui (535-602 AD), *Xu huapinlu* [*Continuation of the Classification of Painters*], emended, annotated and translated by Wang Bomin, Beijing: People's Fine Arts Publishing House, 1962.

徐坚《初学记》,点校本,北京：中华书局,1962年。

许嵩《建康实录》,张忱石点校,北京：中华书局,1986年。

Xu Song, *Jiankang shilu* [*True Records of Jiankang*], punctuated and emended by Zhang Chenshi, Beijing: Zhonghua Book Company, 1986.

《宣和画谱》,俞剑华标点注译,北京：人民美术出版社,1964年。

颜之推《颜氏家训》,王利器集解,北京：中华书局,1993年。

颜之推《颜氏家训》,周法高汇注,二版,台北：中研院历史语言研究所,1993年。

杨仪修、王开沃纂《(乾隆)盩厔县志》。清乾隆五十年(1785年)刻本。

姚最《续画品录》。明王世贞万历初年郧阳初刻《王氏画苑》本。

姚铉纂《唐文粹》,《四部丛刊》初编缩印本,上海：商务印书馆,1936年。

俞琰《席上腐谈》卷上。宝颜堂秘笈本。

叶昌炽《语石》,柯昌泗评,北京：中华书局,1994年。

叶廷珪《海录碎事》,李之亮点校,北京：中华书局,2002年。

元好问编《中州集》,影印本,台北：台湾商务印书馆,1973年。

Yuan Hong [袁宏 328-376 AD], *Houhanji: Xiaominghuangdiji* [后汉纪·孝明皇帝纪, *History of the Eastern Han Dynasty: Memoir of Emperor Xiaoming*], Beijing: Zhonghua Book Company, 2002.

曾公亮等编《武经总要前集》,影印本,北京：中华书局,1959年。

张耒《张耒集》,李逸安、孙通海、傅信点校,北京：中华书局,1990年。

《张说之文集》。《四部丛刊》本。

张彦远《历代名画记》。明王世贞万历初年郧阳初刻《王氏画苑》本。

张彦远《历代名画记》,秦仲文、黄苗子点校,北京：人民美术出版社,1963年。

张彦远《历代名画记》,俞剑华注释,上海：上海人民美术出版社,1964年。

Zhang Yanyuan (815-877 AD), *Lidai minghua ji* [*Record of Famous Painters of All the Dynasties/On Chinese Paintings through the Ages*], emended and annotated by Yu Jianhua, Shanghai: Shanghai People's Fine Arts Publishing House, 1964.

张鷟《朝野佥载》,赵守俨点校,北京：中华书局,1979年。

赵汝愚编《名臣奏议》。《文渊阁四库全书》本。

赵明诚《金石录》,影印本,北京: 中华书局,1983 年。

赵明诚《金石录》,金文明校证,桂林: 广西师范大学出版社,2005 年。

赵钺、劳格《唐御史台精舍题名考》,张枕石点校,北京: 中华书局,1997 年。

郑樵《通志》,影印本,北京: 中华书局,1987 年。

郑樵《通志二十略》。乾隆己巳年 (1749 年) 钱塘汪启淑校刻本。

朱景玄《唐代名画录》。明万历庚寅金陵 "王氏淮南书院重刻"《王氏画苑》本。

朱景玄《唐朝名画录》,温肇桐注,成都: 四川美术出版社,1985 年。

祝穆撰、祝洙增订《方舆胜览》,施和金点校,北京: 中华书局,2003 年。

C. 佛典

阿地瞿多译《陀罗尼集经》,参见《大正新脩大藏經》(100 卷,高楠順次朗、渡邊海旭都監,東京: 大正一切經刊行會,1924-1934 年,下文简作《大正藏》),No. 901,第 18 卷,第 785-897 页。

宝唱《名僧传》,见宗性《名僧传抄》,载《大日本續藏經》(前田慧雲原編、中野達慧增訂,京都: 藏經書院,1905-1912 年,150 套,750 冊,下文简作《續藏經》),第壹輯第貳編乙第七套第壹冊,第 1-17 叶。

Baochang, *Mingseng Zhuan* [*Biographies of Famous Monks* or *Lives of Famous Bhikṣus*], partly preserved in the Japanese *Meisōden-shō* [*A Transcript of Biographies of Famous Monks*] by Shū-shō, in: *Dainihon Zoku Zōkyō* [*Continued Tripiṭaka of Japan*], Vol. 7, No. 1: 1-17.

宝云译《佛本行经》,参见《大正藏》,No. 193,第 4 卷,第 54-115 页。

布顿大师著《佛教史大宝藏论》,郭和卿译,北京: 民族出版社,1986 年。

Bu-ston rin-chen grub, *Bde-bar-gšegs-pahi bstan-pahi gsal-byed, Chos-kyi hbyuń-gnas gsuń-rab-rin-po-chehi mdsod ces-bya-ba* [*History of Buddhism*], tr. Guo Heqing, Beijing: Minzu Publishing House, 1986.

布顿 · 仁钦珠《布顿佛教史》,蒲文成译,兰州: 甘肃民族出版社,2007 年。

不空译《大乘密严经》,参见《大正藏》,No. 682,第 16 卷,第 747-776 页。

崔致远《唐大荐福寺故寺主翻经大德法藏和尚传》,参见《大正藏》,No. 2054,第 50 卷,第 280-286 页。

达摩流支译《佛说宝雨经》,参见《大正藏》,No. 660,第 16 卷,第 283-328 页。

道世《法苑珠林》,周叔迦、苏晋仁校注,北京: 中华书局,2003 年; 参见《大正藏》,No. 2122,第 53 卷,第 269-1030 页。

Daoshi, *Fayuan zhulin* [*Forest of Gems in the Garden of the Law/A Grove of Pearls in the Garden of the Dharma*], emended and annotated by Zhou Shujia and Su Jinren, Beijing: Zhonghua Book Company, 2003; *confer: Taishō shinshū daizōkyō* [*Taishō Revised Tripiṭaka,* 100 vols., ed. by Junjirō Takakusu and Kaikyoku Watanabe, Tokyo: Taishō Issaikyō Kankōkai, 1924-1934, hereafter abbreviated to *Taishō*], No. 2122, Vol. 53: 269-1030.

Daoxuan [道宣], "*Miaofa lianhuajing hongchuan xu* [妙法莲花经弘传序, Preface to Dissemination of *the Saddharma-puṇḍarīka-sūtra or Lotus Sūtra of the Wonderful Law*]", in: *Taishō,* Vol. 9: 1.

道宣《四分律删繁补阙行事钞》,参见《大正藏》,No. 1804,第 40 卷,第 1-156 页。

Daoxuan, *Sifenlü shanfan buque xingshi chao* [*The Essentials of "The Fourfold Rules of Discipline"*], in: *Taishō,* No. 1804, Vol. 40: 1-156.

Daoxuan, *Lüxiang gantong zhuan* [律相感通传, *Responses to Dreamlike Dialogues with Devas*], in: *Taishō,* No. 1898, Vol. 45: 874-882.

道宣《关中创立戒坛图经》,参见《大正藏》,No. 1892,第 45 卷,第 807-819 页。

道宣《续高僧传》,参见《大正藏》,No. 2060,第 50 卷,第 425-707 页。

Daoxuan, *Xü gaoseng zhuan* [*Continued Biographies of Eminent Priests* or *The Tang Dynasty Biographies of Eminent Priests* or *A Continuation of the Memoirs of Eminent Monks*] in: *Taishō,* No. 2060, Vol. 50: 425-707.

道宣《广弘明集》,参见《大正藏》,No. 2103,第 52 卷,第 97-361 页。

Daoxuan, *Guang Hongmingji* [*Further Anthology of the Propagation of Light* or *Expanded Collection on the Propagation and Clarification of Buddhism*], in: *Taishō,* No. 2103, Vol. 52: 97-361.

道宣《集古今佛道论衡》,参见《大正藏》,No. 2104,第 52 卷,第 363-397 页。

道宣《集神州三宝感通录》,参见《大正藏》,No. 2106,第 52 卷,第 404-435 页。

Daoxuan, *Ji shenzhou sanbao gantong lu* [*Collection of the Strange and Extraordinary Events and Deeds of the Buddhist Triratna in China/Records of Spiritual Response of the Three Jewels in China*], in: *Taishō,* No. 2106, Vol. 52: 404-435.

道宣《大唐内典录》,参见《大正藏》,No. 2149,第 55 卷,第 219-342 页。

Daoxuan, *Datang neidian lu* [*The Great Tang Dynasty Catalogue of Buddhist Scriptures* or *A Catalogue of the Buddhist Canon compiled under the Tang Dynasty* or *The Great Tang Record of Inner Classics*], in: *Taishō,* No. 2149, Vol.

55: 219-341.

道宣《释迦方志》,范祥雍点校,北京：中华书局,1983 年；参见《大正藏》,No. 2088,第 51 卷,第 948-975 页。

Daoxuan, *Shijia fangzhi* [*A Geographical Record of Buddhist World*], emended and annotated by Fan Xiangyong, Beijing: Zhonghua Book Company, 1983.

道原《景德传灯录》,参见《大正藏》,No. 2076,第 51 卷,第 196-467 页。

Dharmarakṣa [竺法护], tr. *Fo bonihuan jing* [佛般泥洹经, *Buddha's Parinirvāṇa Sūtra*], in: *Taishō,* No. 5, Vol. 1: 160-175.

地婆诃罗译《方广大庄严经》,参见《大正藏》,No. 187,第 3 卷,第 539-617 页。

地婆诃罗译《大乘密严经》,参见《大正藏》,No. 681,第 16 卷,第 723-776 页。

地婆诃罗译《最胜佛顶陀罗尼净除业障咒经》,参见《大正藏》,No. 970,第 19 卷,第 357-361 页。

地婆诃罗译《佛说七俱胝佛母心大准提陀罗尼经》,参见《大正藏》,No. 1077,第 20 卷,第 185-186 页。

多罗那它《印度佛教史》,张建木译,成都：四川民族出版社,1988 年。

法经等《众经目录》,参见《大正藏》,No. 2146,第 55 卷,第 115-150 页。

Fajing, *Zhongjing mulu* [*A Catalogue of Tripiṭaka*], in: *Taishō,* No. 2146, Vol. 55: 15-150.

法立、法炬译《佛说诸德福田经》,参见《大正藏》,No. 683,第 16 卷,第 777-778 页。

Fali and Faju tr., *Foshuo zhude futian jing* [*Sūtra on the Field of Blessedness of all Virtues*], in: *Taishō,* No. 683, Vol. 16: 777-778.

法琳《破邪论》,参见《大正藏》,No. 2109,第 52 卷,第 474-489 页。

法琳《辩正论》,参见《大正藏》,No. 2110,第 52 卷,第 490-550 页。

法贤译《众许摩诃帝经》,参见《大正藏》,No. 191,第 3 卷,第 932-975 页。

法贤译《帝释所问经》,参见《大正藏》,No. 15,第 1 卷,第 246-250 页。

法显《法显传》,章巽校注,上海：上海古籍出版社,1985 年。

Faxian, *Faxian zhuan* [*The Travels of Faxian* or *Record of Buddhist Kingdoms*], emended and annotated by Zhang Xun, Shanghai: Shanghai Chinese Classics Publishing House, 1985; *confer*: *Taishō,* No. 2085, Vol. 51: 857-866.

Faxian tr., *Dabo niepan jing* [大般涅槃经, *Mahāparinirvāṇasūtra*], in: *Taishō,* No. 7, Vol. 1: 191-207.

法云《翻译名义集》,参见《大正藏》,No. 2131,第 54 卷,第 1055-1185 页。

法藏《梵网经菩萨戒本疏》,参见《大正藏》,No. 1813,第 40 卷,第 602-655 页。

Fazang, *Fanwangjing pusa jieben shu*［*Annotation on the Latter Part of the Brahmājāla-sūtra/Sūtra of Brahmā's Net*］, in: *Taishō,* No. 1813, Vol. 40: 602-655.

法藏《华严经传记》,参见《大正藏》,No. 2073,第 51 卷,第 153-173 页。

法藏《大乘密严经疏》,参见《卍新纂大日本續藏經》(東京：日本國書刊行會,1980-1989 年,90 卷),No. 368,第 21 卷,第 127-170 页。

费长房《历代三宝记》,参见《大正藏》,No. 2034,第 49 卷,第 22-127 页。

Fei Zhangfang, *Lidai sanbo ji*［*Record of the Triratna through the Ages* or *Record concerning the Triratna under Successive Dynasties* or *Record of the Three Jewels throughout Successive Dynasties*］, in: *Taishō,* No. 2034, Vol. 49: 22-127.

佛驮跋陀罗译《大方广佛华严经》,参见《大正藏》,No. 278,第 9 卷,第 395-788 页。

Buddhabhadra［佛驮跋陀罗］tr., *Damoduoluo Chanjing*［达摩多罗禅经, *Dharmatrāta dhyāna-sūtra* or *Dhyāna Sūtra of Dharmatrāta* or *Yogācārabhūmi*］/*Lushan chanjing*［庐山禅经, *Dhyāna-sūtra translated at Mt. Lu*］, in: *Taishō,* No. 618, Vol. 15: 300-325.

佛驮跋陀罗译《佛说观佛三昧海经》,参见《大正藏》,No. 643,第 15 卷,第 645-697 页。

Buddhabhadra tr., *Foshuo guanfo sanmeihai jing*［*Buddha-dhyāna-samādhisāgara-sūtra/The Sutra on the Sea of Mystic Ecstasy Attained by Visualizing the Buddha* or *Ocean of Meditation on the Buddha Sūtra*］, in: *Taishō,* No. 643, Vol. 15: 645-697.

佛陀跋陀罗、法显译《摩诃僧祇律》,参见《大正藏》,No. 1425,第 22 卷,第 227-549 页。

Buddhabhadra and Faxian tr., *Mohesengqi lü*［*Mahāsaṃghika-vinaya*］, in: *Taishō,* No. 1425, Vol. 22: 227-549.

佛陀什、竺道生译《弥沙塞部和醯五分律》,参见《大正藏》,No. 1241,第 22 卷,第 1-194 页。

Buddhajiva and Zhu Daosheng tr., *Mishasai lü*［*Mahīśāsaka-vinaya*］/*Wufen lü*［*Fivefold Vinaya* or *Mahīśāsaka Fivefold Vinaya*］, in: *Taishō,* No. 1421, Vol. 22: 1-194.

佛陀耶舍、竺佛念译《长阿含经》,参见《大正藏》,No. 1,第 1 卷,第 1-149 页。

Buddhayaśas and Zhu Fonian tr., *Chang ahanjing*［*Dīrghāgama* or *The Long Āgama Sūtra*］, in: *Taishō,* No. 1, Vol. 1: 1-149.

佛陀耶舍、竺佛念译《四分律》,参见《大正藏》,No. 1428,第 22 卷,第 567-1014 页。

佛陀耶舍译《四分僧戒本》,参见《大正藏》,No. 1430,第 22 卷,第 1023-1030 页。

Buddhayaśas tr., *Sifenseng jieben*［*Fourfold Bhikṣuprātimokṣa-sūtra/Tanwude jieben,*

Bhikṣuprātimokṣa-sūtra of the Dharmaguptaka school/*Dharamaguptaka-bhikṣu-prātimokṣa-sūtra*], in: *Taishō,* No. 1430, Vol. 22: 1023-1030.

佛陀耶舍译《四分比丘尼戒本》,参见《大正藏》,No. 1431,第 22 卷,第 1031-1040 页。

弗若多罗、鸠摩罗什译《十诵律》,参见《大正藏》,No. 1435,第 23 卷,第 1-470 页。

Puṇyatāra and Kumārajīva tr., *Shisong lü* [*Ten Divisions of Monastic Rules*/*Sarvastivāda-vinaya*], in: *Taishō,* No. 1435, Vol. 23: 1-470.

Gao Yun [高允] "*Luyuan fu* [鹿苑赋, *Rhapsody on the Deerpark*]", in: *Guang hongmingji* [*Further Anthology of the Propagation of Light* or *Expanded Collection on the Propagation and Clarification of Buddhism*] by Daoxuan, in: *Taishō*, No. 2103, Vol. 52: 339.

工布查布《佛说造像量度经解》,参见《大正藏》,No. 1419,第 21 卷,第 941-956 页。

Gyōnen [凝然], *Risshū kōyō* [律宗纲要, *The Essentials of the Vinaya School*], in: *Taishō,* No. 2348, Vol. 74: 5-20.

怀海集编《百丈丛林清规》,仪润证义,载《卍新纂大日本续藏经》,No. 1244,第 63 卷,第 373-521 页。

怀信《释门自镜录》,参见《大正藏》,No. 2083,第 51 卷,第 802-822 页。

慧皎《高僧传》,汤用彤校注,北京:中华书局,1992 年;参见《大正藏》,No. 2059,第 50 卷,第 322-423 页。

Huijiao, *Gaoseng zhuan* [*Biographies of Eminent Priests* or *The Liang Dynasty Biographies of Eminent Priests* or *Biographies of Eminent Monks* or *Memoirs of Eminent Monks*], emended and annotated by Tang Yongtong, Beijing: Zhonghua Book Company, 1992; *confer*: *Taishō,* No. 2059, Vol. 50: 322-424.

慧觉等《贤愚经》,参见《大正藏》,No. 202,第 4 卷,第 349-445 页。

慧立、彦悰《大慈恩寺三藏法师传》,孙毓棠、谢方点校,北京:中华书局,2000 年;参见《大正藏》,No. 2053,第 50 卷,第 220-279 页。

慧琳《一切经音义》,参见《大正藏》,No. 2128,第 54 卷,第 311-933 页。

Huilin, *Yiqiejing yinyi* [*Pronunciation and Meaning in the Buddhist Scriptures* or *Pronunciation and Meaning of all the Scriptures*], in: *Taishō,* No. 2128, Vol. 54: 311-933.

慧远《维摩义记》,参见《大正藏》,No. 1776,第 38 卷,第 421-518 页。

Huiyuan, "*Yu yinshi liu yimin deng shu* [与隐士刘遗民等书, A Letter to Hermit Liu Yimin and others]", in: *Guang hongmingji* [*Further Anthology of the Propagation of Light* or *Expanded Collection on the Propagation and Clarification of Buddhism*] by Daoxuan, in: *Taishō,* No. 2103, Vol. 52: 304.

Huiyuan, "*Nianfo sanmei shiji xu*[念佛三昧诗集序, Preface to *A Collection of Poems on Buddhānusmṛti-samādhi*]", in: *Guang hongmingji*[*Further Anthology of the Propagation of Light* or *Expanded Collection on the Propagation and Clarification of Buddhism*] by Daoxuan, in: *Taishō,* No. 2103, Vol. 52: 351.

Huiyuan, "*Lushan chu xiuxing fangbian chanjing xu*[庐山出修行方便禅经序, Preface to *Dhyāna-sūtra of Buddhasena/Dharmatrāta Dhyāna-sūtra translated at Mt. Lu* or General Introduction to *Dhyāna Scriptures produced on Mt. Lu as Means to Religious Cultivation*]", in: *Chu sanzang ji ji*[出三藏记集, *A Collection of Records concerning the Tripiṭaka* or *A Collection of Records of Translations of the Tripiṭaka* or *Compilation of Notices on the Translation of the Tripiṭaka*] by Sengyou, in: *Taishō,* No. 2145, Vol. 55: 65-66.

Huiyuan[惠苑], *Xinyi dafangguangfo huayanjing yinyi*[新译大方广佛花严经音义, *Pronunciation and Meaning for Buddhist Terms in the Buddhāvataṁsaka-mahāvaipulya-sūtra/Pronunciation and Meaning for Buddhist Terms in the Flower Garland Sūtra* or *Avataṃsaka-sūtra*], in: *Taishō,* Vol. 54: 433-457.

吉迦夜、昙曜译《杂宝藏经》,参见《大正藏》, No. 203,第 4 卷,第 447-499 页。

Kikkāya/Kinkara and Tanyao tr., *Za baozang jing*[*Kṣudrakapiṭaka/Storehouse of Various Treasures Sūtra* or *The Scriptural Text: Storehouse of Sundry Valuables*], in: *Taishō,* No. 203, Vol. 4: 447-499.

Kinkara and Tanyao tr., *Fu fazang yinyuan zhuan*[付法藏因缘传, *A History of the Buddha's Successors* or *History of the Transmission of the Dharma-storehouse*], in: *Taishō,* No. 2058, Vol. 50: 297-322.

吉藏《三论玄义》,参见《大正藏》, No. 1852,第 45 卷,第 1-15 页。

净觉《楞伽师资记》,参见《大正藏》, No. 2837,第 85 卷,第 1283-1290 页。

靖迈《古今译经图纪》,参见《大正藏》, No. 2151,第 55 卷,第 348-367 页。

Jingmai, *Gujin yijing tuji*[*Record of the Picture of Ancient and Modern Translations of Sūtras* or *Record of Illustration of Translating Buddhist Tripiṭaka through the Ages*], *Taishō,* No. 2151, Vol. 55: 348-367.

[南唐]静、筠二禅师编撰《祖堂集》,张华点校,郑州:中州古籍出版社,2001 年。

Jingtai[静泰], *Zhongjing mulu*[众经目录, *A Catalogue of the Tripiṭaka*], *Taishō,* No.

2148, Vol. 55: 180-218.

觉岸《释氏稽古略》,参见《大正藏》, No. 2037,第 49 卷,第 737-902 页。

觉禅集《觉禅钞》,参见《大正新脩大藏经・图像》第五卷,第 1-691 页。

康僧会译《六度集经》,参见《大正藏》, No. 152,第 3 卷,第 1-52 页。

康僧铠译《昙无德律部杂羯磨》,参见《大正藏》, No. 1432,第 22 卷,第 1041-1051 页。

窥基《妙法莲华经玄赞》,参见《大正藏》, No. 1723,第 34 卷,第 651-854 页。

Kuiji, *Miaofa lianhuajing xuanzan* [In Praise of *the Lotus Sūtra*], in: *Taishō,* No. 1723, Vol. 34: 651-854.

窥基《大乘法苑义林章》,参见《大正藏》,No. 1861,第 45 卷,第 245-374 页。

窥基《异部宗轮论疏述记》,参见《卍新纂大日本續藏經》,No. 0844,第 53 卷,第 568-590 页。

Kumārajīva [鸠摩罗什] tr., *Miaofa lianhua jing* [妙法莲花经, *Saddharmapuṇḍarīka-sūtra* or *Lotus Sūtra of the Wonderful Law*], in: *Taishō,* No. 262, Vol. 9: 1-62.

Kumārajīva tr., *Mile xiasheng jing* [弥勒下生经, *Maitreyavyākaraṇa, Advent of Maitreya Sūtra*], in: *Taishō,* No. 454, Vol. 14: 423-425.

Kumārajīva tr., *Foshuo mile chengfo jing* [佛说弥勒成佛经, *Sūtra of Maitreya becoming a Buddha*], in: *Taishō,* No. 456, Vol. 14: 428-434.

鸠摩罗什译《禅密要法经》,参见《大正藏》,No. 613,第 15 卷,第 242-269 页。

Kumārajīva tr., *Chanfa yao* [禅法要, *Essentials of the Dhyāna-discipline*]/*Chanmi yaofa jing* [禅密要法经, *Secret Essentials of the Dhyāna-discipline* or *Sūtra about the Secret Essence of Dhyāna*], in: *Taishō,* No. 613, Vol. 15: 242-269.

Kumārajīva tr., *Zuochan sanmei jing* [坐禅三昧经, *Dhyāna-samādhi-sūtra, Sūtra on the Concentration of Sitting Meditation*]/*Guanzhong chanjing* [关中禅经, *Dhyāna-sūtra translated in the Central Shaanxi Plain*], in: *Taishō,* No. 614, Vol. 15: 269-286.

Kumārajīva tr., *Chanfa yaojie* [禅法要解, *Interpretation of the Dhyāna-discipline* or *Essential Explanation of the Way to Meditate*], in: *Taishō,* No. 616, Vol. 15: 286-297.

Kumārajīva?, *Siwei lueyao fa* [思惟略要法, *An Outline of Meditation* or *Outlining the Way to Reflect*], in: *Taishō,* No. 617, Vol. 15: 297-300.

李华《玄宗朝翻经三藏善无畏赠鸿胪卿行状》,参见《大正藏》,No. 2055,第 50 卷,第 290-292 页。

李俨《〈金刚般若经〉集注序》,载道世《广弘明集》卷二十二,参见《大正藏》No. 2103,第

52 卷,第 259c-260a 页。

礼言《梵语杂名》,参见《大正藏》,No. 2135,第 54 卷,第 1223-1241 页。

Li Yan, *Fanyu zaming* [*Sundry Names in Sanskrit*], in: *Taishō*, No. 2135, Vol. 54: 1223-1241

《历代法宝记》,参见《大正藏》, No. 2075,第 51 卷,第 179-196 页。

Lokakṣema [支娄迦谶译], *Bozhou sanmei jing* [般舟三昧经, *Pratyutpanna-buddha-sammukhāvaṣṭhitasamādhi-sūtra* or *Sūtra of the Meditation to behold the Buddhas* or *Sūtra on the Samādhi for Encountering Face-to-Face the Buddhas of the Present*], in: *Taishō,* No. 417, Vol. 13: 902-919.

明佺《大周刊定众经目录》,参见《大正藏》, No. 2153,第 55 卷,第 372-476 页。

Mingquan, *Dazhou kanding zhongjing mulu* [*A Catalogue of the Buddhist Canon compiled in the Reign Period of Empress Wu Zetian*], in: *Taishō,* No. 2153, Vol. 55: 372-476.

冥祥《大唐故三藏玄奘法师行状》,参见:《大正藏》, No. 2052,第 50 卷,第 214-220 页。

念常《佛祖历代通载》,参见《大正藏》, No. 2036,第 49 卷,第 477-735 页。

菩提流志译《大宝积经》,参见《大正藏》, No. 310,第 11 卷,第 1-685 页。

菩提流支译《入楞伽经》,参见《大正藏》,No. 671,第 16 卷,514-586 页。

菩提流支译《佛说法集经》,参见《大正藏》,No. 761,第 17 卷,609-650 页。

庆吉祥《至元法宝勘同目录》,见《昭和法寳總目録》第二卷,第 179-238 页。

僧伽跋陀译《善见律毗婆沙》,参见《大正藏》,No. 1462,第 24 卷,第 673-800 页。

僧伽提婆译《中阿含经》,参见《大正藏》,No. 26,第 1 卷,第 421-809 页。

Sengrui [僧叡], "*Guanzhong chu chanjing xu* [关中出禅经序, Preface to *Dhyāna-sūtra translated in the Central Shaanxi Plain*]", in: *Chu sanzang ji ji* [*A Collection of Records concerning the Tripiṭaka* or *Compilation of Notices on the Translation of the Tripiṭaka*] by Sengyou, in: *Taishō,* No. 2145, Vol. 55: 65.

僧佑《释迦谱》, 参见《大正藏》, No. 2040,第 50 卷,第 1-84 页。

僧佑《弘明集》, 参见《大正藏》, No. 2102,第 52 卷,第 1-96 页。

僧佑《出三藏记集》,苏晋仁、萧錬子点校,北京：中华书局,1995 年；参见《大正藏》, No. 2145,第 55 卷,第 1-114 页。

Sengyou, *Chu sanzang ji ji* [*A Collection of Records concerning the Tripiṭaka* or *A Collection of Records of Translations of the Tripiṭaka* or *Compilation of Notices on the Translation of the Tripiṭaka*], emended and annotated by Su Jinren and Xiao

Lianzi, Beijing: Zhonghua Book Company, 1995; *confer*: *Taishō,* No. 2145, Vol. 55: 1-114.

阇那崛多译《佛本行集经》,参见《大正藏》, No. 190,第 3 卷,第 655-932 页。

神清《北山录》,参见《大正藏》,No. 2113,第 52 卷,第 573-636 页。

Shenqing, *Beishan lu* [*Buddhism recorded at the Northern Mountain* or *North Mountain Record*], in: *Taishō,* No. 2113, Vol. 52: 573-636.

施护译《佛说法集名数经》,参见《大正藏》,No. 764,第 17 卷,第 660-662 页。

Dānapāla, *Foshuo faji mingshu jing* [*Dharma-saṃgraha*], in: *Taishō,* No. 764, Vol. 17: 660-662.

宋之问《登庄严揔持二寺阁》,参见：李昉《文苑英华》卷一七八,影印本,北京：中华书局,1966 年,第 868 页。

Sun Wenchuan [孙文川] and Chen Zuolin [陈作霖], *Nanchao fosizhi* [南朝佛寺志, *Record of the Buddhist Monasteries of the Southern Dynasties*], in: *Jinling suozhi jiuzhong* [金陵琐志九种, *Nine Annals of the Local History of Jinling*], Nanjing: Nanjing Publishing House, 2008: 139-285.

昙谛译《羯磨》,参见《大正藏》,No. 1433,第 22 卷,第 1051-1065 页。

昙无谶译《佛所行赞》,参见《大正藏》,No. 192,第 4 卷,第 1-54 页。

昙无谶等译《大方等大集经》,参见《大正藏》,No. 397,第 13 卷,第 1-407 页。

唐 (武) 则天皇后《三藏圣教序》,载《昭和法寶總目録》第三卷,第 1425b 页。

Wei Shou [魏收], *Weishu: Shilaozhi* [魏书 · 释老志, *History of the Wei Dynasties*: *Treatise on Buddhism and Taoism*], punctuated and emended ed., Beijing: Zhonghua Book Company, 1974: 3025-3062.

玄应《众经音义》,载《大日本校訂縮刻大藏經》(東京：弘教書院,1881-1885 年,40 函 418 册,下文简作《縮刷藏》),函 "为七"。

玄应《一切经音义》,见《一切经音义：三种校本合刊》,徐时仪校注,上海：上海古籍出版社,2008 年。

Xuanying, *Yiqiejing yinyi* [*Pronunciation and Meaning in the Buddhist Scriptures* or *Pronunciation and Meaning of all the Scriptures*], emended by Sun Xingyan [孙星衍] et al., Shanghai: The Commercial Press, 1936.

Xuanzang [玄奘] tr., *Apidamo dapiposha lun* [阿毗达磨大毗婆沙论, *Abhidharmamahāvibhāṣā-śāstra* or *Great Exegesis of Abhidharma*], in: *Taishō* , No. 1545, Vol. 27: 1-1004.

玄奘译《阿毗达磨顺正理论》,参见《大正藏》, No. 1562,第 29 卷,第 329-775 页。

玄奘译《大乘阿毗达磨集论》，参见《大正藏》，No. 1605，第 31 卷，第 663-694 页。

玄奘译《异部宗轮论》，参见《大正藏》，No. 2031，第 49 卷，第 15-17 页。

Xuanzang tr., *Yibu zonglun lun* [*Samayabhedoparacanacakra/The Doctrines of the Different Schools* or *The Wheel of the Formations of Divisions of the Doctrine*] by Vasumitra, in: *Taishō*, No. 2031, Vol. 49: 15-17.

玄奘《大唐西域记》，季羡林等校注，北京：中华书局，1985 年；参见《大正藏》，No. 2087，第 51 卷，第 867-947 页。

Xuanzang, *Datang xiyu ji* [*Record of the Western Regions of the Great Tang Dynasty* or *The Great Tang Record of* (*Travels to*) *the Western Regions*], emended and annotated by Ji Xianlin et al., Beijing: Zhonghua Book Company, 1985.

彦悰纂录《集沙门不应拜俗等事》，参见《大正藏》No. 2108，第 52 卷，第 443-474 页。

彦琮《唐护法沙门法琳别传》，参见《大正藏》，No. 2051，第 50 卷，第 198-213 页。

阎朝隐《唐大荐福寺故寺主翻经大德法藏和尚传》，参见《大正藏》，No. 2054，第 50 卷，第 280-289 页。

杨衒之《洛阳伽蓝记》，周祖谟校释，北京：中华书局，1963 年。

Yang Xuanzhi, *Luoyang qielan ji* [*A Record of Saṃghārāmas in Luoyang* or *Record of the Monasteries of Luoyang*], emended and annotated by Zhou Zumo, Beijing: Zhonghua Book Company, 1963.

杨衒之《洛阳伽蓝记》，范祥雍校注，上海古籍出版社，1978 年。

义净译《根本说一切有部毗奈耶》，参见《大正藏》，No. 1442，第 23 卷，第 627-905 页。

义净译《根本说一切有部毗奈耶药事》，参见《大正藏》，No. 1448，第 24 卷，第 1-97 页。

义净译《根本说一切有部毗奈耶破僧事》，参见《大正藏》，No. 1450，第 24 卷，第 99-206 页。

义净译《根本说一切有部毗奈耶杂事》，参见《大正藏》，No. 1451，第 24 卷，第 207-414 页。

Yijing tr., *Genben shuoyiqieyoubu pinaiye zashi* [*Mūlasarvāstivāda-vinaya-kṣudraka-vastu, Monastic Rules of the Mūlasarvāstivāda School on Various Matters*], in: *Taishō,* No. 1451, Vol. 24: 207-414.

义净译《根本说一切有部百一羯磨》，参见《大正藏》，No. 1453，第 24 卷，第 455-500 页。

义净《大唐西域求法高僧传》，王邦维校注，北京：中华书局，1988 年；参见《大正藏》，No. 2066，第 51 卷，第 1-12 页。

Yijing, *Datang xiyu qiufa gaoseng zhuan* [*Biographies of Eminent Priests of the Great Tang Dynasty Who Sought the Law in the Western Regions* or *The Great Tang*

Biographies of Eminent Monks who Sought the Dharma in the Western Regions], emended and annotated by Wang Bangwei, Beijing: Zhonghua Book Company, 1988. *confer*: *Taishō,* No. 2066, Vol. 51: 1-12.

义净《南海寄归内法传》,王邦维校注,北京：中华书局,1995 年；参见《大正藏》,No. 2125,第 54 卷,第 204-234 页。

Yijing, *Nanhai ji gui neifa zhuan* [*Record of Buddhist Monastic Traditions of Southern Asia* or *A Record of the Buddhist Kingdoms of the Southern Archipelago or Tales of Returning from the South Seas with the Dharma*], emended and annotated by Wang Bangwei, Beijing: Zhonghua Book Company, 1995; *confer*: *Taishō,* No. 2125, Vol. 54: 204-234.

一行《大毗卢遮那成佛经疏》,参见《大正藏》,No. 1796,第 39 卷,第 579-789 页。

Yixing tr., *Da piluzhena chengfojing shu* [大毗卢遮那成佛经疏, *Annotations on the Mahā-vairocanābhisaṃbodhi-vikurvitādhiṣṭhāna-vaipulya-sūtrendra-vāja-nāma-dharmapar yāya* or *Annotation on Mahā-vairocanā-sūtra*], in: *Taishō,* No. 1796, Vol. 39: 579-789.

Yu Xin [庾信], "*Qinzhou tianshuijun maijiya fokan ming bing xu* [秦州天水郡麦积崖佛龛铭并序, Preface and Epigraph to the Buddhist Niches at Maijiya, Tanshui District, Qinzhou Prefecture]" , in: *Wenyuan yinghua* [*The Best Works in the Literature and Art Circles* or *Corpus of the Literary World*], fascimile edition, Beijing: Zhonghua Book Company, 1966: 4149-4150.

元照《四分律行事钞资持记》,参见《大正藏》,No. 1805,第 40 卷,第 157-428 页。

元照《贞元新定释教目录》,参见《大正藏》,No. 2157,第 55 卷,第 771-1048 页。

赞宁《宋高僧传》,范祥雍点校,北京：中华书局,1987 年。

湛然《止观辅行传弘决》,参见《大正藏》,No. 1912,第 46 卷,第 141-446 页。

智炬《双峰山曹侯溪宝林传》,见《景印宋藏遗珍》,上海：影印宋版藏经会,1935 年,上集第四函；中华大藏经编辑局编《中华大藏经 · 汉文部分》,北京：中华书局,1994 年,第 73 册,第 665-675 页。

智昇《续古今译经图纪》,参见《大正藏》,No. 2152,第 55 卷,第 367-372 页。

智昇《开元释教录》,参见《大正藏》,No. 2154,第 55 卷,第 476-723 页。

Zhisheng, *Kaiyuan shijiao lu* (*The Kaiyuan Era Catalogue of the Buddhist Canon* or *A Catalogue of the Buddhist Sacred Books of the Kaiyuan Period* or *A Catalogue of the Buddhist Canon compiled in the Kaiyuan Period* or *Record of Śākyamuni's*

Teachings Compiled during the Kaiyuan Era), in: *Taishō,* No. 2154, Vol. 55: 477-723.

智旭《阅藏知津》,见《昭和法寶總目録》第三卷,第 1007-1252 页。

子璿《起信论疏笔削记》,参见《大正藏》,No. 1848,第 44 卷,第 297-409 页。

宗鉴集《释门正统》,参见《卍新纂大日本续藏经》,No. 1513,第 75 卷,第 254-365 页。

失译《菩萨本行经》,参见《大正藏》,No. 155,第 3 卷,第 108-124 页。

Unknown translator, *Pusa benxing jing* (*Sūtra on Bodhisattva's Own Deeds*), in: *Taishō,* No. 155, Vol. 1: 108-124.

失译《萨婆多毗尼毗婆沙》,参见《大正藏》,No. 1440,第 23 卷,第 503-558 页。

Unknown translator [失译], *Bonihuan jing* [般泥洹经, *Parinirvāṇa Sūtra*], in: *Taishō,* No. 6, Vol. 1: 176-191.

现代论著

八木春生《中国北魏时期的金刚力士像》,载《宿白先生八秩华诞纪念文集》,北京：文物出版社,2002 年,第 353-369 页。

白文固《南北朝隋唐僧官制度探究》,刊《世界宗教研究》,1984 年第 1 期,第 53-59 页。

鲍鼎《唐宋塔之初步分析》,刊《中国营造学社汇刊》,6 卷 4 期 (1937 年),第 1-29 页。

北京图书馆善本组编《敦煌劫余录续编》,石印本,北京：北京图书馆,1981 年。

北京图书馆金石组、中国佛教图书文物馆石经组编《房山石经题记汇编》,北京：书目文献出版社,1987 年。

北京图书馆金石组编辑《北京图书馆藏中国历代石刻拓片汇编》,全 101 册,郑州：中州古籍出版社,1989 年。

伯希和《六朝同唐代的几个艺术家》,冯承钧译,载冯承钧《西域南海史地考证译丛》第二卷《西域南海史地考证译丛八编》,北京：商务印书馆,1995 年,第 120-167 页。

薄小莹《敦煌遗书汉文卷编年》,铅印本,北京大学,1988 年。

薄小莹《敦煌遗书汉文纪年卷编年》,长春：长春出版社,1990 年。

柴俊林《试论响堂石窟的初创年代》,刊《考古》,1996 年第 6 期,第 73-77 页。

岑仲勉《元和姓纂四校记》,景印二版,台北：中研院历史语言研究所,1991 年。

岑仲勉《汉书西域传地理校释》,2 册,北京：中华书局,1981 年。

Cen Zongmian, *Hanshu xiyuzhuan dili jiaoshi* [*Emendation and Annotation to the Monograph on the Western Regions in the History of the Western Han Dynasty*], Beijing: Zhonghua Book Company, 1981.

常青《龙门石窟“北市彩帛行净土堂”》,载龙门石窟研究所编《龙门石窟研究文选》,上海：上海人民美术出版社,1993 年,第 260-275 页。

常青《初唐宝冠佛像的定名问题》,刊《佛学研究》,第 6 期 (1997 年),第 91-97 页。

常青《试论龙门初唐密教雕刻》,载龙门石窟研究院编《龙门石窟研究院论文选》,郑州：中州古籍出版社,2004 年,第 240-279 页。

陈浩《隋禅宗三祖僧璨塔铭砖》,刊《文物》,1985 年 4 期,第 8 页。

陈 明《Richard Salomon, *A Gāndhārī Version of the Rhinoceros Sūtra: British Library Kharoṣṭhī Fragment 5B;* Gandhāran Buddhist Texts Volume 1 书评》,刊《敦煌吐鲁番研究》第七卷,北京：中华书局,2004 年,第 451-456 页。

陈 明《Tomothy Lenz, *A New Version of the Gāndhārī Dharmapada and A Collection of Previous-Birth Stories: British Library Kharoṣṭhī Fragments 16+25;* Gandhāran Buddhist Texts Volume 3 书评》,刊《敦煌吐鲁番研究》第八卷,北京：中华书局,2005 年,第 362-365 页。

陈明达《关于汉代建筑的几个重要发现》,刊《文物参考资料》,1954 年第 9 期,第 91-94 页。

陈清香《龙门看经寺洞罗汉群像考——祖师传承说的石刻例证》,载陈清香《罗汉图像研究》,台北：文津出版社有限公司,1995 年,第 123-153 页。

陈寅恪《武则天与佛教》,载陈寅恪《金明馆丛稿二编》,上海：上海古籍出版社,1980 年,第 137-155 页。

陈寅恪《童受喻鬘论梵语残本跋》,载陈寅恪《金明馆丛稿二编》,上海：上海古籍出版社,1980 年,第 207-211 页。

陈寅恪《敦煌本十诵比丘尼波罗提木叉跋》,载陈寅恪《金明馆丛稿二编》,上海：上海古籍出版社,1980 年,第 258-260 页。

陈寅恪《隋唐制度渊源略论稿》,上海：上海古籍出版社,1982 年。

陈寅恪《魏晋南北朝史讲演录》,万绳楠整理,合肥：黄山书社,1987 年。

Chen Yinke, *Wei jin nanbeichao shi jiangyan lu* [*Lectures on the History of the Wei, Jin and the Southern-and-Northern Dynasties*], ed. by Wan Shengnan, Hefei: Huangshan Publishing House, 1987.

陈寅恪《唐代政治史略稿》,手写本,上海：上海古籍出版社,1988 年。

Chen Yinke [陈寅恪], *Cheny Yinke ji*: *Dushu zhaji san ji* [陈寅恪集：读书札记三集, *Collected Works of Chen Yinke: Reading Notes III*], Beijing: SDX Joint Publishing House, 2001.

陈寅恪《陈寅恪集：讲义及杂稿》,北京：生活 · 读书 · 新知三联书店,2002 年。

Chen Yinke, *Chen Yinke ji*: *Jiangyi ji zagao* [*Collected Works of Chen Yinke*: *Teaching Materials and Essays*], Beijing: SDX Joint Publishing House, 2002.

陈垣《敦煌劫余录》,南京：国立中央研究院历史语言研究所,1931 年。

陈垣《中国佛教史籍概论》,北京：中华书局,1962 年。

陈垣《释氏疑年录》,北京：中华书局,1964 年。

陈垣《记大同武州山石窟寺》,载《陈垣学术论文集》第一集,北京：中华书局,1980 年,第 398-409 页。

Chen Yuan, "*Ji Datong wuzhoushan shikusi* [Notes on the Cave-temple Complex at Wuzhou Hill, Datong]", in: *Chenyuan xueshu lunwenji* [*A Collection of Essays by Professor Chen Yuan*], Vol. I, Beijing: Zhonghua Book Company, 1980: 398-409.

陈垣《云冈石窟寺之译经与刘孝标》,载《陈垣学术论文集》第一集,北京：中华书局,1980 年,第 443-448 页。

陈兆复《剑川石窟》,昆明：云南人民出版社,1980 年。

陈直《西安出土隋唐泥佛像通考》,载陈直《文史考古论丛》,天津：天津古籍出版社,1988 年,第 502-512 页。

陈祚龙《敦煌古钞内典尾记汇校初编》,载陈祚龙《敦煌文物随笔》,台北：商务印书馆,1979 年,第 153-174 页。

成都市文物考古工作队《成都市西安路南朝石刻造像清理简报》,刊《文物》,1998 年第 11 期,第 4-20 页。

Chengdushi wenwu kaogu gongzuodui [Archaeological Team of Chengdu], "*Chengduoshi xi'anlu nanchao shike zaoxiang qingli jianbao* [A Report on the Excavation of the Buddhist Stone Sculptures of the Southern Dynasties Period from a Hoard at Xi'an Road, Chengdu]", in: *Cultural Relics*, 11 (1998): 4-20.

丁明夷《龙门石窟唐代造像的分期与类型》,刊《考古学报》,1979 年第 4 期,第 519-545 页。

丁明夷、马世长、雄西《克孜尔石窟的佛传壁画》,载新疆维吾尔自治区文物管理委员会、拜城县克孜尔千佛洞文物保管所、北京大学考古系编《中国石窟·克孜尔石窟》一,北京：文物出版社,1989 年,第 186-207 页。

Ding Mingyi et al., "*Kezi'er shiku de fozhuan bihua* [Representation of the Buddha's Life-story in the Mural Paintings at Kizil Caves, Kucha]", in: *Zhongguo shiku*: *Kezi'er shiku* [*The Cave-temples of China: Kizil Caves*], Vol. 1, Beijing: Cultural Relics Press, 1989: 185-222.

丁明夷《巩县天龙响堂安阳数处石窟寺》,载《中国美术全集》雕塑编 13《巩县天龙山响堂山安阳石窟雕刻》,北京：文物出版社,1989 年,第 26-51 页。

丁明夷、李治国《焦山、吴官屯(石窟)调查记》,载《中国石窟·云冈石窟》一,北京：文物出版社,1991 年,第 216-221 页。

董玉祥、臧志军《甘肃武山水帘洞石窟群》,刊《文物》,1985 年第 5 期,第 7-16 页。

董玉祥主编《中国美术全集：麦积山等石窟壁画》,北京：人民美术出版社,1987 年。

段文杰《略论敦煌壁画的风格特点和艺术成就》,刊《敦煌研究》,试刊第 2 期(1982 年),第 1-16 页。

敦煌文物研究所考古组《敦煌晋墓》,刊《考古》,1974 年第 3 期,第 191-199 页。

敦煌文物研究所《莫高窟第 220 窟新发现的复壁壁画》,刊《文物》,1978 年第 12 期,第 41-46 页。

敦煌研究院编《敦煌莫高窟供养人题记》,北京：文物出版社,1986 年。

敦煌研究院编《敦煌石窟内容总录》,北京：文物出版社,1996 年。

敦煌研究院编《敦煌遗书总目索引新编》,北京：中华书局,2000 年。

樊锦诗、马世长、关友惠《敦煌莫高窟北朝洞窟的分期》,载《中国石窟·敦煌莫高窟》一,北京：文物出版社,1981 年,第 185-197 页。

樊锦诗、马世长《莫高窟北朝洞窟本生、因缘故事画补考》,刊《敦煌研究》,1986 年第 1 期,第 36-38 页。

范祥雍《唐代中印交通吐蕃一道考》,载范祥雍《范祥雍文史论文集》,上海：上海古籍出版社,2014 年,第 143-181 页。

方豪《中西交通史》,影印本,长沙：岳麓书社,1987 年。

肥田路美《四川地区的触地印如来坐像的造像次第》,载李正刚主编《2004 年龙门石窟国际学术研讨会文集》,郑州：河南人民出版社,2006 年,第 430-435 页。

冯承钧《历代求法翻经录》,上海：商务印书馆,1931 年。

冯承钧《西域南海史地考证论著汇辑》,北京：中华书局,1957 年。

Feng Chengjun, *Xiyu nanhai shidi kaozheng lunzhu huiji* [*Collected Works on the History and Historical Geography of the Western Regions, South Asia and Southeast Asia*], Beijing: Zhonghua Book Company, 1957.

Feng Chengjun, "*Wang Xuance shiji* [王玄策事辑, Collection of Wang Xuance's Deeds and Affairs]", in: *Xiyu nanhai shidi kaozheng lunzhu huiji* [*Collected Works on the History and Historical Geography of the Western Regions, South Asia and Southeast Asia*] by Feng Chengjun, Beijing: Zhonghua Book Company, 1957: 102-128.

富安敦《龙门大奉先寺的起源及地位》，刊《中原文物》，1997 年第 2 期，第 86-89 页。

傅成金《安岳石刻之玄应考》，刊《四川文物》，1991 年第 3 期，第 48-50 页。

傅成金《再识安岳圆觉洞摩崖造像》，刊《四川文物》，1991 年第 6 期，第 36-41 页。

甘肃省文化局文物工作队《调查炳灵寺石窟的新收获》，刊《文物》，1963 年第 10 期，第 1-6、10 页。

Gansusheng wenhuaju wenwu gongzuodui [Archaeological Team of Gansu Cultural Heritage Bureau], "*Diaocha binglingsi shiku de xin shouhuo* [New Discoveries on the Buddhist Cave-temple Complex at Binglingsi]", in: *Cultural Relics*, 10 (1963): 1-6, 10.

甘肃省文物考古研究所等编《河西石窟》，北京：文物出版社，1987 年。

高田修《佛教故事画与敦煌壁画：专论敦煌前期的本缘故事画》，载《中国石窟·敦煌莫高窟》二，北京：文物出版社，1984 年，第 200-208 页。

宫大中《龙门石窟艺术》，上海：上海人民出版社，1981 年。

谷霁光《府兵制度考释》，上海：上海人民出版社，1962 年。

古正美《龙门擂鼓台三洞的开凿性质与定年：唐中宗的佛王政治活动及信仰》，载《龙门石窟一千五百周年国际学术讨论会论文集》，北京：文物出版社，1996 年，第 166-182 页。

关百益《伊阙石刻图表》，开封：河南博物馆，1935 年。

郭良鋆《佛陀和原始佛教思想》，北京：中国社会科学出版社，1997 年。

Guo Liangyun, *Fotuo he yuanshi fojiao sixiang* [*Buddha and Thought of Primitive Buddhism*], Beijing: Chinese Social Science Press, 1997.

郭相颖《安岳石刻考察纪实》，载重庆大足石刻艺术博物馆、大足县文物保管所编《大足石刻研究文集》，重庆：重庆出版社，1993 年，第 308-338 页。

国家文物局主编《2002 中国重要考古发现》，北京：文物出版社，2003 年。

State Administration of Cultural Heritage ed., *Major Archaeological Discoveries in China in 2002*, Beijing: Cultural Relics Press, 2003.

国家文物局主编《2010 中国重要考古发现》，北京：文物出版社，2011 年。

State Administration of Cultural Heritage ed., *Major Archaeological Discoveries in China in 2010,* Beijing: Cultural Relics Press, 2011.

豪普特曼《巴基斯坦北部印度河上游古代文物研究：兼论丝绸之路南线岩画走廊的威胁与保护》，边钰鼎译，载李崇峰主编《犍陀罗与中国》，北京：文物出版社，2019 年，第 421-474 页。

河南省文化局文物工作队编《巩县石窟寺》，北京：文物出版社，1963 年。

贺世哲《敦煌莫高窟供养人题记校勘》,刊《中国史研究》,第三期(1980年),第25-42页。

何士骥、刘厚滋编《南北响堂及其附近石刻目录》,北平：北平研究院,1936年。

何利群《延安地区佛教石窟调查报告》,打印本,北京大学考古系资料室,2001年。

何利群《延安地区宋金石窟分期研究》(硕士学位论文),打印本,北京大学,2001年。

Higuchi, Takayasu［樋口隆康］, “From Bāmiyān to Dunhuang”, in: *Dunhuang shiku yanjiu guoji taolunhui wenji*: *Shiku kaogu bian*［敦煌石窟研究国际讨论会文集：石窟考古编,*Proceedings of 1987 International Conference on Dunhuang Cave Temples; Archaeological Section*］, Shenyang: Liaoning Fine Art Press, 1990: 117-122.

洪业《驳景教碑出土于盩厔说》,载《洪业论学集》,北京：中华书局,1981年,第56-63页。

忽滑谷快天《中国禅学思想史》,朱谦之译,上海：上海古籍出版社,2002年。

胡适《论禅宗史的纲领》,载姜义华主编《胡适学术文集：中国佛学史》,北京：中华书局,1997年,第34-38页。

Hu Shih, “*Chanxue gushi kao*［禅学古史考, On the History of the *Dhyāna*-discipline］”, in: *Hushi xueshu wenji*: *Zhongguo foxueshi*［胡适学术文集：中国佛学史, *Collected Works of Hu Shih*: *A History of Chinese Buddhism*］, Beijing: Zhonghua Book Company, 1997: 38-54.

胡适《〈楞伽师资记〉序》,载姜义华主编《胡适学术文集：中国佛学史》,北京：中华书局,1997年,第54-60页。

胡适《楞伽宗考》,载姜义华主编《胡适学术文集：中国佛学史》,北京：中华书局,1997年,第94-129页。

胡适《跋〈宝林传〉残本七卷》,载姜义华主编《胡适学术文集：中国佛学史》,北京：中华书局,1997年,第171-182页。

黄宝瑜《中国佛教建筑》,载章嘉等著《中国佛教史论集》三,台北：中华文化出版事业委员会,1956年,第849-914页。

黄苗子《克孜尔断想》,载黄苗子《艺林一枝：古美术文编》,北京：生活·读书·新知三联书店,2003年,第302-307页。

黄如英《石钟山石窟》,刊《文物》,1981年第8期,第80-84页。

黄盛璋《关于古代中国与尼泊尔的文化交流》,载黄盛璋《中外交通与交流史研究》,合肥：安徽教育出版社,2002年,第36-66页。

霍旭初、王建林《丹青斑驳　千秋壮观：克孜尔石窟壁画艺术及分期概述》,载新疆龟兹石窟研究所编《龟兹佛教文化论集》,乌鲁木齐：新疆美术摄影出版社,1993年,第201-228页。

Huo Xuchu and Wang Jianlin, "*Danqing banbo qianqiu zhuangguan: Kezi'er shiku bihua yishu ji fenqi gaishu* [Evidence of the Treasure House of a Great Art: A Survey of Kizil Mural Art and its Periodization]", in: *Qiuzi fojiao wenhua lunji* [*Collected Essays on Kucha Buddhist Culture*], ed. Kucha Cave Research Institute, Urumchi: Xinjiang Art & Photograph Publishing House, 1993: 201-228.

季羡林《原始佛教的语言问题》,载季羡林《印度古代语言论集》,北京：中国社会科学出版社,1982 年,第 402-411 页。

季羡林《中世印度雅利安语二题》,载《季羡林学术论著自选集》,北京：北京师范学院出版社,1991 年,第 343-361 页。

季羡林《原始佛教的语言问题》,载《季羡林佛教学术论文集》,台北：东初出版社,1995 年,第 55-67 页。

季羡林《再谈"浮屠"与"佛"》,载《季羡林佛教学术论文集》,台北：东初出版社,1995 年,第 37-54 页。

季羡林《梅呾利耶与弥勒》,载《季羡林佛教学术论文集》,台北：东初出版社,1995 年,第 277-293 页。

Jia Yingyi [贾应逸], "*Kezi'er yu mogaoku de niepan jingbian bijiao yanjiu* [克孜尔与莫高窟的涅槃经变比较研究, A Comparative Study of Kizil and Mogaoku *Nirvāṇa-sūtra* Paintings]," in: *Qiuzi fojiao wenhua lunji* [*Collected Essays on Kucha Buddhist Culture*], ed. Kucha Cave Research Institute, Urumchi: Xinjiang Art & Photograph Publishing House, 1993: 229-240.

Jia Yingyi, "*Jiumoluoshi yijing he beiliang shiqi de gaochang fojiao* [鸠摩罗什译经和北凉时期的高昌佛教, Kumārajīva's Translated Versions of the *Sūtras* and the Turfan Buddhism in the Period of Northern Liang State]", in: *Dunhuang Research*, No. 1 (1999): 146-158.

焦建辉《龙门东山擂鼓台区第 4 窟相关问题探讨》,刊《石窟寺研究》第三辑,北京：文物出版社,2012 年,第 212-223 页。

金克木《再阅〈楞伽〉》,载金克木《梵佛探》,石家庄：河北教育出版社,1996 年,第 413-421 页。

金维诺《〈纨扇仕女图〉与周昉》,载金维诺《中国美术史论集》,北京：人民美术出版社,1981 年,第 178-189 页。

金维诺《中国美术史论集》,北京：人民美术出版社,1981 年。

荆三林《中国石窟雕刻艺术史》,北京：人民美术出版社,1988 年。

雷奈·格鲁塞著《印度的文明》常任侠、袁音译,北京：商务印书馆,1965 年。

雷玉华、王剑平《四川菩提瑞像研究》,载李正刚主编《2004 年龙门石窟国际学术研讨会文集》,郑州：河南人民出版社,2006 年,第 492-497 页。

李崇峰《克孜尔中心柱窟主室正壁画塑题材及有关问题》,载巫鸿主编《汉唐之间的宗教艺术与考古》,北京：文物出版社,2000 年,第 209-233 页。

Li, Chongfeng, *Kezi'er zhongxinzhuku zhushi zhengbi huasu ticai ji youguan wenti* [The Main Image on the Façade of the *Stūpa*-pillar in the *Chētiyagharas* of Kizil, Kucha], in: *Between Han and Tang: Religious Art and Archaeology in a Transformative Period*, ed. Wu Hung, Beijing: Cultural Relics Press, 2000: 209-233.

李崇峰《中印佛教石窟寺比较研究：以塔庙窟为中心》,北京：北京大学出版社,2003 年。

Li, Chongfeng, *Zhongyin fojiao shikusi bijiao yanjiu: Yi tamiaoku wei zhongxin* (*Chētiyagharas in Indian and Chinese Buddhist Cave-temples: A Comparative Study*), Beijing: Peking University Press, 2003.

李崇峰《西行求法与罽宾道》,刊《燕京学报》,新二十一期 (2006 年),第 175-187 页。

Li, Chongfeng, "*Xixing qiufa yu jibindao* [Jibin Route and Propagation of Buddhism into China]", in: *Yenching Journal of Chinese Studies*, New No. 21 (2006): 175-188.

李崇峰《克孜尔部分中心柱窟与〈长阿含经〉等佛典》,载《徐苹芳先生纪念文集》,上海：上海古籍出版社,2012 年,第 419-465 页。

Li, Chongfeng, "*Kezi'er bufen zhongxinzhuku yu Chang'ahanjing deng fodian* [*The Dīrghāgama* Text and *the Chētiyagharas* at Kizil, Kucha]", in: *Xu Pingfang xiansheng ji'nian wenji* [*Papers in Commemoration of Professor Xu Pingfang*], Shanghai: Shanghai Chinese Classics Publishing House, 2012: 419-465.

李崇峰《菩提像初探》,刊《石窟寺研究》第三辑,北京：文物出版社,2012 年,第 190-211 页。

李昆声《云南艺术史》,昆明：云南教育出版社,1995 年。

李霖灿《剑川石宝山石刻考察记》,载李霖灿《中国名画研究》上,台北：艺文印书馆,1971 年,第 119-151 页。

李霖灿《南诏大理国新资料的综合研究》,台北：故宫博物院,1982 年。

李特文斯基主编《中亚文明史》第三卷,马小鹤译,北京：中国对外翻译出版公司,2003 年。

李文生《龙门石窟的新发现及其它》,载李文生《龙门石窟与洛阳历史文化》,上海：上海人民美术出版社,1993 年,第 16-29 页。

李文生《龙门唐代密宗造像》,载李文生《龙门石窟与洛阳历史文化》,上海：上海人民美术出版社,1993 年,第 38-46 页。

李文生《龙门石窟佛社研究》,载龙门石窟研究院编《龙门石窟研究院论文选》,郑州：中州古籍出版社,2004 年,第 62-85 页。

李永翘、胡文和《大足石刻内容总录》,载《大足石刻研究》,成都：四川省社会科学院出版社,1985 年,第 357-575 页。

李玉昆《龙门杂考》,刊《文物》,1980 年第 1 期,第 25-33 页。

李玉昆《龙门碑刻及其史料价值》,载刘景龙、李玉昆主编《龙门石窟碑刻题记汇录》,北京：中国大百科全书出版社,1998 年,上卷第 8-79 页。

Li Yukun, "*Longmen beike ji qi shiliao jiazhi* [Inscriptions of Longmen and Their Historical Value]", in: *Longmenshiku beike tiji huilu* [*Inscriptions of the Longmen Cave Temples*], Beijing: The Encyclopedia of China Publishing House, 1998, Vol. I: 8-79.

李玉珉《中国观音的信仰与图像》,载台北故宫博物院编辑委员会编《观音特展》,台北：故宫博物院,2000 年,第 10-39 页。

李玉珉《试论唐代降魔成道式装饰佛》,刊《故宫学术季刊》,第二十三卷第三期 (2006 年),第 39-90 页。

李玉珉《四川菩提瑞像窟龛研究》,载重庆大足石刻艺术博物馆编《2005 年重庆大足石刻国际学术研讨会论文集》,北京：文物出版社,2007 年,第 548-561 页。

李聿骐《试述李治武则天时期龙门石窟中的神王像：以典型窟龛为例》,刊《石窟寺研究》第 2 辑,北京：文物出版社,2011 年,第 178-190 页。

李裕群《中原北方地区北朝晚期的石窟寺》(博士学位论文),打印本,北京：北京大学,1993 年。

李裕群《北朝晚期石窟寺研究》,北京：文物出版社,2003 年。

Li Yuqun, *Beichao wanqi shikusi yanjiu* [*A Study on the Cave-temples of the Late Northern Dynasties Period*], Beijing: Cultural Relics Press, 2003.

李月伯等《麦积山石窟的主要窟龛内容总录》,载阎文儒主编《麦积山石窟》,兰州：甘肃人民出版社,1983 年,第 156-200 页。

李志夫《中印佛学比较研究》,北京：中国社会科学出版社,2001 年。

Li Zhiguo [李　治　国] and Liu Jianjun [刘　建　军], "*Beiwei pingcheng luyeyuan shiku diaocha ji*［北魏平城鹿野苑石窟调查记，A Survey of Rock-cut Caves at the Deer-park Monastery and Temple of the Northern Wei Dynasty in Pingcheng］”, in: *Zhongguo shiku*: *Yungang shiku*［中国石窟·云冈石窟，*The Cave-temples of China*: *Yungang Caves*］I, Beijing: Cultural Relics Press, 1991: 212-215.

李铸晋《敦煌隋代叙事画的几个问题》(摘要)，刊《敦煌研究》，1988年第2期，第96页。

梁思成《中国建筑史》，载《梁思成文集》三，北京：中国建筑工业出版社，1985年，第1-272页。

梁思成《中国雕塑史》，载《梁思成文集》三，北京：中国建筑工业出版社，1985年，第273-399页。

Liang Sicheng (Ssu-ch'eng), *Zhongguo diaosushi*［*A History of the Chinese Sculpture*］, in: *Liang Sicheng wenji*［*Collected Works of Liang Sicheng* (Ssu-ch'eng)］, III, Beijing: China Building Industry Press, 1985：273-399.

梁思成、林徽音、刘敦桢《云冈石窟中所表现的北魏建筑》，刊《中国营造学社汇刊》，第四卷第三四期合刊本(1934年)，第171-218页。

列维、沙畹《罽宾考》，载冯承钧《西域南海史地考证译丛》第二卷《西域南海史地考证译丛七编》，北京：商务印书馆，1995年，第58-61页。

林玲爱《克孜尔石窟金刚力士的特征及其意义》，刊《艺术史研究》，第八辑(2006年)，第251-268页。

林梅村《法藏部在中国》，载林梅村《汉唐西域与中国文明》，北京：文物出版社，1998年，第343-364页。

林悟殊、荣新江《所谓李氏旧藏敦煌景教文献二种辨伪》，刊《九州学刊》，第4卷4期(1992年)，第19-34页。

林悟殊《西安景教碑研究述评》，刊刘东主编《中国学术》第四辑，北京：商务印书馆，2000年，第253-256页。

刘敦桢《苏州古建筑调查记》，载《刘敦桢文集》二，北京：中国建筑工业出版社，1984年，第257-317页。

刘敦桢《云南古建筑调查记(未完稿)》，载《刘敦桢文集》三，北京：中国建筑工业出版社，1987年版，第359-401页。

刘敦桢《中国之塔》，载《刘敦桢文集》四，北京：中国建筑工业出版社，1992年，第1-15页。

刘慧达《北魏石窟与禅》，刊《考古学报》，1978年第3期，第337-352页。

Liu Huida, “*Beiwei shiku yu chan*［北魏石窟与禅，*Dhyāna* and the Cave-temples of the Northern Wei Dynasty/The Northern Wei Cave-temples and the Ch'an]", in: *Zhongguo shikusi yanjiu* [中国石窟寺研究, *Studies of the Cave-temples of China*] by Su Bai [宿白], Appendix I, Beijing: Cultural Relics Press, 1996: 331-348.

Liu Jianjun [刘建军], "*Luyeyuan shiku diaocha baogao* [鹿野苑石窟调查报告, A Report on Rock-cut Caves at the Deer-park Monastery and Temple in Pingcheng (Datong)]", in: *Shikusi yanjiu* [石窟寺研究, *Studies of the Cave-temples*], Vol. I, Beijing: Cultural Relics Press, 2010: 1-9.

刘景龙、李玉昆主编《龙门石窟碑刻题记汇录》,北京：中国大百科全书出版社,1998年。

刘景龙、杨超杰编《龙门石窟总录》,全12卷,北京：中国大百科全书出版社,1999年。

刘汝醴《关于龙门三窟》,刊《文物》,1959年第12期,第17-18页。

刘志远、刘廷壁《成都万佛寺石刻艺术》,北京：中国古典艺术出版社,1958年。

Liu Zhiyuan and Liu Tingbi, *Chengdu wanfosi shike yishu* [成都万佛寺石刻艺术, *Stone Sculptures from Site of the Wanfo Monastery in Chengdu*], Beijing: China Ancient Arts Publishing House, 1958.

刘玉权《敦煌莫高窟、安西榆林窟西夏洞窟分期》,载敦煌文物研究所编《敦煌研究文集》,兰州：甘肃人民出版社,1982年,第273-318页。

刘玉权《关于沙州回鹘洞窟的划分》,载《敦煌石窟研究国际讨论会文集：石窟考古》,沈阳：辽宁美术出版社,1990年,第1-29页。

龙门保管所编《龙门石窟》,北京：文物出版社,1961年。

龙门文物保管所编《龙门石窟》,北京：文物出版社,1980年。

龙门石窟研究所、中央美术学院美术史系编《龙门石窟窟龛编号图册》,北京：人民美术出版社,1994年。

龙门石窟研究所编《龙门石窟志》,北京：中国大百科全书出版社,1996年。

龙显昭主编《巴蜀佛教碑文集成》,成都：巴蜀书社,2004年。

罗尔纲《金石萃编校补》,北京：中华书局,2004年。

罗世平《广元千佛崖菩提瑞像考》,刊《故宫学术季刊》,第九卷二期(1991年),第117-138页。

罗世平《巴中石窟三题》,刊《文物》,1996年第3期,第58-64,95页。

罗香林《唐代桂林之摩崖佛像》,香港：中国学社,1958年。

罗炤《宝山大住圣窟刻经中的北方礼忏系统》,刊《石窟寺研究》,第一辑,北京：文物出版社,2010年,第161-180页。

罗炤《试论龙门石窟擂鼓台的宝冠-佩饰-降魔印佛像》,载《徐苹芳先生纪念文集》,上海：上海古籍出版社，2012 年，第 466-501 页。

吕采芷《北魏后期的三壁三龛式窟》，载《中国石窟・云冈石窟》二，北京：文物出版社，1994 年，第 213-218 页。

吕澂《印度佛学源流略讲》，上海：上海人民出版社，1979 年。

Lü Cheng, *Yindu foxue yuanliu luejiang* [*A Survey of Indian Buddhism*], Shanghai: Shanghai People's Publishing House, 1979.

吕澂《中国佛学源流略讲》，北京：中华书局，1979 年。

Lü Cheng, *Zhongguo foxue yuanliu luejiang* [*A Survey of Chinese Buddhism*], Beijing: Zhonghua Book Company, 1979.

吕澂《新编汉文大藏经目录》，济南，齐鲁书社，1980 年。

Lü Cheng, *Xinbian hanwen dazangjing mulu* [*A New Catalogue of the Chinese Versions of the Buddhist Tripiṭāka*], Ji'nan: Qilu Publishing House, 1980.

吕澂《阿含经》，载中国佛教协会编《中国佛教》三，上海：知识出版社，1989 年，第 158-163 页。

吕澂《杂阿含经刊定记》，载《吕澂佛学论著选集》一，济南：齐鲁书社，1991 年，第 1-29 页。

吕澂《诸家戒本通论》及附录《论律学与十八部分派之关系》，载《吕澂佛学论著选集》一，济南：齐鲁书社，1991 年，第 89-143 页。

Lü Cheng, "*Lun lüxue yu shibabu fenpai zhi guanxi* [On thet Relationship between Studies of the Discipline and Schism of Eighteen Hīnayāna Schools]", in: *Lü Cheng foxue lunzhu xuanji* [*Collected Works of Lü Cheng on Buddhism*], Ji'nan: Qilu Publishing House, Vol. I, 1991: 131-143.

吕澂《大般涅槃经正法分讲要》，载《吕澂佛学论著选集》二，济南：齐鲁书社，1991 年，第 1146-1213 页。

吕澂《律学重光的先决问题》，刊《法音》，1998 年第 3 期，第 8-11 页。

吕建福《中国密教史》，北京：中国社会科学出版社，1995 年。

洛阳市龙门文物保管所《洛阳龙门香山寺遗址的调查与试掘》，刊《考古》，1986 年第 1 期，第 40-43 页。

马丰《赴磁县武安县南北响堂寺及其附近工作报告》，刊《国立北平研究院院务汇报》，第 7 卷 4 期（1936 年），第 111-119 页。

马世长《克孜尔中心柱窟研究》（硕士学位论文），打印本，北京：北京大学，1982 年。

马世长《克孜尔中心柱窟主室券顶与后室的壁画》，载《中国石窟・克孜尔石窟》二，北京：文物出版社，1996 年，第 174-226 页。

Ma Shichang, *Zhongguo fojiao shiku kaogu wenji*［中国佛教石窟考古文集，*Essays on the Buddhist Cave Temples of China*］, Taipei/Hsinchu: Chueh Feng Buddhist Art & Culture Foundation, 2001.

Ma Shichang, "*Mogaoku di 323 ku fojiao ganying gushihua*［莫高窟第 323 窟佛教感应故事画，Illustration of 'Received Grace' Stories in Cave 323 at Mogaoku］", in: *Zhongguo fojiao shiku kaogu wenji*［*Essays on the Buddhist Cave Temples of China*］by Ma Shichang, Taipei/Hsinchu: Chueh Feng Buddhist Art & Culture Foundation, 2001: 241-263.

马世长《汉式佛像袈裟琐议：汉式佛教图像札记之一》，刊《艺术史研究》第七辑 (2005 年)，第 247-268 页。

马雍《巴基斯坦北部所见"大魏"使者的岩刻题记》，载马雍《西域史地文物丛考》，北京：文物出版社，1990 年，第 129-137 页。

Meng Mo［蒙默］et al., *Sichuan gudaishi gao*［四川古代史稿 *A History of Ancient Sichuan*］, Chengdu: Sichuan People's Publishing House, 1988.

宁夏回族自治区文物管理委员会、中央美术学院美术史系编《须弥山石窟》，北京：文物出版社，1988 年。

潘别桐、方云、王剑峰《龙门石窟碳酸盐岩体溶蚀病害及防治对策》，载潘别桐、黄克忠主编《文物保护与环境地质》，武汉：中国地质大学出版社，1992 年，第 99-125 页。

潘重规编《龙龛手鉴新编》，北京：中华书局，1988 年。

潘玉闪、马世长《莫高窟窟前殿堂遗址》，北京：文物出版社，1985 年。

Pan Yushan and Ma Shichang, *Mogaoku kuqian diantang yizhi*［*Ruins of Frontal Buildings attached the Mogao Caves*］, Beijing: Cultural Relics Press, 1985.

裴珍达《龙门石窟擂鼓台南洞研究》，载《2004 年龙门石窟国际学术研讨会文集》，北京：文物出版社，2006 年，第 165-169 页。

彭金章、王建军《敦煌莫高窟北区石窟》第一卷，北京：文物出版社，2000 年。

Peng Jinzhang and Wang Jianjun, *Dunhuang mogaoku beiqu shiku*［*The Rock-cut Architectures at the Northern Part of Mogao Caves, Dunhuang*］, Vol. I, Beijing: Cultural Relics Press, 2000.

钱文忠《印度的古代汉语译名及其来源》，载《十世纪前的丝绸之路和东西文化交流：沙漠路线考察乌鲁木齐国际讨论会 (1990 年 8 月 19-21 日)》，北京：新世界出版社，1996 年，第 601-611 页。

Qian Wenzhong, “The Ancient Chinese Names of India and their Origins” , in: *Land Routes of the Silk Roads and the Cultural Exchanges between the East and West before the 10th Century*; Desert Route Expedition International Seminar in Urumqi August 19-21, 1990, Beijing: New World Press, 1996: 601-611.

全汉昇《唐宋帝国与运河》,重排版,台北：中研院历史语言研究所,1995 年。

冉云华《试论敦煌与阿旃陀的〈降魔变〉》,载《敦煌石窟研究国际讨论会文集：石窟艺术》,沈阳：辽宁美术出版社,1991 年,第 194-208 页。

饶宗颐《从石刻论武后之宗教信仰》,刊《中研究历史语言研究所集刊》,第 45 卷第 3 本,台北：中研院历史语言研究所,1974 年,第 397-412 页。

饶宗颐《谈敦煌石窟中的誐尼沙(Ganesa)》,刊《学术研究》,1989 年第 3 期,第 62-64 页。

任继愈主编《中国佛教史》第三卷,北京：中国社会科学出版社,1988 年。

任继愈主编《中国道教史》(修订本),北京：中国社会科学出版社,2001 年。

任肇新、路孝愉纂《(民国)盩厔县志》,铅印本,西安：艺林印书社,1925 年。

萨尔吉《Mark Allon, *Three Gāndhārī Ekottarikāgama-Type Sūtras: British Library Kharoṣṭhī Fragments* 12 and 14; Gandhāran Buddhist Texts Volume 2 书评》,刊《中国学术》,第十五辑,北京：商务印书馆,2003 年,第 315-320 页。

沙畹《宋云行纪笺注》,载冯承钧《西域南海史地考证译丛》第二卷《西域南海史地考证译丛六编》,北京：商务印书馆,1995 年,第 1-68 页。

沙畹《西突厥史料》,冯承钧译,北京：中华书局,1958 年。

商务印书馆编《敦煌遗书总目索引》,北京：商务印书馆,1962 年。

上海博物馆、香港中文大学文物馆《敦煌吐鲁番文物》,香港：香港中文大学,1987 年。

石家庄地区革委会文化局文物发掘组《河北赞皇东魏李希宗墓》,刊《考古》,1977 年第 6 期,第 382-390,372 页。

石璋如《莫高窟形》,全 3 卷,台北：中研院历史语言研究所,1996 年。

史苇湘《关于敦煌莫高窟内容总录》,载敦煌研究院编《敦煌石窟内容总录》,北京：文物出版社,1996 年,第 227-258 页。

史苇湘《福田经变简论》,载《向达先生纪念论文集》,乌鲁木齐：新疆人民出版社,1986 年,第 300-312 页。

史岩《敦煌石室画像题识》,石印本,成都：华西大学比较文化研究所、国立敦煌艺术研究所、华西大学博物馆,1947 年。

史岩《杭州南山区雕刻史迹初步调查》,刊《文物参考资料》,1956 年第 1 期,第 9-22 页。

释禅叡编《敦煌宝藏遗书索引》,台北：法鼓文化事业股份有限公司,1996 年。

水野弘元《佛教的真髓》，香光书乡编译组译，嘉义市：香光书鄉，2002 年。

宋伯胤《记剑川石窟》，刊《文物参考资料》，1957 年第 4 期，第 46-55 页。

宋伯胤《剑川石窟》，北京：文物出版社，1958 年。

宿白《参观敦煌第 285 号窟札记》，刊《文物参考资料》，1956 年第 2 期，第 19-21 页。

宿白《敦煌七讲》，油印本，敦煌：敦煌文物研究所，1962 年。

宿白《中国考古学之五：三国——宋元考古》上（铅印本讲义），北京：北京大学历史系考古教研室，1974 年。

宿白《敦煌莫高窟早期洞窟杂考》，载《大公报在港复刊三十周年纪念文集》上，香港：大公报社，1978 年，第 393-415 页。

宿白《调查新疆佛教遗迹应予注意的几个问题》，刊《新疆史学》，1980 年第 1 期，第 29-33 页。

宿白《东阳王与建平公》，载《向达先生纪念论文集》，乌鲁木齐：新疆人民出版社 1986 年，第 155-173 页。

宿白《凉州石窟遗迹和“凉州模式”》，刊《考古学报》，第 4 期 (1986 年），第 435-446 页。

宿白《东阳王与建平公（二稿）》，载《敦煌吐鲁番文献研究论集》第 4 辑，北京：北京大学出版社，1987 年，第 38-57 页。

宿白《北朝造型艺术中人物形象的变化》，载哲敬堂珍藏选辑《中国古佛雕》，新竹：觉风佛教艺术文化基金会，1989 年，第 219-223 页。

宿白《新疆拜城克孜尔石窟部分洞窟的类型与年代》，载宿白《中国石窟寺研究》，北京：文物出版社，1996 年，第 21-38 页。

Su Bai, “*Xinjiang baicheng kezi'er shiku bufen dongku de leixing yu niandai*［Types and Dating of Some Caves at Kizil in Baicheng, Xinjiang］”, in: *Zhongguo shikusi yanjiu*［*Studies of the Cave-temples of China*］by Su Bai, Beijing: Cultural Relics Press, 1996: 21-38.

宿白《〈大金西京武州山重修大石窟寺碑〉校注——新发现的大同云冈石窟寺历史材料的初步整理》，载宿白《中国石窟寺研究》，北京：文物出版社，1996 年，第 52-75 页。

Su Bai, “*Dajin xijing wuzhoushan chongxiu dashikusi bei jiaozhu*［Annotation and Textual Research on a Copy of the ‘*Tablet of the Restoration of the Great Cave-temple Complex at the Wuzhou Hill near the Western Capital of the Jin Dynasty*’］”, in: *Zhongguo shikusi yanjiu*［*Studies of the Cave-temples of China*］by Su Bai, Beijing: Cultural Relics Press, 1996: 52-75.

宿白《云冈石窟分期试论》，载宿白《中国石窟寺研究》，北京：文物出版社，1996 年，第

76-88 页。

Su Bai, "*Yungang shiku fenqi shilun* [Periodization of Yungang Cave-temples]", in: *Zhongguo shikusi yanjiu* [*Studies of the Cave-temples of China*] by Su Bai, Beijing: Cultural Relics Press, 1996: 76-88.

宿白《平城实力的集聚和"云冈模式"的形成与发展》,载宿白《中国石窟寺研究》,北京:文物出版社,1996 年,第 114-144 页。

Su Bai, "*Pingcheng shili de jiju he 'yungang moshi' de xingcheng yu fazhan* [Gathering of Manpower and Material Resources in Pingcheng and the Creation as well as Development of the 'Yungang Style']", in: *Zhongguo shikusi yanjiu* [*Studies of the Cave-temples of China*] by Su Bai, Beijing: Cultural Relics Press, 1996: 114-144.

宿白《洛阳地区北朝石窟的初步考察》,载宿白《中国石窟寺研究》,北京:文物出版社,1996 年,第 153-175 页。

宿白《参观敦煌莫高窟第 285 号窟札记》,载宿白《中国石窟寺研究》,北京:文物出版社,1996 年,第 206-213 页。

Su Bai, "*Canguan dunhuang mogaoku di 285 hao ku zhaji* [Notes on Cave 285 of the Mogao Caves, Dunhuang]" in: *Zhongguo shikusi yanjiu* [*Studies of the Cave-temples of China*] by Su Bai, Beijing: Cultural Relics Press, 1996: 206-213.

宿白《东阳王与建平公》,载宿白《中国石窟寺研究》,北京:文物出版社,1996 年,第 244-259 页。

Su Bai, "*Dongyangwang yu jianpinggong* [Prince Dongyang and Duke Jianping]", in: *Zhongguo shikusi yanjiu* [*Studies of the Cave-temples of China*] by Su Bai, Beijing: Cultural Relics Press, 1996: 244-259.

宿白《敦煌莫高窟密教遗迹札记》,载宿白《中国石窟寺研究》,北京:文物出版社,1996 年,第 279-310 页。

宿白《中国石窟寺研究》,北京:文物出版社,1996 年。

Su Bai, *Zhongguo shikusi yanjiu* [*Studies of the Cave-temples of China*], Beijing: Cultural Relics Press, 1996.

宿白《东汉魏晋南北朝佛寺布局初探》,载《庆祝邓广铭教授九十华诞论文集》,石家庄:河北教育出版社,1997 年,第 31-49 页。

宿白《武威天梯山早期石窟参观记》,刊《燕京学报》,新 8 期 (2000 年),第 215-228 页。

宿白《中国古建筑考古》,北京:文物出版社,2009 年。

宿白《中国佛教石窟寺遗迹——3 至 8 世纪中国佛教考古学》,北京：文物出版社，2010 年。

Su Bai, *Zhongguo fojiao shikusi yiji* [*The Buddhist Cave-temples of China*], Beijing: Cultural Relics Press, 2010.

宿白《汉唐宋元考古：中国考古学下》,北京：文物出版社,2010 年。

宿白《隋唐长安城和洛阳城》,载宿白《魏晋南北朝唐宋考古文稿辑丛》,北京：文物出版社,2011 年,第 40-62 页。

宿白《四川钱树和长江中下游部分器物上的佛像》,载宿白《魏晋南北朝唐宋考古文稿辑丛》,北京：文物出版社,2011 年,第 211-223 页。

Su Bai, "*Sichuan qianshu he changjiang zhongxiayou bufen qiwu shang de foxiang* [The Buddha images on the Money-trees and Figured Jars unearthed from the Tombs of South China]", in: *Wei jin nanbeichao tang song kaogu wengao jicong* [*Collected Papers on the Chinese Archaeology from the Wei down to the Song Dynasties, 3rd to 13th century AD*] by Su Bai, Beijing: Cultural Relics Press, 2011: 211-223.

宿白《东汉魏晋南北朝佛寺布局初探》,载宿白《魏晋南北朝唐宋考古文稿辑丛》,北京：文物出版社,2011 年,第 230-247 页。

Su Bai, "*Donghan wei jin nanbeichao fosi buju chutan* [A Preliminary Study on the Layout of the Buddhist Monasteries from the Later Han down to the Southern and Northern Dynasties, 1st to 6th century AD]", in: *Wei jin nanbeichao tang song kaogu wengao jicong* [*Collected Papers on the Chinese Archaeology from the Wei down to the Song Dynasties, 3rd to 13th century AD*] by Su Bai, Beijing: Cultural Relics Press, 2011: 230-247.

宿白《试论唐代长安佛寺的等级问题》,载宿白《魏晋南北朝唐宋考古文稿辑丛》,北京：文物出版社,2011 年,第 255-269 页。

宿白《青州龙兴寺窖藏所出佛像的几个问题》,载宿白《魏晋南北朝唐宋考古文稿辑丛》,北京：文物出版社,2011 年,第 330-350 页。

Su Bai, "*Qingzhou longxingsi jiaocang suo chu foxiang de jige wenti* [Some Questions Concerning the Buddhist Sculptures unearthed from a Hoard of the Longxing Monastery at Qingzhou]", in : *Wei jin nanbeichao tang song kaogu wengao jicong* [*Collected Papers on the Chinese Archaeology from the Wei down to the Song Dynasties, 3rd to 13th century AD*] by Su Bai, Beijing: Cultural Relics Press,

2011: 333-350.

Sun Fuxi [孙福喜] ed., *Xi'an wenwu jinghua*: *Fojiao zaoxiang* [西安文物精华：佛教造像, *Masterworks of the Antiquities from Xi'an: Buddhist Images*], Xi'an: World Publishing Corporation, 2010.

谭其骧主编《中国历史地图集》第五册,上海：地图出版社,1982 年。

汤用彤《汉魏两晋南北朝佛教史》,长沙：商务印书馆,1938 年；北京：中华书局,1983 年。

Tang Yongtong, *Han wei liang jin nanbeichao fojiao shi* [*A History of Buddhism from the Han down to the Southern and Northern Dynasties, 1st to 6th century AD*], Changsha: The Commercial Press, 1938; 2nd ed., Beijing: Zhonghua Book Company, 1983.

汤用彤《隋唐佛教史稿》,北京：中华书局,1982 年。

汤用彤《佛与菩萨》,载《汤用彤学术论文集》,北京：中华书局,1983 年,第 316-318 页。

汤用彤《印度哲学史略》,北京：中华书局,1988 年。

汤用彤《从〈一切道经〉说到武则天》,载《汤用彤全集》七,石家庄：河北人民出版社,2000 年,第 42-47 页。

唐长孺《魏晋南北朝隋唐史三论》,武汉：武汉大学出版社,1993 年。

唐仲明《晋豫及其以东地区北朝晚期石窟寺研究——以响堂山石窟为中心》(博士学位论文),打印本,北京：北京大学,2004 年。

汪篯《武则天》,载《汪篯隋唐史论稿》,北京：中国社会科学出版社,1981 年,第 118-131 页。

王邦维《Richard Salomon, *Ancient Buddhist Scrolls from Gandhāra: The British Library Kharoṣṭhī Fragments* 书评》,刊《敦煌吐鲁番研究》,第五卷,北京：北京大学出版社,2001 年,第 343-353 页。

王惠民《敦煌水月观音像》,刊《敦煌研究》,1987 年 1 期,第 31-38 页。

王惠民《敦煌写本水月观音经研究》,刊《敦煌研究》,1992 年 3 期,第 93-98 页。

王惠民《敦煌〈密严经变〉考释》,刊《敦煌研究》,1993 年第 2 期,第 15-25 页。

王家佑《安岳石窟造像》,刊《敦煌研究》,1989 年第 1 期,第 45-53 页。

Wang Jianping [王剑平] and Lei Yuhua [雷玉华], "*Ayuwang xiang de chubu kaocha* [阿育王像的初步考察, A Preliminary Investigation on the Aśoka-type Buddha Images]", in: *Xi'nan minzu daxue xuebao* [西南民族大学学报, *Bulletin of Southwest University for Ethnics*], Vol. 28, No. 9 [2007]: 65-69.

王景荃编《河南佛教石刻造像》,郑州：大象出版社,2008 年。

王静如《敦煌莫高窟和安西榆林窟中的西夏壁画》，载《王静如民族研究文集》，北京：民族出版社，1998 年，第 347-355 页。

王文楚《唐代洛阳至襄州驿路考》，载王文楚《古代交通地理丛考》，北京：中华书局，1996 年，第 117-133 页。

王逊《中国美术史》，上海：上海人民美术出版社，1985 年。

王振国《洛阳经幢研究》，载王振国《龙门石窟与洛阳佛教文化》，郑州：中州古籍出版社，2006 年，第 123-187 页。

王振国《唐宋洛阳佛寺、名僧史迹钩沉》，载王振国《龙门石窟与洛阳佛教文化》，郑州：中州古籍出版社，2006 年，第 189-239 页。

王仲荦《北周六典》，北京：中华书局，1979 年。

王仲荦《魏晋南北朝史》，上海人民出版社，1980 年。

Willemen, Charles [魏查理], "*Yindu bupai fojiao 'huadibu' de xin yanjiu* [印度部派佛教"化地部"的新研究, Some New Ideas on Mahīśāsaka of Indian Buddhism]", in: *Renwen zongjiao yanjiu* [人文宗教研究, *Journal of Humanistic Religion*], Vol. I, ed. Li Silong [李四龙], Beijing: Religious Culture Press, 2011: 126-140.

温玉成《记新出土的菏泽大师神会塔铭》，刊《世界宗教研究》，1984 年第 2 期，第 78-79 页。

温玉成《龙门十寺考辨》(上)，刊《中州今古》，1983 年第 2 期，第 30-31 页。

温玉成《略谈龙门奉先寺的几个问题》，刊《中原文物》，1984 年第 2 期，第 53-57 页。

温玉成《龙门唐窟排年》，载《中国石窟 · 龙门石窟》二，北京：文物出版社，1992 年，第 172-216 页。

温玉成《唐代龙门十寺考察》，载《中国石窟 · 龙门石窟》二，北京：文物出版社，1992 年，第 217-232 页。

Wen Yucheng, "*Tangdai longmen shisi kaocha* [A Reconnaissance on the Ten Monasteries of the Tang Dynasty at Longmen, Luoyang]", in: *Zhongguo shiku: longmen shiku* [*The Cave-temples of China: Longmen Caves*], II, Beijing: Cultural Relics Press, 1992: 217-232.

温玉成《中国石窟与文化艺术》，上海：上海人民美术出版社，1993 年。

温玉成《迹旷代之幽潜　托无穷之柄焕——龙门石窟艺术综论》，载龙门石窟研究院编《龙门石窟研究院论文选》，郑州：中州古籍出版社，2004 年，第 1-45 页。

文齐国《绵阳唐代佛教造像初探》，刊《四川文物》1991 年第 5 期，第 47-53 页。

渥德尔《印度佛教史》，王世安译，北京：商务印书馆，1987 年。

西安市文物保护考古所编著《西安文物精华：佛教造像》,西安：世界图书出版西安公司,2010 年。

西藏自治区文管会文物普查队《西藏吉隆县发现唐显庆三年〈大唐天竺使出铭〉》,刊《考古》1994 年第 7 期,第 619-623 页。

夏鼐《赞皇李希宗墓出土的拜赞庭金币》,刊《考古》,1977 年第 6 期,第 403-406 页。

向达《盩厔大秦寺略记》,载向达《唐代长安与西域文明》,北京：生活 · 读书 · 新知三联书店,1957 年,第 110-116 页。

Xiang Da, *Tangdai chang'an yu xiyu wenming* [唐代长安与西域文明, *The Tang Dynasty Chang'an and the Civilization of Central Asia*], Beijing: SDX Joint Publishing Company, 1957.

[法]谢和耐《中国五至十世纪的寺院经济》,耿昇译,兰州：甘肃人民出版社,1987 年。

谢重光《中古佛教僧官制度和社会生活》,北京：商务印书馆,2009 年。

谢稚柳《敦煌艺术叙录》,上海：古典文学出版社,1957 年。

辛嶋静志《汉译佛典的语言研究》,载朱庆之主编《佛教汉语研究》,北京：商务印书馆,2009 年,第 33-74 页。

Karashima, Seishi, "*Hanyi fodian de yuyan yanjiu* [On the Linguistic Form of the Chinese Translated Versions of *Tripiṭaka*]", in: *Fojiao hanyu yanjiu* [*Studies of the Buddhist-Chinese*], ed. Zhu Qingzhi, Beijing: The Commercial Press, 2009: 33-74.

新疆龟兹石窟研究所编《克孜尔石窟内容总录》,乌鲁木齐：新疆美术摄影出版社,2000 年。

延安地区群众艺术馆编《延安宋代石窟艺术》,西安：陕西人民美术出版社,1983 年。

严耕望《唐代交通图考》,第一至五卷,台北：中研院历史语言研究所,1985-1986 年。

严耕望遗著《唐代交通图考》第六卷,李启文整理,台北：中研院历史语言研究所,2003 年。

严耕望遗著《魏晋南北朝佛教地理稿》,李启文整理,台北：中研院历史语言研究所,2003 年。

严耕望《唐人习业山林寺院之风尚》,载《严耕望史学论文选集》,北京：中华书局,2006 年,第 232-271 页。

颜尚文《隋唐佛教宗派研究》,台北：新文丰出版公司,1980 年。

颜娟英《武则天与长安七宝台石雕佛相》,刊《艺术学》,第 1 期 (1987 年),第 40-89 页。

颜娟英《唐长安七宝台石刻的再省思》,载陕西省考古研究所编《远望集：陕西省考古研究所华诞四十周年纪念文集》,西安：陕西人民美术出版社,1998 年,第 829-843 页。

阎文儒主编《中国石窟艺术丛书：麦积山石窟》，兰州：甘肃人民出版社，1983 年。

阎文儒《龙门奉先寺三造像碑铭考释》，刊《中原文物》特刊（《魏晋南北朝佛教史及佛教艺术讨论会论文选集》），铅印本，郑州：河南省博物馆，1985 年，第 154-157 页。

阎文儒《中国石窟艺术总论》，天津：天津古籍出版社，1987 年。

阎文儒、常青《龙门石窟研究》，北京：书目文献出版社，1995 年。

阎文儒《云冈石窟研究》，桂林：广西师范大学出版社，2003 年。

偃师商城博物馆《河南偃师县四座唐墓发掘简报》，刊《考古》，1992 年 11 期，第 1004-1017 页。

杨森富《唐元两代基督教兴废原因之研究》，见林治平主编《基督教入华百七十年纪念集》，台北：宇宙光出版社，1984 年，第 29-79 页。

杨曾文《唐五代禅宗史》，北京：中国社会科学出版社，1999 年。

杨曾文编校《神会和尚禅话录》，北京：中华书局，1996 年。

杨曾文编校《敦煌新本六祖坛经》附编（一）《传法宝记》，北京：宗教文化出版社，2001 年。

杨泓《中国古兵器论丛》（增订本），北京：文物出版社，1985 年。

姚士宏《克孜尔石窟部分洞窟主室正壁塑绘题材》，载新疆维吾尔自治区文物管理委员会、拜城县克孜尔千佛洞文物保管所、北京大学考古系编《中国石窟 · 克孜尔石窟》三，北京：文物出版社，1997 年，第 178-186 页。

姚学谋、杨超杰《龙门石窟极南洞新考》，刊《石窟寺研究》第一辑，北京：文物出版社，2010 年，第 74-81 页。

耀生《耀县石刻文字略志》，刊《考古》，1965 年第 3 期，第 134-151 页。

印顺《中国禅宗史》，南昌：江西人民出版社，1999 年。

余嘉锡《卫元嵩事迹考》，载《余嘉锡论学杂著》，北京：中华书局，1963 年，第 235-265 页。

余太山《塞种史研究》，北京：商务印书馆，2012 年。

羽溪了谛《西域之佛教》，贺昌群译，上海：商务印书馆，1933 年。

贠安志《安岳石窟寺调查记要》，刊《考古与文物》，1986 年第 6 期，第 45-52 页。

Yuan Shuguang［袁曙光］, "*Sichuansheng bowuguan cang wanfosi shike zaoxiang zhengli jianbao*［四川省博物馆藏万佛寺石刻造像整理简报, The Buddhist Sculptures from Site of the Wanfo Monastery in the Collection of Sichuan Museum］", *Cultural Relics*, 10 (2001): 19-38.

云南省剑川县文化体育局编《南天瑰宝——剑川石钟山石窟》，昆明：云南美术出版社，1998 年。

曾布川宽《唐代龙门石窟造像的研究》,颜娟英译,刊《艺术学》第七期(1992年),第163-267页;第八期(1993年),第99-163页。

Zhang Naizhu[张乃翥]et al., "*Luelun longmen shiku xin faxian de ayuwang xiang*[略论龙门石窟新发现的阿育王像, An Aśoka-type Buddha Image found at Longmen Caves, Luoyang]", in: *Dunhuang Yanjiu*[敦煌研究, *Dunhuang Research*], No. 4 (2000): 21-26.

张大千《漠高窟记》,台北:故宫博物院刊行,1985年。

张光直《考古学专题六讲》,北京:文物出版社,1986年。

张丽明《龙门石窟北市香行像窟的考察》,载龙门石窟研究院编《龙门石窟研究院论文选》,郑州:中州古籍出版社,2004年,第360-371页。

张楠《南诏大理的石刻艺术》,载云南省文物管理委员会编《南诏大理文物》,北京:文物出版社,1992年,第140-149页。

张若愚《伊阙佛龛之碑和潜溪寺、宾阳洞》,刊《文物》,1980年第1期,第19-24页。

张星烺《中西交通史料汇编》,全六册,北京:中华书局,1979年,第六册。

Zhang Xinglang/ Chang Hsing-lang, *Zhongxi jiaotong shiliao huibian* (*The Materials for a History of Sino-Foreign Relations*), 6 volumes, Peking: The Catholic University of Peking, 1930; Beijing: Zhonghua Book Company, 1979.

赵超《新唐书宰相世系表集校》,北京:中华书局,1998年。

浙江省文物考古研究所编《西湖石窟》,杭州:浙江人民出版社,1986年。

郑振铎主编《麦积山石窟》,北京:文化部社会文化事业管理局,1954年。

郑州市文物考古研究所、巩义市文物保护管理所《巩义常庄变电站大周时期墓葬发掘简报》,刊《中原文物》,2005年第1期,第4-11页。

中国佛教协会、中国佛教图书文物馆编《房山石经·隋唐刻经》2,北京:华夏出版社,2000年。

中国社会科学院考古研究所《北魏洛阳永宁寺:1979-1994年考古发掘报告》,北京:中国大百科全书出版社,1996年。

Institute of Archaeology, Chinese Academy of Social Sciences, *Beiwei luoyang yongningsi*[*The Yongning Monastery in the Northern Wei Luoyang*: *An illustrated account of archaeological excavations carried out between the years 1979 and 1994*], Beijing: The Encyclopedia of China Publishing House, 1996.

中国社会科学院考古研究所编《六顶山与渤海镇——唐代渤海国的贵族墓地与都城遗址》,北京:中国大百科全书出版社,1997年。

《中国石窟·敦煌莫高窟》一，北京：文物出版社，1981 年。

《中国石窟·敦煌莫高窟》二，北京：文物出版社，1984 年。

《中国石窟·敦煌莫高窟》三，北京：文物出版社，1987 年。

《中国石窟·永靖炳灵寺》，北京：文物出版社，1989 年。

《中国石窟·天水麦积山》，北京：文物出版社，1998 年。

《中国石窟·云冈石窟》一，北京：文物出版社，1991 年。

《中国石窟·云冈石窟》二，北京：文物出版社，1994 年。

《中国石窟·龙门石窟》一，北京：文物出版社，1991 年。

《中国石窟·龙门石窟》二，北京：文物出版社，1992 年。

《中国石窟·巩县石窟》，北京：文物出版社，1989 年。

Zhongguo shiku: Kezi'er shiku［中国石窟·克孜尔石窟，*The Cave-temles of China: Kizil Caves*］, I, Beijing: Cultural Relics Press, 1989.

《中国石窟雕塑全集》第 1 卷《敦煌》，重庆：重庆出版社，2001 年。

周绍良主编《唐代墓志汇编》，上海：上海古籍出版社，1992 年。

周叔迦《释典丛录》，载《周叔迦佛学论著集》，北京：中华书局，1991 年，第 971-1118 页。

周一良《唐代密宗》，钱文忠译，上海：上海远东出版社，1996 年。

朱谦之《中国景教：唐景教碑新探》，铅印本，北京：中国社会科学院世界宗教研究所，1982 年。

朱希祖《西魏赐姓源流考》，载胡适、蔡元培、王云五编《张菊生先生七十生日纪念论文集》，上海：商务印书馆，1937 年，第 525-586 页。

西文部分

（包括汉文论著外译）

史料

Acker, William Reynolds Beal, *Some T'ang and Pre-T'ang Texts on Chinese Painting*, translated and annotated, 2 vols., Leiden: E. J. Brill, Vol. I, 1954; Vol. II, 1974.

Allon, Mark ed., *Three Gāndhārī Ekottarikāgama-Type Sūtras: British Library Kharoṣṭhī Fragments 12 and 14*, Gandhāran Buddhist Texts Volume 2, Seattle and London: University of Washington Press, 2001.

An, Yang-gyu tr., *The Buddha's Last Days: Buddhaghosa's Commentary on the*

Mahāparinibbāna Sutta, Oxford: Pali Text Society, 2003.

Beal, Samuel, tr., *Si-Yu-Ki—Buddhist Records of the Western World; Chinese Accounts of India,* translated from the Chinese of Hiuen Tsiang, London: Trubner, 1884.

Brough, John ed., *The Gāndhārī Dharmapada,* London Oriental Series 7, London: Oxford University Press, 1962.

Chavannes, Édouard, *Documents sur les Tou-kiue (Turcs) Occidentaux: Recueillis et commentés,* St-Pétersbourg: Académie Impériale des Sciences de St-Pétersbourg, 1903.

Chavannes, Édouard、"Voyage de Song Yun dans l'Udyāna et le Gandhāra (518-22)" , in: *Bulletin de l' Ecole française d' Extrēme-Orient,* III (1903): 379-441.

Cowell, E. B ed., *The Jātaka or Stories of the Buddha's Former Births;* translated from the Pāli by various hands, 6 volumes, Cambridge: Cambridge University Press, Vol. I, 1895; Vol. II, 1895; Vol. III, 1895; Vol. IV, 1895; Vol. V, 1905; Vol. VI, 1907.

Cowell, E. B. and R. A. Neil ed., *Divyāvadāna,* Cambridge: Cambridge University Press, 1886.

Deeg, Max tr., *Das Gaoseng-Faxian-Zhuan als religionsgeschichtliche Quelle; Der älteste Bericht eines chinesischen buddhistischen Pilgermönchs über seine Reise nach Indien mit Übersetzung des Textes,* Studies in Oriental Religions 52, Wiesbaden: Harrassowitz Verlag, 2005.

Eggeling, Julius tr, *Śatapatha-brāhmaṇa*: *According to the Text of the Mādhyandina School*, 5 parts, in: *The Sacred Books of the East* (abbreviated as *SBE*, 50 volumes, Oxford: Clarendon Press, 1879-1910), XII, XXVI, XLI, XLIII, XLIV, Oxford: Clarendon Press, Part 1, 1882; Part 2, 1885; Part 3, 1894, Part 4, 1897, Part 5, 1900.

Geiger, Wilhelm ed. & tr., *Cūḷavaṃsa being the more recent part of the Mahāvaṃsa*, translated from the German into English by C. Mabel Rickmers, London: Pali Text Society, 1929.

Giles, H. A. tr., *The Travels of Fa-hsien (399-414 AD), or Record of the Buddhistic Kingdoms* by Faxian, Cambridge: Cambridge University Press, 1923.

Griffith, G. T. K. tr., *The Hymns of the Ṛgveda*, translated with a popular commentary, 4th ed, Varanari: Chowkhamba Sanskrit Series Office, 1963.

Hurvitz, Leon, tr., *Treatise on Buddhism and Taoism* by Wei Shou, in: *Yun-kang; The*

Buddhist Cave-temples of the Fifth Century AD in North China; detailed report of the archaeological survey carried out by the mission of the Tōhōbunka Kenkyūsho 1938-45 by S. Mizuno and T. Nagahiro, Vol. XVI, Supplement and Index, Kyoto: Jimbunkagaku Kenkyūshō, Kyoto University, 1956: 23-103.

Keith, A. B. tr., *The Veda of the Black Yajus School entitled Taittiriya Sanhita*/transl. from the original Sanskrit Prose and Verse, 2 parts (Harvard Oriental Series, 18 & 19), Cambridge, Mass. : The Harvard University Press, 1914.

Kern, H. ed., *The Jātaka-mālā,* Harvard Oriental Series, Cambridge: Harvard University Press, 1914.

Kloppenborg, Ria tr., *The Sūtra on the Foundation of the Buddhist Order (Das Catuṣpariṣatsūtra)*: *Relating the Events from the Bodhisattva's Enlightenment up to the Conversion of Upatiṣya (Śāriputra) and Kolita (Maudgalyāyana),* Leiden: E. J. Brill, 1973.

Lenz, Tomothy ed., *A New Version of the Gāndhārī Dharmapada and a Collection of Previous-Birth Stories: British Library Kharoṣṭhī Fragments 16+25;* Gandhāran Buddhist Texts Volume 3, Seattle and London: University of Washington Press, 2003.

Müller, Friedrich Max ed, *Ṛgveda-saṁhitā*: *the Sacred Hymns of the Brahmans together with the Commentary of Sayanacharya,* 4 vols., London: William H. Allen, 1849-1862.

Rhys Davids, T. W. and J. Estlin Carpenter ed., *The Dīgha Nikāya,* 3 vols., Pali Text Society, London: Oxford University Press, 1938.

Rhys Davids, T. W., tr., *Mahāparinibhāna Sutta,* in: *SBE*, XI, Oxford: Clarendon Press, 1881.

Rhys Davids, T. W. and C. A. F. Rhys Davids tr., *Dialogues of the Buddha*, transl. from the Pāli of *The Dīgha Nikāya*, 2 vols., London: Oxford University Press, Part I, 1899, Part II, 1910.

Salomon, Richard ed., *A Gāndhārī Version of the Rhinoceros Sūtra: British Library Kharoṣṭhī Fragment 5B;* Gandhāran Buddhist Texts Volume 1, Seattle: University of Washington Press, 2000.

Senart, Émile ed., *Mahāvastu,* 3 vols., Paris: Ernest Leroux, 1882-1897.

Stede, W. ed., *The Sumaṅgala-vilāsinī: Buddhaghosa's Commentary on the Dīgha-*

Nikāya, III, London: Oxford University Press, 1932.

Takakusu, J. tr., *A Record of the Buddhist Religion as Practiced in India and the Malay Archipelago* (*AD 671-695*) by I-tsing (Yijing), London: Clarendon Press, 1896.

Walshe, Maurice tr., *The Long Discourses of the Buddha*, Boston: Wisdom Publications, 1995.

Wang, Yi-t'ung, tr., *A Record of Buddhist Monasteries in Lo-yang* by Yang Hsüan-chih, Princeton: Princeton University Press, 1984.

Ware, James R. tr., "Wei Shou on Buddhism" , in: *T'oung Pao*, 30 (1930): 100-181.

Willemen, Charles tr., *Outlining the Way to Reflect/* 思维略要法 (T. XV 617), Mumbai: Somaiya Publications Pvt Ltd, 2012.

Windisch, Ernst ed., *Die Komposition des Mahāvastu: ein Beitrag zur Quellenkunde des Buddhismus* (Abhandlungen der philologisch-historischen Klasse der Königlich Sächsischen Gesellschaft der Wissenschaften, 27, 14), 2 vols., Leipzig: Tübner, 1909.

现代论著

Aall, Ingrid, "The (Ajanta) Murals: Their Art" , in: *Ajanta Murals,* ed. A. Ghose, New Delhi: Archaeological Survey of India, 1967: 40-52.

Agrawal, D. P. and S. Kusumgar, "Tata Institute Radiocarbon Date List IV" , in: *Radiocarbon,* 1966 (8): 448.

Agrawala, V. S., *Sārnāth,* New Delhi: Archaeological Survey of India, 1980.

Alam, Humera, *Gandhara Sculptures in Lahore Museum,* Lahore: Lahore Museum, 1998.

Allon, Mark and Richard Salomon, "Kharoṣṭhī fragments of a Gāndhārī version of the *Mahāparinirvāṇasūtra*" , in: *Manuscripts in the Schøyen Collection 1; Buddhist Manuscripts,* Vol. I, ed. Jens Braarvig, Oslo: Hermes Publishing, 2000: 243-284.

Ariyadhamma, T., "Kammavācā" , in: *Encyclopaedia of Buddhism*, ed. G. P. Malalasekera, Colombo: The Government of Ceylon, 1996, Vol. VI: 124-125.

Bagchi, P. C., "Ancient Chinese Names of India" , in: *India and China: Interactions through Buddhism and Diplomacy; A Collection of Essays by Professor Prabodh Chandra Bagchi*, compiled by Bangwei Wang and Tansen Sen, Delhi: Anthem Press India, 2011: 3-11.

Bagchi, P. C., "Ki-pin and Kashmir" , in: *India and China: Interactions through Buddhism and Diplomacy; A Collection of Essays by Professor Prabodh Chandra Bagchi*, compiled by Bangwei Wang and Tansen Sen, Delhi: Anthem Press India, 2011: 145-154.

Bai, Shouyi, ed., *An Outline History of China*, Beijing: Foreign Languages Press, 1982.

Bailey, H. W., "Gāndhārī" , in: *Bulletin of the School of Oriental and African Studies*, XI (1946): 764-797.

Bareau, André, "L'origine du *Dīrgha-āgama* traduit en Chinois par Buddhayaśas" , in: *Essays Offered to G. H. Luce by His Colleagues and Friends in Honour of His Seventy-fifth Birthday,* Vol. 1, *Papers on Asian History, Religion, Languages, Literature, Music, Folklore and Anthropology, Artibus Asiae* Supplementum 23. 1, eds. Ba Shin, Jean Boisselier and A. B. Griswold, Ascona: Artibus Asiae, 1966: 49-58.

Bareau, André, *Les sectes bouddhiques du Petit Véhicule,* Paris: Publications de l'École française d'Extrême-Orient 38, 1955.

Barker, H. and J. Mackey, "British Museum Natural Radiocarbon Measurements III" , in: *British Museum Quarterly,* XXVII (1963-64): 55.

Barua, Benimadhab, *Barhut*, 3 vols., Book I: *Stone as a Story Teller,* Book II: *Jātaka-scenes,* Book III: *Aspects of Life and Art,* rep., Patna: Indological Book Corporation, 1979.

Barua, D. K., *Vihāras in Ancient India,* Calcutta: Indian Publications, 1969.

Bechert, Heinz, "Notes on the Formation of Buddhist Sects and Origin of Mahāyāna" , in: *German Scholars on India*, I, ed. Cultural Department of Embassy of the Federal Republic of Germany, New Delhi/Varanasi: Chowkhamba Sanskrit Series Office, 1973: 6-18.

Behrendt, Kurt, "Reuse of Images in Ancient Gandhara" , in: *Gandhāran Studies*, ed. M. Nasim Khan, Vol. 2: 17-38.

Bernhard, Franz, "Gāndhārī and the Buddhist Mission in Central Asia" , in: *Aňjali, Papers on Indology and Buddhism: A Felicitation Volume Presented to Oliver Hector de Alwis Wijesekara on His Sixtieth Birthday,* ed. J. Tilakasiri, Peradeniya: University of Ceylon, 1970: 55-62.

Bloch, Jules, *Les inscriptions d'Aśoka* (Collection Émile Senart 8), Paris: Institut de

Civilisation Indienne, 1950.

Bloch, T., "Notes on Bōdh Gayā", in: *Archaeological Survey of India: Annual Report 1908-09*: 139-158.

Boucher, Daniel, "Gāndhārī and the Early Chinese Buddhist Translations Reconsidered: the Case of the *Saddharmapuṇḍarīkasūtra*", in: *Journal of American Oriental Society*, 118 (1998), No. 4: 471-506.

Brough, John, "Comments on Third-Century Shan-shan and the History of Buddhism", in: *Bulletin of the School of Oriental and African Studies*, 28 (1965): 582-612.

Brown, Percy, *Indian Architecture: Buddhist and Hindu Periods*, 3rd rev & enl. ed., Bombay: Taraporevala Sons & Co, 1959.

Burgess, Jas., *Report on the Buddhist Cave Temples and Their Inscriptions; supplementary to the volume on "The Cave Temples of India"*, in: *Archaeological Survey of Western India,* Vol. IV, 1883.

Burgess, Jas. and B. Indraji, *Inscriptions from the Cave Temples of Western India,* in: *Archaeological Survey of Western India,* Vol. X, Bombay: Government Central Press, 1881.

Burgess, Jas., *The Buddhist Stūpas of Amarāvatī and Jaggayapeṭa in Krishna District, Madras Presidency, surveyed in 1882,* in: *Archaeological Survey of Southern India*, VI, London: 1886.

Burrow, Thomas, *The Language of the Kharoṣṭhi Documents from Chinese Turkestan*, Cambridge: Cambridge University Press, 1937.

Burrow, Thomas, *A Translation of the Kharoṣṭhi Documents from Chinese Turkestan,* James G. Forlong Fund 20, London: Royal Asiatic Society, 1940.

Buswell, Robert E., Jr., "Prakritic Phonological Elements in Chinese Buddhist Transcriptions: Data from Xuanying's *Yiqiejing Yinyi*", in: *Collection of Essays 1993: Buddhism Across Boundaries—Chinese Buddhism and Western Religions* by Erik Zürcher, Lore Sander and others, ed. John R. McRae and Jan Nattier, Taipei: Foguang Cultural Enterprise Co., Ltd, 1999: 187-217.

Callieri, Pierfrancesco, *Saidu Sharif I (Swat, Pakistan)* 1, *The Buddhist Sacred Area; The Monastery*, Rome: IsMEO, 1989.

Chandra, Lokesh, "Introduction", in: G. Tucci, *Stupa: Art, Architectonics and Symbolism* tr. by U. M. Vesci, New Delhi: Aditya Prakashan, 1988: V-XXXVI.

Chavannes, É'douard, *Mission archéologique dans la Chine septentrionale*. Paris: Leroux, Publications de l'Ecole française d'Extréme-Orient, Tome XIII, XIX, 1909-15.

Ch'en, Kenneth, *Buddhism in China: A Historical Survey*. Princeton: Princeton University Press, 1973.

Chhabra, B. Ch., "The Incised Inscriptions", in: *Ajanta: The colour and monochrome reproductions of the Ajanta frescoes based on photography,* ed. G. Yazdani, London: Oxford University Press, Part IV, 1955, Appendix: 112-124.

Chung, Jin-il und K. Wille, "Einige Bhikṣuvinayavibhaṅga-Fragmente der Dharmaguptakas in der Sammlung Pelliot", in: *Untersuchungen zur buddhistischen Literatur zweite Folge: Gustav Roth zum 80 Geburtstag gewidmet,* eds. Heinz Bechert, Sven Bretfeld und Petra Kieffer-Pülz, Sanskrit-Wörterbuch der buddhistischen Texte aus den Turfan-Funden, Beiheft 8, Göttingen: Vandenhoeck & Ruprecht, 1997: 49-94.

Coomaraswamy, A. K., *History of Indian and Indonesian Art*, New York: E. Weyhe/ London: E. Goldston, 1927.

Coomaraswamy, A. K., "Early Indian Iconography: I. Indra, with special reference to 'Indra's Visit'", in: *Eastern Art*, 1928, I (1): 33-41.

Cousens, H., "An Account of the Caves at Naḍsur and Karsambla", in: *ASWI*, 1891, XII.

Cunningham, Alexander, *Archaeological Survey of India: Four Reports made during the years 1862-63-64-65*/ Volume I, 1872.

Cunningham, Alexander, *Archaeological Survey of India: Report for the Year 1872-73*/ Volume V, 1875.

Cunningham, Alexander, *Archaeological Survey of India: Report of a Tour in the Punjab in 1878-79*/ Volume IX, 1883.

Cunningham, Alexander, *The Stūpa of Bhārhut: A Buddhist Monument ornamented with numerous sculptures illustrated of Buddhist legend and history in the third century BC*, London: W. H. Allen & Co., 1879.

Cunningham, Alexander, *Mahabodhi or The Great Buddhist Temple under the Bodhi Tree at Buddha Gayā.* London: W. H. Allen & Co., 1892.

Dani, A. H., *Chilas: The City of Nanga Parvat*, Islamabad; Quaid-i-Azam University, 1983.

Dani, A. H., *Human Records on Karakorum Highway*, Lohore: Sang-e-Meel Publications, 1995.

Das Gupta, C. C., "Shelārwādi Cave Inscription" , in: *Epigraphia Indica*, XXVIII (1950).

Dehejia, V., *Early Buddhist Rock Temples: A Chronological Study*, London: Thames and Hudson, 1972.

de Jong, Jan Willem, *Buddha's Word in China*, The Twenty-eighth George Ernest Morrison Lecture in Ethnology, Canberra: The Australian National University, 1968.

Demiéville, Paul、"*La Yogācārabhūmi* de Saṅgharakṣa" , in: *Bulletin de l'Ēcole française d'Extrême-Orient*, XLIV (1954): 339-436.

Deshpande, M. N., "The Rock-cut Caves of Pitalkhora in the Deccan" , in: *Ancient India* (Bulletin of the Archaeological Survey of India), No. 15 (1959): 66-93.

Deshpande, M. N., "Important Epigraphical Records from the Chaitya Cave, Bhaja" , in: *Lalita Kala,* 1959 (6).

Deshpande, M. N., "The (Ajanta) Caves: Their Historical Perspective" , in: *Ajanta Murals*, ed. A. Ghosh, New Delhi: Archaeological Survey of India, 1967: 14-21.

Deshpande, M. N., "The (Ajanta) Caves: Their Sculpture" , in: *Ajanta Murals*, ed. A. Ghosh, New Delhi: Archaeological Survey of India, 1967: 22-34.

Deshpande, M. N., "The (Ajanta) Murals: Their Theme & Content" , in: *Ajanta Murals*, ed. A. Ghosh, New Delhi: Archaeological Survey of India, 1967: 35-39.

Deva, Krishna、"Northern Buddhist Monuments" , in: *Archaeological Remains, Monuments & Museums,* Part I, New Delhi: Archaeological Survey of India, 1964: 85-99.

Dschi, Hiän-lin [季羡林], "On the Oldest Chinese Transliteration of the Name of Buddha [浮屠与佛]",载季羡林《印度古代语言论集》(*Selected Papers on the Languages of Ancient India/Ausgewählte Kleine Schriften zur altindischen Philologie*),北京：中国社会科学出版社,1982 年,第 334-347 页。

Duroisell, Charles, "The Stone Sculptures in the Ānanda Temple at Pagan" , in: *Archaeological Survey of India: Annual Report 1913-14* (1917): 63-97.

Durt, Hubert、"The Long and Short *Nirvāṇa Sūtras*" , in: *Problems of Chronology and Eschatology*, Four Lectures on the *Essay on Buddhism* by Tominaga Nakamoto (1715-1746), Kyoto: Istituto Italiano di Cultura Scuola di Studi sull' Asia Orientale, 1994: 57-74.

Eliade, Mircea, *Shamanism: Archaic Techniques of Ecstasy,* transl. from the French by W. R. Trask, London: Arkana, 1989.

Enomoto, Fumio, "A Note on Kashmir as Referred to in Chinese Literature: Jibin" , in: *A Study of the Nīlamata: Aspects of Hinduism in Ancient Kashmir,* ed. Yasuke Ikari, Kyoto: Kyoto University, 1994: 357-365.

Faccenna, Domenico, *Butkara I* (*Swāt, Pakistan*) *1956-1962*, Part 1, Part 3, Text, Rome: IsMEO, 1980.

Faccenna, Domenico, *Saidu Sharif I* (*Swat, Pakistan*) 2, *The Buddhist Sacred Area; The Stūpa Terrace*, Text, Rome: IsMEO, 1995.

Falk, Harry, *Aśokan Sites and Artefacts: a source-book with bibliography*, Mainz am Rhein: Verlag Philipp von Zabern, 2006.

Fergusson, James, *Tree and Serpent Worship* or *Illustrations of Mythology and Art in India in the first and fourth centuries after Christ from the Sculptures of the Buddhist Topes at Sāñchī and Amrāvatī*, London: Indian Office, 1873.

Fergusson, James and James Burgess, *The Cave Temples of India*, London: W. H. Allen & Co., 1880.

Fergusson, James et al., *History of Indian and Eastern Architecture*, 2 vols, rev. ed., London: Murray, 1910.

Forte, Anotonino, *Political Propaganda and Ideology in China at the End of the Seventh Century: Inquiry into the Nature, Authors and Function of the Tunhuang Document S. 6502*, Napoli: Istituto Universitario Orientale-Seminario di Studi Asiatici, 1976.

Foucher, Alfred, *L'Art gréco-bouddhique du Gandhâra: étude sur les origines de l'influence classique dans l'art bouddhique de l'Inde et de l'Extréme-Orient*, 2 Bde, Paris: E. Leroux/Imprimerie Nationale, Tome I, 1905; Tome II, 1, 1918; Tome II, 2, 1922; Tome II, 3, 1951.

Fussman, Gérard, "Documents épigraphiques kouchans" , in: *Bulletin de l'École française d'Extrême-Orient,* 61 (1974): 1-76.

Fussman, Gérard, "Gāndhārī écrite, Gāndhārī parlée" , in: *Dialectes dans les littératures indo-aryennes*, ed. Colette Caillat, Publications de l'Institut de Civilisation Indienne, série in-8°, fasc. 55, Paris: Collège de France, 1989: 433-501.

Gemet, Jacques, *Catalogue des Manuscrits Chinois de Touen-Houang* (*Fonds Pelliot Chinois*), Vol. I, Paris, 1970.

Ghosh, A., *Nālandā*, 6th ed., New Delhi: Archaeological Survey of India, 1986.

Ghosh, A. ed., *Ajanta Murals*, New Delhi: Archaeological Survey of India, 1967.

Ghosh, A., "Two Early Brāhmī Records from Ajaṇṭā", in: *Epigraphia Indica*, 37 (1968).

Ghose, Rajeshwari, "Introduction: Kizil on the Silk Road", in: *Kizil on the Silk Road: Crossroads of Commerce & Meeting of Minds*, ed. Rajeshwari Ghose, Mumbai: Marg Publications, 2008: 8-23.

Ghose, Rajeshwari, "The Kizil Caves: Dates, Art, and Iconography", in: *Kizil on the Silk Road: Crossroads of Commerce & Meeting of Minds,* ed. Rajeshwari Ghose, Mumbai: Marg Publications, 2008: 40-65.

Giles, Lionel, *Descriptive Catalogue of the Chinese Manuscripts from Tunhuang in the British Museum*, London: The Trustees of the British Museum, 1957.

Gray, Basil, *Buddhist Cave Paintings at Tun-huang*, photographys by J. B. Vincent, with a preface by Arthur Waley, London: Faber and Faber Limited, 1959.

Griswold, A.B., "Prolegomena to the Study of the Buddha's Dress in Chinese Sculpture", in: *Artibus Asiae*, Vol. XXVI (1963), No. 2: 85-131, Vol. XXVII (1964/65), No. 4: 335-348.

Grünwedel, Albert, *Bericht über archäologische Arbeiten in Idikutschari und Umgebung im Winter 1902-1903*, München: G. Franz'scher Verlag, 1906.

Grünwedel, Albert, *Altbuddhistische Kultstätten in Chinesisch-Turkistan: Bericht über archäologische Arbeiten von 1906 bis 1907 bei Kuča, Qarašahr und in der oase Turfan*, Königlich Preussische Turfan-Expeditionen, Berlin: Druck und Verlag von Georg Reimer, 1912.

Hargreaves, H., "Excavations at Takht-i-Bāhī", in: *Archaeological Survey of India: Annual Report 1910-11* (1914): 33-39.

Harle, J. C., *Gupta Sculpture: Indian Sculpture of the Fourth to Sixth Century* AD, Oxford: Clarendon Press, 1974.

Hartmann, Jens-Uwe, "Buddhist Sanskrit Texts from Northern Turkestan and their Relation to the Chinese *Tripiṭaka*", in: *Collection of Essays 1993: Buddhism Across Boundaries—Chinese Buddhism and Western Religions* by Erik Zürcher, Lore Sander and others, eds. John R. McRae and Jan Nattier, Taipei: Foguang Cultural

Enterprise Co., Ltd, 1999: 107-136.

Hartmann, Jens-Uwe, "Buddhism along the Silk Road: On the Relationship between the Buddhist Sanskrit Texts from Northern Turkestan and those from Afghanistan" , in: *Turfan Revisited—The First Century of Research into the Arts and Cultures of the Silk Road,* ed. Desmond Durkin-Meisterernst, et al, Berlin: Dietrich Reimer Verlag, 2004: 125-128.

Hartmann, Jens-Uwe, "Contents and Structure of the *Dīrghāgama* of the (Mūla-) Sarvāstivādins" , *Annual Report of The International Research Institute for Advanced Buddhology at Soka University*, 7 (2004): 119-137.

Heirman, Ann, "Can we trace the early Dharmaguptakas?" in: *T'oung Pao* (通报), Vol. LXXXVIII (2002), Fasc. 4-5: 396-429.

Hinüber, Oskar von、"Upali's Verses in the Majjhimanikāya and the Madhyamāgama," in: *Indological and Buddhist Studies, Volume in Honour of Professor J. W. de Jong on his Sixtieth Birthday,* ed. L. A. Hercus et al., Canberra 1982: 243-251.

Hinüber, Oskar von, "Sanskrit und Gāndhārī in Zentralasien" , in: *Sprachen des Buddhismus in Zentralasien: Vorträge des Hamburger Symposions vom 2. Juli bis 5. Juli 1981*, eds. Klaus Röhrborn und Wolfgang Veeker, Veröffentlichungen der Societas Uralo-Altaica, Band 16, Wiesbaden: Otto Harrassowitz, 1983: 27-34.

Hinüber, Oskar von, "Origin and Varieties of Buddhist Sanskrit" , in: *Dialectes dans les littératures indo-aryennes,* ed. Colette Caillat, Publications de l'Institut de Civilisation Indienne, śerie in 8, fasc. 55, Paris: Collège de France, 1989: 341-367.

Hinüber, Oskar von, "Expansion to the North: Afghanistan and Central Asia" , in: *The World of Buddhism, Buddhist Monks and Nuns in Society and Culture,* eds. H. Bechert and R. Gombrich, London: Thames and Hudson, 1993: 99-107.

Hirakawa, Akira, *A History of Indian Buddhism: From Śākyamuni to Early Mahāyāna,* tr. Paul Groner, Asian Studies at Hawaii 36, Honolulu: University of Hawaii Press, 1990.

Hoernle, A. F. Rudolf, *Manuscript Remains of Buddhist Literature found in Eastern Turkestan,* Oxford: Clarendon Press, 1916.

Howard, Angela F., Li Kunsheng & Qiu Xuanchong, "Nanzhao and Dali Buddhist Sculpture in Yunnan" , in: *Orientations*, 23 (2): 51-60.

Howard, Angela F., "The Development of Buddhist Sculpture in Yunnan: Syncretic

Art of A Frontier Kingdom" , in: *The Flowering of A Foreign Faith: New Studies in Chinese Buddhist Art,* ed. Janet Baker, Mumbai: Marg Publications, 1998: 134-145.

Howard, Angela F., "Buddhist Art in China" , in: *China Dawn of a Golden Age, 200-750 AD,* ed. James C. Y. Watt et al, New York: The Metropolitan Museum of Art, New Haven and London: Yale University Press, 2004: 89-99.

Howard, Angela F., "Standing Ashoka-type Buddha" , in: *China Dawn of a Golden Age, 200-750 AD,* ed. James C. Y. Watt et al, New York: The Metropolitan Museum of Art, New Haven and London: Yale University Press, 2004: 227-229.

Indian Archaeology 2000-01—A Review, New Delhi: Archaeological Survey of India, 2006.

Ingholt, Harald, *Gandhāran Art in Pakistan; with 577 illustrations photographed by Islay Lyons and 77 pictures from other sources, Introduction and Descriptive Catalogue by Harald Ingholt*, New York: Pantheon Books, 1957.

Joshi, M. C., "Buddhist Rock-cut Architecture: A Survey" , in: *Proceedings of the International Seminar on Cave Art of India and China*, Theme I: Historical Perspective, New Delhi: Indira Gandhi National Centre for the Arts, November 25, 1991: 1-28.

Kao Kuan-ju, "Abhidharma-mahāvibhāṣā" , in: *Encyclopaedia of Buddhism*, ed. G. P. Malalasekera, Colombo: The Government of Ceylon, Vol. I (1961-1965): 80-84.

Khan, Muhammad Ashraf et al, *A Catalogue of the Gandhāra Stone Sculptures in the Taxila Museum,* Islamabad: Department of Archaeology and Museums, Government of Pakistan, 2 vols., 2005.

Konow, Sten, *Kharoshṭhī Inscriptions with the Exception of those of Aśoka*; Corpus Inscriptionum Indicarum II, Part 1, London: Oxford University Press, 1929.

Lal, B. B., "The (Ajaṇṭā) Murals: Their Composition and Technique", in: *Ajanta Murals,* ed A. Ghosh, New Delhi: Archaeological Survey of India, 1967: 53-55.

Lamotte, Étienne, *Histoire du Bouddhisme Indien: des origines à l'ére Śaka,* Bibliothȩque du Muséon 43, Louvain: Institut Orientaliste de Louvain, 1958.

Lamotte, Étienne, *History of Indian Buddhism from the Origins to the Śaka era*, tr. Sara Webb-Boin, Louvain-la-Neuve: Institut Orientaliste de l'Université Catholique de Louvain/Louvain: Peeters Press, 1988.

Le Coq, Albert von and Ernst Waldschmidt, *Die Buddhistische Spätantike in Mittelasien*, VI , Neue Bildwerke II, Berlin: D. Reimer, 1928.

Lee, Sonya S., *Surviving Nirvana: Death of the Buddha in Chinese Visual Culture*, Hong Kong: Hong Kong University Press, 2010.

Legge, James, *The Nestorian Monument of Hsi-An Fu in Shen-hsi, China*, London: Trübner & Co., 1888.

Leidy, Denise P., *The Art of Buddhism: An Introduction to its History and Meaning*, Boston & London: Shambhala Publications, Inc., 2008.

Lèvi, S. and É. Chavannes, "L'Itinéraire d'Ou-k'oung" , in: *Journal Asiatique*, Octobre (1895): 371-384.

Lévi, Sylvain, "Le sūtra du sage et du fou dans la littérature de l'Asie Centrale" , in: *Journal Asiatique,* Sér. 12, 6, Vol. 207/2 (Octobre-Décembre, 1925): 304-332.

Li, Chongfeng, *Chētiyagharas in Indian and Chinese Buddhist Caves: A Comparative Study* (Dissertation submitted to the University of Delhi for the Award of the Degree of Doctor of Philosophy), Delhi: University of Delhi, 1993.

Li, Chongfeng, "The Representation of *Jātakas* in Kizil Caves, Kucha" , in: *Turfan Revisited—The First Century of Research into the Arts and Cultures of the Silk Road,* ed. Desmond Durkin-Meisterernst et al, Berlin: Dietrich Reimer Verlag, 2004: 163-168.

Li, Chongfeng, "The Geography of Transmission: The 'Jibin' Route and Propagation of Buddhism in China" , in: *Kizil on the Silk Road: Crossroads of Commerce & Meeting of Minds,* ed. Rajeshwari Ghose, Mumbai: Marg Publications, 2008: 24-31.

Li, Chongfeng, "Gandhāra, Mathurā and Buddhist Sculptures of Mediaeval China" , in: *Glory of the Kushans: Recent Discoveries and Interpretations*, ed. Vidula Jayaswal, New Delhi: Aryan Books International, 2012: 378-391.

Li, Chongfeng, "Representation of the Buddha's *Parinirvāṇa* in the *Cetiyagharas* at Kizil, Kucha" , in: *Buddhist Narrative in Asia and Beyond,* Vol. I, eds. Peter Skilling and Justin McDaniel, Bangkok: Institute of Thai Studies, Chulalongkorn University, 2012: 59-81.

Li, Chongfeng, "The Image of Maitreya in the *Chētiyagharas* of Kizil, Kucha" , in: *Gandhāran Studies,* Vol. VII: 11-22.

Li, Chongfeng, "*Kumārajīva* and the Early Cave-temples of China: the Case of *Dhyāna-sūtras*", in: *Kumārajīva: Philosopher and Seer*, ed. Shashibala, New Delhi: Indira Gandhi National Centre for the Arts, 2015: 190-221.

Li, Chongfeng, "Jibin and China as seen from Chinese Documents", in: *Archaeology of Buddhism in Asia*, ed. B. Mani, New Delhi: Archaeological Survey of India (in press).

Lin Meicun, "Kharoṣṭhī Bibliorapihy: The Collections from China (1897-1993)", in: *Central Asiatic Journal*, 40 (2): 188-221.

Lin Meicun, "A Formal Kharoṣṭhī Inscription from Subashi", 载敦煌研究院编《段文杰敦煌研究五十年纪念文集》,北京：世界图书出版公司,1996 年,第 328-347 页。

Litvinsky, B. A. ed., *History of Civilizations of Central Asia*, Vol. 3: *The Crossroads of Civilization: AD 250-750*, Multiple History Series, Paris: UNESCO, 1996.

Lohuizen-de Leeuw, J. E. Van, *The "Scythian" Period: An approach to the history, art, epigraphy and palaeography of north India from the 1st century BC to the 3rd century AD*, Leiden: E. J. Brill, 1949.

Longhurst, A. H., *The Story of the Stūpa*, rep., New Delhi: Asian Educational Services, 1979.

Lü Chêng, "Āgama", in: *Encyclopedia of Buddhism*, ed. G. P. Malalasekera, Colombo: The Government of Ceylon, Vol. I (1961-1965): 241-244.

Lü Chêng, "Buddhabhadra", in: *Encyclopaedia of Buddhism*, ed. G. P. Malalasekera, Colombo: The Government of Ceylon, Vol. III (1971): 382-384.

Lüders, Heinrich, "*A List of Brāhmī Inscriptions from the Earliest Times to about A.D. 400 with the Exception of those of Aśōka*", in: *Epigraphia Indica and Record of the Archaeological Survey of India*, Volume X (1909-10), Appendix, Calcutta: Superintendent Government Printing, India, 1912.

Lüders, Heinrich, "Zu und aus den Kharoṣṭhī-Urkunden", in: *Acta Orientalia* 18 (1940): 15-49.

Lüders, Heinrich, *Mathurā Inscriptions: Unpublished Papers Edited by Klaus L. Janert*, Abhandlungen der Akademie der Wissenschaften in Göttingen, Philologisch-historische Klasse, 3. 47, Göttingen: Vandenhoeck & Ruprecht, 1961.

Lüders, Heinrich ed., *Bhārhut Inscriptions*, revised by E. Waldschmidt and M. A. Mehendale, New Delhi: Archaeological Survey of India, 1963.

MaCdonell, A. and A. B. Keith, *Vedic Index of Names and Subjects*, rep., New Delhi: Motilal Banersidass, 1984.

Mair, Victor, "The Khotanese Antecedents of *the Sūtra of the Wise and Foolish* (*Xianyujing*)", in: *Collection of Essays 1993: Buddhism Across Boundaries—Chinese Buddhism and Western Religions* by Erik Zürcher, Lore Sander and others, eds. John R. McRae and Jan Nattier, Taipei: Foguang Cultural Enterprise Co., Ltd, 1999: 361-420.

Majumdar, R. C., et al, *An Advanced History of India*, 4th ed., Madras: Macmillan India Limited, 1978.

Malalasekera, G. P., *The Pāli Literature of Ceylon*, Colombo: M. D. Gunasena & Co., Ltd, 1928.

Marshall, John. H. and S. Konow, "Sārnāth", in: *Archaeological Survey of India: Annual Report 1906-07* (1909): 68-101.

Marshall, John, "The Monuments of Sanchi: Their Exploration and Conservation", in: *Archaeological Survey of India; Annual Report 1913-14* (1917): 1-39.

Marshall, John, *Excavations at Taxila: The Stūpas and Monastery at Jauliāñ; Memoir No. 7 of the Archaeological Survey of India*, Calcutta: Archaeological Survey of India, 1921.

Marshall, John and Alfred Foucher, *The Monuments of Sāñchī*, Calcutta: Manager of Publications/Archaeological Survey of India, 1940.

Marshall, John, *Taxila: An illustrated account of archaeological excavations carried out at Taxila under the orders of the government of India between the years 1913 and 1934*, 3 vols, London: Cambridge University Press, 1951.

Marshall, John, *Buddhist Art of Gandhara: The Story of the Early School; its birth, growth and decline*, London: Cambridge University Press, 1960.

Ma Yong, "The Chinese Inscription of the 'Da Wei' Envoy of the 'Sacred Rock of Hunza'", in *Antiquities of Northern Pakistan: Reports and Studies,* Vol. 1, *Rock Inscriptions in the Indus Valley,* ed. Karl Jettmar et al, Mainz: Verlag Philipp von Zabern, 1989: 139-157.

McNair, Amy, *Donors of Longmen: Faith, Politics and Patronage of Medieval Chinese Buddhist Sculpture*, Honolulu: University of Hawaii Press, 2007.

Под редакцией Л. Н. Меньшикова, ОПИСАНИЕ КИТАЙСКИХ РУКОПИСЕЙ

ДУНЬХУАНСКОГО ФОНДА ИНСТИТУТА НАРОДОВ АЗИИ, вьпіуск I, II, ИЗДАТЕЛЬСТВО ВОСТОЧНОЙ ЛИТЕРАТУРЫ, Москва, 1963, 1967.

Meunié, Jacques, *Shotorak, Mémoires de la Délégation Archéologique Française en Afghanistan*, X, Paris: Les Éditions d'Art et d'Historie, 1942.

Minayeff, Von Joh, "Buddhistische Fragmente", in: *Bulletin de l'Académie Impériale des Sciences de Saint-Pétersbourg*, 1871: 70-85.

Mirashi, V. V. ed., *Inscriptions of the Vākāṭakas: Corpus Inscriptionum Indicarum* V, Ootacamund: Government Epigraphist for India, 1963.

Mitra, Debala, *Buddhist Monuments*, Calcutta: Sahitya Samsad, 1971.

Mitra, Debala, *Ajanta*, 10th ed., New Delhi: Archaeological Survey of India, 1992.

Mitra, R., *Bodh Gayā: The Great Buddhist Temple, the Hermitage of Sakyamuni*, Calcutta: Bengal Secretariat Press, 1878.

Monier-Williams, Monier, *A Sanskrit-English Dictionary*, London: Oxford University Press, 1899.

Nagaraju, S., *Buddhist Architecture of Western India (C. 250 BC-C. AD 300)*, Delhi: Agam Kala Prakashan, 1981.

Nakamura, Hajime, *Indian Buddhism: A Survey with Bibliographical Notes*, Delhi: Motilal Banarsidass Publishers, 1987.

Narain, A. K., *The Indo-Greeks*, Oxford: The Clarendon Press, 1957.

Narain, A. K., *The Tokharians: A History without Nation-State Boundaries*, RGF-NERC-ICSSR Lecture-Series, Shillong: North-Eastern Hill University Publications, 2000.

Nattier, Jan, "Church Language and Vernacular Language in Central Asian Buddhism", in: *Numen* (International Review for the History of Religion), Vol. 37 (1990), No. 2: 195-219.

Noci, Francesco, et al, *Saidu Sharif I* (*Swat, Pakistan*) 3, *The Graveyard*, Rome: IsIAO, 1997.

Oertel, F. O., "Excavations at Sārnāth", in: *Archaeological Survey of India: Annual Report 1904-05* (1908): 50-104.

Patil, D. R., *Kuśīnagara*, New Delhi: Archaeological Survey of India, 1957.

Pelliot, Paul, *Mission Paul Pelliot documents archéologiques XI; Grottes de Touen-houang: Carnet de Notes de Paul Pelliot, inscriptions et peintures murales, V*, eds., N. Vandier-Nicolas et M. Maillard. Paris: Collège de France, 1986.

Petech, L., *Northern India According to the Shui-jing-chu*, Rome: IsMEO, 1950.

Pinault, Georges-Jean, "Épigraphie koutchéenne" , in: *Mission Paul Pelliot Documents conservés au Musée Guimet et à la Bibliothèque Nationale;* Documents Archéologiques VIII, Sites divers de la région de Koutcha, ed. Chao Huashan, S. Gaulier, M. Maillard et G. Pinault, Paris: Center de Recherche sur l'Asie Centrale et la Haute Asie, Collège de France, 1987: 59-196.

Piggot, S., "The Earliest Buddhist Shrines" , in: *Antiquity*, 1943, XVII (65).

Pulleyblank, E. G., "Stages in the Transcription of Indian Words in Chinese from Han to Tang" , in: *Sprachen des Buddhismus in Zentralasien: Vorträge des Hamburger Symposions vom 2. Juli bis 5. Juli 1981*, eds. Klaus Röhrborn und Wolfgang Veenker, Veröffentlichungen der Societas Uralo-Altaica, Band 16, Wiesbaden: Otto Harrassowitz, 1983: 73-102.

Puri, B. N., *Buddhism in Central Asia*, Delhi: Motilal Banarsidass Publishers, 1987.

Rahman, Abdur, "Excavation at Chatpat" , in: *Ancient Pakistan* (Bulletin of the Department of Archaeology, University of Peshawar), Vol. IV (1968-69).

Rhie, Marylin M., *Early Buddhist Art of China & Central Asia.* Vol. 2. Leiden: Brill, 2002.

Rhys Davids, T. W., *Buddhist India*, rev. ed., Delhi: Bharatiya Kala Prakashan, 2007.

Rhys Davids, T. W. and William Stede, *Pali-English Dictionary*, London: Pali Text Society, 1925.

Rong Xinjiang, "Juqu Anzhou's Inscription and the Daliang Kingdom in Turfan" , in: *Turfan Revisited—The First Century of Research into the Arts and Cultures of the Silk Road*, ed. Desmond Durkin-Meisterernst et al., Berlin: Dietrich Reimer Verlag, 2004: 268-275.

Rosenfield, John M., *The Dynastic Arts of the Kushans*, Berkeley: University of California Press, 1967.

Rowland, B., *The Pelican History of Art; The Art and Architecture of India: Buddhist/ Hindu/Jain*, reprinted with revisions and updated bibliography by J. C. Harle, New York: Penguin Books, 1977.

Saeki, P. Y., *The Nestorian Documents and Relics in China*, Tokyo: The Academy of Oriental Culture, Tokyo Institute, 1937.

Sahni, D. R., *Archaeological Remains and Excavations at Bairat*, Jaipur: Department of Archaeology & Historical Research, Jaipur State, 1937.

Salomon, Richard, "New Evidence for a Gāndhārī Origin of the Arapacana Syllabary", in: *Journal of the American Oriental Society,* 110 (1990): 255-273.

Salomon, Richard, *Ancient Buddhist Scrolls from Gandhāra: The British Library Kharoṣṭhī Fragments,* Seattle: University of Washington Press, 1999.

Sander, Lore, "Early Prakrit and Sanskrit Manuscripts from Xinjiang (second to fifth/sixth centuries C.E.): Paleography, Literary Evidence and Their Relation to Buddhist Schools", in: *Collection of Essays 1993: Buddhism Across Boundaries-Chinese Buddhism and Western Religions* by Erik Zürcher, Lore Sander and others, eds. John R. McRae and Jan Nattier, Taipei: Foguang Cultural Enterprise Co., Ltd, 1999: 61-106.

Sander, Lore, "Ernst Waldschmidt's Contribution to the Study of the 'Turfan Finds'", in: *Turfan Revisited—The First Century of Research into the Arts and Cultures of the Silk Road*, ed. Desmond Durkin-Meisterernst et al., Berlin: Dietrich Reimer Verlag, 2004: 303-309.

Schlingloff, Dieter, *Die Buddhastotras des Mātṛceṭa, Faksimilewiedergabe der Handschriften* (Abhandlungen der Deutschen Akademie der Wissenschaften zu Berlin 1968, Nr. 2), Berlin: Akademie-Verlag, 1968.

Schlingloff, Dieter, *Studies in the Ajanta Paintings: Identifications and Interpretations*, Delhi: Ajanta Publications (India), 1987.

Senart, É., "The Inscriptions of the Caves at Kārlē", in: *Epigraphia Indica,* VII (1903).

Seoul Arts Center ed., *The Exhibition of Gandhara Art of Pakistan,* Seoul: Joong-Ang Ilbo, 1999.

Sharma, R. C., *Buddhist Art*: *Mathurā School*, New Delhi: Wiley Eastern Limited & New Age International Limited, 1995.

Sharma, R. C. "Mathurā and Gandhāra: The Two Great Styles", in: *Buddhism and Gandhāra Art,* eds. R. C. Sharma and Pranati Ghosal, Shimla: Indian Institute of Advanced Study, Varanasi: Jñāna-Pravāha and New Delhi: Aryan Books International, 2004: 66-72.

Silva, Roland, *Thūpa, Thūpaghara and Thūpa-pāsāda*; Memoirs of the Archaeological Survey of Ceylon, Volume X, Part II, Colombo: The Department of Archaeology, Sri Lanka, 2004.

Sims-Willams, Nicholas and Joe Cribb, "A New Bactrian Inscription of Kanishka the Great", *Silk Road Art and Archaeology*, Journal of the Institute of Silk Road Studies, Kamakura, 4 (1995/96): 75-142.

Siren, Osavld, *Chinese Sculpture from the fifth to the fourteenth century*, London: Ernest Benn, 1925.

Snellgrove, David L., ed., *The Image of the Buddha*, New Delhi: Vikas Publishing House Pvt Ltd/UNESCO, 1978.

Soper, A. C., "Aspects of Light Symbolism in Gandhāran Sculpture", in: *Artibus Asiae,* 1949, XII (3): 252-283; (4): 314-330; 1950, XIII (1/2): 63-85.

Soper, A. C., *Literary Evidence for Early Buddhist Art in China, Artibus Asiae* Supplementum XIX, Ascona: *Artibus Asiae* Publishers, 1959.

Sorensen, Henrik H., "The Buddhist Sculptures at Feixian Pavilion in Pujiang, Sichuan", in: *Artibus Asiae*, Vol. 58, No. 1/2 (1998): 33-67.

Soundara Rajan, K. V., "Keynote Address (at the National Seminar on Ellorā Caves)", in: *Ellorā Caves: Sculptures and Architecture* (Collected papers of the Unverisity Grants Commission's National Seminar), ed. Ratan Parimoo et al, New Delhi: Books & Books, 1988: 29-51.

Spink, Walter M., *Ajanta : A Brief History and Guide*, Ann Arbor: Asian Art Archives, University of Michigan, 1994.

Spooner, D. B., "Excavations at Takht-i-Bāhī", in: *Archaeological Survey of India: Annual Report 1907-08* (1911): 132-48.

Srinivasan, K. R., "Southern Buddhist Monuments", in: *Archaeological Remains, Monuments & Museums*, Part I, New Delhi: Archaeological Survey of India, 1964: 100-108.

Strong, John S., "Buddha's Funeral", in: *The Buddhist Dead: Practices, Discourses, Representations*, ed. Bryan J. Cuevas and Jacqueline I. Stone, Honolulu: University of Hawaii Press, 2007: 32-59.

Su Bai, "Buddha Images of the Northern Plain, 4th-6th century, " in: *China Dawn of a Golden Age, 200-750 AD,* ed. James C. Y. Watt et al, New York: The Metropolitan Museum of Art, New Haven and London: Yale University Press, 2004: 79-87.

Tarn, W. W., *The Greeks in Bactria and India*, Cambridge: Cambridge University Press, 1951.

Taw Sein Ko, "Some Excavations at Pagan", in: *Archaeological Survey of India: Annual Report 1905-06* (1909): 131-134.

Tissot, Francine, *Gandhâra*, 2e éditon revue et corrigée; Dessins d'Anne-Marie Loth et de l'auteur, Paris: Librairie d'Amérique et d' Orient/Jean Maisonneuve, 2002.

Tiwari, U. R., *Sculptures of Mathura and Sarnath, A Comparative Study* (*Up to Gupta Period*), Delhi: Sundeep Prakashan, 1998.

Tucci, Giuseppe, "Preliminary Report on an Archaeological Survey in Swāt", in: *East and West*, IX/4 (1958): 279-348.

Vats, M. S., "Unpublished Votive Inscriptions in the Chaitya Cave at Kārlē", in: *Epigraphia Indica*, XVIII (1925-26).

Vogel, J. Ph., "The Mathurā School of Sculpture", in: *Archaeological Survey of India: Annual Report 1906-7* (1909): 137-160 and *Archaeological Survey of India: Annual Report 1909-10* (1914): 63-79.

Vogel, J. Ph., *Catalogue of the Archaeological Museum at Mathurā*, Allahabad: 1910.

Vogel, J. Ph., "Explorations at Mathurā", in: *Archaeological Survey of India: Annual Report 1911-12* (1915): 120-133.

Vogel, J. Ph., *La sculpture de Mathurā*, Paris et Bruxelles: Les Editions G. van Oest, 1930.

Warder, A. K., *Indian Buddhism*, 2nd rev. ed., Delhi: Motilal Banarsidass Publishers Pvt. Ltd., 1980.

Waldschmidt, Ernst, *Bruchstücke des Bhikṣuṇī-Prātimokṣa der Sarvāstivādins: Mit einer Darstellung der Überlieferung des Bhikṣuṇī-Prātimokṣa in den verschiedenen Schulen* (Kleinere Sanskrittexte III), Leipzig: Deutschen Morgenländische Gesellschaft, 1926.

Waldschmidt, Ernst, "Über die Darstellungen und den Stil der Wandgemälde aus Qyzil bei Kutscha I", in: A. von Leq und E. Waldschmidt (ed.), *Die buddhistische Spätantike in Mittelasien*, VI: Neue Bildwerke II, Berlin, 1928: 9-62.

Waldschmidt, Ernst, *Bruchstücke buddhistischer Sūtras aus dem zentralasiatischen Sanskritkanon I: herausgegeben und im Zusammenhang mit ihren Parallelversionen bearbeitet* (Königlich Preußische Turfan-Expeditionen, Kleinere Sanskrit-texte IV), Leipzig: Deutschen Morgenländische Gesellschaft, 1932.

Waldschmidt, Ernst, "Beiträge zur Textgeschichte des *Mahāparinirvāṇasūtra*", in:

Nachrichten der Akademie der Wissenschaften in Göttingen, 1939: 55-94.

Waldschmidt, Ernst, *Die Überlieferung vom Lebensende des Buddha: Eine vergleichende Analyse des Mahāparinirvāṇasūtra und seiner Textentsprechungen*, Teil 1 und 2 (Abhandlungen der Akademie der Wissenschaften in Göttingen, Philologisch-historische Klasse, 3. Folge, Nr. 29, 30), Göttingen: Vandenhoeck & Ruprecht, 1944, 1948.

Waldschmidt, Ernst, *Das Mahāparinirvāṇasūtra: Text in Sanskrit und Tibetisch, verglichen mit dem Pāli nebst einer Übersetzung der chinesischen Entsprechung im Vinaya der Mūlasarvāstivādins*, Teil I-III (Abhandlungen der Deutschen Akademie der Wissenschaften zu Berlin, Klasse für Sprachen, Literatur und Kunst, No. 1, 1949; No. 2, 3, 1950), Berlin: Akademie-Verlag, 1950-1951.

Waldschmidt, Ernst, *Das Mahāvadānasūtra: Ein kanonischer Text über die sieben letzten Buddhas; Sanskrit, verglichen mit dem Pāli, nebst einer Analyse der in chinesischer Übersetzung überlieferten Parallelversionen, auf Grund von Turfan-Handschriften herausgegeben und bearbeitet,* Teil 1, 2 (Abhandlungen der Deutschen Akademie der Wissenschaften zu Berlin, Klasse für Sprachen, Literatur und Kunst, 1952, 8; 1954, 3), Berlin: Akademie-Verlag, 1953, 1956.

Waldschmidt, Ernst, *Das Catuṣpariṣatsūtra: Eine kanonische Lehrschrift über die Begründung der buddhistischen Gemeinde*. Teil I-III (Abhandlungen der Deutschen Akademie der Wissenschaften zu Berlin, Klasse für Sprachen, Literatur und Kunst, 1952, 2; 1956, 1; 1960, 1), Berlin: Akademie-Verlag, 1952, 1957, 1962.

Waldschmidt, Ernst, "Die Einleitung des *Saṇgītisūtra*" , in: *Zeitschrift der Deutschen Morgenländischen Gesellschaft*, 105 (1955): 298-318.

Waldschmidt, Ernst, "Drei Fragmente buddhistischer *Sūtras* aus den Turfanhandschriften" , in: *Nachrichten der Akademie der Wissenschaften in Göttingen,* Nr. 1, Philologisch-historische Klasse, Jg. 1968, Göttingen: Vandenhoeck & Ruprecht, 1968: 3-26.

Waldschmidt, Ernst, *Sanskrithandschriften aus den Turfanfunden*. Teil 1, Verzeichnis der orientalischen Handschriften in Deutschland, unter Mitarbeit von Walter Clawiter und Lore Holzman hrsg. und mit einer Einleitung versehen von Ernst Waldschmidt, Wiesbaden: Franz Steiner Verlag, 1965.

Waldschmidt, Ernst, Lore Sander, and Klaus Wille, ed., *Sanskrithandschriften aus den Turfanfunden,* pts. 1-8, Wiesbaden/Stuttgart: Franz Steiner Verlag, 1965-2000.

Waldschmidt, Ernst, "Central Asian *Sūtra* Fragments and their Relation to the Chinese *Āgamas*", in: *Die Sprache der ältesten buddhistischen Überlieferung; The Language of the Earliest Buddhist Tradition* (Symposien zur Buddhismusforschung II), Abhandlungen der Akademie der Wissenschaften in Göttingen: Philologisch-historische Klasse, Ser. 3, Vol. 117, Heinz Bechert, hrsg, Göttingen: Vandenhoeck & Ruprecht, 1980: 136-174.

Watters, Thomas, *On Yuan Chwang's Travels in India AD 629-645*, London: Royal Asiatic Society, Vol. I, 1904; Vol. II, 1905.

Willemen, Charles, "A Chinese *Kṣudrakapiṭaka* (T. IV. 203)", in: *Asiatische Studien Études Asiatiques* XLVI. 1 (1992): 507-515.

Willemen, Charles, et al., *Sarvāstivāda Buddhist Scholasticism*, Leiden: Brill, 1998.

Willemen, Charles, "Sarvāstivāda Developments in Northwestern India and in China", in: *The Indian International Journal of Buddhist Studies* (New Series in continuation of the *Indian Journal of Buddhist Studies*, Vol. X, Varanasi: B. J. K. Institute of Buddhist and Asian Studies), No. 2 (2001): 163-169.

Willemen, Charles, "Kumārajīva's 'Explanatory Discourse' about Abhidharmic Literature", in: *Kokusai Bukkyōgaku Daigaku-in Daigaku Kenkyū Kiyō* [国際仏教大学院大学研究紀要第 12 号 (平成 20 年)/*Journal of the International College for Postgraduate Buddhist Studies*], Vol. XII (2008): 37-83 (156-110).

Willemen, Charles, "Kaniṣka and the Sarvāstivāda Synod", in: *Glory of the Kushans: Recent Discoveries and Interpretations*, ed. Vidula Jayaswal, New Delhi: Aryan Books International, 2012: 218-222.

Wu, N. I., *Chinese and Indian Architecture: the City of Man, the Mountain of God and the Realm of the Immortals*, New York: George Braziller Inc., 1963.

Yaldiz, Marianne, ed., *Dokumentation der Verluste,* Band III, Museum für Indische Kunst, Berlin: Staatliche Museen zu Berlin, 2002.

Yaldiz, Marianne, "Maitreya in Literature and in the Art of Xinjiang", in: *Kizil on the Silk Road: Crossroads of Commerce & Meeting of Minds*, ed. Rajeshwari Ghose, Mumbai: Marg Publications, 2008: 66-83.

Yampolsky, Philip B., *Platform Sūtra: The Text of the Tunhuang Manuscript*, New York:

Columbia University Press, 1967.

Yazdani, G., *Ajanta: The colour and monochrome reproductions of the Ajanta frescoes based on photography*, London: Oxford University Press, Part I, 1930; Part II, 1933, Part III, 1946, Part IV, 1955.

Yen Chuan-ying, *The Sculptures from the Tower of Seven Jewels: The Style, Patronage and Iconography of the Tang Monument* [Ph. D Dissertation], Harvard University, 1986.

Zürcher, Erik, *The Buddhist Conquest of China: The Spread and Adaptation of Buddhism in Early Medieval China*, Leiden: E. J. Brill, 1972.

Zwalf, W., *A Catalogue of the Gandhāra Sculpture in the British Museum*, 2 vols, London: British Museum Press, 1996.

日文部分

（按照黑本 /Hepburn 系次第排列）

足立喜六《法顯傳：中亞、印度、南海紀行の研究》，東京：法藏館，1940 年。

赤沼智善《佛教經典史論》，名古屋：三寶書院，1939 年。

松本榮一《燉煌畫の研究：圖像篇・附圖》，東京：東方文化學院東京研究所，1937 年。

ジャック・ジェス編，秋山光和監修《西域美術：ギメ美術館ペリオ・コレクション；ジャン・フランソヮ・ジャリージエ》，東京：講談社，1994 年。

《大日本校订大藏经》/《大日本校订缩刻大藏经》/《缩刷藏》/《缩刻藏》/《弘教藏》，東京：弘教書院，1881-85 年，40 函 418 册。

《大日本校订藏经》/《日本藏经书院大藏经》/《卍字藏》/《卍字正藏》，前田慧云、中野达慧主持，京都：京都藏经书院，1902-05 年，36 套（函）347 册。

《大日本續藏経 / 日本藏经书院续藏经 / 卍续藏 / 续藏经》，前田慧云原编、中野达慧增订，京都：藏经书院，1905-1912 年，150 套，750 册。

段文杰《敦煌壁画の様式の特色と芸术的成果》，载日中国交正常化十周年記念《中国敦煌壁画展》图录，東京：每日新聞社，1982 年。

圓仁《日本國承和五年（838 年）入唐求法目録》，載《大正藏》第 55 卷，第 1074-1076 頁。

榎本文雄《阿含經典の成立》，刊《東洋學術研究》，23 卷 1 期，第 93-108 頁。

榎本文雄《罽賓一インド仏教の一中心地の所在》，载《知の邂逅一仏教と科学：塚本啓

祥教授還曆紀念論文集》,東京：佼成出版社,1993 年,第 265-266 頁。

Enomoto, Fumio, “Keihin-Indo Bukkyō no Ichichūshinchi no Shozai [Kipin: The Central Area of Indian Buddhism]” , in: *Chi no Kaikō-Bukkyō to Kagaku; Tsukamoto Keishō Kyōju Kanreki Kinen Ronbunshū Kankōkai*, Tōkyō: Kōsei Publishing, 1993: 265-266.

樋口隆康《バーミヤーン：アフガニスタンにおける仏教石窟寺院の美術考古学的調查 1970-1978 年；京都大學中央アシア學術調查報告》,第 I 巻図版篇 (壁画),第 II 巻図版篇 (石窟構造)1983 年；第 III 巻本文篇,第 IV 巻英文 / 実測図篇,1984 年,京都：同朋舍,1983-84 年。

Higuchi, Takayasu, *Bāmiyān: Art and Archaeological Researches on the Buddhist Cave Temples in Afghanistan 1970-1978*, 4 vols., Vol. I: Plates/Murals, Vol. II: Plates/ Construction of Caves, 1983; Vol. III: Text, Vol. IV: Summary/Plans, 1984, Kyoto: Dōhōsha, 1983-84.

肥田路美《唐代における仏陀伽耶金剛座真容像の流行について》,載：町田甲一先生古稀紀念會編《論叢　仏教美術史》,東京：吉川弘文館,1986 年,第 157-186 頁。

久野美樹《龍門石窟擂鼓台南洞中洞試論》,載《美學美術史論集》第 14 輯 (2002 年),第 93-119 頁。

辛嶋靜志《〈長阿含経〉の原語の研究——音写語分析を中心として》,東京：平河出版社,1994 年。

Karashima, Seishi, *Jō-agonkyō no Gengo no Kenkyū-Onshago Bunseki o Chūshin tosite* [*A Study of the Underlying Language of the Chinese Dirghâgama—Focusing on an Analysis of the Translations*], Tokyo: Hirakawa Shuppansha, 1994.

桑山正進《罽賓と佛》,见《展望アジアの考古學——樋口隆康教授退官記念論集》,東京：新潮社,1983 年,第 598-607 頁。

栗田功《ガンダーラ美術》, I 佛伝,II 佛陀の世界,東京：二玄社,1988-1990 年。

Kurita, Isao, *Gandhāra bijutsu* [*Gandhāran Art*], Vol. I *The Buddha's Life Story*, Vol. II The World of the Buddha, Tokyo: Nigensha, 1988-1990.

松原三郎《改訂東洋美術全史》,東京：株式會社東京美術,1981 年。

松原三郎《中国仏教彫刻史論》,東京：吉川弘文館,1995 年。

Matsubara, Saburō, *A History of Chinese Buddhist Sculpture*, Tokyo: Yoshikawa Kōbunkan, 1995.

宮治昭《涅槃と弥勒の図像学——インドから中央アジアへ》,東京：吉川弘文館,

1992年。

Miyaji, Akira, *Nehan to Miroku no zuzōgaku: Indo kara Chūō Ajia e* [*Iconology of Parinirvāṇa and Maitreya: from India to Central Asia*], Tokyo: Yoshikawa Kōbunkan, 1992.

宮治昭，"涅槃と彌勒菩薩"，載東武美術館編集《ブッダ展——大いなる旅路 /*Buddha: The Spread of Buddhist Art in Asia*》，東京：NHK (Japan Broadcasting Corporation) and NHK Promotions, 1998年。

Miyaji, Akira, "Death of Buddha (*Nirvāṇa*) and Maitreya Bodhisattva", in: *Buddha: The Spread of Buddhist Art in Asia,* ed. Tobu Museum of Art et al, Tokyo: NHK (Japan Broadcasting Corporation) and NHK Promotions, 1998.

宮治昭等《佛傳美術の傳播と變容—— シルクロードに沿つて》，刊《シルクロード學研究》，1997年，第3辑。

水野弘元《別譯雜阿含について》，刊《印度學佛教學研究》，18卷2號，第41-51頁。

水野弘元《國譯一切經：四阿含解題の補遺・長含》，東京：大東出版社，1968年，第499-515頁。

水野清一、长广敏雄《河北磁县河南武安响堂山石窟》，京都：东方文化学院京都研究所，1937年。

水野清一、長廣敏雄《龍門石窟の研究》，東京：座右寶刊行會，1941年。

水野清一、長廣敏雄《雲岡石窟：西曆五世紀における中國北部佛教窟院の考古學的調查報告》；東方文化研究所調查，昭和十三年—昭和二十年，16卷，京都：京都大學人文科學研究所，1951-1956年；《雲岡石窟續補；第十八洞實測圖：西曆五世紀における中國北部の佛教窟院》，調查時間　昭和十三年——昭和二十年，水野清一、田中重雄實測 / 製圖，日比野丈夫解说，京都：京都大學人文科學研究所，1975年。

水野清一《雲岡發掘記 1&2》，載水野清一、長廣敏雄《雲岡石窟：西曆五世紀における中國北部佛教窟院の考古學的調查報告》；東方文化研究所調查，昭和十三年—昭和二十年，京都：京都大學人文科學研究所，第七卷，本文 (1952年) 第57-68、123-129頁，第29-56圖；第十五卷，本文 (1955年) 第91-99、185-90頁，第50-53、56-107圖。

Mizuno, S., "Report on the Yünkang Excavations I & II", in: S. Mizuno and T. Nagahiro, *Yun-kang; The Buddhist Cave-temples of the Fifth Century* AD *in North China; detailed report of the archaeological survey carried out by the mission of the Tōhōbunka Kenkyūsho 1938-45*, Kyoto: Jimbunkagaku Kenkyūshō, Kyoto University, Vol. VII (1952): 57-68, 123-129, Figs. 29-56; Vol. XV (1955): 91-99, 185-190, Figs. 50-53, 56-107.

水野清一《敦煌石窟ノート》,載水野清一《中國の仏教美術》,東京：株式会社平凡社,1968年,第386-444頁。

長廣敏雄《雲岡石窟における仏像の服制》,載長廣敏雄《中國美術論集》,東京：株式会社講談社,1984年,第431-445頁。

岡教邃《梵語の阿含經と漢譯原本の考察》,刊《哲學雜誌》482號(1927),第354-357頁；483號(1927),第421-425頁。

荻原雲來《漢訳対照梵和大辭典》,東京：鈴木学術財団/講談社,1974年。

Ogiwara, Unrai, *Bon-wa Daijiten*［*A Sanskrit-Chinese-Japanese Dictionary*］, Tōkyō: Kōdansha, 1974.

小野胜年《中国隋唐長安寺院史料集成》,《史料篇》,《解説篇》,京都：法藏館,1989年。

大村西崖《密教發達志》,東京：佛書刊行會圖像部,1918年。

大阪市立美術館编集《中国の石仏：荘厳なる祈り》/*Chinese Buddhist Stone Sculpture: Veneration of the Sublime*, 大阪市立美術館,1995年。

佐伯好郎《清朝基督教の研究：附錄》,東京：春秋社,1949年,第1-24頁。

白鳥庫吉《罽賓國考》,载白鳥庫吉《西域史研究》上,東京：岩波書店,1944年,第377-462頁。

Shiratori, Kurakichi, "*Keihinkou ku* (On the Jibin kingdom)", in: *Seiiki shi kenkyu* (*Collected Papers on the History of the Western Regions*), Vol. 1, Tokyo: Iwanami Shoten, 1944: 377-462.

靜谷正雄《漢譯〈增一阿含經〉の所屬部派》,刊《印度學佛教學研究》22卷1號,第54-59頁。

曾布川寛《龍門石窟における唐代造像の研究》,刊《東方學報》,第60冊,京都：京都大学人文科学研究所,1988年,第199-397頁。

Taishō shinshū daizōkyō［大正新脩大藏經, *Taishō Revised Tripiṭaka*］, 100 vols., ed. by Junjirō Takakusu［高楠順次朗］and Kaikyoku Watanabe［渡邊海旭］, Tokyo: Taishō Issaikyō Kankōkai, 1924-1934, hereafter abbreviated to *Taishō.*

《大正新脩大藏经勘同目录》,见《昭和法寶總目録》第一卷,第153-656页。

高田修《佛像の起源》,東京：岩波書店,1967年。

高楠順次郎《新文化原理としての佛教》,東京：大藏出版社：1946年。

東武美術館 (Tobu Museum of Art) et al., ed., ブッダ展：大いなる旅路 /*Buddha: The Spread of Buddhist Art in Asia*, Tokyo: NHK, 1998.

《燉煌本古逸經論章疏並古寫經目錄》,載《昭和法寶總目錄》,第一卷,第 1055-1068 頁。

常盤大定、關野貞《支那佛教史蹟》第二輯,東京：佛教史蹟研究會,1926 年。

常盤大定、關野貞《支那佛教史蹟評解》第二集,東京：佛教史蹟研究會,1926 年。

常盤大定、關野貞《支那佛教史蹟評解》第三集,東京：佛教史蹟研究會,1926 年。

塚本善隆《望月佛教大辭典》,增訂版,東京：世界聖典刊行協會,1973-1978 年。

渡邊海旭《新發見の阿含諸經の梵语》,载渡邊海旭《壺月全集》上,東京：壶月全集刊行会,1933 年,第 564-569 頁。

渡邊海旭《真言秘經の起源及發達の實例》,载渡邊海旭《壺月全集》上,東京：壶月全集刊行会,1933 年,第 357-404 頁。

柳田聖山《初期の禪史》I《楞伽師資記、傳法寶記》,東京：築摩書房,1971 年。

插图目录

一、印度寺塔：天竺宗源

塔与塔庙窟

图 1　印度纳西克 (Nāsik) 第 3 窟平面图 (据 J. Burgess 原图绘制)

图 2　印度根赫里 (Kāṇhēri) 第 3 窟平面及纵向垂直剖面图 (据 J. Burgess 原图绘制)

图 3　印度桑吉大塔立面及平面图 (据 *Buddhist Monuments*, Fig.1 绘制)

图 4　印度阿默拉沃蒂大塔塔基饰板浮雕佛塔 (据 *History of Indian and Eastern Architecture*, Vol. I Fig.44 绘制)

图 5　犍陀罗曼吉亚拉 (Mankīyala) 大塔出土的塔形舍利盒 (据 *History of Indian and Eastern Architecture*, Vol. I Fig.24 绘制)

图 6　河南登封嵩岳寺塔平面及立面图 (据《中国古代建筑史》图 60 绘制)

图 7a　张掖郭家沙滩东汉墓出土的陶楼院 (据《敦煌建筑研究》图 53 绘制)

图 7b　山东高唐汉墓出土的陶望楼 (据《中国古代建筑史》图 51 绘制)

图 8　印度帕鲁德大塔栏楯上浮雕的无壁塔

图 9　印度拜拉特圆形塔庙遗址平面图 (据 D. R. Sahni 原图绘制)

图 10　印度杜尔贾莱纳第 3 窟平面及横向垂直剖面图 (据 J.Burgess 原图绘制)

图 11　云冈石窟第 39 窟平面及纵向垂直剖面图 (据水野清一、長廣敏雄《雲岡石窟》第 XV 卷 16c 图绘制)

西印度塔庙窟的分期与年代

图 1　珀贾第 26 窟平面图 (据 *Buddhist Architecture of Western India*, 以下简作 *BAWI*, Fig.25 绘制)

图 2　杜尔贾莱纳第 3 窟平面及横向垂直剖面图（据 J. Burgess 原图绘制）
图 3　贡迪维蒂第 9 窟平面及纵向垂直剖面图（据 *BAWI*, Fig.48 绘制）
图 4　珀贾第 12 窟横向垂直剖面图（据 J. Burgess 原图绘制）
图 5　纳西克第 18 窟平面及纵向垂直剖面图（据 *BAWI*, Fig.56 绘制）
图 6　比德尔科拉石窟连续平面图（采自 *Ancient India*, No. 15 Plate XLVI)
图 7　根赫里第 2、3 窟连续平面图（据 J. Burgess 原图绘制）
图 8　埃洛拉第 10 窟平面图（据 J. Burgess 原图绘制）
图 9　门莫迪第 2 窟平面图
图 10　古达第 15 窟平面图（据 J. Burgess 原图绘制）
图 11　古达第 6 窟平面图（据 J. Burgess 原图绘制）
图 12　格拉德第 48 窟平面及横向垂直剖面图（据 J. Burgess 原图绘制）
图 13　珀贾第 12 窟外立面
图 14　阿旃陀第 9 窟外立面（采自 *Report on the Buddhist Cave Temples and Their Inscriptions*, Plate 17)
图 15　格拉德第 5 窟外立面图（据 J. Burgess 原图绘制）
图 16　明窗演变示意图（采自 *Buddhist Cave Temples of India*, Fig.5)
图 17　阿旃陀第 9 窟横向垂直剖面图（据 J. Burgess 原图绘制）
图 18　格拉德第 5 窟平面及纵向垂直剖面图（据 J. Burgess 原图绘制）
图 19　根赫里第 2e 窟横向垂直剖面图
图 20　门莫迪第 2 窟平面及纵向垂直剖面图（据 *BAWI*, Fig.28 绘制）
图 21　锡万内里第 43 窟平面及纵向垂直剖面图（据 *BAWI*, Fig.37 绘制）
图 22　伯瓦拉第 2 窟平面及纵向垂直剖面图（据 *BAWI*, Fig.57 绘制）
图 23　石柱类型示意图（采自 *BAWI* 及 *Buddhist Cave Temples of India*)
图 24　埃洛拉第 10 窟前室石柱（采自 J. Burgess 原图）
图 25　西印度塔庙窟内佛塔结构示意图
图 26　佛塔（据 *BAWI*, Fig.5 绘制）
图 27　佛塔（据 *BAWI*, Figs.6, 7 绘制）
图 28　佛塔（据 *BAWI*, Fig.8 绘制）
图 29　佛塔（采自 J. Burgess 原图）
图 30　帕鲁德大塔栏楯上浮雕无壁塔（采自 *History of Indian and Eastern Architecture*, Fig.81)
图 31　苏达玛石窟平面及纵向垂直剖面图

图 32 贡德恩第 1 窟外立面双身像

图 33 比德尔科拉第 3 窟外立面药叉

图 34 阿旃陀第 10 窟左侧壁佛传故事画 (采自 *Studies in Ajanta Paintings*, Fig.1-1)

图 35 柱头类型示意图 (a. 采自 J. Burgess 原图；b. 采自 *The Cave Temples of India*, plate xii；c. 出处同上；d. 采自 *Tree and Serpent Worship*, Plate XI)

图 36 伽尔拉第 8 窟前室后壁浮雕 (采自 *The Cave Temples of India*, Plate XIV)

图 37 伽尔拉第 8 窟前廊左壁双身像 (采自 J. Burgess 原图)

图 38 桑吉大塔西门右柱内侧田园浮雕 (采自 *Tree and Serpent Worship*, Plate XXVII)

图 39 古达第 6 窟浮雕动物与牧人 (采自 J. Burgess 原图)

图 40 古达第 6 窟浮雕双身像

阿旃陀石窟参观记

图 1 阿旃陀石窟远景

图 2 阿旃陀石窟连续平面图 (采自 *Report on the Buddhist Cave Temples and Their Inscriptions*, Plate XIV)

图 3 阿旃陀第 6 至 10 窟外景

图 4 阿旃陀第 26 窟 “阿折罗” 题铭 (采自 *Report on the Buddhist Cave Temples and Their Inscriptions*, Plate LVIII, No. 6)

图 5 阿旃陀第 10 窟平面及纵向垂直剖面图 (采自 *The Cave Temples of India*, Plate XXVIII, Nos. 1, 2)

图 6 阿旃陀第 10 窟内景

图 7 阿旃陀第 15A 窟平面图 (采自 *Buddhist Monuments*, Fig.4)

图 8 阿旃陀第 12 窟平面及纵向垂直剖面图 (采自 *The Cave Temples of India*, Plate XXVII)

图 9 阿旃陀第 12 窟内景

图 10 阿旃陀第 12 窟后壁小室 (僧房) 内石床

图 11 阿旃陀第 26 窟外立面

图 12 阿旃陀第 26 窟平面图 (采自 *The Cave Temples of India*, Plate XXXVII)

图 13 阿旃陀第 1 窟外立面

图 14 阿旃陀第 1 窟 (佛殿僧坊混成式窟) 平面图 (采自 *Buddhist Monuments*, Fig.7)

图 15 阿旃陀第 26 窟佛塔正面主像

图 16 阿旃陀第 17 窟佛殿正面
图 17a 阿旃陀第 26 窟右壁涅槃浮雕 (1883 年伯吉斯测绘，采自 *The Cave Temples of India*, Plate L)
图 17b 阿旃陀第 26 窟右侧列柱及右壁涅槃浮雕
图 18 阿旃陀第 26 窟右壁降魔浮雕 (a. 采自 *The Cave Temples of India*, Plate LI)
图 19 阿旃陀第 26 窟前庭左侧龛像
图 20 阿旃陀第 19 窟前庭右侧壁龙王及王后
图 21 阿旃陀第 16 窟门道上方河神
图 22 阿旃陀第 1 窟大厅前壁
图 23 阿旃陀第 17 窟平面及壁画题材分布示意图 (采自 *Inscriptions of the Vākāṭakas: Corpus Inscriptionum Indicarum* V, Plate K)
图 24 阿旃陀第 17 窟柱式大厅后壁
图 25 阿旃陀第 10 窟右壁壁画线描 (采自 *Report on the Buddhist Cave Temples and Their Inscriptions*, Plate XVI)
图 26 阿旃陀第 1 窟柱式大厅后壁左侧龙王本生 (a. 采自 *The Cave Temples of India*, Plate XLIII)
图 27 阿旃陀第 17 窟柱式大厅左侧壁狮子国因缘
图 28 阿旃陀第 1 窟佛殿前室右壁降魔变 (a. 采自 *Ajanta Murals*, Fig.8)
图 29 阿旃陀第 17 窟中央门道上部雕刻及绘画
图 30 阿旃陀第 2 窟佛殿前廊右侧壁及后壁千佛壁画
图 31 阿旃陀第 1 窟佛殿前廊门道两侧，即柱式大厅后壁壁画
图 32 阿旃陀第 17 窟前廊右侧壁轮回图 (b. 据 *Studies in the Ajanta Paintings*, P.383/ Fig.1 绘制)
图 33 阿旃陀第 1 窟柱式大厅顶部壁画 (a. 采自 *The Cave Temples of India*, Plate XLIV, No. 1)
图 34 阿旃陀第 2 窟前廊顶部装饰图案

二、龟兹石窟：西域传法

克孜尔中心柱窟主室正壁画塑题材及有关问题

图 1 帕鲁德大塔栏楯浮雕帝释窟［采自 *Eastern Art*, 1928, I (1), Fig.1］

图 2　秣菟罗博物馆藏陀兰纳（塔门）横梁浮雕佛传
图 3　加尔各答印度博物馆藏帝释窟浮雕（采自 *La Sculpture de Mathurā*, Pl. LIIIb)
图 4　秣菟罗博物馆藏建筑构件上的帝释窟浮雕（采自上引书，Pl. LIb)
图 5　拉合尔博物馆藏锡克里佛塔塔身饰板上的帝释窟
图 6　加尔各答印度博物馆藏帝释窟浮雕（采自 *L'Art gréco-bouddhique du Gandhâra*, Vol. I, Fig.246)
图 7　白沙瓦博物馆藏帝释窟浮雕（采自 *Buddhist Art of Gandhara*, Pl. 85)
图 8　克孜尔第 196 窟主室正壁佛龛上部悬塑菱形山峦
图 9　克孜尔第 80 窟主室正壁佛龛左侧壁画
图 10　克孜尔第 99 窟主室正壁佛龛两侧壁画
图 11　克孜尔第 80 窟主室正壁佛龛及两侧壁画
图 12　柏林亚洲艺术博物馆收藏的帝释窟木雕
图 13　克孜尔第 163 窟主室窟顶菱格构图

The *Jātakas* in the Cave Temple Complex of Kizil, Kucha

Fig.1　Mural of the *jātakas* on the ceiling of Cave 17 at Kizil, Kucha
Fig.2　Mural of the *jātakas* on the side wall of Cave 186 at Kizil
Fig.3　Mural of the *Vessantarajātaka* on the side wall of Cave 81 at Kizil
Fig.4　*Mṛgajātaka* in bas-relief on the *toraṇa* of the Bhārhut *stūpa*
Fig.5　*Mṛgajātaka* in bas-relief from Gandhāra (from *Studies in the Ajanta Paintings: Identifications and Interpretations,* P.403, Fig.32)
Fig.6　*Mṛgajātaka* painted on the ceiling of Cave 38 at Kizil (from *Altbuddhistische Kultstätten in Chinesisch-Turkistan*, Fig.154)
Fig.7　*Śyāmajātaka* in bas-relief on the *toraṇa* of Sāñcī (from *Tree and Serpent Worship,* Plate XXXVI, Fig.1)
Fig.8　*Haṃsajātaka* painted on the side wall of Cave 17 at Ajaṇṭā (from *Ajanta Murals,* Fig.18)
Fig.9　*Śyāmajātaka* painted on the side wall of Cave 10 at Ajaṇṭā (from *Studies in the Ajanta Paintings: Identifications and Interpretations,* P.355-356, Fig.1)
Fig.10a　Mural of the *Naḷapānajātaka* on the ceiling of Cave 17 at Kizil
Fig.10b　line-drawing of *Naḷapānajātaka* on the ceiling of Cave 17 at Kizil (from *Essays on the Buddhist Cave Temples of China* by Ma Shichang, P. 50, Fig.34)

The Representation of Buddha's *Parinirvāṇa* in the *Chētiyagharas* of Kizil, Kucha

Fig.1 Typical iconographic program of a *chētiyaghara* (central pillar cave) at Kizil (from *Kizil on the Silk Road: Crossroads of Commerce & Meeting of Minds,* Fig.5)

Fig.2a *Parinirvāṇa* of the Buddha, mural painting from the rear wall of the back corridor of Cave 171 at Kizil (from *Die Buddhistische Spätantike in Mittelasien*, VI, Tafel 11)

Fig.2b *Śārīra stūpas*, mural on the front wall of the back corridor of Cave 171 at Kizil, *in situ*

Fig.3a *Parinirvāṇa* of the Buddha, mural painting on the rear wall of the back corridor of Cave 205 at Kizil, *in situ*

Fig.3b Cremation of the Buddha, mural painting from the front wall of the back corridor of Cave 205 at Kizil (from *Dokumentation der Verluste,* Band III, 145, IB 8439)

Fig.4a *Parinirvāṇa* of the Buddha, mural painting on the front wall of the back corridor of Cave 58 at Kizil, *in situ*

Fig.4b Distribution of the relics, mural painting on the rear wall of the back corridor of Cave 58 at Kizil, *in situ*

Fig.5a *Parinirvāṇa* of the Buddha, painted clay sculpture on a rock-cut couch against the rear wall of the rear chamber of Cave New No. 1 at Kizil, *in situ*

Fig.5b Distribution of the relics, mural painting on the front wall of the rear chamber of Cave New No. 1 at Kizil, *in situ*

Fig.6a Cremation of the Buddha and great lamentation, mural painting from the front wall of the rear chamber of Cave 224 at Kizil (from *Die Buddhistische Spätantike in Mittelasien*, VI, Tafel 15)

Fig.6b Great lamentation, detail of upper part of Fig.6a, line-drawing (from *Altbuddhistische Kultstätten in Chinesisch-Turkistan: Bericht über archäologische Arbeiten von 1906 bis 1907 bei Kuča, Qarašahr und in der oase Turfan*, Fig.415)

Fig.7a *Parinirvāṇa* of the Buddha, bas-relief, Peshawar Museum, Peshawar (from *The Exhibition of Gandhara Art of Pakistan*, Pl. 104)

Fig.7b *Parinirvāṇa* of the Buddha, bas-relief, British Museum, (from *A Catalogue of the Gandhāra Sculpture in the British Museum*, Pl. 230)

Fig.7c *Parinirvāṇa* of the Buddha, bas-relief, National Museum of Afghanistan, Kabul (from *The Image of the Buddha*, Pl. 138)

Fig.8a *Parinirvāṇa* of the Buddha, bas-relief, Pakistan (from *The Art of Buddhism: An Introduction to its History and Meaning*, Fig.2.7)

Fig.8b The Expired Buddha covered by a drapery, bas-relief from Swāt, Royal Ontario Museum (from *Gandhāran Art*, Vol. I: *The Buddha's Life Story*, Pl. 489)

Fig.8c The Buddha's body wrapped in multiple layers of cloth, bas-relief, Museum für Asiatische Kunst, Berlin

Fig.9a Coffin of the Buddha, bas-relief, Institute of Silk Road Studies (from *Buddha: The Spread of Buddhist Art in Asia*, Pl. 97)

Fig.9b Transporting of the Coffin, bas-relief, National Museum of Pakistan (from *The Exhibition of Gandhara Art of Pakistan*, Pl. 105)

Fig.9c Cremation of the Buddha, bas-relief, Museum für Asiatische Kunst (from *Buddha: The Spread of Buddhist Art in Asia*, Pl. 98)

Fig.10a Mahāsudarśana and his *strī-ratna* (jade-like) concubine, mural painting on the right wall of the back corridor of Cave 7 at Kizil, *in situ* (copied from *The Cave-temples of China: Kizil Caves,* I, Pl. 14)

Fig.10b Mahāsudarśana and his *strī-ratna* concubine, line-drawing of mural painting on the right wall of the back corridor of Cave 13 at Kizil (from *The Cave-temples of China: Kizil Caves,* I: 196, Fig.26)

Fig.11a *Parinirvāṇa* of the Buddha, mural painting on the rear wall of the back corridor of Cave 38 at Kizil, *in situ* (from *The Cave-temples of China: Kizil Caves,* I, Pl. 143)

Fig.11b Details of the scene of the Buddha's *parinirvāṇa*, Subhadra perishing before the *parinirvāṇa* of the Buddha, mural painting on right section of the rear wall of the back corridor of Cave 38 at Kizil, *in situ* (from *The Cave-temples of China: Kizil Caves,* I, Pl. 144)

Fig.11c Details of the scene of the Buddha's *parinirvāṇa*, Mahākāśyapa's worship of the Buddha's feet, mural painting on the left section of the rear wall of the back corridor of Cave 38 at Kizil, *in situ* (from *The Cave-temples of China: Kizil Caves,* I, Pl. 145)

Fig.12a *Stūpa* 1 at Sāñcī

Fig.12b Circular wall-less roofed *caityagṛha*, drawing of a bas-relief from Bhārhut (from *History of Indian and Eastern Architecture*, rev. ed., Vol.1, Fig.81)

Fig.12c Circular *caityagṛha* at Bairāṭ, plan (from *Buddhist Monuments*, Fig.12)

Fig.13a A rock-cut circular *caityagṛha* (*chētiyaghara*) at Guntupalli, section (from *Buddhist Monuments*, Fig.14)

Fig.13b Interior of Cave 8 (*chētiyaghara*) at Kārlā

Fig.13c Interior of Cave 38 (*chētiyaghara*) at Kizil

Fig.13d Interior of Cave 2 (*chētiyaghara*) at Yungang (from *The Cave-temples of China: Yunkang Caves,* I, Pl. 11)

Fig.14 *Stūpa* inside the *chētiyagharas in situ*

The Image of Maitreya in the *Chētiyagharas* of Kizil, Kucha

Fig.1 Typical iconographic program of a *chētiyaghara* (central pillar cave) at Kizil (from *Kizil on the Silk Road: Crossroads of Commerce & Meeting of Minds,* Fig.5)

Fig.2 Maitreya's manifestation and preaching in the lunette above the entrance in Cave 17 at Kizil, in situ.

Fig.3 Maitreya's manifestation and preaching in Tuṣita, from Chārsadda, Gandhāra, Museum für Asiatische Kunst, SMPK, Berlin

Fig.4 Maitreya's manifestation and preaching in Tuṣita, from Shotorak, Afghanistan, Musée Guimet, Paris

Fig.5 Buddha's *parinirvāṇa* along with Maitreya's manifestation and preaching, Archaeological Museum at Taxila, Taxila

Fig.6 A sketch map of Xuanzang's pilgrimage to India [drawn by Chongfeng Li on the basis of *Datang xiyu ji* (*Record of the Western Regions of the Great Tang Dynasty*) by Xuanzang and *Reader's Digest Atlas of the World*]

Fig.7 A sketch map of Greater Gandhāra (copied from *Gandhara: Das buddhistische Erbe Pakistans Legenden, Klöster und Paradiese*, Karte 3)

Fig.8 *Indraśālaguhā* in conjunction with Buddha's *parinirvāṇa*, from Chatpat, Archaeological Museum at Dir, Chakdara

克孜尔部分中心柱窟与《长阿含经》等佛典

图 1 克孜尔第 38 窟中心柱正壁“帝释窟”雕塑遗迹

图 2 克孜尔第 80 窟中心柱正壁“帝释窟”壁画(采自《中国石窟·克孜尔石窟》二,图版 43)

图 3 秣菟罗“帝释窟”浮雕,出土地不详,现藏印度秣菟罗博物馆(采自 *La Sculpture de*

Mathurā, Pl. LIb)

图 4　犍陀罗“帝释窟”浮雕，出土于 Loriyān Tangai，现藏加尔各答印度博物馆（采自 L'Art gréco-bouddhique du Gandhâra, Vol. I, Fig.246)

图 5　克孜尔第 17 窟侧壁“因缘佛传”壁画（采自《中国石窟・克孜尔石窟》一，图版 59)

图 6　犍陀罗佛塔塔基“吉祥施草”浮雕，出土于 Sikri，现藏巴基斯坦拉合尔博物馆

图 7　克孜尔第 171 窟右壁“吉祥施草”壁画

图 8　克孜尔第 17 窟券顶“本生故事”壁画（采自《中国石窟・克孜尔石窟》一，图版 60)

图 9　克孜尔第 38 窟券顶“因缘故事”壁画（采自上引书，图版 112)

图 10　克孜尔第 38 窟后室“涅槃”壁画（采自上引书，图版 143)

图 11　犍陀罗“涅槃”浮雕，出土地不详，现藏伦敦不列颠博物院（采自 *A Catalogue of the Gandhāra Sculpture in the British Museum*, Pl. 231)

图 12　克孜尔第 224 窟前壁门道上方“弥勒菩萨兜率天说法”壁画，现藏德国柏林亚洲艺术博物馆（采自《中国石窟・克孜尔石窟》三，图版 222)

图 13　克孜尔第 17 窟前壁门道上方“弥勒菩萨兜率天说法”壁画（采自《中国石窟・克孜尔石窟》一，图版 56)

图 14　犍陀罗“佛说法图与弥勒菩萨兜率天示现”浮雕，约 1865-1880 年拍摄（采自 *Gandhara-Das buddhistische Erbe Pakistans: Legenden, Klöster und Paradiese*, 46, Abb.2)

图 15　犍陀罗“佛说法图与弥勒菩萨兜率天示现”浮雕细部，原藏巴基斯坦拉合尔博物馆，现藏印度昌迪加尔博物馆（采自 *Gandhara-Das buddhistische Erbe Pakistans: Legenden, Klöster und Paradiese*, Abb.4)

图 16　犍陀罗“弥勒菩萨兜率天示现”浮雕，出土于 Chārsada，原藏巴基斯坦拉合尔博物馆，现藏德国柏林亚洲艺术博物馆

图 17　大犍陀罗区示意图（采自 *Ancient Buddhist Scrolls from Gandhāra: The British Library Kharoṣṭhī Fragments*, Map I)

图 18　克孜尔第 114 窟券顶“勒那阇耶本生”壁画（采自《中国石窟・克孜尔石窟》二，图版 145)

图 19　克孜尔第 114 窟券顶壁画“勒那阇耶本生”线描（采自《克孜尔石窟志》插图 55)

图 20　犍陀罗“*Viśvantara Jātaka*（普护本生）”浮雕，出土于 Jamālgaṛhī，现藏伦敦不列颠博物院（采自シルクロード大美术展；*Grand Exhibition of Silk Road Buddhist Art*, 図版 134)

图 21　克孜尔第 184 窟主室侧壁“须大拏本生”壁画，现藏德国柏林亚洲艺术博物馆（采自

《中国石窟·克孜尔石窟》三，图版 207)

图 22　克孜尔第 38 窟券顶“须大拏本生”壁画，现藏德国柏林亚洲艺术博物馆 (采自《中国石窟·克孜尔石窟》三，图版 184)

图 23　克孜尔第 38 窟后甬道侧壁舍利塔壁画 (采自《中国石窟·克孜尔石窟》一，图版 142)

图 24　巴基斯坦斯瓦特地区 (乌苌国) 布特卡拉 I 号遗址

龟兹与犍陀罗的造像组合、题材及布局

图 1　克孜尔第 38 窟题材布局 (a. 采自《中国石窟·克孜尔石窟》一，图版 82；b. 采自上引书，图版 99；c. 采自上引书，图版 112；d. 采自上引书，图版 143；e. 采自上引书，图版 83)

图 2　克孜尔中心柱窟题材布局示意图 (据 *Kizil on the Silk Road: Crossroads of Commerce & Meeting of Minds*, 45, Fig.5 绘制)

图 3　锡克里佛塔，拉合尔博物馆犍陀罗艺术展厅

图 4　“帝释窟”与“佛涅槃”浮雕，杰德伯特遗址出土，迪尔考古博物馆

图 5　帝释窟浮雕，锡克里佛塔，拉合尔博物馆

图 6　帝释窟浮雕，马曼内·得里 (Mamāne-Dheṛī) 遗址出土，白沙瓦博物馆

图 7　佛涅槃浮雕，现藏于白沙瓦博物馆 (采自 *The Exhibition of Gandhara Art of Pakistan*, Pl. 104)

图 8　“佛涅槃”与“弥勒示现”，现藏于塔克西拉考古博物馆 (采自ブッダ展——大いなる旅路 /*Buddha: The Spread of Buddhist Art in Asia*, Fig.96)

图 9a　兜率天弥勒，法王塔遗址出土，塔克西拉考古博物馆

图 9b　兜率天弥勒，迪尔考古博物馆 (采自 *The Exhibition of Gandhara Art of Pakistan*, Fig.79)

图 10　玄奘西行求法路线示意图 (前半)(李崇峰据玄奘《大唐西域记》及 *Reader's Digest Atlas of the World* 绘制)

图 11　克孜尔第 38 窟圣像组合，即“帝释窟”与“佛涅槃”和“未来佛弥勒”

图 12　柏林亚洲艺术博物馆藏帝释窟木雕

Gandhāra and Kucha: the Case of an Iconological Relationship (refer to the illustrations of 龟兹与犍陀罗的造像组合、题材及布局)

Fig.1　Iconographic scheme in Cave 38 at Kizil: a) façade of the *stūpa* (from *The Cave-temples of China: Kizil Caves,* I, Pl. 82), b) lateral wall (from *opera citato*, Pl. 99),

c) barrel vault (from *opera citato*, Pl. 112), d) back wall of the back corridor (from *opera citato*, Pl. 143), e) lunette above the entrance (from *opera citato*, Pl. 83)

Fig.2 Typical iconographic program of a *chētiyaghara* (*stūpa* cave/central pillar cave) at Kizil (from *Kizil on the Silk Road: Crossroads of Commerce & Meeting of Minds*, Fig.5)

Fig.3 *Stūpa* from Sikri, Gandhāra Gallery, Lahore Museum

Fig.4 "The *Indraśālaguhā*" in conjunction with "the Buddha's *parinirvāṇa*", from Chatpat, Chakdara, Archaeological Museum at Dir

Fig.5 The *Indraśālaguhā*, from Sikri *Stūpa*, Lahore Museum

Fig.6 The *Indraśālaguhā*, from Mamāne-Dheṛī near Chārsada, Peshāwar Museum

Fig.7 Buddha in *Parinirvāṇa*, from Guides' Mess Collection, Peshawar Museum, Peshawar (from *The Exhibition of Gandhara Art of Pakistan*, Plate 104)

Fig.8 "Buddha's *Parinirvāṇa*" in combination with "Maitreya's preaching", Archaeological Museum at Taxila (from ブッダ展——大いなる旅路 /*Buddha: The Spread of Buddhist Art in Asia*, Fig.96)

Fig.9a Bodhisattva in Tuṣita Heaven, from Dharmarājikā, Archaeological Museum at Taxila

Fig.9b Bodhisattva in Tuṣita, Archaeological Museum at Dir (from *The Exhibition of Gandhara Art of Pakistan*, Fig.79)

Fig.10 A sketch map of Xuanzang's pilgrimage to India [drawn by Chongfeng Li on the basis of *Datang xiyu ji* (*Record of the Western Regions of the Great Tang Dynasty*) by Xuanzang and *Reader's Digest Atlas of the World*]

Fig.11 Joint iconographic scheme, viz., "The *Indraśālaguhā*" and "the *Parinirvāṇa*" in combination with "Buddha-to-be" in cave 38 at Kizil

Fig.12 A wooden niche showing scene of the *Indraśālaguhā*, from Kucha, Asian Art Museum, Berlin

三、北方佛寺：中土弘通

从犍陀罗到平城：以地面佛寺布局为中心

图 1　云冈石窟西部冈上遗址（采自《2010 中国重要考古发现》第 128 页）

图 2　云冈石窟西部冈上遗址平面示意图（李崇峰据上引书第 127-130 页绘制）

图 3　云冈石窟西部冈上遗址中央塔基（采自上引书，第 130 页）

图 4　云冈石窟西部冈上遗址北侧廊房遗迹（采自上引书，第 129 页）

图 5a　塔赫特巴希佛寺遗址 (采自 *Archaeological Survey of India: Annual Report 1907-08*, Pl. XLa)

图 5b　塔赫特巴希佛寺遗址中庭 (采自上引书，图版 XLb)

图 5c　塔赫特巴希佛寺遗址 (2004 年)

图 6　塔赫特巴希佛寺遗址平面图 (a. 采自 *Archaeological Survey of India: Report for the Year 1872-73* by A. Cunningham, Pl. VII；b. 采自 *Archaeological Survey of India: Annual Report 1907-08*, Pl. L；c. 采自 *Archaeological Survey of India: Annual Report 1910-11*, Pl. XVII)

图 7a　塔赫特巴希佛寺遗址塔院平面图 (采自 *Archaeological Survey of India: Report for the Year 1872-73* by A. Cunningham, Pl. VIII)

图 7b　塔赫特巴希佛寺遗址塔院周匝佛龛立面图 (采自上引书，图版 IX)

图 8　白沙瓦博物馆展示的塔赫特巴希寺院遗址出土的佛教造像 (采自 *Archaeological Survey of India: Annual Report 1907-08*, Pl. XLIIIa)

图 9a　塔赫特巴希佛寺遗址布萨处及“地下房舍”顶部 (采自 *Archaeological Survey of India: Annual Report 1910-11*, Pl. XIXa)

图 9b　塔赫特巴希佛寺遗址“大像院”(采自上引书，图版 XXIA)

图 10a　赛度·谢里夫 I 号遗址塔院与僧院平面图 (采自 *Saidu Sharif I, 2 The Buddhist Sacred Area; The Stūpa Terrace* by Domenico Faccenna, Text, Fig.22)

图 10b　赛度·谢里夫 I 号遗址复原图 (第一期)(采自上引书，图 23)

图 10c　赛度·谢里夫 I 号遗址复原图 (第二期)(采自上引书，图 23)

图 11　焦莲佛寺遗址平面图 (采自 *Excavations at Taxila: The Stūpas and Monastery at Jauliāñ* by John Marshall; *Memoir No. 7 of the Archaeological Survey of India*, Pl. I)

图 12a　巴伯尔·汗纳塔寺 (金迪亚尔 B 丘) 遗址平面图 (采自 *Archaeological Survey of India: Report for the Year 1872-73* by A. Cunningham, Pl. XX)

图 12b　金迪亚尔 B 丘遗址平面图 (采自 *Taxila: An illustrated account of archaeological excavations carried out at Taxila under the orders of the Government of India between the years 1913 and 1934*, Vol. III: Pl. 91)

图 13　毕钵罗遗址平面图 (采自上引书，图版 98a)

From Gandhāra to Pingcheng: The Layout of a Free-standing Buddhist Monastery (refer to the illustrations of 从犍陀罗到平城：以地面佛寺布局为中心)

Fig.1　General view of a free-standing monastery and temple site unearthed on the western part of the summit of the Wuzhou hill (from *Major Archaeological Discoveries in China in 2010*, 128)

Fig.2 Sketch plan of the free-standing monastery and temple unearthed on the western part of the summit of the Wuzhou hill (drawn by Chongfeng Li on the basis of some plates from *Major Archaeological Discoveries in China in 2010*)

Fig.3 Basement of a *stūpa* in the center of the free-standing monastery and temple (from *opere citato*, 130)

Fig.4 Details of the monk's cells along the northern flank of the free-standing monastery and temple (from *opere citato*, 129)

Fig.5a General view of the ruins at Takht-i-Bāhī, the central court in foreground, from south-west (from *Archaeological Survey of India: Annual Report 1907-08*, Pl. XLa)

Fig.5b The central court after excavation, from north-east (from *opere citato*, Pl. XLb)

Fig.5c General view of the ruined monastic complex at Takht-i-Bāhī, from south, 2004

Fig.6a General plan of Buddhist buildings at Takht-i-Bāhī (from *Archaeological Survey of India: Report for the Year 1872-73* by A. Cunningham, Pl. VII)

Fig.6b Plan of the main monastery, Takht-i-Bāhī, showing excavations in 1908 (from *Archaeological Survey of India: Annual Report 1907-08*, Pl. L)

Fig.6c Plan of the main monastery, Takht-i-Bāhī, showing excavations in 1911 (from *Archaeological Survey of India: Annual Report 1910-11*, Pl. XVII)

Fig.7a Enlarged plan of the *stūpa* court (from *Archaeological Survey of India: Report for the Year 1872-73* by A. Cunningham, Pl. VIII)

Fig.7b Interior view of the *stūpa* court, east side, restored (from *opere citato*, Pl. IX)

Fig.8 Buddhist sculptures in Peshawar Museum (from *Archaeological Survey of India: Annual Report 1907-08*, Pl. XLIIIa)

Fig.9a West wall of the low-level chambers, from north-west (from *Archaeological Survey of India: Annual Report 1910-11*, Pl. XIXa)

Fig.9b Court of the six colossi, from north (from *opere citato*, Pl. XXIa)

Fig.10a Schematic general plan of the *stūpa* court and *vihāra* court at Saidu Sharif I (from *Saidu Sharif I, 2 The Buddhist Sacred Area; The Stūpa Terrace* by Domenico Faccenna, Fig.22)

Fig.10b Reconstructive sketch of the sacred area of Saidu Sharif I (Period I) (from *opere citato*, Fig.23)

Fig.10c Reconstructive sketch of the sacred area of Saidu Sharif I (Period II) (from *opere citato* Fig.23)

Fig.11 Plan of the excavation at Jauliāñ (from *Excavations at Taxila*: *The Stūpas and Monastery at Jauliāñ* by John Marshall; *Memoir No. 7 of the Archaeological Survey of India*, Pl. I)

Fig.12a Plan of mound B at Jaṇḍiāl/*stūpa* and monastery at Babar-Khāna (from *Archaeological Survey of India: Report for the Year 1872-73* by A. Cunningham, Pl. XX)

Fig.12b Plan of mound B at Jaṇḍiāl (from *Taxila: An illustrated account of archaeological excavations carried out at Taxila under the orders of the Government of India between the years 1913 and 1934*, Vol. III: Pl. 91)

Fig.13 Plan of the remains at Pippala, Taxila (from *opere citato*, Pl. 98a)

Kumārajīva and Early Cave-temples of China: the Case of *Dhyāna-sūtras*

Fig.1 Remains of the rock-cut temple at Deer-park, Datong (from *Studies of the Cave-temples,* No. I, Fig.2)

Fig.2 The cave temple complex at Mogaoku, Dunhuang (from *The Cave-temples of China: Mogaoku Caves of Dunhuang*, Vol. I, Pl. 1)

Fig.3 The cave temple complex at Binglingsi, Yongjing (from *The Cave-temples of China: Binglingsi Caves of Yongjing*, Pl. 3)

Fig.4 Amitāyus-niche dated to 420 AD, Cave 169 at Binglingsi (from *The Cave-temples of China: Binglingsi Caves of Yongjing*, Pl. 21)

Fig.5 Portrait of Monk Tanmopi (Dharmapriya?), mural painting, Cave 169 at Binglingsi (from *The Cave-temples of China: Binglingsi Caves of Yongjing*, Pl. 25)

Fig.6 The cave temple complex at Maijishan, Tianshui (from *The Cave-temples of China: Maijishan Caves of Tianshui*, Pl. 1)

Fig.7 The cave temple complex at Yungang, Datong

Fig.8 The cave temple complex at Qixia, Nanjing

Fig.9 *Lēṇa*, plan and longitudinal section of Cave 285 at Mogaoku, Dunhuang (from *The Cave-temples of China: Mogaoku Caves of Dunhuang*, Vol. I, P. 225)

Fig.10 *Stūpa-cave*, viz, *chētiyaghara*, Cave 2 at Yungang, Datong (from *The Cave-temples of China: Yungang Caves*, Vol. I, Pl. 11)

Fig.11 Buddha-hall-cave, Cave 272 at Mogaoku, Dunhuang (from *The Cave-temples of China: Mogaoku Caves of Dunhuang*, Vol. I, Pl. 7)

Fig.12 *Lēṇa*, plan, Cave 5 at Subashi, Kucha

Fig.13 Typical iconographic program of a *chētiyaghara* (central pillar cave) at Kizil (from *Kizil on the Silk Road: Crossroads of Commerce & Meeting of Minds*, 45, Fig.5)

Fig.14 A monk in *dhyāna* meditation, Cave 285 at Mogaoku (from *The Cave-temples of China: Mogaoku Caves of Dunhuang*, Vol. I, Pl. 146)

Fig.15 Main Buddha, cave 20 at Yungang

Fig.16 Maitreya image, Cave 13 at Yungang (from *The Cave-temples of China: Yungang Caves*, Vol. II, Pl. 111)

Fig.17 Śākyamuni and Prabhūtaratna, Cave 6 at Yungang (from *The Cave-temples of China: Yungang Caves*, Vol. I, Pl. 62)

Fig.18 Śākyamuni comforting Ānanda, Cave 38 at Yungang (from *Studies of the Cave-temples of China* by Su Bai, 87, Fig.4)

关于鼓山石窟中的高欢柩穴

图 1　鼓山石窟（北响堂山石窟）北洞外立面示意图

图 2　北洞平面及纵向垂直剖面图

图 3　北洞中心塔柱正壁龛内佛像

图 4　北洞中心塔柱右侧（北）壁龛内佛像

图 5　北洞中心塔柱左侧（南）壁龛内佛像

图 6　北洞北侧壁塔形龛

图 7　北洞侧壁塔形龛立面图

图 8　北洞 3-33 龛室外立面

图 9　北洞 3-33 龛室平面、剖面及立面示意图

图 10　北洞 3-33 龛室入口封门石下部

图 11　北洞 3-33 龛室内残存石块 A、B

图 12　麦积山第 43 窟外立面、平面及纵向垂直剖面图（采自《中国石窟 · 麦积山石窟》，第 204 页，图 5）

僧璨、定禅师与水浴寺石窟

图 1　水浴寺西窟窟门东侧（左侧）上排第一身供养比丘僧璨

图 2　水浴寺西窟窟门西侧（右侧）上排第一身供养比丘神定禅师

敦煌莫高窟北朝晚期洞窟的分期与研究

图 1　莫高窟北朝至隋代部分洞窟连续平面图
图 2　第 461 窟平面及纵向垂直剖面图
图 3　第 430 窟平面及纵向垂直剖面图
图 4　第 296 窟平面及纵向垂直剖面图
图 5　第 461 窟龛梁尾部与龛柱头装饰
图 6　第 430 窟龛梁尾部与龛柱头装饰
图 7　第 297 窟龛梁尾部与龛柱头装饰
图 8　第 438 窟彩塑佛像
图 9　第 430 窟彩塑佛像
图 10　第 301 窟彩塑佛像
图 11　第 297 窟彩塑佛像
图 12　第 438 窟彩塑菩萨像
图 13　第 430 窟彩塑菩萨像
图 14　第 296 窟彩塑菩萨像
图 15　第 297 窟彩塑菩萨像
图 16　第 439 窟彩塑菩萨像
图 17　第 430 窟彩塑弟子像
图 18　第 297 窟彩塑弟子像
图 19　莫高窟彩塑佛像衣纹断面示意图
图 20　第 461 窟侧壁壁画题材布局示意图
图 21　第 430 窟侧壁壁画题材布局示意图
图 22　第 297 窟侧壁壁画题材布局示意图
图 23　第 301 窟侧壁壁画题材布局示意图
图 24　第 296 窟侧壁壁画题材布局示意图
图 25　第 430 窟东壁壁画题材布局示意图
图 26　第 296 窟东壁壁画题材布局示意图
图 27　第 461 窟窟顶壁画题材布局示意图
图 28　第 296 窟窟顶壁画题材布局示意图
图 29　第 297 窟窟顶壁画题材布局示意图

图 30　第 430 窟窟顶壁画题材布局示意图
图 31　第 461 窟壁画菩萨像
图 32　第 296 窟壁画菩萨像
图 33　第 301 窟壁画菩萨像
图 34　第 439 窟壁画菩萨像
图 35　第 438 窟壁画千佛
图 36　第 294 窟壁画千佛细部
图 37　第 294 窟壁画千佛
图 38　第 438 窟天宫形制
图 39　第 461 窟天宫伎乐
图 40　第 301 窟天宫伎乐
图 41　第 438 窟飞天
图 42　第 439 窟飞天
图 43　第 296 窟飞天
图 44　第 297 窟飞天
图 45　第 439 窟飞天
图 46　第 299 窟飞天
图 47　第 294 窟男供养人
图 48　第 430 窟男供养人
图 49　第 296 窟男供养人
图 50　第 299 窟男供养人
图 51　第 297 窟女供养人
图 52　第 301 窟女供养人
图 53　第 297 窟女供养人
图 54　第 461 窟菩萨面部晕染方式
图 55　第 301 窟菩萨面部晕染方式
图 56　第 432 窟平面及纵向垂直剖面图
图 57　第 428 窟平面及纵向垂直剖面图
图 58　第 290 窟龛梁尾部与龛柱头装饰
图 59　第 428 窟龛梁尾部与龛柱头装饰
图 60　第 432 窟彩塑佛像
图 61　第 432 窟彩塑佛像

图 62　第 428 窟彩塑佛像
图 63　第 428 窟彩塑佛像
图 64　第 290 窟彩塑佛像
图 65　第 432 窟彩塑佛像
图 66　第 428 窟彩塑菩萨像
图 67　第 290 窟彩塑菩萨像
图 68　第 428 窟彩塑菩萨像
图 69　第 290 窟彩塑菩萨像
图 70　第 432 窟彩塑菩萨像
图 71　第 432 窟彩塑菩萨像
图 72　第 432 窟彩塑菩萨像
图 73　第 290 窟彩塑菩萨像
图 74　第 428 窟彩塑弟子像
图 75　第 290 窟彩塑弟子像
图 76　第 432 窟化生童子
图 77　第 290 窟侧壁壁画题材布局示意图
图 78　第 428 窟侧壁壁画题材布局示意图
图 79　第 290 窟西壁壁画题材布局示意图
图 80　第 428 窟西壁壁画题材布局示意图
图 81　第 428 窟东壁壁画题材布局示意图
图 82　第 290 窟东壁壁画题材布局示意图
图 83　第 428 窟飞天
图 84　第 428 窟男供养人
图 85　第 428 窟女供养人
图 86　第 442 窟女供养人
图 87　第 438 窟佛像头部
图 88　第 432 窟菩萨像头部
图 89　第 461 窟壁画弟子像
图 90　第 438 窟纹样
图 91　第 461 窟纹样
图 92　第 461 窟纹样
图 93　第 432 窟纹样

图 94　第 438 窟纹样
图 95　第 428 窟佛像头部
图 96　第 290 窟菩萨像头部
图 97　第 430 窟弟子像头部
图 98　第 428 窟壁画佛像
图 99　第 428 窟纹样
图 100　第 428 窟纹样
图 101　第 428 窟纹样
图 102　第 294 窟纹样
图 103　第 290 窟纹样
图 104　第 439 窟纹样
图 105　第 442 窟纹样
图 106　第 296 窟纹样
图 107　第 301 窟壁画佛像
图 108　第 297 窟乐舞壁画（欧阳琳临本）
图 109　第 297 窟羽人塑像
图 110　第 305 窟佛像
图 111　第 302 窟菩萨塑像
图 112　敦煌写本 S.2732 号尾题

龙门石窟唐代窟龛分期试论

图 1　敬善寺平面图（采自阎文儒、常青著《龙门石窟研究》图 42)
图 2　大卢舍那像龛平面图（采自上引书，图 81)
图 3　极南洞平面图（采自上引书，图 106)
图 4　高平郡王洞平面图（采自上引书，图 125)
图 5　擂鼓台南洞平面图（李晓霞、谷宏耀测绘）
图 6　擂鼓台南洞纵向垂直剖面图（李晓霞、谷宏耀测绘）
图 7　万佛洞造像题材示意图（采自阎文儒、常青上引书，图 45)
图 8　龙华寺造像题材示意图（采自上引书，图 103)
图 9　擂鼓台中洞造像题材示意图（路伟、白超绘）
图 10　宾阳南洞造像组合示意图（采自阎文儒、常青上引书，图 26)
图 11　药方洞造像组合示意图（采自上引书，图 82)

图 12　八作司洞造像组合示意图(采自上引书,图 97)

图 13　擂鼓台北洞造像组合示意图(采自上引书,图 115)

图 14　天竺三衣及僧祇支披覆图 (a. 采自栗田 功《ガンダーラ美術》, I 佛伝, 東京：二玄社, 1988 年, 図 164；b. 采自 A. B. Griswold, "Prolegomena to the Study of the Buddha's Dress in Chinese Sculpture" , in: *Artibus Asiae*, Vol. XXVI (1963), No. 2: 85-131, Fig.1；c. 采自 A. B. Griswold, *opere citato*, Fig.2a；d. 采自 A. B. Griswold, *opere citato*, Fig.3；e. 采自 A. B. Griswold, *opere citato*, Fig.2b；f. 采自 A. B. Griswold, *opere citato*, Fig.2c；g. 采自 A. B. Griswold, *opere citato*, Fig.2d；h. 采自 A. B. Griswold, *opere citato*, Fig.4a；i. 采自 A. B. Griswold, *opere citato*, Fig.4b；j. 采自 A. B. Griswold, *opere citato*, Fig.4c；k. 采自 A. B. Griswold, *opere citato*, Fig.4d；l. 采自 A. B. Griswold, *opere citato*, Fig.4e；m. 采自 A. B. Griswold, *opere citato*, Fig. 5a,b)

图 15　药方洞主尊佛像(采自阎文儒、常青上引书,图 83)

图 16　宾阳南洞主尊佛像(白超绘)

图 17　潜溪寺主尊佛像(采自阎文儒、常青上引书,图 38)

图 18　万佛洞主尊佛像(白超绘)

图 19　惠简洞主尊佛像(白超绘)

图 20　擂鼓台北洞主尊佛像(贺志军绘)

图 21　八作司洞主尊佛像(白超绘)

图 22　极南洞主尊佛像(白超绘)

图 23　药方洞佛像头光(白超绘)

图 24　宾阳北洞佛像头光(白超绘)

图 25　大卢舍那像龛佛像头光

图 26　奉南洞佛像头光(白超绘)

图 27　唐字洞佛座(白超绘)

图 28　潜溪寺佛座(白超绘)

图 29　二莲花北洞佛座(白超绘)

图 30　敬善寺佛座(白超绘)

图 31　万佛洞佛座(白超绘)

图 32　奉南洞佛座(白超绘)

图 33　高平郡王洞佛座(采自阎文儒、常青上引书,图 126)

图 34　宾阳南洞左侧弟子(白超绘)

图 35　潜溪寺左侧弟子（白超绘）
图 36　敬善寺左侧弟子（白超绘）
图 37　二莲花南洞左侧弟子（白超绘）
图 38　极南洞左侧弟子（白超绘）
图 39　八作司洞左侧弟子（白超绘）
图 40　宾阳南洞右侧弟子（白超绘）
图 41　宾阳北洞右侧弟子（白超绘）
图 42　惠简洞右侧弟子（白超绘）
图 43　万佛洞右侧弟子（白超绘）
图 44　二莲花南洞右侧弟子（白超绘）
图 45　极南洞右侧弟子（白超绘）
图 46　大卢舍那像龛弟子头光（白超绘）
图 47　奉南洞弟子头光（白超绘）
图 48　药方洞弟子像座（白超绘）
图 49　宾阳北洞弟子像座（白超绘）
图 50　敬善寺弟子像座（白超绘）
图 51　二莲花北洞弟子像座（白超绘）
图 52　奉南洞弟子像座（白超绘）
图 53　八作司洞弟子像座（白超绘）
图 54　高平郡王洞弟子像座（白超绘）
图 55　宾阳南洞左侧菩萨（谷宏耀绘）
图 56　宾阳北洞左侧菩萨（谷宏耀绘）
图 57　惠简洞左侧菩萨（谷宏耀绘）
图 58　清明寺左侧菩萨（谷宏耀绘）
图 59　大卢舍那像龛左侧菩萨（谷宏耀绘）
图 60　擂鼓台北洞左侧菩萨（贺志军绘）
图 61　奉南洞左侧菩萨（谷宏耀绘）
图 62　火上洞左侧菩萨（谷宏耀绘）
图 63　宾阳南洞右侧菩萨（谷宏耀绘）
图 64　药方洞右侧菩萨（谷宏耀绘）
图 65　敬善寺右侧菩萨（谷宏耀绘）
图 66　惠简洞右侧菩萨（谷宏耀绘）

图 67　龙华寺右侧菩萨（谷宏耀绘）
图 68　擂鼓台北洞右侧菩萨（贺志军绘）
图 69　奉南洞右侧菩萨（谷宏耀绘）
图 70　极南洞右侧菩萨（谷宏耀绘）
图 71　宾阳南洞菩萨头光（谷宏耀绘）
图 72　万佛洞菩萨头光（谷宏耀绘）
图 73　净土堂菩萨头光（谷宏耀绘）
图 74　二莲花南洞菩萨头光（谷宏耀绘）
图 75　潜溪寺菩萨像座（谷宏耀绘）
图 76　敬善寺菩萨像座（谷宏耀绘）
图 77　二莲花南洞菩萨像座（谷宏耀绘）
图 78　八作司洞菩萨像座（谷宏耀绘）
图 79　高平郡王洞菩萨像座（谷宏耀绘）
图 80　宾阳北洞左侧神王（谷宏耀绘）
图 81　大卢舍那像龛左侧神王（谷宏耀绘）
图 82　八作司洞左侧神王（谷宏耀绘）
图 83　极南洞左侧神王（谷宏耀绘）
图 84　奉南洞左侧神王（谷宏耀绘）
图 85　宾阳北洞右侧神王（谷宏耀绘）
图 86　敬善寺右侧神王（谷宏耀绘）
图 87　万佛洞右侧神王（谷宏耀绘）
图 88　龙华寺右侧神王（谷宏耀绘）
图 89　奉南洞右侧神王（谷宏耀绘）
图 90　极南洞右侧神王（谷宏耀绘）
图 91　潜溪寺药叉像（谷宏耀绘）
图 92　龙华寺药叉像（谷宏耀绘）
图 93　三佛洞药叉像（谷宏耀绘）
图 94　药方洞左侧金刚（谷宏耀绘）
图 95　二莲花北洞左侧金刚（谷宏耀绘）
图 96　奉南洞左侧金刚（谷宏耀绘）
图 97　高平郡王洞左侧金刚（谷宏耀绘）
图 98　二莲花南洞左侧金刚（谷宏耀绘）

图 99　敬善寺左侧金刚(谷宏耀绘)
图 100　万佛洞左侧金刚(谷宏耀绘)
图 101　药方洞右侧金刚(谷宏耀绘)
图 102　八作司洞右侧金刚(谷宏耀绘)
图 103　奉南洞右侧金刚(谷宏耀绘)
图 104　极南洞右侧金刚(谷宏耀绘)
图 105　双窑北洞右侧金刚(谷宏耀绘)
图 106　敬善寺右侧金刚(谷宏耀绘)
图 107　万佛洞右侧金刚(谷宏耀绘)
图 108　擂鼓台中洞窟顶装饰(白超绘)
图 109　四雁洞窟顶装饰(常青绘)
图 110　万佛洞伎乐(白超绘)
图 111　八作司洞伎乐(白超绘)
图 112　极南洞伎乐(白超绘)
图 113　药方洞飞天(白超绘)
图 114　万佛洞飞天(白超绘)
图 115　龙华寺飞天(白超绘)
图 116　奉南洞飞天(白超绘)
图 117　龙门第 101 龛(王师德龛)造像(采自《龙门石窟总录》第壹卷《实测图》176)
图 118　龙门第 331 龛(韩氏洞)内景(采自《中国石窟·龙门石窟》二,图版 47)
图 119　龙门第 1058 窟(采自《龙门石窟总录》第陆卷《实测图》397、398)
图 120　龙门第 1817 窟(采自上引书,第拾壹卷《实测图》359、360)
图 121　龙门第 1674 窟(采自上引书,第拾卷《实测图》687、685)
图 122　龙门第 1950 窟(采自上引书,第拾壹卷《实测图》721、723)

地婆诃罗、香山寺与“石像七龛”

图 1　擂鼓台三洞(采自《龙门石窟考古报告：擂鼓台卷》)
图 2　擂鼓台北洞窟前岩面蹬道台阶
图 3　擂鼓台北洞主尊(贺志军测绘)
图 4　擂鼓台北洞窟口右侧高僧像(贺志军测绘)
图 5　擂鼓台中洞外立面
图 6　擂鼓台中洞主尊佛像(关野贞拍摄)

图 7　擂鼓台南洞外立面

图 8　擂鼓台南洞内景（关野贞拍摄）

图 9　擂鼓台窟前踏道遗迹

图 10　高平郡王洞窟门右侧金刚像

图 11　高平郡王洞主室正壁

图 12　高平郡王洞平面图

图 13　高平郡王洞像座及铭文

图 14　看经寺外立面

图 15　看经寺主室右壁（北壁）

图 16　看经寺主室左壁（南壁）高僧像

图 17　看经寺主室右壁（北壁）高僧像

图 18a　二莲花洞外景

图 18b　二莲花北洞主室窟顶

石窟寺中国化的初步考察

图 1　比德尔科拉石窟连续平面图（采自 *Ancient India*, No. 15, Plate XLVI)

图 2　均讷尔地区门莫迪五室窟（第 21 窟）平面图（采自 *Buddhist Architecture of Western India* by S. Nagaraju, 以下简作 *BAWI*, Fig.29)

图 3　根赫里第 58 窟平面图（采自 *BAWI*, Fig.41)

图 4　均讷尔伽内什 · 伯哈第 17-20a 窟连续平面图（采自 *BAWI*, Fig.34)

图 5　阿旃陀第 12 窟平面图（采自 *The Cave Temples of India*, Plate XXVII)

图 6　阿旃陀第 16 窟平面图（采自 *Inscriptions of the Vākāṭakas: Corpus Inscriptionum Indicarum* V, Plate I)

图 7　那烂陀寺遗址平面图（采自 *Nālandā* by A. Ghosh)

图 8a　纳西克第 3 窟平面图（采自 *The Cave Temples of India*, Plate XIX, No. 1)

图 8b　呾叉始罗焦莲僧坊遗址平面图（采自 *Buddhist Monuments*, Fig.10)

图 9a　伽尔拉第 8 窟平面及水平剖面、纵向垂直剖面及透视图（采自 *Indian Architecture: Buddhist and Hindu Periods* by Percy Brown, Plate XIX)

图 9b　伽尔拉第 8 窟内景

图 10a　均讷尔地区锡万内里第 64 窟平面图（采自 *BAWI*, Fig.38)

图 10b　均讷尔地区杜尔贾莱纳第 13 窟内景

图 11a　贝德萨第 3、4 窟外景

图 11b　贝德萨第 4 窟（水窖）
图 12　阿旃陀第 17 窟平面图（采自 *The Cave Temples of India*, Plate XXXIII, No. 2）
图 13　格拉德第 48 窟平面及横向垂直剖面图（采自 *The Cave Temples of India*, Plate VI）
图 14　库车苏巴什第 5 窟平面图
图 15　敦煌莫高窟第 285 窟平面及水平剖面、纵向垂直剖面图（采自《中国石窟·敦煌莫高窟》一，第 225 页测绘图）
图 16　莫高窟第 285 窟后壁壁画局部（采自《中国石窟·敦煌莫高窟》一，图版 119）
图 17　拜城克孜尔第 24 窟平面图及第 15 窟炉灶细部
图 18　伽内什·伯哈第 24 窟平面图（采自 *BAWI*, Fig.35）
图 19　纳西克第 23 窟平面图及正壁造像
图 20a　云冈第 7、8 窟平面及纵向垂直剖面图（采自宿白《中国石窟寺研究》第 60 页，图 7）
图 20b　云冈第 7 窟后壁主像（采自水野清一、長廣敏雄《雲岡石窟》第四卷，实测图 VIII）
图 21　龙门万佛洞平面图及正壁造像
图 22　杜尔贾莱纳第 3 窟平面及横向垂直剖面图
图 23　拜拉特（波里夜呾罗国）木构塔殿遗址平面图（采自 *Buddhist Monuments*, Fig.12）
图 24　珀贾第 12 窟外立面及窟内佛塔
图 25　古达第 15 窟平面图及窟内佛塔 (a. 采自 *Report on the Buddhist Cave Temples and Their Inscriptions* by Jas. Burgess, Plate VIII, No. 5)
图 26　埃洛拉第 10 窟外立面、平面图及塔前主像 (b. 采自 *Buddhist Monuments*, Fig.17)
图 27　克孜尔第 38 窟平面及水平剖面、纵向垂直剖面图及内景
图 28　克孜尔第 17 窟侧壁说法图
图 29　克孜尔新 1 窟后室后壁涅槃台上涅槃残像
图 30　莫高窟第 254 窟平面及水平剖面、纵向垂直剖面及透视图和内景 (a. 采自《中国石窟·敦煌莫高窟》一，第 224 页测绘图）
图 31　云冈第 2 窟内景（采自《中国石窟·云冈石窟》一，图版 11）
图 32　巩县石窟第 1 窟平面及水平剖面图、纵向垂直剖面及透视图和内景（采自《中国石窟·巩县石窟》，第 238 页图 2；图版 9、3）

The Sinicizing Process of the Cave-temples: Evolution of the *Lēṇa, Maṭapa* and *Chētiyaghara* (refer to the illustrations of 石窟寺中国化的初步考察）

Fig.1　Ground plan of the cave temple complex at Pitalkhōrā, Aurangābād (from *Ancient*

India, No. 15, Plate XLVI)

Fig.2 Plan of a five-celled cave (Cave 21) at Manmodi, Junnar (from *Buddhist Architecture of Western India* by S. Nagaraju, hereafter abbreviated as *BAWI*, Fig.29)

Fig.3 Plan of Cave 58 at Kaṇhēri (from *BAWI*, Fig.41)

Fig.4 Plan of Cave Nos. 17-20a at Ganesh Pahar, Junnar (from *BAWI*, Fig.34)

Fig.5 Plan of Cave 12 at Ajaṇṭā (from *The Cave Temples of India*, Plate XXVII)

Fig.6 Plan of Cave 16 at Ajaṇṭā (from *Inscriptions of the Vākāṭakas: Corpus Inscriptionum Indicarum* V, Plate I)

Fig.7 Plan of the remains at Nālandā saṃghārāma/Nālandā Mahāvihāra (from *Nālandā* by A. Ghosh)

Fig.8a Plan of Cave 3 at Nāsik (from *The Cave Temples of India*, Plate XIX, No. 1)

Fig.8b Plan of a free-standing *vihāra* at Jauliāñ, Taxila (from *Buddhist Monuments*, Fig.10)

Fig.9a Plan, longitudinal section, section in perspective and *stūpa* of Cave 8 at Kārlā, Poone (from *Indian Architecture: Buddhist and Hindu Periods* by Percy Brown, Plate XIX)

Fig.9b Interior of Cave 8 at Kārlā

Fig.10a Plan of Cave 64 at Sivaneri, Junnar (from *BAWI*, Fig.38)

Fig.10b Interior of Cave 13 at Tūljā-lēnā, Junnar

Fig.11a Caves 3 and 4 at Bēdsā, Poone

Fig.11b Cistern in Cave 4 at Bēdsā

Fig.12 Plan of Cave 17 at Ajaṇṭā (from *The Cave Temples of India*, Plate XXXIII, No. 2)

Fig.13 Plan and transverse section of Cave 48 at Karādh, Satara (from *The Cave Temples of India*, Plate VI)

Fig.14 Plan of Cave 5 (*lēṇa*) at Subashi site, Kucha

Fig.15 Plan and longitudinal section of Cave 285 at Mogao, Dunhuang (from *Cave-temples of China: Mogaoku Caves of Dunhuang*, Vol. I, P. 225)

Fig.16 Detail of mural on the west wall of Cave 285 (from *opere citato*, Plate 119)

Fig.17 Plan of Cave 24 at Kizil and line drawing of a stove in Cave 15 at Kizil, Kucha

Fig.18 Plan of Cave 24 at Ganesh Pahar, Junnar (from *BAWI*, Fig.35)

Fig.19 Plan and main images on the back wall of Cave 23 at Nāsik, Nashik

Fig.20a Plan and longitudinal section of caves 7 and 8 at Yungang (from *Studies of the Cave-temples of China* by Su Bai, P. 60, Fig.7)

Fig.20b　Main images on the back wall of Cave 7 at Yungang (from *Yun-kang: The Buddhist Cave-temples of the Fifth Century* AD *in North China; detailed report of the archaeological survey carried out by the mission of the Tōhōbunka Kenkyūsho 1938-45*, Vol. IV, Plan VIII)

Fig.21　Plan and main images on the back wall of the Wanfodong Cave (Ten Thousands Buddhas' Cave dated to 680 AD) at Longmen, Luoyang

Fig.22　Plan and transverse section of Cave 3 at Tūljālēnā, Junnar

Fig.23　Plan of a free-standing *caitya-gṛha* site at Bairāṭ, Jaipur (from *Buddhist Monuments*, Fig.12)

Fig.24　Façade and *stūpa* of Cave 12 at Bhājā, Poone

Fig.25　Plan and *stūpa* of Cave 15 at Kuḍā, Alibag(a. from *Report on the Buddhist Cave Temples and Their Inscriptions* by Jas. Burgess, Plate VIII, No. 5)

Fig.26　Façade, plan and main image on the *stūpa* of Cave 10 at Ēlūra, Aurangābād (b. from *Buddhist Monuments*, Fig.17)

Fig.27　Plan, longitudinal section and interior of Cave 38 at Kizil, Kucha

Fig.28　Scenes of Buddha delivering his sermon on the lateral wall of Cave 17 at Kizil

Fig.29　Buddha in *Parinirvāṇa,* painted clay sculpture on a rock-cut couch against the rear wall of the rear chamber of Cave New No. 1 at Kizil, *in situ*

Fig.30　Plan, longitudinal section and interior of Cave 254 at Mogao, Dunhuang (a. from *Cave-temples of China: Mogaoku Caves of Dunhuang*, Vol. I, P. 224)

Fig.31　Interior of Cave 2 at Yungang (from *Cave-temples of China: Yungang Caves*, Vol. I, Plate 11)

Fig.32　Plan, longitudinal section and interior of Cave 1 at Gongxian, Zhengzhou (from *Cave-temples of China: Gongxian Caves*, P. 238, Fig.2; Pls. 9, 3)

陕西周至大秦寺塔记

图 1　周至大秦寺塔

图 2　大秦寺塔第二层平面

图 3　大秦寺塔第七层平面

图 4　大秦寺塔阑额及斗拱

图 5　大秦寺塔第二层西壁雕塑

图 6　大秦寺塔第二层西壁雕塑局部

图 7　大秦寺塔第三层南壁雕塑
图 8　苏州罗汉院西塔第一层平面图（采自《刘敦桢文集》二，第 297 页，插图 11）
图 9　西安玄奘塔外景
图 10　安西榆林窟第 2 窟前壁北侧壁画水月观音（采自《中国石窟·安西榆林窟》，图版 138）

四、川滇窟龛：汉化余韵

安岳圆觉洞调查记

图 1　安岳云居山圆觉洞第 71 号龛
图 2　云居山圆觉洞第 71 号龛左侧题铭
图 3　安岳千佛崖第 38 号龛三观音
图 4　云居山圆觉洞第 58 号龛
图 5　云居山圆觉洞第 58 号龛前左侧碑记
图 6　云居山圆觉洞第 59 号龛
图 7　云居山圆觉洞前山（北崖）窟龛示意图
图 8　云居山圆觉洞第 13 号龛
图 9　云居山圆觉洞第 13、14 号龛外景
图 10　云居山圆觉洞第 9 号窟前左侧碑记
图 11　云居山圆觉洞第 7 号龛
图 12　云居山圆觉洞第 7 号龛右侧壁榜题

剑川石窟：1999 年考古调查简报

图 1　剑川石宝山石窟位置示意图
图 2a　沙登箐区 1 号龛上排浮雕（张总绘）
图 2b　沙登箐区 1 号龛上排浮雕局部（王梦祥拍摄）
图 3a　沙登箐区 2 号龛立面图（张总绘）
图 3b　沙登箐区 2 号龛主像
图 4　狮子关 1 号龛主像 (a. 王梦祥拍摄）
图 5　狮子关 10 号龛主像 (b. 张总绘）
图 6　石钟寺区 2 号龛测绘图（张总绘）
图 7a　石钟寺区 8 号龛平面图（张总绘）

图 7b 石钟寺区 8 号龛外立面图（张总绘）

图 8 石钟寺区 8 号龛外“盛德四年”题记

图 9a 石钟寺区 8 号龛内左侧壁坐佛（王梦祥拍摄）

图 9b 石钟寺区 8 号龛内右侧壁坐佛（王梦祥拍摄）

图 10 石钟寺区 9 号龛摩崖壁画（张总绘）

五、史料、遗迹：透视交流

Jibin and China as seen from Chinese Documents

Fig.1 A Map of Greater Gandhāra (from *Ancient Buddhist Scrolls from Gandhāra: The British Library Kharoṣṭhī Fragments* by Richard Salomon, Map I)

Fig.2a A gilded bronze image of Buddha, from site of Shifo Monastery at Huangliang, Chang'an (from *Masterworks of the Antiquities from Xi'an: Buddhist Images*, Plate 2)

Fig.2b A Kharoṣṭhī inscription carved on the back of the pedestal of the above image

西行求法与罽宾道

图 1 玄奘西行求法路线示意图（前半）（李崇峰据玄奘《大唐西域记》及 *Reader's Digest Atlas of the World* 绘制）

图 2 罽宾道示意图（李崇峰据《北史》及 *Mountaineering Map of Pākistān* 绘制）

图 3 中巴公路“洪扎灵岩二号”题铭及摹本（版权属于海德堡科学院）

The Geography of Transmission: The “Jibin” Route and the Propagation of Buddhism in China (refer to the illustrations of 西行求法与罽宾道)

Fig.1 A Sketch Map of Xuanzang's Pilgrimage to India [drawn by Chongfeng Li on the basis of *Datang xiyu ji* (*Record of the Western Regions of the Great Tang Dynasty*) by Xuanzang and *Reader's Digest Atlas of the World*]

Fig.2 A Sketch Map of Jibin Route (drawn by Chongfeng Li on the basis of *Beishi* (*History of the Northern Dynasties*) by Li Yanshou and *Mountaineering Map of Pākistān*)

Fig.3 Inscription and the copy on “Sacred Rock II”, Hunza, 5th century (copyright of Heidelberger Akademie der Wissenschaften)

犍陀罗、秣菟罗与中土早期佛像

图 1 布施祇园，出自 Guides Mess，Mardan，现藏卡拉奇国家博物馆

图 2 立佛，出土于 Mamāne Dheṛi，现藏白沙瓦考古博物馆（采自パキスタン・ガンダーラ彫刻展，Pl. 2）

图 3 乘公羊车上学，出土于 Chārsada，现藏伦敦 Victoria and Albert Museum

图 4 立佛，出土地不详，现藏新德里国家博物馆

图 5 树下观耕，出土于 Sahr-ī-Bahlol，现藏白沙瓦考古博物馆（采自パキスタン・ガンダーラ彫刻展，Pl. 7）

图 6 佛头像，出土于 Tapa Kalān，哈达（Haḍḍa），原藏喀布尔博物馆（采自 *The Image of the Buddha*，Pl. 133）

图 7 坐佛，*Stūpa* 11，哈达 Tapa Shotor 遗址（采自 *The Image of the Buddha*，Pl. 134）

图 8 阎膏珍雕像，出土于 Māṭ，现藏秣菟罗博物馆

图 9 迦腻色迦雕像，出土于 Māṭ，现藏秣菟罗博物馆

图 10 耆那教供施板，出土于秣菟罗 Kankālī，现藏勒克瑙博物馆

图 11 佛与净饭王，出土于秣菟罗 Kankālī，现藏勒克瑙博物馆（采自 *Buddhist Art: Mathura School*，Pl. 57）

图 12 坐佛，出土于 Kaṭrā，现藏秣菟罗博物馆

图 13 菩萨 / 佛立像，出土于萨尔那特，现藏萨尔那特考古博物馆

图 14 坐佛，出土于 Maholī，现藏秣菟罗博物馆（采自 *Buddhist Art: Mathura School*，Pl. 90）

图 15 坐佛，出土于 Govindnagar（戈温德讷格尔），现藏秣菟罗博物馆（采自 *Buddhist Art: Mathura School*，Pl. 104）

图 16 佛头像，出土于 Chāmuṇḍā，现藏秣菟罗博物馆（采自 *The Image of the Buddha*，Pl. 54）

图 17 立佛，出土于 Jamalpur，现藏秣菟罗博物馆（采自 *Buddhist Art: Mathura School*，Pl. 128）

图 18 坐佛，出土于萨尔那特，现藏萨尔那特考古博物馆（采自 *The Image of the Buddha*，Pl. 63）

图 19 立佛，出土于戈温德讷格尔，现藏秣菟罗博物馆（采自 *Buddhist Art: Mathura School*，Pl. 126）

图 20 坐佛，阿旃陀第 1 窟佛殿

图 21 立佛，出土于加德满都 Cā-bāhī，现藏勒克瑙博物馆（采自 *The Image of the Buddha*，Pl. 125）

图 22　鎏金铜佛，出土地不详（采自松原三郎《中国仏教彫刻史論》図版 5a）

图 23　立佛，炳灵寺第 169 窟（采自《中国石窟 · 永靖炳灵寺》图版 34）

图 24　云冈第 18 窟立佛（采自《中国石窟 · 云冈石窟》二，图版 171、172）

图 25　立佛，云冈第 16 窟正壁（采自《中国石窟 · 云冈石窟》二，图版 141）

图 26　坐佛，云冈第 20 窟正壁

图 27　育王像，成都西安路出土（雷玉华摄）

图 28　立佛像，青州龙兴寺出土，现藏山东青州博物馆（采自《山东青州龙兴寺出土佛教石刻造像精品》，图版 92、98、111、114）

Gandhāra, Mathurā and the Buddha Images of Medieval China (refer to the illustrations of 犍陀罗、秣菟罗与中土早期佛像）

Fig.1　Gift of the Jetavanārāma, from Guides Mess, Mardan, National Museum, Karachi

Fig.2　Standing Buddha, from Mamāne Dheṛi, Archaeological Museum, Peshawar (from パキスタン・ガンダーラ彫刻展, Pl. 2)

Fig.3　The child Bodhisattva going to school in a ram-cart, from Chārsada Tehsīl, Victoria and Albert Museum, London

Fig.4　Standing Buddha, site unknown, National Museum, New Delhi

Fig.5　Bodhisattva Siddhartha's meditation, from Sahr-ī-Bahlol, Archaeological Museum, Peshawar(from パキスタン・ガンダーラ彫刻展, Pl. 7)

Fig.6　Head of Buddha, from Tapa Kalān, Haḍḍa, Kabul Museum (from *The Image of the Buddha*, Pl. 133)

Fig.7　Seated Buddhas, *Stūpa* 11, sacred ground of Tapa Shotor, Haḍḍa (from *The Image of the Buddha*, Pl. 134)

Fig.8　Headless statue of the Kuṣāṇa emperor Vima I Taktu or Vima II Kadphises, from Māṭ, Mathurā, Mathura Museum

Fig.9　Headless statue of the Kuṣāṇa emperor Kaniṣka, from Māṭ, Mathurā, Mathura Museum

Fig.10　Ayāgapaṭṭa, from Kankālī, State Museum, Lucknow

Fig.11　Stele representing conversation between Buddha and Śuddodana, from Kankālī, State Museum, Lucknow (from *Buddhist Art: Mathura School*, Pl. 57)

Fig.12　Seated Buddha/Bodhisattva image, from Kaṭrā mound, near Mathurā, Archaeological Museum, Mathura

Fig.13 Colossal image of Bodhisattva/ Buddha, installed by Friar Bala in the 3rd year of Kaniṣka, from Sārnāth, Archaeological Museum, Sārnāth

Fig.14 Seated Buddha, from Maholī, Archaeological Museum, Mathura (from *Buddhist Art: Mathura School*, Pl. 90)

Fig.15 Seated Buddha with *abhaya* pose, webbed hand, from Govindnagar, Archaeological Museum, Mathura (from *Buddhist Art: Mathura School*, Pl. 104)

Fig.16 Head of Buddha, from Chāmuṇḍā, Archaeological Museum, Mathura (from *The Image of the Buddha*, Pl. 54)

Fig.17 Standing Buddha, from Jamalpur, Mathurā, Archaeological Museum, Mathura (from *Buddhist Art: Mathura School*, Pl. 128)

Fig.18 Seated Buddha, from Sārnāth, Archaeological Museum, Sārnāth (from *The Image of the Buddha*, Pl. 63)

Fig.19 Standing Buddha in *abhaya* pose, foldless drapery remarkable, from Govindnagar, Archaeological Museum, Mathura (from *Buddhist Art: Mathura School*, Pl. 126)

Fig.20 Preaching Buddha flanked by attendants, cave 1 at Ajaṇṭā

Fig.21 Standing Buddha, from Cā-bāhī, Katmandu, State Museum, Lucknow (from *The Image of the Buddha*, Pl. 125)

Fig.22 Seated Buddha, provenance unknown, gilt bronze (from *A History of Chinese Buddhist Sculpture*/ 中国仏教彫刻史論), Pl. 5a

Fig.23 Clay sculptures of standing Buddha in Cave 169 at Binglingsi, Yongjing

Fig.24a Stone Sculpture of standing Buddha against the west wall of Cave 18 at Yungang, Datong

Fig.24b Standing Buddha against the east wall of Cave 18 at Yungang

Fig.25 Standing Buddha against the back wall of Cave 16 at Yungang

Fig.26 Seated Buddha in Cave 20 at Yungang

Fig.27 A Aśoka-type Buddha image dated 551 AD, from Xi'an road, Chengdu (Photo: Lei Yuhua)

Fig.28 Stone sculptures of standing Buddha, from the site of Longxing Monastery, Qingzhou Museum, Qingzhou

The Aśoka-type Buddha Images found in China

Fig.1 Aśoka-type Buddha image, height 48 cm, from a hoard at Xi'an Road, Chengdu

Fig.2 Rubbing copy of the inscription carved at the back of the image

Fig.3 Head of an Aśoka-type Buddha image, from the site of Wanfo Monastery in Chengdu, Sichuan

Fig.4 A headless Aśoka-type Buddha image, from the same site

Fig.5 Standing Buddha in *abhaya-mudrā*, from Govindnagar, Archaeological Survey of India

Fig.6 Torso of a Buddha image, from Govindnagar, Mathurā Museum

Fig.7 Mural on the western section of the south wall of Cave 323 at Mogao, Dunhuang

Fig.8 Detail of the aforesaid mural [8a. from *Dunhuang Research*, No. 2 (2013), Pl. 24]

Fig.9 Aśoka-type Buddha image carved on the west wall of Tangzi Cave at Longmen, Luoyang

Fig.10 Aśoka Temple at Yinxian, Zhejiang

Fig.11 A Sculpture of King Aśoka's portrait in the same temple

金刚力士钩稽

图 1 龙门奉南洞前庭正壁金刚力士

图 2 桑吉大塔塔门门柱浮雕门神像

图 3 印度比德尔科拉第 4 窟门道两侧门神

图 4 云冈第 39 窟门道两侧金刚、力士

图 5 龙门宾阳中洞门道两侧金刚、力士

图 6 北魏神龟三年 (520 年) 造像碑，日本京都国立博物馆收藏 (采自《中国の石仏：莊厳なる祈り》/*Chinese Buddhist Stone Sculpture: Veneration of the Sublime*，第 87、148 页)

图 7 龙门宾阳南洞主室前壁示意图 (采自《龙门石窟总录》，第壹卷，实测图 289)

菩提像初探

图 1 龙门石窟擂鼓台北洞主尊 (贺志军测绘)

图 2 龙门擂鼓台区第 5-32 龛 (原编 2071 号，焦建辉测绘)

图 3 印度伽耶摩诃菩提寺平面图 (采自 *Archaeological Survey of India: Four Reports made during the years 1862-63-64-65*/ Volume I, Pl. IV)

图 4 摩诃菩提寺金刚座及大塔西侧面成道像 (采自 *Archaeological Survey of India: Annual Report 1908-09*, Pl. L)

图 5　摩诃菩提寺藏成道像(采自 *Bodh Gayā: The Great Buddhist Temple* by R. Mitra, Pl. XI)

图 6　勒克瑙博物馆藏佛传浮雕(采自 *Archaeological Survey of India: Annual Report 1909-10*, Pl. XXVa)

图 7　萨尔纳特遗址出土造像碑(采自 *Archaeological Survey of India: Annual Report 1904-05*, Pl. XXVIIIa)

图 8　加尔各答印度博物馆藏菩提像(采自 *Buddhist Monuments*, Pl. 32)

图 9　缅甸摩萨博物馆藏银质舍利盒(采自 *The Image of the Buddha*, Fig.100)

图 10　四川广元千佛崖第 366 窟菩提像

图 11　四川巴中西龛第 73 号菩提像、弥勒像合龛(雷玉华摄)

图 12　日本文化厅藏长安七宝台雕像(采自松原三郎《中国仏教彫刻史論》図版 663b)

图 13　龙门擂鼓台南洞"主尊"

后　　记

2013年11月看完本书校样后，需要补充说明编辑、付印过程中的一些情况：

一、本书所收文章，前后撰著时间跨度较长，最早者系1989年写就，最晚者乃不久前草成；所涉内容时空范围较大，从公元前2世纪到公元后14世纪，地跨印度、中亚和中国。因此，体例既不能斠若划一，行文亦难期前后一致，所用资料及观点亦略有差异。为了维持原文的完整及表明作者修正看法之趋势，尽管前后有些繁琐和重复，但各篇文章的论点大体照旧，有些补正主要是资料的变动。现在把这些初步看法汇集起来，目的是便于国内外同好审阅，期望得到各方面的批评指正。

二、书中以英文撰写的论文，原本皆应邀参加相关国际学术会议所做。英语不是我的母语，尝试用英文撰写，只是为了研讨和交流世界性佛教文化遗产。不过，我的每篇英文论文草成后都请外国同道润色；这次重刊前，美国何恩之(Angela F. Howard)教授把全部英文论文再审校一遍，使笔者深为感动。

三、全书后附《本书征引论著目录》和《插图目录》。这样安排，既可避免正文注释过多重沓，力求插图说明简洁，也便于读者据此核查或以此为索引进一步研讨佛教考古及相关问题。其中，除少量汉文史料采纳传统的征引方式外，如张彦远《历代名画记》(明王世贞万历初年郧阳初刻《王氏画苑》本)，本书绝大多数引证论著方式，按照国际学术规范主要分作两种：

第一种为"专著中析出的文献"，著录格式为：析出责任者．析出题名．析出其他责任者．见：原文献责任者．原文献题名．版本．出版地：出版者，出版年．在原文献中的位置。例如：

(1) 向达《盩厔大秦寺略记》，见：向达《唐代长安与西域文明》，北京：生活·读书·新知三联书店，1957年，第110-116页；

(2) M. N. Deshpande, "The (Ajanta) Caves: Their Historical Perspective", in: *Ajanta Murals*, ed. A. Ghosh, New Delhi: Archaeological Survey of India, 1967:

14-21.

第二种为“连续出版物中析出的文献”，著录格式为：析出责任者．析出题名．析出其他责任者．见：原文献题名．版本．在原文献中的位置［依次为年，卷（期、部分号）：页数］。例如：

(1) 梁思成等《云冈石窟中所表现的北魏建筑》，见：《中国营造学社汇刊》，1933年，第四卷第三·四期合刊，第171-218页；

(2) Alexander. C. Soper, “Aspects of Light Symbolism in Gandhāran Sculpture”, in: *Artibus Asiae,* 1949, XII (3): 252-283, (4): 314-330; 1950, XIII (1/2): 63-85.

上述著作引征体例只适于每篇首次引用，该文再次征引时按照通用规范从略。

1982年应聘到敦煌文物研究所（敦煌研究院前身）任职，自此开始了佛教文化与艺术的学习，瞬间已逾三十年，其间真正引导我走上科研之路的是宿师季庚先生。多年来，不断得到季庚师的教诲和鞭策；我的多数文稿，都曾得到本师的审读和教示。先生道德文章，令人敬仰。此外，在我从事佛教考古的过程中，得到了国内外许多师友的帮助，责任编辑缪丹女士更为本书梓行付出了辛勤的汗水。谨此致谢。

李崇峰

2013年11月18日

写于北京大学

修订本后记

《佛教考古：从印度到中国》，2014年1月由上海古籍出版社精装印行。2015年2月，责任编辑缪丹女史电告书已售罄，出版社拟印平装本。鉴于时间紧迫，在不改动版面的前提下，我仅订正了少量失误，后平装本于2015年7月面世。2019年3月，缪丹告知出版社拟对此书修订再版。接到通知后，我计划在6月初之前把原书校阅一过，但由于教学、科研及其他杂务，一直拖至8月底才告一段落。

本书出版后，在教学和科研工作中我陆续发现了不少欠妥或失误之处，故随时订正补遗，这次再版前做了统一处理。又，我国古籍纪年皆用年号及干支，这次接受国外同行建议，参照陈垣《二十史朔闰表》和《中西回史日历》，把书中所有年号及干支转为西历年月日。修订过程中，责任编辑缪丹女史做了非常耐心的校阅。谨致谢忱！

2015年7月，《佛教考古：从印度到中国》被全国文化遗产十佳图书评选推介活动办公室“评为2014年度全国文化遗产优秀图书”。2016年《人文宗教研究》第1册（总第七辑）第326—331页刊发了何利群博士撰写的书评。他写道：“本书是作者根据实地调查资料探讨印度地上塔寺和石窟的发生与发展及其在中国的流变和演化，是研究中印文化交流的重要成果，但其意义并不仅限于具体事例的分析与考证，在佛教考古的学科定位、研究思路与阐释方法等方面也给予了我们许多有益的启示。”作为学术著作，本书出版一年后重印、五年后修订再版，超出了上海古籍出版社及作者本人的预想，这或许从另一方面表明了此书的价值。

李崇峰

2019年9月16日

记于北京大学德斋1106室

图书在版编目(CIP)数据

佛教考古:从印度到中国/李崇峰著.--修订本
.--上海:上海古籍出版社,2020.9(2023.11重印)
ISBN 978-7-5325-9724-6

Ⅰ.①佛… Ⅱ.①李… Ⅲ.①佛教考古-印度②佛教考古-中国 Ⅳ.①K883.51②K87

中国版本图书馆CIP数据核字(2020)第154307号

佛教考古:从印度到中国
(修订本　全二册)
李崇峰 著
上海古籍出版社出版发行
(上海市闵行区号景路159弄1-5号A座5F 邮政编码201101)
(1)网址:www.guji.com.cn
(2)E-mail:guji1@guji.com.cn
(3)易文网网址:www.ewen.co
上海展强印刷有限公司印刷
开本 787×1092 1/16 印张 59.5 插页 17 字数 1,097,000
2020年9月第1版 2023年11月第3次印刷
印数:2,301—3,100
ISBN 978-7-5325-9724-6
K·2888 定价:298.00元
如有质量问题,请与承印公司联系
电话:021-66366565